ArtScroll Mishnah Series®

A rabbinic commentary to the Six Orders of the Mishnah

Rabbi Nosson Scherman / Rabbi Meir Zlotowitz
General Editors

A PROJECT OF THE

Mesorah Heritage Foundation

BOARD OF TRUSTEES

LORD IMMANUEL JAKOBOVITS ל"ז*
*Emeritus, Chief Rabbi
British Empire*

RABBI DAVID FEINSTEIN
*Rosh HaYeshivah
Mesivtha Tifereth Jerusalem*

ABRAHAM BIDERMAN
Executive Vice President, Lipper & Co.

JOEL L. FLEISHMAN
First Sr. Vice President, Duke University

JUDAH I. SEPTIMUS, ESQ., C.P.A.

JAMES S. TISCH
President, Loews Corp.

RABBI NOSSON SCHERMAN
General Editor, ArtScroll Series

RABBI MEIR ZLOTOWITZ
Chairman

INTERNATIONAL BOARD OF GOVERNORS

JAY SCHOTTENSTEIN *(Columbus, OH)*
Chairman

YOSEF DAVIS *(Chicago)*
REUVEN D. DESSLER *(Cleveland)*
BENJAMIN C. FISHOFF
HOWARD TZVI FRIEDMAN *(Baltimore)*
SHIMMIE HORN
LESTER KLAUS
ARTHUR LUXENBERG
RABBI MEYER H. MAY *(Los Angeles)*
ALAN PEYSER
BARRY M. RAY *(Chicago)*
KALMAN RENOV
J. PHILIP ROSEN
ZVI RYZMAN *(Los Angeles)*
ELLIS A. SAFDEYE
A. GEORGE SAKS
ALEXANDER SCHARF
FRED SCHULMAN

HOWARD SCHULMAN
ELLIOT SCHWARTZ
HERBERT E. SEIF *(Englewood, N.J.)*
BERNARD SHAFRAN
NATHAN B. SILBERMAN
SOLI SPIRA *(Jerusalem / Antwerp)*
ALAN STAHLER
A. JOSEPH STERN *(Edison, N.J.)*
IRVING I. STONE* *(Cleveland)*
ELLIOT TANNENBAUM
JAY TEPPER
THOMAS J. TISCH
GARY H. TORGOW *(Detroit)*
STEVEN WEISZ
HIRSCH WOLF
HOWARD J. ZUCKERMAN

---

* *Deceased*

ששה סדרי משנה

THE COMMENTARY HAS BEEN NAMED **YAD AVRAHAM**
AS AN EVERLASTING MEMORIAL AND SOURCE OF MERIT
FOR THE *NESHAMAH* OF
אברהם יוסף ע"ה בן הר"ר אליעזר הכהן גליק נ"י
AVRAHAM YOSEF GLICK ע"ה
WHOSE LIFE WAS CUT SHORT ON 3 TEVES, 5735

Published by
Mesorah Publications, ltd

the mishnah

ARTSCROLL MISHNAH SERIES / A NEW TRANSLATION WITH A COMMENTARY **YAD AVRAHAM** ANTHOLOGIZED FROM TALMUDIC SOURCES AND CLASSIC COMMENTATORS.

INCLUDES THE COMPLETE HEBREW TEXT OF THE COMMENTARY OF **RAV OVADIAH BERTINORO**

FIRST EDITION
Eight Impressions . . . May 1982 — April 1998

REVISED EDITION
First Impression . . . April 2000
Second Impression . . . December 2002
Third Impression . . . November 2005

Published and Distributed by
MESORAH PUBLICATIONS, Ltd.
4401 Second Avenue
Brooklyn, New York 11232

Distributed in Europe by
LEHMANNS
Unit E, Viking Business Park
Rolling Mill Road
Jarrow, Tyne & Wear NE32 3DP
England

Distributed in Australia & New Zealand by
GOLDS WORLD OF JUDAICA
3-13 William Street
Balaclava, Melbourne 3183
Victoria Australia

Distributed in Israel by
SIFRIATI / A. GITLER — BOOKS
6 Hayarkon Street
Bnei Brak 51127

Distributed in South Africa by
KOLLEL BOOKSHOP
Shop 8A Norwood Hypermarket
Norwood 2196, Johannesburg, South Africa

THE ARTSCROLL MISHNAH SERIES ·
SEDER MOED Vol. I(a): *SHABBOS*
© Copyright 1982, 1985, 1986, 1988, 1994, 2000
by MESORAH PUBLICATIONS, Ltd.
4401 Second Avenue / Brooklyn, N.Y. 11232 / (718) 921-9000 / www.artscroll.com

---

All rights reserved. *This text, the new translation, commentary, and prefatory comments
— including the typographic layout, illustrations, charts, appendices, and cover design —
have been edited and revised as to content, form and style
and are fully protected against copyright infringement.*

No part of this book may be reproduced **in any form**
— **including** *photocopying and retrieval systems* —
without **written** *permission from the copyright holder,
except by a reviewer who wishes to quote brief passages in connection with a review
written for inclusion in magazines or newspapers.*

THE RIGHTS OF THE COPYRIGHT HOLDER WILL BE STRICTLY ENFORCED.

ISBN
0-89906-250-4 (hard cover)

Typography by CompuScribe at ArtScroll Studios, Ltd.
4401 Second Avenue / Brooklyn, N.Y. 11232 / (718) 921-9000
Printed in the United States of America by Noble Book Press
Bound by Sefercraft, Quality Bookbinders, Ltd. Brooklyn, N.Y.

❧ Seder Moed Vol. Ia

Tractate Shabbos / מסכת שבת

Mr. and Mrs. Philip Amin,
Mr. & Mrs. Lee R. Furman

lovingly dedicated this volume

to the memory of their son and brother

קלמן בן ר' פסח ע"ה
KALMAN AMIN

December 15, 1942 — ז' טבת תשי"ג

May the Torah learned from this volume

be a source of merit to the soul

that was taken while still rich

in unfulfilled potential.

תנצב"ה

הסכמה

הנה ידידי הרב הגאון ר' אברהם יוסף ראזענבערג שליט"א אשר היה מתלמידי החשובים ביותר וגם הרביץ תורה בכמה ישיבות ואצלינו בישיבתנו בסטעטן אײלאנד, ובזמן האחרון הוא מתעסק בתרגום ספרי קדש ללשון אנגלית המדוברת ומובנת לבני מדינה זו, וכבר איתמחי גברא בענין תרגום לאנגלית וכעת תרגם משניות לשפת אנגלית וגם לקוטים מדברי רבותינו מפרשי משניות על כל משנה ומשנה בערך, והוא לתועלת גדול להרבה אינשי ממדינה זו שלא התרגלו מילדותם ללמוד המשנה וגם יש הרבה שבעזר השי"ת התקרבו לתורה ויראת שמים כשכבר נתגדלו ורוצים ללמוד ללמוד משניות בנקל בשפה המורגלת להם, שהוא ממזכי הרבים בלמוד משניות וזכותו גדול. ואני מברכו שיצליחהו השי"ת בחבורו זה. וגם אני מברך את חברת ארטסקרול אשר תחת הנהלת הרב הנכבד ידידי מוהר"ר מאיר יעקב בן ידידי הרב הגאון ר' אהרן שליט"א זלאטאוויץ אשר הוציאו כבר הרבה חבורים חשובים לזכות את הרבים וכעת הם מוציאים לאור את המשניות הנ"ל.

ועל זה באתי על החתום בז' אדר תשל"ט בנוא יארק.

נאום משה פיינשטיין

מכתב ברכה

יעקב קמנצקי
RABBI J. KAMENECKI
38 SADDLE RIVER ROAD
MONSEY, NEW YORK 10952

בע"ה

יום ה' ערב חג השבועות תשל"ט, פה מאנסי.

כבוד הרבני איש החסד שוע ונדיב מוקיר רבנן מר אלעזר נ"י גליק שלו' וברכת כל טוב.

מה מאד שמחתי בהודעי כי כבודו רכש לעצמו הזכות שייקרא ע"ש בנו המנוח הפירוש מבואר על כל ששת סדרי משנה ע"י "ארטסקרול" והנה חברה זו יצאה לה מוניטין בפירושה על תנ"ך, והנה נקוה שכשם שהצליחה בתורה שבכתב כן תצליח בתורה שבע"פ. ובהיות שאותיות "משנה" הן כאותיות "נשמה" לפיכך טוב עשה בכוונתו לעשות זאת לעילוי נשמת בנו המנוח אברהם יוסף ע"ה, ומאד מתאים השם "יד אברהם" לזה הפירוש, לדמצינו במקרא (ש"ב י"ח) כי אמר אין לי בן בעבור הזכיר שמי וגו'. ואין לך דבר גדול מזה להפיץ ידיעת תורה שבע"פ בקרב אחינו שאינם רגילים בלשון הקדש. וד' הטוב יהי' בעזרו ויוכל לברך על המוגמר. וידוה רוב נחת מכל אשר אתו כנפש מברכו.

יעקב קמנצקי

Approbation/מכתב ברכה

מכתב ברכה

בע"ה – ד' בהעלותך – לבני א"י – תשל"ט – פה קרית טלז, באה"ק

מע"כ ידידי האהובים הרב ר' מאיר והרב ר' נתן, נר"ו, שלום וברכה נצח!

אחדשה"ט באהבה ויקר,

לשמחה רבה היא לי להודע שהרחבתם גבול עבודתכם בקדש לתורה שבע"פ, בהוצאת המשנה בתרגום וביאור באנגלית, וראשית עבודתכם במס' מגילה.

אני תקוה שתשימו לב שיצאו הדברים מתוקנים מנקודת ההלכה, וחזקה עליכם שתוציאו דבר נאה ומתוקן.

בפנותכם לתורה שבע"פ יפתח אופן חדש בתורת ה' לאלה שקשה עליהם ללמוד הדברים במקורם, ואלה שכבר נתעשרו מעבודתכם במגילת אסתר יכנסו עתה לטרקלין חדש וישמשו להם הדברים דחף ללימוד המשנה, וגדול יהי' שכרכם.

יהא ה' בעזרכם בהוספת טבעת חדשה באותה שלשלת זהב של הפצת תורת ה' להמוני עם לקרב לב ישראל לאבינו שבשמים בתורה ואמונה טהורה.

אוהבכם מלונ"ח,
מרדכי

מכתב ברכה

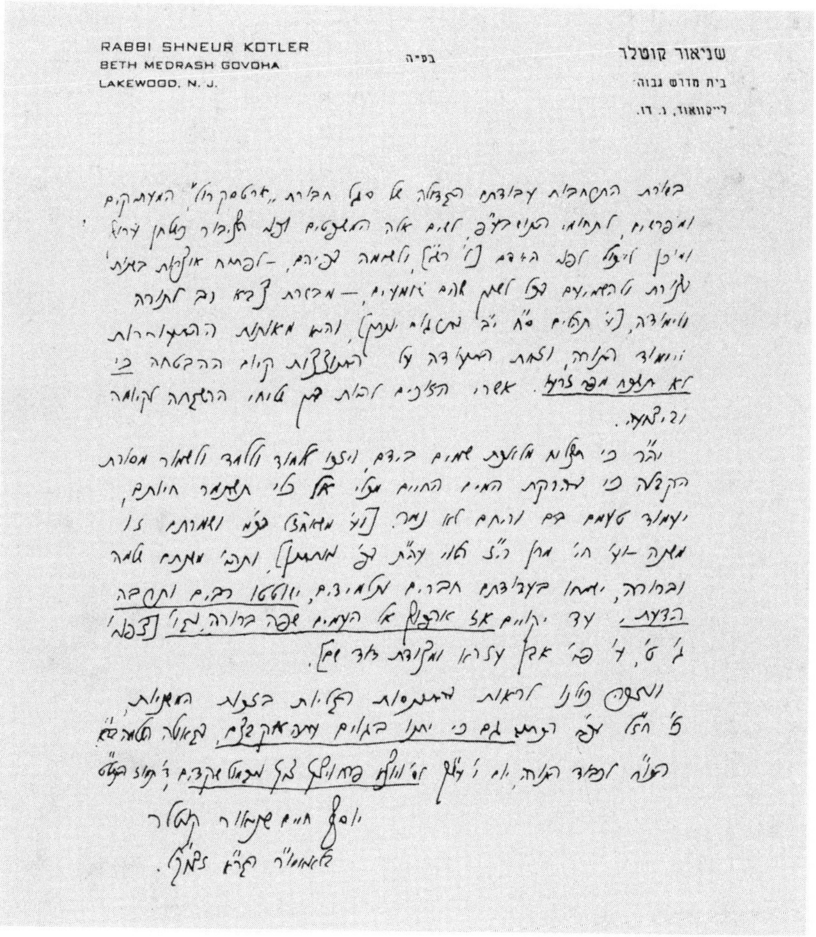

RABBI SHNEUR KOTLER
BETH MEDRASH GOVOHA
LAKEWOOD, N.J.

בס"ד

שניאור קוטלר
בית מדרש גבוה
לייקוואוד, נ. דז.

[handwritten letter]

בשורת התרחבות עבודתם הגדולה של סגל חבורת "ארטסקרול", המעתיקים ומפרשים, לתחומי התושבע"פ, לשים אלה המשפטים לפני הציבור כשלחן ערוך ומוכן לאכול לפני האדם [ל' רש"י], ולשימה בפיהם – לפתוח אוצרות בשנות בצורת ולהשמיעם בכל לשון שהם שומעים – מבשרת צבא רב לתורה ולימודה [ע' תהלים ס"ח י"ב בתרגום יונתן], והיא מאותות ההתעוררות ללימוד התורה, וזאת התעודה על התנוצצות קיום ההבטחה "כי לא תשכח מפי זרעו". אשרי הזוכים להיות בין שלוחי ההשגחה לקיומה וביצועה.

יה"ר כי תצליח מלאכת שמים בידם, ויזכו ללמוד וללמד ולשמור מסורת הקבלה כי ברזק המים החיים מכלי אל כלי תשתמר חיותם, יעמוד טעמים בם וריחם לא נמר. [וע' משאחז"ל בכ"מ ושמרתם זו משנה – וע' חי' מרן רי"ז הלוי עה"ת בפ' ואתחנן]. ותהי משנתם שלמה וברורה, ישמחו בעבודתם חברים ותלמידים, "ישוטטו רבים ותרבה הדעת", עד יקויים "אז אהפוך אל העמים שפה ברורה וגו' " [צפני' ג' ט', ע' פי' אבן עזרא ומצודת דוד שם].

ונזכה כולנו לראות בהתכנסות הגליות בזכות המשניות, כל חז"ל עפ"י הכתוב "גם כי יתנו בגוים עתה אקבצם", בגאולה השלמה בב"א.

הכו"ח לכבוד התורה, יום ו' עש"ק לס' "ויוצא פרח ויצץ ציץ ויגמול שקדים", ד' תמוז התשל"ט

יוסף חיים שניאור קוטלר
בלאאמו"ר הגר"א זצוק"ל

מכתב ברכה

[תמונת מכתב בכתב יד על נייר מכתבים של "ישיבה דפילאדעלפיא"]

ב"ה
לכבוד ידידי וידיד ישיבתנו, מהראשונים לכל דבר שבקדושה
הרבני הנדיב המפורסם ר' אליעור הכהן גליק נ"י
אחדשה"ט באהבה

בשורה טובה שמעתי שכב' מצא את המקום המתאים לעשות יד ושם להנציח זכרו של בנו **אברהם יוסף ע"ה** שנקטף בנעוריו. "ונתתי להם בביתי ובחומתי יד ושם". אין לו להקב"ה אלא ד' אמות של הלכה בלבד. א"כ זהו בית ד' לימוד תורה שבע"פ וזהו המקום לעשות יד ושם לנשמת בנו ע"ה.

נר ד' נשמת אדם אמר הקב"ה נרי בידך ונרך בידי. נר מצוה ותורה אור, תורה זהו הנר של הקב"ה וכששומרים נר של הקב"ה שעל ידי הפירוש "**יד אברהם**" בשפה הלועזית יתרבה ויתפשט לימוד ושקידת התורה בבתי ישראל. ד' ישמור נשמת אדם.

בנו אברהם יוסף ע"ה נתברך בהמדה שבו נכללות כל המדות, לב טוב והיה אהוב לחבריו. בלמדו בישיבתנו היה לו הרצון לעלות במעלות התורה וכשעלה לארצנו הקדושה היתה מבוקשו להמשיך בלמודיו. ביקוש זה ימצא מלואו על ידי הרבים המבקשים דבר ד', שהפירוש "**יד אברהם**" יהא מפתח להם לים התלמוד.

התורה נקראת "אש דת" ונמשלה לאש יש לה הכח לפעפע ברזל לקצץ כוחות האדם, הניצוץ שהאיר בך רבנו הרב שרגא פייוועל מנדלוויץ זצ"ל שמרת עליו, ועשה חיל. עכשיו אתה מסייע להאיר נצוצות בנשמות בני ישראל שיעשה חיל ויהא לאור גדול.

תקותי עוה שכל התלמידי חכמים שנדבתם רוחם להוציא לפועל מלאכה ענקית זו לפרש המשניות כולה, יצא עבודתם ברוב פאר והדר ויכוונו לאמיתה של תורה ויתקדש ויתרבה שם שמים על ידי מלאכה זו.

יתברך כב' ובנ"ב לראות ולרוות נחת רוח מצאצאיו.
הכו"ח לכבוד התורה ותומכיה עש"ק במדבר תשל"ט

אלי' שוויי

[xii] מכתב ברכה/*Approbation*

מכתב ברכה

דוד קאהן ביהמ״ד גבול יעבץ
ברוקלין, נוא יארק

בס״ד כ״ה למטמונים תשל״ט

כבוד רחימא דנפשאי, עושה ומעשה
ר' אלעזר הכהן גליק נטריה רחמנא ופרקיה

שמוע שמעתי שכבר תקעת כפיך לתמוך במפעל האדיר של חברת ארטסקרול — הידוע בכל קצווי תבל ע״י עבודתה הכבירה בהפצת תורה — לתרגם ולבאר ששה סדרי משנה באנגלית. כוונתך להנציח זכר בנך הנחמד אברהם יוסף ז״ל שנקטף באבו בזמן שעלה לארץ הקודש בתקופת התרוממות הנפש ושאיפה לקדושה, ולמטרה זו יכונה הפירוש בשם ,,יד אברהם״; וגם האיר ה' רוחך לגרום עילוי לנשמתו התורה שע״י יתרבה לימוד התורה שניתנה בשבעים לשון, על ידי כלי מפואר זה.

מכיון שהנני מכיר היטיב שני הצדדים, אוכל לומר לדבק טוב, והנני תקוה תקוה שיצליח המפעל הלזה לתת יד ושם וזכות לנשמת אברהם יוסף ז״ל. חזקה על חברת ארטסקרול שתוציא דבר נאה מתוקן ומתקבל מתחת ידה להגדיל תורה ולהאדירה.

והנני מברך אותך שתמצא נוחם לנפשך, שהאבא זוכה לברא, ותשבע נחת — אתה עם רעיתך תחיה — מכל צאצאיכם היקרים אכי״ר

ידידך עז
דוד קאהן

[xiii]   Approbation/מכתב ברכה

Preface To The First Edition

אָמַר ר' יוֹחָנָן: לֹא כָרַת הקב״ה בְּרִית עִם יִשְׂרָאֵל אֶלָּא עַל־תּוֹרָה
שֶׁבְּעַל פֶּה שֶׁנֶּאֱמַר "כִּי עַל־פִּי הַדְּבָרִים הָאֵלֶּה כָּרַתִּי אִתְּךָ בְּרִית...".
R' Yochanan said: The Holy One, Blessed is He, sealed a covenant with Israel only because of the Oral Torah, as it is said [Exodus 34:27]: For according to these words have I sealed a covenant with you ... (Gittin 60b).

In presenting the Torah public with this first volume of the Seder Moed in the ARTSCROLL MISHNAH SERIES, we extend a בִּרְכַּת הוֹדָיָה, a blessing of thanksgiving, to Hashem Yisbarach for endowing Mesorah Publications with the awesome privilege of serving as His vehicle for Torah dissemination. Simultaneous with the ongoing work on Tanach, the Siddur, and other classics of Torah literature, the new Mishnah Series has ב״ה become a major service to the English-speaking public. We are proud that such venerable luminaries as MARAN HAGAON HARAV YAAKOV KAMINECKI and MARAN HAGAON HARAV MORDECHAI GIFTER שליט״א have declared that this series should be translated into Hebrew. Baruch Hashem it has provoked readers to echo the words of King David: גַּל־עֵינַי וְאַבִּיטָה נִפְלָאוֹת מִתּוֹרָתֶךְ, Uncover my eyes that I may see wonders of Your Torah [Psalms 119:18].

Heretofore, there has been a serious lack of adequate English treatment of the Mishnah. In the view of roshei hayeshivah and Torah scholars, there exists a need for a work that willl treat the Mishnah with depth and scope. Like the ARTSCROLL TANACH SERIES, this Mishnah series draws upon large cross-sections of Talmudic, rabbinic, and halachic sources. The purpose is to enable the reader to study each mishnah as though he were sitting in a study hall, participating in the give and take of Talmudic scholarship.

The initiative for this series came from a couple whose unassuming but boundless involvement and visionary concern for important causes has won them the respect and admiration of multitudes. MR. AND MRS. LOUIS GLICK have dedicated the commentary of the entire ARTSCROLL MISHNAH SERIES. It bears the name YAD AVRAHAM, in memory of their son AVRAHAM YOSEF ע״ה. An appreciation of the niftar will appear in Tractate Berachos. May this dissemination of the Mishnah in his memory be a source of merit for his soul. תנצב״ה.

Both in his role as an outstanding patron of Torah and as a major figure in Yeshiva Torah Vodaath, Mr. Glick displays a constant and dedicated interest in our work. We are inspired by him and resolve to live up to his hopes for the ArtScroll Mishnah Series. May he and Mrs. Glick be blessed for their generous dedication to Torah, of which this project is but one instance.

We are grateful to the officers and directors of YESHIVA TORAH VODAATH AND MESIVTA, *whose assistance has done much to make the Mishnah Series possible. One of America's oldest and greatest Torah centers, Torah Vodaath now adds the printed word of the Mishnah to its honor roll of distinguished service to Jewry.*

May we inject two words of caution:

First, although the mishnah, by definition, is a compendium of laws, the final halachah does not necessarily follow the Mishnah. The development of halachah proceeds through the Gemara, commentators, codifiers, responsa, and the acknowledged Torah poskim. Even when our commentary cites the Shulchan Aruch, the intention is to sharpen the reader's understanding of the Mishnah, but not to be a basis for actual practice. In short, this work is meant as a study of the first step of our recorded Oral Law — no more.

Second, as we have stressed in our other books, an ArtScroll commentary is not meant as a substitute for study of the sources. While this commentary, like others in the various series, will be immensely useful even to accomplished scholars and will often bring to light ideas and sources they may have overlooked, we strongly urge those who are able to study the classic sefarim in the original to do so. Whether in Hebrew or English, such commentaries cannot distill every nuance and shade of meaning from the classic expounders of the Torah. It has been said that every droplet of ink coming from Rashi's pen is worthy of seven days' contemplation. Despite the exceptional caliber of our authors, none of us pretend to compensate for study of the greatest minds in Jewish history.

The pattern of the commentary and the style of transliteration follow those of the ARTSCROLL TANACH SERIES.

Hebrew terms connoting concepts for which there are no exact English translations are generally defined the first time they appear and transliterated thereafter.

For the reader's convenience, every word of the Mishnah has been included in the commentary headings. Therefore, the readers may study the commentary continuously without constantly referring back to the text, should he so desire.

The translation attempts to follow the text faithfully. Variations have been made when dictated by the need for clarity in English usage and syntax. Any words that have been added for the sake of flow and clarity are bracketed.

Some of the classic sources from which the commentary have been culled are: the GEMARA *(abbreviated Gem.) with its commentaries, such as* RASHI *(1040-1105);* TOSAFOS *(Tos.). Talmudic glosses by the school of scholars known collectively as Tosafists, who flourished after Rashi];* RITVA *[R' Yom Tov Ishbili (1250-1330)];* RAN *[R' Nissim Gerondi (mid-14th cent.)];* NIMUKEI YOSEF *[R' Yosef Chaviva (early 15th cent.)]; the classical Mishnah commentaries;* RAMBAM *[R' Moshe ben Maimon (Maimonides: 1135-1204)];* R' MENACHEM MEIRI *(1249-1306);* RAV *[R' Ovadiah of Bertinoro (late 15th cent.)];* TOSEFOS YOM TOV *(Tos. Yom Tov) [R' Yom Tov Lipman Heller (1579-1659)]; and more recent commentators:* TOSEFOS R' AKIVA *[R' Akiva Eiger (1761-1837)];* TIFERES YISRAEL *(Tif. Yis.) [R' Israel Lipschutz (1782-1860)]; and many others. A major source is* SHULCHAN ARUCH ORACH CHAIM *and its various commentaries and responsa. For the sake of brevity, the term Orach Chaim has been omitted when referring to these sources.*

Generally, the commentary first offers the interpretation of Rav — Rabbeinu Ovadiah of Bertinoro — the premier commentator to the Mishnah. We attempt to show Rav's sources for his comments, including the various discussions of the Gemara in the classic commentators. Where the preponderance of authorities compels us to deviate from Rav's interpretation, we attempt to show why. Other comments or more involved discussions are given in a smaller-type size; the reader seeking only a basic understanding of the Mishnah may limit his study to the comments given in larger type.

No such work can serve the need for which it is intended unless the author is a talmid chacham of a very high caliber. We are particularly gratified, therefore, to have engaged authors of high scholarship and accomplishment. Although anthologized from numerous sources, each commentary is original in the sense that it reflects the author's own understanding, selection, and presentation.

This volume was written by RABBI YOSEIF ROSENBERG, *a distinguished talmid chacham and rosh yeshivah. His earlier contribution to the ArtScroll Mishnah Series was volume IV of Moed. Self-effacing though he is, his work proclaims his stature. Mesorah Publications is proud to make his Torah knowledge available to Klal Yisrael.*

A work of such magnitude is not done singlehandedly, though the scholarship is the author's. As editors, researchers, and contributors to this volume, RABBI YEHEZKEL DANZIGER *and* RABBI AVIE GOLD *contributed immeasurably to the beauty of the commentary and the general completeness of this volume.* RABBI AVRAHAM KLEINKAUFMAN, *too, read and commented on much of the manuscript.*

RABBI SHEAH BRANDER *has displayed so consistently high a standard of graphic skill that one runs the danger of taking his artistry for granted. We do not. We repeat our admiration and declaration that* only one who has worked with him can appreciate his brilliance and dedication.

We are grateful to the staff of Mesorah Publications whose diligence and dedication finds expression in this sefer; MRS. SHIRLEY KIFFEL, LEA FREIER, CHANEE FREIER, EDEL STREICHER, ESTHER GLATZER, MRS. FAYGIE WEINBAUM, *and* MRS. JUDI DICK. STEPHEN BLITZ *bears gracefully and skillfully the responsibility of disseminating the ArtScroll Series to the public.*

We express our thanks to RABBI DAVID FEINSTEIN שליט״א *and* RABBI DAVID COHEN שליט״א, *whose constant concern and interest throughout the history of the ArtScroll Series have been in further evidence in the course of this work.*

Rabbi Nosson Scherman / Rabbi Meir Zlotowitz

כ״ד אייר תשמ״ב / May 1982
ל״ט למ״טמונים

↫ Seder Moed

Seder Moed [the Order of Festivals] is the second of the Six Orders of the Mishnah. It deals with the sacred days of the Jewish year — the Sabbath, festivals, and fast days — and the laws and activities relating to them. These laws, like the days with which they deal, are varied. Thus we find tractates — in whole or in part — that deal with forbidden labors of the Sabbath; the less-stringent prohibitions of festivals; the Intermediate Days [*Chol HaMoed*]; Temple offerings of those days; such festival *mitzvos* as the *Passover Seder*, the *succah* and Four Species of Succos, the *shofar* and prayer order of Rosh Hashanah, and the Temple service of Yom Kippur; the manner in which funds were collected for communal offerings; the definition of *chametz* and the manner of its disposition; fasts and prayers in time of national crisis; and so on. Varied though they are, these laws share the characteristic of relating to days of the year that are distinguished by their sanctity and by the fact that generally they relate to the calendar.

Seder Moed contains twelve tractates. There are differences of opinion regarding their precise order, but the generally accepted listing is that of *Rambam* in the Introduction to his *Commentary on the Mishnah*:

1. **Shabbos** — which deals primarily with the thirty-nine Scripturally forbidden labors and the additional precautionary prohibitions imposed by the Sages.

2. **Eruvin** — the Sabbath laws relating to private domains where carrying is forbidden by Rabbinical decree, the 2,000 cubit radius around one's "place of dwelling" beyond which one may not walk on the Sabbath, and the means by which domains may be merged, and by which one may extend his walking radius in one direction.

3. **Pesachim** — the laws of *chametz* and *matzoh*, the *Pesach* offering, and the *Seder*.

4. **Shekalim** — the annual half-shekel head tax that was used to finance communal offerings in the Temple.

5. **Yoma** — the laws of Yom Kippur, primarily the Temple service of the day.

6. **Succah** — the laws of Succos, such as the construction of the *succah*, the Four Species, *Simchas Beis HaShoevah* and Hoshanah Rabbah.

7. **Beitzah** — the laws of *muktzeh*, which apply to the Sabbath and all festivals.

8. **Rosh Hashanah** — the procedure for declaring and announcing the New Moon, and the order of *shofar* blasts and prayers of Rosh Hashanah.

9. **Taanis** — the prophetically ordained fast days and those that must be

proclaimed in time of drought, war, or general danger.

10. **Megillah** — the laws of Purim and the reading of *Megillas Esther*.

11. **Moed Kattan** — the laws of the Intermediate Days of Festivals and, tangentially, the laws of mourning.

12. **Chagigah** — the obligation to appear in the Temple for the three pilgrimage festivals [שָׁלֹשׁ רְגָלִים] and the special festive offering that is brought by individuals when they make such appearances.

There is no tractate dealing with the festival of Shavuos, because the only law unique to it — the offering of Two Loaves — does not require a full tractate. (It is discussed in chapter 11 of *Menachos* in *Seder Kodashim*.)

∙≈§ מסכת שבת §≈∙

∙≈§ Tractate Shabbos

Translation and anthologized commentary by
Rabbi Avrohom Yoseif Rosenberg

Contributing editors:
Rabbi Yehezkel Danziger / Rabbi Avie Gold

Mesorah Publications, ltd

The Thirty-nine Melachos

*sowing	1	זוֹרֵעַ
*plowing	2	חוֹרֵשׁ
*reaping	3	קוֹצֵר
*gathering	4	מְעַמֵּר
*threshing	5	דָּשׁ
*winnowing	6	זוֹרֶה
*sorting	7	בּוֹרֵר
*grinding	8	טוֹחֵן
*sifting	9	מְרַקֵּד
*kneading	10	לָשׁ
*baking (*cooking)	11	אוֹפֶה (מְבַשֵּׁל)
*shearing	12	גּוֹזֵז
*whitening	13	מְלַבֵּן
*combing	14	מְנַפֵּץ
*dyeing	15	צוֹבֵעַ
*spinning	16	טוֹוֶה
*mounting the warp	17	מֵסֵךְ
*setting two heddles	18	עוֹשֶׂה שְׁנֵי בָתֵּי נִירִין
*weaving	19	אוֹרֵג
*removing threads	20	פּוֹצֵעַ
*tying	21	קוֹשֵׁר
*untying	22	מַתִּיר
*sewing	23	תּוֹפֵר
*tearing	24	קוֹרֵעַ
*trapping	25	צָד
*slaughtering	26	שׁוֹחֵט
*skinning	27	מַפְשִׁיט
*salting/*tanning[1]	28	מוֹלֵחַ/מְעַבֵּד
[*tracing lines]	29	[שִׂרְטוּט]
*smoothing	30	מוֹחֵק [עוֹר]
*cutting	31	מְחַתֵּךְ
*writing	32	כּוֹתֵב
*erasing	33	מוֹחֵק [כְּתָב]
*building	34	בּוֹנֶה
*demolishing	35	סוֹתֵר
*extinguishing	36	מְכַבֶּה
*kindling	37	מַבְעִיר
*striking the final blow	38	מַכֶּה בַפַּטִּישׁ
*transferring from domain to domain	39	הוֹצָאָה

*Throughout the introduction and commentary we have used an asterisk and italics to indicate an *av melachah*.

1. The list of *melachos* in 7:2 includes *salting hides* and *tanning* as separate *melachos*. The *Gemara* 75b states that these are really the same *melachah*, and inserts שרטוט, *tracing lines*, as the twenty-ninth *melachah*.

General Introduction to Tractate Shabbos
by Rabbi Yehezkel Danziger

זָכוֹר אֶת־יוֹם הַשַׁבָּת לְקַדְּשׁוֹ. שֵׁשֶׁת יָמִים תַּעֲבֹד וְעָשִׂיתָ כָּל־מְלַאכְתֶּךָ. וְיוֹם הַשְּׁבִיעִי שַׁבָּת לַה׳ אֱלֹהֶיךָ לֹא־תַעֲשֶׂה כָל־מְלָאכָה . . .

Remember the Sabbath day to sanctify it. Six days you are to work and accomplish all your tasks. But the seventh day is Sabbath to HASHEM, your God; you may not do any work . . . (Exodus 20:8,9).

The Torah places two obligations upon a person with regard to the Sabbath — *to remember the Sabbath day* (which is fulfilled with the recitation of the prayers and the *kiddush*), and to *refrain from performing any labor*. With the exception of the prohibition of kindling a fire, though, the Torah does not explicitly state what constitutes a labor.

However, the Torah prefaces the section describing the construction of the מִשְׁכָּן [*Mishkan*], *Tabernacle* (*Exodus 35:4ff*), with a repetition of the prohibition against performing labor on the Sabbath (ibid., vs. 1-3). [The *Mishkan* served as the Temple during the Israelites' forty-year journey through the wilderness. The structure and all its utensils were designed so as to be portable.] From this juxtaposition the Sages derived that the labors prohibited on the Sabbath are those which were necessary for the construction of the *Mishkan* and the preparation of its components (*Gem.* 49b, Rashi, s.v. בנגד; *Chagigah* 10a,b, Rashi, s.v. מלאכת מחשבת; cf. *Mechilta* 20:10).

I. The 39 Categories of Prohibited Labor

The mishnah in 7:2 lists these labors and gives their total as thirty-nine.[1] [See chart on facing page.]

אָבוֹת וְתוֹלָדוֹת — Avos and Tolados

Though the thirty-nine labors enumerated here comprise the list of activities necessary to construct the *Mishkan*, they do not exclude other similar activities from being prohibited on the Sabbath. On the contrary, any other activity similar either in method or function to any of these thirty-nine activities is equally prohibited. The formulation of these thirty-nine labors is not intended as a ban on thirty-nine specific acts of labor but rather as a ban on thirty-nine categories of labor. They are therefore known as אֲבוֹת מְלָאכוֹת, *avos melachos*, *primary labors* [lit. *fathers of labors*], in the sense that they constitute the headings of whole categories of labor. Activities whose prohibition is derived

---

1. The *Gemara* (49b) cites various verses from which this number may be derived. This number, however, was clearly stated to Moses at Sinai. See statement of *Rebbi* in *Gem.* 97a.

from one of these thirty-nine are known as תּוֹלָדוֹת, *tolados, secondary* [lit. *descendant*] labors.

[The term *melachah* refers to any prohibited labor; *av melachah* (sometimes shortened to just *av*) is the singular form of *avos melachos* while *toladah* is the singular form of *tolados*.]

There is no difference in the stringency of the prohibition as to whether an act is an *av* or a *toladah*. Both are equally prohibited. Both bear the same penalty (סְקִילָה, *stoning*) for willful transgression (in the presence of two witnesses) and the same atonement (sin offering) for inadvertent transgression. The classification of the *melachos* into *avos* and *tolados* is only to make it possible to group them into identifiable categories. The formulation of categories is significant for the following reason: One who, in his ignorance of a certain prohibited category of labor, performed several different activities all in violation of that one category, is obligated to bring but one sin offering (see 7:1). This is true whether he did an *av* and its *toladah* or several *tolados* of one category. If, however, his activities violated more than one category, he is required to bring a separate sin offering for each category violated. It is, therefore, necessary to know which activities fall into which category in order to determine how many sin offerings one is obligated to bring (*Bava Kamma* 2a).[1]

The activities which actually took place in the construction of the *Mishkan* were accorded the status of *avos* (*Gem.* ibid.). Other activities, however, may also be considered *avos* if they are so similar in nature to the *Mishkan* activity as to be nearly identical. If they are somewhat less similar, they are considered *tolados*. The precise delineation is subject to different opinions. It is, however, generally agreed that any activity which is designed to achieve the same result as the *av* and whose method is basically the same as that of the *av* should also be considered an *av*. E.g., *sowing is an *av*. Grafting, since it is designed to achieve the same result as the *av*, i.e., to promote growth, and since it involves basically the same method, i.e., placing a plant in an area suited to its growth (either a seed into the ground or a branch to another tree) is also considered an *av*.[2]

Pruning, on the other hand, though it is designed to achieve the same results as *sowing (to promote growth), since it does not involve the same method (cutting away rather than adding) is considered a *toladah* rather than an *av* (*Rashi* 73b).

---

1. Actually, there is another practical difference. It is based on the rule that a person cannot be executed for even a willful transgression of a capital crime unless he has been properly warned prior to his commission of that crime. An improperly phrased warning invalidates the warning because the perpetrator may then claim that he did not take the warning seriously, due to its obvious inaccuracy. If witnesses were to warn a person about to transgress the Sabbath that the act he was about to perform was prohibited under a certain category (e.g., that pruning a tree was prohibited as a toladah of *reaping) when in fact it was prohibited under a different category (*sowing, see 12:2), they would thereby invalidate that warning. Though it is actually unnecessary to refer at all to the *av* when issuing a warning for the *toladah*, an incorrect reference would nevertheless suffice to invalidate the warning. The person could not then be punished by the *beis din* (*Tos.* 73b).
2. There is, however, an opinion which disputes even this and seems to hold that only the activities listed in the mishnah may be considered *avos*. See *R' Chananel* (73b).

Rambam (*Hil. Shabbos* 7:3) considers even pruning an *av*. According to him, as long as the activity is designed to achieve the same function and operates on the same object as the *av* (the plant or seed), though the actual process may differ, it is considered an *av*. Where, however, it operates on a different object, e.g., watering the soil around the seed, though it achieves the same function (promoting growth), it is, according to all opinions, a *toladah* (*Kalkalas HaShabbos* in explanation of *Rambam*).

Where the method is the same as that of the *Mishkan* but the function differs *slightly*, it is also a *toladah*. An example of this is shaving a metal bar to make filings. This is a *toladah* of *grinding. Whereas the *av* of *grinding is done for the purpose of making a substance used for food, the purpose of filing metal is to make a substance for industrial use. Though very similar, it is not identical. It is, therefore, a *toladah* rather than an *av*. If the activity is for a function other than that of the *Mishkan* entirely, it is classified, according to most opinions, as a מְלָאכָה שֶׁאֵינָהּ צְרִיכָה לְגוּפָהּ, *labor not done for its defined purpose*, which will be explained below.

The delineation of these categories of labor in all their details occupies the major part of this tractate. This analysis begins for the most part in Chapter 7, although certain aspects of the *melachos* of *transferring from domain to domain* and *cooking are discussed in the first six chapters.

☙ Liable and Exempt

All thirty-nine *melachos*, both *avos* and *tolados*, are prohibited by the Torah as part of the Oral Tradition. [These will be referred to as Biblical or Torah prohibitions.] As in all areas of Torah law, however, the Rabbis enacted further prohibitions to safeguard the Biblical law. [These will be referred to as Rabbinical prohibitions.] The Mishnah's terms for distinguishing between them are *liable* and *exempt*. These terms actually refer to the legal consequences of inadvertent violation of these prohibitions; in the case of one who performed a *melachah* on the Sabbath because he either forgot or never knew that it was forbidden or because he forgot that it was the Sabbath day. Although there is no penalty for the inadvertent violation of even a Biblical prohibition, one is still *liable* for a sin offering to atone for this violation. In the case of a Rabbinical prohibition, however, one is *exempt* from any sin offering. [Although the violator must still repent his sin, no sin offering is required to atone for it.] Therefore, wherever the mishnah with regard to the Sabbath laws states that one who does a certain act is *liable* it means that the act is Biblically prohibited. Where the mishnah states that one is *exempt* it means that though he is exempt from bringing a sin offering the act is nevertheless Rabbinically prohibited. Where the act is actually permissible, the mishnah will say that *one may do* such and such on the Sabbath. [There are, however, three exceptions where the *Tanna* states that one is exempt for a certain act but means that it is permissible. These are mishnah 13:7 and two other statements quoted by the *Gemara* on 107a.]

Aside from Rabbinical decrees prohibiting acts which resemble Biblical prohibitions (and which might, therefore, lead to violation of the Biblical prohibitions), the Rabbis enacted other decrees to reinforce the concept of rest on the Sabbath and to enhance the sanctity of the day. These will be discussed below.

◆§ Penalties

מֵזִיד, *willful*, desecration of the Sabbath through the commission of a Torah-prohibited act carries the penalty of סְקִילָה, *death by stoning* (Sanhedrin 7:8). A court, however, may only impose this penalty if the act took place (a) in the presence of two acceptable witnesses, and (b) immediately after the perpetrator had been warned by them of the transgression and its consequences. If either of these conditions is not met, the matter no longer falls under the jurisdiction of the court (בֵּית דִּין שֶׁל מַטָּה), but is subject to the Divine punishment known as כָּרֵת [*kares*], *excision*.

שׁוֹגֵג, *inadvertent*, violation of these laws, i.e., where the violation was the result of a lack of knowledge rather than a willful disregard of the law, must be atoned for by bringing a קָרְבַּן חַטָּאת, *sin offering*, in the *Beis HaMikdash*. Such inadvertent violation may be the result of one of three errors: (a) One was unaware of the very law of Sabbath; (b) one knew the general law of Sabbath but was unaware that a specific act was prohibited on the Sabbath; or (c) one knew the laws of Sabbath but simply forgot that it was the Sabbath day. These rules will be explained in 7:1.

The penalty for willfully violating the Rabbinic safeguards is a form of flogging known as *makkas mardus* (*Rambam*, *Hil. Shabbos* 1:3; see *Maggid Mishneh* and *Mishneh LaMelech*, there, for discussion of which Rabbinic violations rate this punishment).

There is neither penalty nor sin offering required for inadvertent violation of a Rabbinic prohibition.

II. The Principal Rules of Melachah

◆§ מְלֶאכֶת מַחֲשֶׁבֶת — Calculated Labor

There is one overriding conceptual principle to the laws of the Sabbath which is unique to these laws. This is the principle of מְלֶאכֶת מַחֲשֶׁבֶת אָסְרָה תוֹרָה, *the Torah prohibited only a calculated labor*.[1] In essence this principle means that the Torah does not consider the performance of a *melachah* on the Sabbath as a Biblical transgression unless it conforms to certain general principles. If it does not, it is not Biblically prohibited (although in most cases it is still Rabbinically prohibited). This concept is so broad that there are several major, and seemingly disparate, principles derived from it. These are mentioned by the *Gemara* as individual principles, with only rare or even no references to the basic concept at all. For this reason, only a general explanation of this principle is possible; the specifics of it can be understood only within the context of the corollary principles derived from it by the Sages.

As are the thirty-nine *melachos* themselves, this principle is derived from construction of the *Mishkan*. In describing the unique talents of the master artisan Betzalel for executing the intricate patterns decreed for the utensils of the *Mishkan*, the Torah states (*Exodus* 35:31-33): *And He [Hashem] filled him with the spirit of God, in wisdom, in understanding, in knowledge and in all manner of workmanship . . . to execute in all manner of* מְלֶאכֶת מַחֲשֶׁבֶת. This is

---

1. See *Beitzah* 13b, *Chagigah* 10b, *Bava Kamma* 26b, 60a, *Sanhedrin* 62b, *Kerisos* 19b, *Zevachim* 47a. Curiously, it is not explicitly stated in tractate *Shabbos* at all.

translated by *Targum* as *craftsmanship*. However, its more literal meaning is a thought-out or *calculated labor*, and it is in this sense that the Sages applied the term to the laws of Sabbath. By having us derive the thirty-nine principal forms of labor from construction of the *Mishkan*, the Torah makes clear that these labors are prohibited on the Sabbath only when performed in the manner in which they were executed in the construction of the *Mishkan*. Performed in an essentially different manner, they are not Biblically prohibited (although they are usually still Rabbinically prohibited).

In qualifying the Biblical prohibition of *labor* with the requirement that it be *calculated*, two concepts seem to be implied — *intent* and *design*. The concept of *intent* requires that the act be planned and that the plan be accomplished. The concept of *design* requires that the labor be an activity requiring design, i.e., that it be either creative or part of a creative process rather than merely laborious; it implies that it be focused toward achieving some specified design, and assumes that it will be done in the designed manner.

Both these factors were evident in the construction of the *Mishkan*, whose components had to be made according to specification. To properly construct the *Mishkan*, it was insufficient merely to collect raw materials; these had to be processed and fashioned according to plan into a useful and designed form. For example, to make the woolen coverings of the *Mishkan* it was necessary to shear wool, process it into thread and then weave it. To make the leather coverings it was necessary to slaughter animals, skin them and then process the hides into leather. Indeed, even procuring the raw materials themselves required calculation. The vegetable dyes used on the variegated coverings had to be planted, cultivated, harvested and carefully processed into a usable dye. All these activities were calculated; all were executed with intent to achieve a specific design.

The concepts of *intent* and *design*, as well as the various factors implicit in them, are expressed in several fundamental rules. Since these must be taken into account in virtually every discussion of *melachah*, they will be explained here and the commentary will refer to these definitions.

The requirement of *intent* leads to the following corollary principles:

◆§ מִתְעַסֵּק — An Unwitting Act

When a person does a prohibited act accidentally, since he had no intention of doing a prohibited act, and he did not realize that one might occur as a result of what he intended to do, he is completely free of any responsibility in the matter. [If he did foresee the possibility of such an act occurring, the act is classified as דָּבָר שֶׁאֵינוֹ מִתְכַּוֵּן, *an unintentional act*, see below.] (*Mirkeves HaMishneh, Hil. Shabbos* 1:1). [For example: One set out to cut a vegetable which had already been picked and his hand slipped causing him to cut a vegetable which was still growing (thereby unwittingly transgressing the *melachah* of **reaping*). Since cutting that vegetable was entirely accidental, he is exempt (*Gem.* 72b quoting *Rava*, as explained by *Rashi*).]

This type of act is exempted from liability in most categories of sin [except where the person derives physical pleasure from the unwitting act (*Kerisos* 19b)] and is not derived from מְלֶאכֶת מַחֲשֶׁבֶת. However, certain instances of this exemption are derived from מְלֶאכֶת מַחֲשֶׁבֶת and are therefore unique to the laws of Sabbath, such as if one intends to perform a certain *melachah* and succeeds in doing so but not to the object to which he intended. An example of this would be attempting to pick one vegetable but accidentally picking a different one instead (*Tosafos* 72b; but see *Rashi* there who disputes this ruling).[1]

The particulars of this principle are very involved and the subjects of several disputes. They are not, however, discussed by the mishnah in this tractate (although the *Gemara* does discuss them on 72a,b). Their place is in tractate *Kerisos*.

◆§ דָּבָר שֶׁאֵינוֹ מִתְכַּוֵּן — An Unintentional Act

When a person performs a permissible act and as a result a second, forbidden, act also takes place, this second act is classified as דָּבָר שֶׁאֵינוֹ מִתְכַּוֵּן, *an unintentional act*. In contrast to מִתְעַסֵּק, the *unwitting act* mentioned above, in our case the person was aware that the prohibited act might occur but he did not intend for it to occur.

[For example: A person drags a chair across a lawn in such a manner that he may possibly make a furrow in the lawn (a violation of the *melachah* of *plowing*). Although he is aware that this may occur, he does not intend for it to occur. His sole intent is to move the chair from one place to another.]

This matter is subject to a dispute. R' Yehudah asserts that since the person realized that a prohibition may be violated as a result of his action, he is responsible for that violation should it actually occur. Consequently, he is not permitted to engage in the permissible act because of the possibility that he will violate the prohibition. [I.e., he may not drag the chair because of the possibility that he will perform the *melachah* of *plowing* by making a furrow.]

R' Shimon's opinion, however, is that one is not responsible for a prohibition violated unintentionally. Consequently, as long as one does not intend for the prohibited act to occur, one is permitted to engage in a permissible act even though it may lead to the violation of a prohibition. [I.e., according to R' Shimon one is permitted to drag a chair across a lawn even though it may leave a furrow, as long as he does not intend to make one (*Gem.* 29b; *Beitzah* 2:10, 23b).]

◆§ פְּסִיק רֵישֵׁיהּ — The Inevitable Consequence

There is one important qualification. R' Shimon permits the unintentional act only if the forbidden consequence is a *possible* result, not an *inevitable* one. If the performance of the intended permissible act must *inevitably* result in the violation of a prohibition, even R' Shimon agrees that it is forbidden. This is known as פְּסִיק רֵישֵׁיהּ וְלֹא יָמוּת, *the inevitable consequence* [lit. *can one cut off its (a chicken's) head and it shouldn't die?*].

---

1. According to *R' Akiva Eiger*, there is another difference, too. Although the unwitting performance of a prohibited act in areas other than the Sabbath is also generally exempted from a sin offering, one is nevertheless considered to have sinned unintentionally. One who unwittingly violates a *melachah*, however, is (Biblically) not considered to have sinned at all (although it is Rabbinically prohibited). There are several practical results to this legal distinction which cannot be discussed here. See *Teshuvos R' Akiva Eiger*, vol. I, responsum 8.

With regard to this rule there is yet another qualification. The *Gemara* (ibid.) states that the rule of פְּסִיק רֵישֵׁיהּ, *the inevitable consequence,* applies only when the consequence is נִיחָא לֵיהּ, *beneficial to him,* i.e., the performer benefits from, and is satisfied with, the *inevitable consequence* of his act. If, however, the consequence is לֹא נִיחָא לֵיהּ, i.e., the one performing the act does not benefit from the *inevitable consequence* [either because it is bad for him or because he is indifferent to it (*Rashi* 103a; *Tos.* 75a; but cf. *Rashi* 75a)], he is not liable for it.

According to *Aruch* (quoted by *Tos.* 103a) the act is therefore permissible; according to *Tosafos* it is nevertheless Rabbinically prohibited.

The dispute concerning דָּבָר שֶׁאֵינוֹ מִתְכַּוֵּן, *an unintentional act,* is not restricted to the laws of the Sabbath; it is equally applicable to all Torah transgressions. However, *Tosafos* (4lb) state that even R' Yehudah, who considers the *unintentional act* Biblically prohibited with regard to most prohibitions, agrees that with regard to Sabbath laws it is only Rabbinically prohibited because it does not constitute a מְלֶאכֶת מַחֲשֶׁבֶת, *calculated labor.*

Neither מִתְעַסֵּק, *an unwitting act,* nor דָּבָר שֶׁאֵינוֹ מִתְכַּוֵּן, *an unintentional act,* incurs any liability for a sin offering. In this they differ from שׁוֹגֵג, an *inadvertent transgression,* for which one does incur liability for a sin offering. The reasoning behind this is that in the case of the *unwitting* or *unintentional* act there is no intent to perform the prohibited act. For this reason the Torah does not hold him responsible for what transpires. In the case of the *inadvertent transgression,* however, the person did intend to perform the prohibited act. Although, due to his being ignorant of the prohibition or of the fact that it was the Sabbath, he did so without any intent to transgress, he did nevertheless do exactly what he intended to do. Consequently, he cannot claim a lack of *responsibility* for that act, only a lack of *culpability.* In this the Torah does not consider him completely blameless but assigns to this act a diminished degree of guilt; exempting him from any punishment but still requiring atonement through a sin offering.

The second quality implicit in the concept of a *calculated labor* is *design.* This too gives rise to several corollary principles:

◆§ מְקַלְקֵל — A Destructive Act

Work done in a destructive manner is not considered a *melachah* and one is exempt for it (although it is Rabbinically prohibited). A labor must be geared toward a purposeful design to qualify as a *melachah.* Therefore, in order for one to be liable for a *melachah* it must be performed for a constructive purpose (13:3). In those instances where destruction is a necessary prerequisite for creativity, e.g., *demolishing a structure in order to build a new one in its place, or *erasing writing in order to write something else in its place, the destructive act is also considered a *melachah* since in that context it is part of a purposeful design.

◆§ מְלָאכָה שֶׁאֵינָהּ צְרִיכָה לְגוּפָהּ — A Labor Not Needed [or, Performed] for Its Defined Purpose

As seen in the previous principle, a labor must serve a constructive purpose to qualify as *melachah.* There is a question, though, whether any constructive purpose suffices or whether the Torah considered only certain specific purposes sufficient to qualify a labor as a *melachah.*

This, too, is the subject of a dispute between R' Yehudah and R' Shimon (see 2:5). According to R' Yehudah, a labor done for *any* constructive purpose is considered a *melachah* and one is liable for its performance. According to R' Shimon, however, a labor is only considered a Biblically prohibited *melachah* if it is done to achieve certain *defined purposes*. If it is done for any other reason, it does not violate the Torah prohibition (although it is still Rabbinically prohibited). Accordingly, it is possible for a person to perform a constructive labor and yet be exempt from a sin offering.

In determining the *defined purposes* of various *melachos*, we again return to the linkage of the laws of the Sabbath to the construction of the *Mishkan*. The exact manner by which those laws are linked to the *Mishkan* is a subject of dispute among the *Rishonim*.

A) *Tosafos* (94a) understand this link in a very strict sense. According to them, a labor is only a Biblically prohibited *melachah* when it is done to achieve a purpose similar to that for which it was done in the *Mishkan*. For example, in the construction of the *Mishkan* the boards (which comprised the walls) were transferred from a private domain (the wagons in which they were transported) to a public domain (where the *Mishkan* was erected). The purpose of this act was to transport the boards to the place where they were needed. Consequently, the *defined purpose* of the *melachah* of *transferring from one domain to another* is defined as transferring an object to the domain in which it is needed. One who transfers an object to another domain only to *remove* it from the domain in which it is in is not liable. Although this too may be constructive and even necessary it is not the *defined purpose* of this *melachah*; i.e., it is not the purpose for which this *melachah* was done in the *Mishkan*. For this reason, one who carried a corpse out of a house on the Sabbath to a public domain for burial is, in the opinion of R' Shimon, not liable. This is because one does not need to have the corpse in the cemetery; his purpose in burying it is only to remove it from the premises of the living.

Similarly, the *melachah* of *extinguishing* was done in the construction of the *Mishkan* for the purpose of making charcoal. Consequently, one who extinguishes a flame on the Sabbath in order to conserve fuel is not liable according to R' Shimon, although it is certainly a constructive act (2:5).

The *melachah* of *trapping* was done in the construction of the *Mishkan* for the purpose of using the animals caught for their hides or (in the case of the *chilazon*) for their blood. Consequently, the *melachah* of *trapping* is defined as trapping living creatures to secure their use — either their hides, or their meat, in the case of game animals, or their labor in the case of draft animals such as horses and camels. One who traps a creature in order to prevent its attacking him (e.g., a snake) is not liable because he has not done the *melachah* for its *defined purpose* (14:1).

B) *Rashi* (93b), however, seems to have understood this differently.[1] According to him, the defined purpose of a labor is not necessarily the one for which it was performed in the construction of the *Mishkan*.

---

1. *Aruch HaShulchan* 242:30 states that *Rashi* is in agreement with *Tosafos*. This is, however, not the generally accepted view.

משניות / שבת

It is rather the creative purpose inherent in the labor itself which is considered the *defined purpose* of the *melachah*. A labor performed only in reaction to an undesirable condition — either to prevent it or rectify it — is not an inherently creative purpose and one is therefore not liable for it. To be liable a labor must contribute toward the achievement of a creative or productive goal. This is defined as the inherent purpose of this labor.[1]

According to *Rashi*, the analogy to the *Mishkan* is a looser one; just as in the construction of the *Mishkan* all *melachos* were done to achieve a higher order of design rather than to respond to external difficulties, so too, the *melachos* prohibited on the Sabbath must be to achieve a higher order of design.

Consequently, one who carries boards from the domain they are in to the domain in which they are needed is performing a labor which contributes toward a creative design, namely the erection of a building. One who carries out a corpse, however, is not contributing toward any creative design since he does not need this corpse in the cemetery. He is merely resolving the problem of having a corpse in his house.

Similarly, one who extinguishes a flame to conserve fuel is not involved in a creative process but is rather preventing a loss. The labor therefore is not being done for its [inherently] defined purpose. This is also the case with one who traps a snake to prevent its biting him. Only one who extinguishes a flame to produce charcoal (the only way in which it can be produced) or who traps a snake to use its skin or to extract its venom is engaged in achieving a creative design.

C) *Baal HaMaor* (Ch. 3) has yet a third interpretation of this principle, which is that the labor must be performed to enhance the usefulness of the object to which it is being done. A labor done for the improvement of an object other than the one to which it is done is considered *a labor not needed for its defined purpose*. One who carries out a corpse to remove it from the house or who extinguishes a flame to conserve fuel or who traps a snake to prevent it from biting is not making the subject of that labor more useful to him.

§⊱ שנוי or כְּלְאַחַר יָד — **An Act Performed in an Unusual Manner**

An act of labor must be done in the manner in which it is usually done. If it is done in a manner *significantly* different from the norm it is not Biblically prohibited (although it is Rabbinically prohibited). This is categorized as an act performed in an unusual manner — with a שִׁנּוּי, literally, *change*, or כְּלְאַחַר יָד, literally *with the back of his hand*. [See *Chelkas Mechokeik* to *Even HaEzer* 123:1 that this is derived from the general principle of מְלֶאכֶת מַחֲשֶׁבֶת; see also introduction to *Eglei Tal* subsection 3. Such an act, although meeting all the requirements of purpose and intent, lacks the proper method of design.]

The degree of variance from the usual must be significant, and for this reason it must be determined on a *melachah-by-melachah* basis. A right-handed person *writing with his left hand is considered to be writing in an *unusual manner*

---

1. Similarly, a labor which does not in itself enhance the production of an item, even if it is an unavoidable part of that process, is not an inherently creative labor and does not therefore constitute a Biblically prohibited *melachah*. For this reason, one who digs a hole in order to use the dirt is not liable (*Gem.* 73b). The *melachah* here is making a hole (a *toladah* of *plowing*). The creative purpose of this *melachah* is to make use of the hole. Although making a hole may be an unavoidable part of extracting dirt, it does not in itself enhance the production of dirt, since the person needing the dirt does not necessarily need the hole.

(12:3). But for the same person *transferring an object from domain to domain with his left hand is not considered unusual (10:3). The difference is that writing requires a great deal of dexterity, for which reason right-handed people almost invariably write with their right hand only. Carrying, however, is done almost equally well with both hands and for this reason it is not unusual for even right-handed people to carry things with their left hands (*Chidushei HaRan* to *Gem.* 103a). This is true not only of *transferring, but of almost all *melachos* other than *writing (*Chayei Adam, Hil. Shabbos* 9:2; *Kalkeles HaShabbos* 2:3). The basic criterion for this principle is that deviation from the norm must be sufficiently great to adversely affect the performance of the labor (*Avnei Neizer* 209:9).

The *Gemara* also uses this concept of a *calculated labor* to mean that it must be a labor requiring a minimal degree of proficiency. For this reason, merely stacking gourds or onions into one large pile (the form in which they are stored) is not considered a *melachah* although it is a significant labor relative to the laws of tithes (*Beitzah* 13b).

The *Gemara* also uses this concept to explain why certain labors are considered *melachos* even though one does not directly perform them but harnesses the forces of nature to do them for him. This type of activity, relative to other laws, is considered causative rather than active and does not qualify as action. With regard to the laws of Sabbath, however, it does constitute a *melachah*, as in the case of *winnowing where one tosses the grain in the air to have the wind blow away the chaff while the grain itself falls straight down (*Bava Kamma* 60a). [The *melachah* here is not the tossing but the separating. This is the only instance where the concept of a *calculated labor* makes the person more responsible rather than less.]

III. The Melachah of Transferring

The *melachah* of *transferring from one domain to another* is an unusual *melachah* in the sense that whether the act is forbidden or not is determined not so much by the quality of the act as by where it takes place. Transfer of objects between domains may be either permissible, Rabbinically prohibited or liable for sin offerings, depending on which domains are involved. Since much of this tractate deals with this *melachah* the basic definitions and rules will be given here so as not to necessitate the repetition of the definitions of these ubiquitous terms.

◆§ The Four Domains

The four domains are (A) רְשׁוּת הַיָּחִיד, *private domain*; (B) רְשׁוּת הָרַבִּים, *public domain*; (C) מְקוֹם פְּטוּר, *exempt area*; and (D) כַּרְמְלִית, *karmelis*. [This term, although sometimes translated as a semipublic domain, is a purely legal term which has no simple translation.]

The basic rules determining into which of the four domains a given area falls are:

A) רְשׁוּת הַיָּחִיד, *private domain* — an area at least four טְפָחִים, *handbreadths*, square, and demarcated by walls at least ten handbreadths high. It may be ground level enclosed by a wall of the proper height; a pit ten handbreadths deep; a pit less than ten handbreadths deep but surrounded by a wall that reaches at least ten handbreadths above the floor of the pit; or an elevation whose sides are nearly perpendicular to the ground.

B) רְשׁוּת הָרַבִּים, *public domain* — highways, city streets and squares, and open roads leading to any of the aforementioned. These streets must measure at least sixteen cubits wide,[1] not be roofed, pass through the city entirely and be frequented by many people. Some rule that unless 600,000 people traverse the thoroughfare, it is not judged a public domain (*Shulchan Aruch* 345:7).[2] It must also not be enclosed by walls.

The airspace above a public domain is regarded as a public domain only up to ten handbreadths. Above this, it is regarded as an exempt area (see below).

C) מְקוֹם פְּטוּר, *exempt area* — a place in a public domain whose area is less than four by four handbreadths, and whose height is at least three handbreadths. [If the height is less it is considered the level ground of the public domain.] As in the case of the private domain the height can be either a mound, a ditch or an enclosure.

D) כַּרְמְלִית, *karmelis* — The *karmelis* is an entirely Rabbinic concept. Although sometimes translated as *semipublic domain*, the word *karmelis* is a purely legal term which has no simple translation.[3] Biblically, a *karmelis* is generally an exempt area. Since, however, it in certain respects resembles a private domain and in others a public one, the Rabbis decreed upon it many of the stringencies of both a private and a public domain. This, in order to avoid confusion with true private or public domains.

A *karmelis* is: (1) Any open (unenclosed) land not meeting the specifications of a public domain; (2) a place with an area at least four by four handbreadths, enclosed by walls whose height ranges from three to ten handbreadths, a mound of that height or a ditch of that depth; (3) a sea (see 11:4). The airspace above a *karmelis* is judged as a *karmelis* up to a height of ten handbreadths. Above this height it is an exempt area.

The rules governing *transferring objects between the four domains are:

A) Transfer from a private domain to a public domain or vice versa renders one liable to a sin offering;

---

1. Between twenty-four and thirty-two feet, depending on the various halachic opinions.

2. This is based on the fact that the rules of the domains are derived from the encampment of the Israelites in the desert. It is for this reason that a street meeting all the specifications of a public domain but which is roofed is not deemed a public domain "for it does not resemble the encampment of the desert" (*Gem.* 5a). On this basis, many authorities state that a public domain must also have 600,000 people traversing it. Though in the desert there were considerably more than 600,000 traveling (the number 600,000 refers only to the men between twenty and sixty years of age), since the Torah does not specify how many people there were in total, the number 600,000 is used, that being the only number clearly stated (*Tos., Eruvin* 6a).

3. The etymology of the word *karmelis* is a matter of dispute. *Rashi* (3b ד"ה בעי אביי) maintains that it is adapted from the verse *Isaiah* 10:18) יַעְרוֹ וְכַרְמִלּוֹ, *his forest and great forest*. A forest is neither a public domain (since people do not regularly travel through it) nor a private domain (since it is used privately). This is the model for a *karmelis*.

Tosafos (6a), citing *Yerushalmi* (1:1; see also *Aruch* ע' כרמלית) explain the term to be derived from a combination of two words, רַךְ מַל, *soft* and *crushed*, i.e., grain of medium hardness that is neither hard nor soft (but becomes *soft* when *crushed* between the fingers). Likewise, the *karmelis* is neither a public nor a private domain.

Rambam explains the term as a derivation from כְּאַרְמְלִית, *like a widow*, neither a virgin nor a married woman. Similarly, a *karmelis* is neither a public nor a private domain (commentary 1:1; see also *Rav* 11:1).

B) transfer from a private domain to a *karmelis*, from a public domain to a *karmelis*, or from a *karmelis* to either a private or public domain is Rabbinically prohibited but there is no liability involved;

C) transfer between an exempt area and any other domain is permissible;

D) carrying four cubits (1) in a public domain renders one liable to a sin offering, (2) in a *karmelis* is prohibited but there is no liability, and (3) in a private domain or exempt area is permissible.

৵§ Additional Requirements

There are several Rabbinic requirements to be met before one is actually permitted to carry in a private domain:

A) It must have been enclosed for residential purposes, i.e., to serve as an adjunct to a house or group of houses. Excluded by this rule are enclosed fields, gardens, or corrals which are 70 ⅔ cubits or larger (*Eruvin* 2:3. See *Shulchan Aruch* 358 for the details of this rule).

B) It must be an enclosure belonging to one person. Courtyards common to several homes may not be carried in unless an *eruv chatzeiros* has been made (see below). These and other less common disqualifying factors are the subject of tractate *Eruvin* and will be more fully discussed there. All of them, however, have one common factor; though they are, Biblically speaking, private domains, they are treated Rabbinically with the stringencies of a *karmelis*, i.e., one may not carry a distance of four cubits in them,[1] while they retain the stringencies of a private domain, i.e., one is liable for *transferring* between them and a private domain.

C) Alleys must be enclosed by either three walls or two walls and a side post, with the side post attached to the end of one of the walls and facing the open end (as long as a public domain does not pass through it). This is the opinion of most authorities. *R' Chananel* and *Rambam* (*Hil. Shabbos* 14:1), however, rule that an alley must have at least three walls *plus* a side post to be a private domain. (See *Beur Halachah* beginning of 363 for a full discussion of the various opinions.) According to all opinions, however, one is Rabbinically prohibited from carrying in such an alley unless it has three walls and a side post or crossbar at its open end and the open end does not exceed ten cubits (*Eruvin* 1:1, see *Rav* there).

D) Most halachic authorities rule that the desert was a public domain only during Israel's wanderings there. At any other time, it is a *karmelis*, since it is not frequented by many people (see *Rashi, Tos.* 6b). *Rav* following *Rambam* (14:1), however, rules that deserts are indeed regarded as a public domain in our times. His view is that since during Israel's wanderings the Israelite camps dominated the desert it was not free for all. It was, therefore, not considered a public domain for anyone but the Israelites encamped there. In our times, however, since the desert is free for all to traverse it, it is regarded as a public domain.[2]

---

1. An exception to this rule is an item which was already in the courtyard at the onset of the Sabbath which may be carried anywhere in the courtyard (cf. footnote 11:4).

2. This dispute is based on a difference of interpretation of the *Gemara* 6b which, in regard to its being a public domain or a *karmelis*, differentiates between the desert at the time of Israel's travels through it and the desert today. The *Gemara*, however, does not state which is which.

It is obvious that *Rambam* considers the desert a place frequented by many people (*R' David Arama, Sefer HaLikutim*).

E) If a public domain runs through an enclosure, it remains a public domain unless there are gates where it passes through the walls, which are closed every night (*Rama* 345:7; *Shulchan Aruch* 364:2). The added requirement that the gates be closed every night is not universally held (see second opinion quoted in *Shulchan Aruch*, ibid.). *Mishnah Berurah* 8, however, states that the halachah is in accord with the first opinion.

IV. Eruv

⊷§ עֵירוּב חֲצֵירוֹת — Eruv Chatzeiros

There is a Rabbinic decree that a yard or other enclosed area which is the joint property of more than one dwelling not be considered a private domain unless an *eruv chatzeiros* is made.

A *chatzeir* is a courtyard or other enclosed area common to several dwellings, e.g., the hall of an apartment house. Though it is enclosed by walls and is therefore, strictly speaking, a private domain, it nevertheless resembles a public domain in the sense that its use is not restricted to an individual but is common to several dwellings. Since in the perception of the masses it is more a public domain than a private domain, the Rabbis recognized that permission to carry in what people mistakenly consider to be a public domain might lead them to carry in areas that are truly public domains. The Rabbis therefore prohibited carrying in a common courtyard unless the idea of its being a private domain was reinforced. The mechanism for doing this is the *eruv chatzeiros*, lit. *merging of the courtyards*. This consists of collecting a loaf of bread (or matzah) before the Sabbath from each of the dwellings which open to that yard and placing it in one of those dwellings for the duration of the Sabbath. This then symbolizes that all the contributing residents are actually residing in one dwelling (the place where they left their bread) and the yard is therefore the province of only one dwelling rather than of several. It consequently reverts, in the common perception, to being a private domain rather than a public one (*Rambam, Hil. Eruvin* 1:1-7).

It should be noted that the courtyard must still be enclosed on all four sides by a proper wall or one of the proper substitutes enumerated above or in Chapter 1 of tractate *Eruvin*. What is today colloquially referred to as an *eruv* is still a prerequisite for carrying in the common yard and is indeed a prerequisite for making the *eruv chatzeiros* itself.

⊷§ עֵרוּב תְּחוּמִין — Eruv Techumin

One is Rabbinically prohibited from walking on the Sabbath or *Yom Tov* more than two thousand cubits away from *his place of dwelling*. This distance is known as the תְּחוּם שַׁבָּת, *Sabbath boundary*. The *place of dwelling* is defined as the place in which he found himself at the onset of the Sabbath regardless of whether or not that is his usual dwelling. If that place was: (a) a city,[1] his *place of dwelling* is considered to be the entire city and he may, therefore, walk

---

1. For the definition of what constitutes a city and its limits see *Shulchan Aruch* 398:10,11.

two thousand cubits in any direction from the city limits; (b) a house out in the open[1] or any enclosed encampment,[2] his *place of dwelling* is considered to be the entire area within the walls and he may therefore walk two thousand cubits from the walls of his house or camp; (c) an unenclosed camp or open area in which he happened to be at the onset of the Sabbath, his *place of dwelling* is considered to be a square eight cubits by eight cubits with himself at the center[3] and he may walk two thousand cubits from there.

If one contemplates walking farther he may do so by legally establishing his dwelling at any distance up to two thousand cubits from his present place of dwelling. He must do so before the Sabbath. This is done by placing food at that location on Friday, thereby making that spot his halachic dwelling and allowing him to walk two thousand cubits in any direction from his new dwelling. [Since the prohibition is in the first place only Rabbinic, the Rabbis could decree that the place of his food be considered his dwelling.] However, he may not walk two thousand cubits from where he is now if that will take him out of the two thousand-cubit range of his new dwelling. This food is called עֵרוּב תְּחוּמִין, *eruv techumin* [lit. *merging of boundaries*] (*Rambam, Hil. Eruvin* 6:1).

V. Additional Rabbinical Decrees

◆§ שְׁבִיתָה — Resting

Aside from Rabbinical decrees prohibiting acts which resemble Biblical prohibitions (and which might, therefore, lead to violation of the Biblical prohibitions), the Rabbis enacted other decrees to reinforce the concept of rest on the Sabbath and to enhance the sanctity of the day.

A strict adherence to the laws of *melachah* could still allow a person to work the entire Sabbath as he does everyday, thereby making a mockery of the concept of the Sabbath as a day of rest and sanctity. There is, for example, no Biblical prohibition against loading goods and hauling them to market if this is done entirely inside a private domain, e.g., a walled city. There is no Biblical prohibition against weighing, measuring and packaging; buying and selling; paying and receiving money; engaging workers to perform tasks which are not *melachos* — in short, many of the major activities of commerce are Biblically permissible. [It is even arguable that this would result in an increase in commercial activity since people, prohibited from many other activities, would find the Sabbath a convenient time to shop.]

To prevent this, the Rabbis enacted numerous decrees, the sum total of which serve to insure that the Sabbath be observed as the unique and holy day it is. Therefore, while the individual enactments are certainly only Rabbinic they are, as a body, the fulfillment of the Biblical commandment of "rest" (*Ramban, Lev.* 23:24, *Rambam, Hil. Shabbos* 21:1, see *Maggid Mishneh*).

Included in this are such prohibitions as מוּקְצֶה, *muktzeh* (items set aside from use; see prefatory note to Chapter 17); מִמְצוֹא חֶפְצְךָ וְדַבֵּר דָּבָר, *seeking your*

---

1. A house more than 70 ⅔ cubits removed from any other house is considered to be out in the open (*ibid.* 398:5,6).

2. I.e., by walls ten handbreadths high or deep (*ibid.* 297:2).

3. *Rama* 396:1, *Mishnah Berurah* there: §9.

wants and discussing the forbidden (discussed in Chapter 23); and עוּבְדָא דְחוֹל, *weekday activity.*

עוּבְדָא דְחוֹל — Weekday Activity

In addition to those Rabbinic prohibitions which form the safeguards to the law, the Rabbis prohibited any activity classified as עוּבְדָא דְחוֹל, *weekday activity.* Obviously, this prohibition does not ban every activity which one engages in during the week. The rule refers only to those activities which fall into one of three categories.[1]

A) *Activities resembling a melachah.* Activities which are similar to a *melachah* but fail to qualify as one for some technical reason, e.g., מְלָאכָה שֶׁאֵינָהּ צְרִיכָה לְגוּפָהּ, *a labor not done for its defined purpose*, and a labor performed כִּלְאַחַר יָד, *in an unusual manner*, are included in the general safeguards to the law since they are easily mistaken for Biblically prohibited acts. This new category prohibits activities which only faintly resemble *melachos* and whose prohibition is only because they are reminiscent of a *melachah*.

An example of this is the prohibition of suspending a strainer which, according to most opinions, is prohibited because of making a temporary tent (see 20:1). Although suspending a strainer is not really akin to erecting a tent, and is unlikely to be mistaken for it, it was banned because it is reminiscent of making a tent and is therefore a *weekday activity* (*Gem.* 138a; see *Meiri* and *Chidushei HaRan* there).

B) *Activities which may lead to a melachah.* Although these activities do not in themselves resemble a *melachah*, they are part of a process leading up to a *melachah*. The Rabbis therefore prohibited them out of concern that a person engaging in a weekday routine would forget that it was the Sabbath and conclude the process by doing the *melachah*.

An example of this category is the prohibition against moving a dovecote ladder from one dovecote to another because this is a weekday activity and might lead one to trap the doves (*Rambam, Hil. Shabbos* 26:7).

An additional example is the prohibition against regathering into a basket fruit that had been scattered about in a yard. This activity could possibly lead one to press the fruit together in violation of the *melachah* of מְעַמֵּר, **gathering* (*Gem.* 143b; *Rambam, Hil. Shabbos* 21:11; but cf. *Maggid Mishneh* there).

C) *Activities which detract from the aura of the Sabbath*, either because they involve unnecessary or excessive טִירְחָא, *strain*, or because they make the Sabbath day appear like an ordinary day.

An example of this is the prohibition against a vigorous massage (22:1), or clearing out a storehouse (18:1, according to explanation of Rav Chisda, the halachically accepted reason). This category is the most prevalent not only in this tractate but throughout *Beitzah*, as well.

Many of the activities prohibited as *weekday activities* contain elements of more than one category. For this reason the commentators will occasionally give differing reasons for their being considered weekday activities. Since the practical differences between these categories are slight, the commentary will generally restrict itself to stating that an act is a *weekday activity* without discussing the reasons why.

---

1. See *Kalkalas HaShabbos.* Cf. *Igros Moshe, Orach Chaim* vol. 4 §74 טוֹחֵן 4.

פרק ראשון
Chapter One

שבת
א/א

[א] יְצִיאוֹת הַשַּׁבָּת שְׁתַּיִם שֶׁהֵן אַרְבַּע בִּפְנִים,

---
ר' עובדיה מברטנורא

פרק ראשון – יציאות השבת. (א) יציאות השבת. הוצאות שמרשות לרשות האמורות אגב שבת, והכנסות נמי קא קרי יציאות הואיל ומוציא מרשות לרשות. והאי דתני יציאות ולא תני הוצאות, לישנא דקרא נקט ללקוט המן: שתים שהן ארבע. שתים מן התורה, הוצאה והכנסה לבעל הבית העומד בפנים ברשות היחיד, ועל שתים אלו חייב על שגגתו חטאת, ועל זדונו כרת, ועל התראתו סקילה.

יד אברהם

1.

◆§ The Melachah of *Transferring from Domain to Domain

The first mishnah of this chapter deals with the *melachah* of removing an object from its place and transferring it to another location. This *melachah* is commonly called הוֹצָאָה, literally, *taking out*, and will be referred to below as *transferring.[1]

Not every transfer of an object from place to place is considered a forbidden labor. The Scriptural injunction only applies to: (a) transferring from a public domain to a private domain, or vice versa [these domains are defined in the General Introduction, p. 12]; and (b) transferring an object over a distance of

---

1. Since *transferring appears last on the list of the thirty-nine *melachos* as enumerated in 7:2, it is curious that the *Tanna* begins our tractate with laws pertaining to this final category of work instead of taking one of the more obvious courses of dealing with the categories either in order of the *melachos* as listed in 7:2 or commencing with the laws pertaining to the eve of the Sabbath, as we shall see in 1:3.

Several reasons have been given for this order:

❑ *Transferring of objects from place to place is so common that it is done more frequently than any of the other types of melachos (Tos. 2a quoting *Rabbeinu Tam*).

❑ *Rambam* gives the above reason and adds that since it is accomplished easily and requires no special implements, people are more apt to inadvertently violate it than other types of Sabbath work. Hence the *Tanna* felt the need to stress that this *melachah* is as serious an offense as any other.

❑ Another reason for the need to stress that the transfer from domain to domain has the status of a *melachah* is that at first glance this activity seems too trivial to be forbidden. People would reason that there should be no difference between carrying an object from room to room — which is permitted — to carrying from the house into the street which is forbidden. [It is for this reason that the commentators call it מְלָאכָה גְרוּעָה, an *inferior labor*.] Therefore, the *Tanna* discusses this *melachah* first (*Rambam; Tos.*).

❑ Essentially, the *Tanna's* plan is to commence with the laws pertinent to Sabbath eve, as can be seen from 1:3 which prohibits a tailor to carry his needle close to nightfall lest he forget and continue carrying it on the Sabbath. Thus, in order to provide the necessary background information for that law, the *Tanna* found it necessary to begin with the laws pertaining to *transferring (Tos. Yom Tov).

❑ See also last paragraph of commentary on the first mishnah for another interpretation of the *Tanna's* intention.

1. The [types of] transfers on the Sabbath are two which are [in reality] four within, and two

YAD AVRAHAM

four *amos*[1] within a public domain. [Transfer between a public or private domain and a *karmelis* is only Rabbinically prohibited; transfer between these areas and an exempt area is permissible. See General Introduction, p. 13.]

Every act of **transferring* contains three elements: (a) עֲקִירָה [*akirah*], lit. *uprooting*; i.e., removing an object from its present location; and (b) הֲנָחָה [*hanachah*], *placing*; i.e., setting down the object in its new place; and (c) שִׁינּוּי רְשׁוּת, *change of domain*. As regards a public domain, both the *akirah* and the *hanachah* of the object must be from and to a place measuring at least four handbreadths by four handbreadths. As regards a private domain, only the *akirah* must be from a place of those dimensions (*Gem.* 7b, 8a; cf. *Rashi* 7a; *Maggid Mishneh, Hil. Shabbos* 14:17).

As in the case of all Sabbath labor, one is liable only if he performed the entire act himself; if two people share in an act that, by its nature, should be performed by one person, neither is liable — although the act is forbidden by Rabbinic law. Therefore, if one person effects the *akirah* and another effects the *hanachah*, the labor is considered as being performed by two people, and both are exempt from penalty. In the following mishnah, we will discuss which one is guilty of the Rabbinic infraction.

יְצִיאוֹת הַשַּׁבָּת — *The [types of] transfers on the Sabbath*

This refers to the methods of transgressing the *melachah* of **transferring articles from domain to domain*, which are forbidden on the Sabbath. The expression יְצִיאוֹת, literally *goings out*, is used — rather than the more grammatically accurate and more common form, הוֹצָאוֹת, *takings out* — in keeping with the Biblical passage, אַל יֵצֵא אִישׁ מִמְּקֹמוֹ בַּיּוֹם הַשְּׁבִיעִי, *Let no man go out of his place on the seventh day* (*Exodus* 16:29), which the Rabbis interpret to mean that no one was permitted to go out of the tribal encampments in the wilderness while carrying a vessel to gather manna (*Rav; Tos.* 2a).

שְׁתַּיִם — *are two*

I.e., two types of transfer from domain to domain are prohibited by the Torah to the person standing within the private domain. These are punishable by *stoning*, if committed in the presence of witnesses after having been warned; or by *kares*, if committed intentionally without prior warning or not in the presence of witnesses. If committed inadvertently, they require the sacrifice of a sin offering (*Rav*; see also General Introduction, p. 6).

These two means of transfer are:

(a) הוֹצָאָה, *hotza'ah*, carrying *out* from a private domain to a public domain; and

(b) הַכְנָסָה, *hachnassah*, carrying *in* from a public domain to a private domain. In both these instances the person in the private domain performs both the removal and the setting down.

שֶׁהֵן אַרְבַּע — *which are [in reality] four*

In addition to the two Scripturally prohibited modes mentioned above, there are two modes of transfer which, although permitted by the Torah, are prohibited by the Rabbis. Thus there are a total of four — two forbidden by the Torah and two more forbidden

---

1. Halachic opinions regarding the length of an *amah* [plural, *amos*] range between eighteen and twenty-four inches.

שבת א/א

וּשְׁתַּיִם שֶׁהֵן אַרְבַּע בַּחוּץ. כֵּיצַד? הֶעָנִי עוֹמֵד בַּחוּץ וּבַעַל הַבַּיִת בִּפְנִים: פָּשַׁט הֶעָנִי אֶת יָדוֹ לִפְנִים וְנָתַן לְתוֹךְ יָדוֹ שֶׁל בַּעַל הַבַּיִת, אוֹ שֶׁנָּטַל מִתּוֹכָהּ וְהוֹצִיא — הֶעָנִי חַיָּב

ר' עובדיה מברטנורא

כמו בכל שאר מלאכות של שבת: **שהן ארבע.** מדבריהם הוסיפו שתים, לאסור להתחלה היכא שהתחלת המלאכה נעשית על ידי שנים, זה עוקר וזה מניח, דשנים שעשאוה פטורים, שנאמר (ויקרא ד) בעשותה אחת מכל מצות ה', העושה את כולה ולא העושה מקצתה, וכן בכל מלאכות של שבת אמרינן יחיד שעשאה חייב, שנים שעשאוה פטורים: **ושתים שהן ארבע בחוץ.** שתים מן התורה, הוצאה והכנסה לעני העומד בחוץ ברשות הרבים: **שהן ארבע.** מדבריהם הוסיפו שתים לאסור להתחלה, כשזה עוקר וזה מניח: **פשט העני את ידו.** ובתוכה קופה או הסל שמקבל בו ככרות מבעל הבית. ולהכי נקט הולאה בלשון עני ועשיר, דאגב אורחיה קא משמע לן דמלוה הבאה בעבירה אסורה וחייבין עליה: **ונתן לתוך ידו של בעל הבית.** דעביד ליה עקירה מרשות הרבים והנחה ברשות היחיד: **או שנטל מתוכה והוציא.** החפץ, והניח ברשות הרבים, דעביד עקירה והנחה: **העני חייב.** שעשה מלאכה שלימה. והרי שתים מן התורה לעומד בחוץ. ואף על גב דבעינן עקירה ממקום שיהיה בו ארבעה טפחים על ארבעה טפחים והנחה במקום שיהיה בו ארבעה על ארבעה, וליכא, יד הטני ובעל הבית אין בה מקום שיהיה ארבעה על ארבעה, אמרינן בגמרא ידו של אדם חשובה כארבעה על ארבעה, כיון שהיא עשויה להניח בה וליטול ממנה חפצים ואפילו גדולים הרבה:

יד אברהם

forbidden by Rabbinic enactment, viz., when the one standing in the public domain performs only the removal or only the placing (*Rav; Rashi*).

Apparently the acts committed by the person in the public domain parallel the acts committed by the one in the private domain. Why, then, does the *Tanna*, seemingly, repeat these laws concerning the person standing in the public domain?

Tosafos, quoting *Rabbeinu Tam*, answers that since transferring is considered an "inferior labor," as mentioned in the footnote above, and does not necessarily conform to our notions as to what should constitute forbidden labor, we could not, on our own, infer the laws pertaining to the person in the public domain from the laws pertaining to the one in the private domain, and it is, therefore, necessary for by the Rabbis.

The latter two are instances in which a person standing in a private domain does either the removal or the setting down, but not both.

בִּפְנִים, — *within,*

I.e., for the person standing in a private domain (*Rav; Rashi*).

[This will be explained at length further on in the mishnah.]

וּשְׁתַּיִם שֶׁהֵן אַרְבַּע בַּחוּץ. — *and two which are [in reality] four outside.*

I.e., two methods of transfer by the person standing in the public domain are Scripturally forbidden: (a) carrying *out [hotza'ah]*, and (b) carrying *in [hachnassah]*. These two are forbidden because the one standing in the public domain effects both, the removing and the setting down.

In addition to these there are two more methods of transfer which are

1 which are [in reality] four outside.
1 How is this so? The poor man is standing outside and the householder inside: If the poor man extended his hand inside and placed [an object] into the householder's hand, or if he took [an object] from it and brought [that object] out — the poor man is liable

YAD AVRAHAM

the *Tanna* to state them clearly.

(A more elaborate explanation by the *Shenos Eliyahu* follows below in the footnotes to this mishnah.)

כֵּיצַד? הֶעָנִי עוֹמֵד בַּחוּץ וּבַעַל הַבַּיִת בִּפְנִים — *How is this so? The poor man is standing outside and the householder inside:*

The mishnah speaks in terms of a poor man and a householder to teach us that although it is a mitzvah to give charity, this mitzvah does not have priority over the obligation to observe the Sabbath. If one violates the Sabbath by giving charity, his act is in the category of מִצְוָה הַבָּאָה בַּעֲבֵרָה, *a mitzvah that is performed by means of a transgression*, an act for which the transgressor is liable (*Rav*).

A second explanation: The *Tanna* uses the example of a householder and a poor man for the sake of brevity, so that it should not be necessary to repeat "the person in the private domain" and the person standing in the public domain." The former is referred to as the householder and the latter as the poor man (*Rambam*).

פָּשַׁט הֶעָנִי אֶת יָדוֹ לִפְנִים — *If the poor man extended his hand inside*

I.e., the poor man extended his hand, in which he held an object, to where the householder was standing (*Rav*).

וְנָתַן לְתוֹךְ יָדוֹ שֶׁל בַּעַל הַבַּיִת, — *and placed [an object] into the householder's hand,*

By doing this, the poor man performs the entire act of transferring an object from a public domain to a private one. First he picks it up in the public domain — removal — and then, he places it in the householder's hand which is in the private domain — setting down. He is now liable to the penalties of one who commits a forbidden Sabbath labor (*Rav*).

אוֹ שֶׁנָּטַל מִתּוֹכָהּ — *or if he took [an object] from it*

I.e., if the poor man removed an object from the householder's hand [rather than having it placed in his hand] (*Rav*).

וְהוֹצִיא — *and brought [that object] out —*

I.e., he transferred it from the private domain to the public domain, thereby performing both the removal and the setting down of the article (*Rav*).

הֶעָנִי חַיָּב — *the poor man is liable*

Thus, there are two cases in which the poor man standing outside is liable; one in which he commits the entire act of carrying *in*, i.e., transferring an object from a public domain to a private domain, and one in which he commits the entire act of carrying *out*, i.e., transferring an object from a private domain to a public domain (*Rav and Rashi*).

In keeping with the sequence of the outset of the mishnah, the *Tanna* ought first to have explained the "two that are four" of the householder. However, the *Tanna* of-

שבת
א/א

וּבַעַל הַבַּיִת פָּטוּר;
פָּשַׁט בַּעַל הַבַּיִת אֶת יָדוֹ לַחוּץ וְנָתַן לְתוֹךְ יָדוֹ שֶׁל עָנִי, אוֹ שֶׁנָּטַל מִתּוֹכָהּ וְהִכְנִיס — בַּעַל הַבַּיִת חַיָּב וְהֶעָנִי פָּטוּר;

ר' עובדיה מברטנורא

ובעל הבית פטור. פטור ומותר גמור, דהא לאו מידי עבד: **פשט בעל הבית וכו' בעל הבית חייב.** הרי שתים מן התורה לעומד בפנים:

יד אברהם

ten begins his explanation of a series with the last thing mentioned. Here, too, the *Tanna* last mentioned the poor man on the outside. Thus, he proceeds to enumerate the acts committed by the poor man (*Tos. Yom Tov* from *Ran*).

Although one is not liable for transferring an object from one domain to another, unless the removal is from a place measuring at least four handbreadths by four handbreadths and the dimensions of both the poor man's and the householder's hands are obviously not four by four, he is, nevertheless, liable. The reason for this is that since a person's hand can hold large objects it is considered as if it measures four by four handbreadths (*Rav* from *Gem.* 5a).

וּבַעַל הַבַּיִת פָּטוּר; — *and the householder is exempt;*

Since the householder was entirely passive, having performed neither the removal nor the setting down, he has not violated even a Rabbinic prohibition (*Rav* and *Rashi* 3a).

It would seem from the statement above that the householder is completely innocent of any wrongdoing.

This raises a question. The Torah admonishes us, *Do not place an obstacle before a blind man* (*Lev.* 19:14). This is interpreted halachically as: Do nothing to make it possible for one who is blinded by ignorance or temptation to transgress the laws of the Torah (*Pesachim* 22b; see *Rambam*, *Sh'viis* 5:6). Since, in this instance, the householder is aiding the poor man in his act of desecrating the Sabbath by allowing his hand to be used for doing a prohibited labor, he should not be considered completely innocent.

The *Ran* and *Tosafos Yeshanim* answer that when the mishnah states that the householder is completely exempt, it refers only insofar as the laws of the Sabbath are concerned. It *is* true, however, that the householder has violated the negative commandment of "not placing an obstacle before a blind man" (cited in *Tos. Yom Tov*).

Tosefos R' Akiva adds that there is a significant difference whether the deed is considered a Sabbath transgression or a violation of a negative commandment unrelated to the Sabbath. A habitual transgressor of the Sabbath laws is considered an apostate and his ritual slaughter of animals is invalid. According to some authorities this applies even to one who is a habitual transgressor of Rabbinic laws concerning the Sabbath. This disqualification, however, does not apply to a transgressor of a law unrelated to the Sabbath.

פָּשַׁט בַּעַל הַבַּיִת אֶת יָדוֹ לַחוּץ — *if the householder extended his hand outside*

This is the illustration of the two cases of transferring in which the one standing in the private domain is liable (*Rav*; *Rashi*).

וְנָתַן לְתוֹךְ יָדוֹ שֶׁל עָנִי, — *and placed [an object] into the poor man's hand,*

Thus effecting the removal and the

and the householder is exempt;

if the householder extended his hand outside and placed [an object] into the poor man's hand, or if he took [an object] out of it and brought [that object] in — the householder is liable and the poor man is exempt;

YAD AVRAHAM

setting down from a private domain to a public one while performing both the removal and the setting down (*Tif. Yis.*).

אוֹ שֶׁנָּטַל מִתּוֹכָהּ וְהִכְנִיס — *or if he took [an object] out of it and brought [that object] in —*

I.e., into the private domain, thus effecting a carrying in while performing both the removal and the setting down (*Tif. Yis.*).

בַּעַל הַבַּיִת חַיָּב — *the householder is liable*

Since he performed the entire transfer he is liable to any of the aforementioned penalties prescribed for violation of the laws of the Sabbath (*Tif. Yis.*).

Thus, we have two cases of transfer from one domain to another in which the one standing inside is liable, viz., one case of carrying *out* in which the householder performs both the removal from the private domain and the setting down in the public domain, and one case of carrying *in*, in which he makes the removal in the public domain and the setting down in the private domain (*Rav*).

There is an apparent inconsistency in the mishnah. When the person extends his hand into the domain other than the one in which he is standing, he must place the object either in another's hand or on an area four by four handbreadths, to be liable. However, when he brings the object *into* the domain in which he is standing he need not place the object anywhere to be liable. Just having it in his hand is sufficient. This difference is based on the principle that the hand has the same properties as an area of four by four. This rule holds true only when the hand can be considered subordinate to the rest of the body; only then does the hand acquire the stature of a significant area. However, when the hand is extended beyond the domain of the body, the object cannot be considered at rest (set down) until it is placed either in another's hand or an area which is *actually* four by four.

As a result there is a significant difference between the acts of transfer by the poor man and by the householder. The poor man takes out the object and just holds it in his hand and is immediately liable. The householder, however, must take the object out and first place it into another's hand or an area of four by four before he can become liable.[1]

וְהֶעָנִי פָּטוּר; — *and the poor man is exempt;*

Since he was passive, neither removing the object nor setting it down, he is exempt completely from any violation of the laws of the Sabbath, including

---

1. It is now obvious why we could not infer the laws of the householder from the laws of the poor man as was previously asked by *Tosafos* quoting *Rabbeinu Tam* for the circumstances are not identical.

A difficulty still persists, however: Why not derive the laws of carrying *in* as related to the poor man — where the hand is extended to a domain away from the body — from

שבת א/א

פָּשַׁט הֶעָנִי אֶת יָדוֹ לִפְנִים וְנָטַל בַּעַל הַבַּיִת מִתּוֹכָהּ, אוֹ שֶׁנָּתַן לְתוֹכָהּ וְהוֹצִיא – שְׁנֵיהֶם פְּטוּרִין.
פָּשַׁט בַּעַל הַבַּיִת אֶת יָדוֹ לַחוּץ וְנָטַל הֶעָנִי מִתּוֹכָהּ, אוֹ שֶׁנָּתַן לְתוֹכָהּ וְהִכְנִיס – שְׁנֵיהֶם פְּטוּרִין.

ר' עובדיה מברטנורא

פשט העני וכו'. דעביד העני עקירה מרשות הרבים: **ונטל בעל הבית מתוכה.** והניח בפנים, ועביד ליה בעל הבית הנחה ברשות היחיד: **או שנתן לתוכה.** דעביד ליה בעל הבית עקירה מרשות היחיד: **והוציא.** העני והניח ברשות הרבים: **שניהם פטורים.** שלא עשה שום אחד מהם מלאכה שלימה, אבל אסורים לעשות כן, שמא יבואו כל אחד בפני עצמו לעשות מלאכה שלימה בשבת. הרי שתים מדבריהם, אחת לעני בחוץ ואחת לבעל הבית בפנים. והא דלא חשיב שנים לכל אחד, עקירה לעני ועקירה לבעל הבית, הנחה לעני והנחה לבעל הבית, משום דלא חשיב אלא עקירות שהן תחלת המלאכה ואיכא למיחש למיתי לגמרינהו, אבל הנחות שהן סוף המלאכה לא קתשיב:

יד אברהם

Rabbinic injunctions (Gem. 3a). [See comm. above s.v., וּבַעַל הַבַּיִת פָּטוּר.]

The *Tanna* now proceeds with his explanation of the term: "which are, in reality, four," i.e., the additional two Rabbinic prohibitions for each, the householder and the poor man.

In the following illustrations of the mishnah no one person commits the entire transfer. Rather, it is completed by the combined acts of two people. One removes the object and the other sets it down. It is this factor that reduces the act from a Scriptural transgression to a Rabbinic one (*Tif. Yis.*).

פָּשַׁט הֶעָנִי אֶת יָדוֹ לִפְנִים — *if the poor man extended his hand inside* —

Thereby effecting a removal from the public domain (*Rav*).

וְנָטַל בַּעַל הַבַּיִת מִתּוֹכָהּ, — *and the householder took [an object] from it,*

In this case, the poor man did only the removal and the householder did only the setting down (*Rav; Rashi; Tif. Yis.*).

אוֹ שֶׁנָּתַן לְתוֹכָהּ — *or placed [an object] into it*

The householder placed an object into the poor man's hand, i.e., he removed the object from its place (*Rav; Rashi*).

וְהוֹצִיא — *and he [the poor man] brought [that object] out* —

the laws of carrying *out* as related to the householder — where the hand is also extended away from the domain of the body?

Similarly, why not derive the laws of carrying *in* of the householder — where the hand is in the same domain as the body — from the laws of carrying *out* as related to the poor man — whose hand is also together with his body?

These were the questions that *Rabbeinu Tam* (see above, s.v., וּשְׁתַּיִם שֶׁהֵן אַרְבַּע בַּחוּץ) meant to answer when he said that *transferring is an "inferior labor," and no inferences can be made (Shenos Eliyahu).

1
1

if the poor man extended his hand inside and the householder took [an object] from it, or placed [an object] into it and he [the poor man] brought [that object] out — both are exempt;

if the householder extended his hand outside and the poor man took [an object] from it, or placed [an object] into it and he [the householder] brought [that object] in — both are exempt.

YAD AVRAHAM

I.e., he set the object down in the public domain (*Rav; Rashi*).

שְׁנֵיהֶם פְּטוּרִין — *both are exempt;*
Since neither the poor man nor the householder performed the entire transfer (*Rashi; Rav; Tif. Yis.*).

פָּשַׁט בַּעַל הַבַּיִת אֶת יָדוֹ לַחוּץ וְנָטַל הֶעָנִי מִתּוֹכָהּ, — *if the householder extended his hand outside and the poor man took [an object] from it,*
[Thus the householder removed the object from the private domain, and the poor man set it down in the public domain.]

אוֹ שֶׁנָּתַן לְתוֹכָהּ וְהִכְנִיס — *or placed [an object] into it and he [the householder] brought [that object] in —*
[I.e., the poor man placed an object in the householder's hand, and the householder transferred the object into his private domain. Thus the poor man effected the removal from the public domain, and the householder effected the setting down in the private domain.]

שְׁנֵיהֶם פְּטוּרִין — *both are exempt.*
Since the transfer was effected by two people, neither one having done both the removal and the setting down, they are both exempt from the Scriptural penalties.

Both are exempt would seem to imply that the householder and the poor man are equally exempt.

However, we know that these four illustrations include only two Rabbinic transgressions for the poor man and two for the householder. But since the statement "both are exempt" means that both are equally transgressing a Rabbinic decree, we should have a total of four for the poor man and four for the householder!

We are, therefore, forced to conclude that two of the above for each, the householder and the poor man, are less significant acts, even though they qualify as Rabbinic transgressions, and the *Tanna* therefore chose not to count them.

Which are the two?

We encounter a difference of opinion concerning this question. Some hold that of the three elements of transfer — removal, setting down and changing of the domain — changing of the domain is the primary one and where the transfer is performed by two people, the one causing the changing of the domain, regardless of whether he removes the object or sets it down, is considered the more serious Sabbath transgressor. Thus, only his violation of the Rabbinic injunction is counted by the *Tanna* (*Tos. Yom Tov* from *Tos.* 3a; *Tif. Yis.*).

Others are of the opinion that the *Tanna's* count is directed only at the *initiator* of the transfer — the one who does the removal — for he is more apt to complete the entire *melachah* and thereby come to commit a Scriptural transgression (*Rav; Rashi*).

The wealth of information transmitted in this mishnah is matched by

שבת א/ב

[ב] **לֹא יֵשֵׁב** אָדָם לִפְנֵי הַסַּפָּר סָמוּךְ לַמִּנְחָה, עַד שֶׁיִּתְפַּלֵּל —

ר' עובדיה מברטנורא

(ב) **לא ישב אדם לפני הספר.** ואפילו בחול. ומשום דבעי למתני לא יצא החייט במחטו וכו' שמא ישכח ויצא, דדמי לגזרה דלא ישב אדם לפני הספר סמוך למנחה שמא ישכח ולא יתפלל, משום הכי תנא להו הכא, ואיידי דזוטרן מילייהו פסיק ותני להו ברישא, והדר מפרש מילי דשבת ומאריך בהן: **סמוך למנחה.** מנחה גדולה, משש שעות ומחצה ולמעלה, וסמוך למנחה היינו מתחלת שעה שביעית. ואף על פי שעונתה מרובה, גזרה שמא ישב אצל הזוג של ספרים אחר שהתחיל להסתפר, ותעבור עונת התפלה קודם שיתקננו וישלים התספורת:

יד אברהם

few mishnayos in this tractate. We have learned of carrying *out* [הוֹצָאָה, *hotza'ah*] and carrying *in* [הַכְנָסָה, *hachnassah*] of both the poor man and the householder; the concepts of removal [עֲקִירָה, *akirah*] and setting down [הֲנָחָה, *hanachah*]; the laws concerning two who do one *melachah*; the laws of the hand as being the equivalent of an area four handbreadths square; as well as other laws. Some offer this as yet another reason (see footnote to prefatory remarks) why the *Tanna*, being anxious to impart all this knowledge, decided to commence this tractate with this mishnah (*Riva* quoted by *Tos.* 2a).

2.

In anticipation of mishnah 3, which prohibits certain acts even before the Sabbath, lest they be continued into the Sabbath, the Tanna lists here a number of activities one may not engage in on any day of the week shortly before the time of *Minchah*, lest he forget to pray.[1] Since these laws are very few in comparison to the laws of the Sabbath, he wishes to finish these first, and then to dwell on the laws of the Sabbath (*Rav*).

Alternatively, the Tanna wishes to teach us that even if someone wishes to cut his hair or bathe in honor of the Sabbath, and if he waits to recite the *Minchah* prayer first, he will be delayed in doing so, he may, nevertheless, not commence his haircut or his bath shortly before the time of *Minchah* (*Tif. Yis.*).

לֹא יֵשֵׁב אָדָם לִפְנֵי הַסַּפָּר סָמוּךְ לַמִּנְחָה, עַד שֶׁיִּתְפַּלֵּל — *A person may not sit down before a barber shortly before [the time of] Minchah until he prays* —

In *Berachos* 4:1, it is explained that one may recite the *Minchah* prayer at the earliest, one half-hour after midday, and at the latest, until sunset,[2] or, according to some authorities, until the stars come out. This period is called מִנְחָה גְדוֹלָה [*Minchah gedolah*], *the greater Minchah*, i.e., the longer period in which the prayer may be recited, as opposed to מִנְחָה קְטַנָּה [*Minchah ketannah*], *the lesser*

---

1. This organization by association is a common Mishnaitic mnemonic device, evidence of the time when the entire Mishnah had to be memorized.
2. In regard to laws determined by sunset, there is a dispute among the authorities as to the precise halachic definition of that term.

2. A person may not sit down before a barber shortly before [the time of] *Minchah*, until he prays

YAD AVRAHAM

Minchah, the period commencing from nine and one-half hours[1] after sunrise, and continuing until sunset.

These two periods are derived from the times of the daily afternoon offering, which was called the *Minchah* [lit. gift or offering] as in *II Kings* (16:15), *the morning burnt offering and* מִנְחַת הָעֶרֶב, *the afternoon offering*, and in *Psalms* 141:2. By association, the time period in which the afternoon sacrifice was offered also acquired the name *Minchah*, as did the afternoon prayer. [See ArtScroll *comm.* to *Daniel* 9:21 for reasons why the afternoon offering and prayer are specifically called *Minchah*.] According to the Torah law, the afternoon sacrifice could be slaughtered as early as one half-hour after midday and immediately offered up on the Altar. Indeed, this was the procedure when Passover fell on the Sabbath. Since the Passover sacrifice had to be slaughtered and roasted before evening, the daily sacrifice was therefore slaughtered at the earliest possible time, and the Passover sacrifice slaughtered after the daily service. (See *Pesachim* 5:1.) This period is known as the *Minchah gedolah* or the greater *Minchah*.

The usual procedure was, however, not to slaughter the afternoon sacrifice until eight and one-half hours after daybreak, and to offer it up on the Altar at nine and one-half hours. This delay was made to allow time for the sacrifice of vow offerings and gift offerings, which could be brought only *before* the daily afternoon sacrifice. The period, starting nine and one-half hours after daybreak, is known as *Minchah ketannah* or lesser *Minchah*.

A different derivation of the term *Minchah* is given by *Ramban* (*Exodus* 12:6). The name *Minchah* is not connected to the sacrifice, but refers to the gradual setting of the sun beginning at noon. The term *Minchah* is thus derived from נחה, *to rest*.

The *Gemara* concludes that the *Minchah* meant here is the greater *Minchah*. Even though the greater *Minchah* extends through the entire afternoon, which may be as long as eight hours during the summer, one may, nevertheless, not sit down before a barber a half-hour before the greater *Minchah*, i.e., from noon on, without having first recited the *Minchah* prayers. The Rabbis took this precaution lest the scissors break during the haircut, and the entire period of *Minchah* elapse before it is repaired, leaving him no time to recite the *Minchah* prayers (*Rav; Rif; Rambam* from *Gem.* 9b).

Others explain that, in the final ruling, the *Gemara* means to explain the mishnah as referring to the lesser *Minchah* (*Baal HaMaor, Hagahos Mordechai*). Consequently, the period when one may not sit down before the barber, or enter into any of the other activities listed here, begins one half-hour before the lesser *Minchah*, i.e., nine hours after daybreak.

The Rabbis did not prohibit these activities during the half-hour preceding the time of *Shacharis*. Since it is

---

1. The hours referred to here are *shaos zemaniyos*, or prorated hours, a system in which the daytime is divided into 12 equal units (hours) regardless of the actual length of daylight. In practice, therefore, this actually means nine twelfths, or three fourths, of the daytime. According to some authorities, these twelve units are reckoned from sunrise to sunset (*Gra*), and according to others (*Magen Avraham*), from dawn to the coming out of the stars.

שבת א/ב

לֹא יִכָּנֵס אָדָם לְמֶרְחָץ, וְלֹא לְבֻרְסְקִי, וְלֹא לֶאֱכֹל, וְלֹא לָדִין – וְאִם הִתְחִילוּ, אֵין מַפְסִיקִים.

ר' עובדיה מברטנורא

ולא יכנס למרחץ. סמוך למנחה שמא יתעלף: **ולא לבורסקי.** מקום עבוד העורות, דלמא חזי פסידא וקלקול בעורות אם לא יניעם ממקומס ויתקנס, וימשך במלאכתו עד שתעבור עונת התפלה: **ולא לאכול.** אפילו בסעודה קטנה, שמא ימשך בסעודתה: **ולא לדין.** אפילו בגמר דין, שכבר שמעו טענות בעלי דיניו ולא נשאר עליהן אלא לפסוק הדין בלבד, דלמא חזי טעמא ויסתרו מה שהיו רוצים לפסוק, וחוזר להיות תחלת הדין: **ואם התחילו.** בחד מכל הני דאמרינן, אין מפסיקין.

יד אברהם

unusual for anyone to go to a barber or to enter a bathhouse or a tannery at that time, the Rabbis did not deem it necessary to enact a safeguard (*Rambam, Hil. Tefillah* 6:7).

לֹא יִכָּנֵס אָדָם לְמֶרְחָץ, — *neither may a person enter a bathhouse,*

One half-hour before the greater *Minchah*, even if he intends to use only the sauna, since he may possibly become faint and not recover until the time of prayer has passed (*Rav* from *Gem.* 9b).

וְלֹא לְבֻרְסְקִי, — *nor a tannery,*

I.e., one may not enter a tannery even if he intends only to inspect it, lest he detect a flaw in the process and occupy himself the whole afternoon rectifying this flaw (*Rav; Rambam*).

Some authorities rule that not only may one not enter a tannery, but he may not commence to do any work one half-hour before the greater *Minchah* (*Magen Avraham*[1] 232:8). Others rule that this applies only to work that people usually complete without interruption, like tanning, which one would not interrupt for prayer if he sees that his skins are becoming ruined. Moreover, tanners wear soiled clothing when they work. One would have to bathe and change his clothing before prayer. He would not do this and then go back to his work. Other types of work, such as sewing or writing, which can be interrupted and later resumed, may be commenced (*Meiri* quoting *Rashba*. See *Be'ur Halachah* 232). [If the tannery is not his, and he has no responsibility for the skins, he may inspect them.]

Alternatively, he may see that the skins have been ruined and be troubled the whole afternoon. In his anguish he might forget to pray (*Rashi, Gem.* 9b).

וְלֹא לֶאֱכֹל, — *nor [may he begin] to eat,*

I.e., even to eat a small meal, lest he become preoccupied with his meal and extend it through the afternoon (*Rav; Rambam*).

וְלֹא לָדִין — *nor to judge —*

Even to announce the verdict, lest he find evidence to upset the verdict he had in mind, and be forced to reopen the case. This may take the entire afternoon until after the time of *Minchah* has passed (*Rav; Rambam*).

Aside from the dispute as to whether the *Minchah* time mentioned by the

---

1. For brevity's sake, all citations from *Tur, Shulchan Aruch,* or any of their commentaries (e.g., *Magen Avraham*) refer to the section *Orach Chaim* unless specified otherwise.

1
2
— neither may a person enter a bathhouse, nor a tannery, nor [may he begin] to eat, nor to judge — but if he started, he need not interrupt.

YAD AVRAHAM

mishnah refers to the greater or the lesser *Minchah*, there is another dispute as to the *type* of activity meant by the mishnah. In the preceding paragraphs, we have presented the view of *Rif*, *Rambam*, and others, adopted by *Rav* and *Shulchan Aruch* 232:2. There are, however, other views among the *poskim* [halachic authorities]. Some maintain that these activities are defined differently. The haircut known as "the haircut of Ben Elashah" was copied from that of the *Kohen Gadol*. Since this required exacting work, there was danger that it would not be finished until after the time of *Minchah* had passed. One may, however, go to the barber for a conventional haircut.

Similarly, the prohibition of entering the bathhouse refers only to entering the bathhouse for the complete process of the baths, i.e., to wash the hair, to bathe with hot and cold water, and to use the sauna. Ordinary bathing is permitted even just prior to *Minchah*.

Similarly, the prohibition of entering a tannery before *Minchah* refers only to a large tannery, where there are many skins. Since the number of skins in a large tannery will entail a lengthy period of work one might forget to recite the *Minchah* prayer.

The prohibition of entering to eat a meal involves only a large festive meal, such as a wedding or betrothal feast. A small everyday meal may be eaten during the time of *Minchah*.

Similarly, one may not commence to judge a lawsuit before *Minchah*. He may, however, deliver the verdict.

The combination of these two questions, i.e., whether the *Minchah* period of the mishnah refers to the greater *Minchah* or to the lesser *Minchah*, and whether the type of activity banned is the larger-scaled version (e.g., a wedding feast) or even the smaller-scaled one (e.g., an ordinary meal), makes for a broad spectrum of opinion:

❏ The opinion of *Rif* and *Rambam* (adopted by *Rav* and *Shulchan Aruch* 232:2) is that the period banned is from one half-hour before the greater *Minchah* — in effect, from noon — and that the type of activity banned is even the small-scale one, i.e., even an ordinary meal. This is the most stringent of all possible permutations.

❏ Other authorities rule that, although even small-scale activities are banned, they are banned only from just prior to the lesser *Minchah*. During the interval between the greater and the lesser *Minchahs* all types of activity are permitted (*Baal HaMaor*; *Hagahos Mordechai*).

Still others maintain that the time period banned is only the lesser *Minchah* and that even then only large-scale activities, such as wedding feasts, are prohibited. However, prior to and during the greater *Minchah* period, even large-scale activities are permissible. This is the most lenient of all possible permutations (*Tur* quoting *Rabbeinu Yitzchok*).

This final lenient ruling has been generally adopted in practice. Some say that the reason this has been

שבת א/ב

מַפְסִיקִים לִקְרוֹת קְרִיאַת שְׁמַע, וְאֵין מַפְסִיקִין לִתְפִלָּה.

ר' עובדיה מברטנורא

אלא יגמור ואחר כך יתפלל, והוא שהות ביום לגמור קודם שיעבור זמן התפלה. והתחלת התספורת משיניח מטפורת של ספרים בין ברכיו, הוא הסודר שנותן המתגלח על ברכיו כדי שלא יפול השער על בגדיו. והתחלת המרחץ משיפשוט הבגד הסמוך לבשרו, ואית דמפרשי משיסיר הסודר שעליו שהוא ראשון להפשטת בגדיו. והתחלת הבורסקי משיחגור בין כתפיו את בתי זרועותיו כדי להתעסק בעורות. והתחלת אכילה משיטול ידיו. והתחלת הדין משיתעטפו הדיינין בטליתן לשבת לדין באימה ובירא ה. ואם היו מטופים ויושבים בדין ובא אחר סמוך למנחה, הויא התחלת אותו הדין משפתחו בעלי הדין בטענותם: **מפסיקין לקריאת שמע**. מלתא אתחריתי נקט, והכי קאמר, חברים העוסקים בתורה מפסיקים לקריאת שמע, דזמנה קבוע, דכתיב (דברים ו) ובשכבך ובקומך: **ואין מפסיקין לתפלה**. שאין לה זמן קבוע דאורייתא. ולא שנו אלא כגון רבי שמעון בן יוחאי וחביריו שתורתן אומנותן, אבל אנו הואיל ואנו מפסיקין תורתנו לאומנותנו כל שכן שנפסיק לתפלה:

יד אברהם

The point at which one is considered to have "started" the activity varies from activity to activity. For a haircut it is when one spreads the barber's cloth over himself (to protect his clothing from the hair). For the bath, it is when one removes his headgear (*Rav* from *Rashi*). Others maintain that it is not until he removes his underwear (*Rav* from *Rambam*). For the tannery, it is when he puts on the tanner's apron. For the meal, it is when he washes his hands in preparation for the meal. For sitting in judgment, it is when the judge wraps himself in his *tallis*. [The judge wore a *tallis* while hearing a case in order to impress upon himself and upon the others involved the solemnity of the matter and the reverence to be displayed in a *beis din* (court)] (*Rav* from *Gem.* 9b).]

According to our custom, if the judges sit down with the intention of trying the case, it is considered that they have commenced (*Shulchan Aruch* 232:2, *Rabbeinu Yerucham*, from *Yerushalmi*).

adopted is because people rely on the beadle who calls them to the synagogue, and will remind them to pray. It is, however, preferable to adopt the more stringent ruling as far as a large meal is concerned and not to begin one during the half-hour preceding the greater *Minchah* (*Rama*, 232:2).

וְאִם הִתְחִילוּ — *but if he* [lit. *they*] *started*,

I.e., even if they commenced one of these activities when it was already forbidden to do so (*Tos.* 9b).

אֵין מַפְסִיקִים. — *he* [lit. *they*] *need not interrupt.*

They may complete their activities and then pray. If, however, they see that there will be no time to pray after they have finished, they are required to interrupt their activities in order to recite *Minchah* (*Rav*). In such a case, they may not wait until the end of the day, but must interrupt their activities at the beginning of the lesser *Minchah*, and recite the *Minchah* prayer (*Magen Avraham* 232:4).

1 **They must interrupt for the recitation of *Shema*,**
2 **but they need not interrupt for prayer.**

YAD AVRAHAM

מַפְסִיקִים לִקְרוֹת קְרִיאַת שְׁמַע — *They must interrupt for the recitation of Shema,*

This refers to scholars who are engaged in the study of the Torah day and night and do not engage in any work to earn a livelihood. They must, nevertheless, interrupt their studies to recite the *Shema* [the three portions of the Torah delineated in *Berachos* 2:2 — *Deuteronomy* 6:4-9, 11:13-21, *Numbers* 15:37-41]. Since it is a Biblical commandment to recite these passages, even devoted scholars must cease their learning to perform this mitzvah as soon as it is time to recite the *Shema*. Since the Torah prescribes a specific time for this mitzvah, namely, *when you lie down and when you rise up* (*Deut.* 6:7), it is necessary to interrupt even one's Torah studies to perform this mitzvah (*Rav*).

וְאֵין מַפְסִיקִין לִתְפִלָּה. — *but they need not interrupt for prayer.*

I.e., they need not interrupt their learning to recite *Shemoneh Esrei*, the eighteen blessings of silent prayer, usually referred to simply as *tefillah*, prayer. Since the times prescribed for this prayer are of Rabbinic origin, Torah scholars need not interrupt their learning to comply with them. As mentioned before, the mishnah applies exclusively to such scholars whose Torah is their sole occupation, and who do not engage in any type of employment, such as R' Shimon bar Yochai and his colleagues. Others, who sometimes interrupt their studies in order to earn a livelihood, must also do so to recite the *Shemoneh Esrei* as well (*Rav*).

[It appears that *Rav* follows *Rambam's* view (*Tefillah* 1:1) that "there is a positive mitzvah in the Torah to pray every day, as it is said (*Exodus* 23:25): *And you shall serve* HASHEM *your God.* From tradition, they learned that this service is prayer, as it is said (*Deut.* 11:13): *. . . and to serve Him with all your heart.* The Sages said: What is service that is in the heart? This is prayer. The number of prayers was, however, not set down by the Torah; neither is the form of this prayer set down by the Torah. And prayer has no set time according to the Torah."

It follows that if a scholar has not recited any prayer for the past twenty-four hours, he is required to interrupt his learning to recite some sort of prayer, in order to fulfill the Biblical requirement of prayer. *Rambam* himself, however, words the halachah thus, *". . . he need not stop, for the mitzvah of learning Torah is greater than the mitzvah of prayer"* (*Tefillah* 6:8). Apparently, *Rambam* means that it is greater even than the Biblical mitzvah of prayer.

According to other authorities, the entire mitzvah of daily prayer is Rabbinic in origin (*Ramban, Sefer HaMitzvos* 5). Consequently, a scholar is not required to stop his learning even if he has not prayed for the past twenty-four hours.]

3.

The following mishnah deals with a number of precautionary laws concerning carrying things on the eve of the Sabbath, so that one not forget and transfer them from one domain to another on the Sabbath. From here the mishnah will go on to other precautions applicable to the Sabbath itself.

שבת
א/ג

[ג] לֹא יֵצֵא הַחַיָּט בְּמַחֲטוֹ סָמוּךְ לַחֲשֵׁכָה, שֶׁמָּא יִשְׁכַּח וְיֵצֵא. וְלֹא הַלַּבְלָר בְּקֻלְמוֹסוֹ. וְלֹא יְפַלֶּה אֶת כֵּלָיו וְלֹא

───────────── ר' עובדיה מברטנורא ─────────────

(ג) **לא יצא החייט במחטו.** אפילו תחובה לו בבגדו, שמא ישכח ויצא, ואומן חייב שדרך האומנים לתוחבן בבגדיו כשיוצאים לשוק: **שמא ישכח ויצא.** משתחשך: **הלבלר.** הסופר: **בקולמוסו.** התחוב אחורי אזניו כדרך הסופרים: **ולא יפלה את כליו.** מבער כנים מבגדיו.

יד אברהם

לֹא יֵצֵא הַחַיָּט בְּמַחֲטוֹ סָמוּךְ לַחֲשֵׁכָה, — A tailor may not go out with his needle shortly before nightfall,

I.e., on Friday before dusk (*Tif. Yis.*).

שֶׁמָּא יִשְׁכַּח וְיֵצֵא. — *lest he forget and go out.*

I.e., lest he forget that he is carrying the needle and go out after nightfall while still carrying it. If he were to do so he would be guilty of transferring an object from the private domain (his home) to the public domain (the street).

He may not go out even with the needle pinned to his clothes lest he forget to remove it and go out with it in this manner after dark too. Since it is the normal practice for people of this craft to carry their needles in such a manner, it is considered the conventional manner for them to transfer needles from place to place, and one who does so on the Sabbath is liable. The Rabbis therefore enacted a גְּזֵרָה, *preventive measure,* and forbade a tailor from going out into a public domain with his needle stuck in his clothes shortly before nightfall on Friday. To one who is not a tailor, transporting a needle by pinning it to his garment would be an unconventional manner of transportation and he would therefore be exempt from a sin offering in accordance with the rule that one is liable for a *melachah* only if he performs it in its conventional manner (see below, 10:6). Consequently, there is no ban against a person who is not a tailor going out before nightfall with a needle pinned to his garment, since even if he forgot and continued to do so on the Sabbath, he would be violating a Rabbinical prohibition (performing a *melachah* in an unconventional manner) not a Scriptural one. This is in accordance with the rule of אֵין גּוֹזְרִין גְּזֵרָה לִגְזֵרָה — *The Rabbis do not decree a preventive measure to safeguard* [that which is itself only] *a preventive measure* (*Rav; Shenos Eliyahu*).

This explanation follows R' Yehudah's opinion in the *Gemara*. R' Meir, however, maintains that even for craftsmen who sometimes stick needles into their garments, the normal manner of carrying a needle is by hand, and only in such a manner is one liable. Consequently, even a tailor who transports a needle by pinning it to his garment is considered to have performed the *melachah* in an unconventional manner and is not liable. Therefore, the mishnah's prohibition against going out shortly before nightfall with a needle must refer to carrying the needle in one's hand. Furthermore, prohibiting one from going out with a needle stuck in his garment out of fear that it may lead to carrying

משניות / שבת — פרק א: יציאות השבת [34]

3. A tailor may not go out with his needle shortly before nightfall, lest he forget and go out. Neither may a scribe [go out] with his pen. One may neither delouse his garments nor

YAD AVRAHAM

the needle in his hand which might, in turn, lead to carrying on the Sabbath, is also known as "a preventive measure to safeguard that which is itself only a preventive measure," a measure which the Rabbis do not enact. This is the ruling followed by *Rambam* (*Hil. Shabbos* 19:26).

Accordingly, since the prohibition includes only carrying the needle in one's hand, there is no difference between a tailor and anyone else. Indeed, *Shulchan Aruch* (252:6) states, "A person may not go out on the eve of the Sabbath shortly before dark, with his needle in his hand . . ." According to this explanation, the mishnah gives the example of the tailor and the scribe [see below] only because they are the ones who customarily carry such objects (*Tif. Yis.*).

According to the rule that the Rabbis do not decree a safeguard to a safeguard, we are compelled to assume that if the tailor forgets and goes out he will be liable for a sin offering. Otherwise, the Rabbis would not have prohibited going out with the needle before nightfall. Yet, according to the Talmud (*Bava Kamma* 26b), one is not liable unless he is aware of the presence of the object but forgets that it is the Sabbath day and carries it out. In this case, however, since he was unaware that he was carrying the needle, he ought not to be liable.

Tosafos (11a) offers the following explanation: The Rabbis feared that the tailor may forget to remove the needle from his person and may first remember the needle after the onset of the Sabbath, but at that point may forget that it is the Sabbath day and carry the needle into the public domain. *Tiferes Yisrael* adds that he may, alternatively, forget that carrying out of one domain to another is forbidden. Since he is aware of the needle, he is liable for a sin offering.

וְלֹא הַלַּבְלָר בְּקֻלְמוּסוֹ. — *Neither may a scribe [go out] with his pen.*

I.e., a scribe may not go out into a public domain on Friday before dark, with his pen behind his ear, as scribes are accustomed to doing (*Rav*). However, anyone other than a scribe would be permitted to carry the pen in this fashion before nightfall, since even if he forgot and continued carrying it on the Sabbath, he would only be committing a Rabbinic transgression. (This is again because of the rule that a *melachah* done in an unconventional way is only a Rabbinic prohibition.)

The discussion concerning the tailor with his needle applies just as well to the scribe with his pen. Therefore, according to R' Meir, no person is allowed to carry his pen in his hand to a public domain just prior to nightfall, regardless of whether he is a scribe (a scribe merely being an example of one who is likely to do so). Anyone, including a scribe, is permitted to carry a pen behind his ear, however, since even continuing to do so on the Sabbath would result only in a Rabbinical transgression [this method of transfer being considered unconventional even for a scribe]. This is the ruling followed as the halachah (*Shulchan Aruch* 252:6).

The addition of the case of the scribe and his pen is to teach us that

שבת א/ג

יִקְרָא, לְאוֹר הַנֵּר. בֶּאֱמֶת אָמְרוּ: הַחַזָּן רוֹאֶה הֵיכָן הַתִּינוֹקוֹת קוֹרְאִים, אֲבָל הוּא לֹא יִקְרָא. כַּיּוֹצֵא בוֹ, לֹא יֹאכַל הַזָּב עִם הַזָּבָה, מִפְּנֵי

ר' עובדיה מברטנורא

תרגום בטרתי הקדש פליתי: **ולא יקרא לאור הנר.** בספר, שמא יטה הנר להביא השמן לפי הפתילה כדי שידלוק יפה, ונמלא מבעיר בשבת. ואפילו היה הנר גבוה שתים ושלש קומות, לטולס אסור לקרות לאור הנר אלא אם כן יש עמו אדם אחר לשמרו, או אם הוא אדם חשוב שאינו רגיל לעולם לתקן הנר. **החזן.** מלמד תינוקות: **מחויבן התינוקות קורין.** מהיכן יתחילו לקרות, דבטיון מוטט כי האי לא גזרינן שמא יטה. והתינוקות קוראין לפני רבן לאור הנר, שאימת רבן טליהס: **אבל הוא לא יקרא.** כל הפרשה, מפני שאין אימתן עליו, ושמירתן לא הויא שמירה. ומהאי טעמא נמי איכא למימן דאמר דאשה שומרת לבעלה אין שמירתה שמירה, שאין אימתה עליו: **כיוצא בו.** לעשות הרחקה מן העבירה, אמרו לא יאכל הזב עם השתו זבה, ואף על פי שניהם טמאים.

יד אברהם

not only is one apt to forget an object as small as a needle, but even an object as large as a pen may also be forgotten and inadvertently carried out on the Sabbath. It, too, is therefore banned (*Tos. R' Akiva*).

וְלֹא יְפַלֶּה אֶת־כֵּלָיו וְלֹא יִקְרָא, לְאוֹר הַנֵּר. — *One may neither delouse his garments nor read, by the light of a lamp.*

It frequently occurs that the oil draws away from the wick causing the light to grow dim. If one is engaged in activities requiring a strong light, he might inadvertently tilt the lamp to cause the oil to run into the wick, thus causing the light to shine brighter. *Kindling is a principal type of labor forbidden on the Sabbath (*Rav* from *Gem.* 12b).

Although the cause for this prohibition is that one might unintentionally tilt the lamp, nevertheless, the Rabbis did not differentiate between a lamp which is within reach and a lamp which is out of reach (*Gem.* 12b).

It is however permitted for two people to read together from one book by the light of a lamp since if one will forget and attempt to tilt the lamp, the other will remind him (*Rama* 275:2). Likewise, a prominent person, who never adjusts his own lamps but has his servants attend to such matters, does not fall under this prohibition (*Rav* from *Gem.* 12b).

Wax candles are not included in this prohibition. The *Shulchan Aruch* does, however, prohibit reading by the light of a wax candle because one may trim the wick in order to make it burn better and in doing so, cause the candle to flicker and temporarily extinguish a bit of the fire. Extinguishing a fire is a principal type of labor forbidden on the Sabbath (*Shulchan Aruch* 275:1). The custom, however, is to permit reading by candlelight because one is liable for extinguishing a fire only if he intends to make charcoal (see below, 2:5). Otherwise, the prohibition is only Rabbinical. A prohibition not to read by a wax candle would therefore be regarded as a "preventive measure to safeguard that which for itself is only a preventive measure" (*Magen Avraham ibid.* 3, *Turei Zahav* 2).

בֶּאֱמֶת אָמְרוּ: — *Indeed they said:*

Although this expression usually denotes הֲלָכָה לְמֹשֶׁה מִסִּינַי, *a halachah revealed to Moses on Mt. Sinai*, in this case, the entire prohibition is Rabbinic in nature (*Rav* to *Terumos* 2:1).

1 3 read, by the light of a lamp. Indeed they said: The teacher may see where the children are reading, but he may not read.

Similarly, a *zav* may not eat with a *zavah*, since

YAD AVRAHAM

הַחַזָּן — **The teacher**

This word חַזָּן, *chazzan*, stems from the root חזה, *to see*. It refers to the person who is responsible to oversee the children in their studies and watch where they are reading. Similarly, the person leading the prayers is called *chazzan*, since it was also his duty to watch where those called to the Torah would read. See *Megillah* 4:1 (*Tos. Yom Tov*).

רוֹאֶה הֵיכָן הַתִּינוֹקוֹת קוֹרְאִים, — *may see where the children are reading*,

The children themselves may study by lamplight. Since they sit in awe of their teacher, they are not likely to touch the lamp (*Rav* from *Gem.* 12b).

According to *Yerushalmi*, the children are permitted to read by lamplight because they hope the light will go out so that they will not have to study, and will, therefore, not adjust it.

Additionally, the teacher may look into the scroll to determine where the children will read on the morrow. He merely glances at the scroll to see the beginning of the chapters the children will learn, and he studies the rest from memory. Since he does not read for any length of time from the scroll, he is unlikely to tilt the lamp (*Tif. Yis.*).

אֲבָל הוּא לֹא יִקְרָא. — *but he may not read*.

I.e., he may not read the entire portion by lamplight lest he forget the Sabbath and tilt the lamp. Since he does not fear the children, their presence will not deter him from tilting the lamp. Moreover, they will not admonish him should he forget. For this reason, some rule that even if one instructs his wife to remind him should he forget and attempt to tilt the lamp, he may still not read by lamplight (*Rav*). The halachah is, however, that in that case, one may read by lamplight (*Shulchan Aruch* 275:3).

Although the practical application of this law rarely occurs today, it has, nevertheless, left its imprint on Jewish customs. As mentioned above, if two people read from two books, they may not do so by lamplight. For this reason, those congregations that recite *Maaravis*, special poems inserted in the blessings recited during the *Maariv* service on holidays, omit them on holidays falling on the Sabbath. Since each worshiper had his own *machzor*, one would not see what his neighbor was doing and would not remind him not to tilt the lamp. Though we do not pray by lamplight, the custom still prevails (*Rama* 275:2).

כַּיּוֹצֵא בּוֹ, — *Similarly*,

I.e., just as the rabbis promulgated prohibitions as safeguards for the law of the Sabbath, they also enacted safeguards to family purity (*Rav*).

לֹא יֹאכַל הַזָּב עִם הַזָּבָה, — *a zav may not eat with a zavah*,

The law of *zav* is found in *Leviticus* 15:1-15: אִישׁ אִישׁ כִּי יִהְיֶה זָב מִבְּשָׂרוֹ זוֹבוֹ טָמֵא הוּא, *Any man who will have an issue from his flesh, his issue is ritually unclean...* The Torah teaches that a male who has experienced a gonorrheal issue becomes טָמֵא *[tamei]*, *ritually contaminated*. The details of

שבת
א/ד

הֶרְגֵּל עֲבֵרָה.

[ד] וְאֵלּוּ מִן הַהֲלָכוֹת שֶׁאָמְרוּ בַּעֲלִיַּת חֲנַנְיָה בֶן חִזְקִיָּה בֶן גֻּרְיוֹן כְּשֶׁעָלוּ לְבַקְּרוֹ. נִמְנוּ וְרַבּוּ בֵית שַׁמַּאי עַל בֵּית הִלֵּל.

—— ר' עובדיה מברטנורא ——

מפני הרגל עבירה. שמתוך שהם מתיחדים יבא לבטול זבה שהיא בכרת. וזב וזבה לרבותא נקט שהתשמיש קשה להן ואיכא למימר דודאי לא יבואו לידי הרגל עבירה, אפילו הכי לא יאכלו זה עם זו: (ד) [**ואלו**] **מהלכות.** אין פולין ואין קורין לאור הנר דתנן במתניתין: **בעליית חנניה בן חזקיה.** שבקשו חכמים לגנוז ספר יחזקאל שדבריו נראים כסותרים דברי תורה, כגון, כל נבלה וטרפה מן העוף ומן הבהמה לא יאכלו הכהנים (יחזקאל מד), כהנים הוא דלא אכלי, הא ישראל אכלי. וכגון, וכן תעשה בשבעה בחדש (שם מה), היכן נרמז קרבן זה בתורה. ונטמן חנניה בן חזקיה בעלייה וישב שם ופירש ספר יחזקאל:

—— יד אברהם ——

these laws are discussed in *Megillah* 1:7. See also Appendix, "The Eighteen Decrees," at the end of this volume.

The law of *zavah* is found in *Leviticus* 15:19-33. The Torah delineates the laws of the נִדָּה [*niddah*], menstruant, who experiences a flow during her monthly periods, and the זָבָה, *zavah*, who experiences a flow between the usual time of her periods. (The details are discussed at length in *Chochmas Adam* 107:1, based on *Niddah* 72,73.)

Intercourse with a woman who experienced a flow and did not immerse herself in a valid *mikveh* [ritualarium] after the prescribed preparations is punishable by *kares* [a form of excision meted out by the Heavenly Tribunal] — as it is written (*Lev*. 20:18) וְאִישׁ אֲשֶׁר־יִשְׁכַּב אֶת־אִשָּׁה דָוָה... וְנִכְרְתוּ שְׁנֵיהֶם מִקֶּרֶב עַמָּם, *And a man who will lie with a woman who had a flow ... both of them shall be cut off from among their people*.

The Rabbis enacted safeguards to prevent intimacy during the time a woman is either a *niddah* or a *zavah*.

One of these safeguards is the prohibition of the husband and wife eating together from one plate or even at the same table without a reminder of the woman's state of *tamei*, such as separate tablecloths or an object not usually found on the table set between them.

Although both the *zav* and the *zavah* are *tamei*, and will consequently not increase their contamination through contact, the rabbis, nevertheless, prohibited them from eating together from one plate (*Rav*).

מִפְּנֵי הֶרְגֵּל עֲבֵרָה. — *since it might lead to sin* [lit. *because of habitual sin*].

The physical closeness may lead to intercourse which is a transgression punishable by *kares* (*Rashi*).

Although the physical condition of this couple makes intercourse painful, still the rabbis prohibited their proximity. We therefore conclude that they certainly prohibited a healthy male from eating together with his wife during the time she was a *niddah* or *zavah* (*Rashi; Rav; Tif. Yis.*).

1 it might lead to sin.

4

4. And these are of the *halachos* that they stated in the upper chamber of Chananyah ben Chizkiah ben Gurion when they went up to visit him. They were counted and Beis Shammai outnumbered Beis Hillel

YAD AVRAHAM
4.

וְאֵלּוּ — *And these*
I.e., the aforementioned laws, not to delouse clothing or read by lamplight on the Sabbath (*Rav, Rashi, Gem.* 13b).

מִן הַהֲלָכוֹת שֶׁאָמְרוּ בַּעֲלִיַּת חֲנַנְיָה בֶן חִזְקִיָּה בֶּן גֻּרְיוֹן כְּשֶׁעָלוּ לְבַקְּרוֹ — *are of the halachos that they stated in the upper chamber of Chananyah ben Chizkiah ben Gurion* [the mishnah in the Gemara reads: *ben Garon*] *when they went up to visit him.*

When the Sages sought to suppress the Book of *Ezekiel* because some of its statements seemed to contradict precepts of the Torah, Chananyah ben Chizkiah isolated himself in a chamber in the the upper story of his house and had three hundred barrels of oil brought up to him [for light, to enable him to study through the night

(Rashi)] and compiled a commentary to reconcile the differences (*Menachos* 45a).[1] The Sages often came to visit him to pass judgment on his commentary. On this occasion, all of the great scholars of the time were present and they used the opportunity to enact necessary laws (*Rambam; Rav*).

Rambam explains the expression, כְּשֶׁעָלוּ לְבַקְּרוֹ, to mean *when they went up to test him,* the word בקר meaning *to examine or criticize,* i.e., they went up to pass judgment on his commentary.

נִמְנוּ — *They were counted*
I.e., they voted on the eighteen decrees that they wished to enact (*Tif. Yis.*).

וְרַבּוּ בֵית שַׁמַּאי עַל בֵּית הִלֵּל — *and Beis Shammai outnumbered Beis Hillel*
When they voted, Beis Shammai

---

1. An example of Chananyah ben Chizkiah's reconciliations is given by the Talmud (*Menachos* 45a):
   Ezekiel 44:31 states: *Any neveilah or treifah of fowl or livestock the Kohanim may not eat.* Neveilah is the carcass of an animal which died without proper *shechitah* [ritual slaughter]. *Treifah* is the carcass of an animal which is *torn* — injured internally or externally — in a way that makes it halachically unfit for eating. Now since the Torah clearly forbids all Jews to eat *neveilah* or *treifah* (*Leviticus* 22:8), Ezekiel's limitation of this prohibition to *Kohanim* seems to contradict the Torah's words. Why is it necessary to explicate these prohibitions for the *Kohanim* when they apply equally to all Jews?
   The Talmud explains that the prohibition against *neveilah* was waived for *Kohanim* in the instance of a bird brought for a sin offering. The manner of ritual slaughter in that instance was of a nature that would render the bird *neveilah* in *non*-sacrificial circumstances. Nevertheless, *Kohanim* were permitted to eat from it (see *Leviticus* 5:8ff). Since the prohibition against *neveilah* was waived in this instance it might have been thought that *Kohanim* were not bound by these prohibitions at all. For this reason the prohibition is repeated here, specifically mentioning the *Kohanim*.
   The Talmud also cited apparent contradictions in *Ezekiel* 45:18,20; 46:6,7, and resolves them. [See ArtScroll *Yechezkel*, volume III.]

שבת א/ד

וּשְׁמוֹנָה עָשָׂר דְּבָרִים גָּזְרוּ בּוֹ בַיּוֹם.

ר' עובדיה מברטנורא

ושמונה עשר דברים גזרו בו ביום. שנחלקו בית שמאי ובית הלל, ועמדו למנין, ורבו בית שמאי ופסקו כמותם, כדכתיב (שמות כג) אחרי רבים להטות. וכולהו שמונה עשר דברים מייתי להו בגמרא, ואלו הן, האוכל אוכל ראשון לטומאה או שני לטומאה, גזרו שיהא נעשה גופו שני לטומאה, ופוסל את התרומה במגעו, שפני פוסל בתרומה. הרי אלו שתי גזירות, אוכל אוכל ראשון, ואוכל שני. והשותה משקין טמאים נעשה גם כן שני לטומאה ופוסל את התרומה. הרי שלש. וטעמא דגזור בהני, דזמנין דאכיל אוכלין טמאים וסדי משקין דתרומה בפומיה בעוד שהאוכלים טמאים בפיו ופסיל להו, וזמנין דשתי משקין טמאים ובעודן בפיו שדי אוכלין דתרומה בפיו ופסיל להו. וגזרו על הבא ראשו ורובו, לאחר שטבל מטומאתו בו ביום, במים שאובים, ועל טהור שנפלו על ראשו שלשה לוגין מים שאובין. הרי חמש גזירות. וטעמא דגזור טומאה על הני לטמאה אדם, לפי שהיו טובלין במי מערות סרוחים והיו נותנין עליהם אחר כך מים שאובין להעביר סרחון המים, התחילו ועשאום קבע לומר לא מי המערות מטהרים אלא המים שאובים מטהרים, עמדו וגזרו עליהם טומאה, דלמא אתי לבטולי טורת מקוה וטבלי בשאובים. והגזירה הששית, שיהיו הספרים של כתבי הקדש פוסלים את התרומה במגע. שבתחלה היו מצניעין אוכלין דתרומה אצל ספר תורה, אמרי האי קדש והאי קדש. כיון דחזו דקא אתו אתו ספרים לידי פסידא, שהעכברים המצויים אצל האוכלין היו מפסידים את הספרים, גזרו שיהיו הספרים, דהיינו תורה נביאים וכתובים, במגען פוסלין את התרומה. והגזירה השביעית, גזרו על סתם ידים שפוסלות את התרומה, מפני שהידים עסקניות הן ונוגעות בבשרו במקום הטנופת, וגנאי לתרומה אם יגע בה בידים מזוהמות והיא נמאסת על אוכליה. והגזירה השמינית, האוכלין שנטמאו במשקין שאינן המשקין טמאו מחמת ידים שנגעו בהן קודם נטילה, גזרו על המשקין שיטמאו את האוכלין, שכל הדברים הפוסלים את התרומה מטמאין את המשקין להיות תחלה, גזירה משום משקין הבאים מחמת שרץ, דאשכחן בהן שהן ראשונים מדאורייתא, והאי דגזור בכל טומאת משקין להיות תחלה ולא גזור נמי באוכלין גזירה משום [אוכלין] הבאים מחמת שרץ, היינו טעמא דאמור רבנן במשקין, משום דעלולים לקבל טומאה, שאינן צריכין תיקון הכשר להביאן לידי קבלת טומאה כמו האוכלין שצריכין נתינת מים להכשירן לקבל טומאה. והגזירה התשיעית, כלים שנטמאו במשקין שנטמאו המשקים בשרץ, אף על פי שהם ראשון לטומאה דאורייתא אין יכולין לטמא אדם וכלים, שאין אדם וכלים מקבלין טומאה אלא מאב הטומאה, ולא ממשקין שנטמאו בשרץ שהם ראשונים, ורבנן גזור עלייהו שיטמאו כלים, גזירה משום משקה דזב וזבה שהן רוקו ומימי רגליו, שהן אב הטומאה ומטמאין כלים מדאורייתא. והגזירה העשירית, שיהו בנות כותיים נדות מעריסתן, כלומר מיום שנולדה, שתינוקת בת יומא מטמאה בנדה, וכותים לית להו מדרש זה וכי חזיין לא מפרשי להו הלכך גזור בהו רבנן. והגזירה האחת עשרה, שיהו כל המטלטלין מביאין את הטומאה בטובי המרדע, והוא מלמד הבקר, ויש בהקיפו טפח אבל אין בעביו טפח, ואף על פי שמן התורה אין אהל פחות מטפח, גזר רבנן על כל המטלטלים שיש בהקיפן טפח שאם ראשו אחד האהיל על המת וראשו אחד על הכלים מביאין להם טומאת אהל, גזירה אטו מי שיש בעביו טפח שמביא את הטומאה מן התורה. והגזירה השתים עשרה הבוצר ענבים לדרכן בגת, המשקה היוצא מהן בשעת בצירה מכשירן לקבל טומאה, ואף על פי שהולך לאבוד ולא ניחא ליה, גזירה שמא יבצור בקופות מזופפות, דלא ניחא ליה במשקה היוצא מהן שהרי אינו הולך לאבוד, ומכשיר מן התורה. והגזירה השלש עשרה, שיהיו גידולי תרומה תרומה, גזירה משום תרומה טמאה ביד כהן שאסורה באכילה ובא לזרעה, וגזור שתהא הראשונה והרי היא תרומה טמאה, דחיישינן דלמא משהי לה עד זמן זריעה ואתי למיכלה

1 and they decreed eighteen measures on that day.

ר' עובדיה מברטנורא

בטומאה. והגזירה הארבע עשרה, מי שהחשיך לו בדרך נותן כיסו לנכרי, ולא יטלטלנו פחות מארבע אמות. והגזירה החמש עשרה והשש עשרה, אין פולין ואין קורין לאור הנר דתנן במתניתין. והגזירה השבע עשרה, גזרו על פתן של עובדי כוכבים, ועל שמנן ועל יינן ועל בנותיהן, וכולהו גזירה חדא היא, כדאמרינן גזרו על פתן משום שמנן ועל שמנן משום יינן ועל יינן ועל בנותיהן משום דבר אחר, כלומר משום עבודת כוכבים. והגזירה השמונה עשרה, גזרו על תינוק עובד כוכבים שיהא מטמא בזיבה, כדי שלא יהא תינוק ישראל רגיל אצלו במשכב זכור:

YAD AVRAHAM

were found to be in the majority, and consequently, the halachah was decided in their favor, according to the principle (*Exodus* 23:2): אַחֲרֵי רַבִּים לְהַטֹּת, *Follow the majority* (*Rav*).

וּשְׁמוֹנָה עָשָׂר דְּבָרִים גָּזְרוּ בּוֹ בַיּוֹם — *and they decreed eighteen measures on that day.*

Beis Shammai, outnumbering Beis Hillel, were able to pass eighteen measures over the objections of Beis Hillel.

The eighteen measures are listed here in brief. An expanded discussion appears in an appendix at the end of this tractate.

The first nine measures involve the ritual purity of *terumah*, the share of produce due the *Kohanim*.

(i-vii) The following seven people or objects render *terumah* invalid upon contact: (i) One who eats or drinks food which is a first degree of *tumah*-contamination, or (ii) a second degree of *tumah*, or (iii) a contaminated beverage; (iv) a person who immerses his head and the major portion of his body into water that was drawn by a vessel, on the same day that he cleansed himself in a *mikveh* [ritualarium], or (v) a ritually clean person over whom such water is spilled; (vi) scrolls of Scripture; and (vii) unwashed hands.

(viii) An object or person with any degree of *tumah* capable of invalidating *terumah* renders a liquid a first degree of *tumah* upon contact.

(ix) Contaminated liquid renders a vessel a second degree of *tumah* upon contact.

(x) The daughters of Cuthites are considered menstruants from the cradle.

(xi) Round objects with a circumference of one handbreadth transmit *tumah* as an *ohel*-tent.

(xii) Juice exuding from grapes picked for the wine-press renders the grapes susceptible to contracting *tumah*.

(xiii) The offshoots of seeds that were *terumah* are considered *terumah* even after the original seeds have disintegrated.

(xiv) A traveler who has not reached town before the onset of the Sabbath may not carry his purse less than four *amos* distance at a time, but must give it to a gentile to carry, if one is available.

One may neither (xv) delouse his garments nor (xvi) read, by lamplight, on the Sabbath.

(xvii) The bread, oil, wine and daughters of gentiles are all forbidden.

(xviii) A gentile boy is considered as a *zav*.

שבת
א/ה-ו

[ה] **בֵּית** שַׁמַּאי אוֹמְרִים: אֵין שׁוֹרִין דְּיוֹ וְסַמְמָנִים וְכַרְשִׁינִים, אֶלָּא כְדֵי שֶׁיִּשּׁוֹרוּ מִבְּעוֹד יוֹם. וּבֵית הִלֵּל מַתִּירִין.

[ו] **בֵּית** שַׁמַּאי אוֹמְרִים: אֵין נוֹתְנִין אוּנִין

— ר' עובדיה מברטנורא —

(ה) **אין שורין דיו.** סממנים שעושים מהם דיו לכתיבה: **וסממנים.** ללבוע: **וכרשינים.** מאכל בהמה, ורגילים לשרות אותן במים תחלה, וקורין להם בערבי כרסנ"ה, ובלט"ז ויל"ש, וסבירי בית שמאי אדם מוזהר על שביתת כלים כמו על שביתת בהמתו, והיינו טעמא דאין נותנין אונין טעמא דאין פורשין מצודות. ונר הדולק בשבת וקדרה שעל גבי כירה דמודו בהו בית שמאי, [בדמפקר] אפקורי לכלים ושוב אינו מצווה על שביתתן: **ובית הלל מתירין.** משנתן המים מבעוד יום, אף על פי שהן נשרין והולכין בשבת, דסברי על שביתת בהמה אדם מוזהר, דאית בה לער בעלי חיים, אבל לא על שביתת כלים: (ו) **אונין.** אגודות של פשתן מנופץ, ונותנין אותן בתנור ומתלבנים:

— יד אברהם —

5.

The next seven mishnayos deal with work begun before the Sabbath which will continue unaided on the Sabbath. These *halachos* were also discussed on the day of the meeting in the upper chamber of Chananyah ben Chizkiah ben Gurion. They were not, however, voted on, as were those in the series discussed above. The *melachos* involved in these mishnayos are: לִישָׁה, *kneading*, צְבִיעָה, *dyeing*, לִבּוּן, *whitening*, and צִידָה, *trapping*.

בֵּית שַׁמַּאי אוֹמְרִים: אֵין שׁוֹרִין דְּיוֹ וְסַמְמָנִים — *Beis Shammai say: We may not soak ink, dyes*

I.e., the ingredients to make ink or dyes (*Rav*).

The *melachah* involved in making ink and dyes is לִישָׁה, *kneading*. Adding water to the ingredients is considered kneading even though they are not blended together manually (*Tos.* 18a; *Meiri; Ravad, Hil. Shabbos* 9:14).

Others hold that adding water to form a mixture which does not require manual blending is not considered kneading. According to this opinion, the prohibition involved in ink and dye making is צְבִיעָה, *dyeing*. One is as liable for coloring water as he is for dyeing cloth (*Rambam, Hil. Shabbos* 9:14; see also 8:16).

Ravad maintains that since his purpose of soaking ink or dye is not to color the water itself but to create a means of coloring other things, he is not liable for *dyeing*, but for *kneading*.

וְכַרְשִׁינִים, — *or vetch,*

A species of beans used for fodder. They must be soaked in water to be of any use (*Rav*).

Alternatively, this is another species, which, when peeled, dissolves in water and thickens it (*Meiri*). In either case, here, too, the *melachah* involved is kneading.

אֶלָּא כְדֵי שֶׁיִּשּׁוֹרוּ מִבְּעוֹד יוֹם. — *unless there is sufficient [time] for them to become completely soaked while it is yet day.*

Beis Shammai are of the opinion that שְׁבִיתַת כֵּלִים דְּאוֹרַיְתָא [*shevisas*

1
5-6

5. Beis Shammai say: We may not soak ink, dyes or vetch, unless there is sufficient [time] for them to become completely soaked while it is yet day. But Beis Hillel permit [this].

6. Beis Shammai say: We may not place bundles

YAD AVRAHAM

keilim], *resting* (non-use for the purpose of *melachah*) *of utensils* (instruments, foods) *is a Scriptural commandment*, i.e., just as one is obliged to rest his livestock on the Sabbath, so too is he obliged to rest his utensils. Beis Shammai hold that by placing ingredients for making ink or dyes with water in a vessel before the Sabbath he is causing the work to take place in his vessel on the Sabbath. It is, therefore, prohibited for him to do so (*Rav* from *Gem.* 18a).

Similarly, unless there is enough time for the vetch to be partially softened before the Sabbath, work is being performed with one's vessels on the Sabbath.

The *Gemara* questions this ruling in view of the common practice of lighting candles and setting pots on the stove before the Sabbath and allowing them to continue to burn and cook during the Sabbath.

As a result, the *Gemara* concludes that, according to Beis Shammai, these things are permitted only when ownership is relinquished from the candles and pots prior to the Sabbath. One is responsible for *shevisas keilim* only for vessels which he owns (*Rav* from *Gem.* 18b). Although people do not actually go through the formal procedure of relinquishing ownership, it is, nevertheless, understood to have been their intent (and legally recognized) since there is no other way that the above would be permitted to them (*Tos. Yom Tov* from *Tos.* 18b).

Alternatively, the *beis din* abolishes everyone's ownership from his candlesticks and pots (*Tos. Yom Tov* from *Ran*). [See *Gittin* 36b for source of the *beis din's* power to abolish private ownership.]

וּבֵית הִלֵּל מַתִּירִין. — *But Beis Hillel permit [this].*

Beis Hillel permit soaking ink, dyes, and vetch on the Sabbath as long as one adds the water while it is still day. According to them, there is no objection to the work being performed on the Sabbath since it is unaided by man. Beis Hillel do not agree to the precept of *shevisas keilim*. They maintain that the Torah's concern is for the animal's benefit and that, therefore, only in the case of animals who can suffer pain and fatigue does the Torah command that they be allowed to rest. In the case of inanimate objects this obviously does not apply (*Rav*). (See Commentary of *Sforno* to *Deut.* 5:12 for a different explanation.)

6.

בֵּית שַׁמַּאי אוֹמְרִים: אֵין נוֹתְנִין אוּנִין שֶׁל פִּשְׁתָּן לְתוֹךְ הַתַּנּוּר, — *Beis Shammai say: We may not place bundles of flax into the oven,*

I.e., bundles of combed flax may not be placed in a pot in the oven to

שבת א/ו

שֶׁל פִּשְׁתָּן לְתוֹךְ הַתַּנּוּר, אֶלָּא כְּדֵי שֶׁיַּהֲבִילוּ מִבְּעוֹד יוֹם. וְלֹא אֶת הַצֶּמֶר לַיּוֹרָה, אֶלָּא כְּדֵי שֶׁיִּקְלֹט הָעַיִן. וּבֵית הִלֵּל מַתִּירִין. בֵּית שַׁמַּאי אוֹמְרִים: אֵין פּוֹרְשִׂין מְצוּדוֹת חַיָּה וְעוֹפוֹת וְדָגִים, אֶלָּא כְּדֵי שֶׁיִּצּוֹדוּ מִבְּעוֹד יוֹם. וּבֵית הִלֵּל מַתִּירִין.

ר' עובדיה מברטנורא

שיהבילו. שיתחממו שיעלה בהם ההבל: **ליורה.** של צבעים: **אלא כדי שיקלוט את העין.** שיקלוט הצבע מבעוד יום: **ובית הלל מתירים.** לתתן לתוכו מבעוד יום ותהא קולטת כל הלילה. ולא שרו בית הלל אלא ביורה עקורה מן האש, שאם יש תחתיה אש בשבת אסור, גזירה שמא יחתה בגחלים. וצריך נמי שתהא היורה סתומה וטוחה בטיט, גזירה שמא יגיס ויהפך בה בשבת ויתחייב משום מבשל:

יד אברהם

be bleached by the heat of the oven (Rashi, Rav; Meiri).

Others render אונין as spun threads of flax (Tos. R' Akiva from Rash to Negaim 11:8; Meleches Shlomo; Shenos Eliyahu). [This, if done on the Sabbath, would violate the melachah of מְלַבֵּן, *whitening (see 7:2).]

אֶלָּא כְּדֵי שֶׁיַּהֲבִילוּ מִבְּעוֹד יוֹם — unless there is sufficient [time] for them to become heated while it is yet day.

[At that point, the process of bleaching has been basically completed.]

As in the previous mishnah, Beis Shammai again prohibit this because they maintain the principle of shevisas keilim is a Biblical commandment.

וְלֹא אֶת הַצֶּמֶר לַיּוֹרָה — Nor [may we place] wool into the vat,

Into a dyer's vat (Rav; Tif. Yis.). [*Dyeing is one of the thirty-nine melachos. See 7:2.]

אֶלָּא כְּדֵי שֶׁיִּקְלֹט הָעַיִן — unless there is sufficient [time] for it to absorb the color.

[Since the dyeing process has been completed, there is no objection to the wool remaining in the dyers' vat.]

וּבֵית הִלֵּל מַתִּירִין — But Beis Hillel permit [these acts].

Since Beis Hillel do not agree to the principle of shevisas keilim, they permit the bleaching of the flax and the dyeing of the wool to be completed on the Sabbath, provided they are placed in the oven or the vat before the Sabbath.

Although the Rabbis do not permit leaving a pot on a fire where there is the possibility that one may stir up the coals on the Sabbath (see 3:1), they nevertheless, in the case of the flax, do not prohibit this. This is because it is unlikely that one would uncover the flax to stir the coals, because a draft is detrimental to the flax (Gem. 18b).

It is to teach us this lesson concerning the coals that the mishnah was not satisfied with just the illustrations concerning soaking ink, dyes, and vetch (Tos. Yom Tov from Ran).

In the case of placing wool in the dyer's vat, we do, indeed, fear that one may stir up the coals. As a result, the Gemara (ibid.) requires that the dye pot be removed from above the fire. Also, the pot must be sealed, lest he stir the dyes (while the pot is still hot) and be liable for the melachah of מְבַשֵּׁל, *cooking (Rav from Gemara 18b). Since he will have to go to the trouble of unsealing the pot to stir the dye, he will remember

of flax into the oven, unless there is sufficient [time] for them to become heated while it is yet day. Nor [may we place] wool into the vat, unless there is sufficient [time] for it to absorb the color. But Beis Hillel permit [these acts].

Beis Shammai say: We may not spread snares for beasts, birds or fish, unless there is sufficient [time] to be captured while it is yet day. But Beis Hillel permit [this].

YAD AVRAHAM

the prohibition before he has a chance to commit a transgression (*Tos. Yom Tov* from *Rashi*).

בֵּית שַׁמַּאי אוֹמְרִים: אֵין פּוֹרְשִׂין מְצוּדוֹת חַיָּה וְעוֹפוֹת וְדָגִים, — *Beis Shammai say: We may not spread snares for beasts, birds or fish,*

Again, Beis Shammai follow their principle of *shevisas keilim* (*trapping being one of the thirty-nine *melachos*. See 7:2). This part of the mishnah is added to clarify Beis Hillel's view, as will be explained below (*Tos. Yom Tov* from *Ran*).

אֶלָּא כְּדֵי שֶׁיִּצּוֹדוּ מִבְּעוֹד יוֹם. — *unless there is sufficient [time] to be captured while it is yet day.*

The reasoning of Beis Shammai here is difficult to follow. Since Beis Shammai's reason for prohibiting snares is *shevisas keilim*, then the ability of the snares to trap the game before the advent of the Sabbath ought to be of no consequence. Granted that an animal *may* be caught before the Sabbath, it is, however, equally possible that it may occur *on* the Sabbath.

To answer this problem, the Talmud (*Yerushalmi*) states that Beis Shammai permit setting out snares before the Sabbath only under two conditions: The snares (a) may be set only in forests or lakes abounding in game or fish, and (b) must have a capacity for only one or two animals or fish. In such cases it is more than likely that the snares will complete their work *before* the Sabbath, after which they will be incapable of repeating their work *on* the Sabbath (*Tos.* 17b).

וּבֵית הִלֵּל מַתִּירִין. — *But Beis Hillel permit [this].*

Not only do Beis Hillel permit one's utensils to perform labor on the Sabbath when they are passive, but they do so even when the utensils perform actively, as in the case of a trap (*Tos. Yom Tov* from *Ran*).

7.

The following mishnayos, 7 and 8, introduce the Rabbinic prohibition of אֲמִירָה לְנָכְרִי, *telling a gentile,* to do work for a Jew on the Sabbath. The Rabbis found support for this law in the Torah: כָּל־מְלָאכָה לֹא יֵעָשֶׂה בָהֶם, *no work shall be done in them.* The Torah does not state "Do not perform work," but, rather, "No work shall be done"; suggesting that a Jew shall not be the cause of a *melachah* even when it is being done by a non-Jew (*Mishnah Berurah* 243:5).

שבת
א/ז-ח

[ז] **בֵּית** שַׁמַּאי אוֹמְרִים: אֵין מוֹכְרִין לְעוֹבֵד כּוֹכָבִים, וְאֵין טוֹעֲנִין עִמּוֹ, וְאֵין מַגְבִּיהִין עָלָיו, אֶלָּא כְּדֵי שֶׁיַּגִּיעַ לְמָקוֹם קָרוֹב. וּבֵית הִלֵּל מַתִּירִין.

[ח] **בֵּית** שַׁמַּאי אוֹמְרִים: אֵין נוֹתְנִין עוֹרוֹת לְעַבְּדָן וְלֹא כֵלִים לְכוֹבֵס עוֹבֵד כּוֹכָבִים, אֶלָּא כְּדֵי שֶׁיֵּעָשׂוּ מִבְּעוֹד יוֹם. וּבְכוּלָּן

―― ר' עובדיה מברטנורא ――

(ז) **ולא טוענין עמו.** על החמור. **ולא מגביהים.** עליו משאוי על כתפו, דמיחזי כמסייעו להוליך המשאוי בשבת: **אלא כדי שיגיע למקום קרוב.** כלומר שיהא המקום שרוצה להוליכו קרוב שיוכל להגיע שם מבעוד יום: **ובית הלל מתירין.** כדי שילא מפתח ביתו מבעוד יום: (ח) **לעבדן.** מעבד העורות:

―― יד אברהם ――

בֵּית שַׁמַּאי אוֹמְרִים: אֵין מוֹכְרִין לְעוֹבֵד כּוֹכָבִים, — *Beis Shammai say: We may not sell to a gentile,*

I.e., it is not permitted to sell to a gentile on Friday lest when the gentile leaves the Jew's home or shop carrying his purchases it seem to observers that the load he is carrying is an errand for a Jew on the Sabbath.

This halachah is not related to the dispute concerning *shevisas keilim* of the two previous mishnayos (*Tos. Yom Tov* from *Ran*).

וְאֵין טוֹעֲנִין עִמּוֹ, — *nor help him load,*

[Lit. *and we may not load with him.*] I.e., we may not help him load his donkey on Friday for the same reason. It may appear as though we are helping him to continue transporting his load on the Sabbath as an errand for a Jew (*Rav, Tos. Yom Tov* and *Ran*).

וְאֵין מַגְבִּיהִין עָלָיו, — *nor lift [a load] upon him,*

I.e., we may not lift a load onto his shoulders since it may appear that we are assisting him to carry it on the Sabbath for a Jew (*Rav*).

אֶלָּא כְּדֵי שֶׁיַּגִּיעַ לְמָקוֹם קָרוֹב. — *unless there is sufficient [time] for him to reach a nearby place.*

I.e., we may not do so unless his destination is near enough to enable him to arrive there before the advent of the Sabbath (*Rav*). [Beis Shammai forbids the mere appearance that the gentile is doing work at the request of the Jew.]

וּבֵית הִלֵּל מַתִּירִין. — *But Beis Hillel permit [these acts].*

Beis Hillel are of the opinion that these acts are permitted provided the gentile leaves the Jew's home before the Sabbath (*Rav, Tos. Yom Tov* from *Gem.* 18b). However, if he does not leave before the Sabbath, it will appear that a business transaction between Jew and gentile has taken place on the Sabbath and these acts are, therefore, prohibited (*Tos. Yom* from *Rambam, Hil. Shabbos* 6:19).

The *Gemara* (18b, 19a) cites a *baraisa* which enumerates three other disputes between Beis Shammai and Beis Hillel which parallel our mishnah:

7. Beis Shammai say: We may not sell to a gentile, nor help him load, nor lift [a load] upon him, unless there is sufficient [time] for him to reach a nearby place. But Beis Hillel permit [these acts].

8. Beis Shammai say: We may not give hides to a [gentile] tanner nor clothing to a gentile launderer, unless there is sufficient [time] that they be completed while it is yet day. In all these [cases]

YAD AVRAHAM

(a) Beis Shammai say: It is not permitted to sell, lend,[1] nor give a gift to a gentile [before the Sabbath] unless the gentile has sufficient time to reach his home before the Sabbath begins.

Beis Hillel say: [It is only necessary] that he be able to reach the house nearest the wall of the city [in which he resides].

Rabbi Akiva says: [It is only necessary that] he leave the Jew's home [before the Sabbath].

(b) Beis Shammai say: It is not permitted to sell one's חָמֵץ, *chametz*, leaven, to a gentile unless the Jew knows that it will be totally consumed before *Pesach*.

Beis Hillel say: As long as it is permitted to be eaten it is permitted to be sold (i.e., even if it is known that the *chametz* will be in the gentile's possession on *Pesach*).

(c) Beis Shammai say: [A Jew] may send a letter with a gentile [before the Sabbath] only if a fee has been agreed to and only if the letter will reach its destination before the Sabbath.

Beis Hillel say: [It is only necessary that the letter] be able to reach the house nearest the wall of the city [of the letter's destination].

The significance of setting a fee according to Beis Hillel is that once this is done the gentile's actions regarding the letter are in his own interest. Thus, he is, technically, doing the work for himself and not for the Jew. This allows the letter to be delivered on the Sabbath proper. However, where no fee has been set he is considered working for the Jew and, consequently, cannot deliver on the Sabbath. I.e., until a fee has been set, he is doing the Jew a favor, and consequently, he may not do so on the Sabbath.

Beis Shammai disallow delivery of the letter regardless of whether a fee has been set unless it can possibly reach its destination before sunset. Beis Shammai consistently disallow any act which would arouse the suspicion that the gentile may be working on the Sabbath at the behest of the Jew. As in the case of selling to the gentile the Jew must be certain that the gentile will reach his home before the Sabbath, so too, in regard to the letter, the Jew must be certain of the possibility of the letter's arrival before the Sabbath (*Rashi*, ibid.).

8.

בֵּית שַׁמַּאי אוֹמְרִים: אֵין נוֹתְנִין עוֹרוֹת לְעַבְּדָן וְלֹא כֵלִים לְכוֹבֵס עוֹבֵד כּוֹכָבִים,
Beis Shammai say: We mat not give hides to a [gentile] tanner nor clothing

to a gentile launderer,

Gentile refers to both the *tanner* and the *launderer*. I.e., we may not give either hides to a gentile tanner or

---

1. Two types of loan are included: שְׁאֵלָה, *she'eilah:* — the loan of an object for temporary use after which the object itself is to be returned (e.g., a plow); and הַלְוָאָה, *halva'ah:* — the loan of an object for consumptive use after which an equivalent object or equivalent value is to be returned (e.g., cash or foodstuffs).

שבת
א/ט

בֵּית הִלֵּל מַתִּירִין עִם הַשֶּׁמֶשׁ.

[ט] אָמַר רַבָּן שִׁמְעוֹן בֶּן גַּמְלִיאֵל: נוֹהֲגִין הָיוּ בֵּית אַבָּא שֶׁהָיוּ נוֹתְנִין כְּלֵי לָבָן לְכוֹבֵס עוֹבֵד כּוֹכָבִים שְׁלֹשָׁה יָמִים קֹדֶם לַשַּׁבָּת.

──────── ר' עובדיה מברטנורא ────────

מתירין עם השמש. בעוד שהחמה על הארץ קודם שתשקע: (ט) כלי לבן. שהוא קשה לכבס, צריך שלשה ימים, ומחמירין על עצמן כבית שמאי. ואין הלכה כרבן שמעון בן גמליאל, אלא כבית הלל שמתירין עם השמש:

──────── יד אברהם ────────

clothing to a gentile launderer on the eve of the Sabbath (*Tif. Yis.*).

[The *melachos* involved in this mishnah are *tanning, and *whitening. See 7:2.]

אֶלָּא כְּדֵי שֶׁיֵּעָשׂוּ מִבְּעוֹד יוֹם. — *unless there is sufficient [time] that they be completed while it is yet day.*

Beis Shammai permit this even when the work may actually be done on the Sabbath. When there is sufficient time for the work to be completed before the Sabbath, then even if the gentile does it on the Sabbath, he is not doing so at the behest of the Jew, but for his own convenience.

There is an apparent inconsistency in the position of Beis Shammai. Previously, they maintained that *shevisas keilim* [the prohibition of allowing one's utensils to be used on the Sabbath for the performance of a *melachah*] is a Scriptural injunction. How can they now be of the opinion that a Jew's clothing and hides may be laundered and tanned on the Sabbath by a gentile (when he had sufficient time before the Sabbath)? Are not the *keilim* (clothing and hides) of the Jew being used for the performance of a *melachah*?

Tos. (18a) and *Ran* solve the problem thus: *Shevisas keilim* does not allow for vessels and utensils to engage in work on the Sabbath. However, there is nothing that prohibits work being done to them on the Sabbath while they remain passive (*Tos. Yom Tov*). [Even if the utensils do the work passively, e.g., traps (see end of mishnah 6), Beis Shammai prohibit it. If work is being done to a Jew's article, but not *by* a Jew's utensil, even Beis Shammai permit it.]

וּבְכֻלָּן בֵּית הִלֵּל מַתִּירִין עִם הַשֶּׁמֶשׁ. — *In all these [cases] Beis Hillel permit [the act] while the sun is still up.*

All these cases refers to mishnayos 5-8 (*Tos. Yom Tov*). Beis Hillel permit the action before the Sabbath has begun.

9.

אָמַר רַבָּן שִׁמְעוֹן בֶּן גַּמְלִיאֵל: נוֹהֲגִין הָיוּ בֵּית אַבָּא שֶׁהָיוּ נוֹתְנִין כְּלֵי לָבָן לְכוֹבֵס עוֹבֵד כּוֹכָבִים שְׁלֹשָׁה יָמִים קֹדֶם לַשַּׁבָּת. — *Rabban Shimon ben Gamliel said: My father's household used to give white clothes to a gentile launderer three days before the Sabbath.*

They allowed three days because

1 Beis Hillel permit [the act] while the sun is still up.
9

9. **R**abban Shimon ben Gamliel said: My father's household used to give white clothes to a gentile launderer three days before the Sabbath.

YAD AVRAHAM

white clothes are more difficult to clean than colored and their cleaning required three days. Rabban Gamliel's family conducted themselves in accordance with the more stringent opinion of Beis Shammai, despite the fact that the halachah follows Beis Hillel and permits giving laundry to a gentile until sunset (*Rav*).

The Halachah generally rules strictly according to Beis Hillel; so much so that R' Tarfon related (*Berachos* 1:5) that when he once attempted to recline in order to recite the evening *Shema* (in accordance with the more stringent opinion of Beis Shammai there) the Sages considered him to have almost forfeited his life. This incident illustrates the severity of acting in accordance with the rulings of Beis Shammai where opposed by Beis Hillel.

The question, therefore, arises as to why Rabban Gamliel's family acted according to the dictates of Beis Shammai and insisted on sending their whites to the gentile launderer at least three days before the Sabbath.

Some commentators draw the following distinction between the two cases. In the case of *Shema*, Beis Shammai say that one must recline while reciting the evening *Shema* and stand while reciting the morning *Shema*, in accordance with the literal meaning of *Deuteronomy* 6:7, *When you lie down and when you rise*. Beis Hillel interpret these words as alluding to the time of day when people retire and arise, and no particular posture is required. Thus, when R' Tarfon reclined he committed a blatant act in contradiction to Beis Hillel's view. However, in our mishnah it is Beis Hillel's opinion that the whites may be brought to the launderer at *any* time before the onset of the Sabbath. As a result, bringing the whites three days before in no way indicates any disagreement with Beis Hillel's position. In such a manner, it is therefore permissible for one to act in accordance with Beis Shammai's opinion, if he so desires.

We find, however, an instance which would seem to refute these distinctions. The Mishnah (*Berachos* 8:7) states that Beis Shammai requires a person who forgot to recite *Bircas HaMazon* [Grace After Meals] to return to the place where he ate to recite it. Beis Hillel say that he may recite *Bircas HaMazon* wherever he finds himself. The *Gemara* then relates that a person once returned to where he ate to comply with Beis Shammai's opinion and, as a result, was rewarded from heaven by finding a purse full of gold coins.

Now, here this person actively and blatantly acted according to the ruling of Beis Shammai. Why, then, did he deserve to be rewarded?

Another distinction must, therefore, be added. There are two types of disputes between Beis Shammai and Beis Hillel:

(a) Those in which Beis Shammai make a stringent requirement and Beis Hillel agree that Beis Shammai's is the better way, but the Rabbis did not make it absolutely necessary, e.g., returning to the place of eating to recite the *Bircas HaMazon*. Here it is praiseworthy to act in accordance with Beis Shammai since even Beis Hillel admit that it is the better way.

(b) Those in which Beis Hillel's opinion is that there is absolutely no reason to adhere to Beis Shammai's opinion, there being no advantage whatever in Beis Shammai's way, as in the case of reclining for *Shema*. Beis Hillel interpret *when you lie down* as the *time* for the reciting of *Shema* and there is, therefore, no reason whatever for reclining. In this

שבת א/י

וְשָׁוִין אֵלּוּ וָאֵלּוּ שֶׁטּוֹעֲנִים קוֹרוֹת בֵּית הַבַּד וְעִגּוּלֵי הַגַּת.

[י] **אֵין צוֹלִין** בָּשָׂר, בָּצָל, וּבֵיצָה, אֶלָּא כְּדֵי שֶׁיִּצוֹלוּ מִבְּעוֹד יוֹם.

ר' עובדיה מברטנורא

וְשָׁוִין. בֵּית שַׁמַּאי וּבֵית הִלֵּל, שֶׁטּוֹעֲנִין אֶת הַזֵּיתִים מִבְּעוֹד יוֹם בְּקוֹרַת בֵּית הַבַּד, לְאַחַר שֶׁטָּחֲנוּ הַזֵּיתִים טוֹעֲנִין עֲלֵיהֶם קוֹרוֹת כְּבֵדִים וְהַמַּשְׁקֶה זָב וְהוֹלֵךְ מֵאֵלָיו כָּל הַשַּׁבָּת: **וְעִגּוּלֵי הַגַּת.** הָכִי דְּגַת קָרֵי עִגּוּלִין, שֶׁהָיוּ דַפִּין עָבִין עֲשׂוּיִין בְּעִגּוּל, וּבָהָא מוֹדוּ בֵּית שַׁמַּאי לְבֵית הִלֵּל, מִשּׁוּם דְּאִי נַמִּי עָבִיד לֵהּ בְּשַׁבָּת לֵיכָּא חִיּוּב חַטָּאת, דְּאֵין נוֹתְנִין קוֹרָה עַל גַּבֵּי זֵיתִים עַד שֶׁטָּחֲנָן תְּחִלָּה בָּרֵחַיִם, וְכֵן בַּעֲנָבִים דּוֹרְכִים אוֹתָן בָּרֶגֶל תְּחִלָּה, וּלְאַלּוּ קוֹרָה נַמִּי מַשְׁקֶה נָפֵיק מִמֵּילָא, אֶלָּא דְּלָא נָפֵיק שַׁפִּיר כִּי הַשְׁתָּא, הִלְכָּךְ לֹא דָּמֵי לְדָשׁ: (י) **בִּכְדֵי שֶׁיִּצוֹלוּ.** כְּמַאֲכַל בֶּן דְּרוּסַאי, וְהוּא שְׁלִישׁ בָּשׁוּל, וּבְכָךְ הוּא רָאוּי לַאֲכִילָה וְתוּ לֵיכָּא לְמִגְזַר שֶׁמָּא יְחַתֶּה בַּגֶּחָלִים:

יד אברהם

oil was as follows: The olives were first ground, releasing the majority of their oil, then heavy beams were placed on the olives to facilitate the extraction of the remaining oil. Similarly, grapes were first trampled, then heavy wooden rollers were placed over the trampled grapes. This, too, would cause the remaining juice to flow more readily. However, even unaided, the oil and juice would eventually ooze out. Thus, placing the beams or rollers on the fruit serves only to speed up and facilitate the process and is, therefore, not considered a Scripturally prohibited work, even if done on the Sabbath. [It is, however, Rabbinically prohibited to press the beams on the Sabbath to extract the remaining oil. See *Gem.* 19a.]

Beis Shammai, therefore, agree to Beis Hillel's more lenient ruling in these situations and allow the placing of the beams and rollers on the fruit before the Sabbath despite the fact that the juice and oil will continue to ooze on the Sabbath (*Rashi, Rav*).

Thus, we discern here a guiding instance it is wrong to follow the ruling of Beis Shammai and one who does is exposing himself to potential danger (*Tos. Yom Tov* from *Rosh; Tif. Yis.; Shenos Eliyahu*).

וְשָׁוִין אֵלּוּ וָאֵלּוּ — *And both concur*
I.e., Beis Hillel and Beis Shammai both agree (*Rav*).

שֶׁטּוֹעֲנִים קוֹרוֹת בֵּית הַבַּד וְעִגּוּלֵי הַגַּת. — *that we may place the beams of the olive-press and the rollers of the wine-press.*

The pressing of olives or grapes to extract their juice is prohibited as a derivative of the *melachah* of *threshing* (see 7:2), called מְפָרֵק, *extracting,* or as *Rashi* expresses it, ''unloading'' the fruit of the burden that grows within it. If, however, the fruit has been previously crushed, it has already become unburdened, so to speak, of most of its juice and it is no longer considered a *melachah* to extract the remaining juice or oil, since it will eventually come out by itself, even without laying the beam on it as below (*Rav*).

The process of pressing olives for

1
10
And both concur that we may place the beams of the olive-press and the rollers of the wine-press.

10. We may not roast meat, onions or eggs, unless there is sufficient [time] for them to become roasted while it is yet day.

YAD AVRAHAM

principle of Beis Shammai's opinion, viz., any act, which if committed on the Sabbath would constitute a Scripturally prohibited *melachah*, may not be begun before the Sabbath and allowed to continue on the Sabbath. If, however, the act is prohibited only by Rabbinic injunction, then it may be begun before the Sabbath and allowed to continue on the Sabbath.

10.

אֵין צוֹלִין בָּשָׂר, בָּצָל, וּבֵיצָה, — *We may not roast meat, onions or eggs,*

I.e., it is not permitted to set these foods to roast on Friday ... even according to Beis Hillel (*Tif. Yis.*).

This refers to food roasted directly over the fire. Food roasted in a pot or pan has the same rules as food cooked in a pot, which will be discussed in 3:1 (*Shulchan Aruch* 254:1 with *Magen Avraham*).

אֶלָּא כְּדֵי שֶׁיִּצוֹלוּ מִבְּעוֹד יוֹם. — *unless there is sufficient [time] for them to become roasted while it is yet day.*

I.e., unless there is time for them to become roasted enough to be edible, before the Sabbath. The *Gemara* refers to this amount of cooking as כְּמַאֲכַל בֶּן־דְּרוּסַאי, *like the food of Ben Derusai*. (Ben Derusai was a notorious bandit who, to avoid detection, ate his food hastily when it was only one-third[1] cooked.) We shall learn in 3:1 that it is not permitted to place food on an oven before the Sabbath where there is a chance that one may, in order to increase the heat, stir up the coals on the Sabbath. (For this reason, this prohibition applies even according to Beis Hillel.) However, once the roasted food has reached the state of food of Ben Derusai, no such prohibition applies (*Rav; Ran; Rashi*).

The injunction against placing uncooked meat over the fire before the Sabbath varies with the type of oven and the type of food.

The following distinctions are delineated by some authorities (*Ramban, Hil. Shabbos* 3:16, *Shulchan Aruch* 254:1,2):

(a) *When the meat is placed directly on the coals.* Since he is not troubled by the possibility of the meat's becoming singed, it is obvious that his prime consideration is that the meat be quickly roasted. For this reason, we are concerned that in order to speed up the cooking process he may forgetfully stir up the coals on the Sabbath to increase the heat. Here the Rabbis decreed that if the meat is not at least prepared to the level of the food of Ben Derusai, one may not place it on the fire.

(b) *When the meat is placed near the fire*

---

1. This follows the opinion of *Rashi, Rav* and others. *Ramban's* opinion is, however, that this means one-half cooked (see *Hil. Shabbos* 9:5 and *Ravad* there; cf. *Maggid Mishneh* to 3:16). This opinion, though, is adopted by *Shulchan Aruch* 254:2 although *Yoreh Deah* 113:8 follows *Rashi*. See *Ba'eir Hetev* 254:2 and *Eliyah Rabbah* 253:15.

שבת א/יא

אֵין נוֹתְנִין פַּת לַתַּנּוּר עִם חֲשֵׁכָה, וְלֹא חֲרָרָה עַל גַּבֵּי גֶחָלִים, אֶלָּא כְדֵי שֶׁיִּקְרְמוּ פָנֶיהָ מִבְּעוֹד יוֹם. רַבִּי אֱלִיעֶזֶר אוֹמֵר: כְּדֵי שֶׁיִּקְרֹם הַתַּחְתּוֹן שֶׁלָּהּ.

[יא] **מְשַׁלְשְׁלִין** אֶת הַפֶּסַח בַּתַּנּוּר עִם חֲשֵׁכָה,

---
ר' עובדיה מברטנורא

חררה. עוגת רלפיס: **שיקרמו.** תחלת אפיה טושין כמו קרוס: **פניה.** שהם כלפי אויר התנור: **כדי שיקרום התחתון.** המדובק לחרס התנור, דהוא נאפה תחלה קודם שיקרמו הפנים שכלפי אויר התנור, ובהכי סגי. ואין הלכה כרבי אליעזר: **(יא) משלשלין את הפסח.** התנורים שלהן פיהן למעלה ומורידין הללי לתוכו, להכי תני משלשלין: **עם חשיבה.** ואף על גב דבטלמא אין טולין כדאמרן, הכא שרי, דבני חבורה זריזין הן ומדכרי אהדדי, ולא אתו לחתויי בגחלים:

יד אברהם

of clay and were cone shaped with the wide end at the bottom. This served to intensify the heat as it rose towards the narrow opening at the top. Bread and cakes were baked by pressing the dough to the inside walls of the oven.

וְלֹא חֲרָרָה עַל גַּבֵּי גֶחָלִים, אֶלָּא כְדֵי שֶׁיִּקְרְמוּ פָנֶיהָ מִבְּעוֹד יוֹם. — *nor a cake upon coals, unless there is sufficient [time] for its upper surface to form a crust while it is yet day.*

If the outer surface of the bread, i.e., the surface opposite the one adhering to the wall of the oven, forms a crust, the baking is legally completed and there is no fear that he may stir up the coals, for, if he were to do so, the bread would burn (*Rav; Ramban, Hil. Shabbos* 3:18)

רַבִּי אֱלִיעֶזֶר אוֹמֵר: כְּדֵי שֶׁיִּקְרֹם הַתַּחְתּוֹן שֶׁלָּהּ. — *R' Eliezer says: Sufficient [time] for its bottom [surface] to form a crust.*

I.e., the surface adhering to the oven wall forms a crust before nightfall (*Rashi* 20a).

There is a dispute whether R' Eliezer's opinion is the more stringent or the more lenient.

Tosafos (20a) and the *Rav* hold that

(but not directly on it). Here there are two considerations: (1) Food which requires a great deal of cooking, e.g., beef or goat's meat, may not be placed near the fire before the Sabbath (except under the conditions where cooking food may be left on a fire, see 3:1); (2) food which requires little cooking, e.g., vegetables or kid's meat cut into pieces, are permitted to be placed near the fire. At this stage, it is unlikely that anyone would risk burning the meat by stirring up the coals on the Sabbath when it is already edible.

(c) *Placing food in a sealed oven to roast.* This is permitted for all types of food because opening the oven will cool it and adversely affect the meat.

Other authorities (*Rama* 254:1,2 *Tur* and others) do not differentiate between *on* the fire or *near* the fire. The determining factor is whether the oven is open or sealed. *All* meats are permitted to be placed in a sealed oven before the Sabbath. *All* meats may not be placed in an open oven before the Sabbath.

(d) *In an oven that is closed, but not sealed,* one may place tender meat, but not tough meat before the Sabbath.

(e) *Food cooking in a pot* — will be discussed in 3:1.

אֵין נוֹתְנִין פַּת לַתַּנּוּר עִם חֲשֵׁכָה, — *We may not place bread in the oven near nightfall,*

The ovens of that period were made

1   We may not place bread in the oven near night-
11   fall, nor a cake upon coals, unless there is sufficient [time] for its upper surface to form a crust while it is yet day.

R' Eliezer says: Sufficient [time] for its bottom [surface] to form a crust.

11. We may lower the *pesach* sacrifice into the oven near nightfall, and we may ignite

YAD AVRAHAM

the inner crust is formed first. Accordingly, the *Tanna Kamma* [the first Tanna, i.e., the unidentified speaker of the first opinion disputed by R' Eliezer] holds that it is not sufficient for only the surface adhering to the wall of the oven to have formed a crust. Both surfaces must have a crust before the Sabbath. R' Eliezer, on the other hand, holds that it is sufficient even if only the surface adhering to the wall has formed a crust.

According to this explanation R' Eliezer's view is the more lenient.

Rashi's opinion is that the outer crust is formed before the crust of the surface adhering to the wall. As a result, the *Tanna Kamma* is the more lenient opinion.

Tosefos R' Akiva finds it difficult to accept that *Rashi* and *Tosafos* would dispute a factual process. He, therefore, attributes *Rashi's* and *Rav's* opinions to different situations. *Rashi's* statement deals with an oven whose coals are still present at the bottom. As a result, the greater heat intensity of heat will cause the outer surface, which faces the coals, to form a crust first. *Rav* is dealing with an oven whose coals have been removed, the bread being baked by residual heat. In such a case, the surface of the oven wall will be hotter than the air in the oven and the dough adhering to it will form a crust first.

Shulchan Aruch (254:5) rules in accordance with *Tosafos'* opinion: It is permitted to place bread in an oven even if only the inner crust will have sufficient time to form a crust before the Sabbath. (See *Mishnah Berurah* 29.)

11.

מְשַׁלְשְׁלִין אֶת הַפֶּסַח בַּתַּנוּר עִם חֲשֵׁכָה, — *We may lower the pesach sacrifice into the oven near nightfall,*

During the afternoon of the fourteenth of Nissan, the *pesach* sacrifice was slaughtered and parts were offered up on the Altar. The remaining meat was roasted over the fire, to be eaten in the evening. See *Exodus 28:8-9*.

If the first night of Passover falls on the Sabbath, it is permitted to lower the sacrifice into the oven immediately before nightfall, though it will continue to roast on the Sabbath. Although mishnah 10 states that we may not roast meat unless there is time for it to become roasted while it is still day, the Rabbis made an exception in this case since those engaged in roasting the Pesach sacrifice are extremely careful and will remind one another should one forget and

[53]   THE MISHNAH/SHABBOS — Chapter One: *Yetzios HaShabbos*

שבת
א/יא

וּמַאֲחִיזִין אֶת הָאוּר בִּמְדוּרַת בֵּית הַמּוֹקֵד. וּבַגְּבוּלִין, כְּדֵי שֶׁתֶּאֱחֹז הָאוּר בְּרֻבָּן. רַבִּי יְהוּדָה אוֹמֵר: בְּפֶחָמִין כָּל שֶׁהוּא.

───── ר' עובדיה מברטנורא ─────

ומאחיזין את האור. מעט, בעליל של מדורת בית המוקד, ולא חיישינן שמא יבואו הכהנים להבעירה משתחשך דכהנים זריזין הן: **בית המוקד.** לשכה גדולה היתה בעזרה שמסיקין בה מדורה תמיד והכהנים מתחממים שם, לפי שהולכים יחפים על הרצפה של שיש: **ובגבולין.** צריך האדם להבעיר מדורתו מבעוד יום כדי שתאחוז האור ברובה, וכמה ברובה, כדי שתהא שלהבת עולה מאליה ואינה צריכה לקסמין דקין תחתיה להבעירה: **אף בפחמין כל שהוא.** כי היכי דבמדורת בית המוקד מקילין בבית המוקד לכהנים, כמו כן במדורת פחמים מקילין לכל אדם, ואין צריך להאחיז בהן האור אלא כל שהוא, שאין דרכה להיות כבה והולכת, ולא אתו לחתויי בהו. והלכה כרבי יהודה דליכא מאן דפליג עליה:

───── יד אברהם ─────

attempt to rake the coals. [The entire ban was instituted only to prevent one from stoking the fire unthinkingly. The ban was not necessary to forestall someone from willfully violating the Sabbath laws, nor, obviously, would it be effective (*Rav from Gem.* 20a).]

וּמַאֲחִיזִין — *and we may ignite* [*with chips*]

Thin chips were used to start the fire in the Temple. No precautions are necessary against the *Kohanim* stoking the fire, for the *Kohanim* in the Temple were alert (*Rav from Gem.* 20a).

אֶת הָאוּר בִּמְדוּרַת בֵּית הַמּוֹקֵד. — *the fire of the pyre in the* [*Temple*] *fire chamber.*

There was a large chamber in the Temple court where a fire was constantly kept burning. The *Kohanim*, who walked barefoot on the marble floor, would warm themselves in this chamber (*Rashi; Rav*).

Alternatively, this fire was used to keep the fire on the Altar burning continuously. Although there was always a miraculous fire that descended from heaven on the Altar, it was obligatory to supplement it with a man-made fire. This man-made fire was taken from the fire room (*Ramban*). [See also commentary to *Tamid* 25b and *Tos. Yom Tov* to *Tamid* 1:1.]

[with chips] the fire of the pyre in the [Temple] fire chamber. But in the country, [this may not be done unless there is] sufficient [time] for the fire to take hold of most of them.

R' Yehudah says: With charcoal [it is permitted as long as there is sufficient time for the fire to take hold of] any amount.

YAD AVRAHAM

וּבַגְּבוּלִין, — *But in the country* [lit. *within the borders*],

I.e., in the entire country outside the Temple, one may not ignite a fire before the Sabbath unless it has time to take hold, as described below (*Rav*).

כְּדֵי שֶׁתֶּאֱחֹז הָאוּר בְּרֻבָּן. — [*this may not be done unless there is*] *sufficient* [*time*] *for the fire to take hold of most of them.*

I.e., if before the Sabbath sets in, the fire has caught on to the wood to the extent that no more chips are necessary and the flame rises spontaneously (*Rav, Tif. Yis.* from *Gem.* 20a).

If the fire contains only one log, most of its thickness and most of its circumference must be alight while it is still day on Friday (*Tif. Yis.* from *Gem.* 20a).

If these requirements are not met then, one is not permitted to warm himself by the fire lest he forget and rake the fire or move the sticks to make the flames rise (*Ramban, Hil. Shabbos* 3:19).

רַבִּי יְהוּדָה אוֹמֵר: בְּפֶחָמִין כָּל שֶׁהוּא. — *R' Yehudah says: With charcoal* [*it is permitted as long as there is sufficient time for the fire to take hold of*] *any amount.*

Rav reads: אַף בְּפֶחָמִין, *also with charcoal*. He therefore explains as follows:

Just as the *Kohanim* are permitted to ignite a fire in the Temple fire room shortly before the Sabbath, so too may anyone ignite a charcoal fire shortly before the Sabbath. Once the fire has caught on to any minute bit of the charcoal it will usually continue to burn and it will not be necessary to rake or move the sticks. Since no one disputes R' Yehudah's ruling, the halachah is so decided (*Rav*).

Rav's view is shared by *Tur* (255) and *Rabbeinu Yerucham* (12:3). *Rambam*, however, understands the mishnah to mean that R' Yehudah alone permits the charcoal fire, in opposition to the *Tanna Kamma*, who does not mention this lenient ruling. He, therefore, decides the halachah in accordance with the *Tanna Kamma* (*Tos. Yom Tov*).

פרק שני
Chapter Two

The Rabbis declared an obligation to light a lamp or a candle before the Sabbath so that one may conduct his Sabbath meal in a lighted room. They based this enactment on the prophet's proclamation (*Isaiah* 58:13), וְקָרָאתָ לַשַּׁבָּת עֹנֶג לִקְדוֹשׁ ה' מְכֻבָּד, *And if you proclaim the Sabbath "a delight," the holy one of Hashem "honored one"* ...

Hence, we are required (a) to enjoy the Sabbath, and (b) to honor it. The mitzvah of enjoying the Sabbath is called עֹנֶג שַׁבָּת [*oneg Shabbos*], *delight in the Sabbath*. Some maintain that lighting the Sabbath candles for the Sabbath meal is a fulfillment of *oneg Shabbos*. It is difficult for someone to enjoy the Sabbath when his house is dark and he can neither see where he is going nor what he is eating (*Tos.* 25b). [It is a common experience that one has more enjoyment from food he can see than from food he cannot. Additionally, one who eats in the dark worries about insects falling into his food (*Shibbolei HaLeket*).]

Others base this obligation on כְּבוֹד שַׁבָּת, *honor of the Sabbath*. A feast is always served in a brightly illuminated room. Kindling lights for the Sabbath, therefore, is a mark of honor (*Rashi* 25b).

The Talmud adds that a brightly lit home is conducive to a peaceful atmosphere since it prevents injury from unseen obstacles (*Rashi* 25b).

Rambam's position regarding candle-lighting seems to be inconsistent. In *Hilchos Shabbos* 5:1 he states that the Sabbath light is included in the category of *oneg Shabbos*. Further on (ibid. 30:5), however, he includes candle-lighting among the practices of "honor of the Sabbath."

Aruch HaShulchan (263:2) explains that *Rambam* is discussing different lights. (a) We must light candles in the room where we eat in order to bestow a festive air to our meal. These lights are kindled in "honor of the Sabbath." (b) We must also light candles in the other rooms of the house so that no one will stumble. This is required in order to enjoy the Sabbath. These latter are lit for "joy of the Sabbath."

R' Yitzchak Zev Soloveitchik is reported to have offered an alternate solution to this difficulty:

Just as preparations prior to the arrival of an illustrious guest are all considered an honor for the guest, so too, everything done on Friday in anticipation of the Sabbath is considered honoring the Sabbath. Lighting the candles Friday evening would also fall into this category. The actual enjoyment of the candles, i.e., the partaking of the Sabbath meal in an illuminated room would, however, be classified as enjoyment of the Sabbath. Hence, the two separate *halachos* of *Rambam* (see *Beur HaGra* 529:5).

Chapter 2 discusses the Sabbath lights. It opens with a listing of the materials that are acceptable or disqualified for wicks and oils to be used for the Sabbath lights. The wicks must be made of material that draws oil well, so that the flame will burn with a steady flame, not flicker nor sputter. Oils, too, must be of a variety that is easily absorbed by the wick so that the flame burns steadily.

שבת
ב/א

[א] **בַּמֶּה** מַדְלִיקִין וּבַמָּה אֵין מַדְלִיקִין? אֵין מַדְלִיקִין לֹא בְלֶכֶשׁ, וְלֹא בְחֹסֶן, וְלֹא בְכָלָךְ, וְלֹא בִפְתִילַת הָאִידָן, וְלֹא בִפְתִילַת הַמִּדְבָּר, וְלֹא בִירוֹקָה שֶׁעַל פְּנֵי הַמָּיִם; וְלֹא בְזֶפֶת, וְלֹא בְשַׁעֲוָה, וְלֹא בְשֶׁמֶן קִיק,

---
ר' עובדיה מברטנורא

פרק שני – במה מדליקין. (א) במה מדליקין. נר של שבת; במה טושין פתילות ושמנים להדליק: **לא בלבש.** כמין למר יש באלרז בין הקליפה לעץ, וקרוי לכש: **בחוסן.** פשתן שאינו מנופץ: **בכלך.** פסולת של משי: **בפתילת האידן.** כמין למר יש [בטרבזה] בין הקליפה לעץ: **בפתילת המדבר.** עלי עשב ארוך שגודלין אותם ומדליקין בהן: **בירוקה שעל פני המים.** כמין למר שגדל בדופני הספינה ששהתה זמן מרובה במים. עד כאן פסול פתילות, מכאן ואילך פסול שמנים: **לא בזפת ולא בשעוה.** שלא יתן זפת נמס ושעוה נתכת בנר במקום שמן וידליק, אבל לעשות כמין פתילה ארוכה שרגילין לעשות משטוה שרי: **ולא בשמן קיק.** שמן היולא מגרטעינים שבתוך הלמר גפן שקורין קוטו"ן. ויש מפרשים קיקיון דיונה והוא עשב שעליו גדולים ונקרא בערבי כרו"ע, והשמן היולא ממנו עב ביותר. ופתילות שאמרו חכמים אין מדליקין בהס, מה טעם, מפני שהאור מסכסכת בהס, כלומר שאין האור נכנסת תוך הפתילה [אלא] סביב מבחון. ושמנים שאמרו חכמים אין מדליקין בהס, לפי שאין נמשכים אחר הפתילה, ומתוך שאין הנר דולקת יפה חייסינן שמא יטה השמן על פי הנר ונמלא מבעיר. אי נמי שמא יניח הנר וילא, ואנן קיימא לן דנר של שבת חובה:

יד אברהם

1.

בַּמֶּה מַדְלִיקִין וּבַמָּה אֵין מַדְלִיקִין — With what may we light [the Sabbath lamp], and with what may we not light?

From what materials may we make the wick and what oils may we use as fuel? (*Rav; Tif. Yis.*).

◆§ **Unacceptable Wicks**

אֵין מַדְלִיקִין לֹא בְלֶכֶשׁ — We may light neither with cedar bast,

[Lit. *We may not light, not with cedar bast.* In Hebrew, the double negative is frequently used. See also 4:1; 6:1,3.]

This is the fibrous inner bark of the cedar tree which can be made into wicks (*Rav* from *Gem.* 20b).

וְלֹא בְחֹסֶן — nor with uncarded flax,

I.e., with flax whose stems have been crushed but whose fibers have not yet been carded (*Gem.* ibid.).

Before carding, the flax does not draw the oil well (*Rashi; Gem.* ibid.).

וְלֹא בְכָלָךְ — nor with floss silk,

An inferior grade of silk made from the cocoon of the silkworm which is carded, spun, and woven into cloth. It is unsuitable for wicks because the flame will not burn evenly, but flicker (*Rashi; Gem.* ibid.).

Rambam renders merely: nor with silk.

Alternatively, this is a woolly substance found on stones in the sea, identified with the cissaros-blossom (*Shenos Eliyahu*).

וְלֹא בִפְתִילַת הָאִידָן — nor with willow bast,

A woolly substance found beneath

1. **With** what may we light [the Sabbath lamp], and with what may we not light? We may light neither with cedar bast, nor with uncarded flax, nor with floss silk, nor with willow bast, nor with desert fiber, nor with sea moss; nor [may we light] with pitch, nor with wax, nor with cottonseed oil,

YAD AVRAHAM

the bark of the willow tree (*Rav*).

וְלֹא בִּפְתִילַת הַמִּדְבָּר — *nor with desert fiber*,

Nettle, a long grass that can be braided and used for wicks (*Rashi; Rav; Tif. Yis.*).

וְלֹא בִּירוֹקָה שֶׁעַל פְּנֵי הַמָּיִם — *nor with sea moss* (lit. *the green which is on the surface of the water*);

The dark green moss that accumulates on the bottom of ships (*Rav* from *Gem*. 20b).

◈§ Unacceptable Oils

This mishnah has thus far enumerated the materials unfit for *wicks*. What follows are the *oils* unfit for the Sabbath lamp (*Rav* from *Gem*. ibid.).

וְלֹא בְזֶפֶת, וְלֹא בְשַׁעֲוָה, — *nor [may we light] with pitch, nor with wax*,

I.e., we may not use molten pitch or molten wax as fuel for the lamp. Candles, however, may be made of these materials (*Rashi; Tos.; Rav; Rosh; Rif; Shulchan Aruch* 264:7).

The Rabbis disallowed these because they are not drawn well into the wick. However, when made into candles, they burn evenly and may be used (*Mishnah Berurah* 264:24).[1]

וְלֹא בְשֶׁמֶן קִיק, — *nor with cottonseed oil*,

This is one explanation offered by the *Gemara* (21a). Another identifies *kik* with the *kikayon* mentioned in the Book of Jonah. It is similar to the ricinus plant — a grass with large leaves and very thick oil (*Rav*).

There is still another opinion in the *Gemara* that *kik* is a bird sighted by merchants from overseas.[2] Oil was extracted from them and used in lamps. The term קִיק is identified with קָאָת, mentioned among the unclean fowls in *Lev*. 11:18 (*Shenos Eliyahu; Radak* in *Sefer HaShorashim*).

The Rabbis ruled certain wicks unfit for the Sabbath lights because the flame remains on the outside and does not catch onto them. Alternatively, it does not burn with a steady flame but flickers (*Rashi* 21a). The Rabbis ruled certain oils unfit for the Sabbath lights because they are not drawn freely into the wick. As a result the lamp will sputter and we are concerned that one may inadvertently tilt the lamp to improve its light, in which case he would violate the *melachah* of *kindling (*Rashi*).

Alternatively, he may be displeased with the inadequacy of light and leave

---

1. Some authorities (the *Geonim*, the sages of Narbonne, and several others) prohibited such candles. However, their view is not cited in *Shulchan Aruch* and the more lenient ruling has been adopted. *Bach* maintains that even according to the *Geonim* and the sages of Narbonne, pure pitch and pure wax *are* drawn well by the wick and are permissible for use as candles.

2. *Doros HaRishonim* states that these were merchants who journeyed to India from Babylon (what is today Iraq).

שבת ב/א

וְלֹא בְשֶׁמֶן שְׂרֵפָה, וְלֹא בְאַלְיָה, וְלֹא בְחֵלֶב.

ר' עובדיה מברטנורא

ולא בשמן שריפה. שמן של תרומה שנטמאת. ואמאי קרי ליה שמן שריפה הואיל ולשריפה עומד שהרי אסור באכילה. וביום טוב שחל להיות בערב שבת עסקינן, שכשמדליק הנר מבעוד יום נמצא שורף שמן טמא של תרומה ביום טוב, ואין קיימא לו אין שורפין קדשים ביום טוב דכתיב (שמות יב) והנותר ממנו עד בקר באש תשרופו, ודרשינן קרא הכי, והנותר ממנו עד בקר ראשון, עד בקר שני עמוד ותשרפנו. והוא הדין לכל שאר קדשים הטעונים שריפה:

יד אברהם

the room. As a result, he will not have fulfilled his obligation of the Sabbath light, which requires that he derive benefit from the light (*Rambam*; *Rav*).

Rashash disagrees with the latter opinion since it is unlikely that a person would leave even a dimly lit room to go to a completely dark one. Furthermore, the Rabbis who disagree with R' Ishmael permit lighting with tar which emits a foul odor (mishnah 2) and are not concerned that it may cause the person to leave the room.

He, therefore, suggests that these wicks and oils do not produce enough light to illuminate the room sufficiently for one to be able to avoid tripping over any obstacles on the floor. Since the obligation to light candles was instituted for this purpose, one cannot fulfill his obligation with such inferior materials.

וְלֹא בְשֶׁמֶן שְׂרֵפָה, — *nor with oil that must be burnt*,

This refers to oil which is *terumah* and which has become *tamei*.

One who harvests olives and produces oil from them must set aside *terumah* from that olive oil. [*Terumah* is part of one's crop (between 1/40 and 1/60) that the owner must set aside and give to a *Kohen*.] Upon designating a given quantity of oil as *terumah*, it attains that status and becomes subject to special laws governing *terumah*. Primarily these are: (a) *Terumah* may not be eaten by anyone except a *Kohen*; (b) a *Kohen* may not eat *terumah* except in a state of *taharah*, ritual purity, i.e., uncontaminated by contact with any of the objects (e.g., human or animal corpse) and free of any of the personal conditions (e.g., *zav*, *zavah*, see 1:3) or contact with one who has that condition which, according to the Torah, contaminates a person, rendering him *tamei* and (c) the *terumah* itself must also be in a state of *taharah*, i.e., not having come in contact with any of the above objects or people. [For a discussion about how a person, vessel, or foodstuff becomes *tamei*, see appendix "The Eighteen Decrees" at the end of this volume.]

If *terumah* has become *tamei*, it may not be eaten, but must be destroyed by burning.[1] For this reason *terumah* oil which has become contaminated is called שֶׁמֶן שְׂרֵפָה, *oil which must be burnt*.

The prohibition for use as a Sabbath light, however, is difficult to understand since the law requires only that such contaminated oil be burnt but does not prohibit the *Kohen* from making use of its light while it is burning.

---

1. Unlike people or utensils which have become *tamei*, foodstuffs cannot be purified by immersion in a *mikveh*. There is therefore no recourse but to burn them.

2 **nor with oil that must be burnt, nor with [fat from]
1 a sheep's tail, nor with tallow.**

YAD AVRAHAM

We are compelled to conclude that our mishnah is dealing with a *Yom Tov* (festival) that fell on a Friday and the candle-lighting for the Sabbath would thus be taking place on *Yom Tov* (since it must take place before sunset). There is a halachah which states: אֵין שׂוֹרְפִין קָדָשִׁים בְּיוֹם טוֹב, i.e., *sacrifices that have become disqualified* [and must therefore be destroyed by burning (away from the Altar) *may not be burnt on* Yom Tov.[1]

Contaminated *terumah* is also governed by the above and cannot be burned on *Yom Tov*. Since our mishnah is dealing with a festival which fell on a Friday, lighting the Sabbath candles with *terumah* oil which has become *tamei* and must be burnt would violate this prohibition (*Rav* from *Gem*. 23b).

Tosafos point out a difficulty regarding this matter. The cases of *terumah* oil which must be burnt and sacrifices that have become disqualified and must be burnt seem to be not at all comparable. Since one is not permitted to derive benefit from the burning of disqualified sacrifices, it follows that burning them on *Yom Tov* would not afford benefit to the person of a Jew but would merely be for the performance of the mitzvah. Since the Torah permits kindling a fire on *Yom Tov* only for the personal benefit of a Jew (e.g., for cooking his food or illuminating his house), it is reasonable that burning solely for the purposes of a mitzvah be excluded. In the case of a *Kohen* who lights Sabbath candles with contaminated *terumah* oil, however, no such exclusion should apply. Since the *Kohen* is allowed to derive benefit from the fire which is destroying the contaminated *terumah*, burning such oil on *Yom Tov* does provide benefit (illumination) to the *Kohen* in addition to the fulfillment of a mitzvah. It should be no worse than lighting oil which is not *terumah*. Why then does the mishnah prohibit it?

There are two possible reasons:

(1) Since the Torah prohibits all possible benefits from oil which must be burned, other than that which may be gained while it is being burnt, it is obvious that the primary purpose of the *melachah* is the fulfillment of the mitzvah. The benefit derived is only secondary. Thus, the *melachah* as a whole must be viewed as being done primarily for the mitzvah, and not for one's personal benefit. It is, therefore, prohibited on *Yom Tov*. This is akin to the law which states that one is not permitted to offer voluntary sacrifices on *Yom Tov*, despite the fact that most of the

---

1. This is derived from the verse that discusses the remainder of the meat of the *pesach* sacrifice after the *seder* (*Ex.* 12:10): וְלֹא־תוֹתִירוּ מִמֶּנּוּ עַד־בֹּקֶר וְהַנֹּתָר מִמֶּנּוּ עַד־בֹּקֶר בָּאֵשׁ תִּשְׂרֹפוּ, *And you shall let nothing of it (the meat of the pesach sacrifice) remain until the morning, and that which remains of it until the morning you shall burn with fire.* The repetition of the phrase *until the morning* of this verse seems to be redundant. Our Rabbis learn from this that the verse is referring to a second morning and interpret the verse thus:

Do not let anything (i.e., the parts one is supposed to eat) of the *pesach* offering remain *until the morning* of the fifteenth of the month of Nissan. That which *is* left shall be burnt but not *until the following morning*, i.e., the sixteenth of Nissan.

It is clear from this that the Torah objects to disqualified parts of the sacrifice being burnt on *Yom Tov* (fifteenth of Nissan) and requires waiting until after *Yom Tov* (sixteenth of Nissan).

שבת
ב/ב

נַחוּם הַמָּדִי אוֹמֵר: מַדְלִיקִין בְּחֵלֶב מְבֻשָּׁל. וַחֲכָמִים אוֹמְרִים: אֶחָד מְבֻשָּׁל [וְ]אֶחָד שֶׁאֵינוֹ מְבֻשָּׁל, אֵין מַדְלִיקִין בּוֹ.

[ב] **אֵין** מַדְלִיקִין בְּשֶׁמֶן שְׂרֵיפָה, בְּיוֹם טוֹב. רַבִּי יִשְׁמָעֵאל אוֹמֵר: אֵין מַדְלִיקִין בְּעִטְרָן,

---

ר' עובדיה מברטנורא

וחכמים אומרים אחד מבושל ואחד שאינו מבושל אין מדליקין בו. ותנא קמא נמי אמר "ולא בחלב" כל חלב במשמע. אלא איכא בין חכמים לתנא קמא דת"ק מיירייהו סבר דשרי להדליק בחלב מבושל כשמערב בו שמן כל שהוא, וחד חוסר אפילו על ידי תערובת שמן. ולא נתברר לחכמי התלמוד מי משניהם החוסר ומי המתיר. והלכה כחכמים: **(ב) אין מדליקין בשמן שריפה ביום טוב.** טעמא דמתניתין דלטעי קאמר, מה טעם תקן ולא בשמן שריפה, לפי שאין מדליקין בשמן שריפה ביום טוב, שאין שורפין קדשים ביום טוב: **אין מדליקין בעטרן.** פסולת של זפת וריחו רע ביותר, ומיהו נמשך אחר הפתילה יותר מן הזפת מפני שהוא רך, הילכך אלמלא מפני כבוד שבת היו מדליקין בו:

יד אברהם

meat of such sacrifices is eaten by the one offering it. Although one is permitted to slaughter an animal for meat on *Yom Tov*, since the major purpose in the sacrifice is the fulfillment of a mitzvah, it is not permitted on *Yom Tov*.

(2) There is no reason to impose a Torah prohibition on the burning of contaminated *terumah* on *Yom Tov* since we do receive personal benefit from the burning. The Rabbis, however, concerned lest people confuse burning contaminated *terumah* with burning disqualified sacrifices, which is Biblically prohibited, banned the latter as well (*Tos. R' Akiva* from *Tos.* 24b).

וְלֹא בְאַלְיָה, — *nor with [fat from] a sheep's tail,*

The tail fat mentioned here is permitted to be eaten and is not to be confused with the fatty suet and tallow, the eating of which is forbidden by Torah law (see *Lev.* 7:23). Although this tail fat is drawn more easily into the wick than the tallow mentioned next in the mishnah, it is, nevertheless, not drawn easily enough to make it acceptable for the Sabbath lamp (*Tos. R' Akiva*).

[Assuredly *Tosefos R' Akiva* holds that the mishnah lists the most unacceptable fuels first, for he continues:] We would expect tallow to be listed before tail fat in the mishnah, thereby running a gamut from more objectionable to less objectionable fuels. The order, however, is reversed so that the listing is not interrupted by the dispute regarding tallow.

Some explain that the sheep's tail is dried and used as a torch (*Tif. Yis.*).

וְלֹא בְחֵלֶב — *nor with tallow.*

This refers to the hard fatty tissues which the Torah forbids for consumption (*Lev.* 7:23).

נַחוּם הַמָּדִי אוֹמֵר: מַדְלִיקִין בְּחֵלֶב מְבֻשָּׁל. — *Nachum the Mede says: We may light with boiled tallow.*

Rashi (24b) understands חֵלֶב מְבֻשָּׁל to be tallow which has been boiled and is presently still in its molten state. Others (*Rashba; Ritva; Ran*) hold

**2
2**   Nachum the Mede says: We may light with boiled tallow. But the Sages say: Whether boiled or not boiled, we may not light with it.

2. **W**e may not light with oil that must be burnt, on *Yom Tov*.
R' Yishmael says: We may not light with tar,

YAD AVRAHAM

that it refers to tallow which was melted by boiling and then solidified once again as it cooled.

Nachum the Mede only disallows tallow in its original state (according to *Rashi* — solid; according to the others — raw) for in its processed state it *is* drawn easily by the wick. The *Tanna Kamma*, however, forbids even the processed tallow lest people confuse it with tallow in its natural state (*Tif. Yis.* from *Gem.* 21a).

וַחֲכָמִים אוֹמְרִים: אֶחָד מְבֻשָּׁל [וּ]אֶחָד שֶׁאֵינוּ מְבֻשָּׁל, אֵין מַדְלִיקִין בּוֹ. — *But the Sages say: Whether boiled or not boiled, we may not light with it.*

Seemingly, the Sages merely echo the *Tanna Kamma* who also does not differentiate between processed and unprocessed tallow. The *Gemara* 24b, however, explains that they differ regarding the permissibility of using boiled tallow into which a small quantity of acceptable oil has been mixed. The *Gemara*, however, adds that it is unclear whether it is the *Tanna Kamma* or the Sages who follow the stricter ruling.

The opinion which prohibits this mixture of oil and tallow does so out of concern that people may forget to add it. The opinion which permits the mixture reasons that since boiled tallow is itself only disallowed out of concern that some may use solid tallow, to disallow a mixture out of concern that some may not add the suitable oil would constitute a גְּזֵרָה לִגְזֵרָה, *a safeguard to a safeguard,* which the Rabbis are not empowered to enact (see 1:4). [The opinion which does prohibit the mixture seems to have understood that the original ban on tallow was enacted without any exceptions, to avoid confusion. This would not constitute a *safeguard to a safeguard* (*Tif. Yis.* from *Gem.* 21a, 24b).]

2.

אֵין מַדְלִיקִין בְּשֶׁמֶן שְׂרֵפָה, בְּיוֹם טוֹב. — *We may not light with oil that must be burnt, on Yom Tov.*

The *Tanna* now gives the reason for disallowing *oil which must be burnt* from use in the Sabbath lights (see mishnah 1), namely, that on a Friday that falls on a *Yom Tov*, oil which must be burnt may not be used because of the prohibition against burning disqualified sacrifices or *teru-* *mah* on *Yom Tov* (*Rav* from *Gem.* 24b, 25a).

רַבִּי יִשְׁמָעֵאל אוֹמֵר: אֵין מַדְלִיקִין בְּעִטְרָן. — *R' Yishmael says: We may not light with tar,*

The עִטְרָן, *tar,* of our mishnah is a liquid by-product of the distillation of the זֶפֶת, *pitch,* mentioned in mishnah 1. [Others explain that this is a thinner liquid which flows from the

שבת ב/ג

מִפְּנֵי כְבוֹד הַשַּׁבָּת. וַחֲכָמִים מַתִּירִין בְּכָל הַשְּׁמָנִים: בְּשֶׁמֶן שֻׁמְשְׁמִין, בְּשֶׁמֶן אֱגוֹזִים, בְּשֶׁמֶן צְנוֹנוֹת, בְּשֶׁמֶן דָּגִים, בְּשֶׁמֶן פַּקּוּעוֹת, בְּעִטְרָן, וּבְנֵפְטְ. רַבִּי טַרְפוֹן אוֹמֵר: אֵין מַדְלִיקִין אֶלָּא בְּשֶׁמֶן זַיִת בִּלְבָד.

[ג] **כָּל־הַיּוֹצֵא** מִן הָעֵץ אֵין מַדְלִיקִין בּוֹ,

ר' עובדיה מברטנורא

שומשמין. כך שמו בערבי והוא זרע דק מתוק, ובאלו ישראל יש ממנו הרבה: **שמן צנונות.** שמן היוצא מזרע לפת: **פקועות.** דלעת מדברית: **נפט.** מין זפת הוא, ולבן וריחו רע. והלכה כחכמים שמדליקין בכל השמנים, חוץ מאותן הפסולות שנמנו לעיל במתניתין, וחוץ משמן אפרסמון ונפט לבן, שכל אחד מאלו מצאני השמנים הוא עף ושורף, וחיישינן שמא יניחנו וילך. ועוד יש טעם אחר לאסור בשמן אפרסמון גזירה שמא יסתפק ממנו מפני חשיבותו, וקיימא לן הנותן שמן בנר חייב משום מבעיר, והמסתפק ממנו חייב משום מכבה: (ג) **בל היוצא מן העץ אין מדליקין בו.** לעשות ממנו פתילה:

יד אברהם

tree after the thicker pitch has been extracted.]

Unlike pitch, the thinner consistency of tar allows it to be satisfactorily drawn by a wick. We would therefore be inclined to permit its use in the Sabbath lamp. Indeed, the Sages [see below] do permit its use. R' Yishmael, however, objects to using tar for another reason (Rav; Ran; Rashi).

מִפְּנֵי כְבוֹד הַשַּׁבָּת — *because of honor due the Sabbath.*

Because it gives off a foul odor which may cause one to leave the room in which it is burning and eat his Sabbath meal in a dark one. That would constitute a lack of כְּבוֹד שַׁבָּת, *honor of the Sabbath* (Rav; Tif. Yis.).

וַחֲכָמִים מַתִּירִין בְּכָל הַשְּׁמָנִים: בְּשֶׁמֶן שֻׁמְשְׁמִין, בְּשֶׁמֶן אֱגוֹזִים, — *But the Sages permit [lighting] with all oils: [namely,] with sesame oil, with nut oil,*

בְּשֶׁמֶן צְנוֹנוֹת, — *with radish oil,*

I.e., oil extracted from radish seeds (Rav; Tif. Yis.).

בְּשֶׁמֶן דָּגִים, בְּשֶׁמֶן פַּקּוּעוֹת, — *with fish oil, with colocynth oil,*

Colocynth is a member of the gourd family. This follows Rashi and Rav. See Aruch. Some maintain that it is a bitter melon, whose seeds yield oil (Rav; Rash, Keilim 17:17; Uktzin 3:4; Radak, Il Kings 4:39).

בְּעִטְרָן, וּבְנֵפְטְ. — *with tar, or with naphtha.*

Naphtha, too, is a derivative of pitch. It is white and malodorous.

The halachah is in accordance with the ruling of the Sages that all oils are suitable except the oils mentioned in mishnah 1. Exceptions, too, are naphtha and balsam oil which are extremely flammable and may pose a danger. Balsam oil is also unsuitable because one may be tempted to draw off some of this fragrant oil while it is burning, for

2 because of honor due the Sabbath. But the Sages
3 permit [lighting] with all oils: [namely,] with sesame oil, with nut oil, with radish oil, with fish oil, with colocynth oil, with tar, or with naphtha.

R' Tarfon says: We may light only with olive oil.

3. We may not light with any product of a tree,

YAD AVRAHAM

other use. This would constitute בבוי, the *melachah* of *extinguishing* a flame (*Rav* from *Gem.* 25b). [See prefatory remarks to mishnah 4.]

Rav permits the use of tar for the Sabbath light. However, the halachic ruling in *Shulchan Aruch* 264:3 is in accordance with R' Ishmael, who disallows it because of its foul odor. This is the view of a great majority of the *poskim*.

On festivals the following rules apply:

All oils are permitted, even those that are not drawn easily by the wick. Kindling a fire is permitted on *Yom Tov* and there is, therefore, no need to be concerned that one may tilt the lamp to cause the flame to burn brighter.

Contaminated *terumah* oil may not be used (*Gem.* 24a).

The use of tar is questionable due to its foul odor. On *Yom Tov* too, it is preferable to eat the meals in a brightly lit room and therefore, preferable not to kindle a lamp whose odor may drive a person from the room (*Be'ur Halachah* 264 from *Pri Megadim*).

רַבִּי טַרְפוֹן אוֹמֵר: אֵין מַדְלִיקִין אֶלָּא בְשֶׁמֶן זַיִת בִּלְבָד. — *R' Tarfon says: We may light only with olive oil.*

The *Gemara* 26a relates that R' Yochanan ben Nuri rose to his feet and said (to R' Tarfon): "What shall the Babylonians do, who have nothing but sesame oil? What shall the Medians do, who have nothing but nut oil? What shall the Alexandrians do, who have nothing but radish oil? And what shall the Capadocians do, who have none of these but naphtha? The only oils that should be disallowed are those that the Sages declared unfit."

The *Tannaim* who disagree with R' Tarfon and allow other oils do agree, however, that olive oil is preferable because it is drawn into the wick more easily and therefore produces a better flame than any of the other oils (*Tos.* 23a).

3.

כָּל הַיּוֹצֵא מִן הָעֵץ אֵין מַדְלִיקִין בּוֹ, — *We may not light with any product of a tree* [lit. *anything that comes from a tree, we may not light with it*],

I.e., a wick made from any derivative of a tree, e.g., wood, cannot be used for the Sabbath lamp (*Rashi; Rav; Tif. Yis.*).

שבת ב/ג

אֶלָּא פִּשְׁתָּן. וְכָל הַיּוֹצֵא מִן הָעֵץ אֵינוֹ מְטַמֵּא טֻמְאַת אֹהָלִים, אֶלָּא פִּשְׁתָּן.

ר׳ עובדיה מברטנורא

אלא פשתן. דאיקרי עץ כדכתיב (יהושע ב) ותטמנם בפשתי העץ, ואפילו הכי מדליקין בפתילה שעושין ממנו. וקנבוס וצמר גפן לאו יוצאין מן העץ נינהו, אלא מיני זרע הן הילכך מדליקין בהן. ופשתן נמי מין זרע הוא, ולא איצטריך לרבויי אלא משום דאיקרי עץ, דכתיב ותטמנם בפשתי העץ: **אינו מטמא טומאת אהלים.** אם עשה מהן אהל והמת תחתיו, הוי כשאר בית ואינו טעון הזאה וטבילה, דאהל עצמו אינו מקבל טומאה אלא כלים שתחתיו: **אלא פשתן.** שהאהל עצמו טמא, כדכתיב (במדבר יט) וזאת על האהל, וילפינן אהל אהל ממשכן, דכתיב בית אהל ממשכן (שמות מ) ויפרוש את האהל על המשכן, ולא היה באהל משכן דבר יוצא מן העץ אלא פשתן כדכתיב (שם כו) עשר יריעות שש משזר:

יד אברהם

אֶלָּא פִּשְׁתָּן. — *except flax.*
Either carded flax or linen cloth may be used as a wick, since the flame adheres firmly to them (*Rambam, Hil. Shabbos* 5:5).

The *Tanna* found it necessary to exclude flax, though it does not grow on a tree, because in *Joshua* 2:6 we find flax stalks referred to as פִּשְׁתֵּי הָעֵץ, literally *flax of the tree.* He was therefore compelled to add that, despite this designation of the flax plant as a tree, we may fashion wicks for Sabbath lights from flax (*Rav* from *Tos.* 27b).

Hemp and cotton, which are similar to flax in that they are derived from seeds rather than wood, are obviously suitable for wicks (*Rav*).

Rashi disagrees and categorizes hemp and cotton as tree derivatives (since their stalks harden like wood) and therefore unsuitable for wicks (*Rashi* 27b as explained by *Shibbolei HaLeket* 62).

Tosafos (27b) questions *Rashi's* opinion on two counts: (a) It is common practice to use cotton wicks for Sabbath lights; moreover, they make superior wicks; and (b) since the stalk grows anew every year it is considered a plant rather than a tree according to the guidelines set by the *Gemara* in *Berachos* 40b.[1]

Although this is true of flax, too, its mention by the *Tanna* is due to it being referred to in *Joshua* as a tree.

The accepted halachah is that cotton and hemp are both suitable for wicks (*Shulchan Aruch* 264:1). It is preferable, however, where other wicks are available not to use hemp (*Mishnah Berurah* 264:2, quoting *Eliyah Rabbah*).

וְכָל הַיּוֹצֵא מִן הָעֵץ אֵינוֹ מְטַמֵּא טֻמְאַת אֹהָלִים, אֶלָּא פִּשְׁתָּן. — *And no tree-product can contract tumah-contamination from sheltering [a contaminated object* (lit. *anything that comes from a tree cannot contract the tumah of tents)], except flax.*

The Torah states: זֹאת הַתּוֹרָה אָדָם כִּי־יָמוּת בְּאֹהֶל כָּל־הַבָּא אֶל־הָאֹהֶל וְכָל־אֲשֶׁר בָּאֹהֶל יִטְמָא שִׁבְעַת יָמִים, *This is the law: When a man dies in a tent, all that come into the tent, and all that is*

---

1. The *Gemara* (*Berachos* 40b) establishes the guideline for reciting the *berachah* (blessing), בּוֹרֵא פְּרִי הָעֵץ, *Who creates the fruit of the tree,* as follows: That which, when its fruit is picked, produces another in its place on the same stalk or branch is considered a tree and the required *berachah* is בּוֹרֵא פְּרִי הָעֵץ, *Who creates the fruit of the tree.* Otherwise the proper *berachah* is בּוֹרֵא פְּרִי הָאֲדָמָה, *Who creates the fruit of the earth.* Hemp and cotton are of the latter variety and, therefore, ought not to be considered tree derivatives.

2 except flax. And no tree-product can contract
3 *tumah*-contamination from sheltering [a contaminated object], except flax.

YAD AVRAHAM

within the tent, shall be tamei seven days ... (Numbers 19:14). Another verse (ibid. v. 18) states: וְלָקַח אֵזוֹב וְטָבַל בַּמַּיִם אִישׁ טָהוֹר וְהִזָּה עַל־הָאֹהֶל וְעַל־כָּל־הַכֵּלִים וְעַל הַנְּפָשׁוֹת אֲשֶׁר הָיוּ־שָׁם, *And a clean person shall take hyssop and dip it into the water and sprinkle it upon the tent, and upon all the vessels and upon the persons that were there ...*

Verse 14 teaches that anything in the same tent [i.e., under the same roof] as a corpse contracts *tumah* from the corpse. However, the Torah stresses that *all that is "within" the tent* is *tamei,* implying that the tent itself does not contract *tumah.* Verse 18, on the other hand, requires that the purifying waters be sprinkled *upon the tent,* implying that the tent has indeed contracted *tumah.*

The Sages (*Gem.* 28a) derive the following halachos from the above: (a) Any fixed structure, regardless of what material (including wood and tree products) was used in its construction [with the exception noted below], does not contract *tumah* from a corpse lying within it; and (b) there is one exception to this rule, namely, a tent made of linen. This exception is based upon the fact that elsewhere (*Exodus* 40:19) the Torah refers to a structure of linen by the general term הָאֹהֶל, *the tent.* Since the Torah refers to such a structure as *the tent* without modifying it by the adjective *linen,* we deduce that elsewhere, too, the term *the tent* refers to a *linen tent* unless otherwise specified (*Rav*).

◆§ Diminution of a Cloth by Twisting

A piece of cloth measuring three אֶצְבָּעוֹת, *fingerbreadths,* in each direction is considered to be of intrinsic value [for it is worth saving to be used as a patch]. A cloth of this minimum size is called a בֶּגֶד, *beged* [lit. *an article of clothing*], and is capable of contracting *tumah.* If its size is diminished to less than three by three, it is no longer considered a *beged,* and cannot contract *tumah.* A dispute between *Tannaim* whether twisting a *beged* of minimum size into a wick is considered as decreasing its size has ramifications regarding Sabbath and *Yom Tov.*

Objects which at the onset of the Sabbath or *Yom Tov* did not stand to be used on that Sabbath or *Yom Tov* are known as *muktzeh* [lit. *set aside* from use]. By Rabbinic decree, these objects are banned from use for the remainder of that Sabbath or *Yom Tov* and indeed may not even be moved. [See General Introduction to this tractate.] One form of *muktzeh* is נוֹלָד, *nolad,* lit. *newborn.* Any object that was not in existence in its present form before the Sabbath or *Yom Tov* is considered *nolad,* and cannot be used for the remainder of that Sabbath or that *Yom Tov.*

If a cloth exactly three by three which has been twisted into a wick is not considered diminished in its size but remains a *beged,* then as one kindles this wick he causes the cloth to become less than three by three. Now that its size

שבת ב/ג

פְּתִילַת הַבֶּגֶד שֶׁקִּפְּלָהּ וְלֹא הִבְהֲבָהּ — רַבִּי אֱלִיעֶזֶר אוֹמֵר: טְמֵאָה, וְאֵין מַדְלִיקִין בָּהּ. רַבִּי עֲקִיבָא אוֹמֵר: טְהוֹרָה, וּמַדְלִיקִין בָּהּ.

ר' עובדיה מברטנורא

שֶׁקִּפְּלָהּ. כדרך שגודלין הפתילות: **הִבְהֲבָהּ.** על השלהבת כדי שתהיה מחורכת ותדליק יפה. ובבגד שיש בו שלש אצבעות על שלש אצבעות מצומצמות עסקינן: **טְמֵאָה הִיא.** דקפולה אינו מבטלה מתורת בגד, הואיל ולא הבהבה: **טְהוֹרָה הִיא.** דקפולה בטלה מתורת בגד והיא כאילו אין בה כאילו על שלש, וכל פחות משלש על שלש טהור מלטמא לא בנגעים ולא בטומאת מת: **וְאֵין מַדְלִיקִין בָּהּ.** ביום טוב שחל להיות בערב שבת עסקינן, דשייך ביה איסור מוקצה, ואין מסיקין בשברי כלים שנשברו בו ביום דהוו להו נולד, אבל בכלים מסיקין דהא חזו לטלטול, ודכולי עלמא אית להו המדליק צריך להדליק רוב היוצא מן הפתילה חוץ לנגד שיסלק ידיו, הילכך טעמא דרבי אליעזר דאמר אין מדליקין בה קסבר קפולה לא בטלה מתורת מתורת כלי, וכי אדליק בה פורתא כיון דשלש על שלש מצומצמות היו הוה ליה שבר כלי, דפחות משלש על שלש לאו כלי הוא, וכי מדליק בידים להשלים רוב היוצא גמלא שמדליק בשבר כלי שנשבר ביום טוב, דכי אמרינן מסיקין בכלים דוקא שלא יגע בו אחר שנפחת. ורבי עקיבא אומר מדליקין בה, קסבר קפולה בטלה מתורת כלי, מכי קפלה מערב יום טוב, דאין גודלין פתילה ביום טוב, ונמצא כאן אין שבר כלי שנשבר ביום טוב, הילכך מדליקין בה. והלכה כרבי עקיבא:

יד אברהם

has been diminished it can no longer be considered a cloth, but merely a fragment of a cloth. If this igniting is done on *Yom Tov*, the wick is considered *nolad*, newly created, and may not be used for the remainder of that *Yom Tov* for any purpose, including as a wick for the Sabbath lamp (if *Yom Tov* fell on a Friday).

If, however, once the wick has been twisted before *Yom Tov* the cloth is already deemed a fragment, then igniting this wick on Friday — *Yom Tov* — does not give it a new status and it is not *nolad*. Therefore, one would be allowed to use it for the Sabbath lamp even when Friday is a *Yom Tov*. As we shall see below, R' Eliezer is of the opinion that twisting a *beged* does not alter its size, while R' Akiva maintains that it does (*Rav* from *Gem.* 28b).

פְּתִילַת הַבֶּגֶד שֶׁקִּפְּלָהּ — A wick made from a cloth that one twisted

I.e., a piece of cloth that was twisted into a wick, and which now (in its twisted state) measures less than three fingers by three fingers (*Rav* from *Gem.* 28b).

וְלֹא הִבְהֲבָהּ — but did not singe —

I.e., it was not singed over a flame to char it. (This was generally done to new wicks to make them easier to light.) Had it been singed, it would have become less than three finger- breadths by three fingerbreadths and would not be subject to the following dispute (*Rashi; Rav*).

רַבִּי אֱלִיעֶזֶר אוֹמֵר: טְמֵאָה, — R' Eliezer says: It is susceptible to tumah-contamination,

R' Eliezer maintains that twisting a cloth into the shape of a wick does not diminish its dimensions (see prefatory notes). Consequently, it is still considered as having the required minimum size for susceptibility to *tumah* (*Rav* from *Gem.* 28b).

2 3 A wick made from a cloth that one twisted but did not singe — R' Eliezer says: It is susceptible to *tumah*-contamination, and we may not light with it. R' Akiva says: It is not susceptible to *tumah*-contamination, and we may light with it.

YAD AVRAHAM

וְאֵין מַדְלִיקִין בָּהּ. — *and we may not light with it.*

This mishnah deals with a Yom Tov which falls on a Friday, and the lighting of the Sabbath candles is therefore done on Yom Tov. Furthermore, the mishnah is discussing a cloth measuring exactly three fingerbreadths square (before being twisted). Therefore, as soon as he touches the flame to the wick he diminishes it from the minimum size of a *beged* and now renders it a mere fragment of a cloth. (This change is significant inasmuch as the halachah accords a different status to a whole cloth than to a fragment.) Since this change in status occurs on Yom Tov, the resulting fragment is deemed *nolad*, i.e., it is in a *legal* sense a newly created object, and may not be handled on Yom Tov.

This in itself would not create a problem since after touching the flame to the wick (at which point it becomes *nolad*) he is no longer handling it. However, the rule is that one must hold the flame to the wick of the Sabbath lights until most of the protruding part of the wick has been ignited. Since the wick becomes *nolad* the first instant the flame touches it, at this point it may no longer be handled on Yom Tov; and since, as mentioned above, we are discussing a case of a Friday which is also Yom Tov, he cannot continue to ignite the rest of the wick. Consequently, he may not use such a wick at all.

רַבִּי עֲקִיבָא אוֹמֵר: טְהוֹרָה, — *R' Akiva says: It is not susceptible to tumah-contamination* [lit. *it is* tahor],

R' Akiva maintains that the twisting itself reduces the cloth's dimensions so that it is no longer able to contract *tumah* (*Rav* from *Gem.* ibid.).

וּמַדְלִיקִין בָּהּ. — *and we may light with it.*

Since it was twisted before Yom Tov, it was even then no longer a cloth, but a fragment. Having already been reduced to the status of a fragment before Yom Tov, no change of status occurs on Yom Tov. Consequently, *nolad* is not involved, and it may be used for the Sabbath lamp (*Rav* from *Gem.* ibid.).

As stated, the above explanation of the dispute between R' Eliezer and R' Akiva is based on Yom Tov falling on Friday. Others are of the opinion that this dispute applies to all Fridays, and is based on a different consideration.

R' Eliezer holds that an unsinged wick does not burn well, thereby creating the concern that one may come to tilt the lamp to increase the light (see mishnah 1).

R' Akiva believes that there is no need for such concern and an unsinged wick may be used for the Sabbath lamp (*Meiri* from *Gem.* 29a).

This, obviously, refers only to the dispute regarding *lighting* with an unsinged wick. As regards the dispute of whether such a wick is susceptible to *tumah*, this second explanation also follows the first interpretation (*Tos.* ibid.).

The halachah is in accordance with R' Akiva, that the wick does not need to be

שבת
ב/ד

לא [ד] יָקֹב אָדָם שְׁפוֹפֶרֶת שֶׁל בֵּיצָה, וִימַלְאֶנָּה שֶׁמֶן, וְיִתְּנֶנָּה עַל פִּי הַנֵּר בִּשְׁבִיל שֶׁתְּהֵא מְנַטֶּפֶת, אֲפִלּוּ הִיא שֶׁל חֶרֶס. וְרַבִּי יְהוּדָה מַתִּיר.

─── ר' עובדיה מברטנורא ───

(ד) **שפופרת של ביצה.** הקליפה הקשה העליונה שהבילה מונחת בתוכה: **בשביל שתהא מנטפת.** טפה טפה לתוך הנר, וטעמא גזירה שמא יסתפק ממנו, וכיון שהקלוהו לגר חייב משום מכבה: **ואפילו היא של חרס.** דמחים, אפילו הכי גזרינן, שכיון שאין הפתילה הדולקת בתוך הכלי שיש בו השמן, אתי לאסתפוקי מיניה, דסבר אין כאן משום מכבה: **ורבי יהודה מתיר.** דלא גזר דילמא אתי לאסתפוקי מיניה, שהרי הוא רוחה השמן נוטף על הפתילה שתחתיו:

יד אברהם

singed (Tos. 29a, Shulchan Aruch 264:9). However, it is customary to light the wick and to extinguish it (so that it be easier to light) before performing the mitzvah of lighting the Sabbath lights (Rama from Tur 264).

4.

◆§ **The Melachah of *Extinguishing**

*Extinguishing a fire is an *av melachah*. The *Gemara* (*Beitzah* 22a) states that even the removal of some oil from a burning lamp makes one liable for *extinguishing*. There is a difference of opinion among the *Rishonim* as to the reason. *Tosafos* (ad loc.) hold that the decrease in the amount of oil causes a decrease in the intensity of the flame, which is tantamount to extinguishing that portion of the flame. *Rosh's* opinion is that the removal of oil will cause the lamp to extinguish itself sooner.

Tosafos reject *Rosh's* view because the removal of the oil, according to him, has no immediate effect. He is, therefore, not directly extinguishing the flame, but only *causing* this to happen. This is called גְּרַם כִּבּוּי, *causing to be extinguished* — which is not a *melachah*.

The *Rosh*, however, holds that anything done *directly* to the fire or to the fuel which eventually causes the flame to be extinguished is considered *extinguishing*, notwithstanding the fact that the flame is not immediately extinguished. The exception of "causing to be extinguished" applies only where nothing was done *directly* to the flame or the fuel; for example, placing a pitcher of water in the fire's path to keep it from spreading. Although the heat from the fire will eventually crack the pitcher, releasing the water to extinguish the fire, since the person himself has done nothing to either the fuel or the flame directly, no transgression has been committed.

Our mishnah will teach that it is not permitted to set up the Sabbath lamp in a manner that may bring about the removal of some oil, for this will result in a violation of the *melachah* of *extinguishing*.

לֹא יָקֹב אָדָם שְׁפוֹפֶרֶת שֶׁל בֵּיצָה — **One** (lit. *a person*) **may not pierce an eggshell** (lit. *a pipe of egg*),

This reading follows most commentaries (*Rav, Tif. Yis.* et al.). *Tosafos R' Akiva* cites *Maharil* who reads

4. One may not pierce an eggshell, fill it with oil, and put it over the mouth of a lamp so that it [the oil] will drip, even if it [the container] is of earthenware. But R' Yehudah permits [this].

YAD AVRAHAM

שְׁפוֹפֶרֶת שֶׁל בֵּיצָה, *a swamp reed.*

וִימַלְאֶנָּה שֶׁמֶן, וְיִתְּנֶנָּה עַל פִּי הַנֵּר בִּשְׁבִיל שֶׁתְּהֵא מְנַטֶּפֶת, — *fill it with oil, and put it over the mouth of a lamp so that it [the oil] will drip,*

I.e., one may not do so before the Sabbath (*Tif. Yis.*).

To prevent the flame from consuming more oil than necessary, lamps were constructed of two pieces: a shallow dish or pan in which the wick would sit with a minimum of oil, and a reservoir of oil suspended above the dish. A small hole on the bottom of this reservoir would allow just enough oil to drip down to the dish to assure the wick a constant fuel supply (*Tif. Yis.*). These reservoirs were sometimes made of eggshells. The Rabbis prohibited their use for the Sabbath lamp lest one remove oil from the shell [or even the whole shell with its contents (*Tif. Yis.*)], thus performing the *melachah* of מְכַבֶּה, *extinguishing (*Rashi; Ramban; Rav;* see preface).

Although the use of oil lamps is permitted on the Sabbath (because people are aware of the prohibition of removing oil from them), the Rabbis forbade them where the oil and wick are not in one dish because to the unlearned it appears as a two-piece arrangement from which one *should* be permitted to remove the oil (*Rav*).

According to *Rosh* (discussed in the preface to this mishnah) this halachah is clear. Removing oil from the eggshell will certainly cause the lamp to go out earlier than previously intended. Therefore, the Rabbis prohibited the use of the eggshell since there is the possibility that he may come to use the oil.

Tosafos' position, however, presents a difficulty. They are of the opinion that to be liable for *extinguishing there must be an immediate effect on the flame. Obviously, the removal of some oil from the eggshell, which is dripping into the lamp, will not show results until some time later. Why, then, should the use of the eggshell be disallowed?

As a result of this problem *Hagahos Mordechai* concludes that although causing a flame to be extinguished is Biblically permitted, it is nevertheless Rabbinically prohibited except in emergencies, such as preventing the spread of a fire (*Shenos Eliyahu*).

Alternatively, since the oil has been set apart for burning, it is *muktzeh*, and may not be used for any other purpose even if the lamp goes out or the oil drips out of the lamp (*Ramban, Hil. Shabbos* 5:12).

אֲפִלּוּ הִיא שֶׁל חֶרֶס. — *even if it [the container] is of earthenware.*

Even if the vessel is made of earthenware (in place of the eggshell), which tends to make the oil repugnant, there is, nevertheless, concern that he may come to use the oil (*Rav, Rashi* from *Gem.* 29b).

וְרַבִּי יְהוּדָה מַתִּיר. — *But R' Yehudah permits [this].*

He sees no need to decree any precautionary measures. The sight of the

שבת ב/ד

אֲבָל אִם חִבְּרָהּ הַיּוֹצֵר מִתְּחִלָּה, מֻתָּר, מִפְּנֵי שֶׁהוּא כְלִי אֶחָד. לֹא יְמַלֵּא אָדָם אֶת־הַקְּעָרָה שֶׁמֶן, וְיִתְּנֶנָּה בְּצַד הַנֵּר, וְיִתֵּן רֹאשׁ הַפְּתִילָה בְּתוֹכָהּ בִּשְׁבִיל שֶׁתְּהֵא שׁוֹאֶבֶת. וְרַבִּי יְהוּדָה מַתִּיר.

ר' עובדיה מברטנורא

אם חברה היוצר מתחלה בו'. והוא הדין אם חברה בעל הבית בסיד או בחרסית מערב שבת ליכא למיחש, דמשום איסורא דשבת בדיל מיניה: **ויתן ראש הפתילה.** שהוא יוצא מן הצד לשאוב השמן ונמשך דרך הפתילה לראש הדולק. ואשמעינן מתניתין פלוגתא דרבי יהודה ורבנן בשפופרת של ביצה, וחרס, ובקערה. דהני אשמעינן. דאי בשפופרת של ביצה בהא קאמרי רבנן, דכיון דלא מאיסא אתי לאסתפוקי מינה, אבל של חרס דמאים אימא מודו ליה לרבי יהודה. ואי אשמעינן של חרס, בהא קאמר רבי יהודה, אבל בהאי אימא מודה להו לרבנן. ואי אשמעינן הני תרתי, בהא קאמר רבי יהודה מפני שהשפופרת של ביצה והחרס מונחים בתוך חלל הנר למעלה, ולא מפסיק מידי בין הנר וביניס, וליכא למגזר שמא יסתפק דבדיל מיניה, אבל בקערה דמפסקא, שהרי אצל הנר מונחת ויש כאן הפסק וליכא למימר גופיה הוא אימא מודה דנגזור. ואי אשמעינן בהאי, בההיא קאמרי רבנן, אבל בהנך תרתי מודו לרבי יהודה, צריכא. והלכה כחכמים:

יד אברהם

one would not remove oil from an ordinary lamp, one would not remove oil from this shell either (*Rav; Rashi*).

לֹא יְמַלֵּא אָדָם אֶת־הַקְּעָרָה שֶׁמֶן, וְיִתְּנֶנָּה בְּצַד הַנֵּר, — *One* [lit. *a person*] *may not fill a bowl with oil, (and) put it beside a lamp,*

[The mishnah describes a two-piece, makeshift lamp. A bowl used as a reservoir is placed next to the lamp which holds a long wick. The unlit end of the wick is extended from the lamp to the bowl thus affording an additional supply of fuel.] The Rabbis disallow the use of such a setup for the Sabbath lamp for the same reason as they disallow the two-piece lamp in which the oil drips from a suspended reservoir, namely, for fear that one might remove some of the oil (*Gem.* 29b).

וְיִתֵּן רֹאשׁ הַפְּתִילָה בְּתוֹכָהּ — *and put the end of the wick into it* [*the bowl*]

I.e., the end that is not lit (*Tif. Yis.*).

oil dripping into the lamp will itself make one aware of the prohibition to remove the oil (*Rav*).

R' Yehudah permits the use of both the eggshell and the earthenware (*Gem.* 29b).

אֲבָל אִם חִבְּרָהּ הַיּוֹצֵר מִתְּחִלָּה, מֻתָּר, — *However, if the potter attached it originally, it is permitted,*

If, before firing the lamp in his kiln, the potter joined the reservoir to the dish, thus forming a one-piece lamp (*Tif. Yis.*), or even if the owner subsequently cemented the two pieces together (*Rav; Tif. Yis.* from *Gem.* 29b), then even the Rabbis permit using the lamp on the Sabbath. The mishnah mentions the potter to indicate that the piece must be joined together in a permanent, professional manner (*Gem.* 29b).

מִפְּנֵי שֶׁהוּא כְלִי אֶחָד. — *because it is a single vessel.*

Since the shell and the lamp are joined, they become one, and just as

2 4 However, if the potter attached it originally, it is permitted, because it is a single vessel.

One may not fill a bowl with oil, put it beside a lamp, and put the end of the wick into it [the bowl] so that it will draw [oil]. But R' Yehudah permits [this].

YAD AVRAHAM

בִּשְׁבִיל שֶׁתְּהֵא שׁוֹאֶבֶת. — *so that it will draw [oil]*.

I.e., in order that the wick draw additional oil from the bowl to the end which is lit (*Tif. Yis.*).

וְרַבִּי יְהוּדָה מַתִּיר. — *But R' Yehudah permits [this]*.

Even where the bowl is entirely separate from the lamp there is no fear that one may use the oil.

The mishnah lists three instances of the same dispute: an eggshell reservoir suspended just above a lamp; an earthenware reservoir similarly suspended; and a bowl placed near a lamp to serve as its reservoir. In each case the *Tanna Kamma* speaking for the Rabbis disallows its use lest one remove oil from the reservoir, while R' Yehudah permits its use. This is not redundant, for, as the *Gemara* (29b) explains, the cases are dissimilar. Had the mishnah only listed the case of the eggshell, one would apply the stringent ruling of the Rabbis only to that instance, for the eggshell is clean and one would be tempted to draw off some oil. The repugnancy of the earthenware reservoir, on the other hand, would, we would think, dissuade anyone wishing to use its oil. This would lead to the erroneous conclusion that in the case of an earthenware reservoir the Rabbis defer to R' Yehudah. To prevent this misconception the mishnah mentions the dispute in regard to the earthenware reservoir, too.

Conversely, had the dispute been given only in terms of the earthenware reservoir, one would think that R' Yehudah's lenient ruling was due to the reservoir's repugnancy. Hence both instances need be cited.

Had the mishnah listed only these two cases, omitting the bowl placed near the lamp, a different misconception would arise. The reservoir suspended above the lamp and dripping directly into it is easily recognized as a part of the lamp, and we would conclude that this is the basis for R' Yehudah's leniency. We would then mistakenly assume that R' Yehudah agrees to the stricter view with regard to a bowl placed near the lamp, which less obviously forms one unit with it.

Conversely, were the mishnah to discuss only the bowl, one would base the stringent opinion of the Rabbis on this lack of unity, and mistakenly assume that in the case of the eggshell the Rabbis defer to R' Yehudah. Hence all three cases must be cited (*Rav* from *Gem.* 29b).

Tosefos Yom Tov carries the question one step further. Why not omit the case of the eggshell? From the above arguments we may rate the three cases as follows:

(a) most obviously permitted (according to R' Yehudah) — earthenware reservoir [due to its repugnancy];

(b) most obviously prohibited (according to the Rabbis) — bowl placed near lamp [it is a totally separate vessel (or, according to *Rambam*, it is in contact with the wick)];

(c) neither obviously permitted nor obviously prohibited — eggshell.

Therefore, the mishnah's mention of R' Yehudah's leniency regarding the bowl would logically be extended to the eggshell; while mention of the Rabbis' stringent ruling regarding the earthenware would also be extended to the eggshell. Why, then, are all three cases mentioned?

He answers that we might think that R' Yehudah permits the earthenware vessel because it becomes repugnant, and the bowl because it is joined to the lamp by the wick.

שבת
ב/ה

[ה] **הַמְכַבֶּה** אֶת־הַנֵּר מִפְּנֵי שֶׁהוּא מִתְיָרֵא מִפְּנֵי גוֹיִם, מִפְּנֵי לִסְטִים, מִפְּנֵי רוּחַ רָעָה, וְאִם בִּשְׁבִיל הַחוֹלֶה שֶׁיִּישַׁן, פָּטוּר.

— ר' עובדיה מברטנורא —

(ה) **מפני עובדי כוכבים.** כגון פרסיים שאין מניחין להדליק אור ביום אידם אלא בבית עבודת כוכבים שלהם: **מפני לסטים.** שלא יראו שיש שם אדם ויבואו עליו: **מפני רוח רעה.** השורה עליו, וכשאינו רואה נוח לו. ורמב"ס פירש רוח רעה, מין ממיני החולי הבא לבעלי המרה השחורה, שלא ינוחו אלא כשישבו בחשך ובהסתרה מבני אדם: **ואם בשביל החולה שיישן פטור.** האי חולה חולה שיש בו סכנה הוא, דאילו מכבה בשביל חולה שאין בו סכנה חייב, מסתבר האי תנא דמלאכה שאינה צריכה לגופה עליה. וכן מפני עובדי כוכבים, מפני לסטים, מפני רוח רעה, כולהו אית בהוא סכנה. ובדין הוא דלתני מותר, אלא משום דבעי למתני סיפא חייב, תנא רישא פטור:

— יד אברהם —

In the case of the eggshell, however, which is not repugnant, nor is it joined to the lamp by the wick, perhaps R' Yehudah, too, fears that one will use the oil. It is, therefore, necessary to state the case of the eggshell.

Rambam (Comm.) offers another approach: Where the bowl is joined to the lamp by the wick, removal of the oil from the bowl would constitute a true *melachah* of *extinguishing*. In the first two situations, removal of the oil would result only in a Rabbinic transgression, viz., causing a fire to be extinguished. [In this he is obviously concurring with the opinion of *Tosafos* as explained by *Hagahos Mordechai*, mentioned above and disputing that of *Rosh*.] One might think therefore that R' Yehudah would not be lenient in a situation where a possible violation of a true *melachah* is involved; thus, the need for the mishnah to tell us that R' Yehudah allows even the separate bowl joined by the wick.

Conversely, one might conclude the reverse, namely, that R' Yehudah is lenient only where the possibility of a true Biblical *melachah* exists, for then we are sure that a person will be properly mindful not to remove the oil, thus, obviating the necessity for the Rabbis to ban such a lamp. The other two cases would need greater safeguards for a person might tend to become lax since, at most, only a Rabbinic transgression is involved; thus, the need for the mishnah to tell us that R' Yehudah is lenient even in the first two cases (*Tos. Yom Tov; Abudraham*).

The halachah rules like the *Tanna Kamma* that all these arrangements are prohibited (*Rav; Rambam; Shulchan Aruch* 265:1,2).

The *Gemara* (29b) relates that R' Yehudah based his lenient ruling on an incident. He once spent the Sabbath in the upper chamber of Nithzeh's house in Lydda. An eggshell was perforated, filled with oil and put over the opening of the lamp. R' Tarfon and the Sages were present and did not object. From their silence R' Yehudah concluded that they considered it permissible. Actually, they felt that the house of Nithzeh was different as they were heedful and needed no safeguards.

Rambam explains that the presence of the Sages served as a deterrent to touching the eggshell.

5.

⊷§ **Work Not Needed for Its Defined Purpose**

As explained in the General Introduction, p. 9, some *Tannaim*, most notably R' Shimon (*Gem.* 105b), hold that a מְלָאכָה שֶׁאֵינָהּ צְרִיכָה לְגוּפָהּ, *work not needed*

5. One who extinguishes a lamp because he fears idolaters, because of bandits, because of melancholia, or so that a sick person may fall asleep, he is exempt.

YAD AVRAHAM

for its defined purpose, is not Biblically prohibited. [It does, nevertheless, remain Rabbinically prohibited.] Others, led by R' Yehudah (ibid.), maintain that *a work not needed for its defined purpose* is considered a *calculated labor*, and one who performs such work is liable for desecration of the Sabbath.

There are three opinions among the *Rishonim* as to what constitutes work not needed for its defined purpose.

(a) A *melachah* whose purpose is different from the purpose for which it was done in the *Mishkan* (*Tos.* 94a). An example of this is *extinguishing*. Extinguishing a flame was performed in the *Mishkan* for the purpose of creating charcoal. Thus, should one extinguish a flame in order to salvage the rest of the oil or to keep the lamp from cracking it would be classified *a work not needed for its defined purpose* (*Tos.* 94a).

(b) A *melachah* performed only in reaction to an undesirable condition — either to prevent or rectify it. To be liable a labor must contribute to the achievement of a creative or productive goal. This is defined as the inherent purpose of this labor. In producing charcoal it is necessary to have a flame extinguished. Therefore, *extinguishing* is considered inherently necessary for the production of charcoal. Extinguishing a flame in order to salvage its oil, however, is not an inherently creative act, since the person would be just as satisfied if there were no flame to extinguish. Put simply, extinguishing a flame is not inherently necessary for the stockpiling of oil (*Rashi* 31b; *Rav* as explained by *Tos. R' Akiva*).

(c) A *melachah* whose purpose is to benefit an object other than the one to which it is being done, e.g., extinguishing the flame of the wick not for the wick's sake but for the oil (*Baal HaMaor* Ch. 3).

הַמְכַבֶּה אֶת־הַנֵּר — *One who extinguishes a lamp*
[I.e., on the Sabbath.]

מִפְּנֵי שֶׁהוּא מִתְיָרֵא מִפְּנֵי גּוֹיִם, — *because he fears idolaters,*
Some religions, e.g., certain Persian sects, prohibited lighting lamps on the day of their festival other than in their place of worship (*Rashi; Rav*).
They were fire worshipers and, on their festivals, allowed fire only in their temples (*Tif. Yis.*).

מִפְּנֵי לִסְטִים, — *because of bandits,*
... lest they see him and attack him (*Rashi; Rav*).

מִפְּנֵי רוּחַ רָעָה, — *because of melancholia* (lit. *an evil spirit*),
I.e., one who suffers melancholia and feels relief in the dark (*Rambam; Rav*).

וְאִם בִּשְׁבִיל הַחוֹלֶה שֶׁיִּישַׁן, פָּטוּר. — *or so that a sick person may fall asleep, he is exempt.*
[I.e., in all of the above cases he is not liable.]
This *Tanna* holds [along with R' Yehudah] that one *is* liable for work not needed for its defined purpose (as is evidenced by the fact that he concludes by saying that if one extinguished

[75] THE MISHNAH/SHABBOS — Chapter Two: *Bameh Madlikin*

שבת ב/ה

כְּחָס עַל הַנֵּר, כְּחָס עַל הַשֶּׁמֶן, כְּחָס עַל הַפְּתִילָה, חַיָּב. וְרַבִּי יוֹסֵי פּוֹטֵר בְּכֻלָּן, חוּץ מִן הַפְּתִילָה, מִפְּנֵי שֶׁהוּא עוֹשֶׂה פֶּחָם.

ר' עובדיה מברטנורא

כחס על הפתילה חייב. ואף על גב דאינו צריך לגוף הכבוי אלא לצורך דבר אחר, שלא תדלק הפתילה או שלא יפקע הנר חייב, דמלאכה שאינה צריכה לגופה חייב עליה: **פוטר בכולן חוץ מן הפתילה.** שאין לך כבוי הצריך לגופו, אלא כבוי של פחמים, וכבוי של הבהוב פתילה, שעושה הכבוי להחייה האור מהר כשירצה להדליקו. ואין הלכה כרבי יוסי: **שהוא עושה פחם.** שהוא מתכוין לעשותה עכשיו בכבוי זה פחם, שתהא מהובהבת להאיר יפה:

יד אברהם

the light to salvage the oil or the lamp he is liable; see below). Why, then, does he exempt extinguishing out of fear of heathens, robbers, etc.?

We must assume that these are situations where פִּקּוּחַ נֶפֶשׁ, *protection of life*, i.e., an act done to prevent or to overcome a mortal danger, is involved. Such cases override the prohibitions of the Sabbath (*Rav*).

Rav and *Rashi* disagree as to what level of danger must be evident in the first three situations of the mishnah, i.e., Persians, robbers and melancholia. *Rav's* opinion is that these situations are inherently dangerous and that therefore no *specific* indications of imminent danger need be evidenced to permit extinguishing the light. In the case of the ill person, however, the light may not be extinguished unless there is some specific indication of at least an indirect threat to his life. *Rashi's* opinion is that in *all* of the cases of the mishnah there must be some specific indication of danger to life to permit extinguishing the light; barring that, the general existence of the situation is not in itself sufficient grounds to violate the prohibition of *extinguishing* (*Tos. R' Akiva*).

If one is not critically ill, but there is danger that if he does not sleep his condition will deteriorate and his life will become endangered, he is considered as one who is already critically ill. In the case of one already critically ill, however, we may, as a general rule, assume that sleep will be beneficial, and extinguish the light. In the case of one not critically ill, we may do so only if a physician states that lack of sleep may endanger his life (*Beur Halachah* 278:1).

Usually in this tractate the term פָּטוּר indicates that although one is not liable, the activity is, nevertheless, Rabbinically prohibited. It is obvious, however, that where danger to life is involved one is not only permitted to, but is obligated to, perform the *melachah* to prevent loss of life. Why, then, does the mishnah use the term פָּטוּר?

The *Gemara* answers that the term פָּטוּר was used to keep the terminology consistent with the term חַיָּב, *he is liable* (the opposite of which is פָּטוּר, *he is not liable*), used later in the mishnah. In point of fact, however, one should perform a *melachah* where danger to life is involved (*Rav*).

Since the rule that danger to life overrides Torah law applies to *all* laws of the Torah except idolatry, immorality (i.e., adultery or incest) and murder (*Sanhedrin* 74a), why is it necessary for the *Tanna* to restate this rule here?

Ritva and *Ran* explain that the *Tanna* teaches that even in cases such as those recorded here, where there is no assurance

2 5

[But if he does so] to spare the lamp, to spare the oil, or to spare the wick, he is liable. R' Yose exempts in all of these [cases], except that of the wick, because he makes it [into] charcoal.

YAD AVRAHAM

that doing the *melachah* will save a life, the mere possibility that a life will be saved is considered sufficient grounds to allow doing *a melachah* on the Sabbath.

Alternatively, even where it is possible to carry away the light or to cover it, which would not involve violation of a Biblical law, one may, nevertheless, extinguish the light if resorting to the other methods would take more time.

Rambam disagrees with this latter point and specifies that the fire may be extinguished only if no other method is available. (See *Beur Halachah* 278:1.)

כְּחָס עַל־הַנֵּר, — *[But if he does so] to spare the lamp,*

I.e., if he fears that the lamp will crack because of the intense heat (*Rambam, Hil. Shabbos* 1:7).

כְּחָס עַל־הַשֶּׁמֶן, — *to spare the oil,*

I.e., if he extinguished the fire to salvage the remaining oil to use at a later time (*Rambam*, ibid. and *comm.*).

כְּחָס עַל־הַפְּתִילָה, — *or to spare the wick,*

I.e., to salvage what remains of the wick (*Rambam,* ibid.).

The כ prefixed to the word חָס is an unusual construction. The translation follows *Tosefos Yom Tov* who, citing *Ran*, renders *if,* or *when*.

Alternatively, *Tosefos Yom Tov* suggests that the repeated כ prefix is an abbreviated form of comparison, here used to compare the cases of the lamp and the oil to the case of the wick. Just as he is liable when his purpose is to save the wick (to which everyone agrees, since it is *work done for its defined purpose,* see below), so is he liable if he does so to salvage the lamp or the oil.[1]

חַיָּב. — *he is liable.*

Though the *melachah* was not done for its defined purpose, i.e., for making charcoal, he is, nevertheless, liable. This *Tanna* follows the view of R' Yehudah that work not done for its defined purpose is liable (*Rav* from *Gem.* 32b).

וְרַבִּי יוֹסֵי פּוֹטֵר בְּכֻלָּן, — *R' Yose exempts in all of these [cases],*

R' Yose follows the view of R' Shimon, that a work not needed for its defined purpose is *not* liable. Therefore, in all these cases there is no liability (*Rav* from *Gem.* ibid.) ... even when there is no danger to life and limb. It is, however, Rabbinically prohibited, even according to this view (*Gem.* 30a).

חוּץ מִן הַפְּתִילָה, מִפְּנֵי שֶׁהוּא עוֹשָׂה פֶּחָם. — *except that of the wick, because he makes it [into] charcoal.*

This refers to an unsinged wick,

---

1. The Vilna Gaon is quoted as having explained the comparative prefix in a homiletical manner: It is *as though* he wishes to spare the lamp or the oil. In reality, however, he is sparing nothing since everything a person is destined to have for the year is allotted to him on Rosh Hashanah, exclusive of expenses of Sabbaths and festivals (*Beitzah* 16a). Thus, if this person had faith that the expense incurred to replace the lamp or to buy more oil would be reimbursed by the Almighty, he would realize that he is saving nothing, and would not extinguish the light. He did so only because *it seemed* to him that he was saving the lamp or the oil. Hence the כ indicating comparison. He is *like* one who saves the lamp, etc. (*Shitah Mekubetzes,* quoting *Otzeros Yerushalayim*).

שבת
ב/ו

[ו] **עַל** שָׁלֹשׁ עֲבֵרוֹת נָשִׁים מֵתוֹת בִּשְׁעַת לֵדָתָן: עַל שֶׁאֵינָן זְהִירוֹת בְּנִדָּה וּבְחַלָּה וּבְהַדְלָקַת הַנֵּר.

ר' עובדיה מברטנורא

(ו) **בשעת לידתן.** בשעת סכנה מזומן פורענותא: **ובחלה ובהדלקת הנר.** לפי שצרכי הבית הן והיא מצויה בבית, תלויין בה:

יד אברהם
---

which was ignited expressly to singe it for future use. This is considered a *work done for its defined purpose*, since this was the purpose of extinguishing fire in the *Mishkan*. Moreover, extinguishing a lit flame is a necessary step in the creation of charcoal, unlike the cases of extinguishing the fire to salvage the lamp or the oil, where he would be satisfied not to have any flame at all (*Rav, Tos. Yom Tov* from *Gem.*).

Rav, following *Rambam*, states that the halachah is not in accordance with R' Yose. Many authorities, however, maintain that the halachah *is* in accordance with R' Yose who follows R' Shimon and exempts *melachah* not done for its defined purpose (*Ravad; Maggid Mishneh* quoting *Rabbeinu Chananel; Ramban; Rashba*).

[As explained above, this is, for the most part, an academic question, since, in any case, we are forbidden to perform *a melachah* even if we do not intend it for its defined purpose. Though it is not Biblically prohibited, it is Rabbinically prohibited.]

6.

עַל שָׁלֹשׁ עֲבֵרוֹת נָשִׁים מֵתוֹת בִּשְׁעַת לֵדָתָן: — *For three trangressions*[1] *women die during their childbirth:*

A woman in childbirth is in peril

---

1. The Talmud explains the relationship of these three mitzvos thus: An inhabitant of Galilee expounded to R' Chisda:
   God said, "I have given you lifeblood and I have commanded you on matters of blood [i.e., the laws of *niddah* menstruation]; I have designated you as 'first' [i.e., chosen] and I have commanded you on matters of 'first' [i.e., the laws concerning *challah* referred to in the Torah as רֵאשִׁית עֲרִיסוֹתֵיכֶם, *the first of your dough* (Numbers 15:20)]; I have given you a soul called 'light' [גֵּר ה' נִשְׁמַת אָדָם, *the candle (light) of God is the soul of man* (Proverbs 20:27)], and I have commanded you on matters of 'light' [i.e., to kindle the Sabbath lights].
   "If you fulfill these precepts — good and well. But if not, I shall take your soul" (*Gem.* 32a). [As a result, your lifeblood will be lost, your light will be extinguished, and your designation as "first" will be nullified (*Rashi*).]
   Rashi explains that the reason women were given special responsibility for these three mitzvos is because these mitzvos are household duties and it is the woman upon whom the household depends (ibid.).
   Additionally, Eve, by persuading Adam to transgress the will of God, brought about Adam's death. As a result she (a) spilled the blood of Adam; (b) destroyed the "dough" of the world [i.e., Adam who was formed from earth and water as dough is formed from flour and water]; and (c) extinguished the "light" of life by bringing death to the world.
   To atone for these calamities, brought about by Eve, women were made especially responsible for these mitzvos (ibid.).

6. For three transgressions women die during their childbirth: because they are not careful regarding [the laws of] *niddah*, *challah*, and kindling the [Sabbath] light.

YAD AVRAHAM

and requires special kindness from God to come through safely. Although her merit may be sufficient to see her through ordinary situations, it may be insufficient to gain for her the *special* protection necessary to overcome moments of danger. It is, therefore, a time when, in effect, she is more vulnerable to punishment for wrongdoing, i.e., the withholding of God's special kindness (*Rav*). [This is equally true of anyone who is in danger.]

עַל שֶׁאֵינָן זְהִירוֹת בְּנִדָּה — *because they are not careful regarding* [*the laws of*] *niddah*,

I.e., they are not scrupulous in their observance of the laws prescribed for the נִדָּה [*niddah*], *menstruant*, as they are delineated in *Leviticus* 15:9. [See commentary to 1:3.]

וּבְחַלָּה — (*regarding*) *challah,*

I.e., they are not scrupulous in their observance of the laws of separating *challah* from the kneaded dough, as is prescribed *in Numbers* 15:17-21. [See preface to mishnah 7.]

וּבְהַדְלָקַת הַנֵּר. — *and* (*regarding*) *kindling the* [*Sabbath*] *light.*

The *Tanna* here refers to the act of candle-lighting in contrast to *challah* where he omits the act (i.e., he does not refer to it as the *separation of challah*). This is taken as an allusion to the statement of the *Tikkunei HaZohar* that it is the husband's mitzvah to *prepare* the candles and the wife's to *light* the candles (*Tos. R' Akiva*).

7.

◈§ **The Portions Separated from Produce**

The following terms are relevant to the discussion of tithes found in this mishnah.

טֶבֶל — Tevel

Tevel is the name given to every commodity that requires that one or more tithes be removed from it. Prior to the separation of the particular tithe the food is called *tevel*, a contraction of two words, טַב לֹא, *not good*, meaning it lacks the process that will make it fit for consumption (*Rav, Berachos* 7:1). Alternatively, the word may be derived from the word טַבְלָא, *board* or *table*, suggesting that this food is as inedible as a board (*Aruch*).

תְּרוּמָה גְדוֹלָה — Terumah

The first portion separated is the *terumah* (usually between a fortieth and sixtieth of the total) which is given a *Kohen* and is forbidden to a non-*Kohen*. This portion is sometimes called תְּרוּמָה גְדוֹלָה, *the great terumah*, to differentiate it from תְּרוּמַת מַעֲשֵׂר, *terumah from the* [*first*] *tithe*, which is given by Levites and which is also a form of *terumah* as described below.

שבת
ב/ז

[ז] **שְׁלֹשָׁה** דְּבָרִים צָרִיךְ אָדָם לוֹמַר בְּתוֹךְ בֵּיתוֹ עֶרֶב שַׁבָּת עִם חֲשֵׁכָה: "עִשַּׂרְתֶּם? עֵרַבְתֶּם? הַדְלִיקוּ אֶת הַנֵּר!"

―――――― ר' עובדיה מברטנורא ――――――

(ז) **צריך אדם לומר בתוך ביתו.** ולריך למימרינהו בניחותא כי היכי דלקבלו מיניה: **עם חשיכה.** כשהוא סמוך לחשיכה ויש עדיין שהות ביום לעשר ולערב, אבל קודם לחשיכה הרבה לא, דלמא פשעי ואמרי עדיין יש שהות ביום: **עשרתם.** לסעודת שבת, שאף אכילת ערבית של שבת קובעת למעשר: **ערבתם.** ערובי תחומין וחלרות. והני תרתי שייך למימרינהו בלשון שאלה דשמא כבר עשו, אבל בנר לא שייך למימר הדלקתם את הנר, דדבר הנראה לעין הוא אי אדליק אי לא אדליק:

יד אברהם

מַעֲשֵׂר רִאשׁוֹן — First Tithe

After the *terumah* has been separated, the first tithe is taken from the remainder and presented to a Levite. This tithe is exactly a tenth of the crop.

מַעֲשֵׂר מִן הַמַּעֲשֵׂר — Tithe from the Tithe

From his first tithe, the Levite separates an additional *terumah* that he gives to a *Kohen*. The amount of his *terumah* is exactly one tenth of his first tithe. It is also called תְּרוּמַת מַעֲשֵׂר, *terumah of the tithe*, and is subject to all the laws peculiar to *terumah*.

מַעֲשֵׂר שֵׁנִי — Second Tithe

In the first, second, fourth and fifth years of the seven-year Sabbatical cycle, a second tithe, a tenth of the remaining produce, is separated from what remains of the produce after the *Kohen* and Levite's shares have been removed. This tithe must be brought to Jerusalem by the owner and eaten there by him, his household, and guests. If this is not convenient, the owner may redeem the produce for money, which he takes to Jerusalem and uses there for the purchase of food. The food assumes the sanctity previously resident in the produce and redemption money.

מַעֲשֵׂר עָנִי — Tithe of the Poor

In the third and sixth year of the Sabbatical cycle, a tenth of the produce is separated for distribution to the poor. It has no sanctity or special requirements, but the produce is *tevel* until this tithe is removed from it.

חַלָּה — Challah

Dough requires yet an additional *terumah*. This is called חַלָּה, *challah* [lit. *loaf*], and has all the laws of *terumah*.

דְּמַאי — Demai

With the passage of time, it became apparent to the Sages that many עַמֵּי הָאָרֶץ, *ignorant* [and avaricious] *people*, were becomng less scrupulous in the separation of the various tithes. Although they continued to separate *terumah* carefully and to treat it with the proper seriousness, and most of them were just as careful with the other tithes, significant numbers of them no longer separated any tithes except for *terumah*. As a result, anyone who purchased produce from

7. A man must say three things in his home on the eve of the Sabbath just before dark: "Have you tithed? Have you prepared the *eruv*? Kindle the [Sabbath] light!"

YAD AVRAHAM

an ignorant person — unless he was known to be fully observant — could not know whether or not the produce was *tevel*, and the seller could not be trusted to give an honest answer even if he were asked directly. Such a produce was called דְּמַאי [*demai*], a contraction of דָּא מַאי, *what is this?* In view of the possibility that the *demai* might be *tevel*, the Sages forbade purchasers to eat it unless they separated the doubtful tithes. However, they did *not* impose this burden upon poor people. In view of the compliance of *most* ignorant people with the laws of tithes and the great need of the poor, the Sages allowed them to use *demai* without tithing.

שְׁלֹשָׁה דְבָרִים צָרִיךְ אָדָם לוֹמַר — *A man must say three things*

I.e., he must remind the members of his household of the following three mitzvos. Since these mitzvos affect the peace and harmony of the household, one should be sure that they have been duly performed before the onset of the Sabbath (*Abudraham*).

בְּתוֹךְ בֵּיתוֹ — *in his home*

The *Tanna* does not use the expression *to the members of his household* but rather the expression *in his house*. Although their meaning is identical, the latter is used to indicate that when issuing his reminder he should speak quietly, i.e., that his voice should be heard only within his house. By speaking softly, he will increase the likelihood of his words being accepted (*Tif. Yis.* based on *Gem.* 34a).

עֶרֶב שַׁבָּת עִם חֲשֵׁכָה: — *on the eve of the Sabbath just before dark:*

He should allow sufficient time for them to be done before nightfall. However, he should not allow too much time lest members of his household neglect and eventually forget to do these things, thinking that they still have ample time (*Rashi; Rav*).

"עִשַּׂרְתֶּם?" — "*Have you tithed?*"

I.e., have you tithed the produce we need for the Sabbath? It is not permitted to eat untithed produce as part of אֲכִילַת קֶבַע, *a meal.* Under certain circumstances, however, before produce has been completely processed, e.g., it was harvested and threshed but not yet winnowed, it may be eaten אֲכִילַת עֲרַאי, *as a snack* (*Rambam, Hil. Maaser* 3:1). On the Sabbath even a snack is considered a meal and untithed produce may not be eaten in any circumstance. Tithing, however, is not permitted on the Sabbath. Thus, if one wishes to partake of any produce on the Sabbath, he must be sure that the tithing has already taken place before the Sabbath arrives (*Rav*).

"עֵרַבְתֶּם?" — "*Have you prepared the eruv?*"

This refers to the *eruv techumin* [the mechanism by which one may be allowed to walk more than the usually permitted 2000 cubits from his dwelling (see General Introduction p. 15)] and the *eruv chatzeiros* [the mechanism which allows people to

שבת ב/ז

סָפֵק חֲשֵׁכָה, סָפֵק אֵין חֲשֵׁכָה, אֵין מְעַשְּׂרִין אֶת הַוַּדַּאי, וְאֵין מַטְבִּילִין אֶת הַכֵּלִים, וְאֵין

ר' עובדיה מברטנורא

ספק חשיכה. מתחלת שקיעת החמה כל זמן שנראה כוכב אחד בלבד ודאי יום, וכל זמן שנראים שני כוכבים בינונים הוא ספק חשיכה, וקרוי בין השמשות, ונותנים עליו חומרי יום וחומרי לילה, ומשיראו שלשה כוכבים בינונים הוא ודאי לילה לכל דבר: **אין מעשרין את הודאי.** דתקון מעליא הוא. ואף על גב דאינו אסור אלא משום שבות, קסבר האי תנא גזרו על השבות אף בין השמשות: **ואין מטבילין את הכלים.** להעלותן מידי טומאתן, דהוי כמתקן כלי, ואית ביה נמי שבות:

יד אברהם

carry in an enclosed courtyard which is jointly used by the occupants of more than one dwelling (see General Introduction p. 15)].

"הַדְלִיקוּ אֶת הַנֵּר!" — "*Kindle the [Sabbath] light!*"

[Lighting the Sabbath lights is important for a peaceful, harmonious Sabbath, since without them, one is prone to stumbling in the dark.]

"*Have you tithed?*" and "*Have you prepared the eruv?*" are said in question form. "*Kindle the light!*" is said as a command. This is because it is normally not obvious whether produce has been tithed and the *eruv* has been placed. Thus he must inquire about them. It is, however, obvious whether or not the lamp has been lit and therefore, when he finds the negative to be true, he commands, "*Kindle the light!*" (*Rashi; Rav*).

סָפֵק חֲשֵׁכָה, סָפֵק אֵין חֲשֵׁכָה, — *If there is a doubt whether it is dark or it is not dark,*

This refers to the time period known as בֵּין הַשְּׁמָשׁוֹת [*bein hashemashos*], *twilight,* i.e., the transition between day and night. From the beginning of sunset and as long as only one star is visible, it is surely day. When two stars appear, it is *bein hashemashos*. When three medium stars appear, it is surely night (*Rav*).

There is a dispute between the *poskim* concerning this period. According to *Rabbeinu Tam* (*Tos.* 35a) there are two sunsets, the first when the sun disappears below the horizon, the second when all illumination from the sun ceases $58\frac{1}{2}$ minutes later. It is at this point that "day" ends. Then begins the period of *bein hashemashos*, this lasting $13\frac{1}{2}$ minutes, during which time there is doubt as to whether it is yet day or already night. Seventy-two minutes after the first sunset, it becomes definitely night.

The *Geonim*, however, maintain that *bein hashemashos* commences with the setting of the sun and lasts $13\frac{1}{2}$ minutes. Immediately following this period, night begins. See *Mishnah Berurah* 261:2, 20, 23.[1]

---

1. Regarding the onset of the Sabbath, present-day halachic authorities are unanimous that the "day" of Friday ends at sunset, at which time Sabbath restrictions begin. The duration of *bein hashemashos*, however, is not unanimously agreed upon. Since the time span between sunset and darkness is directly related to proximity from the equator, many authorities recognize the halachic validity of the *Geonim's* view only for Babylon where the *Gemara* [upon which it is based] was compiled. According to this view the length of *bein hashemashos* must be measured independently for each area. In New York City

2 7 If there is a doubt whether it is dark or it is not dark, we may not tithe definite[ly untithed produce], nor may we immerse vessels, nor may we

YAD AVRAHAM

אֵין מְעַשְּׂרִין אֶת הַוַּדַּאי, — *we may not tithe definite[ly untithed produce]*,

Untithed produce is called טֶבֶל, *tevel*. (See prefatory note to this Mishnah.) Tithing *tevel* produce on the Sabbath is prohibited because it resembles repairing a vessel. It is, in a sense, repairing the produce by rendering it fit for consumption. Unlike actual repair of a vessel, there is no physical change in the produce, and therefore the prohibition is only Rabbinic. This *Tanna* rules that during the *bein hashemashos* period even a Rabbinic prohibition is forbidden (*Rav*).

Others maintain that a Rabbinic prohibition is permitted during *bein hashemashos* where it is necessary for a mitzvah. Thus, if the food that needs to be tithed is essential for the proper enjoyment of the Sabbath, it may be tithed during *bein hashemashos*.

According to this opinion, our mishnah deals only with a situation where the produce is not greatly needed for this Sabbath (*Tif. Yis.* from *Taz* 261:1).

This dispensation may be utilized where there is no alternative. However, if other food is available or the food can be made permissible by other means, it is not permitted.

For example: Separating *challah* from dough outside of *Eretz Yisrael* is but a Rabbinic requirement. They, therefore, permitted one to eat the bread even before separating *challah*, provided that he leave over a piece from which he will later separate *challah*.

Therefore, outside of *Eretz Yisrael*, if one forgot to separate *challah* he may not do so during *bein hashemashos* for he has the alternative of eating from the bread on the Sabbath, even without first removing the *challah* as long as he makes sure to leave a little for after the Sabbath from which to separate *challah* (*Mishnah Berurah*, ibid. 4).

וְאֵין מַטְבִּילִין אֶת הַכֵּלִים, — *nor may we immerse vessels*,

Vessels that have become *tamei* [ritually contaminated] may not be immersed in a *mikveh*. This, too, resembles the repairing of vessels and is Rabbinically proscribed *bein hashemashos* (*Rav*).

According to the second opinion mentioned in the previous section, this too is only where the use of this utensil is not essential for the Sabbath, e.g., where he has another plate from which to eat (*Tif. Yis.*).

Just as ritually unclean vessels require immersion in a *mikveh* to purify them, vessels used for the preparation or serving of food that have been bought from non-Jews require immersion as well. [This immersion is similar to that of a proselyte who, in changing his status from non-Jew to Jew, must undergo immersion in a *mikveh*. Likewise, the change in

night begins fifty minutes after sunset and it is at this time Saturday night that the Sabbath ends (*Igros Moshe, Orach Chaim,* vol. 4, §62). Many other authorities accept *Rabbeinu Tam's* view, regardless of geographical location. According to them, the Sabbath does not end until seventy-two minutes after sunset.

שבת ב/ז

מַדְלִיקִין אֶת הַנֵּרוֹת; אֲבָל מְעַשְּׂרִין אֶת הַדְּמַאי, וּמְעָרְבִין, וְטוֹמְנִין אֶת הַחַמִּין.

ר' עובדיה מברטנורא

ואין מדליקין את הנרות. כל שכן, דספיקא דאורייתא הוא, וזו ואין צריך לומר זו קתני. ורבותי פירשו ואין מדליקין את הנרות אין אומרים לנכרי להדליק: **אבל מעשרים את הדמאי.** ולא דמי למתקן דרוב עמי הארץ מעשרין הן: **ומערבין.** עירובי תחומין, דחומרא בעלמא הוא, אבל לא עירובי תחומין דיש להם סמך מקראי: **וטומנין את החמין.** בדבר שאינו מוסיף הבל, דאילו בדבר המוסיף הבל אפילו מבעוד יום אסור. וטעמא דטומנין את החמין בין השמשות בדבר שאינו מוסיף הבל, שלא אסרו להטמין את החמין בשבת בדבר שאינו מוסיף הבל אלא גזירה שמא ימלא קדרתו שנצטננה ויראה בשר ונמצא מבשל בשבת, ובין השמשות ליכא למגזר בהכי, דסתם קדרות בין השמשות רותחות הן וליכא למיחש שמא נצטננה ויראה, הילכך טומנין את החמין בין השמשות אף על פי שאין טומנין בשבת:

יד אברהם

ownership of these vessels, from being in the possession of a non-Jew to being in the possession of a Jew, requires them to be immersed in a *mikveh* (*Yerushalmi, Avodah Zarah* 5:15).] Since they may not be used before immersion, immersing them resembles repair of a utensil and is Rabbinically forbidden on the Sabbath and *Yom Tov* (*Beitzah* 18). Accordingly, such immersion is also forbidden *bein hashemashos* (*Mishnah Berurah* 261:1,5 *Tif. Yis.*)

וְאֵין מַדְלִיקִין אֶת הַנֵּרוֹת; — *nor may we kindle the lights;*

Lighting the lamps is a *melachah* and is forbidden *bein hashemashos*. The *Tanna* merely draws for us the obvious conclusion that if a Rabbinic prohibition may not be set aside *bein hashemashos* then certainly a Biblical one may not.

Alternatively, we may not tell a gentile to light the lamps *bein hashemashos*, even though this, too, is only a Rabbinic prohibition (*Rav*; see 1:8). However, if no light at all has been lit for the Sabbath, he may tell a gentile to light one for him (*Shulchan Aruch* 261:1).

אֲבָל מְעַשְּׂרִין אֶת הַדְּמַאי, — *but we may tithe demai,*

Demai [see prefatory note to this mishnah] is not as strict as *tevel* because most ignorant people do tithe (a statistic which may be relied upon, Biblically speaking). Since the ban on eating *demai* before retithing is only

kindle the lights; but we may tithe *demai*, make an *eruv*, and insulate hot food.

YAD AVRAHAM

Rabbinic, the tithing of it is not as great a repair as the tithing of *tevel*, which before tithing is Biblically banned. The Rabbis, therefore, were more lenient and permitted tithing *demai* during the period of *bein hashemashos*, when the arrival of the Sabbath is still in doubt (*Rav*).

וּמְעָרְבִין, — (*and we may*) *make an eruv*,

I.e., we may make ready an *eruv chatzeiros* during the period of *bein hashemashos*. The prohibition of carrying to and from a common courtyard or from one house to another is of Rabbinic origin and is without the support of a Biblical verse. Thus, the preparation of the *eruv* which allows such carrying is not considered a true repair, and is permitted during *bein hashemashos*.

However, the prohibition against walking more than two thousand cubits does have a Biblical support; i.e., although the ban on walking more than two thousand cubits is only Rabbinical, the phraseology of certain verses in the Torah tends to support such a concept. Therefore, the *eruv techumin* which serves to make such walking permissible is considered comparable to repairing vessels and its preparation is not permitted during *bein hashemashos* (*Rav* from *Gem.* 34a).

וְטוֹמְנִין אֶת הַחַמִּין. — *and* (*we may*) *insulate* [lit. *conceal*] *hot food.*

The Rabbis prohibited insulating or covering hot food on Friday (to be kept warm on the Sabbath) with substances which tend to increase the heat. They were concerned that if this were allowed some might use a mixture of hot ash and coals for this purpose and might come to stir the coals on the Sabbath, which would be a violation of the *melachah* of *kindling (see 4:1).

On the Sabbath proper, they added to this prohibition even materials which only preserve the heat without increasing it. They feared that if the person will find the food cooled he may forgetfully heat it, thereby committing the *melachah* of *cooking.

During *bein hashemashos* most pots are still hot and there need be no concern of finding cooled food. They therefore allowed insulating the food with anything that will preserve the heat provided it does not increase the heat (*Rav* from *Gem.* 34a).

פרק שלישי
Chapter Three

Since *cooking is one of the thirty-nine prohibited categories of labor (listed in 7:2 as *baking), one must cook any food he intends eating on the Sabbath before it begins. That being the case, one who wishes to eat hot food on the Sabbath must resort to one of two devices. He must either allow it to remain over a fire [שְׁהִיָה, shehiyah] or envelop it while it is still hot in some insulating material [הַטְמָנָה, hatmanah (lit., hiding)] thereby preserving its heat.

Woodcoal fires, if left unattended, form a crust of ash as they burn. This crust diminishes the level of heat radiated by the fire. Therefore, if one wishes to maintain the heat level of the fire, he must stoke the coals from time to time.

The Rabbis, recognizing that people have a tendency to stoke their fires unthinkingly — an act prohibited as a form of the *melachah* of *kindling — restricted the conditions under which a person may leave his pot over a fire, *shehiyah*, or insulate it, *hatmanah*, to those which make it unlikely for him to stoke the fire forgetfully.

Each of the above-mentioned methods for keeping food warm is governed by a separate set of rules. The conditions under which *shehiyah* is permitted and whether, after once removing the pot from that fire, one may replace it on the Sabbath are the subject of this chapter. The rules of *hatmanah* are discussed in Chap. 4.

שבת ג/א

[א] **כִּירָה** שֶׁהִסִּיקוּהָ בְּקַשׁ וּבִגְבָבָא, נוֹתְנִים עָלֶיהָ תַבְשִׁיל; בְּגֶפֶת וּבְעֵצִים, לֹא יִתֵּן עַד שֶׁיִּגְרֹף אוֹ עַד שֶׁיִּתֵּן אֶת הָאֵפֶר. בֵּית שַׁמַּאי אוֹמְרִים: חַמִּין אֲבָל לֹא תַבְשִׁיל.

ר' עובדיה מברטנורא

פרק שלישי – כירה. (א) בירה. מקום עשוי באורך כדי שפיתת שתי קדרות והאש עוברת תחת שתי הקדרות: **בגבבא.** עלים דקים כקש שגובבין מן השדה: **נותנים עליה תבשיל.** מערב שבת להשהותו שם בשבת: **בגפת.** פסולת של זיתים ושומשמין לאחר שהוציאו שמנן: **לא יתן.** מערב שבת כדי להשהותה שם בשבת: **עד שיגרוף.** הגחלים ויוליאם מן הכירה: **או שיתן האפר.** על גבי גחלים לכסותם ולצננם, וטעמא גזירה שמא יחתה בגחלים בשבת כדי למהר בשולו. ודוקא בתבשיל שלא בשל כל צרכו, או אפילו בשל כל צרכו ומצטמק ויפה לו, הוא דגזרינן שמא יחתה, אבל תבשיל שלא בשל כלל או בשל כל צרכו ומצטמק ורע לו מותר להשהותו על גבי כירה אף על פי שאינה גרופה וקטומה ולא חיישינן שמא יחתה, הואיל והסיח דעתו ממנו. וכן תבשיל שבשל כל צרכו והשליך בתוכו אבר חי סמוך לבין השמשות, נעשה הכל כתבשיל שלא בשל כלל שהרי הסיח דעתו ממנו: **בית שמאי אומרים.** מים חמין נותנין על גבי כירה לאחר שגרף, דלא צריכי לבשולי וליכא למגזר שמא יחתה: **אבל לא תבשיל.** אף על פי שגרף, שאי אפשר לגרף כל הגחלים עד שלא ישאר שם ניצוץ אחד, ואתי לחתויי מאחר דניחא ליה בבשוליה:

יד אברהם

1.

Mishnah 1 outlines the basic rules for where and how *shehiyah* is permitted. The *Gemara* (36b), however, offers two very different explanations of the mishnah, based on a dispute between Chananyah and the Rabbis. Since the *Gemara* concludes that the mishnah may be reconciled with either of these opinions, and since the later authorities down to and even within the *Shulchan Aruch* are in dispute as to which opinion the halachah follows, both explanations will be presented. For the sake of clarity, the entire mishnah will first be explained according to the Rabbis, and will then be repeated according to the explanation of Chananyah. The various opinions as to the halachah will be discussed at the end of the mishnah.

כִּירָה — *A double stove*

This stove was set into the ground. Upon it was place for two pots, under which the fire burned (*Rav*). It was made of earthenware (*Tos. Yom Tov*).

Rashi, however, describes a pot-shaped structure into which a pot is placed.

Others explain this stove as a semicircular structure open at the top and on one side. The stove is large enough to accommodate two pots, which may be placed either on top of the stove or in it (*Ritva*, ms.; *Chiddushei HaRan*).

Tiferes Yisrael describes an inverted pot, whose rim is cemented to the ground with mud, and in whose narrow upper end were two holes upon which pots could be set.

שֶׁהִסִּיקוּהָ בְּקַשׁ וּבִגְבָבָא — *that was heated with straw or with stubble,*

This translation follows *Rashi*. Straw

1. A double stove that was heated with straw or with stubble, we may place a cooked food upon it; [if it was heated] with marc or with wood, one may not place [cooked food upon it] until he has swept away [the coals], or until he has put ashes [over them]. Beis Shammai say: Hot water but not cooked food.

YAD AVRAHAM

is the upper part of the grain stalk, which is harvested together with the grain. Stubble is the lower part of the stalk which remains attached to the ground after the the harvest. *Tosafos* reverses the translation, stating that קַשׁ is *stubble* and גְּבָבָא is *straw* (*Maharsha*). *Rav* explains גְּבָבָא as *small wood rakings*.

נוֹתְנִים עָלֶיהָ תַּבְשִׁיל — *we may place a cooked food upon it;*

I.e., we may place a pot of cooked food on the stove on Friday in order that it remain hot for the Sabbath (*Rav*).

Straw and splinters do not form coals, but are quickly consumed. Thus, there is no concern that one may stir the coals and be guilty of the *melachah* of *kindling.

בְּגֶפֶת — *[if it was heated] with marc*

That which remains after fruits have been pressed is called marc. In our mishnah it refers to a by-product of olive and sesame oils. After the oil has been extracted, the residue can be used for fuel (*Rav*).

וּבְעֵצִים, — *or with wood*,

[I.e., if the double stove is heated with either marc or wood.]

לֹא יִתֵּן — *one may not place [cooked food upon it]*

I.e., one may not place food on the stove on the eve of the Sabbath to keep it there for the Sabbath. Since wood and marc form coals, there is concern

that he may stir the coals to hasten the cooking process (*Rav*). [This obviously applies only to foods which will benefit from further cooking. This will be discussed below, s.v., וּבֵית הִלֵּל אוֹמְרִים.]

עַד שֶׁיִּגְרֹף — *until he has swept away [the coals],*

According to *Rav*, the coals must be completely removed. According to *Ran* and *Baal HaMaor* it is sufficient to move the coals from directly under the pot to the side of the double stove.

אוֹ עַד שֶׁיִּתֵּן אֶת הָאֵפֶר. — *or until he has put ashes [over them].*

I.e., until he puts ashes over the burning coals, diminishing their heat and thereby serving as a reminder not to stoke the fire (*Rav; Tif. Yis.*). Since *shehiyah* is prohibited lest one forgetfully stoke the coals, the Rabbis permitted *shehiyah* where either of the two safeguards has been enacted.

בֵּית שַׁמַּאי אוֹמְרִים: חַמִּין — *Beis Shammai say: Hot water*

I.e., Beis Shammai state that the previously stated rule applies only to hot water. Since water needs no additional cooking, there is no concern about stirring coals (*Rav*).

אֲבָל לֹא תַבְשִׁיל. — *but not cooked food.*

I.e., cooked food may not be left on a stove under any conditions. Although the coals have been swept away it is likely that some embers remain. We are, therefore, still concerned

THE MISHNAH/SHABBOS — Chapter Three: *Kirah She'hisikuhah*

שבת ג/א

וּבֵית הִלֵּל אוֹמְרִים: חַמִּין וְתַבְשִׁיל. בֵּית שַׁמַּאי אוֹמְרִים: נוֹטְלִין אֲבָל לֹא מַחֲזִירִין. וּבֵית הִלֵּל אוֹמְרִים: אַף מַחֲזִירִין.

ר' עובדיה מברטנורא

בית שמאי אומרים נוטלים וכו'. אפילו חמין דשריין להשהות על גבי כירה גרופה וקטומה את האפר, לאחר שנטלן אין מחזירין דמיחזי כמבשל בשבת: **ובית הלל אומרים.** בין חמין בין תבשיל יכולין להחזיר לאחר שנטלן. ולא שרו בית הלל להחזיר אלא בעודן בידו שלא הניחן על גבי דבר אחר, אבל לאחר שהניחן בקרקע או על גבי דבר אחר אסור להחזירן אפילו לבית הלל, דהוי כמטמין לכתחלה בשבת: (ב) **תנור.** מתוך שלו. למעלה ורחב למטה נקלט חומו לתוכו טפי מכירה, ואפילו

יד אברהם

that if allowed to leave food he may stir the remaining coals (*Rav*).

וּבֵית הִלֵּל אוֹמְרִים: חַמִּין וְתַבְשִׁיל — *But Beis Hillel say: Both hot water and cooked food.*

[The previously stated rule applies both to hot water and cooked food. Since the coals have been swept, we have no reason to fear any possible violations.]

Since the prohibition of *shehiyah* is based entirely on the concern that one may stir the coals to hasten the cooking process, the *Gemara* reasons that in situations where increasing the heat is detrimental to the food (referred to as מִצְטַמֵּק וְרַע לוֹ) no such prohibition is necessary. Thus, if the food is completely done and further cooking is harmful, *shehiyah* is permitted even without sweeping away or covering the coals, since he is unlikely to stir the coals. The same applies to completely raw food, which under no circumstances can be made ready in time for the evening meal (see *Beur Halachah* 253:5).

Since by the time of the morning meal, it will be thoroughly cooked in any case, stirring the coals at night would serve no useful purpose and consequently, we need not take any precautions to prevent such action.

Shehiyah, therefore, is permitted even without sweeping away or covering the coals. Accordingly, the mishnah, in the opinion of Beis Hillel, is discussing only foods for which further cooking is beneficial.

בֵּית שַׁמַּאי אוֹמְרִים: נוֹטְלִין אֲבָל לֹא מַחֲזִירִין. — *Beis Shammai say: We may remove [the food] but not replace [it].*

Furthermore, not only does the rule of the mishnah according to Beis Shammai apply only to hot water, it also applies only to *leaving* the hot water on the fire. Once removed, however, it may not be *replaced* on the stove because that gives the appearance of cooking on the Sabbath. [It is not actually cooking because the water is still hot at the time he replaces it on the stove.] Therefore, on the Sabbath one may only remove hot water from the stove but not replace it (*Rav*).

וּבֵית הִלֵּל אוֹמְרִים: אַף מַחֲזִירִין. — *But Beis Hillel say: We may even replace [it].*

Beis Hillel, however, hold that if the stove has been swept clear of coals, or if its coals have been covered with ash, not only may one leave both hot water and cooked food on it before the Sabbath but he may even, if he removed them on the Sabbath, replace them (*Rav*).

This applies only when one is still

**3
1**   But Beis Hillel say: Both hot water and cooked food. Beis Shammai say: We may remove [the food] but not replace [it]. But Beis Hillel say: We may even replace [it].

YAD AVRAHAM

holding the pot in his hand. Once it has been put down, however, he may no longer replace it (*Rav*). This is because it appears as though one is first placing it there on the Sabbath. Even where leaving food on the stove is permitted, it is permitted only if one placed it on the stove before the Sabbath.

Tos. R' Akiva cites two opinions on this matter found in the *Gemara* 38b.

The first requires that two conditions be met before one is allowed to replace the pot:

(a) He must still be holding the pot in his hand;

(b) at the time he removed the pot, it was his intention to replace it.

The second opinion is more lenient and prohibits the replacing of the pot only if:

(a) he has placed the pot elsewhere;

(b) *and* he did not have in mind to return the pot.

Thus, he points out, *Rav* should have stated either, that having placed the pot elsewhere, he may not replace it if he did not have in mind to do so; or, if he is still holding it he may return it *only* if he had in mind to do so.

Rama (253:2) rules in accord with the first position that both requirements (i.e., holding the pot in his hand and having in mind to replace it) must be met before one is allowed to replace the pot on the stove.

Beis Yosef, following *Rambam's* opinion which omits the above two positions entirely, rules that holding it in one's hand is sufficient to permit the returning of the pot. Obviously, *Rav*, too, follows the ruling of *Rambam*.

Up to this point, we have explained the mishnah according to the Rabbis. According to them, we may not keep any cooked food over the Sabbath on a *double stove*, unless the coals have been removed or covered with ash.

⋅ঌ Chananyah's Interpretation

As explained in the prefatory note, however, the *Gemara* (36b) offers another explanation of the mishnah which follows the opinion of the *Tanna* Chananyah. He rules that food which has been cooked as much as the food of Ben Derusai [a notorious bandit who, due to the uncertainties of his profession, only allowed his food to cook one third (*Rashi*) or one half (*Rambam*) its normal time] may be placed on a double stove to remain there during the Sabbath even though the coals have neither been swept nor covered with ash. The mishnah, which prohibits this, is referring, not to leaving food there over the Sabbath (*shehiyah*), but to *replacing* on the stove food which had been previously removed. In order for replacement to be permitted on the Sabbath, the coals must have been swept away or covered in ash prior to the Sabbath. Thus, whereas according to the Rabbis there is no difference between the rules of leaving something on the fire and replacing it (except according to Beis Shammai), according to Chananyah the rules of replacing are more stringent than those governing leaving it there in the first place. [It should be noted that as regards food cooked less than that of Ben Derusai, Chananyah is in agreement with the first opinion that it may not be left on an unswept stove (unless it is something

שבת
ג/ב

[ב] **תַּנּוּר** שֶׁהִסִּיקוּהוּ בְּקַשׁ וּבִגְבָבָא, לֹא יִתֵּן בֵּין מִתּוֹכוֹ בֵּין מֵעַל גַּבָּיו. כּוּפָח שֶׁהִסִּיקוּהוּ בְּקַשׁ וּבִגְבָבָא, הֲרֵי זֶה כְּכִירַיִם;

────── ר' עובדיה מברטנורא ──────

הסיקוהו בקש ובגבבא חיישינן שמא יחתה דלטולה אינו מסיח דעתו ממנו: **בין מעל גביו.** לסמוך אצל דופנו: **כופח.** עשוי ככירה, אלא שאין כרחבו ואין בו אלא מקום שפיתת קדרה אחת, והאש עוברת תחתיה והבלו רב מהבל הכירה, שהכירה פתוחה מלמעלה שיעור שתי קדרות והכופח אין פתוח אלא שיעור קדרה אחת, ופחות מהבל התנור:

────── יד אברהם ──────

which cannot be ready in time for the evening meal, see above). According to Chananyah, however, the mishnah is *only* discussing food which *has* been cooked to the degree of that of Ben Derusai.]

According to Chananyah, the mishnah is to be understood as follows:

A double stove that was heated with straw or with stubble — we may replace cooked food on it; with marc or with wood, one may not replace [cooked food on it] until he has swept away the coals, or until he has put ashes [over them].

Since the mishnah formulates the prohibition only in terms of *replacing* a pot on an unswept stove, it implies obviously that leaving a pot, *shehiyah*, is permitted even on an unswept stove. The unstated but implicit rule of the mishnah is therefore: We may, however, keep pots on a double stove even if the coals have not been swept away or ashes placed upon them.

Assuming our having properly inferred the above rule, the mishnah comments upon it: What may we *keep* on such a stove? *Beis Shammai say: Hot water but not cooked food. But Beis Hillel say: Both hot water and cooked food.*

[The ruling concerning *replacing* pots on the stove is, however, not unanimous for] *Beis Shammai say: We may remove [the food] but not replace [it]. But Beis Hillel say: We may even replace [it].*

◆§ The Halachah Regarding Shehiyah

Rif, Rambam, and *Rav* adopt the first explanation, obviously ruling in accord with it. *Rashi, Tosafos,* and others, however, adopt the second explanation. *Shulchan Aruch* (253:1) quotes both opinions without stating a decision. *Rama,* however, states that the custom is to follow the more lenient ruling, i.e., that *shehiyah,* leaving a pot to remain on the fire over the Sabbath, is permissible even without sweeping away or covering the coals provided the food has been cooked at least to the extent of that of Ben Derusai; replacing a pot on the Sabbath is permitted only if the coals have been swept away or covered.[1]

[As for the practical rules concerning present-day stoves, see comments at the end of mishnah 2.]

---

1. *Rama* states that the custom goes so far as to permit placing the pot directly upon the coals. This is in opposition to *Beis Yosef,* who considers this an act of *hatmanah* (insulating) with a substance which adds heat (see 4:1), unless there is a separation between the pot and the coals, such as a tripod or stones. *Rama* adds that it is customary to remove the pot from directly on the coals before the Sabbath, in order to allow for removal of the pot without moving the coals.

2. An oven that was heated with straw or with stubble, one may neither place [food] in it nor on it.

A single stove that was heated with straw or with stubble is like a double stove; with marc

YAD AVRAHAM

2.

תַּנּוּר — *An oven*
This refers to a structure wider at the bottom than at the top with room for only one pot. As a result it retains intense heat for a longer period than does the double stove and has, therefore, a more stringent rule (*Rav; Rashi*).

שֶׁהִסִּיקוּהוּ בְקַשׁ וּבִגְבָבָא, — *that was heated with straw or with stubble,*
[See mishnah 1 for a discussion of these fuels.]
Since the heat of this oven lasts longer, a person is able to cook on it even if it is heated with straw or stubble. Consequently, we fear he may rake even such a fire (*Rav*), i.e., there may be sparks left from the straw even though it has been swept away (*Tif. Yis.*).
Since this prohibition applies even to an oven which had been heated with straw or stubble, it certainly applies to one heated with marc or wood. Moreover, even if the coals have been swept away or covered with ash the prohibition still applies. Since owing to the intensity of the heat remaining in the oven it is still possible for one to cook, we still fear that he may rake some remaining spark (*Tos. Yom Tov*).

לֹא יִתֵּן — *one may neither place [food]*
According to the first explanation in mishnah 1 this means one may not place food there before the *Sabbath to remain* there on the Sabbath. According to Chananyah's explanation this means that one may not *replace* food which has been removed (*Tos.* 38b).

[He may, however, leave it there in the first place.]

בֵּין מִתּוֹכוֹ — *in it*
[I.e., inside the oven next to the fire.]

בֵּין מֵעַל גַּבָּיו. — *nor on it.*
I.e., to place the pot over the opening at the top of the oven, or even to place it against the outer wall of the oven (*Rav* from *Gem.*).

כּוּפָּח — *A single stove*
This stove is constructed in the same manner as the double stove of mishnah 1, except that it has room for only one. Because it has only one opening on top, its heat is more intense than that of a double stove. It is, however, still less intense than the heat of an oven (*Rashi* and *Rav* from *Gem.*). As a result, it is sometimes accorded the rules of a double stove and sometimes those of an oven. The differentiation is based on the type of fuel used to heat it, as the mishnah proceeds to explain.

שֶׁהִסִּיקוּהוּ בְקַשׁ וּבִגְבָבָא, — *that was heated with straw or with stubble*

הֲרֵי זֶה כְּכִירַיִם; — *(it) is like a double stove;*
I.e., the rules of a double stove apply to it. If it is *swept or covered with ash*, a pot may be left on top of it or leaning against its outer wall (*Gem.* 38b). [According to the first explanation of the previous mishnah; while according to Chananyah's explanation a pot may even be replaced upon it.]

[93] THE MISHNAH/SHABBOS — Chapter Three: *Kirah She'hisikuhah*

שבת ג/ג

בְּגֶפֶת וּבְעֵצִים, הֲרֵי הוּא כְתַנּוּר.

[ג] **אֵין** נוֹתְנִין בֵּיצָה בְּצַד הַמֵּחַם בִּשְׁבִיל שֶׁתִּתְגַּלְגֵּל, וְלֹא יַפְקִיעֶנָּה בְּסוּדָרִין. וְרַבִּי יוֹסֵי מַתִּיר. וְלֹא יַטְמִינֶנָּה בְּחוֹל וּבַאֲבַק דְּרָכִים.

ר' עובדיה מברטנורא

(ג) **אין נותנין.** בשבת: **ביצה בצד המיחם.** קומקוס של נחושת שמחממים בו המים ט"ג. החם: **שתתגלגל.** שתצלה קלת עד שתהא מגולגלת כלומר מטורפת: **ולא יפקיענה בסודרין.** לא יצברנה על סודר שהוחם בחמה כדי שתצלה בו, דגזרינן תולדות חמה אטו תולדות האור: **ורבי יוסי מתיר.** דסבר לא גזרינן תולדות חמה אטו תולדות האור. ואין הלכה כרבי יוסי: **לא יטמיננה בחול ובאבק דרכים.** שהוחמו מכח החמה, ובהא לא שרי רבי יוסי דגזר חול אטו רמן, הואיל ותרוייהו

יד אברהם

בְּגֶפֶת וּבְעֵצִים — *with marc or with wood,* [i.e., if it was heated with marc or with wood.]

הֲרֵי הוּא כְתַנּוּר. — *it is like an oven.*

It is considered as an oven and *shehiyah* is not permitted even if one removes the coals or covers them with ashes. [Here, too, according to Chananyah's explanation, *shehiyah* is permitted and only replacing it is forbidden.] Hence, no pot may be placed on the top or leaned against the walls of a single stove. Again, due to the intensity of the heat, we fear he will rake the coals or remaining sparks (*Gem*.).

Where the coals are completely removed from the oven, there is a dispute as to whether the oven may be used. *Rav* states that even so the oven may not be used. *Ran* and *Baal HaMaor*, however, are of the opinion that an oven is more stringent than a double stove only where the coals have not been completely removed but have only been covered with ashes or swept aside to where they are not directly under the pot. Since there is still heat being produced and since the oven retains a greater degree of heat, its use is banned. Where, however, the coals have been completely removed, even an oven may be used (*Tif. Yis.* from *Ran*).

Our present-day ovens have their openings on the side; their heat is not as intense as that of the oven of the mishnah, nor are they as narrow as the single stove, which had space for only one pot. As a result, our ovens are most comparable to the double stove, and it is these laws which apply to them (*Rama* 253:1). Similarly, the tops of our gas ranges and electric stoves are considered a double stove (*Igros Moshe, Orach Chaim,* vol. I §93; vol. 4 §74, *bishul* 26).

The custom is to place a *blech* (Yiddish for tin), i.e., a sheet of metal, over the burners, thereby covering the flame. The *blech* on our stoves is considered the equivalent of covering the coals with ashes.

3.

◆§ Cooking with an Indirect Source of Heat

Objects whose heat is not self-generated but derives from their having been heated by a fire are known as תּוֹלְדוֹת הָאוּר, *derivatives of fire.* If their heat has come from baking in the sun, they are known as תּוֹלְדוֹת הַחַמָּה, *derivatives of the sun.*

3 or with wood, it is like an oven.

3. We may not place an egg beside a kettle for it to become slightly cooked, nor may one break it open upon [hot] scarves. But R' Yose permits [this]. Nor may one cover it in sand or in the dust of the roads

YAD AVRAHAM

On a Scriptural level, the *melachah* of *cooking applies only to cooking by the heat of a fire or its derivative. Cooking by the direct heat of the sun [e.g., to set an egg or a glass of water in a place where it will receive the full heat of the sun's rays] is permissible. Cooking by the heat of a *derivative of the sun* is forbidden by Rabbinical decree, for since the heat of the derivative is removed from its source, it is not always apparent whether that source was a fire or the sun. The Rabbis therefore forbade cooking by the heat of a solar derivative lest one cook by the heat of a fire derivative. Cooking by the heat of the sun is even Rabbinically permissible since it is apparent that one is not cooking with a fire (*Shulchan Aruch* 318:3; based on *Gem.* 39a and *Rashi*).

אֵין נוֹתְנִין בֵּיצָה בְּצַד הַמֵּחַם — *We may not place an egg beside a kettle*

On the Sabbath, we may not place an egg beside a hot kettle which has been removed from the fire.

מֵחַם refers to a copper or other metal *kettle* used for heating water, and which retains its heat well (*Rav; Rambam; Rashi*).

בִּשְׁבִיל שֶׁתִּתְגַּלְגֵּל, — *for it to become slightly cooked*,

I.e., for it to become slightly roasted. The term שֶׁתִּתְגַּלְגֵּל is derived from גלגל, which can mean *to mix* or *to roll* (*Rav; Rambam*). When an egg is slightly roasted, the white and the yolk tend to mix (*Aruch HaShalem*).

Alternatively, a raw egg does not roll freely. As the egg becomes hardened by cooking or roasting it rolls more easily (*Musaf HeAruch*).

Cooking or roasting an egg by placing it next to a heated kettle makes one liable to a sin offering. Cooking by the heat of a derivative of *fire* is equivalent to cooking by fire itself (*Rambam, Hil. Shabbos* 9:3).

וְלֹא יַפְקִיעֶנָּה בְּסוּדָרִין. — *nor may one break it open upon [hot] scarves*.

I.e., one may not crack open an egg over scarves which have been heated by the sun in order to roast the egg. As explained above, there is no Biblical prohibition involved, since this heat was not brought about by fire, but is a *derivative of the sun.* However, the Rabbis prohibited cooking even with heat deriving from the sun lest one cook with heat deriving from a fire (*Rav;* from *Gem.* 39a).

However, cooking by the heat of the sun itself is permissible, since the sun and fire will not be confused (*Tos. R' Akiva* from *Gem.* ibid.).

וְרַבִּי יוֹסֵי מַתִּיר. — *But R' Yose permits [this].*

R' Yose is of the opinion that there need be no concern that people will confuse heat deriving from the sun with heat deriving from a fire (*Rav* from *Gem.* 39a).

The halachah does not follow the opinion of R' Yose (*Rav*).

וְלֹא יַטְמִינֶנָּה בְּחוֹל וּבַאֲבַק דְּרָכִים — *Nor may one cover it in sand or in the dust of the roads*

I.e., which have baked in the sun (*Rav*).

שבת ג/ד

[ד] **מַעֲשֶׂה** שֶׁעָשׂוּ אַנְשֵׁי טְבֶרְיָא וְהֵבִיאוּ סִילוֹן שֶׁל צוֹנֵן לְתוֹךְ אַמָּה שֶׁל חַמִּין. אָמְרוּ לָהֶם חֲכָמִים: ״אִם בְּשַׁבָּת, כְּחַמִּין שֶׁהוּחַמּוּ בְשַׁבָּת, אֲסוּרִין בִּרְחִיצָה וּבִשְׁתִיָּה; בִּשְׁבִיל שֶׁתִּצָּלֶה.

ר׳ עובדיה מברטנורא

דרך הטמנה אתי למימר מה לי רמץ מה לי חול. אי נמי גזר רבי יוסי שמא יזיז עפר ממקומו, שמא לא יהא שם חול עקור ככל הצורך ואתי לאחוזי עפר הדבוק, והוי תולדה דחורש: (ד) **סלון.** צינור שממשיכין המים לתוכו, והיה אותו צינור משוקע בחמי טבריא ומתחמם מכח אותם המים החמים, וכשהיו המים צונין נמשכין בתוכו מתחממין באותו סלון שנתחמם בתוך חמי טבריא. ואמרו חכמים שהמים שנמשכו באותו צינור בשבת דינם כחמין שהוחמו בשבת שאסורים לרחוץ בהן אפילו אבר קטן, ואסורים אף בשתיה. והמים שעוברים בו ביום טוב דינם כחמין שהוחמו ביום טוב שאסורים לרחוץ בהם כל הגוף, אבל מותר לרחוץ בהן ידיו ורגליו, ומותרין בשתיה והלכה כחכמים. וחזרו בהם אנשי טבריא ושברו את הסלון:

יד אברהם

בִּשְׁבִיל שֶׁתִּצָּלֶה — in order that it be roasted.

As in the case of boiling an egg in sun-heated scarves, this too is prohibited as a derivative of the sun.

R' Yose, however, concurs with the Tanna Kamma in prohibiting this latter case. The Gemara (39a) offers two reasons for this. According to one opinion this is because this is akin to hatmanah [insulating], i.e., people may tend to confuse heated sand with heated ashes and might go ahead and cook with the ash, which would constitute the melachah of *cooking. According to the other opinion, we are concerned that he may move the sand or soil for this purpose. Rashi explains that the concern is that he may loosen tightly packed sand for this purpose and thereby be guilty of digging, which is a toladah of חוֹרֵשׁ, *plowing.

Tosafos, in one opinion, however, understands that the concern is that he may use sand not designated for use prior to the Sabbath, thus violating the prohibition against moving muktzeh, objects set aside from use on the Sabbath and whose handling is, in consequence, Rabbinically prohibited (see below introd. to mishnah 6 and General Introduction).

According to the opinion which explains R' Yose as being concerned with his moving the sand, if there is sufficient soft earth, the egg may be covered (Gem. ibid.). [According to Rashi because there is no longer a concern that he will dig; according to Tosafos because the earth is so loosely packed that the egg will sink in by itself.] The Tanna Kamma, prohibits any cooking with a derivative of the sun (Magen Avraham 318:9).

4.

מַעֲשֶׂה — [There was] an incident: [This is an expression signifying a precedent in support of a previously stated ruling.]

4. [T]here was] an incident: The people of Tiberias ran a pipe of cold water through a canal of hot springs.

The Sages said to them: "If [it was done] on the Sabbath, it is like hot water that was heated on the Sabbath, [namely,] it is forbidden for [both] bathing and drinking; [if it was done] on

YAD AVRAHAM

שֶׁעָשׂוּ אַנְשֵׁי טְבֶרְיָא וְהֵבִיאוּ סִילוֹן שֶׁל צוֹנֵן לְתוֹךְ אַמָּה שֶׁל חַמִּין. — *The people of Tiberias ran* (lit. *that the people of Tiberias did, they brought*) *a pipe of cold water through a canal of hot springs.*

Tiberias is a city noted for its thermal springs. The cold water was cleaner than the water of the hot springs and was preferable for bathing. This pipe carried the cold water through a canal of hot springs, thus heating the water. The water then ran from the pipe into a *mikveh* which was used by the Tiberians on the Sabbath (*Tif. Yis.*).

Also, they found their drinking water too cold and used this method to heat the water (*Meiri*).

Others explain that the purpose for drawing the water through the pipe was to cool the hot springs. The pipe had holes to permit the cool water to mix with the hot, thereby cooling the hot and enabling the people to bathe in the hot springs (*Meiri*).

אָמְרוּ לָהֶן חֲכָמִים: — *The Sages said to them:*

[I.e., to the Tiberians.]

אִם בְּשַׁבָּת, — *"If [it was done] on the Sabbath,*

I.e., if the water ran into the *mikveh* on the Sabbath, though it entered the pipe *before* the Sabbath (*Tif. Yis.*) and

remained within the pipe for some time on the Sabbath until the tap was opened (*Mishnah Berurah* 326:14).

כְּחַמִּין שֶׁהוּחַמּוּ בְשַׁבָּת, — *it is like hot water that was heated on the Sabbath,*

[I.e., we apply to it the same rules as those of hot water heated on the Sabbath.]

אֲסוּרִין בִּרְחִיצָה — *[namely,] it is forbidden for [both] bathing*

I.e., in water which has been heated before the Sabbath it is permissible to bathe one's hands, face, and feet (though not one's entire body). Since, however, this water was heated on the Sabbath, this too is forbidden. The water may not be used until enough time has elapsed after the Sabbath to heat it (so that no benefit will be derived from the water having been heated on the Sabbath) (*Tif. Yis.*).

וּבִשְׁתִיָּה; — *and drinking;*

[I.e., it is also forbidden for drinking.]

As previously mentioned, the incident of the people of Tiberias was meant as a precedent for a ruling mentioned in the preceding mishnah. Some interpret this as a precedent for R' Yose's ruling against covering an egg in hot sand on the Sabbath. Just as the Rabbis prohibited the use of the cold-water pipe on the Sabbath because it is

שבת
ג/ד

בְּיוֹם טוֹב, כְּחַמִּין שֶׁהוּחַמּוּ בְּיוֹם טוֹב, אֲסוּרִין בִּרְחִיצָה וּמֻתָּרִין בִּשְׁתִיָּה."
מֵילְיָאר הַגָּרוּף, שׁוֹתִין הֵימֶנּוּ בְּשַׁבָּת. אַנְטִיכִי, אַף־עַל־פִּי שֶׁגְּרוּפָה, אֵין שׁוֹתִין מִמֶּנָּה.

ר' עובדיה מברטנורא

מוליאר. פירשו בגמרא מים מבפנים וגחלים מבחוץ, והוא כלי שיש לו בית קיבול קטן חלל דופנו מבחוץ מחובר לו ונותנים שם גחלים, והמים בקבולו הגדול, ואם גרפוהו מן הגחלים מבעוד יום שותין מן המים שבקבולו הגדול בשבת, ואף על פי שהוחמו קלת מחמת כלי, לפי שאינו מוסיף הבל אלא משמר ומקיים חום שלהם שלא ילטננו: **אנטיכי.** הוא כלי נחושת שיש לו שתי שולים ומשימין המים למעלה והאש למטה בין שתי השולים, ומתוך שהאש למטה בין שתי השולים חומו נשאר הרבה, ואף על פי שגרף הגחלים מע"ש המים מתחממים בו בשבת, לפיכך אין שותים מהם בשבת:

יד אברהם

considered *hatmanah*, so did R' Yose consider covering an egg in hot sand as *hatmanah*. Since the pipe passed through a thermal spring, it was considered insulated in a substance that increases its heat, which is forbidden even when placed there before the Sabbath (see 4:1).

Those who attribute Yose's ruling to the fear that one may move earth when he buries the egg (a ruling to which the incident in Tiberias bears no relationship) interpret this as a precedent for the Rabbis' prohibition of using derivatives of the sun. They cite the incident of the pipe being conducted through the hot springs of Tiberias as evidence that although the water was *not* heated by a fire or its derivative, it was, nevertheless, forbidden to be used. Similarly, derivatives of the sun, which are also not derived from fire, may *not* be used to cook on the Sabbath. R' Yose, who permits cooking in a *derivative of the sun*, is of the opinion, however, that the hot water of Tiberias is considered a *fire derivative* because it is heated by subterranean fires referred to in the Talmud (*Eruvin* 19a) as "the entrance of Gehinnom." Heat coming from a *solar derivative*, however, may be used on the Sabbath (*Tos. R' Akiva* from *Gem.* 30a). The halachah does not follow R' Yose's opinion (*Rav*).

בְּיוֹם טוֹב, כְּחַמִּין שֶׁהוּחַמּוּ בְּיוֹם טוֹב — *[if it was done] on a festival, it is like hot water that was heated on a festival,*

I.e., if the water passed through the pipe on a festival, we apply to it the same rules as those of hot water heated on a festival.

אֲסוּרִין בִּרְחִיצָה — *[namely,] it is forbidden for bathing*

It is forbidden to be used for bathing the entire body, but it may be used for washing one's face, hands, and feet (*Rav*).

Had the water been heated before the festival, one would be permitted to bathe even his entire body in it. In this, *Rav* follows the ruling of *Rambam*, *Yom Tov* 1:16, and *Rif*, *Beitzah* 21b, who rule that on festivals one may bathe his entire body with water that was heated before the festival. *Tosafos* (*Shabbos* 39b) rules, however, that one may not bathe his entire body in hot water on *Yom Tov*, regardless of when it was heated. *Tosafos* differentiates only where rinsing is concerned. One may rinse his entire body with water heated before *Yom Tov*, but not with water heated on

3
4

a festival, it is like hot water that was heated on a festival, [namely,] it is forbidden for bathing but permitted for drinking."

A *miliarium* that was cleared [of its coals], we may drink from it on the Sabbath. An *antichi*, even if it was cleared, we may not drink from it.

YAD AVRAHAM

Yom Tov. (This is in accordance with R' Shimon; see *Gem*. 39b.) The halachah, however, is in accordance with R' Yehudah, who prohibits even rinsing the entire body with any hot water on *Yom Tov* (*Tos. R' Akiva; Rama* 511:2).

וּמֻתָּרִין בִּשְׁתִיָּה. — *but permitted for drinking."*

Since one is permitted to cook liquids or food on *Yom Tov* for the purpose of consuming them on *Yom Tov*, he may certainly drink water heated in the above manner.

As mentioned above, heating water to wash the hands, face, and feet is also permitted on festivals (see *Beitzah* 2:8).

מְלְיָאר — *A miliarium*

I.e., a vessel with a large bowl for water, surrounded by a narrow receptacle for coals (*Rav* from *Gem*. 41a). [*Miliarium* is a Greek word.]

According to *Rabbeinu Chananel* and *Rambam*, the *Gemara* (ibid.) reads, the coals are in the middle and are surrounded by the water (*Kehati*).

הַגָּרוּף, — *that was cleared [of its coals]*,
Before the Sabbath (*Rashi*).

שׁוֹתִין הֵימֶנּוּ בְשַׁבָּת. — *we may drink from it on the Sabbath.*

Without its coals the *miliarium's* purpose is only to retain heat, not to increase it and no prohibited *hatmanah* is involved. We may, therefore, keep water in it on the Sabbath and drink from it (*Rav; Rashi*).

אַנְטִיכִי, — *An antichi,*

A copper vessel with a double bottom, with space for coals between the two bottoms (*Rav; Rambam*). [*Antichi* is a Greek word.]

אַף־עַל־פִּי שֶׁגְּרוּפָה, — *even if it was cleared,*

[Even though the coals were cleared away before the Sabbath.]

אֵין שׁוֹתִין מִמֶּנָּה. — *we may not drink from it.*

Since the coals are kept between the two bottoms, even after they have been cleared from there the heat remains trapped in that space. It therefore effectively continues to heat the water even after the coals have been removed. The water is, therefore, considered as if it were heated on the Sabbath (*Rav; Rambam*).

Alternatively, this is prohibited because it is considered *hatmanah* with a substance that increases heat (*Rashi*).

Tosafos maintains that this is not related to *hatmanah* because the prohibition of *hatmanah* applies only to a case where it may lead people to cover food with hot ashes. An *antichi* is so unlike hot ashes that we need not be concerned that some people may confuse the two. The mishnah's intent is that we may not use the water to dilute wine. Since an *antichi* retains intense heat, the water will cook the wine. A *miliarium*, however, does not retain such intense heat, and its water is unable to cook the wine (*Tos.* quoting *R' Poras*).

שבת
ג/ה

[ה] **הַמֵּחַם** שֶׁפִּנָּהוּ, לֹא יִתֵּן לְתוֹכוֹ צוֹנֵן בִּשְׁבִיל שֶׁיֵּחַמּוּ, אֲבָל נוֹתֵן הוּא לְתוֹכוֹ אוֹ לְתוֹךְ הַכּוֹס כְּדֵי לְהַפְשִׁירָן. הָאִלְפָּס וְהַקְּדֵרָה שֶׁהֶעֱבִירָן מֵרְתָחִין, לֹא

ר' עובדיה מברטנורא

(ה) **המיחם.** קומקוס של נחושת שמשימין אותו על גב האש לחמם המים שבתוכו: **שפינהו.** מעל הכירה ויש בתוכו מים חמין: **לא יתן לתוכו.** מים מועטים כדי שיתחממו מן המים החמין שנשארו בתוך המיחם, דהוה ליה כמבשל בשבת: **אבל נותן לתוכו.** מים מרובים עד שישובו הכל פושרין: **או לתוך הכוס.** ואף על פי שהוא כלי שני דוקא להפשירן מותר, אבל מועטים כדי שיחמו לא, דסבירא ליה להאי תנא דכלי שני מבשל. ולקמן תנינן אבל נותן הוא לתוך הקערה דמשמע דכלי שני אינו מבשל. והלכה דכלי שני אינו מבשל: **שהעבירן.** מן האור: **מרותחין.** בין השמשות:

יד אברהם

5.

⋠§ The Melachah of *Cooking / Primary and Secondary Vessels

Hot water, even when removed from the fire, is still capable of cooking other things if it is hot enough that יָד סוֹלֶדֶת בּוֹ, *one's hand is scalded by it.*[1]

Hot water, or any other cooked substance, which is still in the vessel in which it was cooked is referred to as being in a כְּלִי רִאשׁוֹן [kli rishon], *primary vessel.* If it has been transferred to another vessel, this second vessel is called a כְּלִי שֵׁנִי [kli sheini], *a secondary vessel.* Most opinions maintain that the transfer of the water from its primary vessel (pot) to the secondary vessel renders it halachically unfit for cooking and placing food in it cannot, therefore, come under the prohibition of *cooking.

הַמֵּחַם — *A kettle*
A copper kettle which one placed on a stove to heat the water in (*Rav*).

שֶׁפִּנָּהוּ, — *that was removed [from the fire],*
After the water had been heated the kettle was removed from the stove (*Rav*).

לֹא יִתֵּן לְתוֹכוֹ צוֹנֵן בִּשְׁבִיל שֶׁיֵּחַמּוּ, — *one may not add cold water to it to heat it up,*
I.e., one may not add a small amount of cold water to heat it.
This is prohibited because heating cold water in a *kli rishon* constitutes *cooking (*Rav* from *Gem.* 42a).

אֲבָל נוֹתֵן הוּא לְתוֹכוֹ — *but he may add to it,*
I.e., he may put a large amount of cold water into a kettle (*Rav* from *Gem.* ibid.).

אוֹ לְתוֹךְ הַכּוֹס — *or into a [hot] cup*
Or even a small amount of water (*Tos.*; *Ran*; *Rashba*) into a *kli sheini*, secondary vessel (*Tif. Yis.*).

כְּדֵי לְהַפְשִׁירָן. — *to make it (the cold water) lukewarm.*
I.e., where the net result will be that

---

1. There is a dispute between contemporary *poskim* as to the temperature of יָד סוֹלֶדֶת בּוֹ. The opinions range from 110 degrees Fahrenheit to 120 degrees Fahrenheit.

5. A kettle that was removed [from the fire], one may not add cold water to it to heat it up, but he may add to it, or into a [hot] cup to make it lukewarm.

A sealed pot or an [ordinary] pot which was removed [from the fire] while boiling, one may not

YAD AVRAHAM

the entire mixture is only lukewarm (*Rav*).

The kettle is a primary vessel. Thus, only a large amount of cold water, which we can be certain will not become hot, may be added. A cup of hot water, on the other hand, is only a secondary vessel, which is considered incapable of cooking other things. Therefore, we may add even a small amount of cold water to it (*Tos.; Ran; Rashba*).[1]

Rav adds (from *Gem.* 42b) that according to the mishnah there is an addtional stipulation. We may add a large amount of water to a kettle which has been removed from the stove only if that kettle contains water of its own. If it is empty, however, it is forbidden since adding cold water to it will contract and therefore harden the metal of the kettle — an act forbidden on the Sabbath as a *toladah* of *striking the final blow* (Rashi). This is deduced from the fact that the mishnah states that one removed the kettle from the stove without adding that one removed the water from the kettle indicating that the original water still remains in the kettle. Although the person's intent when adding the water is to warm the water and not to harden the metal, and the hardening of the metal therefore constitutes a דָּבָר שֶׁאֵינוֹ מִתְכַּוֵּן, an

unintended labor, which many opinions permit (see General Introduction p. 8), this mishnah was stated by R' Yehudah who rules that an unintended labor is prohibited. Accordingly, we must conclude that although it is the opinion of *this* mishnah that one may add a large amount of cold water to the kettle only if there is hot water still in it, the halachah is that one may add cold water to the kettle in any case (since the halachah rules that an unintended labor is permissible). It is strange, therefore, that *Rav* does not add this (*Tos. R' Akiva*). *Ohr Gadol* answers that *an unintended labor* is prohibited by everyone where it is a case of פְּסִיק רֵישָׁא, i.e., where, despite the lack of intent, the *melachah* will *inevitably* follow. Since in our situation, though he does not intend to harden the metal, it is usually inevitable that he will, *Rav* lets stand the ruling prohibiting the addition of even a large amount of cold water into an empty kettle.

הָאִלְפָּס וְהַקְּדֵרָה שֶׁהֶעֱבִירָן מְרֻתָּחִין, — *A sealed pot or an [ordinary] pot which was removed [from the fire] while boiling,*

I.e., pots which were removed from the fire and which are still boiling during *bein hashemashos* [twilight] (*Rav; Rashi*).

לֹא יִתֵּן לְתוֹכָן תְּבָלִין, — *one may not*

---

1. *Rav* proposes a complicated explanation. He assumes that this *Tanna* is of the opinion that *a kli sheini* can cook other things and, therefore, even into a *kli sheini* only a large amount of cold water, which cannot possibly become hot, may be added. The mishnah which later states that spices may be put into a bowl of hot water [which is a *kli sheini*, demonstrating that a *kli sheini* cannot cook other things] is attributed by *Rav* to a different *Tanna*.

שבת ג/ה

יִתֵּן לְתוֹכָן תְּבָלִין, אֲבָל נוֹתֵן הוּא לְתוֹךְ הַקְּעָרָה אוֹ לְתוֹךְ הַתַּמְחוּי. רַבִּי יְהוּדָה אוֹמֵר: לַכֹּל הוּא נוֹתֵן, חוּץ מִדָּבָר שֶׁיֵּשׁ בּוֹ חֹמֶץ וְצִיר.

ר' עובדיה מברטנורא

לא יתן לתוכן תבלין. משתחשך, דכלי ראשון כל זמן שרותח מבשל: **אבל נותן הוא לתוך הקערה.** דכלי שני אינו מבשל: **תמחוי.** כמין קערה גדולה שמערה כל האילפס לתוכו ומשם מערה לקערות: **לכל הוא נותן.** אפילו לכלי ראשון: **חוץ מדבר שיש בו חומץ או ציר.** הנוטף ממליחת דגים שהם מבשלין התבלין, ואין הלכה כר"י. ודוקא תבלין הוא דאסור ליתן בכלי ראשון אפילו לאחר שהעבירו מן האור, אבל מלח אפילו בכלי ראשון לא בשלה, אלא על גבי האור בלבד, לפיכך מותר לתת מלח אפילו בכלי ראשון לאחר שהעבירו מן האור:

יד אברהם

add spices to them,

I.e., one may not add spices into them after nightfall, since a primary vessel which remains hot enough to scald one's hand retains its ability to cook something else (*Rav; Rashi*).

Alternatively, even if the pots are no longer hot enough to scald one's hand the spices may not be added lest one add them to a pot that is hot (*Ritva ms.; Magen Avraham* 318:28).

Rav and *Rashi* specify that one may not add spices *after nightfall,* implying that during *bein hashemashos* it is permitted. This can be explained as follows: Later in the mishnah R' Yehudah permits adding spices even to a liquid in a primary vessel that has been removed from the fire. It is therefore likely that the *Tanna Kamma* prohibits it only as a Rabbinic enactment and not Biblically, for it is unusual to find a dispute where the participants disagree to such extremes. Where a Rabbinic enactment is involved we permit it *bein hashemashos,* for the purpose of a mitzvah (see above 2:7) (*Tos. R' Akiva* 22:2).

We have until this point been discussing adding spices to a hot liquid. Salt is different. According to one view in the *Gemara* salt can only become cooked when the pot is actually on the fire. Therefore, it may be added even to a primary vessel once that vessel has been removed from the fire. Others maintain that salt can become cooked even in a secondary vessel. The halachah is in accordance with the former view, though it is commendable to observe the more stringent ruling (*Shulchan Aruch* 318:9, *Rama*).

This applies to rock salt, which is prepared without cooking. Sea salt, however, is processed by cooking and the principle of אֵין בִּשּׁוּל אַחַר בִּשּׁוּל, *there is no cooking after cooking* [i.e., once something has been cooked, there is no law prohibiting it from being cooked again, a principle that only applies to dry substances but does not apply to liquids], is applicable.

Some question this ruling as it applies to salt, as well as other substances that dissolve. It is, therefore, advisable not to add such substances to a primary vessel (*Mishnah Berurah* 318:71).

אֲבָל נוֹתֵן הוּא לְתוֹךְ הַקְּעָרָה — *but he may add [spices] into a bowl*

Spices may be added to a bowl into which the contents of the pot have been transferred. The bowl is a secondary vessel and the spices can therefore not be cooked in it (*Rav*).

אוֹ לְתוֹךְ הַתַּמְחוּי. — *or into a tureen.*

A large bowl into which the contents of the sealed pot are transferred to be dished out into the individual bowls. This, too, is a secondary vessel (*Rav; Rashi*).

A secondary vessel does not cook

add spices to them, but he may add [spices] into a bowl or into a tureen.

R' Yehudah says: One may add [spices] to anything, except something containing vinegar or brine.

YAD AVRAHAM

foods even if it is hot enough to scald one's hand (*Mishnah Berurah* 318:87; *Tif. Yis.*).

This ruling applies only where the secondary vessel contains liquids. If, however, there is hot solid food in the secondary vessel many *poskim* rule that we may not add spices to it as long as the food is still hot enough to scald one's hand (*Magen Avraham* 318:45; *Mishnah Berurah*). [Solid food does not lose its heat as rapidly as does liquid.]

רַבִּי יְהוּדָה אוֹמֵר: לַכֹּל הוּא נוֹתֵן, — *R' Yehudah says: One may add [spices] to anything,*

I.e., even into a primary vessel (*Rav; Tif. Yis.* from *Gem.* 42b).

It is R' Yehudah's opinion that spices can be cooked only directly over a fire. Consequently, they may be added even to a primary vessel which is hot enough to scald one's hand as long as it is no longer on the fire. He agrees, however, with the *Tanna Kamma* in regard to other foods (*Tos.* 42b).

חוּץ מִדָּבָר שֶׁיֵּשׁ בּוֹ חֹמֶץ וְצִיר. — *except something containing vinegar or brine.*

I.e., brine of salted fish. These sharp substances will cause spices to cook in a primary vessel even after it has been removed from the fire (*Rav; Tif. Yis.*).

The halachah is not in accordance with R' Yehudah (*Rav*).

6.

◢§ **Muktzeh**

As a general rule, objects that people do not intend to use on the Sabbath are known as מֻקְצֶה [*muktzeh*], *set apart*. The Rabbis [Nehemiah and his court in the early days of the Second Temple (see *Nehemiah* 13:15*ff*)] decreed that such things may not be moved about on the Sabbath (*Shabbos* 123b). The reasons for this law and its details are discussed at length in the preface to Chap. 17.

Generally speaking, anything which is neither a utensil nor a food (for either people or animals) is considered *muktzeh*. For this reason, the flame of a candle or lamp is considered *muktzeh*.

Also *muktzeh* is anything which, though itself not *muktzeh*, serves as a *base to muktzeh*. Since the oil of a lamp serves as a base to the wick which in turn serves as a base to the flame, the oil too is considered a base to the flame and is classified as a *base to muktzeh*. It, too, is therefore *muktzeh* (*Gem.* 47a).

One of the general rules governing all the various categories of *muktzeh* is that anything which was *muktzeh* during *bein hashemashos* (twilight) of Friday remains *muktzeh* for the rest of that Sabbath even if the reasons for its being *muktzeh* are no longer applicable. (This is disputed by Shimon in certain cases.) Therefore, the oil in a lamp which was burning at the beginning of the

[ו] **אֵין** נוֹתְנִין כְּלִי תַּחַת הַנֵּר לְקַבֵּל בּוֹ אֶת הַשֶּׁמֶן, וְאִם נְתָנוֹ מִבְּעוֹד יוֹם, מֻתָּר. וְאֵין נֵאוֹתִין מִמֶּנּוּ, לְפִי שֶׁאֵינוֹ מִן הַמּוּכָן. מְטַלְטְלִין נֵר חָדָשׁ, אֲבָל לֹא יָשָׁן. רַבִּי שִׁמְעוֹן אוֹמֵר: כָּל הַנֵּרוֹת מְטַלְטְלִין, חוּץ מִן הַנֵּר הַדּוֹלֵק בְּשַׁבָּת.

ר' עובדיה מברטנורא

(ו) **אין נותנין.** בשבת: **כלי תחת הנר לקבל בו את השמן.** המטפטף, משום דשמן מוקצה הוא ואסור לבטל כלי מהיכנו, כלומר להושיב כלי במקום שלא יוכל עוד ליטלו משם, דהוה ליה כקובע לו מקום ומחברו בטיט ודמי למלאכה, וכלי זה משיפול בו השמן מוקצה הוא ואסור לטלטלו: **אין ניאותין.** אין נהנין מן השמן המטפטף מן הנר בשבת, לפי שאינו מן המוכן שכבר הוקצה להדלקה: **מטלטלין נר חדש.** שאינו מאוס וחזי לאשתמושי ביה: **אבל לא ישן.** דמוקצה מחמת מיאוס הוא: **חוץ מן הנר הדולק.** בעוד שהוא דולק אסור, גזירה שמא יכבה ואין ליה לרבי שמעון מוקצה מחמת מיאוס, ולא מוקצה מחמת איסור. ואין הלכה כרבי שמעון שמתיר לטלטל כל הנרות

יד אברהם

Sabbath, having been *muktzeh* at that time, remains *muktzeh* even after the flame has gone out (after which it no longer serves as a base to *muktzeh*). Similarly, oil which dripped out of the lamp also remains *muktzeh* despite the fact that it is no longer a base to the flame.

אֵין נוֹתְנִין כְּלִי תַּחַת הַנֵּר — **We may not place a utensil under a lamp**

I.e., on the Sabbath we may not place a utensil near the base of a lighted lamp (*Rav; Tif. Yis.*).

לְקַבֵּל בּוֹ אֶת הַשֶּׁמֶן, — **to catch the [dripping] oil,**

I.e., to catch oil that drips from the lamp. The oil in the lamp is *muktzeh*, and when it drips into the utensil under the lamp that utensil itself becomes unusable because of the *muktzeh* oil in it. The *Gemara* (43a) calls this בִּטוּל כְּלִי מֵהֲכָנוֹ, **nullification of the utensil's availability**. Since the utensil becomes unmovable because of the *muktzeh* in it, it is locked in its place. The Rabbis found this similar to cementing a utensil in place [which is a violation of the *melachah* of בּוֹנֶה, *building* (see 7:2) (*Meiri*)]. They therefore prohibited one to do anything to a utensil on the Sabbath which would render it *muktzeh* (*Rav; Rashi*).

Others explain that *nullifying a utensil's availability* is similar to demolishing it (since it becomes unusable). This was therefore Rabbinically prohibited as a form of the *melachah* of סוֹתֵר, *demolishing* (*Rashi* 128b, 154b; *Rambam, Hil. Shabbos* 25:23).

וְאִם נְתָנוֹ מִבְּעוֹד יוֹם, מֻתָּר. — **but if he places it while it is yet day, it is permissible.**

Rashi explains the phrase *it is permitted* to mean that once one has gone ahead and placed the utensil under the lamp he may leave it there. It would seem from this statement of *Rashi* that even on a Friday it is still preferable that one not place a utensil there because we are fearful that he may inadvertently move the utensil about on the Sabbath after the oil has begun to drip into it. This consideration is, however, not sufficient for us to

6. **We** may not place a utensil under a lamp to catch the [dripping] oil, but if he places it while it is yet day, it is permissible. And we may not benefit from it, since it is not something prepared [for Sabbath use].

We may move a new lamp, but not an old one. R' Shimon says: All lamps may be moved, except a lamp burning on the Sabbath.

YAD AVRAHAM

require him to remove it.

Tosafos and *Tur* (265) disagree with *Rashi* and permit placing the utensil there on Friday without reservation.

Tosafos admit that according to their opinion the mishnah should have read אֲבָל מִבְּעוֹד יוֹם נוֹתְנִין, *but when it is yet day we may place it,* in the present tense, which would imply that one may go ahead and do so (*Tos. Yom Tov*).

This difficulty may be reconciled according to the ruling of *Maharil* (Responsum 32), that one may place a bowl under a table over which a lamp is hanging. Before retiring, one may move the table away, thereby causing the oil to drip into the bowl. Since one is only indirectly nullifying the utensil from its usefulness, this is permissible. Thus we can explain the mishnah: If he placed the utensil under the lamp in such a way that it did not become a base for the oil when it is still daytime (i.e., by placing it beneath a table which was under the lamp), he may even nullify the availability of the utensil on the Sabbath [because he is doing so indirectly — by removing the table] (*Korban Nesanel*).

וְאֵין נֵאוֹתִין מִמֶּנּוּ, — *And we may not benefit from it,*

I.e., we may not benefit on the Sabbath from oil that drips from the lamp (*Rav*).

לְפִי שֶׁאֵינוֹ מִן הַמּוּכָן. — *since it is not something prepared [for Sabbath use].*

I.e., since it was set aside for kin-dling the Sabbath light (*Rav*).

מְטַלְטְלִין נֵר חָדָשׁ, — *We may move a new lamp,*

I.e., we may move a lamp that has not yet been used. Since it has never yet been lit, it has not become grimy and is therefore still usable for other purposes. Consequently, it is not *muktzeh* (*Rav; Rashi*).

אֲבָל לֹא יָשָׁן. — *but not an old one.*

I.e., one that has already been used. Since after having been used as a lamp it is grimy, one would not use it for other purposes. Therefore it becomes *muktzeh* under the category of מֻקְצֶה מֵחֲמַת מִאוּס, *set aside because of repugnance* (*Rav*). [Although it is certainly usable as a lamp, that is a use which is prohibited on the Sabbath. Since because of its repugnance it is not really fit for any permissible use on the Sabbath, the Rabbis declared it *muktzeh*.]

רַבִּי שִׁמְעוֹן אוֹמֵר: כָּל הַנֵּרוֹת מְטַלְטְלִין, — *R' Shimon says: All lamps may be moved,*

R' Shimon does not subscribe to the prohibition of *muktzeh because of repugnance* (*Rav*).

חוּץ מִן הַנֵּר הַדּוֹלֵק בְּשַׁבָּת. — *except a lamp burning on the Sabbath.*

I.e., a lamp may not be moved while lit because the lamp, the oil, and the

שבת
ג/ו
נוֹתְנִין כְּלִי תַּחַת הַנֵּר לְקַבֵּל נִיצוֹצוֹת; וְלֹא יִתֵּן לְתוֹכוֹ מַיִם, מִפְּנֵי שֶׁהוּא מְכַבֶּה.

ר' עובדיה מברטנורא

חוץ מן הנר הדולק, שנר שהדליקוהו לליל שבת אף על פי שכבה אסור לטלטלו כל אותו שבת, דמגו דאיתקצאי לבין השמשות אתקצאי לכולי יומא, אבל בשאר נרות מוקים שאין מוקצה לשבת אלא מוקצה מחמת חסרון כיס דמודה ביה רבי שמעון: **נותנים כלי תחת הנר.** בשבת לקבל ניצוצות של שלהבת הנוטפות מן הנר כדי שלא ידלק מה שתחתיו דניצוצות אין בהם ממש ואין הכלי מבוטל מהיכנו בהכי: **ולא יתן לתוכו מים.** ואפילו מערב שבת, דגזרינן ערב שבת אטו שבת, ובשבת אי הוה עביד כי האי גוונא הוי מכבה וחייב, הילכך בערב שבת אסור:

יד אברהם

wick all become a base for the flame and that which supports *muktzeh* becomes *muktzeh* (*Tos. R' Akiva* from *Gem.* 47a; *Tif. Yis.*).

Rav and *Rashi* explain that it is prohibited because we are afraid he may extinguish the flame while carrying the lamp. Although this reason is suggested by the *Gemara*, 46b, it is ultimately rejected (*Tos. R' Akiva*).

The halachah rules: (a) in accordance with R' Shimon's view that all lamps, new or used, may be moved about on the Sabbath, לְצֹרֶךְ גּוּפוֹ אוֹ מְקוֹמוֹ, *if they are needed for a permis-*sible use or if the space they occupy is needed for something else; but (b) against R' Shimon's view that only a lit lamp is *muktzeh*. Rather, any lamp which was burning during *bein hashemashos* (dusk) is *muktzeh* even after the flame goes out. This is based on the principle: *Anything muktzeh bein hashemashos remains muktzeh for the entire day* (even after the reason for its being *muktzeh* has passed) (*Rav*).

נוֹתְנִין כְּלִי תַּחַת הַנֵּר — *We may place a utensil under a lamp*

3 6   We may place a utensil under a lamp to catch sparks; but one may not place water in it, because he extinguishes [them].

YAD AVRAHAM

We may do so even on the Sabbath (*Rav*).

לְקַבֵּל נִיצוֹצוֹת; — *to catch sparks;*

Sparks, being intangible, do not, upon landing on the utensil, nullify its availability (*Rav* from *Gem.* 47b).

וְלֹא יִתֵּן לְתוֹכוֹ מַיִם, — *but one may not place water in it,*

I.e., even on Friday, one may not pour water into the utensil he places under the lamp (*Rav* from *Gem.* 47b).

מִפְּנֵי שֶׁהוּא מְכַבֶּה. — *because he extinguishes [them].*

Pouring the water in while the sparks are falling would constitute the *melachah* of מְכַבֶּה, *extinguishing. The Rabbis, therefore, enacted a precautionary measure forbidding one to pour in water even before the Sabbath (*Rav; Rashi; Tos.*)

Tosafos maintain that even if one were to do this on the Sabbath, he would not violate the *melachah* of *extinguishing. According to R' Shimon, who rules that a work not done for its defined purpose is not liable, as explained above (2:5), one is not liable for *extinguishing unless his intention is to make charcoal. Obviously, where sparks are involved there is no opportunity for making charcoal. We must, therefore, conclude that in this case the Rabbis enacted a double precautionary measure — a *decree to a decree;* viz., pouring water into the utensil before the Sabbath is not permitted lest he do so on the Sabbath; which is in turn only prohibited lest he extinguish for the purpose of charcoal. Though, normally, the Rabbis do not decree *a decree to a decree*, they, nevertheless, felt that in this case it was necessary (*Tos.* 47b).

Rambam (below 4:1) writes that where the Rabbis felt that there would be laxity in the observance of a precautionary measure, they added an additonal precautionary measure (*Tos. Yom Tov; Tif. Yis.*). [See preface to Chapter 4.]

פרק רביעי
Chapter Four

This chapter deals with *hatmanah*, literally *hiding*, i.e., insulating hot food by wrapping the pot with some material, as a way of preserving its heat for the Sabbath. The general rule is that before the Sabbath we may insulate the food with substances which do not raise the temperature of the food. On the Sabbath proper, however, we may not add *any* insulation.

The mishnah (2:7) has already mentioned that the latest we are permitted to cover food is during *bein hashemashos* (twilight).

The reason for the prohibition of *hatmanah* on the Sabbath proper is the fear that should one find the food to have cooled he might reheat it. During *bein hashemashos*, however, when pots are almost always still hot, we are not concerned that one may come to reheat them.

Before the Sabbath we may not cover food with substances that raise the heat level, lest one cover the food with hot ash mixed with live coals, which, in turn, may lead to his raking them in order to hasten the cooking. *Hatmanah* applies even to foods that are completely done, though one will certainly do nothing to hasten the cooking. This is because of the principle known as לֹא פְּלוּג, non-differentiation, i.e., the Rabbis decree a general prohibition and do not exempt the individual cases where the reason for the decree may not apply (*Tif. Yis.*; *Rashi* 34b).

Rambam (based on the *Geonic* version of the *Gem.*) gives an alternate explanation. On Friday we may not cover substances that raise the heat level because they may cause the pot to boil too vigorously on the Sabbath, which would necessitate the removal of the pot cover to allow the boiling to subside. One would then be tempted to replace the pot cover and, in effect, commit on the Sabbath *hatmanah* that increases heat. Accordingly, we may cover hot food even with substances that add heat during the *bein hashemashos* period because, in general, any food cooked for the Sabbath has already boiled and ceased to froth and there is little likelihood that it will again come to a vigorous boil.

On the Sabbath, however, we may not store hot food even with substances which do *not* raise the temperature. This is so that one not insulate the food on the Sabbath with hot ashes which may still contain live sparks, in which case he will, in effect, be raking coals (*Rambam, Comm.* and *Hil. Shabbos* 4:2,3; see *Lechem Mishneh*).

There are two objections raised against *Rambam's* explanation. (a) An ironic situation is created whereby the restrictions of *hatmanah* in substances that raise the heat levels are more stringent on Friday by day than during *bein hashemashos*, since during *bein hashemashos* this sort of *hatmanah* is permitted whereas during daylight on Friday it is not (*Ravad*). (2) Strangely, *Rambam* considers hot ashes a substance that does not add to the heat (*Maggid Mishneh*).

See also *Ran* and *Ravad* for alternate interpretations of the *Geonic* version of the *Gemara*.[1]

---

1. *Rambam* points out that although there is a general principle of אֵין גּוֹזְרִין גְּזֵרָה לִגְזֵרָה, we do not decree a safeguard to a safeguard, here we seem to be doing just that. We prohibit insulating hot food on the Sabbath in any substance lest we do so with hot ash. In turn, insulating hot food with hot ash is itself only prohibited for fear there may still be a few hot sparks left in it which he will then be, in effect, raking.

Rambam explains that the principle of not decreeing a safeguard to a safeguard applies to a previously existing safeguard, i.e., the Rabbis may not issue a new decree to safeguard a previous one. The Rabbis may, however, issue a decree and, realizing that this decree alone may fail to stand up, may simultaneously issue another decree to support the initial one (*Rambam, Comm.*). [This explanation seems to be the opinion of *Rashi*, too. See *Rashi* to *Beitzah* 3a.]

שבת
ד/א

[א] **בַּמֶּה טוֹמְנִין**, וּבַמָּה אֵין טוֹמְנִין? אֵין טוֹמְנִין לֹא בְגֶפֶת, וְלֹא בְזֶבֶל, לֹא בְמֶלַח, וְלֹא בְסִיד, וְלֹא בְחוֹל, בֵּין לַחִים בֵּין יְבֵשִׁים; לֹא בְתֶבֶן, וְלֹא בְזַגִּים, וְלֹא בְמוֹכִים, וְלֹא בַעֲשָׂבִים, בִּזְמַן שֶׁהֵן לַחִים, אֲבָל טוֹמְנִין בָּהֶן כְּשֶׁהֵן יְבֵשִׁין.

ר' עובדיה מברטנורא

פרק רביעי – במה טומנין. (א) במה טומנין. הבא לסלק קדרה מעל גבי כירה בערב שבת ולטמנה בדבר אחר, ואמרו חכמים אין טומנין בדבר המוסיף הבל אלא בדבר המעמיד הבל, חיזהו דבר המוסיף ואסור: **לא בגפת**. פסולת של זיתים ושומשמין, כשהוא כנוס יחד חם מאד: **לחים**. יש בהן הבל הרבה יותר מיבשין: **זגין**. קליפי הענבים: **חרצנים**, גרעיני הענבים: **מוכין**. כל דבר רך קרוי מוכין, כגון למר גפן ותלושי למר רך של בהמה וגרירת בגדים בלויים: **בזמן שהן לחין**. אכולהו קאי אחתבן וזגין ומוכין ועשבים. ולחין שאמרו לחין מחמת עצמן לא לחין מחמת משקין שנפלו עליהן לאחר שיבשו, ומוכין לחין מחמת עצמן משכחת לה, כגון בלמר הסמוך לאליה או בלמר שבין ירכות הבהמה:

יד אברהם

1.

בַּמֶּה טוֹמְנִין, וּבַמָּה אֵין טוֹמְנִין? — With what may we insulate [hot food], and with what may we not insulate [them]?

If one removes a pot from a stove on Friday and wishes to preserve its heat, what may he use to insulate the pot? (*Rav; Rashi*).

אֵין טוֹמְנִין לֹא בְגֶפֶת, — We may not insulate [them] neither with marc,

[The use of the double negative occurs often in the Mishnah.]

I.e., we may not cover the pot with a mass of the pulp of olives or of sesame. These and the other materials listed below increase the heat of the pot. For this reason the Rabbis prohibited their use for *hatmanah*, as explained above (*Rav; Tif. Yis.; Rambam.*).

וְלֹא בְזֶבֶל, לֹא בְמֶלַח, וְלֹא בְסִיד, וְלֹא בְחוֹל, בֵּין לַחִים בֵּין יְבֵשִׁים; — nor with manure, nor with salt, nor with lime, nor with sand, either wet or dry;

Not only may we not use these substances when they are damp and tend to increase the heat greatly, but even when dry they are not permitted, for they still tend to generate some heat (*Rav; Rashi*).

לֹא בְתֶבֶן, — nor with straw,

See above 3:1 for the difference between תֶּבֶן and קַשׁ.

Rambam deletes לֹא בְתֶבֶן (*Rambam, Hil. Shabbos* 4:1).

וְלֹא בְזַגִּים, — nor with grape skins,

The translation follows *Rav* and *Rambam*.

[A Nazirite is prohibited from partaking of grapes or any grape product including every part of the grape from זָג to חַרְצַנִּים (*Numbers* 6:4). The

[110]

4
1

1. With what may we insulate [hot food], and with what may we not insulate [them]? We may not insulate [them] neither with marc, nor with manure, nor with salt, nor with lime, nor with sand, either wet or dry; nor with straw, nor with grape skins, nor with flocking, nor with grasses, when they are moist, but we may insulate [hot food] with them when they are dry.

YAD AVRAHAM

Mishnah (*Nazir* 6:2) records a difference of opinion regarding the meaning of these terms. R' Yehudah defines the חַרְצַנִּים as the *outside skin* and the זַג as the *inside pits*. R' Yose reverses these definitions.] Thus, *Rav* and *Rambam* here are in accord with R' Yose's view in tractate *Nazir* (*Tos. Yom Tov*).

וְלֹא בְמוֹכִין, — *nor with flocking,*

I.e., any tufts of unprocessed soft material such as cotton, soft wool, or shreds of worn-out clothing (*Rav; Rashi*).

וְלֹא בַעֲשָׂבִים, בִּזְמַן שֶׁהֵן לַחִים, — *nor with grasses, when they are moist,*

I.e., straw, grape skins, flocking and grass may not be used when they are moist (*Rav*).

These cause the temperature to rise only when they are damp, not when they are dry. Furthermore, this is true only of their natural moisture, i.e., if the straw, grape skins, or grasses are damp because they still retain their original, natural moisture [flocking, too, if it is damp from the sweat of the animal]. If the original moisture of these substances had dried out and they subsequently became moist due to external factors, these materials may be used (*Rav; Rif; Rambam, Comm.*).

Rambam (*Hil. Shabbos* 4:1) states that we may not use "grape skins, flocking or grasses, when they are moist even if the moisture is their own," implying that external moisture would cause an even greater increase of heat.[1]

Hence, these moist materials are forbidden regardless of the source of the moisture. *Tur* and *Shulchan Aruch* (257) agree and do not distinguish between native and external moisture.

[This question is actually posed by the *Gemara* (49a). The above-mentioned dispute is over how to rule on the halachah.]

אֲבָל טוֹמְנִין בָּהֶן כְּשֶׁהֵן יְבֵשִׁין. — *but we may insulate [hot food] with them when they are dry.*

[As explained above, when these materials are dry, they do not raise the heat level.]

---

1. According to this, *Rambam* in *Hilchos Shabbos* is at variance with his own commentary on the mishnah where he states that *only* if they are naturally moist are they prohibited (*Tif. Yis.*). Old manuscripts of *Rambam's* code have been discovered, however, which omit the word *even* thus reconciling his code with his commentary. (See *Rambam — Frankel Ed.*, pp. 25, 734.)

שבת ד/ב

טוֹמְנִין בִּכְסוּת, וּבְפֵרוֹת, בְּכַנְפֵי יוֹנָה, וּבִנְסֹרֶת שֶׁל חָרָשִׁים, וּבִנְעֹרֶת שֶׁל פִּשְׁתָּן דַּקָּה. רַבִּי יְהוּדָה אוֹסֵר בְּדַקָּה וּמַתִּיר בְּגַסָּה.

[ב] **טוֹמְנִין** בִּשְׁלָחִין, וּמְטַלְטְלִין אוֹתָן; בְּגִזֵּי צֶמֶר, וְאֵין מְטַלְטְלִין אוֹתָן. כֵּיצַד

ר' עובדיה מברטנורא

נסורת. פסולת שמנסרים הנגרים מן העץ כשמגררים אותו במגירה: **נעורת.** דק דק שמנערין מן הפשתן כשמנפצין אותו: **רבי יהודה אוסר בדקה.** בנעורת של פשתן דקה, אבל בנסורת מודה דשרי בין דקה בין גסה. ואין הלכה כרבי יהודה. ומה שאסרו להטמין מבעוד יום בדבר המוסיף הבל, גזירה שמא יטמין ברמץ ויבא לחתות בגחלים משתחשך. ואסרו להטמין בשבת בדבר שאינו מוסיף הבל ואף על פי שאינו מבשל, גזירה שמא ימלא קדרתו שנצטננה ויריתחנה בחזר בשבת. ובין השמשות מותר להטמין בדבר שאינו מוסיף הבל כדאמרינן בסוף פרק במה מדליקין. דליכא למגזר שמא ימלא קדרתו שנצטננה ויריתחנה, דסתם קדרות בין השמשות רותחות הן. ורמב"ם פירש בסתם קדרות בין השמשות רותחות הן, פירוש שאין הדעת סובלתו, מפני שבוט הגוסחאות וגרסאות מהופכות שנמלא בגמרא שלפניו בפרק במה מדליקין, שהוא היה גורס מפני מה אמרו אין טומנין בדבר שאינו מוסיף הבל משתחשיכה גזירה שמא יטמין ברמץ, ומפני מה אמרו אין טומנין בדבר המוסיף הבל מבעוד יום גזירה שמא ירתיח, ואין הגרסות כן, אלא מפני מה אמרו אין טומנין בדבר שאינו מוסיף הבל משתחשיכה גזירה שמא ירתיח, ואין טומנין בדבר המוסיף הבל מבעוד יום גזירה שמא יטמין ברמץ:
(ב) **שלחין.** עורות. תרגום והפשיט, וישלח: **ומטלטלין אותן.** בין שטמן בהן בין שלא טמן בהן, דחזו למזגא עלייהו, כלומר להשען עליהם: **ואין מטלטלין אותן.** דמוקצות הן לטווח ולארוג, ואף על פי שטמן בהן לפי שעה לא הפקירן לגמרי כשלא להטמנה, אבל הטמנה מטלטלה:

יד אברהם

טוֹמְנִין בִּכְסוּת, וּבְפֵרוֹת — *We may insulate [hot food] with clothing, with produce,*

E.g., wheat or beans (Rashi; Meiri).

בְּכַנְפֵי יוֹנָה, — *with pigeon feathers,*

Other feathers as well may be used for *hatmanah* (Meiri; Tif. Yis. from Rama 257:1). Pigeon feathers are used as an example only because they were the most commonly used in Mishnaic times (Shenos Eliyahu).

וּבִנְסֹרֶת שֶׁל חָרָשִׁים, וּבִנְעֹרֶת שֶׁל פִּשְׁתָּן דַּקָּה. — *with carpenters' sawdust, or with fine flax combings.*

I.e., with the splinters that fall from the flax when it is combed out (Tif. Yis.).

The *Tanna Kamma* permits *hatmanah* even with the fine combings, surely with the coarse ones (Meiri).

Indeed, most exegetes delete the word "fine" (Rif; Rosh; Tif. Yis).

רַבִּי יְהוּדָה אוֹסֵר בְּדַקָּה וּמַתִּיר בְּגַסָּה. — *R' Yehudah prohibits fine [combings] but permits coarse [combings].*

R' Yehudah disputes only flax combings. He agrees with the *Tanna Kamma*, however, that both coarse and fine sawdust are permitted (Rav from Gem.).

The halachah is not in accordance with R' Yehudah (Rambam; Rav).

**4
2**

We may insulate [hot food] with clothing, with produce, with pigeon feathers, with carpenters' sawdust, or with fine flax combings. R' Yehudah prohibits fine [combings] but permits coarse [combings].

2. **W**e may insulate [hot food] with pelts, and we may move them; with wool shearings, but we may not move them. What should

YAD AVRAHAM

2.

The mishnah continues to expound on the laws of *hatmanah*, and teaches us that not only may we use materials that may be moved on the Sabbath, but that we may even use materials that fall under the category of *muktzeh*, items which may not be moved on the Sabbath (see Chap. 17).

טוֹמְנִים בִּשְׁלָחִין, — *We may insulate [hot food] with pelts,*

I.e., animal hides from which the hair has not been removed (*Rav; Tos. Yom Tov*).

וּמְטַלְטְלִין אוֹתָן; — *and we may move them;*

Despite their not having yet been fashioned into a usable utensil, they may be moved about even for purposes other than covering hot food because they can be, and sometimes are, used as a rug upon which to recline (*Rav; Rashi*).

Since they have a useful purpose on the Sabbath, they are not *muktzeh* and may be moved about for any reason.

Rashi stipulates that this is the case only insofar as pelts of cattle are concerned. Pelts of sheep and goats cannot be used unless treated and are, therefore, *muktzeh* in their unfinished state.

Rabbeinu Tam's opinion is that dried pelts, regardless of their species, are useful and thus not *muktzeh*, whereas moist pelts of any kind are useless and *muktzeh* and cannot, therefore, be moved about on the Sabbath (*Tos.*).

בְּגִזֵּי צֶמֶר, וְאֵין מְטַלְטְלִין אוֹתָן. — *with wool shearings, but we may not move them.*

They are generally reserved to be made into thread and are thus deemed *muktzeh*.

Although they *could* be used for *hatmanah*, one *would* not generally do so because he is afraid of their becoming soiled or otherwise damaged and consequently unfit for their primary purpose of thread. This is known as *muktzeh* due to loss of money [see Introduction to Chapter 17 p. 287] (*Mishnah Berurah* 259:3). This is so even where they have previously been used to cover food, since it is still expected that they will be spun into thread. If, however, one permanently designates them for *hatmanah*, they are no longer *muktzeh*, and may be moved about (*Rav* from *Gem.* 50a).

[113] THE MISHNAH/SHABBOS — Chapter Four: *Bameh Tomnin*

שבת
ד/ב

הוּא עוֹשֶׂה? נוֹטֵל אֶת הַכִּסּוּי, וְהֵן נוֹפְלוֹת. רַבִּי אֶלְעָזָר בֶּן עֲזַרְיָה אוֹמֵר: קֻפָּה מַטָּה עַל צִדָּהּ וְנוֹטֵל, שֶׁמָּא יִטֹּל וְאֵינוֹ יָכוֹל לְהַחֲזִיר. וַחֲכָמִים אוֹמְרִים: נוֹטֵל וּמַחֲזִיר: לֹא כִסָּהוּ מִבְּעוֹד יוֹם, לֹא יְכַסֶּנּוּ מִשֶּׁתֶּחְשָׁךְ. כִּסָּהוּ וְנִתְגַּלָּה,

─── ר' עובדיה מברטנורא ───

בּיצד יעשה. זה שטמן בהם כילד יטול קדרתו, הואיל ואסור לטלטלן והרי היא טמונה כולה בהן: **נוטל.** כסוי של קדרה שיש תורת כלי עליו, ואף על פי שהן עליו לא איכפת לן דלא נעשה בסיס להן שאין עשוי אלא לכסות את הקדרה: **רבי אלעזר אומר קופה מטה על צדה ונוטל.** כשבא ליטלה מטה הקופה על לדה, שמא יטול את הקדרה ויפלו הגיזין שמכאן ומכאן לתוך הגומא שיש בה הקדרה ואם יצטרך להחזיר ולהטמינה לא יוכל לטלטל הגיזין לכאן ולכאן ולעשות גומא ולהחזירה לתוכה: **וחכמים אומרים נוטל.** את הקדרה ואם לא נפלו הגיזין שמכאן ומכאן ולא נתקלקלה הגומא מחזיר הקדרה למקומה, ולא אסרינן ליה ליטול את הקדרה לכתחלה גזירה שמא תתקלקל הגומא. ומודים חכמים שאם נתקלקלה הגומא שלא יחזיר. והלכה כחכמים: **לא יבסנו משתחשך:** שאסור להטמין בשבת בין בדבר המוסיף הבל בין בדבר שאינו מוסיף הבל בדרך הטמנה:

─── יד אברהם ───

כֵּיצַד הוּא עוֹשֶׂה? — *What should one do?*

If one stored food inside wool shearings, by what means can he remove the food so as not to handle the *muktzeh* wool shearings? (*Rav; Rashi*).

נוֹטֵל אֶת הַכִּסּוּי, וְהֵן נוֹפְלוֹת — *He removes the lid, and they fall.*

I.e., by lifting the lid he causes them to slide off. This manner of moving *muktzeh* is known as טִלְטוּל מִן הַצַּד, *indirect movement* of *muktzeh*, and is permissible. [This exemption to the general ban of moving *muktzeh* is explained at length in Chap. 21. See also General Introduction.]

Although the wool shearings are being supported by the lid, the lid does not become a base to the shearings (and thus a base for a *muktzeh* object, which is then itself considered *muktzeh*; see introductions to 3:6 and Chap. 17; see also General Introduction) for the lid's primary purpose is to cover the pot, not to hold up the shearings (*Rav; Rashi*).

Furthermore, the wool's function is to keep the pot warm and it, in effect, serves the pot. The pot, is, therefore, not deemed a base to the wool (*Tif. Yis.*).

If the handle of the lid is exposed, one may pick up the lid by its handle. He may not grope through the shearings to get at the handle, since this would constitute direct movement of the *muktzeh* shearings (*Shulchan Aruch* 259:5). However, he may insert a reed or stick through the shearings to get to the handle and thereby lift off the cover (*Magen Avraham* 259:5).

He may also tip the receptacle which contains the pot and the shearings until the upper shearings fall away and expose the lid (*Chidushei HaRan*).

After explaining how to remove the lid, the mishnah now discusses the proper procedure for removing the

משניות / שבת – פרק ד: במה טומנין [114]

4 2 one do? He removes the lid, and they fall. R' Elazar ben Azaryah says: He tilts the box on its side and removes [the food], lest he remove [the pot] and be unable to replace [it]. But, the Sages say: He may remove [it] and replace [it].

If he did not cover it when it was yet day, he may not cover it after dark. If he covered it and it became

YAD AVRAHAM

food that he needs (*Ran*).

רַבִּי אֶלְעָזָר בֶּן עֲזַרְיָה אוֹמֵר: כּוֹפָה מִטָּה עַל צִדָּהּ — *R' Elazar ben Azaryah says: He tilts the box on its side*

[I.e., he should tilt the box containing the shearings in which the pot is covered.]

וְנוֹטֵל — *and removes [the food]*,

I.e., he should remove the food he requires and leave the rest in the pot for the next meal. He should not lift the pot out of the box (*Tif. Yis.*).

שֶׁמָּא יִטּל וְאֵינוֹ יָכוֹל לְהַחֲזִיר. — *lest he remove [the pot] and be unable to replace [it]*.

If he removes the pot, and the shearings on both sides fall into the cavity, he will not be permitted to move them aside when he will want to replace the pot with the remaining food (*Rav; Rashi*).

R' Elazar ben Azaryah is concerned that he will move the shearings to restore the cavity that was previously there, thereby violating the *muktzeh* prohibition (*Tos. Yom Tov*).

Alternatively, rearranging the shearings to form a new cavity constitutes a new act of *hatmanah* which is forbidden on the Sabbath, as was explained above (*Rambam*). Accordingly, even if one stores food, even in a substance that is not *muktzeh*, he may not remove the pot (according to R' Elazar ben Azaryah) for fear he will restore the cavity (*Beis Yosef* 259).

וַחֲכָמִים אוֹמְרִים: נוֹטֵל וּמַחֲזִיר — *But, the Sages say: He may remove [it] and replace [it]*.

I.e., he may replace it into the original cavity, if it is still extant.

However, the Sages agree with R' Elazar ben Azaryah that if the shearings *do* collapse, it is prohibited to rearrange them in order to restore the cavity. They disagree only in that they are concerned that he may want to return the pot after the cavity collapses and thereby violate the *muktzeh* prohibition. The halachah is in accordance with the Sages (*Rav; Tos. Yom Tov*).

לֹא כִסָּהוּ מִבְּעוֹד יוֹם — *If he did not cover it when it was yet day*,

[I.e., if one did not cover the pot of hot food before the Sabbath.]

לֹא יְכַסֶּנּוּ מִשֶּׁתֶּחְשָׁךְ. — *he may not cover it after dark*.

This covering constitutes *hatmanah*, which may not be done on the Sabbath proper even with materials that do not raise the level of the heat (*Rav; Rashi*).

כִּסָּהוּ וְנִתְגַּלָּה, — *If he covered it and it became uncovered*,

If he covered it before the Sabbath and it became uncovered on the Sabbath (*Tif. Yis.*).

שבת ד/ב

מֻתָּר לְכַסּוֹתוֹ. מְמַלֵּא אֶת הַקִּיתוֹן וְנוֹתֵן לְתַחַת הַכַּר אוֹ תַּחַת הַכֶּסֶת.

ר' עובדיה מברטנורא

ונותן. בשבת, תחת הכר שמשים מראשותיו ואף על פי שהוא מלא מוכן או גולש, שאין דרך הטמנה בכך: **בסת.** גדול מכר:

יד אברהם

מֻתָּר לְכַסּוֹתוֹ. — *he may cover it.*

Just as one may remove a pot from its *hatmanah* and then replace it, so may one replace the lid of a pot that has become uncovered on the Sabbath (*Tos.* 51a).

Though the mishnah's expression, *and it became uncovered*, would seem to indicate that one is not allowed to remove the lid in the first place with the intent of then replacing it, this in fact is not the case. One is permitted to do so. The mishnah's stating *it became uncovered* is for the purpose of teaching that had the pot become uncovered *before* the Sabbath even by inadvertence, he may still *not* replace the lid on the Sabbath (*Tif. Yis.* from *Taz* 257:4).

Tosafos disagree and hold that if the pot became inadvertently uncovered before the Sabbath, one may replace the lid on the Sabbath. In that case, it does not resemble the initial *hatmanah*. Should he intentionally uncover it before the Sabbath, however, recovering it on the Sabbath does resemble *hatmanah* (5la).

4
2 uncovered, he may cover it.
One may fill a bottle and place it under a cushion or under a bolster.

YAD AVRAHAM

מְמַלֵּא אֶת הַקִּיתוֹן — *One may fill a bottle*
I.e., one may fill a bottle or jug with cold water or a cooked food that has become cold (*Tif. Yis.* from *Gem.* 51a).

וְנוֹתֵן לְתַחַת הַכַּר אוֹ תַחַת הַכֶּסֶת. — *and place it under a cushion or under a bolster.*

I.e., even on the Sabbath (*Rav*) one may place it under a cushion or under a bolster to keep it cold during the summer (*Rashi*).

Alternatively, this is permissible even to remove the chill (*Ran; Rambam, Hil. Shabbos* 4:4).

Since it is not usual to insulate cold foods the Rabbis did not prohibit it (*Rav*).

They did, however, prohibit *hatmanah* of cold water or cold foods even before the Sabbath in substances that raise the heat level (*Rambam,* ibid.; *Shulchan Aruch* 257:6).

Although the above-mentioned cushions are filled with feathers or flocking which, as explained in mishnah 1, tend to increase the heat, *Rambam* and *Rav* are obviously referring to *dry* feathers or *dry* flocking, which do not increase the heat (*Rashash*). [See mishnah 1.]

פרק חמישי
Chapter Five

One is forbidden to transport a burden on an animal (or to allow his animal to carry a burden) on the Sabbath either through a public domain, from a private to a public domain or vice versa; as it is said: (*Ex.* 23:12) . . . *in order that your ox and your donkey rest*. This includes any other domesticated animal, wild beast, or fowl as well as the ox and donkey (*Rambam, Hil. Shabbos* 20:1).

The Rabbis interpreted this ruling to include any gear unnecessary for controlling the animal, be it either inadequate or excessive for that purpose. If, however, it is usual for the animal to wear such gear, it is not considered a burden and may be worn on the Sabbath. The mishnah enumerates the items considered essential for controlling an animal and those not considered essential.

There are six categories of objects which may not be carried by an animal into a public domain: (a) a burden; (b) gear insufficient for controlling the animal; (c) gear excessive and unnecessary for controlling the animal; (d) gear that may become dislodged and fall from the animal [one may come to inadvertently carry it]; (e) gear normally used for leading an animal to market; (f) objects worn for ornament (*Shenos Eliyahu*).

שבת
ה/א

[א] בַּמֶּה בְהֵמָה יוֹצְאָה, וּבַמָּה אֵינָהּ יוֹצְאָה? יוֹצֵא הַגָּמָל בְּאַפְסָר, וְנָאקָה בַחֲטָם, וְלֻבְדְּקִיס בִּפְרֻמְבִּיָא, וְסוּס בְּשֵׁיר; וְכָל בַּעֲלֵי הַשֵּׁיר יוֹצְאִים בְּשֵׁיר, וְנִמְשָׁכִים בְּשֵׁיר,

ר' עובדיה מברטנורא

פרק חמישי – במה בהמה. (א) במה בהמה יוצאה. לפי שאדם מצווה על שביתת בהמתו בשבת, ומידי דמנטרא ביה הבהמה לא הוי כמשאוי ומידי דלא מנטרא ביה הוי כמשאוי: **אפסר.** חבל שקושרים על פי הבהמה: **והנאקה.** בגמרא מוקי לה בנאקה לבנה דוקא שגריכה נטירותא יתירתא: **בחטם.** לוקחין כמין טבעת של ברזל ונוקבין חוטם הנאקה ומכניסין אותו בתוכו: **לובדקס.** חמור הבא ממדינת לוד, והם קשים וחזקים וצריכין שמירה יותר משאר חמורים הגמלאים בישוב: **בפרומביא.** רסן של ברזל: **בשיר.** כמין אלעדה סביב לוארו וטבעת קבועה בו ומכניסין בטבעת חבל ומושכין הבהמה: **וכל בעלי השיר.** כגון כלבים של ליידים וחיות קטנות: **יוצאים בשיר.** כרוך על לוארן החבל הקבוע בשיר: **ונמשכין בשיר.** ואם רלה מושך הבהמה בחבל שבשיר.

יד אברהם

1.

בַּמֶּה בְהֵמָה יוֹצְאָה — *With what may an animal go out,*

[I.e., with what gear may an animal go out to a public domain on the Sabbath? What types of gear are essential for controlling the animal?]

וּבַמָּה אֵינָהּ יוֹצְאָה? — *and with what may it not go out?*

[I.e., what gear is not considered essential?]

יוֹצֵא הַגָּמָל בְּאַפְסָר, — *A camel may go out with a curb,*

I.e., a rope tied to the mouth of the animal (*Rav*).

Tif. Yis. renders it as a halter.

A camel is a comparatively tame beast and a curb is sufficient to control it. A more powerful restraint, such as a nose ring, would be considered a burden since it is more than the animal requires [see prefatory remarks] (*Gem.* 51b).

וְנָאקָה בַחֲטָם, — *a dromedary with a nose ring,*

I.e., a white female dromedary (*Rashi, Gem.* ibid.).

Since the female dromedary is faster than an ordinary camel and is more apt to break away, it requires a more powerful restraint than does the camel (*Rashi; Tif. Yis.*).

According to *Aruch*, this does not refer to a separate variety of camel but rather to all female camels at the age they become fit to bear burdens (*Tos. Yom Tov*). *Aruch* distinguishes three stages in the life of a camel: (a) *alkaut* (Arabic) — at birth; (b) as it grows — the male is called *bechot*, and the female *bichrah*; (c) when it becomes old enough to bear burdens — the male is called גָּמָל, *gamal*, and the female נָאקָה, *nakah*.

Hence a male camel may only go out with a curb, while a female camel, which cannot be controlled by a curb, may only go out with a nose ring, not with a curb.

וְלֻבְדְּקִיס — *a Libyan ass*

Donkeys from Libya are more powerful than other donkeys and require a more powerful restraint (*Rav*).

Some editions read: לֻבְדְּקִים, a plural noun (*Mishnah in Gem.* 51b; *Rif*).

5
1

1. With what may an animal go out, and with what may it not go out? A camel may go out with a curb, a dromedary with a nose ring, a Libyan ass with a bit, a horse with a neck chain; and all that wear a neck chain may go out with a neck chain, and may be pulled with a neck chain,

YAD AVRAHAM

בְּפְרֻמְבְּיָא, — *with a bit,*

This includes the entire harness enclosing the head and jaws (*Rashi, Gem.* ibid.).

The curb normally used for a camel is insufficient to control the Libyan ass and, if placed on it, is considered merely a burden (*Gem.* ibid.).

Domestic donkeys may not go out with a bit since they are milder in manner than the Libyan strain and do not require such great restraint (*Shulchan Aruch* 305:3, see *Taz*).

Camels too may not go out with this type of bit which is considered excessive and unnecessary for a tamer animal and therefore a burden (*Taz* 305:1).

וְסוּס בְּשֵׁיר; — *a horse with a neck chain;*

Or a neck band to which a ring is attached. A rope is then inserted through the ring by which the animal may be led (*Rav; Rashi*).

A rope tied to a horse's mouth is considered a burden since it is inadequate to control the horse (*Rambam, Hil. Shabbos* 20:8; *Shulchan Aruch* 305:2).

This should not be compared to the curb which is securely fastened to the animal's head, whereas the rope is attached only to the mouth, allowing the horse to easily slip out of it (*Taz* 3).

וְכָל בַּעֲלֵי הַשֵּׁיר — *and all that wear a neck chain*

I.e., all animals which normally wear neck chains for ornament, such as hunting dogs or other smaller animals (*Rashi; Rav*).

Rav follows *Rashi* closely, but deletes the words *for ornament*. Here he follows the view of *Tosafos*, that any adornment worn by an animal is considered a burden. *Rashi*, however, rules that any adornment usually worn by the animal is not considered a burden. Only an unusual adornment is considered a burden (*Ran*).

יוֹצְאִים בְּשֵׁיר, — *may go out with a neck chain,*

I.e., they may go out with a neck chain with a rope attached to it though the rope is wound around the animal's neck (*Rav* from *Gem.* 52a).

Rashi explains that this is done for ornament and is therefore permitted. *Tosafos*, however, maintain that were the purpose only for ornamentation, the animal would not be permitted to go out with it. However, since even when the rope is wound around its neck the animal can still be seized by the rope if it attempts to run away, the rope is not considered a burden.

וְנִמְשָׁכִים בְּשֵׁיר, — *and may be pulled with a neck chain,*

If one wishes, he may lead the animal with the rope attached to the neck chain (*Rav*).

שבת
ה/ב

וּמַזִּין עֲלֵיהֶם וְטוֹבְלִין בִּמְקוֹמָן.

[ב] **חֲמוֹר** יוֹצֵא בְמַרְדַּעַת בִּזְמַן שֶׁהִיא קְשׁוּרָה לוֹ. זְכָרִים יוֹצְאִין לְבוּבִין.

ר' עובדיה מברטנורא

ומזין עליהן. במקומן כמות שהן בצוואר הבהמה, אם נטמאו במת: **וטובלין במקומן.** מכניסים הבהמה במים להטביל השיר. ואף על גב דקיימא לן דכל הכלים המיוחדים לבהמה אין מקבלין טומאה, השיר וכיוצא בו מקבל טומאה וצריך טבילה, הואיל ונעשו לאדם שינהיג בו את הבהמה, ככלי העשוי לתשמיש אדם דמי: (ב) **במרדעת.** כמין אוכף קטן, ומניחים אותו על החמור כל היום כולו כדי שיתחמם: **בזמן שהיא קשורה לו.** מערב שבת, דגלי דעתיה שהחמור צריך לו לחממו, כדאמרי אינשי חמרא אפילו בתקופת תמוז קריר ליה ולאו משאוי הוא. אבל לקשור מרדעת על החמור בשבת אסור, לפי שאי אפשר לקשרה לו אלא אם כן סומך עצמו בצדי הבהמה ונמצא משתמש בבעלי חיים, ואם עבר וקשרו אסור לצאת בו: **לבובין.** בטור שקושרים להם הס כנגד זכרות שלא יעלו על הנקבות:

יד אברהם

וּמַזִּין עֲלֵיהֶם וְטוֹבְלִין בִּמְקוֹמָן — and we may sprinkle upon them and immerse them in their place.

[Some editions of the mishnah insert the word בִּמְקוֹמָן, in their place, after וּמַזִּין עֲלֵיהֶם (Rashi; Tos.; Bach).]

I.e., we may sprinkle water of the פָּרָה אֲדֻמָּה, red cow, on those items while they are in place on the animal's neck, to cleanse them of tumah contracted from a corpse (Rav).

Persons or utensils designated for use by humans which contract ritual contamination from a corpse are tamei [ritually contaminated] for seven days. They are ritually cleaned in the following manner: A hyssop is immersed in the water prepared with ashes of the red cow (see Numbers 19:1-22) and the water is sprinkled on the man or utensil on the third and seventh days of their contamination, after which they are immersed in a mikveh and become tahor [cleansed] after sunset of that day.

If this water is used for other work it becomes unfit for use in cleansing (Rambam, Hil. Parah Adumah 11:1).

The neck chain of our mishnah requires cleansing, though it is worn by an animal. This is so because it serves the purpose of allowing a person to lead the animal. It is, therefore, considered designated for use by humans and contact with a corpse renders it tamei (Rav; Tos. Yom Tov from Gem. 52).

The mishnah needs to teach us that the cleansing water may be sprinkled on the neck chain even while it is on the animal and we need not be concerned that the water may first fall on the animal [rendering it unfit for use in cleansing according to some opinions], or that he may intend to sprinkle the water on the animal and only inadvertently hit the neck chain [which is invalid according to others] (Tos 52a; Tif. Yis., Meleches Shlomo, Parah 12:3).

וְטוֹבְלִין בִּמְקוֹמָן. — and immerse them in their place.

We may submerge them in the mikveh or other body of water qualified for ritual immersion while they are still on the animal's neck. We need not be concerned that they will be fas-

and we may sprinkle upon them and immerse them in their place.

2. A donkey may go out with a saddlecloth when it is tied to it. Rams may go out strapped.

YAD AVRAHAM

tened too tightly to the animal and thereby prevent the water from coming between the neck chain and the animal's neck (*Tos. Yom Tov*).

2.

חֲמוֹר יוֹצֵא בְּמַרְדַּעַת — *A donkey may go out with a saddlecloth*

A small saddle [made of cushions (*Tif. Yis.*)] worn by the donkey throughout the day to keep it warm, since donkeys chronically feel chilled even during the hottest days of summer (*Rav; Rashi*).

בִּזְמַן שֶׁהִיא קְשׁוּרָה לוֹ. — *when it is tied to it.*

I.e., if he tied it to the donkey before the Sabbath, thereby indicating that the donkey needs the saddle pack to keep warm. It is, therefore, considered a garment, not a burden. [Although tying it on the Sabbath indicates this just as well,] if one did not tie the saddlecloth on the donkey before the Sabbath, he may not do so on the Sabbath, because it is impossible to tie it on the donkey without leaning against the animal. This is forbidden on the Sabbath, as in *Beitzah* 5:2. If one did tie it on during the Sabbath, the donkey may not go out with it (*Rav; Rashba; Rosh; Maggid Mishneh* 20:10; from *Yerushalmi*).

Alternatively, if the donkey wears it before the Sabbath, this indicates that it needs it to keep warm, and it is considered a garment. If, however, the donkey does not wear it before the Sabbath, we assume that it does not need it. If then, one ties it on during the Sabbath, it is viewed as a burden (*Rashi*).

Tosafos offer an explanation very similar to *Rashi's*. It differs only insofar as, while according to *Rashi*, if one attaches it during the Sabbath, it is definitely considered a burden, according to *Tosafos* it is forbidden because it gives the *appearance* of being a burden, although this is not truly the case (*Maharsha*).[1]

Alternatively, if one attached a saddlecloth to a donkey on the Sabbath, he appears to be preparing it for a journey (*Rabbeinu Poras* quoted by *Tos.*).

One may, however, lay a saddlecloth on a donkey's back to keep it warm without tying it provided he does not let it leave a private domain (*Tos. Yom Tov; Tif. Yis.;* from *Rosh*, as explained in *Yerushalmi*).

זְכָרִים יוֹצְאִין לְבוּבִין. — *Rams may go out strapped.*

I.e., with a leather pouch tied under their genitals to prevent them from copulating with the ewes (*Rav; Tif. Yis.* from *Gem.* 53b). The pouch was heart shaped, to fit properly around

---

1. Alternatively, *Rashi* holds that since it is not self-evident that the saddlecloth is the donkey's garment, it is automatically considered a burden. *Tosafos*, however, go on to say that it actually appears as though he intends that the donkey carry out the saddlecloth for his use (*Maharam*).

שבת ה/ב

רְחֵלוֹת יוֹצְאוֹת שְׁחוּזוֹת, כְּבוּלוֹת, וּכְבוּנוֹת. הָעִזִּים יוֹצְאוֹת צְרוּרוֹת. רַבִּי יוֹסֵי אוֹסֵר בְּכֻלָּן, חוּץ מִן הָרְחֵלִין הַכְּבוּנוֹת. רַבִּי יְהוּדָה אוֹמֵר: הָעִזִּים יוֹצְאוֹת צְרוּרוֹת לְיַבֵּשׁ, אֲבָל לֹא לְחָלָב.

ר' עובדיה מברטנורא

שחוזות. שאוחזים אליה שלהן קשורה למעלה כדי שיעלו עליהן זכרים: **כבולות.** שכובלים אליה שלהן וקושרים אותה ברגליהן כדי שלא יעלו עליהן זכרים: **כבונות.** שקושרים בגד סביב הכבשים ביום שנולדים לשמור למרן שלא יטנף: **צרורות.** דדיהן צרורות, פעמים ליבש החלב שמהדקים אותן בחוזק, ופעמים קושרין להן כיס בדדיהן שלא יטפטף החלב לארץ ויפסד: **רבי יוסי אוסר בכולן.** דמשאוי הוא: **חוץ מן הרחלין הכבונות.** שהוא שמירת למרן שלא יטנף והוי להו תכשיט: **יוצאות צרורות ליבש.** רבי יהודה סבירא ליה כתנא קמא דלאו משאוי הוא, מיהו ליבש דמיהדק שפיר ליכא למיגזר דלמא נפיל ואתי לאתויי, אבל לחלב דלא מיהדק שפיר אסור, חיישינן דלמא נפיל ואתי לאתויי. והלכה כתנא קמא:

יד אברהם

from becoming soiled (*Rav; Rashi* 54a).

Additionally, this was done to preserve the moisture and the soft texture of the wool. This was done only to the females, whose wool is softer than that of the males (*Rambam*).

הָעִזִּים יוֹצְאוֹת צְרוּרוֹת — *She-goats may go out [with their udders] tied.*

This may be done in either of two manners and for one of two reasons. Sometimes the udders are tied up to cause the milk to dry up — either to allow the she-goats to conceive again or to cause them to become fatter. Other times a pouch is tied on to the udders to prevent the milk from dripping and being wasted (*Rav; Rashi*).

רַבִּי יוֹסֵי אוֹסֵר בְּכֻלָּן, — *R' Yose forbids all of them,*

R' Yose forbids allowing the animals to go out to a public domain with any of this gear, since he considers it a burden (*Rav*).

חוּץ מִן הָרְחֵלִין הַכְּבוּנוֹת — *except the ewes covered up.*

Since the purpose of the cover is to the genitals. Hence the word לְבוּבִין from לֵב (*Tif. Yis.*).

Alternatively, the rams may go out with a piece of skin tied over their heart, to protect them from attack by wolves. The wolves were known to attack the heart rather than any other part of the body. They would only attack the rams, whose aggressive posture incited the wolves, not the ewes (*Gem.* 53b, as explained by *Rashi* cited by *Rambam, Hil. Shabbos* 20:12).

רְחֵלוֹת יוֹצְאוֹת שְׁחוּזוֹת, — *Ewes may go out exposed,*

I.e., they may go out with their tails tied to their backs, exposing their genitals, to encourage copulation with the rams (*Rav* from *Gem.* 53b).

כְּבוּלוֹת, — *tied,*

I.e., they may go out with their tails tied down to their legs, to prevent copulation with the rams (*Rav* from *Gem.* 54a).

וּכְבוּנוֹת. — *or covered up* [lit. *veiled*] (*Tif. Yis.*).

From birth, a cloth is bound around the ewe lambs to protect their wool

5
2

Ewes may go out exposed, tied, or covered up.

She-goats may go out [with their udders] tied.

R' Yose forbids all of them, except the ewes covered up.

R' Yehudah says: She-goats may go out [with their udders] tied to dry up, but not for the milk.

YAD AVRAHAM

keep the wool clean, it is considered an article of attire rather than a burden. The animal may therefore wear it when walking in the public domain (*Rav*).

רַבִּי יְהוּדָה אוֹמֵר: הָעִזִּים יוֹצְאוֹת צְרוּרוֹת לְיַבֵּשׁ, אֲבָל לֹא לֶחָלָב. — *R' Yehudah says: She-goats may go out [with their udders] tied to dry up, but not for the milk.*

I.e., they may go out with their udders tied tightly in order to dry up the milk. R' Yehudah agrees with the first *Tanna*, who considers the pouch an article of attire rather than a burden. He permits this, however, only if the pouch is tied tightly in order to dry up the milk. In the case of a pouch tied on to catch the dripping milk, since the pouch is tied loosely, there is the possibility that the pouch will fall off, and that the goatherd will carry it (*Rashi; Rav*).

Rashi on the *Gemara* (53b), however, explains that the pouch is attached to gather the milk that drips from the udders. The milk that gathers in the pouch is considered a burden. If, however, the pouch is attached tightly to dry up the milk, it is for the benefit of the goat, who loses weight through lactation. Moreover, since it is attached tightly, there is no danger that it will fall off and be carried in a public domain.

Tosafos object to this very strongly, for, if the pouch is attached to gather the milk, even the first *Tanna* would not permit the goats to go out in such a manner,

since the milk would definitely be a burden. *Tosafos*, therefore, quote *Rabbeinu Poras*, who explains that the pouch is not attached to collect the milk, but to prevent it from running out of the udders. The first *Tanna* permits this since it is comparable to the ewes going out covered up which, although not benefiting the ewe, does protect its wool. In our case as well, the pouch preserves the milk inside the ewe's udder by preventing it from running out. R' Yehudah prohibits it because since it is attached somewhat loosely, so as not to dry up the milk, it may fall off and be carried by the goatherd on the Sabbath.

Tosafos also quote the explanation of *Ri* who explains that in both cases the pouch is attached to protect the nipples from being lacerated on thorns and other sharp objects. This should be permissible, since it is for the protection of the animal. However, when the owner is interested that the milk continue to flow, he does not tie the pouch tightly. Therefore, we encounter the risk that it will fall off, and the goatherd will pick it up and carry it in a public domain. When he also wishes to dry up the milk, however, he makes sure to tie the pouch tightly, and there is consequently no danger that it will fall off in a public domain (*Tos.* 53b, quoted by *Tos. R' Akiva*).

Since there are two schools of thought concerning this halachah, *Shulchan Aruch* (305:6) in following *Rambam* and *Rif* adopts the more stringent ruling, i.e., that of R' Yehudah. *Rav*, however, states that the halachah is in accordance with the first *Tanna*.

שבת
ה/ג

[ג] **וּבַמָּה** אֵינָהּ יוֹצְאָה? לֹא יֵצֵא גָמָל בִּמְטוּטֶלֶת, לֹא עָקוּד, וְלֹא רָגוּל; וְכֵן שְׁאָר כָּל הַבְּהֵמוֹת. לֹא יִקְשׁוֹר גְּמַלִּים זֶה בָזֶה וְיִמְשׁוֹךְ, אֲבָל מַכְנִיס חֲבָלִים לְתוֹךְ יָדוֹ וְיִמְשׁוֹךְ, וּבִלְבַד שֶׁלֹּא יִכְרֹךְ.

ר' עובדיה מברטנורא

(ג) **מטוטלת.** חתיכה של מטלית קשורה בזנבו לסימן או לדבר אחר: **עקוד.** שקושרים ידיהם עם הרגלים בכבלים שלא יברחו: **רגול.** שכופפים ידו על זרועו וקושרין: **לא יקשור גמלים זה בזה וימשוך.** אחד, וכולן הולכין, שלא יראה כמוליכן לשוק למכרן: **אבל מכניס הוא חבלים לתוך ידו.** והוא שלא יהיו ראשי החבלים תלויין ויוצאין מתחת ידו לארץ טפח או יותר, כדי שלא יראה כמו שנושא חבלים תלויין בידו: **ובלבד שלא יכרוך.** לאו לענין שבת קא מיירי אלא לענין כלאים, והכי קאמר המכניס חבלים בידו קלנס של פשתן וקלנס של צמר לא יכרוך זו בזו, דכי כריך להו הוו להו כלאים וידו מתחממת באחיזתן ואסור:

יד אברהם

3.

וּבַמָּה אֵינָהּ יוֹצְאָה? — *And with what may it not go out?*

[The *Tanna* now delineates the gear with which an animal may not go out into a public domain on the Sabbath, for the reasons enumerated in the prefatory note of this chapter.]

לֹא יֵצֵא גָמָל בִּמְטוּטֶלֶת, — *A camel may not go out with a patch on its tail,*

I.e., a camel may not go out into a public domain on the Sabbath with a patch of cloth attached to its tail for identification or other purposes (*Rav; Rambam*).

Rashi, however, translates this as a packsaddle, or small cushion attached under the tail to protect the flesh from becoming bruised by the strap that holds the load on the camel's back. This is prohibited lest it fall off in a public domain and someone pick it up and carry it.

לֹא עָקוּד, — *nor with its forelegs and hind legs chained together,*

This is done to prevent the camel from running away (*Rav* from *Gem*. 54a; *Rashi*).

וְלֹא רָגוּל; — *nor with its foreleg bent back to the shoulder;*

The foreleg was bent back toward the shoulder and tied (*Rav; Tif. Yis.* from *Gem* ibid.). This, too, was done to prevent the animal from running away by leaving it only three free legs (*Rashi* on *Gem.*).

This is forbidden since this is an excessive restraint for control of the animal and is therefore considered a burden. See above prefatory remarks (*Tif. Yis.*).

וְכֵן שְׁאָר כָּל הַבְּהֵמוֹת. — *and so [it is] with all other animals.*

[I.e., other animals, too, may not go out on the Sabbath with their forelegs chained to their hind legs or with their foreleg bent toward the shoulder. Since this is an excessive restraint in any animal, it is deemed a burden.]

3. And with what may it not go out? A camel may not go out with a patch on its tail, nor with its forelegs and hind legs chained together, nor with its foreleg bent back to the shoulder; and so [it is] with all other animals. One may not tie camels to one another and lead them, but he may gather ropes into his hand and lead them, provided he does not wind [the ropes one around the other].

YAD AVRAHAM

לֹא יִקְשׁוֹר גְּמַלִּים זֶה בָּזֶה וְיִמְשֹׁךְ — *One may not tie camels to one another and lead them,*

I.e., one may not [tie camels one behind the other and] pull the lead camel so that the others follow since he appears to be taking them to a fair for sale (*Rav; Tif. Yis.* from *Gem.* 54a).

אֲבָל מַכְנִיס חֲבָלִים לְתוֹךְ יָדוֹ וְיִמְשֹׁךְ — *but he may gather ropes into his hand and lead them,*

[I.e., he may gather the tethers of all the camels into his hand, if he does not tie the camels together.]

This is permissible only if less than a handbreadth of rope is left hanging from his hand. If a handbreadth or more of the end of the rope, i.e., the end not attached to the animal, is hanging from his hand he may not go out because he appears to be carrying ropes on the Sabbath (*Rav* from *Gem.* 54a). Furthermore, he must not allow the rope between his hand and the animal to dangle to within a handbreadth of the ground, since it is then not obvious that the animal is being led by this rope (*Gem.* 54b). If the rope is too long, he may wind it around the animal's neck (*Shulchan Aruch* 305:16; see above s.v. יוֹצְאִים בְּשֵׁיר).

וּבִלְבַד ... — *provided ...*

This final clause of the mishnah alludes to the prohibition of wearing or covering oneself with *shaatnez*, a combination of wool and linen. See *Lev.* 19:19 and *Deut.* 22:11. Not only is one guilty of infracting this law if he wears a garment made of wool and linen, but even if one takes two ropes in his hand to lead two animals, and one rope is made of wool while the other is made of linen, he may be guilty of transgressing this prohibition. This occurs only if the ropes are fastened together in such a way as to be considered one, thus becoming *shaatnez*. If one derives benefit by warming his hand with the ropes, he violates the *shaatnez* prohibition. (If one of these conditions is absent, it is permissible to lead two animals with such ropes.) It is to such a case that the Mishnah now addresses itself.

וּבִלְבַד שֶׁלֹּא יִכְרֹךְ — *provided he does not wind [the ropes one around the other].*

Rav explains this as meaning provided he does not twist the ropes together in such a fashion that they will remain permanently entwined — i.e., by knotting together the ends of the ropes. If he does knot together the

שבת
ה/ד

[ד] **אֵין** חֲמוֹר יוֹצֵא בְמַרְדַּעַת בִּזְמַן שֶׁאֵינָהּ קְשׁוּרָה לוֹ; וְלֹא בְזוּג אַף עַל פִּי שֶׁהוּא פָקוּק; וְלֹא בְסֻלָּם שֶׁבְּצַוָּארוֹ; וְלֹא בִרְצוּעָה שֶׁבְּרַגְלוֹ. וְאֵין הַתַּרְנְגוֹלִין יוֹצְאִין

ר' עובדיה מברטנורא

(ד) **בזוג.** כמין פעמון שתולין בצוארו הבהמה שתשמיע קול בהליכתה: **אף על פי שהוא פקוק:** בסומכין דהשתא אין הענבל שלו מקשקש להשמיע קול מפני שנראה כמוליכו למכור בשוק: **בסולם שבצוארו.** כמין לו מכה נותנים בצוארו עלים כמין שתי וערב כדי שלא יחזור ראשו לחכך חבורתו: **ולא ברצועה שברגלו.** בהמה שמכה רגליה זו בזו בהליכתה עושין לה כמין טבעת של רצועה עבה וקושרים אותה במקום שרגליה מנקשות זו בזו: **בחוטין.** שטושים להן לסימנא שלא יתחלפו בתרנגולות אחרים: **ולא ברצועות.** שקושרין שתי רגליהן יחד ברצועה קצרה שלא ידלגו וישברו את הכלים:

יד אברהם
---

ends of the ropes,[1] the two become one rope of *shaatnez*. Consequently, he may not hold them in his hand, since by holding them in his hand he tends to warm his hand. This is akin to wearing a glove of *shaatnez*. [See also *Shenos Eliyahu* and *Meleches Shlomo*.]

Alternatively, this phrase may be translated *provided he does not wind [the ropes around his hand]*. I.e., if the ropes are tied together with a double knot one may, nonetheless, *take* them into his hand as long as he does not *wind* them around his hand. Even though the ropes are of *shaatnez*, according to this opinion holding the ropes does not afford any warmth unless one winds them around his hand (*Rashi* according to *Shenos Eliyahu*; *Chidushei HaGra*; *Rambam*, *Hil. Kilayim* 10:21; *Tif. Yis.*).

Even where one does derive benefit from holding the ropes in his hand, this benefit is, doubtless, unintentional. A secondary, unintentional result occurring as an outgrowth of another activity is called דָּבָר שֶׁאֵינוֹ מִתְכַּוֵּן, *an unintentional act*. We find in numerous places in the Talmud that R' Shimon permits performing a given act, even though it *may* result in another forbidden one, if the second act is unintentional. R' Yehudah, however, rules that even though the second act occurred unintentionally, one is considered to have violated that prohibition. Consequently, one must refrain from performing even the first act wherever there is a possibility of the second forbidden one occurring (see *Beitzah* 2:8).

Rashi (54a) states that our mishnah expresses the opinion of R' Yehudah. Since here, too, the prohibited act (the derivation of warmth from apparel

---

1. There is a dispute among the authorities regarding whether the knot referred to here is a single knot or a double one. Generally, wool and linen tied together do not become *shaatnez* unless fastened by a double knot, which accords a degree of permanency to this combination. Therefore, most authorities explain this knot, too, as being a double knot (*Beis Yosef*, *Yoreh Deah* 300 based on *Rashi*; *Bach* from *Mordechai* et al.; *Taz*, *Yoreh Deah* 300:11; *Aruch HaShulchan* 300:25). Some authorities, however, state that due to the rope being wound round his hand, even a single knot suffices to create *shaatnez* (see *Beis Yosef* and *Bach*, ibid.).

5 4

4. A donkey may not go out with a saddlecloth when it is not tied to it; nor with a bell even if it is plugged; nor with a ladder on its neck; nor with a strap on its leg. Chickens may not go out

YAD AVRAHAM

made from *shaatnez*) is not done intentionally but is merely an outgrowth of his leading the animals by a rope made of *shaatnez*, this activity can only be prohibited according to R' Yehudah who rules that even an unintentional act is prohibited. According to R' Shimon, however, who permits such an act, one is permitted to lead the animals by ropes of *shaatnez* since any warmth he may derive is both secondary and unintentional. The halachah follows R' Shimon (*Ran*; *Rabbeinu Yerucham* 19:2; *Rama*, *Yoreh Deah* 300:6).

Others maintain that even though one does not intend to warm his hand, since he will inevitably derive this benefit from the ropes made of *shaatnez*, it is forbidden. The *Gemara* (133a) calls such cases פְּסִיק רֵישֵׁיהּ וְלֹא יָמוּת [lit. *cut off his head, will he not die?*], i.e., the secondary result is *inevitable*. In such cases, even R' Shimon agrees that the first act is prohibited. Accordingly, the mishnah follows the opinion of both R' Yehudah and R' Shimon and is the accepted halachah (*Rambam*; *Semag*; *Tur*; *Shulchan Aruch*, *Yoreh Deah* 300:6; *Tos. R' Akiva* from *Shiltei Giborim*; *Tif. Yis.*).

4.

אֵין חֲמוֹר יוֹצֵא בְּמַרְדַּעַת — *A donkey may not go out with a saddlecloth*

[As explained in mishnah 2, this is a saddlelike cushion worn by the donkey to keep it warm.]

בִּזְמַן שֶׁאֵינָהּ קְשׁוּרָה לוֹ; — *when it is not tied to it;*

[I.e., when it was not tied to it before the Sabbath, as explained in mishnah 2.]

וְלֹא בְזוּג — *nor with a bell*

[I.e., with a bell hanging from its neck.]

אַף עַל פִּי שֶׁהוּא פָּקוּק; — *even if it is plugged;*

I.e., even if the bell is stuffed with wool or cotton, so that the tongue will not resound against it, it is, nonetheless, prohibited since it appears as though one is leading the donkey to the fair to sell it (*Rashi*; *Rambam*; *Rav*). It was customary to hang a bell on an animal one wished to sell in order to attract prospective customers (*Tif. Yis.*).

וְלֹא בְסֻלָּם שֶׁבְּצַוָּארוֹ; — *nor with a ladder (that is) on its neck;*

When an animal had a wound on its foreleg or on its neck, a ladderlike wooden frame was attached around its head to prevent it from turning its head to scratch the wound with its teeth (*Rav* from *Gem.* 54b). This may not be worn on the Sabbath because it may become detached. Since it is expensive, the owner may forget that it is the Sabbath and carry it (*Rashi*).

וְלֹא בִרְצוּעָה שֶׁבְּרַגְלוֹ. — *nor with a strap (that is) on its leg.*

An animal whose strides were short, causing its feet to knock against each other, would wear a strap around its feet to prevent them from being bruised (*Rav*; *Rashi*). This strap would often fall off, and the owner could forget the Sabbath, and pick it up and carry it in the public domain (*Meiri*).

שבת
ה/ד

בְּחוּטִין, וְלֹא בִּרְצוּעוֹת שֶׁבְּרַגְלֵיהֶם. וְאֵין הַזְּכָרִים יוֹצְאִין בַּעֲגָלָה שֶׁתַּחַת הָאַלְיָה שֶׁלָּהֶן. וְאֵין הָרְחֵלִים יוֹצְאוֹת חֲנוּנוֹת. וְאֵין הָעֵגֶל יוֹצֵא בְגִימוֹן; וְלֹא פָרָה בְּעוֹר הַקֻּפָּד, וְלֹא בִּרְצוּעָה שֶׁבֵּין קַרְנֶיהָ. פָּרָתוֹ שֶׁל רַבִּי אֶלְעָזָר בֶּן עֲזַרְיָה הָיְתָה יוֹצְאָה בִּרְצוּעָה שֶׁבֵּין קַרְנֶיהָ, שֶׁלֹּא בִרְצוֹן חֲכָמִים.

ר' עובדיה מברטנורא

בעגלה שתחת האליה. כמין עגלה קטנה קושרין תחת האליה של הכבשים שאליתים גדולה כדי שלא תלקה באבנים ובסלעים: **חנונות.** עץ אחד יש ששמו יחנון, מביאין קיסם ממנו ומניחין לה בחוטמה כדי שתתעטש ויפלו התולעים שבראשה. ולזכרים אין צריכין לעשות כן שמתוך שמנגחים זה בזה נופלים התולעים מאליהם: **בגימון.** כמין עול של גמי נותנים על צואר העגל כדי שיהא למוד לכוף ראשו כשיגדל: **בעור הקופד.** שרץ שעימיו חדין כמחט, וקושרין עורו בדדי הפרה שלא יינקוה השרצים: **ולא ברצועה שבין קרניה.** בין לנוי בין לשמור אסור, דכל נטירותא יתירתא משאוי הוא: **פרתו של רבי אלעזר בן עזריה.** לא שלו היתה אלא של שכנתו, ועל שלא מיחה בה נקראת על שמו:

יד אברהם

וְאֵין הַתַּרְנְגוֹלִין יוֹצְאִין בְּחוּטִין, — *Chickens may not go out with cords,*

These were attached for identification (*Rav from Gem.* 54b).

This ruling applies to both male and female (*Rambam; Tos. Yom Tov*).

וְלֹא בִּרְצוּעוֹת שֶׁבְּרַגְלֵיהֶם. — *nor with straps (that are) on their legs.*

These were attached to shorten their stride and prevent them from jumping and breaking utensils (*Rav from Gem.* ibid.).

וְאֵין הַזְּכָרִים יוֹצְאִין בַּעֲגָלָה שֶׁתַּחַת הָאַלְיָה שֶׁלָּהֶן. — *Rams may not go out with a wagonette (that is) under their fat tail.*

It was customary to tie a small wagon under the fat tails of the sheep to protect them from becoming lacerated by the stones and boulders (*Rav*).

Rashi explains that the tail of the sheep is very wide, like a small cushion. Since it has no bone, and it is very thick and heavy, it drags on the earth. Consequently, it was in danger of becoming bruised and lacerated. They would, therefore, tie a miniature wagon under it, which the animal would pull along behind it.

וְאֵין הָרְחֵלִים יוֹצְאוֹת חֲנוּנוֹת. — *Ewes may not go out with henna chips in their nose.*

These were chips from a tree known in Hebrew as חֲנוּן or יַחֲנוּן. They were inserted into the nostrils of the ewes to induce sneezing and rid them of worms in their head. The rams, however, did not require this treatment since they would habitually butt each other and the butting would dislodge the worms (*Gem.* ibid.).

Since the worms produced but mild discomfort, this remedy was prohibited on the Sabbath (*Tif. Yis.*). *Meiri* comments that some explain the reason for this prohibition, that the chips may fall out and be carried. Others consider them a burden.

וְאֵין הָעֵגֶל יוֹצֵא בְגִימוֹן; — *A calf may not go out with a little yoke,*

This was placed on the calf's neck to

5
4

with cords, nor with straps on their legs. Rams may not go out with a wagonette under their fat tail. Ewes may not go out with henna chips in their nose. A calf may not go out with a little yoke, nor a cow with a hedgehog skin, nor with a strap between her horns. R' Elazar ben Azaryah's cow used to go out with a strap between her horns, without the consent of the Sages.

YAD AVRAHAM

accustom it to bend its head in order that it be able to bear a yoke when it grew up (*Rashi* on *Gem*. 54b).

It was called גימון because it trained the calf to bend its head like אַגְמוֹן, *a reed* (*Gem*. 54b).

Rambam and *Rav* add that the yoke was actually made from reeds. [The source of this contention is unknown.]

וְלֹא פָרָה בְעוֹר הַקֻּפָּד, — *nor a cow with a hedgehog skin*,

It was customary to cover the cows' udders with hedgehog skin to prevent leeches from sucking the milk while they were asleep. When leeches, snakes, or other reptiles would attempt to suck the milk, they would be repelled by the sharp spines of the hedgehog skin (*Rav*, *Rambam* from *Gem*. ibid.).

This is identified by *Aruch* with קפוד mentioned in *Isaiah* 14:2.3, 34:11. In many editions, however, the word is spelled קִפָּר. (See *Tif. Yis.*)

Tosafos maintain that this was done to discourage hedgehogs from sucking the milk.

According to *Yerushalmi*, this was done to prevent the cow from nursing its own calf.

וְלֹא בִרְצוּעָה שֶׁבֵּין קַרְנֶיהָ. — *nor with a strap (that is) between her horns*.

This is prohibited whether the strap

is intended as an ornament or to control the cow. Since it is excessive, it is considered a burden (*Rav* from *Gem*. 55a).

פָּרָתוֹ שֶׁל רַבִּי אֶלְעָזָר בֶּן עֲזַרְיָה הָיְתָה יוֹצְאָה בִרְצוּעָה שֶׁבֵּין קַרְנֶיהָ, שֶׁלֹּא בִרְצוֹן חֲכָמִים. — *R' Elazar ben Azaryah's cow used to go out with a strap (that was) between her horns, without the consent of the Sages*.

In reality, it was not R' Elazar's cow but his neighbor's. However, since he did not prevent her from letting her cow go out with the strap that was between its horns, he was considered responsible and the cow was referred to as his (*Rav*, *Rambam* from *Gem*. 54b).

The fact that R' Elazar ben Azaryah did allow this, however, indicated that he permitted it. It is, therefore, listed among the three things that R' Elazar permitted, which the Sages prohibited (see *Beitzah* 2:8).

Yerushalmi takes this as an allusion to R' Elazar's wife, who once went out on the Sabbath with a strap on her head that resembled one the cow wears between her horns. Since this was contrary to the view of the Sages (6:1), R' Elazar repented of his sin by fasting until his teeth became black. See *Meleches Shlomo*.

פרק ששי
Chapter Six

As was discussed in the first chapter of this tractate, *transferring* objects on the Sabbath, either from a private domain to a public domain, or from a public domain to a private domain, or for a distance of four cubits within a public domain, is prohibited by the Torah and is the thirty-ninth *melachah* enumerated in the mishnah (7:2). This prohibition applies only to objects being transferred from one domain to another, not to items of apparel worn by a person going from one domain to the other. Since these items serve the function of clothing the person, they are considered as if they were a part of the person rather than as separate objects being transported by the person. Needless to say, only items of apparel actually being worn are exempted from this prohibition. One who *carries* his clothing is just as liable as one who carries any other object.

Not all items worn by a person are considered apparel. The item must serve one of three functions: (a) to clothe, i.e., to cover the person (out of a sense of modesty), e.g., shirt, pants, dress; (b) to protect one's body from the elements (snow, rain, cold, heat) or from injury, e.g., winter coat, raincoat, shoes, boots;[1] (c) to ornament the person, e.g., necktie, jewelry. [Additionally, any item which helps fasten or otherwise abet the wearing of one of these types of garments is also considered an item of apparel; e.g. a belt or tie clip.] Any item which does not serve one of these three functions, e.g., a key, may not be worn from domain to domain even if it is fastened to one's garments (unless it also assists in one of these three functions) (*Shulchan Aruch* 303:11).

This is the Torah law. The Rabbis, however, noticed that people occasionally took off certain items while in the public domain and then forgetfully continued walking while still carrying those items (rather than putting them on again). To prevent this inadvertent desecration of the Sabbath (by carrying four cubits in a public domain), the Rabbis deemed it necessary to prohibit wearing, when going out, those items of apparel which one might normally take off while in the public domain. *Shenos Eliyahu* places these items into six categories: (a) an article having a tendency to fall off (because it is loose, for example); (b) an article often removed by its wearer to display to others; (c) a garment which might subject its wearer to ridicule (thus causing him to remove it temporarily); (d) an article which a person must remove in certain given circumstances; (e) an article which a person objects to wearing; and (f) a hobnailed sandal.

These six categories are the subject of this chapter and will be explained in detail.

The chapter concerning animals' gear precedes the chapter concerning people's apparel because in agricultural societies animals generally went out earlier in the day than did most people (*Tif. Yis.*). Also, the rules regarding animals are fewer and less complex than those regarding people and therefore more easily dealt with (*Meleches Shlomo*).

---

1. An item whose sole purpose is to protect one's clothing from damage or dirt is not considered apparel and may not be worn from one domain to another as this is tantamount to carrying the item. However, an article which is generally worn to protect a person, e.g., a raincoat, may be worn even when the intention is only to protect one's clothing. Only an item never worn except to protect one's clothing is forbidden for such a purpose (*Shulchan Aruch* 301:13,14).

שבת ו/א

[א] **בַּמֶּה** אִשָּׁה יוֹצְאָה, וּבַמֶּה אֵינָהּ יוֹצְאָה? לֹא תֵצֵא אִשָּׁה לֹא בְחוּטֵי צֶמֶר, וְלֹא בְחוּטֵי פִשְׁתָּן, וְלֹא בִרְצוּעוֹת שֶׁבְּרֹאשָׁהּ - וְלֹא תִטְבֹּל בָּהֶן עַד שֶׁתְּתַרְפֵּם;

ר' עובדיה מברטנורא

פרק שישי – במה אשה.(א) במה אשה. שבראשה. אכולהו קאי חוטי צמר ופשתן ורצועה שמקלעת בהן שער שבראשה, ומה טעם לא תצא בהן בשבת מפני שאמרו חכמים בחול לא תטבול בהן עד שתרפם, לפיכך בשבת לא תצא בהן שמא מתרמיא לה טבילה של מצוה ושריא להו ואתיא לאתויינהו ארבע אמות ברשות הרבים: **עד שתתרפם.** שתתירם קלת שיהיו רפויין ויכנסו המים ביניהם שלא יהיו חוצצים בטבילה:

יד אברהם

1.

— בַּמֶּה אִשָּׁה יוֹצְאָה, וּבַמֶּה אֵינָהּ יוֹצְאָה? — *With what may a woman go out, and with what may she not go out?*

[I.e., what may a woman wear when she goes out on the Sabbath, and what may she not wear when going out? Whether this applies to going out only to a public domain or even to her own courtyard will be discussed below, s.v., לִרְשׁוּת הָרַבִּים.]

לֹא תֵצֵא אִשָּׁה — *A woman may not go out*

Having posed two questions the mishnah proceeds to answer the second question first. This differs from the preceding chapter in which the mishnah also poses two questions and answers them in the order asked. *Tiferes Yisrael* accounts for this order as an allusion to the passage in *Psalms* 45:14: כָּל־כְּבוּדָה בַת־מֶלֶךְ פְּנִימָה, *the complete glory of the princess is within*. This verse describes the modesty of the Jewish woman, who is no less a princess than a king's daughter. The glory of the Jewish wife and mother is to hold court in the inner chambers of her own home which is her palace and royal domain. [See *Tehillim*, ArtScroll ed., vol. 2.] To bring out this point, the *Tanna* commences with the words לֹא תֵצֵא אִשָּׁה, *a woman may not go out.*

[This is a plausible homiletic explanation. It does not, however, account for this order in the second and fourth chapters, each of which begins with two questions, the second being answered first. Moreover the Talmud (*Nedarim* 3a) concludes that both forms are acceptable, and there is no particular reason for choosing one instead of the other (*Tos. Yom. Tov*).]

לֹא בְחוּטֵי צֶמֶר, וְלֹא בְחוּטֵי פִשְׁתָּן, וְלֹא בִרְצוּעוֹת שֶׁבְּרֹאשָׁהּ — — *neither with woolen threads, nor with linen threads, nor with straps that are on her head* —

The expression, *that are on her head*, describes all three items mentioned, i.e., a woman may not go out on the Sabbath with either woolen or linen threads on her head, nor with straps on her head (*Rav*). *Rashi* and *Rav* understand the prohibition to apply even when these adornments are braided into her hair. *Tosafos*, however, maintain that such ornaments

1. **W**ith what may a woman go out, and with what may she not go out? A woman may not go out neither with woolen threads, nor with linen threads, nor with straps that are on her head — nor may she immerse herself [in a *mikveh*] with them unless she [first] loosens them;

YAD AVRAHAM

may be worn if they are braided into her hair; the prohibition applies only if the threads or the straps are merely bound around the hair. The reasoning behind each of these views is dependent on an understanding of the next phrase in the mishnah and is given at the end of the commentary to that phrase.

וְלֹא תִטְבֹּל בָּהֶן עַד שֶׁתְּרַפֵּם; — *nor may she immerse herself [in a mikveh] with them unless she [first] loosens them;*

Following the cessation of her menstrual period a woman is still considered a נִדָּה, *menstruant* (see comm. to 2:6), until she immerses herself in a *mikveh*. Such immersion is not valid if any חֲצִיצָה, *interposition*, shields a part of her body from the water. The straps and threads of our mishnah are considered an interposition since they prevent the *mikveh* water from reaching those hairs bound by the straps. Therefore, they must be loosened before her immersion, thereby allowing the water to pass between them and the hair. Often, however, rather than merely loosening the straps or threads, a woman will find it more convenient to remove them entirely. Should the time of her immersion occur on the Sabbath, she might forget to retie them in her hair (especially since her hair is still somewhat wet) and carry them home. To avoid such an unintentional desecration of the Sabbath, the Rabbis prohibited the wearing of such ties on the Sabbath (*Rav* from *Gem.* 57a). [This is an illustration of the fourth category in the prefatory note to this chapter.] This rule applies to all accessories that (a) must be removed before immersion and (b) that a woman will sometimes carry with her rather than put on. Garments are not included in this prohibition since a woman would not walk through the streets without wearing them (*Tos.*).

Once the Rabbis prohibited wearing these hair ties, they did not differentiate between younger women (who must go to the *mikveh*) and older women (who, having experienced menopause, no longer need to go to the *mikveh*). This follows the general rule of לֹא פְּלוּג, *nondifferentiation* (in rabbinic ordinances), i.e., that where rabbinic ordinances are instituted, the Rabbis do not distinguish between individual differences of circumstances or people (*Turei Zahav* 303:2). [This is done to avoid confusion and individual interpretation of the law by the unqualified masses.]

There is a difference of opinion as to whether the mishnah refers only to those threads which are bound around her hair or whether it refers also to the threads braided into her hair. *Tosafos, Rosh, Ran,* and *Ritva* take the view that threads braided into her hair are not included in the prohibition of the mishnah. The reason for this

שבת א/ו

וְלֹא בְטוֹטֶפֶת, וְלֹא בְסַנְבּוּטִין, בִּזְמַן שֶׁאֵינָן תְּפוּרִין; וְלֹא בְכָבוּל לִרְשׁוּת הָרַבִּים; וְלֹא

─────── ר' עובדיה מברטנורא ───────

בטוטפת. כֵּן שֶׁקּוֹשְׁרִין עַל הַמֵּצַח מֵאֹזֶן לְאֹזֶן: **סנבוטין:** תְּלוּיִין בַּטּוֹטֶפֶת וּבָאִין עַל הַלְּדָעַיִם עַד הַלְּחָיַיִם. טַנִּיּוֹת טוּסוֹת אוֹתָן שֶׁל מִינֵי צִבְעוֹנִין, עֲשִׁירוֹת טוּסוֹת אוֹתָן שֶׁל כֶּסֶף וְשֶׁל זָהָב. וּמִתּוֹךְ שֶׁחֲשׁוּבִין הֵן חָיְישִׁינַן דִּלְמָא שָׁלְפָא וּמַחְוְיָא לְחַבְרְתָהּ: **בִּזְמַן שֶׁאֵינָן תְּפוּרִין.** בִּשְׂבָכָה שֶׁבְּרֹאשָׁהּ, אֲבָל תְּפוּרִים לֵיכָּא לְמֵיחַשׁ לְאַחֲוֹיֵי, שֶׁאֵינָהּ נוֹטֶלֶת הַשְּׂבָכָה מֵרֹאשָׁהּ בִּרְשׁוּת הָרַבִּים שֶׁהֲרֵי הִיא מְגַלָּה שְׂעָרָהּ: **בכבול:** חֲתִיכָה שֶׁל בֶּגֶד כְּמוֹ מִגְבַּעַת קְטַנָּה שֶׁקּוֹשְׁרִין אוֹתָהּ עַל הַמֵּצַח וְנוֹתְנִין הַצִּיץ עָלֶיהָ כְּדֵי שֶׁלֹּא יַזִּיק הַצִּיץ בַּמֵּצַח, וּפְעָמִים שֶׁהָאִשָּׁה מִתְקַשֶּׁטֶת בּוֹ בְּלֹא צִיץ: **לִרְשׁוּת הָרַבִּים.** אֲבָל לֶחָצֵר שָׁרֵי. וְכָל הַנִּזְכָּר לְמַעְלָה אֲסוּרִים אַף בֶּחָצֵר, דִּגְזוּר בְּהוּ שֶׁלֹּא תִּתְקַשֵּׁט בַּשַּׁבָּת כְּלָל לֹא בֶחָצֵר וְלֹא בִרְשׁוּת הָרַבִּים, וּבַכָּבוּל הִתִּירוּ, שֶׁלֹּא לֶאֱסֹר אֶת כָּל תַּכְשִׁיטֶיהָ וְתִתְגַּנֶּה עַל בַּעְלָהּ. וּרְמַבַּ"ם פֵּירַשׁ דִּלְרְשׁוּת הָרַבִּים קָאֵי מְכֻלְּהוּ תַּכְשִׁיטִין הָאֲמוּרִים בְּמַתְנִיתִין דְּכֻלְּהוּ לֹא אֲסִירֵי אֶלָּא גְּזֵרָה שֶׁמָּא תַּעֲבִירֵם הָאִשָּׁה אַרְבַּע אַמּוֹת בִּרְשׁוּת הָרַבִּים:

──── **יד אברהם** ────

distinction is because one is not permitted to undo a braid on the Sabbath, just as one is not permitted to braid hair on the Sabbath (see 10:6). Since the braid may not be undone on the Sabbath, the thread braided into it can consequently not be removed on the Sabbath and there is therefore no possibility of her carrying this thread. [Should she have to immerse herself on the Sabbath, she would have had to have previously made sure to unbraid the thread from her hair since she would not be permitted to do so on the Sabbath.] Only a thread bound around her hair, which may be removed on the Sabbath [since the reason for the prohibition, as explained in 10:6, does not apply], presents the possibility of being inadvertently carried from the *mikveh* through the street.

Rashi (followed by *Rav*), on the other hand, understands the prohibition of the mishnah as applying even to threads braided into her hair. The reason for this opinion is that it might be possible to loosen the braid somewhat and extract the thread without actually undoing the braid. [This would be permitted on the Sabbath as long as the braid of hair itself remained intact.] It is therefore conceivable that she might end up carrying even a thread which had been braided (*Bach; Tur* 303; *Magen Avraham* 303:3). Others explain that she would be permitted to ask a non-Jew to undo the braid for her, in order that should be able to immerse in the *mikveh*.[1] Therefore, the possibility of her carrying that thread away from the *mikveh* remains (*Turei Zahav* 303:1).

וְלֹא בְטוֹטֶפֶת, — *nor [may she go out] with a frontlet,*

This is an ornament worn on the forehead from ear to ear [resembling the golden צִיץ, *forehead plate,* worn by the *Kohen Gadol* (see *Yoma* 7:5)] (*Rav; Tif. Yis.* from *Gem.* 57b).

וְלֹא בְסַנְבּוּטִין, — *nor with head bangles,*

Ribbons were sometimes attached to the frontlet, which hung over the temples, reaching down to the cheeks.

---

1. This follows the rule of שְׁבוּת דִּשְׁבוּת בִּמְקוֹם מִצְוָה, *a Rabbinical prohibition of a Rabbinical prohibition in the place of a mitzvah,* i.e., a Jew may ask a non-Jew to do a *Rabbinically* prohibited activity in order to facilitate the performance of a mitzvah.

6 1 nor [may she go out] with a frontlet, nor with head bangles, when they are not sewn; nor with a forehead pad into a public domain; nor with a

YAD AVRAHAM

They were made either of gold, silver or colored cloth, depending upon the wearer's financial status (*Rav* from *Gem.* 57b).

בִּזְמַן שֶׁאֵינָן תְּפוּרִין; — *when they are not sewn;*

Frontlets and head bangles are prohibited only if they are not sewn to the hat, because she might then take them off to show to a friend. [This is an example of the second category listed in the prefatory note to this chapter.] If they are sewn on, however, she could only remove them to show to a friend by removing her hat entirely. Since a married Jewish woman is forbidden to uncover her hair in public, we need not fear that this will happen. Consequently, she may go out with the frontlets or head bangles when they are sewn to her hat (*Rav; Rashi; Ravad, Hil. Shabbos* 19:6). Some opinions rule that a girl who has not yet married, and who is therefore permitted to go in public with her hair uncovered, may not go out with these ornaments even if they are sewn to her hat, for fear she may remove her hat (*Rama* 303:2).

Rambam understands the phrase to mean that if the bangles are sewn either together or to the frontlet it is sufficient (*Comm.* and *Hil. Shabbos* 19:6). He explains that the frontlet and bangles are prohibited not because she might remove them to show to a friend but rather because they might fall off, and the woman would then be apt to pick them up and carry them. [This would then be an example of the first category enumerated in the prefatory note to this chapter.] Therefore, if they are sewn together there is no such fear. [*Rambam* obviously considers it unlikely for a woman to remove this particular ornament in order to show it.] (*Maggid Mishneh*, ad loc.)

וְלֹא בְכָבוּל — *nor with a forehead pad*

This is a cloth pad, usually worn under the frontlet to protect the forehead from irritation, but sometimes worn as an adornment, even without the frontlet (*Rav*).

לִרְשׁוּת הָרַבִּים; — *into a public domain;*

I.e., she may not wear a forehead pad when going out to a public domain, but she may wear it in a courtyard. The adornments mentioned in this mishnah other than the forehead pad, however, are prohibited even in a courtyard (where one is ordinarily permitted to carry) [see comm. to mishnah 5 for proof of this explanation] so that a woman refrain from adorning herself with jewelry on the Sabbath. In this way she will not come to wear them in the street where she might take them off to show her companions. The Rabbis did not prohibit wearing the forehead pad in a courtyard for they did not want to leave women completely unadorned lest they become plain and unattractive in the eyes of their husbands (*Rav* from *Gem.* 64b).

Rambam (*Hil. Shabbos* 19:8) rules that jewelry is prohibited only in a courtyard in which no *eruv chatzeiros* [the mechanism to allow people to carry in an enclosed courtyard which is used jointly by the occupants of more than one dwelling (see General Introduction, p. 15)] has been made. If

[137]   THE MISHNAH/SHABBOS — Chapter Six: *Bameh Ishah*

שבת ו/א

בְּעִיר שֶׁל זָהָב; וְלֹא בְקַטְלָא; וְלֹא בִנְזָמִים; וְלֹא בְטַבַּעַת שֶׁאֵין עָלֶיהָ חוֹתָם; וְלֹא בְמַחַט שֶׁאֵינָהּ נְקוּבָה. וְאִם יָצְאָת; אֵינָהּ חַיֶּבֶת חַטָּאת.

ר' עובדיה מברטנורא

עיר של זהב. עטרת זהב עשויה כמין עיר לורת ירושלים: **ולא בקטלא.** תכשיט שנתון בלוחר בדוחק והאשה חונקת עלמה בו כדי שתראה בעלת בשר, ובערבי מכנק"ז: **ולא בנזמים.** נזמי האף, אבל נזמי האזן יולאין בהם: **חותם.** לורה לחתום בה אגרות או כל דבר סתר, ואף על גב דתכשיט הוא לה אסור, דלמא שלפא ומחויא, אבל יש עליה חותם תכשיט הוא לה אמרינן לקמן דחייבת חטאת, ואף על פי שמוליאתו בטבעת דרך מלבוש, לפי שפעמים שהטבעל מסיר אותו מאלבעו ונותן אותן לאשתו להניעתו והיא נותנתו באלבעתה והולכת בו, ונמלא שדרך הולאתו בכך. וכן טבעת שאין עליה חותם דלא הוי תכשיט לאיש, חייב חטאת אף על פי שמוליאו באלבעו דרך מלבוש, שפעמים שהאשה נותנתו לו שיוליכנו לאומן והוא מוליאו לאומן באלבעו: **ואם יצאת.** האשה בכל הנך דאמרינן עד הכא במתניתין אינה חייבת חטאת, דכולהו תכשיטין נינהו ורבנן הוא דגזור בהו דלמא שלפא ומחויא:

יד אברהם

A clasp engraved with a likeness of Jerusalem (*Rashi*). Alternatively, a golden crown engraved with a likeness of Jerusalem and its walls (*Rav; Rambam; Tos.* 59a).

According to this latter view our mishnah seems to contradict another one (*Sotah* 9:14) which states: At the time of the siege of Titus [which ended with the destruction of the Second Temple] the Sages prohibited the wearing of bridal crowns. The Talmud there (49b) describes the bridal crown as עִיר שֶׁל זָהָב, *a golden city*. Thus, the wearing of a golden city is forbidden at all times, not just on the Sabbath. Yet our mishnah only prohibits it on the Sabbath. Various reconciliations between the two mishnayos are offered:

❐ The prohibition in the mishnah in *Sotah* applies only to brides. A bride's joy knows no bounds, but since the destruction of the Holy Temple, boundless joy is inappropriate. Therefore, the Sages removed some of the bride's jewelry to remind her of the yard has an *eruv chatzeiros*, however, it is just like a house, and all types of jewelry may be worn.[1]

Ran, Ramban, and *Rashba*, however, rule that the law applies even to a yard in which an *eruv* has been made (*Maggid Mishneh*, ad loc.).[2] According to them, the Rabbis innovated a double safeguard. They prohibited wearing jewelry in a yard lest a woman wear it in the public domain. They prohibited wearing jewelry in the public domain lest she take it off to show her friends and carry it four cubits. Since this was enacted at one time as one decree, it does not fall under the rule of אֵין גּוֹזְרִין גְּזֵרָה לִגְזֵרָה, *we may not enact one decree to safeguard another decree* (*Ran*). [See beginning of Ch. 4.]

וְלֹא בְעִיר שֶׁל זָהָב; — *nor with a golden city;*

---

1. Although *Rambam* in his *commentary* states that all adornments may be worn in any courtyard whether or not it has an *eruv chatzeiros,* and are prohibited only in the public domain, he obviously recanted this view, as evidenced by the above quotation from [his later work] *Mishneh Torah (Tos. Yom Tov).*

2. Some opinions rule that the prohibition applies even in a house (*Shulchan Aruch* 303:18).

6
1

golden city; nor with a necklace; nor with nose rings; nor with a ring that bears no signet; nor with a needle without an eye. But if she went out, she is not liable for a sin offering.

YAD AVRAHAM

the national tragedy. However, on the Sabbath any woman is prohibited to wear this crown, lest she remove it and carry it (*Tos. Yom Tov; Tos.* 59a; *Tos., Gittin* 7a, s.v. עטרות חתנים).

☐ A golden likeness of any other city was prohibited; an engraving of Jerusalem, however, serves as a reminder of the destruction of the Holy City and is thus in keeping with the Psalmist's oath (137:5): *If I forget thee, O Jerusalem* ... The permissibility of wearing the golden Jerusalem is evidenced by R' Akiva's buying such an ornament for his wife [see *Nedarim* 50a] (*Reshash*).

☐ [*Rashi's* interpretation of *golden city* as a clasp is intended to reconcile the two mishnayos. Prohibited during the siege of Titus for all time was only a golden crown; a golden clasp, however, was prohibited only on the Sabbath (*Rosh Yosef*).]

וְלֹא בְקַטְלָא — *nor with a necklace;*

I.e., an ornament tied tightly around the neck to give the impression that the wearer is plump. This was accomplished by forcing forward the skin under the chin, giving the impression of a double chin (*Rav; Rashi* 57b).

It appears that this was an ornate bib, fastened high around the neck with wide ribbons so as not to choke its wearer (*Rashi* 59b).

וְלֹא בִנְזָמִים — *nor with nose rings;*

Earrings, however, are permitted. Since the ears are covered with bands [perhaps the bands around her hair], it is burdensome to remove them. We therefore have no fear that she will remove the earrings to show her companions (*Rashi; Tos. Yom Tov*).

וְלֹא בְטַבַּעַת שֶׁאֵין עָלֶיהָ חוֹתָם; — *nor with a ring that bears no signet;*

A signet ring was used by men to sign documents. Women would wear rings bearing no signet. Since women customarily wore their rings as ornaments, the Rabbis prohibited them from being worn on the Sabbath, lest a woman take one off to show to her companions. If a woman wears a signet ring (which is not considered an ornament for her), she transgresses a Torah prohibition and is liable to a sin offering. This will be elaborated upon in mishnah 3 (*Rav*).

וְלֹא בְמַחַט שֶׁאֵינָה נְקוּבָה. — *nor with a needle without an eye.*

This is a pin to which a gold plate is attached. On weekdays, a woman uses the pointed end to part the hair. On the Sabbath, she inserts the pin into her turban, and the gold plate adorns her forehead. The mishnah states that even though this is an ornament, a woman may not go out with it on her head (*Gem.* 60a).

[If she goes out with a needle that has an eye, she is liable to a sin offering. See mishnah 3.]

וְאִם יָצָאת, — *But if she went out,*

I.e., even if she went out into a public domain wearing one of the adornments mentioned above (*Rav*).

אֵינָהּ חַיֶּבֶת חַטָּאת. — *she is not liable for a sin offering.*

Since these restrictions are Rabbinic in nature, enacted lest a woman take off her jewelry to show her friends, no sin offering is required (*Rav*).

שבת
ו/ב

[ב] **לֹא יֵצֵא** הָאִישׁ בַּסַנְדָּל הַמְסֻמָּר; וְלֹא בְיָחִיד בִּזְמַן שֶׁאֵין בְּרַגְלוֹ מַכָּה; וְלֹא בִתְפִלִּין; וְלֹא בְקָמֵיעַ

ר' עובדיה מברטנורא

(ב) **בסנדל המסומר.** של עץ הוא ותוחבים בו מסמרות לחזקו, ואסרוהו בשבת וביום טוב משום מעשה שהיה, שפעם אחת היו נחבאים במערה מפני הגזירה ושמעו קול מעל גבי המערה כסבורין שעליהן הן באים דחקו זה את זה והרגו זה את זה במסמרים שבסנדליהן, ומפני שמעשה זה בשבת היה אסרוהו בשבת וביום טוב שהוא יום של כנופיא כמו שבת: **ולא ביחיד.** ולא בסנדל יחיד: **בזמן שאין ברגלו מכה.** אית דאמרי טעמא שמא יתשדלו שהסנדל השני טמון לו תחת כנפיו ומוליאו בשבת, ואית דאמרי דילמא מחייכי עליה ושליף ליה מזה שברגלו ומייתי ליה בידיה, ומיהו בזמן שיש ברגלו מכה שרי ללאת בסנדל יחידי ברגל שאין בו מכה, מפני שמכתו מוכחת עליו: **ולא בקמיע.** שתולין לרפואה:

יד אברהם

2.

After delineating the women's adornments proscribed by Rabbinic decree, the *Tanna* goes on to the items of men's gear proscribed in the same manner.

לֹא יֵצֵא הָאִישׁ — *A man may not go out*

I.e., a man may not go out on the Sabbath into a public domain (*Tif. Yis.*).

בַּסַנְדָּל הַמְסֻמָּר; — *with a* (lit. the) *hobnailed sandal;*

[*Rif* reads בְּסַנְדָּל מְסֻמָּר, without the definite article.]

These were clogs studded with nails to fasten the soles to the uppers (which were of leather — *Ritva* ms.). The hobnailed sandals were prohibited because of an unfortunate incident that took place during a time of persecution. A group of fugitives were hiding in a cave when they heard a noise of someone walking atop the cave. Suspecting that this was an enemy attack, they started pushing one another in panic, and many of them were killed. More were killed in panic than were killed by the foes (*Gem.* 60a). The noise had actually been made by Jews walking over the cave wearing hobnailed sandals (*Tos.* as explained by *Maharam*). Others explain that they killed each other with the nails of their shoes (*Rashi*).

Lest the memory of this calamity bring sadness to people on the Sabbath, the Sages decreed that no hobnailed sandals be worn on the Sabbath or on holidays, both occasions of gathering when no work may be done (glosses of *Meleches Shlomo*, quoting *Rabbeinu Yehonasan*; *Rav* from *Gem.* 60). On fastdays, such as those described in *Taanis* 1:6, even though it was customary to assemble and work was forbidden, hobnailed sandals were not proscribed since work was permitted the night before. Hence these days do not resemble the Sabbath on which the calamity occurred (*Tos. Yom Tov* from *Gem.* 60; *Tos. R' Akiva*).

Yerushalmi gives another reason for the prohibition against wearing

2. A man may not go out with a hobnailed sandal; nor with a single one when there is no wound on his foot; nor with *tefillin*; nor with an amulet

YAD AVRAHAM

hobnailed sandals. Pregnant women often aborted at the sight or sound of hobnailed sandals, either because it reminded them of the calamity that occurred in the cave (*Pnei Moshe*) or because of their ominous appearance and loud squeak (*Korban HaEdah*). [According to this latter view the prohibition is completely unrelated to the incident in the cave.]

Yerushalmi explains further that by prohibiting the wearing of these sandals on the Sabbath, the Sages effectively prevented their use on weekdays also, since most people did not own more than one pair of shoes or sandals.

וְלֹא בְיָחִיד — *nor with a single one*

One may not go out wearing a sandal only on one foot even if it is not studded with nails (*Rav; Tif. Yis.*).

A person wearing only one shoe will be suspected of carrying its mate under his outer garments (*Rav; Rashi* from *Yerushalmi*).

Alternatively, we fear that people will jeer at him, and he will take off his shoe and carry it (*Rav; Rashi* citing his teachers). [This is an example of the third category listed in the prefatory note to this chapter.]

בִּזְמַן שֶׁאֵין בְּרַגְלוֹ מַכָּה — *when there is no wound on his foot;*

If there is a wound on one foot, he may go out wearing just the shoe on the other foot since people will realize that he cannot wear a shoe on that foot, and that he therefore left the other shoe at home. Moreover, they will not jeer at him for going with only one shoe (*Rav; Rashi* 61a).

וְלֹא בִתְפִלִּין — *nor with tefillin;*

There is a dispute in the Talmud (*Eruvin* 95b) whether *tefillin* may be worn on the Sabbath. According to those who rule שַׁבָּת לָאו זְמַן תְּפִלִּין, *Sabbath is not a time for putting on tefillin*, one may surely not go out while wearing them since they are then neither a garment nor an ornament. Even those who rule שַׁבָּת זְמַן תְּפִלִּין, *the Sabbath is a time for putting on tefillin*, i.e., that one is required to wear *tefillin* on the Sabbath [a view not accepted by halachah], still rule that one may not go out with them. This is based on the rule that one may not wear *tefillin* when he feels the need to relieve himself. Since, if he feels the need while wearing his *tefillin* in the public domain on the Sabbath, he will necessarily remove his *tefillin*, we are apprehensive that he might then carry them four cubits. The Rabbis, therefore, prohibited wearing *tefillin* on the Sabbath in the public domain [this is an example of the fourth category listed in the prefatory note to this chapter] (*Tos. Yom Tov* from *Gem.* 61a).

וְלֹא בְקָמֵיעַ — *nor with an amulet*

קָמֵיעַ [*Kamea*], amulet [lit. bundle or package (*Rashi; Aruch*)], refers to a piece of parchment upon which certain of God's names or certain prayers are written. It may also be composed of roots of herbs reputed to cure certain ailments. It is hung round the neck as either a curative or preventive measure (*Meiri*).

שבת ו/ג

בִּזְמַן שֶׁאֵינוֹ מִן הַמֻּמְחֶה; וְלֹא בְשִׁרְיוֹן; וְלֹא בְקַסְדָּא; וְלֹא בְמַגָּפַיִם. וְאִם יָצָא, אֵינוֹ חַיָּב חַטָּאת.

[ג] **לֹא תֵצֵא** אִשָּׁה בְּמַחַט הַנְּקוּבָה; וְלֹא בְטַבַּעַת שֶׁיֵּשׁ עָלֶיהָ חוֹתָם;

ר' עובדיה מברטנורא

שאינו מן המומחה. מאדם מומחה שריפא שלשה בני אדם, אבל קמיע הנלקח מאדם מומחה שריפא שלשה בני אדם בשאר קמיעות, אף על גב דלאו אתמחי קמיע שרי, דתכשיט הוא לחולה כאחד ממלבושיו: **וקסדא.** כובע של ברזל: **מגיפין.** כמין בתי שוקיים של ברזל שלובשים במלחמה, ולפי שאין לובשין אותן אלא בשעת מלחמה אסור ללבשן בשבת: (ג) **במחט נקובה.** שתופרים בה, דלאו תכשיט הוא, וחייבת חטאת הוא, אף על פי שמוליחה אותה במלבושיה ולא בידיה, שאומן שהוליאה דרך אומנתו חייב חטאת.

יד אברהם

בִּזְמַן שֶׁאֵינוֹ מִן הַמֻּמְחֶה — *when it is not from an expert;*

If the maker of the amulet did not show success with his handiwork at least three times, one may not wear it on the Sabbath. If he was successful with other of his amulets on at least three previous occasions (though this particular amulet has not yet been known to cure), it may be worn on the Sabbath. Since the maker of the amulet has been established as reliable, the new amulets he makes are also considered reliable though they are as yet untested. Since the wearer is secure in the efficacy of the amulet, it is considered an item of apparel for him and may thus be worn on the Sabbath. Where the reliability of the maker (and therefore the amulet) has not been established, the amulet may not be worn on the Sabbath (*Rav* from *Gem.* 6la), for since the wearer does not rely on the therapeutic properties of the amulet, he may remove it and carry it in the street (*Meiri*).

וְלֹא בְשִׁרְיוֹן — *nor with a coat of mail;*

A coat of mail is worn only in battle and never as ordinary dress. That being the case, if one were to wear a coat of mail, people would suspect him of going off to battle. This is forbidden on the Sabbath (except in cases of imminent danger). Therefore, according to the rule of מַרְאִית הָעַיִן (lit. *sight of the eye*), i.e., things which a person is forbidden to do because they cause others to suspect him of engaging in prohibited activities, one is not permitted to wear armor on the Sabbath (*Ran, ad loc.; Rashi* 64b quoted here by *Tos. R' Akiva*). Furthermore, even in the privacy of one's home it is forbidden to wear armor on the Sabbath. This is in accordance with the general rule that anything which is forbidden by reason of מַרְאִית הָעַיִן is forbidden even in the privacy of one's home (*Mishnah Berurah* 301:24 from *Tos. Shabbos*). [See below 22:4 where this matter is discussed at length.]

וְלֹא בְקַסְדָּא — *nor with a helmet;*

This, too, is battle attire and is not to be worn on the Sabbath (*Rambam* ibid.; *Meiri*).

when it is not from an expert; nor with a coat of mail; nor with a helmet; nor with greaves. But if he went out, he is not liable for a sin offering.

3. **A** woman may not go out with a needle that has an eye; nor with a signet ring;

YAD AVRAHAM

וְלֹא בְמַגֵּפַיִם. — *nor with greaves.*
These are iron guards used to protect the legs during battle. Since they are worn only during battle, they may not be worn on the Sabbath (*Rav*).

וְאִם יָצָא, — *But if he went out,*
[I.e., if he went out with one of the items of attire enumerated in this mishnah.]

אֵינוּ חַיָּב חַטָּאת. — *he is not liable for a sin offering.*
Since all these items are really garments which are worn on weekdays, not burdens, and are prohibited only by Rabbinic decree, no sin offering is required (*Tos. Yom Tov* from *Ran*). [As mentioned above, the hobnailed sandal was prohibited because of the unfortunate incident; the single sandal because of either suspicion or the chance one may take it off and carry it; the *tefillin*, too, are considered a garment even if they are not to be worn on the Sabbath (*Gem.* 61a). The *amulet* is worn as an ornament even if it is not efficacious; battle garb is worn as a garment on weekdays when battles are waged (*Rashi*).]

3.

After enumerating the types of adornments proscribed by Rabbinic decree, and for whose infraction no sin offering is brought, the *Tanna* now enumerates those proscribed by the Torah, for which a sin offering is required. He starts with those applying to women just as he did in mishnah 1.

לֹא תֵצֵא אִשָּׁה בְּמַחַט הַנְּקוּבָה; — *A woman may not go out with a* (lit. *the*) *needle that has an eye;*
[*Rif* reads בְּמַחַט נְקוּבָה, without the definite article.]
Since such a needle is used for sewing and not for adornment, it is considered a burden. A tailor, who customarily carries a needle thrust through his garments, is liable to a sin offering for carrying it out in such a manner. Since he is accustomed to carrying the needle this way it is deemed a *melachah* done in its proper fashion. Although not necessarily a seamstress by profession, a woman, who is used to sewing, has the same status in this regard as a tailor (*Rav*; *Tos. Yom Tov*).

This implies that a man who usually does not sew is not liable to a sin offering unless he carries out the needle in his hand. Since he is not a tailor, he is not in the habit of transporting needles thrust through his garments. For him to do so, therefore, is to perform a *melachah* כִּלְאַחַר יָדוֹ, *backhandedly*, i.e., in an unusual fashion, for which one is not liable (see General Introduction and 10:3). This follows the ruling of *Rosh* (*Tos. Yom Tov*).

וְלֹא בְטַבַּעַת שֶׁיֵּשׁ עָלֶיהָ חוֹתָם; — *nor with a signet ring;*
Since it is not customary for women

שבת ו/ד

וְלֹא בִּכְלָיָאר, וְלֹא בְּכוֹבֶלֶת; וְלֹא בִּצְלוֹחִית שֶׁל פְּלָיָטוֹן. וְאִם יָצְתָה, חַיֶּבֶת חַטָּאת — דִּבְרֵי רַבִּי מֵאִיר. וַחֲכָמִים פּוֹטְרִין בְּכוֹבֶלֶת וּבִצְלוֹחִית שֶׁל פְּלָיָטוֹן.

[ד] לֹא יֵצֵא הָאִישׁ לֹא בְסַיִף, וְלֹא

ר' עובדיה מברטנורא

בכליאר. כלי שהאשה מעגלת בראשה כמין טבעת שמסבב הראש, והוא משווי לפי שאין רוב הנשים יוצאות בו: **בכובלת.** קשר של כסף או של זהב שקשור בתוכו בושם להעביר ריח רע שבאשה: **של פליטון.** מור, שקורין מוסק"ו: **וחכמים פוטרין.** דסברי תכשיטין נינהו ולכתחלה לא רשאה דלמא שלפא ומחויא. והלכה כחכמים: **(ד) לא יצא.** אם לא לצורך מלחמה:

יד אברהם

[*Aruch* reads בִּכְלָיָאר.] This is a snail-shaped ring worn on the head (*Rav*; *Rambam*; *Aruch*; *R' Chananel*).

According to others, it is a snail-shaped brooch used to fasten a cloak (*Rashi*).

Since most women do not wear this item, it is considered a burden rather than an adornment (*Rav*).

וְלֹא בְּכוֹבֶלֶת; — nor *with a spice bundle;*

[*Aruch* reads בְּכוֹבֶלֶת.]

This is a vial made of silver or gold, containing spices [balsam (*Rashi*)]. It is worn by women suffering from body odor (*Rav*).

וְלֹא בִּצְלוֹחִית שֶׁל פְּלָיָטוֹן. — nor *with a perfume flask.*

A flask filled with balsam (*Rashi*) or musk (*Rav*; *Rambam*).

וְאִם יָצְתָה, — *And if she went out,*

[I.e., if she went out into a public domain with any of the items mentioned in this mishnah.]

חַיֶּבֶת חַטָּאת — *she is liable for a sin offering —*

[Since all of these items are burdens, she is guilty of an infraction of Torah to wear such rings, they are not considered adornments for a woman. Since the ring is neither a garment nor an adornment it is deemed a burden (*Tif. Yis.*; see also prefatory note to this chapter).

It would appear that a woman wearing a man's ring would be deemed performing work in an unusual manner, and should therefore not be liable (see introduction to this tractate; also 10:3). Nevertheless, since a man often gives his ring to his wife to put away, and she puts it on her finger until she can deposit it in its proper place, it is considered a normal manner of carrying even for her. Similarly, if a man wears a ring that has no signet, though it is uncommon for a man to wear a woman's ring, he is liable. It is, therefore, considered a normal manner of carrying for him because when a woman gives her husband her ring to deliver to a craftsman for repair he will occasionally put it on his finger until he reaches the craftsman's establishment (*Gem.* 62a).

וְלֹא בִּכְלָיָאר; — nor *with a cochlea-shaped head ring;*

6 4 nor with a cochlea-shaped head ring; nor with a spice bundle; nor with a perfume flask. And if she went out, she is liable for a sin offering — [these are] the words of R' Meir.

But the Sages exempt her in [the case of] a spice bundle or a perfume flask.

4. A man may not go out neither with a sword,

YAD AVRAHAM

law, and consequently liable for a sin offering.][1]

דִּבְרֵי רַבִּי מֵאִיר. — [these are] the words of R' Meir.

[R' Meir considers the spice bundle and the perfume flask as burdens, since only women troubled by unpleasant body odors wear them. The overwhelming majority of women do not.]

וַחֲכָמִים פּוֹטְרִין — But the Sages exempt her

[She need not bring a sin offering.]

בְּכוֹבֶלֶת וּבִצְלוֹחִית שֶׁל פְּלַיָטוֹן. — in [the case of] a spice bundle or a perfume flask.

The Sages consider these as adornments. She is, therefore, not liable to a sin offering. She is prohibited from wearing these items only Rabbinically lest she go out with them into the street, and remove them to show to her companions. The halachah is in accordance with the Sages (*Rav*, from *Gem.* 62a).

4.

The following mishnah deals with gear that a man may not go out with on the Sabbath. Unlike those enumerated in mishnah 2, going out with these makes one liable for a sin offering. In particular, the mishnah discusses weaponry and battle gear, those which are neither articles of apparel nor adornments.

לֹא יֵצֵא הָאִישׁ — A man may not go out

I.e., a man may not go out into a public domain on the Sabbath. If he was wearing these articles before the

Sabbath, he may continue to wear them. To take them into his hands on the Sabbath, however, is prohibited because of *muktzeh*. See Chapter 17 and General Introduction:

1. The difference of opinion between *Rambam* and *Rav* noted in mishnah 1 as to whether the phrase *a woman may not go out* refers to going out to a public domain or even to a yard (s.v., לִרְשׁוּת הָרַבִּים), and mishnah 5 (s.v., לְחָצֵר), is not applicable here. That dealt only with the extent of the Rabbinic prohibition banning going out in the first place. According to all opinions, however, no Torah law is violated by going into a חָצֵר, *courtyard*, with these items since according to Torah law one is permitted to actually *carry* into the yard. Only if she went from a private to a public domain or vice versa, or if she went a distance greater than four cubits in the public domain, has she transgressed a Torah prohibition and is liable to a sin offering.

[145]   THE MISHNAH/SHABBOS — Chapter Six: *Bameh Ishah*

שבת
ו/ד

בְּקֶשֶׁת, וְלֹא בִתְרִיס, וְלֹא בְאַלָּה, וְלֹא בְרֹמַח. וְאִם יָצָא, חַיָּב חַטָּאת. רַבִּי אֱלִיעֶזֶר אוֹמֵר: תַּכְשִׁיטִין הֵן לוֹ. וַחֲכָמִים אוֹמְרִים: אֵינָן אֶלָּא לִגְנַאי, שֶׁנֶּאֱמַר, "וְכִתְּתוּ חַרְבוֹתָם לְאִתִּים וַחֲנִיתוֹתֵיהֶם לְמַזְמֵרוֹת; לֹא־יִשָּׂא גוֹי אֶל־גּוֹי חֶרֶב וְלֹא־יִלְמְדוּ עוֹד מִלְחָמָה."

─── ר' עובדיה מברטנורא ───

תריס. מגן עשוי כתבנית משולש: **אלה.** מגן עגול, ושניהם של עץ. ואני שמעתי אלה מל"א בלע"ז, ובעטרבי דסו"ס: **וכתתו חרבותם לאתים.** ואי תכשיטין נינהו לא יהיו בטלים לעתיד:

יד אברהם

לֹא בְסַיִף, וְלֹא בְקֶשֶׁת, וְלֹא בִתְרִיס — neither with a sword, nor with a bow, nor with a shield,

Some interpret תְּרִיס as a triangular wooden shield (Rambam; Rav).

וְלֹא בְאַלָּה — nor with a buckler,

Rambam and Rav translate a round wooden shield. Alternatively, it is a mace (a club with a round ball at its tip), used in combat (Rashi; Aruch; Meiri; Ran; Rav).

וְלֹא בְרֹמַח. — nor with a spear.

[All of these are neither garments nor adornments of any kind. Therefore . . .]

וְאִם יָצָא, — And if he went out,

[Into a public domain on the Sabbath.]

חַיָּב חַטָּאת. — he is liable for a sin offering.

[Being neither garments nor adornments, they are considered burdens. Consequently, he is liable to a sin offering.]

The *Tanna* intentionally chose to enumerate five types of weapons and protectors. This alludes to *Exodus* 13:18: וַחֲמֻשִׁים עָלוּ בְנֵי יִשְׂרָאֵל מֵאֶרֶץ מִצְרָיִם, *And the children of Israel went up armed from Egypt.* The word חֲמֻשִׁים, *armed*, is derived from חֲמִשָּׁה, *five*, alluding to the five armaments enumerated in the mishnah; i.e., each Israelite was armed with these five armaments (*Shenos Eliyahu* from *Yerushalmi*, see *Korban HaEdah*).

רַבִּי אֱלִיעֶזֶר אוֹמֵר: תַּכְשִׁיטִין הֵן לוֹ. — R' Eliezer says: They are adornments for him.

R' Eliezer bases his contention on the words of *Psalms* 45:4: *Gird your sword upon your thigh, O mighty one — your majesty and your splendor.* This indicates that the sword is an object of splendor. Therefore, it is considered an adornment.

The sword discussed here refers to a sword worn hanging from one's belt (in a scabbard, for instance) or strapped to his thigh (*Hagahos Ashri* ad loc.; *Magen Avraham* 301:10; *Eliyah Rabbah* 301:36). Even so, the Sages consider it a burden for which he is liable (as will be explained below). The other weapons mentioned here, however, seem to refer to weapons being carried in one's hand (*Tif. Yis.*; *Machatzis HaShekel* on *Magen Avraham* 301:27).

Eliyah Rabbah 301:36 seems to have understood that all the weapons mentioned here are being worn, not carried. [The mace was often strapped to the belt, the bow strung over the shoulder and even the spear was sometimes strapped to the quiver.]

משניות / שבת – פרק ו: במה אשה [146]

nor with a bow, nor with a shield, nor with a buckler, nor with a spear. And if he went out, he is liable for a sin offering.

R' Eliezer says: They are adornments for him. But the Sages say: They are nothing but a disgrace, as it is said, *And they shall beat their swords into plowshares and their spears into pruning hooks; one nation shall not lift up a sword against another nation, neither shall they learn war anymore* (Isaiah 2:4).

YAD AVRAHAM

Since in the view of R' Eliezer these weapons are adornments, and the common fashion is to carry them, they are considered adornments even when being held rather than worn.[1]

וַחֲכָמִים אוֹמְרִים: אֵינָן אֶלָּא לִגְנַאי, — *But the Sages say: They are nothing but a disgrace*,

[I.e., they cannot be considered adornments because implements of war are a disgrace; as such they are considered burdens. Therefore, one who goes out with any of them is liable to a sin offering.] Even if one girds the sword on his thigh, he is still liable (*Hagahos Asheri*; *Magen Avraham* 301:10).

The garments listed in mishnah 2 are bona-fide garments. A coat of mail is a suit, no less than one made of cloth. A helmet is a hat, no less than one made of felt. Likewise, greaves are stockings, no less than those made of cotton. Therefore, even though the Rabbis prohibited wearing them in the street, one who wears them is, nevertheless, not liable to a sin offering. Swords, shields, maces, and spears, however, are neither garments nor adornments; therefore, going out with them constitutes carrying burdens into a public domain, and requires a sin offering (*Rambam, Hil. Shabbos* 19:1).

שֶׁנֶּאֱמַר, ,,וְכִתְּתוּ חַרְבוֹתָם לְאִתִּים וַחֲנִיתוֹתֵיהֶם לְמַזְמֵרוֹת לֹא־יִשָּׂא גוֹי אֶל־גּוֹי חֶרֶב וְלֹא־יִלְמְדוּ עוֹד מִלְחָמָה." — *as it is said, And they shall beat their swords into plowshares and their spears into pruning hooks; one nation shall not lift up a sword against another nation, neither shall they learn war anymore*[Isaiah 2:4].

The Sages contend that if implements of war were adornments, they would not be abolished in the

---

1. Some authorities deduce from R' Eliezer's view that any adornment that is customarily held in the hand may be carried on the Sabbath. Even the Sages who disagree with R' Eliezer disagree only because they maintain that weaponry is not an adornment. An object that is uncontestedly an adornment, however, such as a cane with a silver handle, may be carried on the Sabbath (*Tif. Yis.*). Others maintain that even R' Eliezer does not actually *permit* one to carry these implements, since even an adornment may not be carried in the hand. R' Eliezer merely rules that if one goes out with them, he is not liable to a sin offering. But it is still Rabbinically forbidden to carry an adornment such as a spear on the Sabbath. Similarly, it is forbidden to carry a cane with a silver handle on the Sabbath (*Magen Avraham*, 301:27). *Eliyah Rabbah* seems to adopt the position of *Tiferes Yisrael*. See *Mishnah Berurah* (301:66) for the final halachah with all its details.

שבת ו/ה

בִּירִית טְהוֹרָה, וְיוֹצְאִין בָּהּ בַּשַּׁבָּת; כְּבָלִים טְמֵאִין, וְאֵין יוֹצְאִין בָּהֶם בַּשַּׁבָּת.

[ה] **יוֹצְאָה** אִשָּׁה בְחוּטֵי שֵׂעָר, בֵּין מִשֶּׁלָּהּ, בֵּין מִשֶּׁל חֲבֶרְתָּהּ, בֵּין מִשֶּׁל

ר' עובדיה מברטנורא

בירית. אצעדה על השוק להחזיק בתי שוקים שלא יפלו ויראו שוקיה, הלכך טהורה דלאו תכשיט לנוי הוא, וכלי תשמיש נמי לא הוי אלא כלי המשמש כלי, דומיא דטבעות הכלים שהן טהורים: **יוצאין בה.** דדרך לבישה היא, וליכא למיתש דלמא שלפא ומחויא דלא מגליא שוקה: **כבלים טמאין.** משפחה אחת היתה בירושלים שהיו פסיעותיהן גסות והיו בתוליהן נושרים, והטילו שלשלת בין בירית לבירית שבשוקיה ונעשה כבלים כדי שלא יהיו פסיעותיהן גסות ולא יהיו בתוליהן נושרים, הילכך שלשלת תשמיש דאדם הוא ולא תשמיש כלי לפיכך היא מקבלת טומאה: **ואין יוצאין בהם.** דלמא שלפא לשלשלת שהיא של זהב ומחויא, דכי שקלא לשלשלת לא מגליא שוקה שהרי בירית במקומה עומדת: (ה) **חוטי שער.** שער תלוש שעושתה אותו כמין חוטין וקולעת בהן שערה, או אפילו קשרה אותן על פדחתה קשר מהודק, דלא דמי לחוטי צמר וחוטי פשתן דלבטיל, לפי שהמים נכנסים בהם, ואי מתרמיא לה טבילה מינה צריכה שתתירם ולא אתיא לאתויינהו: **בין משלה בין משל חברתה בין משל בהמה.** צריכי, דאי תנא משלה משום דלא מאיס לה אבל חברתה דמאיס לה

יד אברהם

Messianic era. The prophet says that not only will wars cease to be fought but that even the very weapons of war will cease to exist (*they shall beat their swords into plowshares, etc.*). We therefore see that the image of a man is not enhanced by carrying a weapon, else the weapons would survive in the form of adornments (*Rav* from *Gem.* 63a).

The Sages do not represent a third view. They merely explain the view of the first *Tanna* (*Tos. Yom Tov*).

The halachah is in accordance with the first *Tanna* (*Rambam*).

בִּירִית טְהוֹרָה — *A garter is not susceptible to tumah-contamination* (lit. *it is tahor*),

It is not susceptible to *tumah*-contamination, since it is not a garment in its own right, but is merely an article that serves another garment, namely the stocking. This is analogous to rings that serve vessels, that are also not susceptible to contamination (*Rav*). [See comm. to 5:1.]

וְיוֹצְאִין בָּהּ בַּשַּׁבָּת — *and we may go out with it on the Sabbath;*

They are considered bona-fide garments. Additionally, there is no danger the wearer will remove them, since to do so would be to bare her leg (*Rav*).[1]

כְּבָלִים — *ankle chains*

There was a family in Jerusalem whose girls were accustomed to walking with long strides, thereby destroy-

---

1. [The crowning glory of the Jewish woman is her צְנִיעוּת *modesty*. Throughout all generations, Jewish woman are scrupulous in their observance of these laws, not to bare any part of the body usually covered. See below 8:3, that woman would go veiled, with one eye covered. See also *Kesubos* 7:6, regarding penalties for married women who go out with their hair or their arms exposed, or otherwise behave immodestly.]

6
5

A garter is not susceptible to *tumah*-contamination, and we may go out with it on the Sabbath; ankle chains are susceptible to *tumah*-contamination, and they may not go out with them on the Sabbath.

5. A woman may go out with bands of hair, whether of her own [hair], or of her companion's [hair],

YAD AVRAHAM

ing the internal membranes that are signs of their virginity. They therefore hung golden chains connecting one garter to the other, thus forcing the girls to take smaller steps (*Rav* from *Gem.* 63b).

טְמֵאִין, — *are susceptible to tumah-contamination,*

Since the chain is used to serve the body, not another item of apparel, in contrast to the garters mentioned above, it is susceptible to ritual contamination (*Rav; Rashi* 63b).

וְאֵין יוֹצְאִין בָּהֶם בַּשַּׁבָּת. — *and they may not go out with them on the Sabbath.*

Since the chains are made of gold and can be removed without exposing the leg, we fear that the woman may remove them to show her friend (*Rav* from *Rashi* 63b).

5.

The following mishnah delineates those items of apparel with which a woman may go out on the Sabbath.

יוֹצְאָה אִשָּׁה — *A woman may go out*

I.e., a woman may go out on the Sabbath even into a public domain (*Rashi* and *Ran* later in the mishnah, s.v. לְחָצֵר).

בְּחוּטֵי שֵׂעָר, — *with bands of hair,*

I.e., with bands made of human hair added now as an artificial braid. Unlike the bands of wool and linen, mentioned in mishnah 1, bands of human hair allow the water to pass through, and may therefore be worn during טְבִילָה, *immersion*. [I.e., if they are wound around her own hair. If they are fastened, however, they must be removed (*Taz, Yoreh Deah* 198:6).] Consequently, they do not necessitate removal on such occasions and we need not fear that a woman will carry them in her hand while walking in a public domain (*Rav*).

בֵּין מִשֶּׁלָּהּ, — *whether of her own [hair],*

If the bands were made out of her own hair which has been previously cut and made into a hairpiece they are certainly not repulsive to her, and she is not apt to remove them and carry them in a public domain (*Rav* from *Gem.* 64b).

בֵּין מִשֶּׁל חֲבֶרְתָּהּ, — *or of her companion's [hair],*

I.e., even if they were made from another woman's hair and may be repulsive to her, we do not fear that she will take them off and carry them in a public domain (*Rav* from *Gem.* ibid.).

[It may be repulsive to her out of worry that the other woman may have been afflicted with a disease of the scalp that causes bald spots (*Tos. Yom Tov; Rambam*).]

בֵּין מִשֶּׁל בְּהֵמָה; — *or of an animal's [hair];*

Even if the bands are of horsehair,

שבת ו/ה

בְּהֵמָה; וּבְטוֹטֶפֶת, וּבְסַנְבּוּטִין, בִּזְמַן שֶׁהֵן תְּפוּרִין; בְּכָבוּל וּבְפֵאָה נָכְרִית לֶחָצֵר;

ר׳ עובדיה מברטנורא

אימא ניחוש דלמא שלפא לה ואתיא לאתויינהו, ולי תנא של תבדתה משום דבת מינה היא לא מינכר ולא מחייכי עלה ומשום הכי ליכא למיחש דלמא שלפא ואתיא לאתויי, אבל דבהמה דלאו בת מינה היא ומינכר אימא דלמא שלפא לה ואתיא לאתויי, צריכא: **בזמן שהן תפורין.** לשבכה שבראשה, דתו לא שלפא לה לאתויי: **לחצר.** אכבול ופאה נכרית קאי, דאסרוה לעיל למיפק ביה לרשות הרבים, והשתא אשמעינן דלחצר מותר: **פאה נכרית.** אשה שאין לה רוב שער, לוקחת שער נשים אחרות ומשימה בראשה ונראה כאילו הוא שערה:

יד אברהם

which does not match her own, she may, nevertheless, wear them, and we do not fear that she will be ridiculed, causing her to remove them and then carry them through the street (*Rav* from *Gem.* ibid.).

Although a woman may wear even horsehair, a young woman may not wear bands of white hair taken from an old woman, nor may an old woman wear bands of black hair taken from a young woman (*Gem.* 64b). Since these bands cause her to look different than her age, we fear that she may be scoffed at by those who see her, causing her to remove the bands and carry them. According to *Rambam's* alternate explanation of the *Gemara*, the rule is that though a young woman may not wear bands of white hair of an old woman, an old woman may wear bands of the black hair of a young woman; since it is pleasing to her to appear youthful, she is unlikely to be offended by any remarks about that youthful appearance (*Hil. Shabbos* 19:9; *Maggid Mishneh*; *Lechem Mishneh*).

וּבְטוֹטֶפֶת, — *or with a frontlet,*

A gold plate worn over the forehead (see comm. to mishnah 1).

וּבְסַנְבּוּטִין, — *or with head bangles,*

Ribbons attached to the frontlet, that hang down over the temples (see comm. to mishnah 1).

בִּזְמַן שֶׁהֵן תְּפוּרִין; — *when they are sewn;*

If these adornments are sewn to her hat, there is then no fear that she will remove them to show to her companions (*Rav;* see also comm. to mishnah 1).

בְּכָבוּל — *or with a forehead pad*

A cloth pad, worn under the frontlet to protect the forehead from irritation. Sometimes a woman wears this pad without the frontlet (see comm. to mishnah 1).

וּבְפֵאָה נָכְרִית — *or with a wig* (lit. *strange locks*)

A piece made of human tresses and worn by women with thinning hair to give the appearance of a full head of hair (*Rashi; Rav; Meiri*).

לֶחָצֵר; — *into a courtyard;*

I.e., though the forehead pad and the wig may not be worn when going out to the public domain,[1] they may be worn when going into a courtyard.

---

1. *Tiferes Yisrael* explains that the woman would wear the wig atop another headress which covered her hair. Therefore, we fear that she may remove it if people scoff at her, and she may not wear it in a public domain. He prohibits wigs alone because of *maris ayin*, i.e., appearance of going bareheaded. *Shiltei Giborim*, however, permits it. This is the basis for

6
5
or of an animal's [hair]; or with a frontlet, or with head bangles, when they are sewn; or with a forehead pad or with a wig into a courtyard;

YAD AVRAHAM

The items mentioned earlier in this mishnah may be worn even when going out to a public domain (*Rashi; Ran*). They are items which a woman would never take off in public, since it would necessitate uncovering her hair (as explained in mishnah 1). The last two are items which she might remove — the forehead pad to show to a friend (since it was also an adornment), the wig because it looked awkward on her and which she might remove if ridiculed by those who see her. They should, therefore, really be prohibited even in a courtyard, the same as all the prohibited items of this chapter. The Rabbis, however, did not want to entirely forbid wearing adornments for fear a woman might become plain and unattractive in the eyes of her husband. They therefore permitted these two items in a courtyard (since no Torah law would be transgressed even were she to carry).

The forehead pad mentioned here is also one of the adornments enumerated in mishnah 1 in the list of ornaments which a woman may not wear when going out. As was explained there, all the other items enumerated in that mishnah are proscribed from being worn even when going out to a courtyard (which is common to several dwellings with the exception of the forehead pad). The phrase which concludes that mishnah, *into a public domain*, refers only to the last-mentioned item on that list, namely, the forehead pad. This explanation of that mishnah is proven by the wording of the mishnah here which declares the permissibility of wearing adornments into a חָצֵר, *courtyard*, only vis-à-vis the forehead pad and the wig but not vis-à-vis any of the other adornments cited in mishnah 1.

As was stated in mishnah 1, there is a difference of opinion as to whether the חָצֵר, *courtyard*, mentioned here refers even to one with an *eruv chatzeiros* or only to one without. See there for full discussion.

There is another opinion mentioned in the *Gemara* (64b) in the name of R' Yishmael son of R' Yose (who was a *Tanna*) which disputes the ruling of the mishnah and states that all adornments may be worn into a courtyard and are forbidden only when going into a public domain. Most authorities (*Rambam, Rif* and others) rule in accordance with our mishnah. *Tosafos* (ad loc.) rules in accordance with the opinion of R' Yishmael son of R' Yose.

◈§ Today's Custom

According to all opinions, women may not wear adornments in a public domain or even in a *karmelis*, a semipublic domain (see General Introduction to this tractate), or a courtyard that has no *eruv*. Yet women since the times of the *Geonim* have been known to wear jewelry even in the street, and the Rabbis

widespread practice to wear wigs in the street, although many authorities are against it. See *Responsa Teshuvah MeAhavah,* 48. [If we assume that in those days they wore something else covering their hair in addition to the wig, we can understand why the Rabbis proscribed wearing it in a public domain lest the wearer remove it and carry it. Nowadays, however, when women wear wigs alone, they would surely not remove them in the street. This may be the justification for wearing wigs in a public domain on the Sabbath.]

שבת ו/ה

בְּמוֹךְ שֶׁבְּאָזְנָהּ, וּבְמוֹךְ שֶׁבְּסַנְדָּלָהּ, וּבְמוֹךְ שֶׁהִתְקִינָה לְנִדָּתָהּ; בְּפִלְפֵּל, וּבְגַרְגִּיר מֶלַח, וּבְכָל דָּבָר שֶׁתִּתֵּן לְתוֹךְ פִּיהָ, וּבִלְבַד שֶׁלֹּא תִתֵּן לְכַתְּחִלָּה בַּשַּׁבָּת —

ר' עובדיה מברטנורא

במוך שבאזניה. שנותנת לבלוע ליחה של אוזן החן: **שבסנדלה.** שלא יזיק הסנדל לכף רגלה: **לנדתה.** באותו מקום שיבלעו בו הדם ולא יטנף בגדיה, ואף על פי שאינו קשור, דאי נפל לא אתיא לאתויי מפני מאיסותו. אבל מוך שבאזנה ושבסנדלה לא תלא בו אלא אם כן קשור ומהודק: **בפלפל.** שנותנת בפיה מפני ריח הפה: **ובגרגיר מלח.** שנותנת לרפואת חולי השינים:

יד אברהם

have searched for the justification of this practice. R' *Baruch* explains that during the time of the Talmud, when cities with streets qualifying as public domains, i.e., 16 cubits wide, and traversed by 600,000 people each day, were common, the Rabbis prohibited wearing jewelry in a *karmelis*, lest they wear it in a public domain too. In our times, however, when such streets are rare and virtually all our streets are only a *karmelis*, they did not prohibit wearing jewelry in a *karmelis* since wearing jewelry in those streets will almost never lead to wearing jewelry in a real public domain (*Tos.* 64 quoted in *Shulchan Aruch* 303:18). Many dispute this reasoning on the grounds that: (a) many authorities do not require 600,000 passersby to qualify a street as a public domain (*Beur Halachah* 303:18); (b) in our times, too, there are streets that do meet these qualifications (*Aruch HaShulchan*).

Others justify the custom on the basis that the Rabbis promulgated their ban on wearing jewelry on the Sabbath only in Talmudic times when jewelry was rare, and women did not wear it on weekdays. There was then, therefore, the apprehension that when they would meet their friends on the Sabbath they would remove their adornments to show them off. In our times, however, when jewelry is more common and is worn even during the week, we have no fear that they will remove it to show to their friends (*Tos.* quoting *R' Shimshon* who found this in the name of *R' Sar Shalom*). *Aruch HaShulchan* compares all jewelry in our time to a crown, worn only by women of rank (*Gem.* 59b). Since only women of rank wear this adornment, and they do not remove their jewelry to show their friends, the Rabbis did not proscribe its being worn. In our times, all women fit into the category of women of rank. He adds that in the time of the Talmud women did not go out of the house all week. Consequently, they never met their friends. Moreover, they did not visit their friends in their homes even on the Sabbath. There was no women's gallery in the synagogue where they could display their finery. The only place they met their friends was on the street. There was, therefore, a great probability that they would remove their jewelry to show it to their friends while meeting in the street. In our times, however, women go out and visit their friends even during the week. Moreover, they see each other in the synagogue. There is, therefore, no danger that they will remove their jewelry in the street to show it to their friends. For other reasons see *Tosafos* ibid. and *Shulchan Aruch* ibid.

בְּמוֹךְ שֶׁבְּאָזְנָהּ, — *with wadding (that is) in her ear,* — Wool or cotton inserted in the ear to absorb the wax when it runs (*Rav; Rashi*).

6
5
with wadding in her ear, or with wadding in her sandal, or with wadding she prepared for her menses; with a pepper, or with a globule of salt, or with anything that she will put into her mouth, provided that she does not put [it in] initially on the Sabbath —

YAD AVRAHAM

וּבְמוֹךְ שֶׁבְּסַנְדָּלָהּ, — *or with wadding (that is) in her sandal,*

Inserted to prevent the sandal from irritating the sole of the foot (*Rav*).

Alternatively, it is more comfortable to walk on the wadding than on the hard sole of the sandal (*Rashi*).

וּבְמוֹךְ שֶׁהִתְקִינָה לְנִדָּתָהּ; — *or with wadding (that) she prepared for her menses;*

I.e., she may go out with the wadding prepared to absorb the menstrual flow, so that it not soil her clothing (*Rashi; Rav*).

Other authorities contend that if her sole intention is to spare her clothing, she may not go out with the wadding on the Sabbath. The mishnah permits it only if she does so to prevent the blood from falling on her skin, where it will dry and cause her discomfort (*Tif. Yis.; Tos.* 64b; *Rama* 303:15).

To go out with wadding in one's ear or sandal is permissible only if it is fastened securely, lest it fall out, and possibly result in her carrying it. To go out with the wadding prepared to absorb the menses, however, is permissible even if it is not tied. Since it is repulsive, even if it were to fall out she would surely not pick it up and carry it through the public domain (*Rav* from *Gem.* ibid.).

בְּפִלְפֵּל, — *with a pepper,*

A woman with bad breath may go out with a pepper in her mouth to combat the halitosis (*Rav; Rashi*).

וּבְגַרְגִּיר מֶלַח, — *or with a globule of salt,*

Used to alleviate a toothache (*Rashi; Rav*).

וּבְכָל דָּבָר שֶׁתִּתֵּן לְתוֹךְ פִּיהָ, — *or with anything that she will put into her mouth,*

I.e., with any spice that she puts into her mouth, such as ginger or cinnamon (*Tif. Yis.* from *Gem.* 65a).

The version appearing in the mishnah in the *Gemara* reads: שֶׁנִּתֵּן, *that was put.* *Rashi's* version reads: שֶׁנְּתָנָהּ, *that she put,* i.e., that she put into her mouth before the Sabbath. These two versions appear to be more accurate than our version, since, being in the past tense, they imply that she had already put the spices into her mouth in the past, i.e., before the Sabbath; not so our version, which is in the future tense (see next paragraph).

וּבִלְבַד שֶׁלֹּא תִתֵּן לְכַתְּחִלָּה בַּשַּׁבָּת — *provided that she does not put [it in] initially on the Sabbath —*

Since these are remedies, one is forbidden to take them, just as one is forbidden to take any medicine on the Sabbath [the particulars of this rule will be discussed at length in 14:3,4] (*Tos.,* quoting *R' Poras; Shenos Eliyahu*).

Tosefos R' Akiva questions this in light of *Tosefta Shabbos* 13:7, which draws a distinction between chewing a type of syrup for remedy and doing so to conceal halitosis (the latter not being considered a malady and its "cure," therefore, not a "remedy").

Others explain that one is prohibited to put spices in his mouth on the Sabbath and go out with them, since it may appear to others as though his true

שבת ו/ו

וְאִם נָפַל, לֹא תַחֲזִיר. שֵׁן תּוֹתֶבֶת וְשֵׁן שֶׁל זָהָב — רַבִּי מַתִּיר, וַחֲכָמִים אוֹסְרִים.

[ו] **יוֹצְאָה** בְּסֶלַע שֶׁעַל הַצִּינִית. הַבָּנוֹת קְטַנּוֹת יוֹצְאוֹת בְּחוּטִין וַאֲפִלּוּ בְּקִיסְמִין

ר' עובדיה מברטנורא

שֵׁן תּוֹתֶבֶת. עשויה בלחיים במקום השן שנפל לה: **וְשֵׁן שֶׁל זָהָב.** שן שנשתנה מראיתו מחמת עפוש, מכסה אותו בזהב: **רַבִּי מַתִּיר.** לצאת בה, דלא שלפה ומחוייא שלא לגלות מומה: **וַחֲכָמִים אוֹסְרִים.** כיון שהוא משונה משאר שיניה, דלמא מחייכי עלה ושלפא לה ואתיא לאתויי. והלכה כחכמים: (ו) **בְּסֶלַע.** מטבע שיש עליו צורה: **שֶׁעַל הַצִּינִית.** מכה שתחת פרסות הרגל, וקושרים בה מטבע שיש עליו צורה לרפואה: **הַבָּנוֹת יוֹצְאוֹת בְּחוּטִין.** הקטנות מנקבות את אזניהן ואין טושין להן נזמין עד שיגדלו, ונותנין חוטין או קסמים באזניהן שלא יסתמו אזניהן: **וַאֲפִלּוּ בְּקִסָמִים.** רבותא קאמר, אף על גב דלאו תכשיט של נוי הוא, אורחייהו בהכי ולאו משאוי הוא:

יד אברהם

The translation follows *Rav* who states: A tooth covered with gold, to conceal the change in its appearance caused by decay.

רַבִּי מַתִּיר — *Rabbi* [*Yehudah HaNassi*] *permits* [*them*],

Rabbi permits a woman to go out with a false tooth or a gold crown. Since her own tooth is disfigured, she would not remove the false tooth or the crown so as not to reveal her blemish (*Rav*).

[רַבִּי יְהוּדָה הַנָּשִׂיא, *R' Yehudah HaNassi*, is referred to as רַבִּי, *Rabbi*, throughout the Mishnah.]

וַחֲכָמִים אוֹסְרִים. — *but the Sages prohibit* [*them*].

Since people may ridicule her, she may remove them from her mouth and carry them (*Rav*).

Alternatively, we are dealing with a false tooth made of wood. Since both the false tooth and the gold crown are different from all her other teeth, the Sages fear that her friends may ask to see them, and she will remove them from her mouth to oblige. Rabbi, however, contends that since she is embar-

intention is to transport them. This stipulation therefore applies to the wadding in the ear and in the sandal, as well (*Tos. Yom Tov* from *Tos.*). [Since all of these are being taken out in the mouth in order to remedy or prevent injury to the body they are considered a part of the body and not a burden, in the same manner as garments (see prefatory note to this chapter). They are forbidden in this instance only because they *appear* to be taken out for the purpose of being transported. If she inserts them before the Sabbath, however, it is not obvious that she is carrying them on the Sabbath.]

וְאִם נָפַל, — *and if it fell* [*out*], [I.e., on the Sabbath.]

לֹא תַחֲזִיר. — *she may not put* [*it*] *back*.

[For the same reasons that she may not put this item in initially, she may not put it back if it fell out. This is true only if it fell on the ground. If she held it in her hand, however, she may put it back (*Tos. Yom Tov*).]

שֵׁן תּוֹתֶבֶת וְשֵׁן שֶׁל זָהָב — *A false tooth or a tooth with a gold crown* (lit. *a golden tooth*)

6 and if it fell [out], she may not put [it] back.

A false tooth or a tooth with a gold crown — Rabbi [Yehudah HaNassi] permits [them], but the Sages prohibit [them].

6. She may go out with the *sela* that is on a wound [on the sole of her foot].

Young girls may go out with the threads or even with the slivers that are in their ears.

YAD AVRAHAM

rassed by her deformity, she will not comply with their wishes (*Ran*).

Rashi understands these two cases as one. *A false tooth of gold, Rabbi permits but the Sages prohibit.* I.e., only if the false tooth is made of gold, which differs in appearance from all her other teeth, do the Sages fear that she will be tempted to remove it from her mouth because of ridicule. If the false tooth looks natural, however, even the Sages permit it. *Rashi* adds that even if we were to read the mishnah as referring to two separate cases, the false tooth of the mishnah would still not be a subject of dispute, since it refers to a natural-looking tooth replacing one she lost.

Thus, the mishnah is to be read: *A woman may go out with bands of hair ... or a with a globule of salt ... [or] with a false tooth. A false tooth, Rabbi permits but the Sages prohibit* (*Rashi*).

A silver crown, which is close in color to her other teeth, may be worn, even according to the Sages. Since she would not be the object of ridicule, she would have no reason to remove it (*Gem.* 65 as interpreted by *Rashi* citing his teachers). *Rashi* himself explains that a gold tooth may not be worn. Since it is expensive, the Sages fear that she may take it out of her mouth to show her friends. A silver tooth, however, since it is not unusual, does not present any such fear.

[Just as the Rabbis did not prohibit wearing jewelry for men, since they are not prone to show off their ornaments, so did they not prohibit going out with a gold tooth (see *Yerushalmi* 6:1). According to *Rashi's* rabbis, we may say that men are not as sensitive as women, and do not tend to remove a false tooth or a gold crown because of ridicule.]

6.

יוֹצְאָה — *She may go out*

[Mishnah 6 continues the list of articles with which a woman may go out, even into a public domain.]

בְּסֶלַע — *with a sela*

A coin of a certain denomination.

שֶׁעַל הַצִּינִית — *that is on a wound [on the sole of her foot].*

As a remedy for wounds on the sole of the foot [calluses or bunions (*Rif* as explained by *Aruch HaShalem*)], an embossed *sela* coin would be bound to the wound (*Rav* from *Gem.* 65a).

הַבָּנוֹת קְטַנּוֹת יוֹצְאוֹת בְּחוּטִין וַאֲפִלּוּ בְּקִיסָמִין שֶׁבְּאָזְנֵיהֶן. — *Young girls may go out with the threads or even with the slivers that are in their ears.*

The ears of young girls were pierced but earrings were not made for them

שבת ו/ז

שֶׁבְּאָזְנֵיהֶן. עַרְבִיּוֹת יוֹצְאוֹת רְעוּלוֹת, וּמָדִיּוֹת פְּרוּפוֹת. וְכָל אָדָם, אֶלָּא שֶׁדִּבְּרוּ חֲכָמִים בַּהֹוֶה.

[ז] **פּוֹרֶפֶת** עַל הָאֶבֶן, וְעַל הָאֱגוֹז, וְעַל הַמַּטְבֵּעַ, וּבִלְבַד שֶׁלֹּא תִפְרֹף לְכַתְּחִלָּה בַּשַּׁבָּת.

ר׳ עובדיה מברטנורא

עַרְבִיּוֹת. בְּנוֹת יִשְׂרָאֵל שֶׁבְּעַרְבִיָּא: **יוֹצְאוֹת רְעוּלוֹת.** מְעוּטָפוֹת בְּרֹאשָׁן וּפְנֵיהֶן מְכוּסוֹת חוּץ מִן הָעֵינַיִם, כְּדֶרֶךְ הָעַרְבִיּוֹת: **מָדִיּוֹת. פְּרוּפוֹת.** בְּנוֹת יִשְׂרָאֵל שֶׁבְּמָדַי: **פְּרוּפוֹת.** שֶׁמִּתְעַטְּפוֹת בַּטַּלִּית וְתוֹלוֹת רְצוּעָה בִּשְׂפָתָהּ אַחַת כְּנֶגֶד אוֹטָרָהּ וּבִשְׂפָתָהּ הַשֵּׁנִית כּוֹרֶכֶת אֶבֶן אוֹ אֱגוֹז וְקוֹשֶׁרֶת הָרְצוּעָה בַּכֶּרֶךְ וְאֵין הַטַּלִּית נוֹפֶלֶת מֵעָלֶיהָ: (ז) **פוֹרֶפֶת.** מְחַבֶּרֶת. תַּרְגּוּם קְרָסִים, פּוֹרְפִין: **וּבִלְבַד שֶׁלֹּא תִפְרֹף לְכַתְּחִלָּה.** אַמַּטְבֵּעַ לְחוּדֵיהּ קָאֵי, שֶׁלֹּא תִפְרֹף לְכַתְּחִלָּה עַל הַמַּטְבֵּעַ מִפְּנֵי שֶׁאָסוּר לְטַלְטְלוֹ:

יד אברהם

until they became older. Threads or slivers were inserted into the holes so that they not close up in the interim (*Rav; Rashi*).

Even though the slivers are in no way considered adornments, they may, nevertheless, be worn, since they are worn all the time (*Rav; Rashi*). Should they fall out, there was little chance the girls would carry them since they were of little value (*Tif. Yis.*).

Others explain this as threads or bands worn around the neck. If they are not colored, they may be worn in the street. If they are colored, however, we fear that she may remove them to show to her companions (*Rambam*).

Rashi quotes another interpretation that the threads are worn to braid the hair, as in mishnah 1. Since it is unusual for young girls to immerse in a *mikveh*, there is no reason for them to remove the threads and carry them in the public domain. [Before the age of menstruation, they did not come under the prohibition of wearing threads in the hair on the Sabbath.] *Rashi* rejects this interpretation, however, since it *was* common for young girls to immerse in mishnaic times when people observed laws of *taharah;* moreover, the word ''even''

does not apply if we are discussing two entirely unrelated cases. [The latter difficulty pointed out by *Rashi* is also inherent in *Rambam's* commentary. Perhaps *Rambam's* reading of the mishnah omitted the word וַאֲפִלּוּ, *even. Shinuyei Nuschaos* cites such a variant reading.]

עַרְבִיּוֹת יוֹצְאוֹת רְעוּלוֹת, — *Arabian women may go out veiled,*

Since Arabian women customarily appear in public with their faces veiled, leaving only their eyes exposed, Jewish women living in Arabia may go out into the public domain on the Sabbath while wearing such veils (*Rav; Rashi*). We do not fear her removing the veil since the custom of these women is to keep their faces covered at all times.

וּמָדִיּוֹת — *and Median women [may go out]*

[Media was in what is today Northwestern Iran.]

פְּרוּפוֹת. — *with their cloaks fastened over their shoulders.*

Median women wore a cloak which had a short strap attached to one of its upper corners. A stone, nut or coin would be wrapped into the opposite

Arabian women may go out veiled, and Median women [may go out] with their cloaks fastened over their shoulders. [Indeed] all people [may do so], but the Sages spoke of the actual custom.

7. She may fasten [her cloak] with a stone, or with a nut, or with a coin, provided she does not fasten [it] initially on the Sabbath.

YAD AVRAHAM

upper corner. The cloak was then fastened by tying the strap around the stone [which functioned as a button]. Since this was the usual manner of dress in Media, the Jewish women of that land were permitted to wear such cloaks on the Sabbath and were not considered to be carrying the makeshift button (*Rav; Rashi*).

וְכָל אָדָם, — [*Indeed*] *all people* [*may do so*],

[Not only Arabian and Median women are permitted to do so, but so too may anyone else.]

אֶלָּא שֶׁדִּבְּרוּ חֲכָמִים בַּהוֶֹה — *but the Sages spoke of the actual custom* [lit. *in the present*].

[The Sages referred to Arabian and Median women only because it was the well-known custom of those women to wear these garments. Since these are legitimate garments, even those who usually do not wear them may do so.]

7.

In the preceding mishnah we learned that the women may go out with their cloaks fastened over their shoulders with makeshift buttons. Mishnah 7 delineates the materials which may be used for such buttons and the circumstances under which they may be utilized on the Sabbath.

פּוֹרֶפֶת — *She may fasten* [*her cloak*]

I.e., she may loop the straps around the makeshift button as a means of fastening the cloak around her neck.

She is not considered to be carrying the makeshift button. Since it serves as a functional part of her garment, it is viewed as a part of that garment and not as an object in its own right being transported.

עַל הָאֶבֶן, וְעַל הָאֱגוֹז, וְעַל הַמַּטְבֵּעַ, — *with a* (lit., *upon the*) *stone, or with a* (lit., *upon the*) *nut, or with a* (lit., *upon the*) *coin,*

As explained above, she may use any of these items as a makeshift button.

Unlike the case in mishnah 5, in which we prohibit carrying a pepper in the mouth since it appears as a ruse to carry the pepper in the public domain, it is obvious here that the woman needs the article to keep her cloak fastened (*Tos. Yom Tov* from *Tos.* 64b).

וּבִלְבַד שֶׁלֹּא תִפְרֹף לְכַתְּחִלָּה בְּשַׁבָּת. — *provided she does not fasten* [*it*] *initially on the Sabbath.*

This statement refers only to a coin. If a coin serves as a button, she may not button it on the Sabbath, since coins are מֻקְצֶה, *set apart from Sanbath use.* See 17:4 and General Introduction. If she was already wearing

שבת
ו/ח

[ח] **הַקִּטֵּעַ** יוֹצֵא בְקַב שֶׁלּוֹ – דִּבְרֵי רַבִּי מֵאִיר. וְרַבִּי יוֹסֵי אוֹסֵר. וְאִם יֵשׁ לוֹ בֵּית קִבּוּל כְּתוּתִים, טָמֵא.

ר' עובדיה מברטנורא

(ח) **הקטע.** שנקטעה רגלו: **יוצא בקב שלו.** עושים לו כמין דפוס רגל וחוקק בו מעט לשום ראש שוקו בתוכו, ואינו נסמך עליו. ומותר בו למנעל דידיה הוי: **ורבי יוסי אוסר.** דלאו תכשיט הוא. והלכה כרבי יוסי: **ואם יש לו בית קבול כתותין.** שנחקק בו כדי קבול של כתיתין דקין ומוכין להניח ראש שוקו עליהן, מקבל טומאה מדרס. אבל אם אין לו אלא בית קבול שוקו בלבד

יד אברהם

the garment buttoned up before the Sabbath, she may go out wearing it on the Sabbath (*Rav* from *Gem.* 65b).

Even though stones are *muktzeh* as well, if they are designated before the Sabbath for Sabbath use they are not *muktzeh* (*Rashi* 65b). [The difference between a stone and a coin is that unlike a coin, a stone has no intrinsic value. A person who designates a properly shaped stone for use as a button will likely continue to use it as such, or at least not decide to use it as something else. It *becomes*, to all intents and purposes, a button, and consequently is no longer *muktzeh*. A coin, on the other hand, though momentarily designated for use as a button, will likely not continue to be used as a button since its value as a coin exceeds its value as a button. It will likely revert to being used as a coin. Therefore, though temporarily designated as a button, it must continue to be considered primarily as currency. Therefore, it does not lose its classification as *muktzeh*.]

[Though as regards the laws of *muktzeh* we view the coin as currency, we do not view it as a burden as regards the prohibition against carrying on the Sabbath. In that respect, we continue to view it as a part of the garment. This is because the delineation of what is a garment and what is a burden is decided on the basis of its present use. The delineation of what is or is not *muktzeh* is based on its general function, which takes into account both present and future use.]

If, however, one designated the coin for permanent use as a button, it becomes a button and is no longer *muktzeh* (*Mishnah Berurah* 303:74). Similarly, if one actually tied it to the garment before the Sabbath, thus making it physically part of the garment (rather than merely designating it for use as such), it is considered as a button and is not deemed *muktzeh* (ibid.) [see 17:4 for further clarification].

8.

הַקִּטֵּעַ יוֹצֵא בְקַב שֶׁלּוֹ – דִּבְרֵי רַבִּי מֵאִיר. — *An amputee may go out with his wooden foot — [these are] the words of R' Meir.*

This refers to an artificial foot constructed from wood, into which the amputee's stump fits. Though he does not use this wooden foot for support, he may still go out with it on the Sabbath, since it is considered his shoe (*Rav; Rashi*).

וְרַבִּי יוֹסֵי אוֹסֵר. — *But R' Yose prohibits [it].*

He does not consider it an adornment (*Rav; Rashi*).

Since he cannot walk on it without using crutches (which he may use on the Sabbath), and he wears it merely to

משניות / שבת – פרק ו: במה אשה [158]

8. An amputee may go out with his wooden foot — [these are] the words of R' Meir. But R' Yose prohibits [it]. If it has a cavity for pads, it is susceptible to *tumah*-contamination.

YAD AVRAHAM

conceal the fact that his foot is missing, it is not considered an adornment or a shoe, and he may not go out with it on the Sabbath (*Tos. Yom Tov* from *Beis Yosef* quoting *R' Yerucham*).

Others explain that R' Yose prohibits going out with the wooden foot, since it may fall off, and the cripple may carry it (*Tos.*).

The halachah is in accordance with R' Yose (*Rav*).

Since we are dealing with wooden feet and supports used by cripples, the mishnah delineates their status as regards *tumah*-contamination, specifically in regard to the following two laws: (a) The law that wooden vessels are not susceptible to *tumah* [even when in direct contact with *tumah*] unless they are receptacles. פְּשׁוּטֵי כְּלֵי עֵץ, *flat wooden vessels*, which have no cavity in which articles may be contained, are not susceptible to contamination (see *Keilim* 2:1). The mishnah delineates which of these various types of gear fall into this category. (b) Their status as מִדְרָס [*midras*], an article which *supports* the weight of a זָב, *zav* [one who experienced a gonorrheal issue (see above 1:3)], or a נִדָּה, *niddah* [menstruant]. The word מִדְרָס, from דרס, *to step*, means *something stepped on.*

◆§ **Midras Contamination**

In delineating the *tumah* of a *zav*, the Torah states: וְהַיּשֵׁב . . . וְאִישׁ אֲשֶׁר יִגַּע בְּמִשְׁכָּבוֹ עַל־הַכְּלִי אֲשֶׁר־יֵשֵׁב עָלָיו הַזָּב יְכַבֵּס בְּגָדָיו, *and a person who touches his bed . . . or who sits on the seat* (lit. *utensil*) *upon which the zav sits shall wash his clothes* (*Lev.* 15:5-6). The wording used in the case of the *niddah* is almost identical (*Lev.* 15:20-22). From these verses we see that such articles as the bed, couch, and chair of the *zav* or *niddah* acquire the same level of contamination as the person from whom the *tumah* emanates. One who touches any of these articles must immerse not only himself, but also his garments. The mishnah calls the contamination of objects upon which one of these people rests or leans by the term *midras*. One may contaminate through *midras* in any of five ways: by standing, sitting, or lying on an object, using leverage to move it (for example a seesaw or balance scale), or leaning against it (*Zavim* 2:4). [By specifying bed and seat, the Torah implies that *midras* contamination only applies to articles which are intended as chairs or similar supports for people. A makeshift seat, such as an inverted pot (about which a worker may say, "Arise! Let us do our job!"), does not acquire *midras*-contamination (*Gem.* 59a).]

וְאִם יֵשׁ לוֹ בֵּית קִבּוּל כְּתוּתִים, — *If it has a cavity for pads*,

I.e., padding upon which to rest his stump (*Rav*).

Rambam explains this to mean that there is room for the jagged edges of the stump (where the amputation was not performed smoothly).

טָמֵא. — *it is susceptible to tumah-contamination* (lit. *is contaminated*).

Since the padding can be carried in this wooden foot, it is deemed a receptacle, and is, consequently, susceptible to contamination. If, however, it has

שבת ו/ח

סָמוֹכוֹת שֶׁלּוֹ טְמֵאִין מִדְרָס, וְיוֹצְאִין בָּהֶן בַּשַּׁבָּת, וְנִכְנָסִין בָּהֶן בָּעֲזָרָה.
כִּסֵּא וְסָמוֹכוֹת שֶׁלּוֹ טְמֵאִין מִדְרָס, וְאֵין יוֹצְאִין בָּהֶם בַּשַּׁבָּת, וְאֵין נִכְנָסִין בָּהֶן בָּעֲזָרָה.

--- ר׳ עובדיה מברטנורא ---

בלא כתיתין, לאו בית קבול הוא לטומאה והוה ליה כפשוטי כלי עץ. דדומיא דשק בעינן דקבול שלו עשוי לטלטל על ידי מה שנותנין בו, אבל שוקו אינו מטולטל על גבי הכלי: **סמוכות שלו.** יש קטע שתי רגליו והולך על שוקיו ועל ארכובותיו ועושה סמוכות של עור בשוקיו: **טמאים מדרס.** אם זב הוא, דהא לסמיכות גופו עבדי ומדרס הן ונעשו אב הטומאה: **ויוצאין בהם בשבת.** דתכשיט דידיה הן: **ונכנסין בהן לעזרה.** ואף על גב דתנן לא יכנס להר הבית במנעלו, הני לאו מנעל מיקרו דלאו ברחש רגליו הן: **בסא.** יש קטע שיבשו וכווצו גידי שוקיו ואף על ארכובותיו אינו יכול לילך ועושה כמין כסא נמוך ויושב עליו וכשהוא מהלך נסמך על ידי בספסלים קטנים ותוקר גופו מן הארץ ונדחף לפניו וחוזר ונח על אחוריו והכסא קשור לאחוריו: **סמוכות.** של אותו קיטע, עושה לו סמוכות של עור או של עץ לראשי שוקיו או רגליו התלויין, וכשהוא נשען על ידי תוקר טלמו נשען גם על רגליו קלה: **ואין יוצאין בהם בשבת.** דהאיידי דתלו ולא מהדקי, זמנין דמשתלפי ואתי לאתויינהו. ואית דאמרי מפני שאין לריכין לו כל כך והוו משאוי: **ואין נכנסין בהן לעזרה.** דמנעל מיקרו:

יד אברהם

If the cripple who uses them is a *zav*, they contract *midras* contamination, since he supports his body on them. They therefore become *av hatumah* — the equivalent of the *zav* himself (*Rav; Rashi*).

וְיוֹצְאִין בָּהֶן בַּשַּׁבָּת, — and he (lit. they) may go out with them on the Sabbath,

They are considered the cripple's adornment (*Rashi; Rav*).

וְנִכְנָסִין בָּהֶן בָּעֲזָרָה. — or enter the [Temple] Courtyard with them.

The mishnah alludes to the prohibition of entering the Temple Mount wearing shoes (*Berachos* 9:5). Since these kneepads are worn on the knee, not on the end of the foot (since part of

no cavity for pads, it is deemed as a פְּשׁוּטֵי כְּלִי עֵץ, *a flat wooden vessel,* which is not susceptible to contamination. Even though the cripple inserts his leg into this foot, his leg cannot be carried by it. The cavity, consequently, cannot be judged a receptacle and the wooden foot is therefore considered a flat wooden vessel (*Rav; Rashi*).[1]

סָמוֹכוֹת שֶׁלּוֹ — *His kneepads*

A cripple who is missing both feet may move by walking on his legs and knees. He makes pads of leather or boards upon which to rest his knees (*Rav; Tif. Yis.*).

טְמֵאִין מִדְרָס, — *are susceptible to midras contamination,*

---

1. *Rav* explains that until this point the mishnah speaks of *contact* contamination [*midras* contamination is first introduced in the next phrase]. This view follows Abaye's opinion cited in the *Gemara* (66a): It is susceptible to contamination by [contact with] a corpse [or any other contact contamination (*Rashi*)] but is not susceptible to *midras* contamination, because he does not rest his weight on this false foot. Rava, however (*Gem.* ibid.), understands that the foot does support his body and is therefore susceptible to *midras* contamination (*Tos. Yom Tov*).

6 8   His kneepads are susceptible to *midras* contamination, and he may go out with them on the Sabbath, or enter the [Temple] Courtyard with them.

His stool and his supports are susceptible to *midras* contamination, and he may neither go out with them on the Sabbath, nor enter the [Temple] Courtyard with them.

YAD AVRAHAM

his leg below the knee still remains), they are not considered shoes (*Rashi; Rav*).

כִּסֵא — *His stool*
Some amputees could not propel themselves by means of kneepads because their legs were atrophied. They therefore sat on a low stool, which was tied to them, and propelled themselves by pressing down with their arms and swinging their bodies forward. To protect their hands, they rested them on small benchlike supports. [This was a primitive form of wheelchair (*Rav; Rashi*).]

וְסָמוֹכוֹת שֶׁלוֹ — *and his supports*
In addition to these supports, the amputee had supports of wood or leather tied to his stumps. When propelling himself with his hands, he would support himself slightly on these leg supports. These latter supports are called סָמוֹכוֹת (*Rav; Rashi*).

טְמֵאִין מִדְרָס, — *are susceptible to midras contamination,*
[If the cripple using them is a *zav*, they contract *midras* contamination since he supports himself on them, as explained above.]

וְאֵין יוֹצְאִין בָּהֶם בַּשַּׁבָּת, — *and he* (lit. *they*) *may neither go out with them on the Sabbath,*
Since the סָמוֹכוֹת, *the* (wood or leather) *supports*, tied to his stump

were not his primary means of propulsion, they were often not attached very well. There was therefore the danger that they would fall off in the street and be carried. Others explain that since they are not necessary [since he can propel himself without them], they may not be worn on the Sabbath (*Rav; Rashi*).

These two reasons would seem to apply only to the leg supports, and not to the stool, since the stool is tied to the cripple and is a necessity. Nor do they apply to the hand supports which are no worse than crutches, which are permitted. Therefore, we must interpret the mishnah as follows: His stool (and crutches) and supports are *both* susceptible to *midras* contamination. As regards his *supports, however*, he is additionally prohibited from going out with them on the Sabbath or entering the Temple Courtyard with them (*Tos. Yom Tov* from *Beis Yosef*, quoting numerous sources).

וְאֵין נִכְנָסִין בָּהֶן בָּעֲזָרָה. — *nor enter the [Temple] Courtyard with them.*
These are considered shoes since they are worn on the stumps (*Rav, Rashi*).

[This is in contradistinction to the previously mentioned kneepads. There the mishnah is referring to an amputee whose legs have been amputated below the knee and who is wearing

שבת ו/ט

[ט] **הַבָּנִים** יוֹצְאִין בִּקְשָׁרִים, וּבְנֵי מְלָכִים אַנְקַטְמִין טְהוֹרִין, וְאֵין יוֹצְאִין בָּהֶן.

ר' עובדיה מברטנורא

אנקטמין. כמין פרצוף אדם משונה שמשימין על הפנים להבעית בו התינוקות. פירוש אחר, חמור שהלצנים עושין ונושאין אותו על כתפיהן: **טהורים.** מקבל טומאה, דלאו כלי תשמיש ולא תכשיט הוא: (ט) **בקשרים.** בן שיש לו געגועים על אביו נוטל האב רצועה של מנעל ימין וקושרה לו לבן בשמאלו וכל זמן שאותו קשר עליו סרים הגעגועים מעליו, בסגולה. ולהכי תני הבנים, שאין לבנות געגועים על אביהן כמו הבנים:

יד אברהם

kneepads in addition to that which he wears to protect his stumps. Since the kneepads are not worn on the end of his leg, they are not deemed shoes and may be worn on the Temple Mount. Only the pads which he wears over the ends of his stumps are deemed shoes.]

This ruling, too, applies only to the leg supports, not to the stool upon which he sits nor the benchlike supports in his hands, since they are not shoes. They are surely no more shoes than kneepads, which may be worn in the Temple Courtyard, since they are not worn on the end of the foot (*Tos. Yom Tov*).

Although the mishnah states that they may not enter the Temple Courtyard with these supports, they may, indeed, not even enter the Temple Mount, as in *Berachos* 9:5, *Bikkurim* 1:8, *Chagigah* 1:1. Why then does the mishnah only speak of the Courtyard? In the preceding case, the mishnah states that they may even enter the Temple Courtyard with their supports, certainly a greater leniency than if it were merely to mention the Temple Mount. Following the word pattern of the previous case the mishnah once again uses the word Courtyard; the prohibition, however, extends to the entire Temple Mount (*Tos. Yom Tov*).

אַנְקַטְמִין — *Masks*

The translation of this word is the subject of many diverse opinions. The *Gemara* (66b) itself offers three opinions. (The *Gemara* in our texts renders the word as לוֹקְטְמִין.) These three translations, given in Aramaic, are in turn subject to different translations by the *Rishonim*. The translation we have offered in our text is the one used by *Rashi* on the mishnah and also by *Rav*. It is based upon *Rashi*'s translation of the third explanation offered by the *Gemara*. *Rashi's* translation of the three explanations offered by the *Gemara* are: (a) a wooden donkey worn over the shoulders of clowns in such a way as to give the appearance of being ridden; (b) wooden stilts worn when walking through muddy areas [or stilts used by clowns (*Tosafos* based on *Aruch*)],[1] (c) masks used to frighten children.

R' Chananel cites only two explanations of the *Gemara* and translates

---
1. *Rashi* himself questions how the mishnah could state, accordiing to this explanation, that they are not susceptible to contamination. Since they are trod upon when walking through the mud, they should at least be susceptible to *midras* contamination. Tosafos answer this objection by stating that an object is not considered a *midras* unless it is used as such in the normal course of events. Objects used as *midras* only to avoid unususal obstacles but otherwise not in common use are not deemed *midras*.

Masks are not susceptible to *tumah*-contamination, and we may not go out with them [on the Sabbath].

9. Boys may go out with laces, and princes [may

YAD AVRAHAM

them as a wooden hand made for an amputee; or, a bib placed on elderly people to absorb their drool. Other explanations are: a musical instrument in the shape of a wooden leg (*Rav, Keilim* 15:6); a wooden shoe, not fit for walking (*Rambam*).

טְהוֹרִין — *are not susceptible to tumah-contamination* (lit. *are tahor*),

They are not considered utensils of any use (*Rav; Rashi*). This refers to the wooden donkey and the mask. *Aruch* states that the wooden donkey is, in fact, not a utensil. *Rashi* and *Tosafos* explain that the stilts are flat wooden vessels. This is probably true of the wooden hand and the musical instrument. The wooden shoe is probably of no use at all, since it is not fit for walking. The problem is why the bib is not considered a garment. Possibly, since it is used only to prevent soiling one's clothes, it is not considered a garment. [This is analogous to the case described in the footnote for the prefatory note at the beginning of this chapter.]

וְאֵין יוֹצְאִין בָּהֶן. — *and we may not go out with them [on the Sabbath].*

[The donkey, the stilts, and the mask are neither adornments nor garments. The bib is used to protect other articles from soil and is not considered a garment. The musical instrument and the shoe cannot be worn. Only the wooden hand presents a problem. Perhaps it is analogous to the wooden foot of the amputee, which, according to *Rashi*, is a burden, and, according to *Tosafos*, is proscribed because it may slip off and he would carry it.]

9.

The following mishnah introduces the concept of רְפוּאָה, *medicinal cure,* and סְגֻלָּה, *chain.* Some cures were found to be efficacious although no natural explanation could be found for their efficacy. Some of these were found to have originated from the superstitions of the Emorites. The status of these practices is discussed here.

הַבָּנִים יוֹצְאִין בִּקְשָׁרִים, — *Boys may go out with laces,*

There was a custom that a man, who upon leaving his home knew that his son would long for him, would take his right shoelace and tie it to his son's left arm.[1] As long as the lace was tied to the arm, it would act as a charm to eliminate the longings. This applied only to boys, because girls would not become so attached to their fathers, and consequently, would not long for

---

1. The *Gemara* (ibid.) gives the procedure of putting on *tefillin* as a mnemonic for this practice. Just as the right hand ties the *tefillin* to the left arm, so does the father tie his right shoelace to his son's left arm. Should he reverse the procedure, the child would be stricken by uncontrollable longing.

שבת
ו/י

בְּזוּגִין; וְכָל אָדָם, אֶלָּא שֶׁדִּבְּרוּ חֲכָמִים בַּהוֶֹה.

[י] **יוֹצְאִין** בְּבֵיצַת הַחַרְגּוֹל, וּבְשֵׁן שׁוּעָל, וּבְמַסְמֵר מִן הַצָּלוּב, מִשּׁוּם רְפוּאָה — דִּבְרֵי רַבִּי מֵאִיר. וַחֲכָמִים אוֹמְרִים: אַף בְּחֹל אָסוּר מִשּׁוּם דַּרְכֵי הָאֱמוֹרִי.

──────── ר' עובדיה מברטנורא ────────

בזוגין. כמין פעמונים קטנים. תרגום פעמון זהב, זַגָּא דְדַהֲבָא: **(י) החרגול.** מין חגב, כדכתיב (ויקרא יא) את החרגול למינהו, ותולין אותו באחן ומרפאים בו כאב האחן: **ובשן של שועל.** דעבדי לשינתא. למאן דניים להקיצו, תולין עליו שן של שועל חי. ולמאן דלא ניים כדי שיישן, תולין עליו שן של שועל מת: **ובמסמר הצלוב.** מסמר שצבען התלוי, אס יניחוהו על נפח שצמכה יסיר הנפח. ורמב"ס פירש שמטמינים אותו בלואר מי שיש לו קדחת שלישית וירפאהו: **ורבי מאיר אומר אף בחול אסור.** ואין הלכה כרבי מאיר, דקיימא לן כל דבר שיש בו משום רפואה אין בו משום דרכי האמורי, ולא קרינן בהו ובחוקותיהם לא תלכו:

──────── יד אברהם ────────

them as much as boys would (*Rav* from *Gem.* 66b).

וּבְנֵי מְלָכִים בְּזוּגִין; — *and princes [may go out] with bells;*

I.e., they may go out with bells, whose clappers have been removed, attached to their clothes. If the clappers have not been removed, they are forbidden, since it is forbidden to jingle a bell on the Sabbath (*Tif. Yis.*). [The bells were worn as ornament on the garments of princes.]

וְכָל אָדָם, — *and all people [may do so],*

I.e., so may anyone else wear bells on the Sabbath. Laces, however, are permissible only for those who require them, as explained above (*Tos. Yom Tov*).

This lenient ruling concerning wearing bells applies only if the bells are woven into the garment, thus assuring us that the wearer will not remove them to display them to his friends (*Gem.* 67a). If they are not woven, however, we fear he may remove them and carry them in a public domain. Also, we fear that the nobility will ridicule those who wear bells if their social status does not warrant such ornamentation (*Rashi* 67a).

According to *Yerushalmi*, we need take no precaution lest a minor carry on the Sabbath. The danger here is only that the father may hear the princes ridiculing his son, take the bells off his son's garment, and carry them in the street. We, therefore, require that the bells be woven into the garment (*Tos.* ibid.).

Since the bells are not fitting for those of lower social status, they are considered a burden, unless they are made part of the garment (*Ritva* ms.; *Chidushei Ha-Ran*).

See *Bach* 301, that even princes may wear bells only if they are woven into their garments. [He offers no source for this ruling.]

אֶלָּא שֶׁדִּבְּרוּ חֲכָמִים בַּהוֶֹה. — *but the Sages spoke of the actual custom* (lit. *in the present*).

[They mentioned princes because it was customary for princes to go out so attired.]

go out] with bells; and all people [may do so], but the Sages spoke of the actual custom.

10. We may go out with a locust's egg, or with a fox's tooth, or with a nail from a gallows, for the purpose of healing — [these are] the words of R' Meir.

But the Sages say: Even on weekdays these are forbidden because of [the prohibition against following in] the ways of the Emorites.

YAD AVRAHAM
10.

יוֹצְאִין בְּבֵיצַת הַחַרְגּוֹל, — *We may go out with a locust's egg,*
A locust's egg hanging from an afflicted ear was considered a remedy for an earache (*Rav* from *Gem.* 67a).

וּבְשֵׁן שׁוּעָל, — *or with a fox's tooth,*
One who had insomnia would wear a tooth of a dead fox; one who was constantly sleepy would wear a tooth of a live fox (*Rav* from *Gem* 67a).

וּבְמַסְמֵר מִן הַצָּלוּב, — *or with a nail from a gallows,*
This was believed to be a remedy for a swelling on a wound (*Rav*; *Rashi*).
Alternatively, it was hung about the neck of one suffering from severe fever (*Rav* quoting *Rambam*).

מִשּׁוּם רְפוּאָה — *for the purpose of healing —*
[This phrase refers back to the first word of this mishnah: *we may go out* with these articles for the purpose of healing.]

דִּבְרֵי רַבִּי מֵאִיר. — *[these are] the words of R' Meir.*
The *Yerushalmi* has a variant reading (followed by *Rambam* and *Rav*) which attributes this view to R' Yose.

וַחֲכָמִים אוֹמְרִים: אַף בְּחוֹל אָסוּר — *But the Sages say: Even on weekdays these are forbidden*
According to the *Yerushalmi* (followed by *Rav*) cited above, R' Meir is the proponent of this stricter ruling forbidding these remedies on weekdays. [This is probably *Rambam's* version of this mishnah also.]

מִשּׁוּם דַּרְכֵי הָאֱמוֹרִי. — *because of [the prohibition against following in] the ways of the Emorites.*
I.e., these practices stem from the superstitions of the Emorites who dwelt in the Holy Land prior to its conquest by Israel. All superstitions of the non-Jews (Emorites being only an example) are forbidden under the prohibition of וּבְחֻקֹּתֵיהֶם לֹא תֵלֵכוּ, *and in their ways you shall not go* (*Rashi*). The halachah is in accordance with the first *Tanna*, since anything found to be effective in healing, i.e., that physicians attest to its efficacy, is not prohibited as following the practices of the Emorites (*Rambam, Hil. Shabbos* 19:13).

Meiri explains that any medicines or dressings for wounds are not considered as following the ways of the Emorites. Incantations and the likes are, however, considered as such.

פרק שביעי
Chapter Seven

מֵזִיד, *willful desecration*, of the Sabbath through the commission of a Torah-prohibited act carries the death penalty (*Sanhedrin* 7:8). A court, however, may only impose this penalty if the act took place (a) in the presence of two acceptable witnesses, and (b) after the perpetrator had been warned by them of the transgression and its consequences. If either of these conditions is not met, the matter no longer falls under the jurisdiction of the court (בֵּית דִּין שֶׁל מַטָּה), but is subject to the Divine punishment known as כָּרֵת [*kares*], *excision*. [See General Introduction, p. 5???.]

שׁוֹגֵג, *inadvertent violation*, of these same laws must be atoned for by bringing a קָרְבַּן חַטָּאת, *sin offering*, in the *Beis HaMikdash*. Such inadvertent violation may be the result of one of three errors: (a) One was unaware of the very law of Sabbath; (b) one knew the general law of Sabbath but was unaware that a specific act was prohibited on the Sabbath; or (c) one knew the laws of the Sabbath but simply forgot that it was the Sabbath day.

In general, though one is theoretically liable for each and every *melachah* one does, one sin offering suffices to atone for all the inadvertent violations committed as a result of any one error. Where various violations resulted from different errors (e.g., one was unaware of several of the Sabbatical prohibitions), one is required to bring a separate sin offering for every error which resulted in a violation.

There is one important qualification of this rule. A sin offering can only atone for all violations committed as a result of any one error provided they were all committed without his ever having realized the error in the interim. If, however, one committed a violation, then realized his error, and then again forgot the prohibition, any new violations committed as a result of this second episode of forgetfulness [even if they were exact repeats of the original violation] will necessitate bringing a second sin offering. This case is akin to committing two violations resulting from two different errors, the first forgetting and then the second forgetting. [For a fuller discussion of this rule see prefatory note to 12:6.]

The exact determination of when one is obligated to bring one sin offering and when one is obligated to bring more than one sin offering depends on which of the above-mentioned errors was the cause of his transgressions. Any determination of the number of errors made can be made only relative to what it is that one did not know. The mishnah, therefore, delineates this rule as it applies to each of the three above-mentioned errors.

The kinds of labor prohibited on the Sabbath are classified as either אָבוֹת [*avos*], *primary labors* (lit. *fathers*), or תּוֹלָדוֹת [*tolados*], *secondary labors* (lit. *descendants*). The *avos* are labors which were necessary for the construction of the *Mishkan*, the Tabernacle built in the desert after the Exodus. The *tolados* are types of work similar to the *avos* in their aim or in their essence. This will be elaborated upon in mishnah 2.

שבת א/ז

[א] **כְּלָל** גָּדוֹל אָמְרוּ בַשַׁבָּת: כָּל הַשׁוֹכֵחַ עִקַּר שַׁבָּת, וְעָשָׂה מְלָאכוֹת הַרְבֵּה בְּשַׁבָּתוֹת הַרְבֵּה, אֵינוֹ חַיָּב אֶלָּא חַטָּאת אֶחָת;

ר' עובדיה מברטנורא

פרק שביעי – כלל גדול. (א) **בלל גדול.** השוכח עיקר שבת. כסבור אין שבת בתורה, ואף על גב דמטיקרא שמע וטעכשיו שכחו: **אינו חייב אלא חטאת אחת.** על כל השבתות שחלל דכולה שגגה חדא היא דכתיב (שמות לא) את שבתותי תשמורו ומשמע שמירה אחת לשבתות הרבה:

יד אברהם

בְּלָל גָּדוֹל אָמְרוּ בַשַׁבָּת: — *A major rule was stated [by the Sages] concerning the Sabbath:*

The special importance accorded this rule is a reflection of its topic, not of the rule itself. Because of the stringency of the laws of the Sabbath, the Tanna uses the expression בְּלָל גָּדוֹל, *a major rule,* rather than the usual זֶה הַבְּלָל, *this is the rule* (Tif. Yis. from Gem. 68a).

[This is as if to say, *a rule of a major law.* Though rules are cited elsewhere in this tractate (see, e.g., 12:1) without being referred to as major rules, this rule deals with the atonement for the desecration of the Sabbath. It is therefore a rule describing the importance and holiness of the Sabbath.]

כָּל הַשׁוֹכֵחַ עִקַּר שַׁבָּת, — *Anyone who forgot* (lit. forgets) *the essence of the Sabbath,*

I.e., one who forgot the entire mitzvah of the Sabbath.

There is a difference of opinion in the *Gemara* (68b) as to whether the mishnah's rule applies to one who once knew about the mitzvah of Sabbath but subsequently forgot it, or whether it applies equally to one who *never* knew about the mitzvah of Sabbath and who is now finding out about it for the first time. (The examples cited by the *Gemara* for this extraordinary ignorance are one who was captured by non-Jews in his childhood and grew up among them, or one who converted to Judaism while living entirely among non-Jews.) According to the first opinion, one who never knew of the existence of the mitzvah of Sabbath is not obligated to bring any sin offering at all. Never having known of even the mitzvah of Sabbath, the transgressions which resulted are deemed unavoidable and therefore require no atonement. One, however, who once knew of the mitzvah of Sabbath and subsequently forgot it may be held responsible for his having forgotten. Though his transgressions were not willful they were, nevertheless, avoidable. They therefore require atonement. The second opinion, on the other hand, does not consider ignorance as a basis for deeming the transgressions unavoidable. Since it was possible for one to have sought out someone who could have taught him about Torah, his transgressions were, at least theoretically, avoidable. They therefore require atonement.[1]

---
1. The philosophical implications of this controversy do not fall within the purview of this work. The explanation offered here is intended only as a definition of a legal principle.

1.

A major rule was stated [by the Sages] concerning the Sabbath: Anyone who forgot the essence of the Sabbath, and performed many labors on many Sabbaths, is liable for but one sin offering;

YAD AVRAHAM

Rav, in his commentary, adopts the first opinion (see *Tos. Yom Tov* to *Krisus* 1:2). *Rambam* (*Hil.. Shegagos* 7:2), however, rules according to the second opinion.

According to the view adopted by *Rambam*, it is necessary to explain why the mishnah gives a case of one who *forgot* the Sabbath rather than a case of one who *never knew* the Sabbath. *Rashi* (68b) explains that had the mishnah given the case of one who *never knew* of the Sabbath, we might have mistakenly inferred that one who once knew the mitzvah of Sabbath but subsequently forgot it would be liable for each Sabbath during which he committed a transgression. [This is actually the rule which applies to one who forgets which day is the Sabbath, as will be explained later in this mishnah.] The mishnah therefore gives the case of one who *forgot* the Sabbath to make clear that even so one is obligated to bring but one sin offering for all his transgressions. The same ruling, however, applies equally well to one who *never knew* the Sabbath and no implication to the contrary is intended.

וְעָשָׂה מְלָאכוֹת הַרְבֵּה בְּשַׁבָּתוֹת הַרְבֵּה, אֵינוּ חַיָּב אֶלָּא חַטָּאת אֶחָת; — *and performed many labors on many Sabbaths, is liable for but one sin offering;*

Although he worked on many Sabbaths, and although he did various types of work, since all his desecrations of the Sabbath stemmed from forgetting only one fact — the very existence of the Sabbath — he is obligated to bring but one sin offering for all his transgressions.

The Sages base this ruling on the verse (*Ex.* 31:13): אֶת־שַׁבְּתֹתַי תִּשְׁמֹרוּ,

My Sabbaths shall you observe, implying one observance for numerous Sabbaths. This is as if to say, that a person, by observing one certain aspect of the Sabbath, causes himself to observe many Sabbaths. The significance of this statement is in its converse; a person by failing to observe one certain aspect of the Sabbath causes himself to fail to observe (to desecrate) many Sabbaths.

It is possible that the Rabbinic interpretation of the word תִּשְׁמֹרוּ, *you shall observe*, follows the other definition of the word; namely, *to heed* or *be careful of*. This would then be used in the sense of the statement of the *Talmud* (*Eruvin* 96a and elsewhere) that wherever the Torah prefaces a mitzvah with the word הִשָּׁמֶר, or פֶּן, אַל, a negative commandment (*you shall not*) is meant (הִשָּׁמֶר and תִּשְׁמֹרוּ being both from the same root — שמר). This would then render the interpretation of the verse as *of My Sabbaths you shall be careful*, i.e., be careful of the one factor which will enable you to heed many Sabbaths (— Ed.).

The one failure which can, in consequence, cause a person to desecrate numerous Sabbaths is the failure to know the very existence of the law of Sabbath. The failure to realize which day is the Sabbath is not one failure but numerous failures. Each week one forgets is a separate failure. [This will be discussed further, below.] Where one knows the basic law of Sabbath the failure to know specific prohibitions of the Sabbath is also more than one failure, each individual prohibition being a separate failure (*Rav* from *Gem.* 69b).

[169] THE MISHNAH/SHABBOS — Chapter Seven: *Klal Gadol*

שבת א/ז

הַיּוֹדֵעַ עִקַּר שַׁבָּת, וְעָשָׂה מְלָאכוֹת הַרְבֵּה בְּשַׁבָּתוֹת הַרְבֵּה, חַיָּב עַל כָּל שַׁבָּת וְשַׁבָּת; הַיּוֹדֵעַ שֶׁהוּא שַׁבָּת, וְעָשָׂה מְלָאכוֹת הַרְבֵּה בְּשַׁבָּתוֹת הַרְבֵּה, חַיָּב עַל כָּל אָב מְלָאכָה וּמְלָאכָה;

ר' עובדיה מברטנורא

היודע עיקר שבת. שיש שבת בתורה ונאסרו בו מלאכות, ועשה מלאכות הרבה בשבתות הרבה ע"י שגגת שבת, שאינו יודע ששבת היום, חייב על כל שבת ושבת חטאת אחת, ועל זה נאמר (שם) ושמרו בני ישראל את השבת, דמשמע שמירה לכל שבת ושבת, כלומר שחייב חטאת על כל שבת ושבת, ואף על פי שלא נודע לו בינתיים והעלם אחד הוא, אמרינן ימים שבינתיים הויין ידיעה, שאי אפשר שלא שמע בינתיים שאותו היום שבת היה, אלא שלא נזכר במלאכות שעשה בו, הילכך כל שבת ושבת שגגה אחת היא: **היודע שהוא שבת ועשה מלאכות הרבה.** שלא ידע שמלאכות הללו אסורות ועשאן כמה פעמים בכמה שבתות, חייב על כל אב מלאכה חטאת אחת, ואף על פי שחזר וכפלן בכמה שבתות, כל אב מהן חדא שגגה היא, דהא לא נודע לו בינתיים, והכא ליכא

יד אברהם

הַיּוֹדֵעַ עִקַּר שַׁבָּת, — *one who knew* (lit. *knows*) *the essence of the Sabbath,*

I.e., he knows that the Torah contains the mitzvah of Sabbath observance, and that various types of work are prohibited (*Rav; Rashi*).

וְעָשָׂה מְלָאכוֹת הַרְבֵּה בְּשַׁבָּתוֹת הַרְבֵּה, — *and performed many labors on many Sabbaths,*

Losing track of the calendar, he did work on the Sabbath, thinking it was a weekday (*Rav; Rashi*).

חַיָּב עַל כָּל שַׁבָּת וְשַׁבָּת; — *is liable for every Sabbath;*

This is based on the verse (*Ex.* 31:16): וְשָׁמְרוּ בְנֵי־יִשְׂרָאֵל אֶת־הַשַּׁבָּת, *and the children of Israel shall observe the Sabbath.* Unlike the verse cited above which had ''Sabbaths,'' this verse speaks in the singular, ''the Sabbath,'' denoting a separate observance for each Sabbath. Since it is highly unlikely for a person to go through an entire week without discovering which day of the week it really is, the law presumes that one did in fact realize his error at some time during the intervening week. Repeating the error on the following Sabbath is therefore considered a reflection of a new error rather than a continuation and consequence of the old one (*Rav; Rashi*).

Though the person has no recollection of having in the interim realized his error, this is attributed to his failure to connect his realization with the events which took place in consequence. That is, having realized at some point during the week that it was really a different day than he had thought, he failed to conclude that he had, in consequence, desecrated the Sabbath (by acting on the Sabbath as if it were Friday or Sunday). Not appreciating the significance of this realization, with the passage of a few more days even the very realization of the error in days fades from his memory. Therefore, though after repeating the error a second time the person himself is under the impression there has been only one long lapse, the law presumes that there have been two separate lapses [since it is indeed likely that this is what actually transpired] (*Rashi; Rav*).

Ri (quoted in *Tos.* 67b) disputes this.

7
1

one who knew the essence of the Sabbath, and performed many labors on many Sabbaths, is liable for every Sabbath;

one who knew that it is the Sabbath, and performed many labors on many Sabbaths, is liable for every primary [category of] labor;

YAD AVRAHAM

Based on his analysis of the *Gemara* (71a), he concludes that the mere realization of a calendarial error without a concomitant realization of the more important religious error (the desecration of the Sabbath) does not constitute a true *realization* of error. Any further error made along the same lines as the first ought, therefore, to be included in the same sin offering as the one brought for the first.

The rule about inclusion of two separate transgressions in one sin offering is based on a certain legal definition of *realization* or *awareness*. For a full explanation of this rule see prefatory note to 12:6.

Ri, therefore, offers the alternative explanation that this rule is a גְּזֵרַת הַכָּתוּב, *Scriptural decree*,[1] that the passage of a week's time be viewed as the legal equivalent of a realization of error (necessitating a separate sin offering), though no such factual realization has taken place.

הַיּוֹדֵעַ שֶׁהוּא שַׁבָּת, וְעָשָׂה מְלָאכוֹת הַרְבֵּה בְּשַׁבָּתוֹת הַרְבֵּה, — *one who knew* (lit. *knows*) *that it is the Sabbath, and performed many labors on many Sabbaths,*

This refers to one who knew the general law of Sabbath, and also knew that it was the Sabbath day but, forgetting that certain types of labor are prohibited, inadvertently performed labors on several different Sabbaths (*Rav*).

חַיָּב עַל כָּל אַב מְלָאכָה וּמְלָאכָה — *is liable for every primary [category of] labor;*

I.e., he is obligated to bring a separate sin offering for every one of the thirty-nine אֲבוֹת מְלָאכוֹת, *primary categories of labor*,[2] he has violated. Though he may have violated one particular category numerous times and over several Sabbaths, he is nevertheless obligated to bring only one sin offering to atone for all violations of that one category. Any violation, however, falling under a different category, though it may have occurred only once, necessitates a separate sin offering. Though this case is similar to the first case of the mishnah — one who forgets the very law of the Sabbath — it differs in one fundamental respect. A person who is ignorant of even the basic idea of the Sabbath, though he is in consequence unaware of each of the

---

1. גְּזֵרַת הַכָּתוּב, *Scriptural decree*, is the name given to a part of a law that does not seem to follow the internal logic of that law. Though possessing discernible philosophical or ethical consistency, it appears, to human eyes, to be an exception to the general *legal* principle of which it forms a part. It is therefore termed a *Scriptural decree*; a Divinely decreed rule for which no further legal justification or explanation is required.

2. Although the term אַב מְלָאכָה usually refers to a *primary labor*, in contrast to a *secondary labor*, it is here used in the sense of the category it represents rather than the specific activity it is.

[171] THE MISHNAH/SHABBOS — Chapter Seven: *Klal Gadol*

שבת
א/ז

הָעוֹשֶׂה מְלָאכוֹת הַרְבֵּה מֵעֵין מְלָאכָה אַחַת אֵינוֹ חַיָּב אֶלָּא חַטָּאת אֶחָת.

ר' עובדיה מברטנורא

למימר ימים שביניתיים הוויין ידיעה לחלק, דמשום ימים שביניתיים אין לו לדעת איזו מלאכה אסורה ואיזו מלאכה מותרת, אלא אם כן ישב ועסק לפני חכמים בהלכות שבת. והוא הדין שחייב על שתי תולדות של שני אבות חלוקות על כל אחת חטאת אחת, אבל אי עביד אב ותולדה דידיה, או שתי תולדות של אב אחד, לא מחייב אלא חדא, כדקתני סיפא העושה מלאכות הרבה מעין מלאכה אחת אינו חייב אלא אחת, כגון שתי תולדות של אב אחד, משום דהוי כעושה וחוזר ועושה בהעלם אחת ואין חלוק חטאות בהעלם אחת, אלא בגופי עבירה שאינן דומים, או בחלוק שבתות לענין שגגת שבת:

יד אברהם

thirty-nine separate categories of labor, is in a more fundamental sense guilty of only one error; namely, not knowing the very concept of the Sabbath. Had he possessed this one crucial piece of information, it is quite possible he would have concerned himself to learn all the various laws derived from it. Since all his actions can be said to have been the result of one error, it suffices for him to bring one sin offering to atone for all violations resulting from that one error. [See prefatory note here and 12:6.] A person, on the other hand, who is aware of the general law of Sabbath but is unaware of various of the specific laws involved cannot blame his different violations on one flaw in his knowledge. Each category of labor of which he is unaware represents a separate piece of incognizance. There is, furthermore, no reason to assume that the discovery of any one category of which he is now ignorant would have in any way inspired or abetted his discovery of any of the other categories of which he is ignorant. He is, therefore, separately accountable for each category of which he is unaware. All violations, however, which are of the *same* category of labor are the result of one error; namely, one's ignorance of a specific prohibition. Therefore, one sin offering is sufficient to atone for all violations within that one category of labor.

Additionally, though the various transgressions were repeated over the course of different Sabbaths, they are all considered as part of one error. Only when an error is chronological in nature, that is, where one did not know which day of the week it was, can the passage of time be presumed to correct the error automatically. As explained above, this is because in the normal course of events one *will* likely discover which day of the week it really is. Where, however, one's error is in a lack of Torah knowledge, i.e., where one did not know either the general law of Sabbath or certain of the specific laws of Sabbath, there is no way for time alone to correct the error. This can be done only through study of the Sabbath laws and there is no reason to assume that one has studied the Sabbath laws during the intervening week. Since the law can make no presumption of an awareness of error having taken place between one Sabbath and the next, all violations are attributed to one's lack of knowledge. One sin offering suffices, therefore, to atone for all violations committed within any one category of labor, no matter over how many Sabbaths they may have been committed (*Rashi; Rav*).

7
1

one who [knew that it is the Sabbath, and] performed many labors of one [category of] labor, is liable for but one sin offering.

YAD AVRAHAM

⋅§ Summary

Though in principle one sin offering suffices to atone for all transgressions committed as a result of one error, the practical determination of how many sin offerings one is obligated to bring depends on what type of error one made, as follows:

(a) If one errs in not knowing the basic law of the Sabbath, one is never obligated to bring more than one sin offering. This is true regardless of the number of different categories of labor one violated and regardless of the number of Sabbaths over which the violations took place. All violations derive from one error; all the violations together, therefore, constitute one long mistake.

(b) If one knows of the general rule of Sabbath but errs in not knowing various specific laws of the Sabbath, one is obligated to bring a separate sin offering for each *category* of labor one has violated. This is true regardless of how many times each category may have been violated and regardless of over how many Sabbaths the violations took place. Each category of which one was unaware constitutes a separate error; all violations *within* each category derive from but one error.

(c) If one knows all the laws of the Sabbath but errs in not knowing the days of the week, one is obligated to bring one sin offering for each Sabbath during which a violation took place. This is true regardless of how many categories of labor were violated. Each Sabbath constitutes a separate error; all violations committed on any given Sabbath derive from but one error.

הָעוֹשֶׂה מְלָאכוֹת הַרְבֵּה מֵעֵין מְלָאכָה אַחַת — *one who [knew that it is the Sabbath, and] performed* (lit. *performs*) *many labors of one [category of] labor,* I.e., if one performs an *av* and its *toladah*, or two *tolados* of one *av* (without becoming aware of his error in the interim) (*Rav; Rashi*).

אֵינוּ חַיָּב אֶלָּא חַטָּאת אֶחָת. — *is liable for but one sin offering.*

As mentioned above, this is analogous to performing the same labor repeatedly in a single period of forgetfulness. Since the *toladah* is a derivative of the *av*, he has violated only one category of labor. Therefore, though one may have committed numerous different acts in violation of that one category, he is obligated to bring but one sin offering.

Rambam understands that even some of the primary labors may comprise more than one specific activity. Sowing seeds, planting or layering trees, grafting and pruning are, according to him, all forms of the *av* of זוֹרֵעַ, *sowing* [see mishnah 2], not *tolados*. In each case the purpose of the task is to promote the growth of the plant and entails physical contact with the plant or seed. Acts which promote the growth of the plant, but do not involve physical contact with it, such as weeding, are called *tolados*. Thus, our mishnah is interpreted: If one does many forms of one primary labor, e.g., he sowed, planted, and layered trees, in one period of forgetfulness, he is liable for but one sin offering, for they are all one *av* (*Rambam, Hil. Shabbos* 7:9). [*Rambam* does not dispute the fact that one who performs an *av* and its *toladah* is obligated to bring but one sin offering (see ibid. 7:7). He merely explains the phraseology of the mishnah as referring to two forms of one *av*, rather than to an *av* and its *toladah*.]

שבת
ז/ב

[ב] **אֲבוֹת** מְלָאכוֹת אַרְבָּעִים חָסֵר אַחַת: [1] הַזּוֹרֵעַ, [2] וְהַחוֹרֵשׁ,

---
ר' עובדיה מברטנורא

(ב) **הזורע החורש.** הא דלא תנא החורש ברישא והדר הזורע כדרך כל הארץ, לאשמועינן שאם היה קרקע קשה ותרשו וזרעו ואחר כך חזר וחרשו, מחייב אחרישה שנייה משום חורש:

יד אברהם

2.

◈ **Avos and Tolados**

As explained at length in the General Introduction (p. 3), all labors performed in the construction of the מִשְׁכָּן [*Mishkan*], *Tabernacle,* are called *avos* or primary labors. [Types of work which are similar in nature to *avos* are called *tolados* or *secondary labors.*] These labors derive not only from the actual construction of the *Mishkan* but also from the activities necessary for the preparation of the components of the *Mishkan.*

Though the thirty-nine labors enumerated here comprise the list of activities necessary to construct the *Mishkan,* they do not exclude other similar activities from being prohibited on the Sabbath. On the contrary, any other activity similar either in method or function to any of these thirty-nine activities is equally prohibited. These thirty-nine form a ban not only on specific acts of labor but on whole categories of labor. They are therefore known as אֲבוֹת מְלָאכוֹת, *avos melachos,* primary labors [lit. *fathers of labors*], in the sense that they constitute the headings of whole categories of labor. Any other activity whose prohibition is derived from one of these thirty-nine is known as a תּוֹלָדָה, *toladah,* secondary [lit., *descendant*], labor.

אֲבוֹת מְלָאכוֹת — *The primary labors*
I.e., the labors used in the construction of the *Mishkan.*

The order of the thirty-nine primary labors, as listed in our mishnah, may be subdivided into four sections: (a) Eleven labors necessary to the baking of bread; (b) thirteen involved in the manufacture of clothing; (c) nine required for the writing of a Torah scroll; and (d) six labors of actual construction and erection of the *Mishkan* itself.

אַרְבָּעִים חָסֵר אַחַת: — *are forty minus one.*

This expression for the number thirty-nine is used elsewhere in the Mishnah (*Makkos* 3:10) in regard to the thirty-nine lashes given as punishment for certain transgressions. It originates from an oral law interpretation of *Deut.* 25:2-3, *with the count of forty* [lashes] *shall he strike him ...* which the Talmud in *Makkos* explains as meaning with the count that leads to forty, i.e., one less than forty. The expression for thirty-nine therefore became forty minus one (*Tos. Yom Tov*).

◈ **Eleven Melachos in the Preparation of Bread**

הַזּוֹרֵעַ, — [1] *sowing* [lit. *the sower*],
In a list of forbidden labors the gerund form (**sowing,* **plowing,* *reaping) would seem more appropriate

משניות / שבת — פרק ז: כלל גדול [174]

2. The primary labors are forty minus one:
[1] sowing,   [2] plowing,

YAD AVRAHAM

than the identification of the perpetrator (*the planter, the plower, the reaper*). Indeed, *Rambam* (*Hil. Shabbos* 7:1) uses that form [הַחֲרִישָׁה וְהַזְּרִיעָה וְהַקְּצִירָה] in enumerating the primary labors. However, in explaining why the *Tanna* finds it necessary to preface this list with a number, the *Gemara* (73a) states that the purpose is to enumerate the maximum number of sin offerings to which an inadvertent volator can be subject. For this reason the *Tanna* speaks of the perpetrator rather than the labors themselves (*Tos. Yom Tov*).

Since the purpose of *sowing is to cause plants to grow, any type of labor that promotes plant growth falls into this category. Planting or layering trees, grafting[1] or removing a perforated flowerpot from a bench to the ground (where it can draw nutrients from the soil) are essentially equivalent activities. They are therefore all considered *avos*. Pruning is an *av* according to *Rambam* but a *toladah* according to all other opinions (see General Introduction, p. 4). Weeding is a *toladah* of *sowing, if it is done to improve the growth of a plant. Where it is done to improve the arability of the ground in preparation for plowing, it is a *toladah* of *plowing. (Cf. below, s.v. הַחוֹרֵשׁ, *plowing*, and also commentary to 12:2.)

As mentioned above, all *avos* were activities used in the construction of the *Mishkan*. The dyes required for the curtains and the priestly garments were of herbal origin. These herbs had, therefore, to first be planted before production of the dyes could take place. Although the Israelites were wandering through an arid wilderness, it miraculously became fertile and produced vegetation (*Tos. Chullin* 88b). It is also possible that they used dyes made from plants grown in Egypt or purchased from nearby peoples. Although the seeds were not sown specifically for the *Mishkan*, the sowing was, nevertheless, a necessary prelude to the manufacture of dye and is thus considered an *av* (*Minchas Chinuch* quoting *Pnei Yehoshua*).

וְהַחוֹרֵשׁ, — [2] *plowing*,

The purpose of *plowing is to soften the earth or to otherwise improve its arability. Therefore, any type of work performed directly upon the earth and designed to achieve these results is equivalent to *plowing. Hence, plowing, digging holes, or agriculturally needed trenches are forms of the *av* of *plowing. All involve digging in the ground, and all are for a similar function (*Kalkalas Shabbos* from *Rambam, Hil. Shabbos* 7:2).

Uprooting weeds at the roots of trees, cropping herbage close to the ground, and thinning out the branches of a tree (which hang too low over the ground) with a view to improving the arability of the ground, are all *tolados* of *plowing (*Kalkalas Shabbos* from *Rambam*, ibid. 8:1). Each of these latter cases is considered

---

1. Grafting may also be forbidden apart from the Sabbath prohibition, where it involves grafting a branch of one species on to a tree of another species. This is the prohibition of כִּלְאַיִם, *mixing two species* (*Kilayim* 1:7). Grafting within one species is normally permitted but is forbidden on the Sabbath because it falls into the category of *sowing.

שבת ז/ב [3] וְהַקּוֹצֵר, [4] וְהַמְעַמֵּר, [5] הַדָּשׁ,
[6] וְהַזּוֹרֶה, [7] הַבּוֹרֵר,

ר' עובדיה מברטנורא

הקוצר. בזרעים, והמלקט באילנות, חייב משום קוצר: **המעמר.** אוסף זרעים תלושים וצוברם אל מקום אחד: **הזורה.** ברחת לרוח: **הבורר.** פסולת, בידיו או בכברה:

יד אברהם

a *toladah* because the work is not performed on the ground itself, yet is intended for its improvement (ibid.).

As with *sowing, *plowing was required in growing the plants used in the manufacture of dyes.

Although *plowing prepares the ground for *sowing, the *Tanna* reverses the order to teach that in places where the earth is hard and requires replowing after the sowing, one is also liable for this second plowing (*Rav* from *Gem.* 73b). Since *plowing must precede *sowing, *Rambam* (*Hil. Shabbos* 7:1) reverses the order.

וְהַקּוֹצֵר, — [3] *reaping,*

Detaching any growing plant from its roots falls under the category of *reaping (*Rambam, Hil. Shabbos* 8:3). If done in a customary manner (e.g., cutting grain with a scythe) the labor is an *av*; if in an unusual manner (e.g., pulling grain by hand) it is a *toladah* (*Rambam* ibid.; *Lechem Mishneh*).

[Although it is not usual to pull out grain by hand rather than with an implement, it is not considered performing the labor in an unusual manner, which is exempt from a sin offering, unless he effects the pulling in an unusual manner, such as throwing a stone at a palm, thereby knocking off dates, as in *Gemara* 73b.]

In describing this labor *Rambam* uses the word הָעוֹקֵר, *one who uproots.* This does not necessarily mean pulling the plant out by the roots as opposed to the *av*, which consists of cutting it off above the ground. It means, rather, that detaching a plant by hand rather than by an implement, no matter how much one pulls off, is a *toladah* since this is not the usual method of reaping (*Magen Avos*).

If one prunes a tree intending also to use the branches, in addition to being liable for a sin offering for planting, i.e., for promoting the tree's growth, he is liable for an additional sin offering for *reaping, i.e., for cutting the branches (*Rambam, Hil. Shabbos* 8:4, from *Gem.* 73b). [For a fuller explanation of this, see comm. to 12:2.)

וְהַמְעַמֵּר, — [4] *gathering together,*

I.e., gathering cut plants into one pile (*Rav*).

This *melachah* applies only to things that grow. Gathering salt from a salt deposit is excluded. However, such labor is subject to a Rabbinical prohibition (*Gem.* 73b) as *Rambam* expresses it, because he appears like one *gathering together* (*Hil. Shabbos* 21:11) [i.e., like one doing the same labor as gathering plants].

Note also that the prohibition applies only to gathering cut plants in the place where they grew (*Tif. Yis; Tos. Beitzah* 31a; *Hagahos Maimonios* 21:11; *Shulchan Aruch* 340:9). Thus, fruits which have fallen from their tree (even before the Sabbath) may not be gathered on the Sabbath. However, if a bag of fruit spills onto the floor, it may be gathered together (*Mishnah Berurah* 340:37).

[3] reaping, [4] gathering together, [5] threshing, [6] winnowing, [7] sorting,

YAD AVRAHAM

הַדָּשׁ, — **[5]** *threshing,*

The purpose of threshing is to extract grain from its husk. Extracting any food from its shell in a similar manner is a *toladah* of *threshing (*Zichru Toras Moshe* 16; *Chayei Adam* 14).

Likewise, extracting liquid from the fruit in which it is absorbed, or converting a solid food into a liquid, such as pressing olives or grapes to make oil or wine, is a *toladah of threshing*. This applies only to extracting food from the shell by pressing the outside. Peeling fruit or shelling nuts does not enter this category (*Shevisas HaShabbos*).

וְהַזּוֹרֶה, — **[6]** *winnowing,*

After the kernels have been extracted from their husks, the mixture is cast into the air with a pitchfork. The wind blows away the chaff, leaving the heavier kernels.

Since *Rashi* and *Rav* explain that *winnowing is done with a pitchfork, it would appear that casting into the wind by hand is permissible. [If *Rashi* means merely that this is the usual manner of *winnowing, but one is liable for *winnowing with the hand as well, we find difficulty of *work done in an unusual manner*, which is exempt. See above, *reaping*.] *Magen Avos*, however, quotes *Semak* (or *Semag*; this is, however, not found in our editions of either of these works) as prohibiting throwing seeds to fowl from a high place, where the wind will scatter them. It is possible that this prohibition is Rabbinical.

The *Yerushalmi* (7:2), however, states that even one who spits into the wind is liable, indicating that the prohibition is Biblical. In any case, it is probable that the *Yerushalmi* and the *Bavli* do not agree on this point, since the *Bavli* regards *winnowing as a labor designed to separate food from chaff, obviously not applying to the case of the *Yerushalmi*. The *Yerushalmi* apparently considers anything into the wind which will scatter it a *toladah* of *winnowing. It is possible that the *Bavli*, too, agrees with the *Yerushalmi*. The *Bavli* means that in the construction of the *Mishkan*, the only winnowing was separating food from chaff (*Shevisas HaShabbos*). *Beur Halachah* cites *Alfei Menashah* that the *Yerushalmi* agrees with the *Bavli*, that *winnowing applies only to separating food from chaff. If one spits into the wind, he is liable only if the spittle flies four cubits in a public place. The analogy to *winnowing is that one is liable for an act performed with the assistance of the wind. The overwhelming majority of halachic authorities permit spitting into the wind (*Mishnah Berurah* 319:67).

הַבּוֹרֵר, — **[7]** *sorting,*

Sorting inedible matter from food by hand or with a sieve (*Rav*).

This prohibition applies not only to unprocessed foodstuffs but even to ready-to-eat food. It thus poses a problem when preparing food for the Sabbath meals and even during the meal itself. The rules of this *melachah* are very complex and cannot be fully dealt with within the limits of this work. The general rule (taken from *Shulchan Aruch* 319), however, is as follows:

A) *Removing inedible matter from food* is prohibited under all circum-

שבת [8] הַטּוֹחֵן, [9] וְהַמְרַקֵּד, [10] וְהַלָּשׁ, [11] וְהָאוֹפֶה;
ז/ב

ר׳ עובדיה מברטנורא

והמרקד. בנפה, ואף על גב דהני כולהו חדא נינהו דלהפריש פסולת מתוך אוכל נעשו שלשתן, משום דשלשתן הוו במשכן אף על גב דדמו להדדי חשיב להו כל חדא באנפי נפשה. אי נמי לפי שאין בבת אחת אלא זה אחר זה: **האופה.** לא הויא במשכן, דאין אפייה אלא בפת ופת לא שייכא במלאכת המשכן, אלא תנא סדורא דפת נקט, ומיהו מבשל שהוא מעין מלאכת אופה הוה במשכן, בסממנין של צבע תכלת וארגמן ותולעת שני. והמגיס בקדרה, והנותן כסוי על גבי קדרה העומדת על האש, וכל הנך קמאי דחשיב במתניתין הזורע הקוצר הדש וכו', כולהו הוו בסממנין בצבע של מלאכת המשכן:

יד אברהם

stances. This is true whether the inedible matter is (1) a foreign substance, such as a pebble or sand which became mixed into the food, or (2) indigenous to the food itself, such as spoiled parts of the food itself or bits of peel or shell mixed in with a plateful of fruit or nuts. This prohibition applies regardless of whether the removal is done by hand or by special implement, either before and during the meal. Its prohibition is a Torah one, i.e., one is liable for a sin offering for having done it inadvertently or for capital punishment for having done it willfully.

B) *Removing food from inedible matter* is sometimes permitted, sometimes prohibited: (1) Removing the food from the inedible matter well in advance of a meal is prohibited, in any manner. This is also a Torah prohibition. (2) Removing the food from the inedible matter just before or during a meal depends on how one does it. If it is done: (a) with an implement designed especially for separating the different substances (e.g., a sieve or sifter) one is liable to a sin offering, i.e., the prohibition is a Torah prohibition; but if it is done (b) with a utensil not especially designed for such a task but whose use makes the task easier (e.g., a reed basket in place of a sieve) it is prohibited Rabbinically (since it resembles a sieve); however, if it is done (c) by hand (or with a fork or spoon) it is permissible.

C) *Separating two varieties of food* which have become mixed together falls into the category of *sorting and follows the same rules as above. In this case, the variety one wishes to use now is considered the food, while the variety one wishes to set aside is given the status of the inedible matter (*Gem.* 74a as explained by *Tos.* [1]).

D) *Selecting the usable from the unusable in non-food substances* also follows the above rules of *sorting (*Mishnah Berurah* 319:15).

There are additional rules which apply to many specific cases. See *Shulchan Aruch* 319.

הַטּוֹחֵן, — [8] *grinding,*

I.e., grinding wheat into flour. This includes also pounding condiments or spices (*Rambam, Hil. Shabbos* 8:15).

In the construction of the *Mishkan*, plant parts were pounded to make dyes for the curtains (*Rashi* 49b).

Cutting vegetables into fine pieces to cook them is a *toladah* of *grinding. Even for the purpose of eating this is

---

1. *Beis Yosef* followed by *Magen Avraham* explain that *Rambam's* opinion in this matter differs slightly. Cf. *Beur Halachah* 319:3.

7 2 [8] grinding, [9] sifting, [10] kneading, and [11] baking;

YAD AVRAHAM

sometimes prohibited (cf. *Shulchan Aruch* 321:8-12).

Similarly, filing a metal bar to obtain metal powder — as gold refiners do — is *a toladah* of *grinding (*Rambam, Comm.* and *Hil. Shabbos* 7:5 from *Gem.* 74b, *Yerushalmi* 7:2). Many authorities rule, however, that *grinding applies only to things that grow from the ground, just as *gathering applies only to such things (*Terumas HaDeshen* 56; *Shulchan Aruch* 321:9 and *Mishnah Betutah*; *Eglei Tal* 8).

וְהַמְרַקֵּד, — [9] *sifting,*

I.e., sifting flour after it has been ground. This is done with a sifter, a sieve with fine holes (*Rav*), in order to remove the bran (*Meiri*). [This too was done in the preparation of the dyes.]

Three of the preceding *melachos* — *winnowing, *sorting, *sifting — are closely related. All have one purpose, separating food from waste. They should rightfully be considered one *av*, since their purpose is similar. Since all three were done separately in the construction of the *Mishkan*, however, the *Tanna* considers them as separate *avos* (*Gem.* 74a).

Each of these *melachos* is in a way distinct: *winnowing separates the straw from the grain; *sorting separates the pebbles from the grain after it has been winnowed; and *sifting is done after the grain has been ground to flour (*Rashi* 75b). Since all three labors are performed at different points in the process of preparing the same material, such as grain, or, in the construction of the *Mishkan*, dye plants, they are counted as three distinct *avos* (*Rav*).

Alternatively, the differences lie in the methods of separating the food from the dross: *winnowing makes use of the wind, *sorting may be done by hand [i.e., for *sorting one is sometimes liable for doing so by hand] and *sifting utilizes a utensil, such as a sieve (*Aruch*; *Rabbeinu Chananel*).

וְהַלָּשׁ, — [10] *kneading,*

The purpose of *kneading is to cause particles to adhere to each other through the addition of liquid to the mixture. (See *Shulchan Aruch* 321, 324.) The *av* consists of pouring water on flour and working it together to form a dough. Kneading earth to use in building materials is a *toladah* (*Gem.* 18a; *Rambam, Hil. Shabbos* 8:16).

Other details of *kneading have already been discussed in 1:5. This *melachah* includes kneading flour, cereal, cement — or any other material which can be kneaded — with water — or any other liquid that will effectively combine with the flour, etc. The consistency of the finished product may be either thick or thin (*Mishnah Berurah* 321:50-54).

וְהָאוֹפֶה; — and [11] *baking;*

Baking itself was not done in the construction of the *Mishkan*. Instead, cooking was performed in the preparation of the dyes. The *Tanna* lists *baking, which is equivalent to *cooking, however, because he uses the bread-making process as a model for his list (*Rav* from *Gem.* 74b, according to *Rashi*). Both baking and cooking are considered *avos*.

Since baking bread is more common than cooking dyes, the *Tanna* follows this order [presumably for mnemonical purposes] even though it was not done in the construction of the *Mishkan* (*Tos. Yom Tov* from *Ran*). [Though the cooking of food is even more common than baking, the other *melachos* leading up to it do not necessarily take place during the preparation of food other than bread. This is most especially true of *threshing, *winnowing, *sifting and

שבת [12] הַגּוֹזֵז אֶת הַצֶּמֶר, [13] הַמְלַבְּנוֹ,
ז/ב [14] וְהַמְנַפְּצוֹ, [15] וְהַצּוֹבְעוֹ, [16] וְהַטּוֹוֶה,

────────────── ר' עובדיה מברטנורא ──────────────

הגוזז צמר. וכל שאר מלאכותיה שייכי בצמר תכלת של מלאכת המשכן: **המלבנו.** מכבסו בנהר: **המנפצו.** חובטו בשבט אי נמי סורקו במסרק:

יד אברהם

kneading. The *Tanna*, therefore, prefers discussing the process of baking, wherein all the above-mentioned *melachos* were an integral part of the process.]

Others explain that the labors of the *Mishkan* include not only those performed in its construction, but also those performed in the preparation of the sacrifices. Hence, all the eleven *avos* listed until this point were performed in conjunction with the meal offering of the *Kohen Gadol*, known as חֲבִתֵּי כֹהֵן גָּדוֹל, *the pan offering of the Kohen Gadol*, consisting of fine flour baked into loaves (see *Lev.* 6:12-15; *Rav Hai Gaon* quoted in the beginning of *Maaseh Rokeach*; see also *Eglei Tal* 1).

One who stirs or covers a cooking pot is liable for a sin offering since by doing so he abets the cooking (*Rav*).

These are forms of the *av* (*Rambam, Hil. Shabbos* 9:4).

The *tolados* of *cooking* are: melting wax, tar, or metal (*Rambam, Hil. Shabbos* 9:6). All of these labors achieve either the softening of a substance or its conversion from a solid to a liquid state. In this way, these labors resemble *cooking*.

Where one hardens a substance by fire, *Rambam* rules that this, too, is a *toladah* of *cooking*. Therefore, if one bakes earthenware vessels in a kiln, he is liable to a sin offering. *Rashi* (94b) apparently does not concur. He rules that only where the fire first softens the object, at least temporarily, is he liable for a sin offering (see *Lechem Mishneh, Hil. Shabbos* 9:6).

⚞ **Thirteen Melachos in the Preparation of Wool**

The following thirteen *melachos* [12]-[24] are those performed in the preparation of wool, used for the curtains of the *Mishkan* (*Rav; Rashi*). Clothing being secondary to food in order of importance to a person, these *melachos* are enumerated after those performed in the preparation of food.

הַגּוֹזֵז אֶת הַצֶּמֶר, — [12] *shearing wool*,

Shearing wool or hair from an animal be it living or dead — or even from the flayed pelt of an animal are forms of the *av* of *shearing*.

Plucking a feather from a bird, paring one's nails, and trimming one's moustache or beard with an instrument are *tolados* of *shearing* and one is liable to a sin offering. If, however, one trims nails or hair by hand, he is exempt from a sin offering (*Rambam,*

Hil. Shabbos 9:8; see below 10:6). Such acts are, nevertheless, Rabbinically proscribed (*Hagahos Maimonios*).

הַמְלַבְּנוֹ — [13] *whitening it*,

I.e., washing the wool in a river (*Rav; Rashi* and *Ran* according to some editions). We have no clear reason for specifying "in a river" except that that was the usual place to wash wool or clothing (*Magen Avos*). Other editions of *Rashi* and *Ran* read, "washing it with nitron." The reason for

7:2 [12] shearing wool, [13] whitening it, [14] combing it, [15] dyeing it, [16] spinning,

YAD AVRAHAM

adding this is not clear, since one is liable for washing clothes in water even without soap or any other cleansing agent. Perhaps this is a *toladah*, while *whitening with a cleansing agent is an *av*. Rambam (*Hil. Shabbos* 9:10,11) calls scouring wool, linen, etc. an *av*, and laundering clothes a *toladah*.

Wringing out wet clothes is a *toladah* of *whitening (*Shabbos* 111; Rambam ibid. 9:11), as is shaking dew off a garment (*Gem.* 147a, *Tos.* ibid.; *Shulchan Aruch* 302:1).

וְהַמְנַפְּצוֹ, [14] — *combing it*,

Combing wool, flax, cotton or the like are all included in this *av*. Combing tendons until they resemble wool, in order to spin them into thread [to sew a *Sefer Torah*], constitutes a *toladah* and renders one liable to a sin offering (*Kalkalas HaShabbos* from Rambam 9:12; *Semag* 65). This rule originates in *Yerushalmi* 7:2, which states that combing bark, straw, or palm leaves is a *toladah* of *combing. *Maaseh Rokeach* theorizes that Rambam's edition of *Yerushalmi* read "tendons." [*Semag*, however, quotes *Yerushalmi* as we have it; nevertheless, he too mentions combing tendons.]

וְהַצּוֹבְעוֹ, — [15] *dyeing it*,

Wool was dyed for use in the curtains and the covers of the *Mishkan* (*Rav; Meiri*). *Yerushalmi*, however, states that *dyeing is an *av* because they would dye the ram skins red for the cover of the *Mishkan*. It is indeed puzzling that the obvious dyeing of the wool for the curtains is not mentioned. (See *Sheyarei Korban*, ad loc.)

The Torah prohibition applies only to application of a permanent dye.

Application of a dye which fades away is prohibited by Rabbinical decree (*Rambam* 9:13). According to *Semag*, however, even a temporary color is a Torah prohibition (*Chayei Adam, Nishmas Adam* 24:1). For this reason the application of cosmetics on the Sabbath is prohibited [either by Torah law or Rabbinical decree (ibid. 24:2)].

According to *Rambam* (9:14), manufacturing dye is a *toladah* of *dyeing, since the water becomes colored by the coloring agents. *Ravad*, however, contends that since the ultimate intent is to produce dyed cloth, not colored water, the work of *dyeing is incomplete. Therefore, one is not liable for *dyeing. According to him one is, however, liable for *kneading the mixture. See above 1:5.

וְהַטּוֹוֶה, — [16] *spinning*,

I.e., twisting fibers together to make threads. One is liable for spinning wool, linen, down, hair, tendons or the like.

Rope making is a *toladah* of *spinning (*Yerushalmi* 7:2).

The following four *avos* constitute the weaving process, which will be explained before going into the details of each *melachah*. A weaving loom is fundamentally a frame, upon which two rollers are mounted; one, at the far end (called the warp beam), away from the weaver, and one at the near end (called the cloth beam). The warp thread is wound around the warp beam and stretched to the cloth beam, upon which the woven fabric will eventually be rolled.

The weaving process consists of setting up the warp threads on the loom and introducing the weft threads between them to produce a woven fabric.

שבת ז/ב

[17] וְהַמֵּסֵךְ, [18] וְהָעוֹשֶׂה שְׁתֵּי בָתֵּי נִירִין, [19] וְהָאוֹרֵג שְׁנֵי חוּטִין, [20] וְהַפּוֹצֵעַ שְׁנֵי חוּטִין, [21] הַקּוֹשֵׁר, [22] וְהַמַּתִּיר,

---
ר' עובדיה מברטנורא

הַמֵּסֵךְ. אורדי"ר בלט"ז: **בתי נירין.** שנותן שני חוטין בתוך בתי ניר: **הפוצע.** מסיר חוטי הערב מעל השתי או השתי מעל הערב, לצורך אריגה: **והקושר והמתיר.** שכן ליד חלונו שמצמו עושין התכלת קושרין ומתירין, שפעמים צריך ליטול חוטין מרשת זו להוסיף על זו, ומתיר מכאן וקושר כאן:

יד אברהם

וְהַמֵּסֵךְ — [17] mounting the warp (lit., the loom dresser),

Rambam (Hil. Shabbos 9:17) describes how a weaving loom is set. First the warp threads are stretched to the desired length and width. A rod is then used to line the threads up side by side so that all lie in the desired direction and none are crossed. This process of stretching the threads is known as *mounting the warp, and the mounter is called מֵסֵךְ, a loom dresser. Pressing the threads to separate them and line them up properly is called שׁוֹבֵט [lit. hitting with a rod] and constitutes a toladah of *mounting the warp (Rambam ibid. 18).

וְהָעוֹשֶׂה שְׁתֵּי בָתֵּי נִירִין — [18] setting (lit. making) two heddles,

Between the two beams and perpendicular to them are two frames (called harnesses), through which the warp threads must pass. Each of these harnesses has numerous threads attached to it. Each pair of adjacent threads on the harness is knotted in two places to form a loop (or eye) at the center. This pair of threads is called a heddle. [Heddles may also be made by tying a ring between two lengths of thread. Modern handlooms often use a metal strip pierced at its center.] One warp thread passes through the eye of a heddle on the first harness and between two heddles on the second harness. The next warp thread passes between two heddles on the first harness and through the eye of a heddle in the second harness.

Threading two threads through the heddle-eyes constitutes the av of *setting two heddles (Rav; Rashi; Tos. Yom Tov).

Alternatively this refers to tying the loops or rings of the heddle (Tif. Yis.).

Rambam has a different interpretation of this melachah. According to him it refers to weaving loosely woven lace or netting. His opinion will be discussed in the commentary to 13:2.

וְהָאוֹרֵג שְׁנֵי חוּטִין — [19] weaving two threads,

The weaver raises the two frames alternately (shedding). First he raises the front frame. In doing so he raises all the odd warp threads and forms a "shed" between the two sets of warp threads. The weft is passed through this shed from right to left (picking). He then raises the even warp threads by lowering the first harness and raising the other, and passes the weft through from left to right.

To complete the basic weaving a comblike device (the reed) is used to press the newly woven weft threads into place. This act simultaneously assures that the warp treads remain evenly spaced and parallel to one another. This action is called מְדַקְדֵּק,

[17] mounting the warp, [18] setting two heddles, [19] weaving two threads, [20] removing two threads, [21] tying [a knot], [22] untying [a knot],

YAD AVRAHAM

beating in, and is a *toladah* of *weaving* (*Gem.* 75b with *Rashi*).

Thus, the *weaving* process consists of these basic steps: shedding, picking and beating in.

Inserting the weft thread twice through the warp [right to left and left to right] constitutes a transgression of the *av* of *weaving* (*Tis. Yis.*).

Further details of this *melachah* are delineated in Chapter 13.

וְהַפּוֹצֵעַ שְׁנֵי חוּטִין, — **[20]** *removing two threads,*

I.e., either removing two threads of the woof from the warp or vice versa, in order to weave [i.e., to aid in the *weaving*] (*Rav*).

[*Rav* qualifies the liability by adding the words, "in order to weave," for otherwise, removing threads would be a destructive act (מְקַלְקֵל) which is not considered a מְלֶאכֶת מַחֲשֶׁבֶת, *purposeful labor,* and therefore not Biblically prohibited (see General Introduction, p. 6). Removing threads from a fabric constitutes purposeful labor only if the intention is to aid in the weaving of the fabric after the threads have been removed.]

Rashi explains this as the removal of excess warp threads to make the fabric narrower.

Rambam reads בּוֹצֵעַ and explains this as a labor performed to reweave a tear in the material: First some of the woof is removed, then the ends of the torn threads are joined and finally the woof previously removed is rewoven, until the two pieces of fabric or the two edges of the tear become united (*Rambam, Hil. Shabbos* 9:20).

Ravad objects to this explanation on the grounds that it very closely resembles *tearing in order to sew two stitches.*[1] He explains it therefore as *cutting two threads;* i.e. when the weaving has been completed, the woven fabric is cut away from the remaining unwoven threads. One who cuts away even two threads is liable.

הַקּוֹשֵׁר, וְהַמַּתִּיר, — **[21]** *Tying [a knot],* **[22]** *untying [a knot],*

The types of knots prohibited from being tied or untied are delineated in Chapter 15.

Those who would hunt the *chilazon,* a small fishlike creature whose blood was used for *techeles* [the blue dye used for the curtains of the *Mishkan*], would both tie and untie their nets, since it was sometimes necessary to remove ropes from one net and attach them to another. Thus we find in the *Mishkan* both *tying* and *untying* (*Rav* from *Gem.* 74b; *Rashi,* ad loc.).

This explanation indicates that one is liable for *untying* a knot only if it is done with the intention of retying

---

1. *Maggid Mishneh* answers *Ravad's* objections by distinguishing between the tearing of two stitches whereby the fabric is taken apart by cutting one thread into two, and where this is accomplished by the removal of entire threads from a weave. Since all the components, in the latter case, remain intact, and only their joining is disturbed, this activity cannot be considered *tearing.* On the contrary, he objects to *Ravad's* interpretation, deeming it an act of מַכֶּה בְּפַטִּישׁ, *striking the final blow.* Since one is cutting off the unheeded threads, he is putting the finishing touches on his work. (See below [38].)

◆§ The Weaving Process

Woven cloth consists of two series of parallel threads that criss-cross each other at right angles. Every second horizontal thread passes over the first vertical thread, under the second, over the third, under the fourth, etc. until it has passed through all the vertical threads. Each remaining horizontal thread passes under the first vertical thread, over the second, under the third, etc.

 In the weaving process, the vertical threads (called שְׁתִי, *warp*) are fixed in place, while a single thread (called עֵרֶב, *weft*) is passed over and under them first from right to left and then from left to right repeatedly. With each pass of the weft thread a new line of cloth is created.

To assure an even weave, the warp must be kept taut while the weft passes through it. This is accomplished by wrapping the warp threads around a beam (called the warp beam) and stretching them to a second beam (called the cloth beam, for it is around this beam that the finished fabric will be wound).

Clearly, the weaving process would be long and tedious unless some means of mechanization could be introduced, especially since the warp often contains as many as one hundred or more threads per inch. A method which would enable the weft thread to make a complete pass in one motion would obviously speed up the weaving process considerably.

 Additionally, since it is advantageous that the weft threads be (a) as long as possible (to avoid an excessive number of knots in the finished cloth), and (b) wound around a spool (to prevent tangling), a way must be found to pass a large bulky amount of weft thread 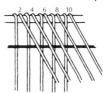 through the closely laid warp threads. These two objectives could be achieved if all the odd-numbered warp threads could be raised simultaneously to allow the weft thread to pass under them, but above the even-numbered threads. By then lowering the raised threads and raising the even-numbered ones, the weft thread could be passed through in the opposite direction.

In a weaving loom, two frames (called harnesses) are placed between the two beams and perpendicular to them (see illustration on next page). Each harness contains a number of threads, equal to half the number of threads in the warp, stretched vertically and looped in the center. The warp threads are then drawn through the loops. The looped threads are called נִירִין, *heddles*. The loops are called בָּתֵּי נִירִין, *heddle-eyes*. [Heddles may also be made by tying a ring between two threads, as in our illustration.]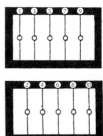

When the harnesses are in place, all odd-numbered warp threads are drawn through the heddle-eyes of one harness and between the heddles of the other,

© Copyright 1982, MPL. Reproduction prohibited.

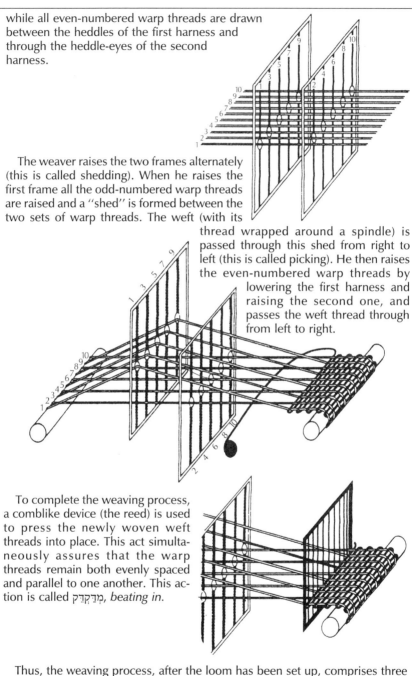

while all even-numbered warp threads are drawn between the heddles of the first harness and through the heddle-eyes of the second harness.

The weaver raises the two frames alternately (this is called shedding). When he raises the first frame all the odd-numbered warp threads are raised and a "shed" is formed between the two sets of warp threads. The weft (with its thread wrapped around a spindle) is passed through this shed from right to left (this is called picking). He then raises the even-numbered warp threads by lowering the first harness and raising the second one, and passes the weft thread through from left to right.

To complete the weaving process, a comblike device (the reed) is used to press the newly woven weft threads into place. This act simultaneously assures that the warp threads remain both evenly spaced and parallel to one another. This action is called מְדַקְדֵּק, *beating in*.

Thus, the weaving process, after the loom has been set up, comprises three steps: shedding, picking and beating in.

© *Copyright 1982, MPL. Reproduction prohibited.*

שבת ז/ב

[23] וְהַתּוֹפֵר שְׁתֵּי תְפִירוֹת, [24] הַקּוֹרֵעַ עַל מְנָת לִתְפֹּר שְׁתֵּי תְפִירוֹת; [25] הַצָּד צְבִי, [26] הַשּׁוֹחֲטוֹ, [27] וְהַמַּפְשִׁיטוֹ, [28] הַמּוֹלְחוֹ, [29] וְהַמְעַבֵּד אֶת

ר' עובדיה מברטנורא

והתופר וקורע. גמי הוי בירוטות, שכן יריעה שאכלה עש ונקבה בו נקב קטן ועגול צריך לקרוע למטה ולמעלה את הנקב שלא תהא התפירה עשויה קמטין קמטין: **והתופר שתי תפירות.** והוא שקשרן, דאי לא קשרן לא קיימי. ומחייב תרתי משום קושר ומשום תופר: **הצד צבי.** וכל מלאכת טורו נוהגת בתחשים בעורותיהן: **המולחו והמעבדו.** בגמרא מקשה דהיינו מולח היינו מעבד, אלא אפיק חד מינייהו ועייל שרטוט במקומו, שמשרטט מאבות מלאכות הוא:

יד אברהם

it, similar to the *melachah* of *tearing in order to sew two stitches* (see below [24]; *Tos. Yom Tov*).

Tosafos (73a) questions whether or not it is necessary for the liability of the *melachah* to be specifically for the purpose of retying or whether any other productive purpose suffices. *Tosafos* inclines to the view that it is necessary. *Rambam*, however, does not add this stipulation to his explanation of *untying*. He apparently rules that one who unties a knot, even without the intention of retying it, is liable (*Olas Shabbos* 317:6).

וְהַתּוֹפֵר שְׁתֵּי תְפִירוֹת, — [23] *sewing two stitches,*

I.e., a minimum of two stitches is required before one is liable for *sewing.* Since it is somewhat surprising that two stitches should be considered significant, the *Tanna* goes out of his way to specify the minimum of this *melachah* more so than in others (*Tif. Yis.*).

Since two stitches cannot hold unless the two ends of the thread are tied, one is not liable unless he ties the two ends (*Rav* from *Gem.* 74b; *Rashi,* ad loc.). Accordingly, he is liable for two sin offerings: one for *sewing* and one for *tying* (*Rav*).

Sefer Yereim states that a single knot, though it is insufficient to make one liable for *tying,* is nevertheless sufficient to make one liable for *sewing* when tied to the ends of a sewn thread.

Magen Avos extends this to include other knots [delineated in Ch. 15] which are exempt from *tying,* such as temporary and non-professional knots.

Gluing papers or hides together is a *toladah* of *sewing;* separating glued papers is a *toladah* of *tearing*

[24] — הַקּוֹרֵעַ עַל מְנָת לִתְפֹּר שְׁתֵּי תְפִירוֹת; *tearing in order to sew two stitches;*

The implication here is that liability for a sin offering is not incurred unless the *tearing* was done as a part of the mending process. Such tearing of the fabric is done when sewing together uneven pieces of fabric to prevent creases and lumps from forming in the area being stitched. [If small round moth holes were found in the curtains of the *Mishkan,* adjacent threads would be torn to broaden and square the hole, thus enabling the tailor to make a neat repair (*Rav* from *Gem.* and *Rashi* 75a). Even though many stitches were used, the Rabbis judged two stitches to be significant enough for liability (*Tos.* ad loc.).]

Tearing, as an *av,* is limited by the *Tanna* to *"tearing in order to sew."* This limitation

7 2 [23] sewing two stitches, and [24] tearing in order to sew two stitches; [25] trapping a deer, [26] slaughtering it, [27] skinning it, [28] salting it, [29] tanning its

YAD AVRAHAM

may be based on the fact that tearing per se is מְקַלְקֵל, *a destructive act*, and therefore not subject to a sin offering (although still Rabbinically prohibited; see General Introduction). *Tearing in order to sew*, on the other hand, is a productive act and, as such, subject to a sin offering. Accordingly, any positive or productive accomplishment effected by *tearing would also render one liable. Thus we find in mishnah 13:3, below, that one who tears his clothing on the Sabbath, in fulfillment of his obligation to rend his garments over the death of a near relative, is liable to a sin offering. Although he did not tear "in order to sew," he nevertheless did effect a positive result. This opinion is upheld by *Olas Shabbos* (317:15).

Others rule, however, that the intention to resew is an absolute requirement of this *av*. Absence of such intention, regardless of any other ends accomplished, renders the act exempt (*Beis Yosef* and *Magen Avraham* 317:10). [Since all *melachos* must be of a constructive nature, and tearing is, per se, a destructive act, we cannot derive from the *Mishkan* a general *melachah* of *tearing. Rather, we can derive only a more limited type of *melachah*; i.e., the act of tearing within the narrow context of its function in the *Mishkan*. Since in the *Mishkan* tearing was done only to facilitate sewing, the only *melachah* of *tearing there can be is for the purpose of *sewing.] This latter view, though, finds difficulty in explaining the ruling of 13:3 cited above (*Tos. R' Akiva;* see also *Tos.* 73b s.v., וצריך לעצים).

◆§ Melachos in the Preparation of a Scroll

The following seven *melachos* pertain to the preparation of hides as scrolls for writing. In the construction of the *Mishkan*, they were performed in the preparation of the hides of the תַּחַשׁ, *tachash* [a species now extinct], for the covering of the *Mishkan* (see *Exodus* 26:14; *Rav*).

הַצָּד צְבִי, — [25] *trapping a deer,*

The *trapping or hunting of any species is a *melachah* provided that the species is one which is normally trapped or hunted (deer is used by the *Tanna* because it is the most common example of such a species). A species not normally trapped or hunted (e.g., a housefly) is not included in this *melachah*. It is, nevertheless, Rabbinically prohibited [see 14:1].

הַשּׁוֹחֲטוֹ, — [26] *slaughtering it,*

This labor is not limited to שְׁחִיטָה, *ritual slaughter*, but also includes taking the life of any creature belonging to any species of wild or domestic beast, fowl, fish, or reptile; whether by slaughtering, stabbing, or battering.

Strangling a living creature, although it causes no loss of blood, is a *toladah* of *slaughtering (*Rambam, Hil Shabbos* 11:1 from *Gem.* 75a;b).

וְהַמַּפְשִׁיטוֹ, וְהַמּוֹלְחוֹ, — [27] *skinning it,* [28] *salting it,*

Salting the hide is the first step in *tanning (*Rashi* 75b).

וְהַמְעַבֵּד אֶת עוֹרוֹ, — [29] *tanning its hide,*

The *Gemara* objects to the separate listing of *salting and *tanning on the grounds that, since *salting is the beginning of the *tanning process, the two are actually one *melachah*. The *Gemara*, therefore, deletes one of these and substitutes שִׂרְטוּט, *tracing of lines*. Before leather is cut, lines are traced to

[187] THE MISHNAH/SHABBOS — Chapter Seven: *Klal Gadol*

שבת ז/ב עוֹרוֹ, [30] וְהַמּוֹחֲקוֹ, [31] וְהַמְחַתְּכוֹ, [32] הַכּוֹתֵב שְׁתֵּי אוֹתִיּוֹת, [33] וְהַמּוֹחֵק עַל מְנָת לִכְתּוֹב שְׁתֵּי אוֹתִיּוֹת; [34] הַבּוֹנֶה, [35] וְהַסּוֹתֵר; [36] הַמְכַבֶּה, [37] וְהַמַּבְעִיר; [38] הַמַּכֶּה בְּפַטִּישׁ,

— ר׳ עובדיה מברטנורא —

הממחקו. מגרד שערו: **מחתכו.** מקליטו ומחתכו לרצועות וסנדלים: **וכותב ומוחק.** הוא במשכן, שכן רושמים בקרסים לידע איזה בן זוגו וכותב אות בזה ואות בזה, ופעמים שטעה ומוחק: **מכבה ומבעיר.** באש שתחת דוד הסממנין: **מכה בפטיש.** הוא גמר מלאכה, שכן אומן מכה בסדן בגמר מלאכה, ואין מכה בפטיש אלא בגמר מלאכה. ומניינא דרישא דמנה אבות מלאכות ארבעים חסר אחת, אף על גב דהדר תשיב להו חדא חדא, אתא לאשמטינן דאפילו עביד אינש כל מלאכות

— יד אברהם —

indicate the desired shape. In the *Mishkan* this was done before cutting the hides of the rams and the *techashim* for the coverings (*Rav; Rashi* 75b).

Although salting meats or other foods to preserve them is akin to *tanning, there is no Biblical prohibition involved, because *tanning does not apply to foodstuffs (*Gem.* 75b). [See 14:2.]

וְהַמּוֹחֲקוֹ — [30] *smoothing it,*

I.e., scraping the hair off the hide (*Rav; Rambam, Comm.; Rashi*).

In the manufacture of parchment or leather, smooth skin is required. The hide must, therefore, be scraped clean (*Meiri*).

Plucking the feathery parts from a quill is a *toladah* of *smoothing (*Gem.* 74b). Similarly, smoothing out a poultice of any size, or wax, pitch, or any other substance whose surface is smoothed renders one liable for *smoothing (75b) (ibid.; *Rambam, Hil. Shabbos* 11:6).

וְהַמְחַתְּכוֹ — [31] *cutting it,*

I.e., trimming it and cutting it for straps or shoes (*Rav; Rashi*).

*Cutting a piece of leather (large enough to make an amulet) incurs liability only if attention is paid to the dimensions of the piece being cut. If, however, one cuts with intent to destroy, or absentmindedly, he is exempt.

Clipping the quill or stem of a feather to a specific size or the ends of wooden poles are *tolados* of *cutting (*Rambam, Hil. Shabbos* 11:7).

Included in this *melachah* are cutting, sawing; tearing or breaking either paper, wood, metal, fabric or any other substance to a specific size. The only stipulation is that one must do it in the manner considered normal for that substance [e.g. cutting paper, sawing wood] (*Kalkalas HaShabbos*).

הַכּוֹתֵב שְׁתֵּי אוֹתִיּוֹת — [32] *writing two letters,*

I.e., the writing of even two letters renders one liable (*Tif. Yis*).

Adjacent wall boards of the *Mishkan* were inscribed with the same letter to facilitate matching them each time the *Mishkan* was re-erected (*Rav* and *Rashi* from *Gem.* 103b). [See below 12:3-6.]

וְהַמּוֹחֵק עַל מְנָת לִכְתּוֹב שְׁתֵּי אוֹתִיּוֹת; — and [33] *erasing in order to write two letters;*

I.e., erasing two letters in order to write two other letters in their place (*Rambam, Hil. Shabbos* 11:9).

If the builders of the *Mishkan* erred

hide, [30] smoothing it, [31] cutting it, [32] writing two letters, and [33] erasing in order to write two letters; [34] building, and [35] demolishing; [36] extinguishing, and [37] kindling; [38] striking the final blow, and

YAD AVRAHAM

in writing the letters on a board, they would erase them in order to write the proper ones (Rav; Rashi from Gem. 103b).

The dispute cited above [24] concerning *tearing for a productive reason other than *sewing would also apply here to *erasing for a beneficial purpose other than *writing. For example, a superfluous letter was written in a passage of a Torah scroll. The scroll may not be used for public Torah reading until this superfluous letter is erased. Thus, erasing this letter would accomplish validating the scroll, although the erasure does not facilitate any new writing (Magen Avos, Beur Halachah 340:3 in name of Pri Megadim). Liability in this case would therefore be subject to the same difference of opinion cited above.

הַבּוֹנֶה, — [34] building,

*Building any amount is a melachah. Leveling the surface of the floor inside a house — e.g., by flattening a bump or filling in a rut or crack — is considered *building.

Making a permanent tent is a toladah of *building, as are making articles out of clay, cheese making, and inserting the handle of an ax into its socket (Rambam, Hil. Shabbos 10:12, 13 from Gem. 73b, 102b, 138a).

וְהַסּוֹתֵר; — and [35] demolishing;

Although the mishnah does not limit this melachah to demolishing in order to rebuild, such limitation is inherent in the labor. Otherwise, the act is a destructive one. The mishnah states this qualification in the cases of *tearing and *erasing, only to teach the amount required for liability. In the case of *demolishing, however, since any amount incurs liability (just as for building) the Tanna did not need to qualify his words (Tos. Yom Tov from Tos. 31b).

הַמְכַבֶּה, — [36] extinguishing,

I.e., extinguishing a fire. Both *extinguishing and the next labor, *kindling, were done in the context of the fire used to cook the dyes (Rashi; Rav).

As explained above (2:5), the purpose of *extinguishing in the construction of the Mishkan was to make charcoal (since otherwise extinguishing is not a constructive act). This was done because wood which has become charcoal ignites faster and burns better than raw wood.

Extinguishing fire for any purpose other than making charcoal is regarded as מְלָאכָה שֶׁאֵינָהּ צְרִיכָה לְגוּפָהּ, a labor not performed for its defined purpose (see General Introduction). As discussed above (2:5) there is a dispute between R' Yehudah and R' Shimon as to whether one is liable for such labor. According to all opinions, it is at least Rabbinically prohibited.

וְהַמַּבְעִיר; — and [37] kindling;

In the Mishkan, fire was kindled to cook the dyes (Rashi; Rav).

הַמַּכֶּה בְּפַטִּישׁ, — [38] striking the final blow (lit. one who strikes with a hammer),

Although the concept of finality is not inherent in the name given to this av, the Gemara (75b) understands it as the finishing touch at the completion of a job. Either it refers to the hammer

שבת ז/ב

[39] הַמּוֹצִיא מֵרְשׁוּת לִרְשׁוּת. הֲרֵי אֵלּוּ אֲבוֹת מְלָאכוֹת — אַרְבָּעִים חָסֵר אֶחָת.

ר' עובדיה מברטנורא

שבטלם בשבת אחת, בהעלם אחת, אי אפשר שיתחייב יותר מארבעים חטאות, דכולהו שאר מלאכות תולדות להנך אבות, ואשתכח דעביד אב ותולדה דיליה ולא מחייב אלא חדא:

יד אברהם

blow which the craftsman delivers to the anvil, leaving him a smooth surface for the next job (*Rashi; Rav*), or the blow dealt a finished utensil to smooth out any rough edges (*Ran* quoting R' *Chananel*; see also 12:1). Others explain it as the last hammer blow used to dislodge a hewn stone from its place when quarrying stone (see 12:1). Hence, the labor of *striking the final blow* comes to mean putting the finishing touch on any object which is essentially complete. If any other labor for which one is liable is still necessary, this *av* is not applicable (*Meiri* 104b).

Thus, putting the finishing touch on any object constitutes a *toladah* of *striking the final blow*. Included in this category are: blowing a glass vessel; carving designs; planing; drilling a hole in wood or metal of a building or utensil (*Rambam, Hil. Shabbos* 10:16); trimming a stone; picking protruding threads from a garment because their presence is disturbing (ibid. 10:18 from *Gem.* 75b).

However, making an opening in a building or utensil is considered a *toladah* of *striking the final blow* only if the opening is used for both entry and exit (ibid. 10:16 from *Gem.* 146a). An opening made for one-way passage, e.g., a hole in the roof of a chicken coop to allow the stagnant air to escape, is Rabbinically proscribed (*Gem.* ibid.).

[39] *and* — הַמּוֹצִיא מֵרְשׁוּת לִרְשׁוּת. *transferring [objects] from one domain to another domain.*

[I.e., either from a private domain to a public domain or vice versa, as has been delineated in the General Introduction. This *melachah* is elaborated upon in 1:1, the following two mishnayos and Chapters 8-11.]

הֲרֵי אֵלּוּ אֲבוֹת מְלָאכוֹת — אַרְבָּעִים חָסֵר אֶחָת. — *These are the primary labors — forty minus one.*

The repetition of this number, already mentioned in the beginning of the mishnah, requires explanation. By enumerating each *melachah* individually, the *Tanna* obviates the need for any number at all, since it is not the style of the *Tanna* to state a number for the sole purpose of sparing us the necessity of calculating it ourselves. *Rav* explains the purpose of the first number as alluding to the maximum number of sin offerings for which one may be liable on any one Sabbath. No matter how many *melachos* one performs, he can never be liable to more than thirty-nine, since beyond that one is, of necessity, repeating certain categories. Though one may perform different labors within one category (e.g., performing the *av* and one or several of its *tolados*), one can never be liable to more than one sin offering for all inadvertent transgressions committed under any one category of labor on any given Sabbath. (See mishnah 1.)[1]

---

1. Though this too might seem obvious from the last rule of mishnah 1, some additional clarification of that rule is still necessary. Left on its own, that rule might be erroneously

[39] transferring [objects] from one domain to another domain. These are the primary labors — forty minus one.

YAD AVRAHAM

Rav, however, does not offer any explanation for the second reference to the number 39 in the mishnah.

Tosefos Yom Tov explains differently. Seemingly, it should be impossible for a person to be liable for even thirty-nine sin offerings on one Sabbath. In order to be liable to a sin offering, a person must have transgressed the prohibition inadvertently. As explained in mishnah 1, this can occur in one of two ways. Either one forgot (or never knew) the laws of Sabbath, or one forgot that it was the Sabbath day. In the latter case, mishnah 1 teaches that one is liable for only one sin offering for all transgressions committed on that one Sabbath. Under no circumstances can this form of inadvertence, then, lead to thirty-nine sin offerings on one Sabbath. This leaves us with only the first type of inadvertence, forgetting the laws of the Sabbath. Mishnah 1, however, further teaches that one who forgets the basic law of Sabbath (i.e., the basic prohibition against working on the Sabbath) is not liable to more than one sin offering. In order for one to be aware of this prohibition, he must be aware of at least one category of labor which is prohibited. Being aware of one prohibited category, it is possible for him to assume mistakenly that the general prohibition against working on the Sabbath applies solely to this one category. In this manner, one could be said to be aware of the basic law of Sabbath but unaware of the many specific prohibitions involved. Consequently, he could be liable for every category transgressed but only up to a maximum of thirty-eight. If, however, one is unaware of all thirty-nine categories then one must, apparently, be unaware of even the basic prohibition against working on the Sabbath, in which case he would be liable for only one sin offering. It is, therefore, seemingly impossible for anyone to be liable to thirty-nine sin offerings on one Sabbath. The Gemara (70b), in dealing with this problem, offers two possibilities. One is that the person was aware of the prohibition but unaware of its severity; i.e., he did not know that it bears the penalty of kares for willful transgression (when not performed in the presence of witnesses and therefore not subject to the punishment of the court). Though committing the transgression willfully, by not being aware of its severity, the person is considered an inadvertently transgressor. This is because the law

interpreted as referring only to the performance of two tolados of one category but not to the performance of an av and its toladah. The literal wording of that mishnah could support such an interpretation. It states, One who performs many labors of one [category of] labor, which could be taken to mean that one performed several labors of the category but not the av itself. If that were true, it would be possible to be liable to up to seventy-eight sin offerings on one Sabbath (by performing each av and one of its tolados). The Tanna, therefore, adds in mishnah 2 the seemingly redundant statement that there are thirty-nine principal categories of labor, thereby indicating that the maximum number of sin offerings possible on any one Sabbath is thirty-nine and laying to rest any possible misinterpretation of mishnah 1 (Tos. Yom Tov from Tos.).

שבת
ג/ז

[ג] **וְעוֹד כְּלָל** אַחֵר אָמְרוּ: כָּל הַכָּשֵׁר לְהַצְנִיעַ, וּמַצְנִיעִין כָּמוֹהוּ, וְהוֹצִיאוֹ בַשַּׁבָּת, חַיָּב עָלָיו חַטָּאת. וְכָל שֶׁאֵינוֹ

───── ר׳ עובדיה מברטנורא ─────

(ג) **כל הכשר להצניע.** שהוא דבר העשוי לצורך האדם:

יד אברהם

assumes that had he, in fact, been aware of the severity of the transgression, he would have refrained from violating any of the prohibitions. By being aware of all thirty-nine prohibitions but by being unaware of their severity, it is possible for a person to transgress all thirty-nine categories of labor on one Sabbath inadvertently while still being aware of the basic prohibition against work on the Sabbath. This explanation follows the opinion of R' Yochanan, quoted by the *Gemara*.

An alternative explanation follows the opinion of R' Akiva. He states that there is a Scriptural prohibition against traveling more that one *mil* away from one's city or campsite on the Sabbath. A *mil* is 2,000 cubits, equal to between approximately one half to two thirds of a mile depending on the various opinions to the proper conversion of cubits to feet. According to the Sages, this is only a Rabbinic prohibition. According to R' Akiva's view, it is possible for a person to have been aware of the prohibition against laboring on the Sabbath but to believe that it applies only to traveling more that a *mil*. Being totally unaware of the thirty-nine categories of labor, he can transgress them all while yet being aware of the basic law of Sabbath. In consequence, he would be liable to thirty-nine sin offerings on one Sabbath. The *Tanna*, by stating the number thirty-nine at the beginning of the mishnah, draws attention to the fact that it is possible to be liable to thirty-nine sin offerings on one Sabbath. The precise manner in which it is possible depends on which of the above-mentioned opinions one follows.

The repetition of thirty-nine at the end of the mishnah is to preclude the opinion of R' Yehudah, who counts two more labors as *avos*, but which the Sages deem *tolados*. The *Tanna* therefore repeats, *these are the primary [categories of] labors, forty minus one*, to emphasize that there are no others.

[The mere listing of the *avos* does not preclude others from being included. In several places the *Gemara* points out that it is the style of the mishnah to list items without intending that list to be complete. See *Sukkah* 54a and *Masores HaShas* there for other references.]

3.

From here on, the mishnah discusses the details of the *avos melachos* enumerated in the preceding mishnah. As is often the case throughout mishnayos, the mishnah begins the detailed analysis of a long list of items by first discussing the last-mentioned item, in this case the *av* of *transferring from one domain to another* (*Tos. Yom Tov*). From here until the beginning of Chapter 11, the mishnah discusses the various minimum amounts, depending on the object involved, for which one is liable for *transferring on the Sabbath. As an introduction to this, the mishnah establishes the general rule governing the minimum amounts for any

משניות / שבת — פרק פרק ז: כלל גדול   [192]

7
3

3. They stated yet another general rule: Whatever is fit to store, and people store such [a quantity], and one carried it out on the Sabbath, he is liable for a sin offering. But whatever is

YAD AVRAHAM

substance for which one is liable for carrying on the Sabbath. It is from this general rule that the Rabbis derived the specific minimums for each substance. [Though even less than the minimum amount is also forbidden by the Torah (*Yoma* 74a), one is not liable for punishment or sin offering for inadvertent transgression unless an at least minimally substantive result has been achieved by the transgression. Less than this amount is too insignificant to warrant any specific Torah judgment. One may, however, still be subject to Rabbinic punishment (see *Rambam, Hil. Shevisas HeAsor* 2:3 and *Maggid Mishneh* there).]

This is true of all Torah prohibitions, be they subject to capital punishment, *kares*, corporal punishment, or any of the various types of sin offerings. The amounts, however, vary not only from prohibition to prohibition but also from item to item within one prohibition. As regards the laws of Sabbath, for instance, the minimums vary not only from category to category but even from one object to another within one category. The variations depend on with which and to which object one is doing the *melachah*. The remainder of this chapter and the next three chapters detail the minimums for many commonly carried objects, while later chapters will delineate minimums for other *melachos*.

וְעוֹד כְּלָל אַחֵר אָמְרוּ: — *They stated yet another general rule:*

[I.e., the Rabbis stated another rule concerning the liability for sin offerings for violation of the Sabbath.]

The rule stated in mishnah 1 applies to all *melachos*, whereas this latter rule applies only to the *melachah* of **transferring from one domain to another* (*Shenos Eliyahu*).

כָּל הַכָּשֵׁר לְהַצְנִיעַ, — *Whatever is fit to store,*

I.e., it is a substance normally used by people (*Rav; Rashi*).

One who carries out something usually discarded by people is not liable to a sin offering. The *Gemara* interprets this to exclude the wood of an *asheirah* (a tree used in pagan worship), because one is forbidden to derive any benefit from it and is obligated to burn it (*Ran*). Also excluded is a woman's menstrual discharge (*Gem.* 75b). Other repulsive substances are also excluded from liability (*Tif. Yis.*).

וּמַצְנִיעִין כָּמוֹהוּ, — *and people store such [a quantity],*

I.e., it is an amount that is worth keeping (*Rav; Rashi*)

Thus, the substance carried out must be both a substance used by people and in an amount worth keeping (*Tif. Yis.; Tos. R' Akiva*).

וְהוֹצִיאוֹ בַשַּׁבָּת, — *and one carried it out on the Sabbath,*

[I.e., one carried it from one domain to another.]

חַיָּב עָלָיו חַטָּאת. — *he is liable for a sin offering.*

I.e., even if the one who carries it is wealthy and this substance is of no importance to him, he is, nevertheless, liable (*Tif. Yis.*). [Being of importance

שבת ז/ד

כָּשֵׁר לְהַצְנִיעַ, וְאֵין מַצְנִיעִין כָּמוֹהוּ, וְהוֹצִיאוֹ בַּשַּׁבָּת, אֵינוֹ חַיָּב אֶלָּא הַמַּצְנִיעוֹ.

[ד] הַמּוֹצִיא תֶּבֶן, כִּמְלֹא פִי פָרָה; עֵצָה, כִּמְלֹא פִי גָמָל; עָמִיר, כִּמְלֹא פִי טָלֶה; עֲשָׂבִים, כִּמְלֹא פִי גְדִי;

ר' עובדיה מברטנורא

ומצניעין כמוהו. שיש בו שיעור הראוי להצניעו: **אין חייב אלא המצניעו.** אם נעשה חביב על אדם אחד והצניעו, חייב על הוצאתו אם הוציאו, אבל אדם אחר אינו חייב עליו, דלגביה לאו מלאכה היא: (ד) **עצה.** תבן של מיני קטניות: **כמלוא פי גמל.** שיעורו גדול ממלוא פי פרה, וכמלוא פי פרה לא מחייב בעצה, דהא לא חזיא לפרה: **עמיר.** קשין של שבלין: **פי טלה.** נפיש מפי גדי, הילכך עמיר דלא חזי לגדי לא מחייב כמלא פי גדי עד דאיכא מלא פי טלה, אבל עשבים הואיל וחזי לגדי ולטלה מחייב אפילו כמלוא פי גדי.

יד אברהם

to the general populace, the law does not take into account the specific circumstances rendering the substance unimportant to a particular individual.]

וְכָל שֶׁאֵינוֹ כָשֵׁר לְהַצְנִיעַ — *But whatever is unfit to store,*

I.e., a substance not used by people. [This does not mean to preclude certain very valuable or rare items not normally available for daily usage. Rather, it precludes items which, though commonly available, are not considered worth using.]

וְאֵין מַצְנִיעִין כָּמוֹהוּ, — *or [people] do not store [it in] such [a quantity],*

I.e., even if the substance is one used by people but it is in a quantity people do not consider worth keeping (*Tif. Yis.; Tos. R' Akiva*).

וְהוֹצִיאוֹ בַּשַּׁבָּת, אֵינוֹ חַיָּב אֶלָּא הַמַּצְנִיעוֹ. — *and one carried it out on the Sabbath, the only one liable (lit., none is liable except) is the one who stores it.*

I.e., if a person took a liking to a certain material and stored it away, though it is either a smaller quantity than usually saved or a material not normally used by people, he is liable for *transferring on the Sabbath. Others, however, are exempt, since, to the population at large, it is not important (*Rav; Rashi*).

[The rule therefore is: An item considered important by most people achieves a legal status of "importance" vis-a-vis all people. An item considered unimportant by most people may yet achieve a status of "importance" to one who actually values it.] There is a dissenting opinion expressed to this rule in mishnah 8:1. It will be explained there.

4.

After stating that one is not liable for a sin offering for *transferring from one domain to another* unless one carries out both a quality and a quantity that people consider of sufficient value to store, the mishnah details the precise minimum quantities of various commonly used substances.

unfit to store, or [people] do not store [it in] such [a quantity], and one carried it out on the Sabbath, the only one liable is the one who stores it.

4. One who takes out straw [is liable if he takes out] as much as a cow's mouthful; bean straw, as much as a camel's mouthful; straw of ears of grain, as much as a lamb's mouthful; grass, as much as a kid's mouthful;

YAD AVRAHAM

הַמּוֹצִיא תֶבֶן, — *One who takes out straw*

I.e., straw taken from the stalks of grain (*Meiri; Shenos Eliyahu* from *Rashi* 140a).

It is the upper part of the stalk, in contrast to the stubble (*Tos. Yom Tov* to *Bava Metzia*; see also 3:1).

כִּמְלֹא פִּי פָרָה; — *[is liable if he takes out] as much as a cow's mouthful;*

Since straw is commonly eaten by cows, a cow's mouthful is the prescribed measure, even if one takes it out to feed a camel [for whom this quantity is insignificant] (*Meiri* from *Gem.* 76a).

עָצָה, — *bean straw,*

[I.e., one who takes out bean straw is not liable unless he took out at least . . .]

כִּמְלֹא פִּי גָמָל; — *as much as a camel's mouthful;*

This measure is larger than a cow's mouthful.

Since bean straw is not generally fit for bovine consumption, one is not liable for taking out as much as a cow's mouthful (*Rav; Rashi*). [Bean straw is hard, as evidenced by the name עָצָה, derived from עֵץ, *wood.*]

One who takes bean straw out expressly to feed a cow, however, is liable for even a cow's mouthful, since a cow can, with difficulty, eat bean straw (*Rambam, Hil. Shabbos* 18:3). [This is a corollary of the rule stated at the end of the previous mishnah. The *general* importance of an item is determined by its common usage. Since in common usage bean straw is used only to feed camels, it generally requires at least a camel's mouthful to incur liability. One, however, who decides to force his cow to eat bean straw, thereby attaches personal value to a smaller measure of it. Since a cow can actually eat bean straw, albeit with difficulty, he personally is liable for carrying out this smaller amount.]

עָמִיר, כִּמְלֹא פִּי טָלֶה; — *straw of ears of grain, as much as a lamb's mouthful;*

This should not be confused with straw mentioned in the beginning of the mishnah. This is a softer straw, which is fit for the consumption of smaller animals (*Tif. Yis.*).

Others render this as straw of fenugreek (*Aruch*).

עֲשָׂבִים, כִּמְלֹא פִּי גְדִי; — *grass, as much as a kid's mouthful;*

A lamb's mouthful is larger than a kid's mouthful. Since the straw of ears of grain is still too hard for a kid, one is not liable unless he carries out a minimum of a lamb's mouthful. For carrying out grass, however, which is

שבת ז/ד

עֲלֵי שׁוּם וַעֲלֵי בְצָלִים לַחִים, כִּגְרוֹגֶרֶת, יְבֵשִׁים, כִּמְלֹא פִי גְדִי. וְאֵין מִצְטָרְפִין זֶה עִם זֶה מִפְּנֵי שֶׁלֹּא שָׁווּ בְשִׁעוּרֵיהֶן. הַמּוֹצִיא אֳכָלִים כִּגְרוֹגֶרֶת חַיָּב. וּמִצְטָרְפִין זֶה עִם זֶה מִפְּנֵי שֶׁשָּׁווּ בְשִׁעוּרֵיהֶן — חוּץ מִקְּלִפֵּיהֶן, וְגַרְעִינֵיהֶן, וְעֻקְצֵיהֶן, וְסֻבָּן, וּמֻרְסָנָן. רַבִּי יְהוּדָה אוֹמֵר: חוּץ מִקְּלִפֵּי עֲדָשִׁים

ר' עובדיה מברטנורא

לחים. הראויין לאדם: **כגרוגרת.** דזה שיעור לכל מאכל אדם בשבת, אבל כמלא פי גדי לא, דלחים לא חזו לגדי: **ומצטרפין.** כל אוכלי אדם זה עם זה: **חוץ מקליפיהן.** שאינן אוכל ואין משלימין השיעור: **ועוקציהן.** זנב הפרי דהוא עץ בעלמא: **וסובן.** קליפת החטים הנושרת מחמת הכתישה: **ומורסנן.** הנשאר בנפה. ורמב"ס פירש איפכא דמורסן הוא עבה וגרוע מסובין: **חוץ מקליפי עדשים.** [שמלטרפין]:

יד אברהם

fit for either a lamb or a kid, one is liable for the smaller measure, namely, a kid's mouthful (Rav; Rashi).

A lamb's mouthful is equal to the bulk of a dried fig, the amount for which one is liable for carrying out foodstuffs fit for human consumption. The *Tanna* worded it in this manner, however, to illustrate the reason for this measure (*Tos. R' Akiva* from *Gem.* 76a, *Tos.*, ad loc.).

עֲלֵי שׁוּם וַעֲלֵי בְצָלִים לַחִים, כִּגְרוֹגֶרֶת, — leaves of garlic or onion [if they are] fresh, the equivalent of a dried fig,

This refers to the tubulated leaves which sprout from the bulb of the onion above ground, and by which the onion can be picked (*Tos. Yom Tov*).

Since these are fit for human consumption, the prescribed measure is the equivalent of a dried fig (i.e., a quantity of leaves equal in volume to a dried fig), as is that of all foodstuffs. If one carried out as much as a kid's mouthful, he is exempt from a sin offering because fresh garlic and onion leaves are not fit for kid's fare (*Rav; Rashi*).

יְבֵשִׁים, — [if they are] dry,

[I.e., dry garlic and onion which are not used for consumption.]

כִּמְלֹא פִי גְדִי. — as much as a kid's mouthful.

[One is liable for carrying out this amount, since they are fit for kids.]

וְאֵין מִצְטָרְפִין זֶה עִם זֶה — And they cannot be combined with one another

E.g., if one carried out one half of a cow's mouthful of grain straw and one half of a camel's mouthful of bean straw, he is not liable (*Tif. Yis.*).

מִפְּנֵי שֶׁלֹּא שָׁווּ בְשִׁעוּרֵיהֶן. — because they are not alike in their prescribed measures.

I.e., since bean straw has less stringent regulations than grain straw (imposing liability only for a larger minimum), it cannot be counted to complete the minimum required for grain straw. On the other hand, if one carried out less than a *camel's mouthful* of bean straw and completed the minimum of a camel's mouthful by adding to it grain straw, he is liable. Since grain straw has more stringent

משניות / שבת – פרק ז: כלל גדול [196]

leaves of garlic or onion [if they are] fresh, the equivalent of a dried fig, [if they are] dry, as much as a kid's mouthful. And they cannot be combined with one another because they are not alike in their prescribed measures.

One who takes out foodstuffs the equivalent of a dried fig is liable. And they can be combined with each other because they are alike in their prescribed measures — excluding their shells, their pits, their stems, their coarse bran, and their fine bran.

R' Yehudah says: Excluding the shells of lentils

YAD AVRAHAM

regulations than bean straw (imposing liability for carrying out a smaller minimum), it can be counted towards meeting the less stringent minimum. One must, however, add a sufficient amount so that, in total, it adds up to the larger amount (*Tif. Yis; Tos. R' Akiva* from *Gem.* 76a).

הַמּוֹצִיא אֲכָלִים — *One who takes out foodstuffs*

I.e., any foodstuffs fit for human consumption (*Tif. Yis.*).

בִּגְרוֹגֶרֶת חַיָּב. — *the equivalent of a dried fig is liable.*

This minimum is a הֲלָכָה לְמֹשֶׁה מִסִּינַי, *a rule told to Moshe at Sinai*, but neither written nor alluded to in the written Torah (*Eruvin* 4b).

וּמִצְטָרְפִין זֶה עִם זֶה — *And they can be combined with each other*

I.e., all foodstuffs fit for human consumption can be combined with each other to make up the minimum of the equivalent of a dried fig (*Rav; Rashi*).

מִפְּנֵי שֶׁשָּׁווּ בְשִׁעוּרֵיהֶן — *because they are alike in their prescribed measures —*

I.e., because they all have the identical minimums for liability.

חוּץ מִקְּלִפֵּיהֶן, וְגַרְעִינֵיהֶן, וְעֻקְצֵיהֶן, — *excluding their shells, their pits, their stems,*

None of these is food and therefore cannot be counted towards the minimum (*Rav; Rashi*).

וְסֻבָּן, — *their coarse bran,*

This is the outer shell of the wheat kernel, which falls off when the wheat is pounded (*Rav; Rashi*).

וּמֻרְסָנָן. — *and their fine bran.*

This is found in the sifter after sifting the flour (*Rashi*).

Rambam reverses these latter two translations (*Rav*). Although bran is eaten along with the grain, it is not considered of any value, and is, therefore, not counted toward the minimum (*Tos. Yom Tov*).

רַבִּי יְהוּדָה אוֹמֵר: חוּץ מִקְּלִפֵּי עֲדָשִׁים — *R' Yehudah says: Excluding the shells of lentils*

I.e., the shells of lentils do count toward the minimum of a fig's bulk to make one liable for carrying out on the Sabbath (*Rav; Rashi*).

[197] THE MISHNAH/SHABBOS — Chapter Seven: *Klal Gadol*

שבת ז/ד שֶׁמִּתְבַּשְּׁלוֹת עִמָּהֶן.

ר' עובדיה מברטנורא

שהן מתבשלות עמהן. לאפוקי הקליפות החיצונות שהן נושרות כשטוחש מהם גורן. וקליפי הפולין בזמן שהן לחים ומתבשלין עם קליפתן, לרבי יהודה מלטרפין עם האוכלין לשיעור גרוגרת, אבל יבשים לא שהרי נאכלין בקליפתן לפי שהן נראין כזבובין בקטרה. ואין הלכה כרבי יהודה:

יד אברהם

שֶׁמִּתְבַּשְּׁלוֹת עִמָּהֶן — *which are cooked with them.* I.e., since people cook the lentils without first shelling them, and the

7 4 which are cooked with them.

YAD AVRAHAM

peels are then eaten, they are considered part of the lentil and can be counted toward making up the minimum.

This excludes the outer shell, which falls off at their harvest time. Also excluded are of the shells of dried beans, which are not eaten with the beans. The shells of fresh beans, however, are eaten like those of lentils, and are, therefore, counted toward the minimum measure of liability (*Rav* from *Gem.* 76b).

פרק שמיני
Chapter Eight

The previous chapter concluded by delineating the minimum measurements of various foodstuffs required before one is held liable for *transferring* them from one domain to another on the Sabbath. This chapter continues by doing the same for various beverages, liquids and other substances (*Chidushei HaRan*).

שבת
ח/א

[א] **הַמּוֹצִיא** יַיִן, כְּדֵי מְזִיגַת הַכּוֹס; חָלָב, כְּדֵי גְמִיעָה; דְּבַשׁ, כְּדֵי לִתֵּן עַל הַכָּתִית;

ר' עובדיה מברטנורא

פרק שמיני – המוציא. (א) המוציא [יין] **כדי מזיגת הכוס.** של ברכת המזון, שהוא רובע רביעית יין חי, כדי שימזגנו לחשבון על חד של יין תלתא ממים ויעמוד על רביעית הלוג שהוא שיעור כוס של ברכה: **כדי גמיעה.** מה שאדם בולע בבת אחת, וחלב בהמה טמאה דלא חזי לשתיה שיעורו כדי לכחול עין אחת: **על הכתית.** מכה שעל גבי הסוסים והחמורים מחמת המשאוי. ומלאתי כתוב שאחין היוצא בטור הבשר, כשמגיע להתבשל הוא עושה ראש למעלה וקרוי פי כתית. ואף על פי שהדבש עיקרו לאכילה, כיון שרפואתו מצויה, והוא משהו, אזלינן בתר שיעורא זוטרא לחומרא:

יד אברהם

הַמּוֹצִיא יַיִן — **One who takes out wine**
[I.e., one who takes wine from one domain to another or carries it a distance of 4 cubits in a public domain.]

כְּדֵי מְזִיגַת הַכּוֹס; — [is liable if he takes out] enough for mixing a cup;
I.e., enough wine for mixing the cup used for reciting בִּרְכַּת הַמָּזוֹן [Bircas HaMazon], Grace After Meals.

[The Bircas HaMazon is properly recited over a cup of wine, the same as Kiddush or Havdalah. There are various opinions as to when this is done. Some rule that it is only done when at least three men recite the Bircas HaMazon together. Others rule that even an individual uses a cup of wine when reciting the Bircas HaMazon. A third opinion rules that one is not obliged to use a cup of wine when reciting the Bircas HaMazon; it is, however, preferable wherever possible (Shulchan Aruch 182:1). The custom of most people follows the third opinion (Mishnah Berurah ibid. 4).]

The actual amount referred to in this mishnah is 1/16 of a log. This figure is arrived at because the minimum size of the cup used for Bircas HaMazon (or Kiddush, Havdalah, and the Four Cups of the Pesach Seder) is one quarter of a log, known as a reviis. Since, however, the wines of that era were very strong, it was necessary to dilute the wine with water, the whole mixture adding up to one cup. This is what is meant by enough for mixing a cup, i.e., the amount of wine needed to mix with water to form one cupful. The prescribed dilution for the wines was three parts water to one part wine. The amount of wine actually used, therefore, was only one quarter of the total volume of the cup. This comes to 1/16[1] of a log (Gem. 76b).

חָלָב, — milk,
I.e., if one carries out the milk of a kosher animal, which is fit for drinking (Rav; Rambam). (The milk of a non-kosher animal, since it may not be drunk, has a different standard, as will be explained below.)

כְּדֵי גְמִיעָה; — enough for a swallow;
I.e., he is liable for carrying out the amount of milk normally swallowed in one gulp (Rav; Rambam).

The Gemara does not define this amount in terms of other measurements. Tosafos quotes R' Poras who

---
1. The conversion of lugin into modern measurements is a matter of controversy. According to the various opinions it ranges from 13.2 to 21.2 fluid ounces. One sixteenth of a log would then be between 0.8 and 1.3 fluid ounces.

Since present-day wines are not as strong as those discussed in the mishnah, wine diluted in the stated proportions might not be considered wine regarding the required blessing.

משניות / שבת – פרק ח: המוציא יין [202]

1. One who takes out wine [is liable if he takes out] enough for mixing a cup; milk, enough for a swallow; honey, enough to apply to a sore;

YAD AVRAHAM

identifies this as the equivalent of the commonly found measurement called מְלֹא לוּגְמָיו, a *cheek full*, which comes to just over half the quarter-*log* necessary for *Bircas HaMazon* or *Kiddush*.

Maggid Mishneh (*Hil. Shabbos* 18:2) quotes *Ramban* who maintains that this is less than a cheek full. See also *Ran*, who differentiates between the two measurements.

As mentioned above, this measurement applies only to the milk of a kosher animal, since it may be used for drinking. If one carries out the milk of a non-kosher animal, he is liable if he carries out an amount sufficient to apply to one eye as medicine (*Rav, Rambam* from *Yerushalmi Shabbos* 8:1).

The amount of milk one needs to apply to one eye is very minute, surely less than a swallow. The question therefore arises as to why one is not equally liable for carrying out this lesser quantity of the milk of even a kosher animal, since it, too, can be used for medicinal purposes.

The answer is that since kosher milk is commonly used for drinking, one is liable only for carrying out the amount regarded as a drink. Since it is not commonly used for medicinal purposes, one is not liable for carrying out an amount useful solely as medicine. Non-kosher milk, however, since it is rarely used for either purpose, and since the smaller amount is indeed useful, is determined by the smaller standard of enough to apply to one eye (*Mareh HaPenim, Yerushalmi*). This follows the rule explained in the previous chapter that the minimums of each item are determined by their common usage. (See Chap. 7. See also the next paragraph for further elaboration.)

דְּבַשׁ, כְּדֵי לִתֵּן עַל הַכָּתִית; — *honey, enough to apply to a sore;*

I.e., one is liable for carrying out honey in an amount sufficient to put on a sore (as a salve). The mishnah refers to one of several types of commonly found small sores whose size was generally known, for which reason the *Tanna* did not bother to elaborate. The commentaries list three possibilities: (a) sores on the backs of camels and horses resulting from the constant rubbing of their packs (*Rashi; Rav*); (b) abrasions on the backs of hands or legs (*Rashi* citing his teachers); (c) boils coming to a head, in this instance honey was placed on the point of the boil (*Rav; Meiri*).

Even though honey is used mainly as a food, whose prescribed measurement is the equivalent of a dried fig (as in 7:4), it is also *commonly* used for medicinal purposes. We therefore adopt the smaller measure of enough to apply to a sore (*Rav, Meiri* from *Gem.* 78a). This is in contradistinction to kosher milk, which though it may be used as an eyewash (a smaller standard), is, nevertheless, reckoned as a beverage (necessitating a larger standard for liability). The *Gemara* (78a) states the following principle: *Any item which has both a common use and an uncommon use, the Rabbis went by its common use, adopting the lenient standard,* i.e., even where following the common use would mean adopting the more lenient standard.

שבת ח/א

שֶׁמֶן, כְּדֵי לָסוּךְ אֵבֶר קָטָן; מַיִם, כְּדֵי לָשׁוּף בָּהֶם אֶת הַקִּילוֹר. וּשְׁאָר כָּל הַמַּשְׁקִין בִּרְבִיעִית; וְכָל הַשּׁוֹפְכִין, בִּרְבִיעִית. רַבִּי שִׁמְעוֹן אוֹמֵר: כֻּלָּן בִּרְבִיעִית. וְלֹא אָמְרוּ כָּל הַשִּׁעוּרִין הַלָּלוּ

ר' עובדיה מברטנורא

אבר קטן. של תינוק בן יומו והוא אלבע קטנה שברגל: **לשוף.** לשפשף ולמחות בהן: **קילור.** שנותנין על העין: **ושאר כל המשקין.** שאין תושין מהם רפואה: **שופכין.** מים סרוחין, וחזו לגבל בהן את הטיט: **כולן ברביעית.** אף יין וחלב ודבש, דלא נאמרו שעורין במשנה אלא למעליתיהן, אבל שאר כל אדם אין חייבין אלא ברביעית. וסבירא ליה לרבי שמעון דמעליט עלמו בעי שיעורא זוטא, ובבליר מהאי שיעורא לא מחייב דלית ליה לרבי שמעון כל שאין כשר להעליט ואין מעליעין עליו מעליעו שיתחייב בכל שהוא, ואין הלכה כרבי שמעון:

יד אברהם

Where both (uses) are common, the Rabbis adopted the common use with the more stringent (i.e., smaller) standard ... with respect to milk, whose use as a beverage is common but whose medicinal use (as eyewash) is uncommon, the Rabbis went by its use as a beverage, adopting the more lenient standard (i.e., not considering him liable unless he carries out the larger measure of enough for a swallow); regarding honey, whose use as food is common and whose use as a medicine (salve) is also common, the Rabbis went by its common use as a medicine, adopting the more stringent standard (i.e., considering him liable for carrying out even the smaller amount of enough to apply to a sore).

It should be noted that although honey is certainly used as a food more often than as a salve, its use as a salve was neither uncommon nor unusual. Since both measures represent common and therefore significant uses of honey, there is no compelling reason to adopt the larger (more lenient) standard rather than the smaller (more stringent) one. We are therefore forced to adopt the more stringent measure as the one applicable to the prohibition of carrying. The use of kosher milk as eyewash, on the other hand, is unusual and we therefore view it as a beverage only. Non-kosher milk, however, was not commonly used for anything whatsoever. There was therefore again no reason to defer to its larger standard (as a beverage) since all its uses were equally uncommon. The smaller standard (as eyewash) was therefore adopted.

שֶׁמֶן, כְּדֵי לָסוּךְ אֵבֶר קָטָן; — *oil, enough to anoint a small limb;*

I.e., one is liable for carrying out oil only if it is an amount at least sufficient to anoint a small limb. [Olive oil was commonly applied after bathing, in olden times. See *Gem.* 41a.]

The *Gemara* (77b, 78a) explains this as an amount sufficient to anoint the smallest limb of a newborn infant. Some explain this as the infant's little toe (*Rav; Rambam*); others as a joint of its little finger (*Rashi*).

מַיִם, כְּדֵי לָשׁוּף בָּהֶם אֶת־הַקִּילוֹר. — *water, enough to rub on an eye plaster.*

I.e., one is liable for carrying out water only if it is an amount at least sufficient to rub on an eye plaster.

8
1
oil, enough to anoint a small limb; water, enough to rub on an eye plaster. **[For] all other liquids [one is liable] for a quarter-log; and [for] all waste water, for a quarter-*log*.**

R' Shimon says: [For] all of them, [one is liable] for a quarter-*log*. They did not state all these measurements

YAD AVRAHAM

Since this use was a common one the Rabbis adopted it as the standard for water just as with honey.

Although other liquids, too, are suitable for this purpose, only water is commonly used, since other liquids form a crust and impede one's vision. The mishnah rules, therefore, that only in the case of water is one liable for this amount; other liquids require an amount suitable for drinking (*Tos. R' Akiva* from *Gem.* 78a).

וּשְׁאָר כָּל הַמַּשְׁקִין בִּרְבִיעִית — **[For] all other liquids [one is liable] for a quarter-log;**

I.e., for all other liquids not used for medicinal purposes (*Rav*), one is liable only if he carries out at least a רְבִיעִית, *quarter-log*. (For the various opinions concerning this amount, see footnote 1, p. 202.)

וְכָל הַשֹּׁפָכִין, בִּרְבִיעִית. — **and [for] all waste water, for a quarter-log.**

I.e., if one carries out dirty or fouled water, unfit for drinking, he is liable only if he carries at least a quarter-*log*. Since the water is fouled, he would not apply it to an eye plaster. He must therefore have at least a quarter-*log* since it is then suitable for kneading clay (*Rav* from *Gem.* 78a).

רַבִּי שִׁמְעוֹן אוֹמֵר: כֻּלָּן בִּרְבִיעִית. — **R' Shimon says: [For] all of them [one is liable] for a quarter-log.**

I.e., for all liquids, including milk, honey, and wine, one is liable only if he carries out at least a quarter-*log* (*Rav; Rashi*).[1]

וְלֹא אָמְרוּ כָל הַשִּׁעוּרִין הַלָּלוּ — **They did not state all these measurements**

I.e., the Rabbis did not state the standards of less than a *reviis* given for wine, milk, and honey as making one liable *except for* ...

[R' Shimon does not dispute the validity of these lesser measures, which were propounded by Rabbis well before R' Shimon's time (as is apparent from his statement *They did not state*[2]...). He disputes only the

---

1. Apparently, *Rashi* and *Rav* understand that R' Shimon disputes the ruling of the Sages only as regards the minimum measurements of wine, milk, and honey. As regards oil and water, however, he concurs that, in the case of oil, one is liable for carrying out enough to anoint a small limb, and in the case of water, one is liable for carrying out enough to rub on an eye plaster. R' Shimon views the small amount of wine required for mixing a cup as insignificant. One swallow of milk is also insignificant. As regards honey, he regards its use for human consumption more common than its use as a salve for camels and horses. Oil, however, is not drunk in its pure state, but combined with foods. Therefore, it cannot be judged as a beverage to make one liable only for carrying out a *reviis*. Consequently, its use for anointing is as common as its use for food. Water, too, is commonly used for an eye plaster (*Tif. Yis.*).

2. This may be an allusion to the pre-Tannaic mishnah mentioned by *Rabbeinu Shimshon of Kinon* in *Sefer HaKereissus*. This theme is developed by R' Isaac HaLevi in *Doros HaRishonim* (v. 1, pp. 206-310, Israeli ed. see especially p. 218). See ArtScroll *Pesachim* 1:1, pp. 5,6.

שבת
ח/ב

אֶלָּא לְמַצְנִיעֵיהֶן.

[ב] הַמּוֹצִיא חֶבֶל, כְּדֵי לַעֲשׂוֹת אֹזֶן לְקֻפָּה. גֶּמִי, כְּדֵי לַעֲשׂוֹת תְּלַאי לְנָפָה וְלִכְבָרָה. רַבִּי יְהוּדָה אוֹמֵר: כְּדֵי לִטֹּל מִמֶּנּוּ מִדַּת מִנְעָל לְקָטָן. נְיָר, כְּדֵי לִכְתֹּב עָלָיו קֶשֶׁר מוֹכְסִין,

―― ר' עובדיה מברטנורא ――

(ב) **אזן לקופה.** לאוחזה בה: **תלאי.** לתלותו בו, ובליר משיעור אזן לקופה: **מדת מנעל.** להראות לאומן כמדה זו אני לריך, ושעורים בליר מתלאי: **נייר.** מטבים עושין אותו: **קשר של מוכסין.** פעמים שאדם נותן מכס בראש הנהר מזה והוא מוסר לו חותם להראות למוכס שבעבר האחר מן הנהר להראותו שכבר פרע המכס, ודרכו לכתוב שתי אותיות גדולות לסימן, והן גדולות משתי אותיות שלנו:

―― יד אברהם ――

application of these standards. Whereas according to the first *Tanna* these standards apply to anyone who carries out wine, milk, etc., according to R' Shimon they apply only to *those who store them*.]

אֶלָּא לְמַצְנִיעֵיהֶן — **except for those who store them.**

I.e., only one who has actually set aside the measure of wine, milk, etc. previously stated in the mishnah is held liable if he subsequently carries it out. One who has not previously stored this small measure of liquid, but who, having such a quantity available to him (e.g., left over from a drink), carries it out, is not liable for such a small measure. In such a case he is not liable unless he carries out at least a *reviis*.

Though people occasionally store small quantities of liquid to be used for specific purposes, R' Shimon does not consider that small quantity significant, in general terms, except to one who has actually set it aside, thereby showing he values it. Even a stored measure, however, is significant only when it is in a quantity which people would on occasion set aside. An amount one stores for himself *never* normally stored by most people is not considered significant even to the one who does actually store it.

This is the opinion of R' Shimon. In this he differs with the *Tanna* of mishnah 3 of the preceding chapter who rules that one who carries out an item he has previously stored is liable for any amount (as long as it is the full amount he set aside). That mishnah reflects the opinion of the *Tanna Kamma* (first opinion) of the mishnah here.

As can be seen, then, there are two areas of disagreement between the *Tanna Kamma* and R' Shimon. The *Tanna Kamma* rules that one who has actually set aside a liquid and then carries it out is liable for any amount he may have set aside. If one has not previously set aside this liquid, he is not liable unless he carries out a certain

8
2

except for those who store them.

2. One who takes out rope, enough to make a handle for a basket.

Reed-grass, enough to make a hanger for a sifter or for a sieve. R' Yehudah says: Enough to take the measure of a child's shoe.

Paper, enough to write on it a tax collector's receipt,

YAD AVRAHAM

minimum amount (delineated in this mishnah), though it may be less than a *reviis*. R' Shimon, on the other hand, rules that even one who has previously stored this liquid is liable only if he carries out at least the minimum amount delineated in this mishnah. If one did not previously store this liquid, he is not liable unless he carries out at least a *reviis*.

2.

הַמּוֹצִיא חֶבֶל, — *One who takes out rope,*

[I.e., one who takes out rope from one domain to another on the Sabbath.]

כְּדֵי לַעֲשׂוֹת אֹזֶן לְקֻפָּה. — *enough to make a handle for a basket.*

I.e., a large basket or barrel (*Tif. Yis.*). Since rope is coarse, it is useful only for heavy utensils such as large baskets or barrels. Lightweight or thin utensils may be damaged by a coarse rope. Consequently, such a large measure is required for liability (*Gem.* 78b).

גֶּמִי, כְּדֵי לַעֲשׂוֹת תְּלַאי לְנָפָה וְלִכְבָרָה. — *Reed-grass, enough to make a hanger for a sifter or for a sieve.*

I.e., a kind of handle by which to hang a sifter or a sieve. This is a smaller measure than to make a handle for a basket (*Rav*).

[A sifter has fine holes used to sift flour to rid it of bran. A sieve has large holes, used to sort kernels of grain from pebbles.]

רַבִּי יְהוּדָה אוֹמֵר: כְּדֵי לִטֹּל מִמֶּנּוּ מִדַּת מִנְעָל לְקָטָן. — *R' Yehudah says: Enough to take the measure of a child's shoe.*

I.e., to show a cobbler the length of the child's foot, so that he can make shoes of the proper size (*Rashi; Rav*).

This is a smaller measurement than that prescribed by the first *Tanna* (*Rav; Meiri*).

R' Yehudah disagrees with the first *Tanna* in the case of rope as well, requiring this smaller measurement for liability. In both cases, his view is not accepted as halachah (*Meiri*).

נְיָר, — *Paper,*

This was made from grass [probably papyrus] (*Rav; Rashi*).

כְּדֵי לִכְתֹּב עָלָיו קֶשֶׁר מוֹכְסִין, — *enough to write on it a tax collector's receipt,*

Toll collectors at one side of a river would issue receipts to be shown at the other side of the river as proof of payment. The receipt was a piece of paper with the collector's seal stamped on it. It generally consisted of two larger than usual letters (*Rav; Rashi*).

וְהַמּוֹצִיא קֶשֶׁר מוֹכְסִין חַיָּב; נְיָר מָחוּק, כְּדֵי לִכְרֹךְ עַל פִּי צְלוֹחִית קְטַנָּה שֶׁל פְּלַיָטוֹן.

[ג] עוֹר, כְּדֵי לַעֲשׂוֹת קָמֵיעַ; קְלָף, כְּדֵי לִכְתֹּב עָלָיו פָּרָשָׁה קְטַנָּה שֶׁבַּתְּפִלִּין, שֶׁהִיא "שְׁמַע יִשְׂרָאֵל"; דְּיוֹ,

---

ר' עובדיה מברטנורא

נייר מחוק. שוב אינו ראוי לכתוב, לפיכך צריך שיעור גדול לכרוך על פי צלוחית: **(ג) לעשות בו קמיע.** לכסות בו את הקמיע: **קלף כדי לכתוב [עליו] פרשה קטנה.** דאיידי דדמיו יקרין לא עבד מיניה קשר מוכסין אלא תפילין ומזוזות, ולא מחייב בשיעורא זוטא:

יד אברהם

וְהַמּוֹצִיא קֶשֶׁר מוֹכְסִין חַיָּב; — *and one who takes out a tax collector's receipt is liable;*

Since one is liable for carrying a blank piece of paper large enough on which to write a toll collector's receipt, it is self-evident that one is certainly liable for carrying out the actual receipt itself. The necessity to add this statement is to cover the case of a receipt written on parchment. Blank parchment has a larger measurement for liability (see mishnah 3), it being generally too valuable to use for such mundane purposes. Nevertheless, where one has in fact stamped a toll collector's receipt on parchment, one is liable for carrying out even this smaller measure, since it is now valuable (*Tos. 78b*).

Alternatively, this phrase refers to an old receipt that one saves to prove one's general integrity to a suspicious tax collector at some future date. Though no longer immediately useful, one is liable for carrying it out. This follows the opinion of R' Yehudah, quoted in the *Gem.* (78b). Though the Sages quoted there dispute this opinion, *Rambam* may have deduced from this reference in the mishnah that the halachah is in accordance with R' Yehudah (*Tos. R' Akiva*).

נְיָר מָחוּק — *erased paper,*

And consequently, paper no longer suitable for writing (*Rav; Rashi*).

כְּדֵי לִכְרֹךְ עַל פִּי צְלוֹחִית קְטַנָּה שֶׁל פְּלַיָטוֹן. — *enough to wrap around the mouth of a small bottle of perfume.*

Since it is no longer suitable for writing, it requires a larger measurement, namely, the amount required to wrap around the mouth of a small bottle of perfume for use as a stopper (*Rav; Rashi; Meiri*).

3.

עוֹר — *Hide,*

I.e., an animal skin that is only partially tanned, i.e., salted but not yet treated with flour or gall-nut (*Tos. Yom Tov from Gem.* 79a).

כְּדֵי לַעֲשׂוֹת קָמֵיעַ; — *enough to make an amulet;*

I.e., to wrap an amulet therein (*Rav*). [As discussed above (6:2), amulets were composed of parchment upon which verses of the Torah dealing with cures were written, or herbs,

**8
3**
and one who takes out a tax collector's receipt is liable; erased paper, enough to wrap around the mouth of a small bottle of perfume.

3. Hide, enough to make an amulet; parchment, enough to write the smallest section of the *tefillin*, namely, *Shema Yisrael*; ink,

YAD AVRAHAM

קְלָף, — *parchment*,
[I.e., from the outer layer of the animal hide, used for writing *tefillin* and *mezuzos*.]

כְּדֵי לִכְתֹּב עָלָיו פָּרָשָׁה קְטַנָּה שֶׁבַּתְּפִלִּין, שֶׁהִיא ,,שְׁמַע יִשְׂרָאֵל״; — *enough to write the smallest section of the tefillin, namely, Shema Yisrael;*

Since parchment is expensive, it is not used for writing tax collector's receipts. Consequently, one is not liable for such a small amount, but only for carrying an amount sufficient for writing the smallest section of the *tefillin* (*Rav; Rashi*).

[As the *Tanna* states, the section of שְׁמַע (*Deut.* 6:4-9) is the smallest section found in the *tefillin*. The other sections, קַדֶּשׁ (*Ex.* 13:1-10), וְהָיָה כִּי-יְבִאֲךָ (ibid. 11-16), and וְהָיָה אִם שָׁמֹעַ (*Deut.* 11:13-21), are all longer. Although שְׁמַע and וְהָיָה כִּי-יְבִאֲךָ each contain six verses, שְׁמַע has less than half the number of words.]

The necessity of specifying that *Shema Yisrael* is the smallest section of the *tefillin*, though this fact is readily apparent to anyone examining *tefillin*, is accounted for in the following ways:

Since *tefillin* are invalid unless they contain all four prescribed sections (*Menachos* 3:7), a piece of parchment large enough for only one section should, in itself, have no

reputed to effect a cure to certain maladies. This was wrapped in a partially tanned hide.]

value. This one section may, however, also be used by someone reciting the *Shema* before retiring, the custom being to recite only the first section of the *Shema*, assuming one has said the *Maariv* at its proper time. This reason by itself is also insufficient, since most people recite it by heart. The two uses taken together are, however, enough to make this small piece of parchment sufficiently valuable to be used as a proper standard for carrying out parchment. The mishnah alludes to this by saying enough for *the smallest section of the tefillin*, referring to its use in *tefillin* and adding *namely Shema Yisrael*, making reference to the reciting of the *Shema* before retiring (*Tos. Yom Tov.*)

Alternatively, the *Shulchan Aruch* 32:14 prescribes that the smallest section be written on the thickest parchment, to assure uniform bulk for all four sections. We might therefore conclude that one is liable only if he takes out a piece of parchment both large enough and thick enough for the section of *Shema Yisrael*. The *Tanna*, therefore, makes it clear that as long as there is room for writing *Shema Yisrael*, it is sufficient for liability since deviation from this rule does not invalidate the *tefillin* (*Tif. Yis.*).

Alternatively, one may misinterpret the "smallest section" to mean the last section (as in *Sotah* 9:15). This could be explained in the following manner: Since *tefillin* must be written in the order they appear in the Torah, a piece of parchment for writing any but the last section could not produce the finished product. We might, therefore, think that one is not liable for carrying it out, since it has no value. If, however, one wrote three sections, and then found that

שבת כְּדֵי לִכְתֹּב שְׁתֵּי אוֹתִיּוֹת; כָּחוֹל, כְּדֵי לִכְחֹל עַיִן אֶחָת.
ח/ד

[ד] דֶּבֶק, כְּדֵי לִתֵּן בְּרֹאשׁ הַשַּׁבְשֶׁבֶת; זֶפֶת וְגָפְרִית, כְּדֵי לַעֲשׂוֹת נֶקֶב (קָטָן); שַׁעֲוָה, כְּדֵי לִתֵּן עַל פִּי נֶקֶב קָטָן. חַרְסִית, כְּדֵי לַעֲשׂוֹת פִּי כוּר שֶׁל צוֹרְפֵי זָהָב.

ר' עובדיה מברטנורא

דיו כדי לכתוב שתי אותיות. לרשום על שתי חוליות של כלי או על שני קרסים לזווגן: כדי לכחול עין אחת. שכן דרכן של נשים ההולכות מעוטפות אין מגלות אלא עין אחת וכוחלות אותה: (ד) השבשבת. הצלמידין מושיבין נסר קטן בראש הקנה ומותנים עליו דבק והעוף יושב עליו ונדבק בו וצריך לתת עליו דבק הרבה כדי שיהא הטוען נדבק בו: [בדי] לעשות בו נקב. קטן. כלי שמטמינין בו כסף חי וסותם פיו בזפת או בגפרית ועושה בסתימה נקב קטן להוציא ממנו הכסף חי: חרסית. לבינה כתושה: לעשות פי כור. שהמפוח נכנס בו:

יד אברהם
---

he had no more parchment, a piece of parchment for writing the final section, would, indeed, be of great value to him. We would, therefore, be inclined to believe that only the last section bears with it liability for carrying on the Sabbath. The *Tanna*, therefore, specifies that the smallest section is *Shema Yisrael*, even though it can be utilized only for a part of the *tefillin*, after which more parchment will be required to complete them (*Lechem Shamayim*).

דְּיוֹ, כְּדֵי לִכְתֹּב שְׁתֵּי אוֹתִיּוֹת; — *ink, enough to write two letters;*

I.e., to write two letters on two sections of a utensil, or on two adjoining boards, to match them (*Rashi; Rav*).

Whether one takes out dry ink, ink on a pen, or in an inkwell, the prescribed measurement is the amount necessary for writing two letters (*Rashi* 80a).

Others contend that this is sufficient only for ink already on the pen. In other cases, it is impossible to write two letters unless there is more ink, so that the pen can pick up enough ink with which to write two letters (*Rabbeinu Chananel; Rambam, Hil. Shabbos* 18:9; *Yerushalmi Shabbos* 8:3).

In any case, if the ink is less than the minimum requirement for liability, one is not liable for carrying out the pen or the inkwell, since they are secondary to the ink which is less than the minimum measurements. See below 10:5 (*Rashi* 80a).

כָּחוֹל, — *stibium,*

Eye paint used for both cosmetic and medicinal purposes (*Gem.* 80a).

כְּדֵי לִכְחֹל עַיִן אֶחָת. — *enough to paint one eye.*

Modest women would go out in the street with veils over their face, exposing but one eye. They would, therefore, paint only that one eye (*Rav* from *Gem.* ibid.).

In villages where the population was sparse and frivolity was at a minimum, women would not cover their faces. In such a case, since no woman would paint just one eye, one would be liable only if he took out enough stibium to paint both eyes (*Gem.* ibid., *Rashi*). If it is fit for medicinal purposes, however, he would be liable for

8 4 enough to write two letters; stibium, enough to paint one eye.

4. Paste, enough to put at the end of a birdcatcher's board; pitch or sulphur, enough to make a (small) hole [therein]; wax, enough to put on the opening of a small hole.

Crushed brick, enough to make the opening of a gold

YAD AVRAHAM

taking out enough to paint one eye. Alternatively, if this is a place where stibium is manufactured for cosmetic purposes, one is liable only if he took out enough to paint both eyes. If it is manufactured for medicinal purposes, he is liable even if he took out just enough to paint one eye (*Tos.* 80a).

4.

דֶּבֶק, כְּדֵי לִתֵּן בְּרֹאשׁ הַשַּׁבְשֶׁבֶת; — *Paste, enough to put at the end of a birdcatcher's board;*

Hunters would attach a small board to the end of a stick, upon which they would put paste. A bird alighting upon it would be caught. The amount of paste necessary for the bird to adhere to the board was considerable (*Rav, Rashi* 80a).

זֶפֶת וְגָפְרִית, כְּדֵי לַעֲשׂוֹת נֶקֶב (קָטָן); — *pitch or sulphur, enough to make a (small) hole [therein];*

[This wording is found in *Rashi* and *Rav*. In our editions, as well as *Meiri's*, the word קָטָן, *small*, does not appear.]

This refers to a phial in which mercury is kept. Its opening is sealed with pitch or sulphur. A small hole is then made in the seal through which the mercury can be removed [without danger of its spilling] (*Rav; Rashi; Tif. Yis.*).

Alternatively, we render, *enough to close a small hole,* i.e., to close the opening of a mercury phial (*Meiri*).

Others explain the hole mentioned here as referring to a large hole in a wine barrel or the like. Although usually wax is used to seal wine barrels (see next paragraph), wax will not adhere to a large crack, and pitch or sulphur is used instead (*Meiri*).

שַׁעֲוָה, כְּדֵי לִתֵּן עַל פִּי נֶקֶב קָטָן. — *wax, enough to put on the opening of a small hole.*

I.e., a small hole in a wine barrel. The *Gemara* specifies wine, because it flows through a very small hole, as opposed to more viscous substances, such as oil and honey, which require a larger hole (*Tos. Yom Tov* from *Rashi* 80a).

As mentioned above, wax is useful only to seal a *small* hole in a wine barrel. To seal a larger hole, pitch or sulphur was used (*Meiri*).

חַרְסִית, כְּדֵי לַעֲשׂוֹת פִּי כוּר שֶׁל צוֹרְפֵי זָהָב. — *Crushed brick, enough to make the opening of a gold refiner's crucible.*

Some translate this as clay rather than crushed brick (*Shenos Eliyahu; Rambam, Comm.*).

I.e., the opening into which the bellows is inserted (*Rav; Rashi*). [The crucible is a vessel used to heat metals to

רַבִּי יְהוּדָה אוֹמֵר: כְּדֵי לַעֲשׂוֹת פִּטְפּוּט. סוֹבִין, כְּדֵי לִתֵּן עַל־פִּי כוּר שֶׁל צוֹרְפֵי זָהָב. סִיד, כְּדֵי לָסוּד קְטַנָּה שֶׁבַּבָּנוֹת. רַבִּי יְהוּדָה אוֹמֵר: כְּדֵי לַעֲשׂוֹת כִּלְכּוּל. רַבִּי נְחֶמְיָה אוֹמֵר: כְּדֵי לַעֲשׂוֹת אַנְדִּיפִי.

[ה] **אֲדָמָה,** כְּחוֹתָם הַמַּרְצוּפִין — דִּבְרֵי רַבִּי עֲקִיבָא. וַחֲכָמִים אוֹמְרִים:

ר' עובדיה מברטנורא

פטפוט. רגל למקום מושב הכור, שמושיבין אותו על כן ובסיס העשוי לכך: **סובין כדי ליתן על פי הכור של צורפי זהב.** במקום שאין פחמין טורפין הזהב באש של סובין. פירוש אחר שרגילים לתת סובין על פי הכור כשמתיכים הזהב: **לסוד קטנה שבבנות.** בנות שהגיעו לפירקן ולא בא להן האחרת, בנות עשירים טופלות אותן בסיד והאחרת ממהר לבא ומשיר נמי את השער, ובנות עשירים טופלות בסולת, ובנות מלכים בשמן זית שלא הביא שליש: **בלכול.** הצדעין, וסדין אותן בסיד להשכיב את השער: **אנדיפי.** למטה מן הצדעין מעט, שקורין בת לדעה. ואין הלכה לא כרבי יהודה ולא כרבי נחמיה: (ה) **אדמה.** טיט אדום: **מרצופין.** שקין גדולות שנושאין בהם פרקמטיא בספינות, וחותמין אותם כדרך שחותמים האגרות. ושיעוריה דרבנן זוטר מדר"ע. והלכה כחכמים:

יד אברהם

intensive heat to refine or fuse them. There is a hole into which the bellows is inserted to start the fire. Around the hole they would place crushed brick.]

Here, too, *Meiri* explains: *to close the opening of a gold refiner's crucible.*

Chidushei HaRan states that since gold is soft and malleable, it does not require intense heat for refining. Therefore, crushed brick is sufficient for the opening of the crucible. For refining copper, however, intense heat is required. Clay is, therefore, used for the opening of the crucible, since crushed brick would crack.

רַבִּי יְהוּדָה אוֹמֵר: כְּדֵי לַעֲשׂוֹת פִּטְפּוּט — *R' Yehudah says: Enough to repair a prop of a tripod.*

I.e., to plaster the cracks of a tripod made to support a small stove (*Shenos Eliyahu, Tos. Chadashim* from *Gem.* 80a).

This is a smaller amount than that required by the first *Tanna*, as are all R' Yehudah's measurements (*Tos. R' Akiva* from *Gem.* ibid.).

Others explain that R' Yehudah requires the amount of crushed brick or clay needed to make a leg of a tripod supporting a crucible (*Rav; Rashi; Rambam*). [This does not follow the *Gemara's* conclusion, however.]

Tiferes Yisrael explains that R' Yehudah requires the amount needed to plaster the base of a crucible. [This, too, does not coincide with the *Gemara's* conclusion, which requires only enough to plaster the cracks of the prop.]

Although crushed brick is used more often to make an opening for a crucible than to repair the prop of a tripod, R' Yehudah regards the amount necessary for this repair as sufficient for liability, since sometimes crushed brick is used for this purpose. The first *Tanna*, however, rules that we judge by the more common use (*Chidushei HaRan*).

8
5 refiner's crucible. R' Yehudah says: Enough to repair a prop of a tripod.

Coarse bran, enough to put on the opening of a gold refiner's crucible.

Quicklime, enough to smear a girl's smallest limb. R' Yehudah says: Enough to flatten out the hair of the temples. R' Nehemiah says: Enough for a [forehead] plaster.

5. **R**ed clay, enough for the seal of packing sacks — [these are] the words of R' Akiva. But the Sages say:

YAD AVRAHAM

סֻבִּין — *Coarse bran,*
[See above 7:4.]

כְּדֵי לִתֵּן עַל־פִּי כוּר שֶׁל צוֹרְפֵי זָהָב. — *enough to put on the opening of a gold refiner's crucible.*

In places where charcoal is scarce, gold refiners smelt gold using bran as a fuel (*Rav; Rashi*).

Alternatively, the opening of the crucible is closed with bran during the smelting (*Rav; Rambam*). This is done to retain the heat (*Tif. Yis.*).

סִיד, כְּדֵי לָסוּד קְטַנָּה שֶׁבַּבָּנוֹת. — *Quicklime, enough to smear a girl's smallest limb.*

Various reasons are given for this practice: to give a ruddy hue to the skin (*Rashi* 80b); as a depilatory (*Rashi* ibid.); as a skin whitener (*Tos.* ibid.); to bring on the menstrual cycle of a pubescent girl (*Rav*).

For whatever reason, it had to be applied to large parts of the body, and it could not safely be applied all at once (*Gem.* ibid.). The custom was, therefore, to apply it to only one limb at a time. Consequently, one who carries out enough for even the smallest limb of a girl is liable.

רַבִּי יְהוּדָה אוֹמֵר: כְּדֵי לַעֲשׂוֹת כִּלְכּוּל. — *R' Yehudah says: Enough to flatten out the hair of the temples.*

The translation follows *Rav, Rashi.*

רַבִּי נְחֶמְיָה אוֹמֵר: כְּדֵי לַעֲשׂוֹת אַנְדִּיפִי. — *R' Nehemiah says: Enough for a [forehead] plaster.*

This was plastered to the forehead to give the forehead a ruddy hue (*Rashi,* ibid.; *Tif. Yis.*).

Alternatively, enough quicklime to remove the fuzzy hair below the temples (*Rav*). This follows the initial explanation of the *Gemara* but it is not the conclusion of the *Gemara* (*Tif. Yis.; Tos. Chadashim*).

[Whatever the purpose of the plaster, it was accomplished upon its removal.]

5.

אֲדָמָה — *Red clay,*
A type of earth used for making seals (*Kehati*).

כְּחוֹתַם הַמַּרְצוּפִין – דִּבְרֵי רַבִּי עֲקִיבָא. — *enough for the seal of packing sacks — [these are] the words of R' Akiva.*

These were large sacks used for shipping merchandise. They were sealed in the same fashion as letters (*Rav; Rashi*). According to some, these sacks were

שבת
ח/ו

כְּחוֹתַם הָאִגְּרוֹת. זֶבֶל וְחוֹל הַדַּק, כְּדֵי לְזַבֵּל קֶלַח שֶׁל כְּרוּב – דִּבְרֵי רַבִּי עֲקִיבָא. וַחֲכָמִים אוֹמְרִים: כְּדֵי לְזַבֵּל כְּרֵישָׁא. חוֹל הַגַּס, כְּדֵי לִתֵּן עַל מְלֹא כַף סִיד; קָנֶה, כְּדֵי לַעֲשׂוֹת קֻלְמוֹס, וְאִם הָיָה עָבֶה אוֹ מְרֻסָּס, כְּדֵי לְבַשֵּׁל בּוֹ בֵּיצָה קַלָּה שֶׁבַּבֵּיצִים, טְרוּפָה וּנְתוּנָה בָּאִלְפָּס.

[ו] **עֶצֶם,** כְּדֵי לַעֲשׂוֹת תַּרְוָד. רַבִּי יְהוּדָה אוֹמֵר: כְּדֵי לַעֲשׂוֹת מִמֶּנּוּ חָף.

───── ר' עובדיה מברטנורא ─────

כדי לזבל כרישא. כרתי. וְשָׁעוּרָיו זוּטָר מִקֶּלַח שֶׁל כְּרוּב. וְהִלְכָה כַּחֲכָמִים: **מלא כף סיד.** כַּף שֶׁל סַיָּדִין: **כדי לעשות קולמוס.** הַמַּגִּיעַ לְקִשְׁרֵי שֶׁל אֶמְצַע אֶצְבְּעוֹתָיו: **עבה.** שֶׁאֵינוֹ רָאוּי לִכְתִיבָה: **מרוסס.** מְרוֹצָץ וְשָׁבוּר: **ביצה קלה.** בֵּיצַת תַּרְנְגוֹלֶת. וְאַמַּאי קָרֵי לָהּ בֵּיצָה קַלָּה שֶׁקַּלָּה לְהִתְבַּשֵּׁל יוֹתֵר מִשְּׁאָר בֵּילִים. וְהַשִּׁעוּר הוּא כְּדֵי לְבַשֵּׁל כִּגְרוֹגֶרֶת מִמֶּנָּה: **טרופה.** מְעוֹרֶבֶת בְּשֶׁמֶן: **ונתונה באלפס.** שֶׁהוּא חַם כְּבָר שֶׁהִיא מְמַהֶרֶת לְהִתְבַּשֵּׁל: (ו) **תרווד.** כַּף: **חף.** שֵׁן מַשִּׁינֵי הַמַּפְתֵּחַ שֶׁפּוֹתְחִים בָּהּ הַדְּלָתוֹת. וְאֵין הֲלָכָה כְּרַבִּי יְהוּדָה.

יד אברהם

made of leather. *Rashi*, however, states that they were made of tree bark (*Meleches Shlomo*).

וַחֲכָמִים אוֹמְרִים: כְּחוֹתַם הָאִגְּרוֹת — **But the Sages say: Enough for the seal of letters.**

This is a smaller amount than required by R' Akiva. The halachah is in accordance with the Sages (*Rav*).

זֶבֶל וְחוֹל הַדַּק, כְּדֵי לְזַבֵּל קֶלַח שֶׁל כְּרוּב – דִּבְרֵי רַבִּי עֲקִיבָא. — **Manure or fine sand, enough to fertilize a cabbage stalk — [these are] the words of R' Akiva.**

[I.e. to fertilize a single cabbage plant.]

וַחֲכָמִים אוֹמְרִים: כְּדֵי לְזַבֵּל כְּרֵישָׁא. — **But the Sages say: Enough to fertilize a leek.**

This is less than R' Akiva's requirement. The halachah is in accordance with the Sages (*Rav*).

חוֹל הַגַּס, כְּדֵי לִתֵּן עַל מְלֹא כַף סִיד; — **Coarse sand, enough to put on a full trowel of lime;**

I.e., enough to fill a plasterer's trowel (*Rav* from Gem. 80b; see also *Meleches Shlomo*).

Although sand diminishes the whiteness of the plaster, it nevertheless strengthens the structure more than pure plaster.

Alternatively, since the destruction of the *Beis HaMikdash*, one is not permitted to plaster his house with pure lime, but must mix in some earth (*Rashi* on Gem. 80b).

קָנֶה, כְּדֵי לַעֲשׂוֹת קֻלְמוֹס, — **A reed, [large] enough to make a pen,**

Reeds were often used as pens, in the same fashion as quills. The length of the reed had to be sufficient to fashion from it a pen long enough to reach the middle joint of the finger (*Rav*; *Tif. Yis.*).

R' Akiva Eiger points out that the

8
6 Enough for the seal of letters.

Manure or fine sand, enough to fertilize a cabbage stalk — [these are] the words of R' Akiva. But the Sages say: Enough to fertilize a leek.

Coarse sand, enough to put on a full trowel of lime; a reed, [large] enough to make a pen, but if it was thick or cracked, enough to cook with it the most easily cooked eggs, beaten and put in a stew pot.

6. Bone, enough to make a spoon. R' Yehudah says: Enough to make with it a tooth [of a key].

YAD AVRAHAM

Gemara questions whether the pen must be long enough to reach the upper joint or the lower joint. Since the question remains unanswered, it would be impossible to make one liable for carrying out a reed unless it was long enough to make into a pen that could reach the upper joint of one's fingers. *Rambam*, indeed, rules accordingly (*Sabbath* 18:4). It is, therefore, puzzling why *Rav* and *Tiferes Yisrael* explain the mishnah as referring to the middle joint.

וְאִם הָיָה עָבֶה — *but if it was thick*

I.e., if the reed was too thick to be used for writing (*Rav*). [Too thick a reed could not be used for writing since its hollow interior would hold too much ink, causing it to smear as one wrote.]

אוֹ מְרֻסָּס, — *or cracked,*

Cracked in many places (*Rashi*). Crushed and broken (*Rav*).

כְּדֵי לְבַשֵּׁל בּוֹ בֵּיצָה קַלָּה שֶׁבַּבֵּיצִים, — *enough to cook with it the most easily*

cooked (lit. *the lightest*) *eggs,*

Since it is not suitable for writing, it is regarded only as wood, and it bears liability only if it is sufficient to provide enough fire to cook an egg [as in 9:5] (*Meiri*).

The amount of egg cooked must be equal to the size of a dried fig. This is less than a whole egg (*Rashi* 80b).

The most easily cooked of eggs is a chicken egg, which cooks faster than all other eggs (*Rav* from *Gem.*). [Apparently, *cooking* means *frying.*]

טְרוּפָה — *beaten*

I.e., beaten and mixed with oil (*Rav* from *Gem.*). When mixed with oil, it cooks faster (*Tif. Yis.*).

וּנְתוּנָה בָאִלְפָּס. — *and put in a stew pot.*

I.e., put into a stew pot preheated with these reeds (*Tif. Yis.*). An egg will cook faster in a preheated pot than it will in a pot which first begins to heat when the egg is placed in it (*Rav*).

6.

עֶצֶם, כְּדֵי לַעֲשׂוֹת תָּרְוָד. — *Bone, enough to make a spoon.*

[Animal bones were dried and then carved into spoons.]

רַבִּי יְהוּדָה אוֹמֵר: כְּדֵי לַעֲשׂוֹת מִמֶּנּוּ חָף. —

R' Yehudah says: Enough to make with it a tooth [*of a key*].

The keys of that era were composed of separate teeth inserted into the main body of the key. Therefore, R'

שבת
ח/ז

זְכוּכִית, כְּדֵי לִגְרֹר בּוֹ רֹאשׁ הַכַּרְכַּר. צְרוֹר אוֹ אֶבֶן, כְּדֵי לִזְרֹק בָּעוֹף. רַבִּי אֱלִיעֶזֶר בַּר יַעֲקֹב אוֹמֵר: כְּדֵי לִזְרֹק בִּבְהֵמָה.

[ז] **חֶרֶס**, כְּדֵי לִתֵּן בֵּין פַּצִּים לַחֲבֵרוֹ – דִּבְרֵי רַבִּי יְהוּדָה. רַבִּי מֵאִיר אוֹמֵר: כְּדֵי לַחְתּוֹת בּוֹ אֶת הָאוּר. רַבִּי יוֹסֵי אוֹמֵר: כְּדֵי לְקַבֵּל בּוֹ רְבִיעִית.

אָמַר רַבִּי מֵאִיר: אַף־עַל־פִּי שֶׁאֵין רְאָיָה לַדָּבָר, זֵכֶר לַדָּבָר: "וְלֹא־יִמָּצֵא בִמְכִתָּתוֹ חֶרֶשׂ לַחְתּוֹת אֵשׁ מִיָּקוּד."

ר' עובדיה מברטנורא

כרכר. של אורגין, ומעבירו על השתי כשמתוח מתוח לפניו ושובט בו החוטין: **כדי לזרוק בבהמה.** דלא טרח אינש למשקל צרור משום עוף, דבקלא בעלמא סגי ליה: (ז) **בין פצים לחבירו.** כשמסדרין פלימין ועומדין וקורות וטושין שורות של קורות על הארץ ויש חלל בין זו לזו סומכו תחתיו שלא יתעקם: **זכר לדבר.** דתשיב חרס בתחיית האור.

יד אברהם

Yehudah views each tooth as important in its own right.

As in all previous cases, R' Yehudah's measurement is smaller than that of the Sages. The halachah is in accordance with the Sages (*Rav*).

— זְכוּכִית, כְּדֵי לִגְרֹר בּוֹ רֹאשׁ הַכַּרְכַּר. — *Glass, enough to scrape the point of a weaver's needle.*

I.e., a piece of glass large enough with which to sharpen the point of a weaver's needle. These needles were used to separate the warp threads of the loom, which sometimes become entangled during the setting of the loom or entangled due to the fuzziness of the threads (see above 7:2, s.v. וְהַמַּסָךְ) (*Rav; Rashi*).

צְרוֹר אוֹ אֶבֶן, כְּדֵי לִזְרֹק בָּעוֹף. — *A pebble or stone, [large] enough to throw at a bird.*

[I.e., large enough to throw at a bird in order to drive it away.]

רַבִּי אֱלִיעֶזֶר בַּר יַעֲקֹב אוֹמֵר: כְּדֵי לִזְרֹק בִּבְהֵמָה. — *R' Eliezer bar Yaakov says: [Large] enough to throw at an animal.*

R' Eliezer bar Yaakov contends that it is unnecessary to use a stone to drive away a bird, since it is just as easily intimidated by a shout. Consequently, the smallest stone a person would normally bother to carry is one sufficiently large to throw at an animal in order to drive it away (*Rav; Rashi*).

In a *baraisa* quoted by the *Gemara* (81a), R' Eliezer delineates this as a stone weighing ten *zuz*.

The halachah is in accordance with R' Eliezer bar Yaakov (*Rambam, Hil. Shabbos* 18:11).

7.

חֶרֶס, כְּדֵי לִתֵּן בֵּין פַּצִּים לַחֲבֵרוֹ – דִּבְרֵי רַבִּי יְהוּדָה. — *A shard, [large] enough to*

8 Glass, enough to scrape the point of a weaver's needle.

A pebble or stone, [large] enough to throw at a bird. R' Eliezer bar Yaakov says: [Large] enough to throw at an animal.

7. A shard, [large] enough to place between one board and another — [these are] the words of R' Yehudah. R' Meir says: [Large] enough to pick up fire therewith. R' Yose says: [Large] enough to contain a quarter-*log*.

Said R' Meir: Although there is no proof to the matter, there is an intimation of the matter: *And there shall not be found among its pieces a shard with which to pick up fire from the hearth* (Isaiah 30:14).

YAD AVRAHAM

place between one board and another — [these are] the words of R' Yehudah.

When boards, pillars, or beams are stacked, there are often gaps between one layer and another. [This is due either to minor variations in the thickness of a board from one end to another, or to the differences in the lengths of the boards.] Where these gaps occur, a shard is placed there to prevent the boards from becoming warped (*Rav; Rashi*).

Rambam translates this as: *Between one half-brick and another.* Where there is a space between one half-brick and another, it is filled in with shards and pebbles. Alternatively, shards were placed between the boards of the window frame, one above the window and one below (*Melechos Shlomo*) from *Rashi, Bava Basra* 20b).

רַבִּי מֵאִיר אוֹמֵר: כְּדֵי לַחְתּוֹת בּוֹ אֶת הָאוּר. — *R' Meir says: [Large] enough to pick up fire therewith.*

I.e., to transfer burning coals from place to place. This is a larger measurement than that required by R' Yehudah [a larger piece is necessary to avoid burning the hands] (*Meiri, Shenos Eliyahu*).

רַבִּי יוֹסֵי אוֹמֵר: כְּדֵי לְקַבֵּל בּוֹ רְבִיעִית. — *R' Yose says: [Large] enough to contain a quarter-*log.

This is a smaller measurement than that of R' Meir (*Meiri*). (See mishnah 1 for explanation of quarter-*log*.)

אָמַר רַבִּי מֵאִיר: אַף־עַל־פִּי שֶׁאֵין רְאָיָה לַדָּבָר, זֵכֶר לַדָּבָר: — *Said R' Meir: Although there is no proof to the matter, there is an intimation of the matter:*

There is no conclusive proof from the following verse but there is at least an indication that a shard large enough to pick up fire has value (*Rav; Rashi*).

"וְלֹא־יִמָּצֵא בִמְכִתָּתוֹ חֶרֶשׂ לַחְתּוֹת אֵשׁ מִיָּקוּד". — *"And there shall not be found among its pieces a shard with which to pick up fire from the hearth"* (Isaiah 30:14).

שבת ח/ז

אָמַר לוֹ רַבִּי יוֹסֵי: מִשָּׁם רְאָיָה? ,,וְלַחְשׂף מַיִם מִגֶּבֶא".

ר' עובדיה מברטנורא

לחשוף. לדלות: מגבא. גומא קטנה שהמים נקבלים בה, אלמא חשיב חרס נמי בקבלת המים והלכה כרבי יוסי:

יד אברהם

[We see, therefore, shards were used to pick up burning coals.]

אָמַר לוֹ רַבִּי יוֹסֵי: מִשָּׁם רְאָיָה? — R' Yose retorted: *Is there proof from there?*

I.e., is there evidence from that verse that a shard too small to pick up fire is of no value?

,,וְלַחְשׂף מַיִם מִגֶּבֶא." — [The verse concludes,] *"Or to scoop up water from a pit."*

I.e., the verse ends with the expression, "Or to scoop up water from a pit."

8
7 R' Yose retorted: Is there proof from there? [The verse concludes,] *Or to scoop up water from a pit* (ibid).

YAD AVRAHAM

This indicates that even a small shard, just large enough to scoop up water from a small pit where water has gathered, is likewise of value (*Rav*).

Thus, the verse means that not only will there not remain a shard large enough to pick up burning coals, but not even one large enough to scoop up water from a pit (*Tif. Yis.*).

R' Meir, for his part, explains the verse as follow: Not only will there not remain a shard of value, viz. one large enough to pick up burning coals from the hearth, but there will not even remain a valueless shard, viz. one only large enough to scoop water from a pit (*Tos. Yom Tov* from *Gem.* 82a).

The halachah is in accordance with R' Yose (*Rambam*).

פרק תשיעי ⁘
Chapter Nine

[Though the grouping of unrelated topics because of verbal associations may seem to us an unusual way of organizing the mishnah, it is, nevertheless, a very prevalent form throughout the Mishnah. (See, for example, *Megillah* 1:4-11; *Chullin* 1:4-7 and elsewhere.) Indeed, this form is so integral a part of the pattern of the Mishnah that about half of tractate *Sotah* (3:7-8, 5:2-5 and all of Chap. 7,8, and 9) is included only because of word and category associations and associations of these associations (see second half of Chap. 9), though the topics have otherwise no connection to *Sotah*, whatever. It must be borne in mind that prior to the days of R' Yehudah HaNassi the Mishnah was not written down. Even after he formalized and wrote down the text of the Mishnah, it was still the practice of scholars to memorize the entire text. These kinds of association were, therefore, a great aid to memory and may account for the popularity of organizing topics according to word or category associations.]

The seven topics discussed in the first four mishnayos of Chapter 9 are unrelated. Six of them are not relevant to tractate *Shabbos*, but would be expected to appear in other tractates; indeed, some of them are repeated elsewhere almost verbatim [see comm.]. Various reasons for their inclusion here have been offered:

❏ The מְצִיעֲתָא, *intermediate clause*, of mishnah 3 speaks of laws pertaining to caring for the incision of circumcision on the Sabbath. Since the other six cases are couched in similar language [each begins with the word מִנַּיִן, *from where do we learn*, and ends with a Scriptural verse which lends support to the law stated, but which is not conclusive proof] they are included here (*Rav*; *Rashi*).

❏ *Tosafos* objects to this reasoning, since it presumes that this chapter is the proper place for discussing the care of a recently circumcised infant on the Sabbath. However, it seems more likely that proper place for this discussion be in Chapter 19, where the special laws of circumcision in regard to the Sabbath are discussed. Since, according to this explanation, all the other topics are added only because of their association to the law of caring for a newly circumcised infant, this entire chapter should have been inserted in Chapter 19 rather than here. *Tosafos* therefore explains that this chapter is added by association to the last mishnah in Chapter 8. That mishnah concludes by citing a verse which seems to lend support to the stated law, but which is not conclusive proof. The *Tanna* then appends seven other cases which follow this same pattern (*Rav.*; *Tos.*).

❏ Since Chapter 8 concludes with two quotes from *Isaiah* 30:14, the *Tanna* goes on to expound on verse 22 of that same chapter [mishnah 1]. He then continues with other similarly phrased mishnayos (*Rav; Tos.*).

❏ The verse cited at the end of Chapter 8 is interpreted midrashically as alluding to idolatry, as is the verse cited in mishnah 1 of Chapter 9. Furthermore, mishnah 6 deals with transporting objects used for idolatry (*Meiri*).

✥ The Tumah of Avodah Zarah

עֲבוֹדָה זָרָה, *avodah zarah* (lit. *strange worship*), is a general term denoting the worship of any and all false deities. In a secondary sense, it has come to mean the object of that worship, i.e., the idol itself. An *avodah zarah* is not necessarily a carved statue. Any object of strange worship, e.g., a building or a tree, may be considered, in this context, an *avodah zarah*. Though there are certain exceptions to this rule (see *Tractate Avodah Zarah* 3:5 and *Gem.* ibid. 45a), as a general rule, any idol of either a gentile or a Jew[1] becomes subject to certain laws. Firstly, it is incumbent upon any Jew into whose possession it comes to destroy it. Secondly, no Jew is permitted to derive any benefit from it (*Avodah Zarah* 3:1) or, after it has been destroyed, from its ashes (*Rambam, Hil. Avodas Kochavim* 7:10). These are the main Biblical laws which apply to it. The Rabbis, however, further decreed that it impart *tumah*, ritual contamination, upon those who come in contact with it.

Most sources of *tumah* contaminate primarily by direct physical contact. Certain forms of *tumah*, however, contaminate in other ways, too. One of these ways is by carrying. Though a person may have no direct contact with the source of *tumah*, nevertheless, he may become *tamei* by carrying the source of *tumah*. An example of this is one who carries a source of *tumah* in a box. Though he has not actually touched the *tumah*, he, nevertheless, becomes *tamei*, ritually contaminated. This mishnah deals with whether or not this manner of contamination is included in the Rabbinic decree of *tumah* on *avodah zarah*.

---

1. For the differences between the idol of a gentile and that of a Jew see *Avodah Zarah* 4:4.

שבת ט/א

[א] **אָמַר** רַבִּי עֲקִיבָא: מִנַּיִן לַעֲבוֹדָה זָרָה שֶׁמְּטַמְּאָה בְמַשָּׂא כְּנִדָּה? שֶׁנֶּאֱמַר: "תִּזְרֵם כְּמוֹ דָוָה, צֵא, תֹּאמַר לוֹ." מַה נִּדָּה מְטַמְּאָה בְמַשָּׂא, אַף עֲבוֹדָה זָרָה מְטַמְּאָה בְמַשָּׂא.

ר' עובדיה מברטנורא

פרק תשיעי — אמר רבי עקיבא. (א) אמר רבי עקיבא. מנין לעבודת כוכבים שמטמאה במשא. איירי דחיירי לטיל באסמכתא לגבי חרס, נקט נמי להני קראי דאסמכתא. וקרא דתזרם כמו דוה הוה סמוך לקראי דלא ימלא במכתתו חרס דחיירי לטיל. אי נמי משום דבעי למיתנא מנין שמרחיצין את המילה וכו' תנא להנך מנין דדמו לה: **מטמאה במשא.** הנושא אותה יכבס בגדיו ואפילו לא נגע בה, כגון שהיתה בקופה וכיוצא בה. ואפליגו רבנן עליה דרבי עקיבא ואמרי אינו מטמא אלא במגע כשרן. והלכה כחכמים: **תזרם כמו (אשה) דוה.** כלומר יהי בעיניך כזרים, כמו דוה, כאשה נדה, כדכתיב (ויקרא טו) והדוה בנדתה, ובעבודת כוכבים משתעי קרא:

יד אברהם

1.

אָמַר רַבִּי עֲקִיבָא: מִנַּיִן לַעֲבוֹדָה זָרָה שֶׁמְּטַמְּאָה בְמַשָּׂא — *Said R' Akiva: From where do we learn that [an object of] idolatry transmits tumah-contamination by carrying,*

R' Akiva seeks Scriptural support for the Rabbinical enactment of *tumah* for objects of idol worship or their accessories, and for the enactment of so stringent a form of contamination that it contaminates by carrying alone, even without physical contact, e.g., in a bowl or a basket (*Rav*).

כְּנִדָּה? — *like a menstruant?*

A *niddah* [see 2:6], in addition to transmitting *tumah* through direct contact, also transmits *tumah* to anyone who carries her, even if he does not touch her (e.g., on a stretcher.)

שֶׁנֶּאֱמַר: "תִּזְרֵם כְּמוֹ דָוָה, צֵא! תֹּאמַר לוֹ." — *For it is stated: "Cast them away like a menstruant. 'Go out!' shall you say to it"* (Isaiah 30:22).

The prophet speaks of estranging oneself from idolatry as one estranges himself from his menstruous wife, not having any physical contact with her (*Rav*).

However, the comparison is not total, for the *niddah* cleanses herself by immersion in a *mikveh*, and may then return to her husband, whereas *avodah zarah* remain contaminated forever. To the idols you only say, "Go out!" You do not say to them, "Come in!" [Therefore, the expression *cast them away* is used with regard to the idols, though not applicable to a *niddah*.] (*Tif. Yis.* from *Gem.* 82b).

מַה נִּדָּה מְטַמְּאָה בְמַשָּׂא, — *Just as a menstruant transmits tumah-contamination by carrying,*

[As explained above, if one carries a *niddah*, he becomes *tamei* even though he has not touched her.]

אַף עֲבוֹדָה זָרָה מְטַמְּאָה בְמַשָּׂא. — *so does [an object of] idolatry transmit tumah-contamination by carrying.*

The prophet compares the imperative of avoiding contact with *avodah zarah* to that of avoiding contact with a *niddah*. The Rabbis therefore, in decreeing *tumah* on *avodah zarah*, saw

1. Said R' Akiva: From where do we learn that [an object of] idolatry transmits *tumah*-contamination by carrying, like a menstruant? For it is stated: *Cast them away like a menstruant. "Go out!" shall you say to it* (Isaiah 30:22). Just as a menstruant transmits *tumah*-contamination by carrying, so does [an object of] idolatry transmit *tumah*-contamination by carrying.

YAD AVRAHAM

fit to impose the same consequences for contact with *avodah zarah* as results from contact with a *niddah*. Since a *niddah* transmits *tumah* through both touching and carrying, so too, *avodah zarah* transmits its *tumah* through both *touching* and carrying.

Though the mishnah does not cite any dissenting opinion, the *Gemara* (82b) states that the Sages dispute this ruling. According to their view *avodah zarah* transmits *tumah* not in the manner of a *niddah* but rather in the manner of a *sheretz*.[1] A dead *sheretz* transmits *tumah* through touching only, in contrast to a *niddah* who transmits through carrying too.

The Sages base their view on the verse (*Deut.* 7:26) which states, in reference to *avodah zarah*, שַׁקֵּץ תְּשַׁקְּצֶנּוּ, *You shall detest it utterly.* The root of the word שֶׁקֶץ means also a detestable creature, specifically a *sheretz*. The Rabbis therefore interpret the verse as if to say: You shall detest it (*avodah zarah*) like a *sheretz*. They therefore apply only the *tumah* of dead *sheratzim* to *avodah zarah*. The halachah is that *avodah zarah* transmits *tumah* through touching only, in accordance with the view of the Sages (*Rav; Rambam, Hil. Avos HaTumah* 6:2).

2.

◈§ **Objects Not Susceptible to Tumah-Contamination**

Not all objects which come in contact with a source of *tumah* become *tamei.* Only three categories of things are susceptible to *tumah:* (a) people, (b) foods and beverages, (c) utensils. Plants, live animals, rivers, rocks and many other things cannot become *tamei.* Furthermore, even utensils must meet certain specifications before they are considered susceptible to *tumah.* The main specification is that any non-metallic utensil must be a receptacle, i.e., possess an interior capable of holding other things. Furthermore, even a utensil possessing an interior must be small enough so that it can be carried even when full. If its capacity is more than 40 *seah* it is again not susceptible to *tumah,* since it cannot be carried when fully loaded. An exception to this second rule is an earthenware utensil, which remains susceptible to *tumah* no matter how large it is.

There are actually several exceptions and complications to these two rules, in

---

1. Eight species of reptiles and rodents are identified in *Leviticus* 11:29-30 and classified as שְׁרָצִים [*sheratzim*, singular *sheretz*], *creepers.* See below, 14:1, for a fuller discussion.

שבת
ט/ב

[ב] **מִנַּיִן** לִסְפִינָה שֶׁהִיא טְהוֹרָה? שֶׁנֶּאֱמַר: "דֶּרֶךְ־אֳנִיָּה בְלֶב־יָם."
מִנַּיִן לַעֲרוּגָה שֶׁהִיא שִׁשָּׁה עַל שִׁשָּׁה טְפָחִים, שֶׁזּוֹרְעִין בְּתוֹכָהּ חֲמִשָּׁה זֵרְעוֹנִין, אַרְבָּעָה בְּאַרְבַּע רוּחוֹת הָעֲרוּגָה וְאֶחָד בָּאֶמְצַע?

---- ר' עובדיה מברטנורא ----

(ב) **שֶׁהִיא טְהוֹרָה.** שאינה מקבלת טומאה: **בלב ים.** ופשיטא דאניה בלב ים היא, אלא לאשמועינן דספינה הרי היא כים, מה ים טהור אף ספינה טהורה, ואפילו היא של חרס ואפילו טענוה ביבשה והורידוה ליס: **שזורעים בה חמשה זרעונים.** ויש בה כדי להפריש ביניהן הפרש הראוי ולא הוי ערבוב: **ארבעה בארבע רוחות הערוגה.** ממלא את כל הרוח עד סמוך לקרן ובאמצע אינו זורע אלא גרעין אחד כדי שיהיה הגרעין שבאמצע רחוק שלשה טפחים מן הזרוע שבכל רוח, דשיעור יניקת כל זרע טפח ומחצה, ואף על פי שאלל הקרנות שברוחות הזרעים קרובים זה לזה ואין ביניהם הרחקה ג' טפחים ויונקין זה מזה, אין כאן בית מיחוש דאכלאים בלבד קפיד קרא דלא להוי ערבוב, וליניקה לא חיישינן, כדתנן היה גדר בינתים זה סומך לגדר מכאן וזה סומך לגדר מכאן, ואף על גב דיניקי מתתאי, וכאן יש היכר גדול שרוח זו זרועה לפון ודרוס, ורוח זו זרועה מזרח ומערב, אבל בין זרע האמצעי לזרעוני הרוחות אין היכר, ואי מקרבי הוי עירבוב, הילכך צריך הרחק כדי יניקה:

---- יד אברהם ----

addition to other rules. These are, however, the province of tractate *Keilim* and are more properly discussed there. Mishnah 2, however, states that a boat, even when it in every respect meets all the requirements of a utensil, is not susceptible to *tumah* by virtue of its being a boat.

מִנַּיִן לִסְפִינָה שֶׁהִיא טְהוֹרָה? — *From where do we learn that a ship is not susceptible to tumah-contamination* (lit. *tahor*)?

שֶׁנֶּאֱמַר: דֶּרֶךְ־אֳנִיָּה בְלֶב־יָם. — *For it is stated: "The way of a ship in the midst of the sea"* (Proverbs 30:19).

Since it is obvious that a ship travels in the midst of the sea, Scripture must be adding this seeming redundancy to teach some specific lesson. The Sages explain this as alluding to the following principle: Just as the sea is immune to *tumah*-contamination, so too is a ship immune to *tumah*-contamination (*Rav* from *Gem.* 83b).

[The sea itself is not susceptible to *tumah* since, on the contrary, it acts as the purifier of *tumah* by virtue of its being a *mikveh*.]

The *Gemara* 83b cites the opinion of Chananyah who explains the exclusion of boats from susceptibility to *tumah* not as a new rule, but rather as part of the general rule which excludes all utensils larger than 40 *seah* from susceptibility to *tumah*.

The dispute regarding the source of the exemption of ships from contamination has several ramifications:

— Earthenware vessels contract contamination even if they cannot be moved when full. According to Chananyah an earthenware ship is susceptible to contamination.

— Small boats, which do not have a forty-*seah* capacity, are also susceptible to *tumah* according to Chananyah (*Gem.* 83b). *Rambam* (*Hil. Keilim* 18:9) rules in accordance with the view expressed in our mishnah.

2. From where do we learn that a ship is not susceptible to *tumah*-contamination? For it is stated: *The way of a ship in the midst of the sea* (*Proverbs* 30:19).

From where do we learn that a garden-bed, that is six by six handbreadths, may be sown with five types of seeds, four on the four sides of the garden-bed and one in the center?

YAD AVRAHAM

◆§ The Prohibition Against Mingled Seeds

כִּלְאֵי זְרָעִים, *mingling of seeds*, is forbidden by Torah law as stated: לֹא־תִזְרַע שָׂדְךָ כִּלְאָיִם, *You shall not sow your field with mingled seeds* (*Lev.* 19:19).

This prohibition takes various forms: (a) grafting a branch of one species of tree or plant onto the body of another species; (b) mingling the seeds of different species together, by planting them at one time and in the same place; (c) planting different species separately, but in close proximity to each other.

Grafting of differing species is prohibited both in *Eretz Yisrael* and outside of *Eretz Yisrael* (*Shulchan Aruch, Yoreh Deah* 295:1 from *Kiddushin* 39a). Mingling seeds is prohibited in *Eretz Yisrael* under almost all circumstances [though there are some exceptions, e.g., non-edible plants (see *Yoreh Deah* 297:3)] but is permitted outside of *Eretz Yisrael*. The only exception is grape seeds, which may not be planted even outside of *Eretz Yisrael* together with the seeds of grain or certain vegetables in one place and at one time. Planting different species in close proximity is forbidden only in *Eretz Yisrael* but is completely permissible outside of *Eretz Yisrael* (ibid. 297:2). The various details of these laws are the subject of tractate *Kilayim*. The next part of this mishnah concerns itself with planting in close proximity in *Eretz Yisrael*.

מִנַּיִן לַעֲרוּגָה שֶׁהִיא שִׁשָּׁה עַל שִׁשָּׁה טְפָחִים, שֶׁזּוֹרְעִין בְּתוֹכָהּ חֲמִשָּׁה זֵרְעוֹנִין, — *From where do we learn that a garden-bed, that is six by six handbreadths, may be sown with five types of seeds,*

What Scriptural evidence do we have for the law which is stated in *Kilayim* 3:1 that it is possible to sow five types of seeds in an area of six handbreadths[1] by six handbreadths and yet leave enough space so that the seeds will not be considered mingled? (*Rav; Rashi*).

אַרְבָּעָה בְּאַרְבַּע רוּחוֹת הָעֲרוּגָה — *four on the four sides of the garden-bed*

[The above being accomplished in the following manner:]

The perimeter of the bed may be sown with four types of seeds, each filling a different side and stopping just short of the corner which is left fallow (*Rav; Rashi*). [See diagram.]

וְאֶחָד בָּאֶמְצַע? — *and one in the center?*

One single seed of yet a fifth species may be planted in the center so that it is

---

1. A handbreadth is the equivalent of between three and four inches, depending on the different opinions of the proper conversion factors.

שבת ט/ב

שֶׁנֶּאֱמַר: ,,כִּי כָאָרֶץ תּוֹצִיא צִמְחָהּ, וּכְגַנָּה זֵרוּעֶיהָ תַצְמִיחַ." ,,זַרְעָהּ" לֹא נֶאֱמַר, אֶלָּא ,,זֵרוּעֶיהָ."

ר' עובדיה מברטנורא

שנאמר כי בארץ תוציא צמחה. תוליא חד, למחה חד, זרועיה תרי, תלמיח חד, הרי חמשה. ושטה טפחים ליכא למילף מקרא, אלא קים להו לרבנן דה' זרעונים בשטה טפחים לא ינקי הרוחות מן האמלטי, ולא האמלטי מן הרוחות, דשטור יניקת כל זרע טפח ומחלה, הילכך כי רמיז לקרא חמשה זרעונים בערוגה בת שטה טפחים קאמר. ובמסכת כלאים פירשתי הלכות ערוגה ופרטותיה ודקדוקיה וכאן קלרתי:

יד אברהם

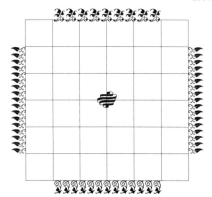

bine to make the species appear distinct from each other and unmingled. One is therefore permitted to plant them in this fashion without separating them by three handbreadths. The seed in the center, whose furrow is not angled away from that of the others, must however be separated by at least three handbreadths in order to appear distinct (*Rav, Rashi*).

שֶׁנֶּאֱמַר: ,,כִּי כָאָרֶץ תּוֹצִיא צִמְחָהּ, וּכְגַנָּה זֵרוּעֶיהָ תַצְמִיחַ." — *For it is stated: "For like the earth, it will give forth its plant, and like a garden, it will cause its seeds to grow"* (Isaiah 61:11).

The *Gemara* 84b explains thus: Each word denoting growth or vegetation is taken as a reference to a separate species of seed. Hence we expound: תּוֹצִיא, *give forth*, denotes one species: צִמְחָהּ, *its plant*, denotes a second species; זֵרוּעֶיהָ, *its seeds*, being plural, denotes two more species, and תַצְמִיחַ, *it will cause to grow*, denotes a fifth species.

The dimensions of the garden-bed are not specified in this passage. The Sages, however, knowing that the minimum space necessary to prevent physical mingling of the roots is three handbreadths (one and a half for the extension of each species), made the corollary calculation that the minimum area required for a garden of five species is a square of six handbreadths by six handbreadths. Though this cal-

separated from the row on each side by three handbreadths. Since the roots of the plants spread one and a half handbreadths, each species must be separated three handbreadths from its neighbor, thus preventing a mingling of the roots.

The measurement of a one and a half handbreadths spread in either direction includes the area taken up by the seed itself. The width of each furrow is only enough to accommodate one seed, thus the parallel furrows are six handbreadths apart (three handbreadths from each side to the center) (*Rashi, Tos.* 85a).

Although the vegetation on each side is not separated by three handbreadths from the species on either of its adjacent sides, the furrows do, nevertheless, run in different directions, i.e., perpendicular to each other. This, together with the fact that the corners are left fallow [see diagram], com-

For it is stated: *For like the earth, it will give forth its plant, and like a garden, it wil cause its seeds to grow (Isaiah 61:11). "Its seed"* is not stated, but *"its seeds."*

YAD AVRAHAM

culation is arrived at without reference to the verse, the verse teaches us that the sowing of five species within one garden-bed is permitted despite its giving a superficial appearance of mingling (*Tos. Yom Tov* from *Tos.* 85a).[1]

"זַרְעָה" לֹא נֶאֱמַר, "אֶלָּא זֵרוּעֶיהָ". — *"Its seed" is not stated, but "its seeds."*

[I.e., *its seeds* being plural is counted as two species rather than one. The total of five species rather than four are indicated.]

3.

◈§ The Tumah of Semen

The following section relates to the laws of טֻמְאָה וְטָהֳרָה [*tumah* and *taharah*], *contamination and purity*. In particular, we are dealing with the *tumah* of שִׁכְבַת זֶרַע, *semen*, listed in *Keilim* 1:1 as an אַב הַטֻּמְאָה, *a primary source of contamination* (see *Appendix: The Eighteen Decrees*). This is based on the Torah law (*Lev.* 15:17) that semen contaminates garments and leather goods. Additionally, the Torah decrees that a couple becomes *tamei* after copulation. It follows, therefore, that a woman who immerses herself in a *mikveh* after coitus becomes *tahor*. If she subsequently emits semen, she again becomes *tamei*. However, if a number of days have elapsed, and the sperm is no longer viable, it does not cause her to become *tamei*. The only evidence we have concerning the time required for sperm to lose its viability is from the episode of the Revelation on Mount Sinai. On that momentous occasion, anyone *tamei* by virtue of coitus was not permitted to be present (*Ex.* 19:15 and *Rashi*, ad loc.). Since women, too, were expected to be present at the Revelation, we can derive from the amount of time couples were ordered to abstain from copulation, the amount of time necessary for sperm to lose its viability.

1. [This derivation seems to be an אַסְמַכְתָּא, *a Biblical allusion cited to lend support* to a law which is actually only of Rabbinic origin, since the entire prohibition of *Kilayim* based on close proximity of species is only of Rabbinic origin. See *Kesef Mishneh*, *Hil. Kilayim* 4:16 who, in his explanation of *Rambam* there, states that Biblically speaking, only actual mingling of seeds [see prefatory note] is prohibited. Planting in close proximity is prohibited by Rabbinic decree because the different species might appear to a passerby to have been planted together simultaneously. Therefore, whenever the intent of the sower is obviously to segregate the various species, such as by separating them by a distance sufficient to prevent their roots from mingling or by angling the furrows away from one another, the Rabbis permitted it. (This statement of *Kesef Mishneh* is quoted also by *Tos. Yom Tov* tractate *Kilayim* 1:9. This appears to be also the opinion of *Rav* (*Kilayim* 3:4). *Aruch HaShulchan* (*Yoreh Deah* 297:3-5), however, disputes *Kesef Mishneh's* interpretation of *Rambam*, though he agrees that *Rashi's* view (84b) is similar to that of *Kesef Mishneh*. According to his explanation of the opinions of *Rambam* and *Tosafos* the derivation here appears to be a true Biblical derivation.)]

שבת ט/ג

[ג] **מִנַּיִן** לְפוֹלֶטֶת שִׁכְבַת זֶרַע בַּיּוֹם הַשְּׁלִישִׁי שֶׁהִיא טְמֵאָה? שֶׁנֶּאֱמַר: ״הֱיוּ נְכֹנִים לִשְׁלֹשֶׁת יָמִים.״

מִנַּיִן שֶׁמַּרְחִיצִין אֶת־הַמִּילָה בַּיּוֹם הַשְּׁלִישִׁי שֶׁחָל לִהְיוֹת בַּשַּׁבָּת? שֶׁנֶּאֱמַר: ״וַיְהִי בַיּוֹם הַשְּׁלִישִׁי בִּהְיוֹתָם כֹּאֲבִים.״

ר' עובדיה מברטנורא

(ג) שהיא טמאה. דיום השלישי אכתי לא מסרחא שכבת זרע וראויה לקלוט ולהיות ולד נוצר ממנה, וקרינן בה שכבת זרע הראוי להזריע: לשלשת ימים. דהקפיד הכתוב על טומאי קרי במתן תורה, לכך הפרישן שלשה ימים ולא חש אם יפליטו אחר כך ביום רביעי להפרשה, דמסרחא ואינו ראוי להזריע. ופסק הלכה שהפולטת ביום השלישי טהורה, ומתניתין משבשתא היא, ותני מנין לפולטת שכבת זרע ביום השלישי שהיא טהורה שנאמר היו נכונים לשלשת ימים, ולשלשת ימים דאמר קרא היינו ליום השלישי, דביום שלישי להפרשה נתנה תורה. אי נמי לא משבשתא היא אלא [רבנן דרבי] אליעזר בן עזריה היא, דסבירא [להו] הפולטת ביום השלישי טמאה, ולית הלכתא [כוותייהו]: **מנין שמרחיצין וכו'.** אפילו בחמין שהוחמו בשבת, דאף ביום שלישי מסוכן הוא, וכל שכן ראשון ושני. והמים חמין מחזיקין לגוף התינוק ומבריאין אותו.

יד אברהם

מִנַּיִן לְפוֹלֶטֶת שִׁכְבַת זֶרַע בַּיּוֹם הַשְּׁלִישִׁי שֶׁהִיא טְמֵאָה? — *From where do we learn that a woman who emits semen on the third day is* tamei?

By what Scriptural verse can we show that on the third day following coitus any semen emitted imparts *tumah* to the woman emitting it? (*Rav, Rashi*).

שֶׁנֶּאֱמַר: ״הֱיוּ נְכֹנִים לִשְׁלֹשֶׁת יָמִים.״ — *For it is stated: "Be prepared for three days"* (Exodus 19:15).

The verse ends אַל־תִּגְּשׁוּ אֶל־אִשָּׁה, *have no intimacy with a woman*. God ordered the Jews to abstain from intercourse for three days prior to the giving of the Torah, lest a woman emit semen on the day of the giving of the Torah and thus be disqualified from participating in this momentous event. Apparently, if she emitted semen that had been deposited within her more than three days prior to this date, it would not render her *tamei*.

The *Gemara* (82a,b) states that there are four opinions regarding how long after coitus the emission of semen imparts *tumah*. Our mishnah follows the opinion of the Sages who state that the limit is 72 hours, i.e., three full days. The other opinions are all of lesser duration. There is, however, a view mentioned in the *Gemara* that our mishnah should properly read *From where do we learn that . . . on the third day is tahor* (rather than *contaminated*). According to this reading, our mishnah follows the opinion of R' Elazar ben Azaryah who states in *Mikvaos* 8:3 that emission of semen can impart *tumah* only the first two days but not the third. This opinion follows the view which explains the above verse to man — *be ready for the third day*. Accordingly, the three days mentioned refer to two days of abstinence with the Revelation coming on the third day. Following this explanation, the verse is proof that any emissions on the third day do not impart *tumah* since only two days of abstinence were required. *Rav,*

3. **From where do we learn that a woman who emits semen on the third day is *tamei*?** For it is stated: *Be prepared for three days* (Exodus 19:15). **From where do we learn that we may bathe a circumcised infant on the third day [even] if it falls on the Sabbath?** For it is stated: *And it came to pass on the third day when they were in pain* (Genesis 34:25).

YAD AVRAHAM

מִנַּיִן שֶׁמַּרְחִיצִין אֶת־הַמִּילָה בַּיּוֹם הַשְּׁלִישִׁי שֶׁחָל לִהְיוֹת בַּשַּׁבָּת? — *From where do we learn that we may bathe a circumcised infant* (lit. *the circumcision*) *on the third day [even] if it falls on the Sabbath?*

The *Tanna* is seeking a verse which indicates that even on the third day after circumcision the baby is still presumptively considered critically ill[1] and that the laws of Sabbath may therefore be suspended on his behalf, as they are for any critically ill Jew. Such suspension would allow us, for instance, to boil water with which to bathe the baby, for bathing him in warm water has a curative effect (*Rav*).

Rav adds that if the boy's condition on the third day permits suspending the laws of the Sabbath, then certainly his condition on the first and second day warrants the same suspension.

שֶׁנֶּאֱמַר: ,,וַיְהִי בַיּוֹם הַשְּׁלִישִׁי בִּהְיוֹתָם כֹּאֲבִים.'' — *For it is stated: "And it came to pass on the third day when they were in pain"* (Genesis 34:25).

following the view of *Rambam*, declares the halachah in accord with this latter opinion. Most authorities, however, rule according to the first opinion, namely, that emission of semen imparts *tumah* for up to 72 hours (*Beis Yosef*, Yoreh Deah 196; *Shulchan Aruch* Yoreh Deah 196:11).

On the third day after the men of the city of Shechem were circumcised, Simeon and Levi seized the opportunity to attack the city. The populace, having witnessed the rape and kidnapping of Dinah by their prince, Shechem the son of Hamor, and not having protested, was held communally accountable [see ArtScroll *Genesis*, pp. 1480-1481]. The two brothers of Dinah did not wait for the fourth day, since by then the post-operative weakness would have passed. It is therefore apparent that the third day after circumcision is one on which post-operative danger still remains.

The question, however, arises as to why they did not attack on the first or second day; presumably the danger to life was even greater then and the level of any resistance by the circumcised men of Shechem even less effective. One view is that even though the danger to life was greater, they had, nevertheless, more strength on those two days, the general condition of weakness being a cumulative effect. Another view is that on the first two days no life-threatening situation yet exists. The danger, however, increases day by day, until it reaches its maximum on the third day, when it becomes life threatening (*Tos. Yom Tov*, quoting *Ran*).

Nowadays, it is not normally considered perilous for a child not to be

---

1. The philosophical implications of this controversy do not fall within the purview of this work. The explanation offered here is intended only as a definition of a legal principle.

מִנַּיִן שֶׁקּוֹשְׁרִין לָשׁוֹן שֶׁל־זְהוֹרִית בְּרֹאשׁ שָׂעִיר הַמִּשְׁתַּלֵּחַ? שֶׁנֶּאֱמַר: ״אִם יִהְיוּ חֲטָאֵיכֶם כַּשָּׁנִים, כַּשֶּׁלֶג יַלְבִּינוּ.״

[ד] **מִנַּיִן לִסִיכָה** שֶׁהִיא כִּשְׁתִיָּה בְּיוֹם הַכִּפּוּרִים? אַף־עַל־פִּי שֶׁאֵין רְאָיָה לַדָּבָר, זֵכֶר לַדָּבָר, שֶׁנֶּאֱמַר: ״וַתָּבֹא כַמַּיִם בְּקִרְבּוֹ, וְכַשֶּׁמֶן בְּעַצְמוֹתָיו.״

ר׳ עובדיה מברטנורא

לשון של זהורית. כמין לשון של צמר אדום, היו קושרין חציו בראש השעיר המשתלח לעזאזל וחציו בסלע, וכשהיה דוחה השעיר למטה היה הלשון ההוא מלבין ויודעין שנתכפרו עונותיהם: **(ד) מנין לסיכה שהיא כשתיה.** לא כשתיה ממש לחיובי עליה כרת, אלא שהיא אסורה.

יד אברהם

bathed in warm water on the third day after circumcision. Therefore, one who wishes to bathe the baby must do so without any desecration of the Sabbath (*Shulchan Aruch* 331:9).

מִנַּיִן שֶׁקּוֹשְׁרִין לָשׁוֹן שֶׁל־זְהוֹרִית בְּרֹאשׁ שָׂעִיר הַמִּשְׁתַּלֵּחַ? — *From where do we learn that a strip of red wool is tied on the head of the goat that is sent out?*

On Yom Kippur, in the *Beis HaMikdash*, there was a sin offering brought on behalf of the entire nation. It consisted of two goats, one of which was slaughtered and whose blood was brought into the Holy of Holies and the other of which was sent out to a wilderness area to be cast off the precipice of a stony mountain. This latter goat is known as the goat of *Azazel* (*Lev.* Chap. 16; *Yoma* Chap. 6). The mishnah in *Yoma* 6:6 says that the one who lead the goat out to the *Azazel* area would take a strip of red wool, divide it in two, tying one half to the goat's head and the other half to the rock at the top of the precipice. He would then push the goat down the mountain. As the goat fell, the wool would turn white. This was a divine sign that the sins of the people were forgiven. Our mishnah inquires as to the Biblical origin of this practice (*Rav*).[1]

שֶׁנֶּאֱמַר: ״אִם יִהְיוּ חֲטָאֵיכֶם כַּשָּׁנִים, כַּשֶּׁלֶג יַלְבִּינוּ.״ — *For it is stated: "If your sins will be like crimson, they will become white as snow"* (Isaiah 1:18).

The mishnah understands the prophet's words as an allusion to the practice of tying the strip of red wool on the head of the goat and of its turning white as a sign of forgiveness for the nation's sins.

---
1. The wool was, according to one explanation, stored at the head of the mountain from before Yom Kippur. This was done to avoid the problem of carrying the wool on Yom Kippur. Another opinion maintains that it was tied onto the horns of the goat and was thus transported in an unusual fashion. Such unusual transportation is not Biblically prohibited, and the Rabbinic injunction against it was set aside for the purposes of the *Beis HaMikdash* (*Tos. R' Akiva, Yoma* 6:6 from *Tos. Yeshanim*).

From where do we learn that a strip of red wool is tied on the head of the goat that is sent out? For it is stated: *If your sins will be like crimson, they will become white as snow* (Isaiah 1:18).

4. From where do we learn that anointing is tantamount to drinking on Yom Kippur? Although there is no proof for the matter, there is an intimation of the matter, for it is said: *And it came like water into his innards, and like oil into his bones* (Psalms 109:18).

YAD AVRAHAM

4.

מִנַּיִן לְסִיכָה שֶׁהִיא כִּשְׁתִיָּה בְּיוֹם הַכִּפּוּרִים? — *From where do we learn that anointing is tantamount to drinking on Yom Kippur?*

Yoma 8:1 teaches: On Yom Kippur eating, drinking, washing [one's body], anointing [one's body with oil], wearing shoes, and cohabitation are prohibited. The *Tanna* here seeks a Scriptural basis for considering anointing tantamount to drinking and thus being prohibited on Yom Kippur. The comparison will prove a limited one, however, for drinking is punishable by *kareis*, excision, whereas anointing is not (*Rav*).

Furthermore, according to many opinions only eating and drinking are Torah prohibitions. The other four are only Rabbinic prohibitions (see ArtScroll Yoma 8:1). Accordingly, the verse is only cited here as an אַסְמַכְתָּא, *to lend support* to a law which is actually of Rabbinic origin.

אַף־עַל־פִּי שֶׁאֵין רְאָיָה לַדָּבָר, זֵכֶר לַדָּבָר, — *Although there is no proof for the matter, there is an intimation of the matter,*

[Despite the lack of conclusive evidence from Scripture, there is a verse in *Psalms* which intimates the rule equating anointing with drinking.]

שֶׁנֶּאֱמַר: ,,וַתָּבֹא כַמַּיִם בְּקִרְבּוֹ, וְכַשֶּׁמֶן בְּעַצְמוֹתָיו." — *For it is said: "And it came like water into his innards, and like oil into his bones"* (Psalms 109:18). Scripture compares anointing the body with oil to drinking water. This is, however, not conclusive evidence, because it is possible that Scripture is only comparing anointing with oil to *washing* with water, which enters the body through the pores (*Tif. Yis.*).

5.

The *Tanna* now resumes his delineation [which began in 7:4 and continued through the entire eighth chapter] of the minimum amounts of various substances, the carrying out of which render one liable to a sin offering.

שבת
ט/ה

[ה] **הַמּוֹצִיא עֵצִים,** כְּדֵי לְבַשֵּׁל בֵּיצָה קַלָּה; תְּבָלִין, כְּדֵי לְתַבֵּל בֵּיצָה קַלָּה; וּמִצְטָרְפִין זֶה עִם זֶה. קְלִפֵּי אֱגוֹזִים, קְלִפֵּי רִמּוֹנִים, אִסְטִיס, וּפוּאָה, כְּדֵי לִצְבֹּעַ בָּהֶן בֶּגֶד קָטָן בִּסְבָכָה. מֵי רַגְלַיִם, נֶתֶר, וּבוֹרִית, קְמוֹנְיָא, וְאַשְׁלָג, כְּדֵי לְכַבֵּס בָּהֶן בֶּגֶד קָטָן בִּסְבָכָה.

---- ר' עובדיה מברטנורא ----

(ה) **בֵּיצָה קַלָּה.** ביצת תרנגולת שהיא קלה לבשל יותר מכל שאר ביצים, ולא כדי לבשל כולה אלא כגרוגרת ממנה, טרופה ונתונה באלפס: **וּמִצְטָרְפִין.** כל מיני תבלין זה עם זה: **אִסְטִיס.** כ"ל בלשון ערבי, ולבעו דומה לתכלת: **וּפוּאָה.** שרשי עשב שצובעין בהם אדום, ובערבי אלפו"ה: **בִּסְבָכָה.** בראש הסבכה שעושיה כקליעה נותנים מטע בגד: **נֶתֶר.** מין אדמה הוא, ומזהיר, וקורחים לו אלו"ם בלט"ז: **בּוֹרִית.** מין למח שמנקה ומטהר: **קְמוֹנְיָא.** עשב שמנקים בעפרו את הידים להעביר את הזוהמא, ובלשון תלמוד קרוי שלוף דוץ, ובערבי קורין לו אלקל"י: **וְאַשְׁלָג.** לא נתפרש לי מה הוא:

---- יד אברהם ----

הַמּוֹצִיא עֵצִים, כְּדֵי לְבַשֵּׁל בֵּיצָה קַלָּה; — One who takes out wood [is liable if he takes out] enough to cook an easily cooked egg (lit. *a light egg*);

This measure is the same as that of thick reeds given in 8:5. See commentary there. Though implicit there, the *Tanna* nevertheless found it necessary to explicitly repeat the ruling regarding wood. One might otherwise think that even a minuscule piece of wood would render one liable to a sin offering, since such a piece can be used as a tooth in a key (*Tos. Yom Tov* from *Gem.* 89b). [Perhaps that is an unusual use of wood.]

תְּבָלִין, — condiments,

Spices such as pepper, ginger, cassia, and the like used to season foods (*Rambam*).

כְּדֵי לְתַבֵּל בֵּיצָה קַלָּה; — enough to season an easily seasoned egg (lit., *a light egg*);

Just as a hen's egg is the easiest egg to cook, it is likewise the most palatable of all eggs and thus requires the least amount of seasoning (*Tif. Yis.*).

וּמִצְטָרְפִין זֶה עִם זֶה. — and they may be combined with one another.

The minimum quantity described here need not be of one condiment. Since all condiments serve the same purpose, to make the food more palatable, they are considered as one substance (*Rambam, Comm.*).

קְלִפֵּי אֱגוֹזִים, — Nutshells,

The fresh outer green shell of the nut is useful for dyeing (*Tif. Yis.*).

קְלִפֵּי רִמּוֹנִים, אִסְטִיס, וּפוּאָה, — pomegranate shells, woad, or madder,

אִסְטִיס [Latin, *Isatis tinctorial*], woad, is a plant that yields a bluish dye. פוּאָה [*Rubia tinctorum*], madder, is a root from which red dye is made (*Rav*).

כְּדֵי לִצְבֹּעַ בָּהֶן בֶּגֶד קָטָן בִּסְבָכָה. — enough to dye the smallest cloth in a headdress.

This refers to a netlike headdress which was usually topped by a small patch of [colorful (*Tif. Yis.*)] cloth (*Rav; Rashi*).

5. One who takes out wood [is liable if he takes out] enough to cook an easily cooked egg; condiments, enough to season an easily seasoned egg; and they may be combined with one another. Nutshells, pomegranate shells, woad, or madder, enough to dye the smallest cloth in a headdress.

Urine, niter, soap, saltwort, or *eshlag*, enough to launder with them the smallest cloth in a headdress.

YAD AVRAHAM

One who carries out enough nutshells, etc., from which to make a quantity of dye sufficient to dye this cloth patch, is liable. One, however, who carries out the dye itself is liable for the amount necessary to make a sample to show to prospective buyers. (The fabric size used for samples is smaller than the cloth patch.) The reason for this difference is that the uses of such a small quantity of dye (enough only for a sample) do not justify the effort required to produce it. Consequently, one is not liable for transporting a quantity of raw materials sufficient only to produce enough dye for a sample, since no one would trouble to make such a small quantity of dye. One, however, would trouble to transport a small quantity of the actual dye itself, if it were sufficient to dye a sample cloth. One is therefore liable for carrying out dye in smaller quantities than for carrying out the raw material of dyes (*Gem.* 90a).

The *Gemara* has a variant reading, פִּי סְבָכָה, *the top* (lit., *mouth*) *of a headdress*, which does not change the meaning of the phrase. Talmud Yerushalmi, however, reads בֶּגֶד קָטָן בִּסְבָכָה, *a garment as small as a headdress* (*Meleches Shlomo*).

מֵי רַגְלַיִם, נֶתֶר — *Urine, niter*,

Urine was used, in olden times, to remove difficult stains (*Tos.* 90a, see *Niddah* 9:6). The translation *niter* for נֶתֶר follows *Rashi* and *Tif. Yis.* [the latter has the synonymous *saltpeter*]. *Rav* renders: a crystalline earth called *alum* [aluminum potassium sulfate].

וּבוֹרִית, — *soap*,

A cleaning agent of vegetable origin (*Rav, Tif. Yis.* from *Gem.* 89b; *Sefer HaShorashim*).

קִמּוֹנְיָא, — *saltwort*,

A plant found in alkaline regions, from which a cleansing agent is made. It is dried and ground, and used to remove dirt embedded in the hands (*Rav; Aruch*).

The mishnah of the *Gemara* reads קִמּוֹלְיָא, *Cimolian earth*. A white earth found on the island of Cimolus, near Crete (*Mosaf HeAruch*).

וְאַשְׁלָג, — *or eshlag*,

A kind of mineral substance used for cleansing. It is found in the cavities of pearls and is removed with an iron nail (*Gem.* 90a). Its precise definition is unknown (*Rav*).

כְּדֵי לְכַבֵּס בָּהֶן בֶּגֶד קָטָן בִּסְבָכָה — *enough to launder with them the smallest cloth in a headdress*.

[For explanation of this quantity see above, this mishnah.]

שבת
ט/ו

רַבִּי יְהוּדָה אוֹמֵר: כְּדֵי לְהַעֲבִיר עַל הַכֶּתֶם.

[ו] **פִּלְפֶּלֶת**, כָּל־שֶׁהוּא; וְעִטְרָן, כָּל־שֶׁהוּא; מִינֵי בְשָׂמִים וּמִינֵי מַתָּכוֹת, כָּל־שֶׁהֵן; מֵאַבְנֵי הַמִּזְבֵּחַ, וּמֵעֲפַר הַמִּזְבֵּחַ, מֶקֶק סְפָרִים, וּמֶקֶק מִטְפְּחוֹתֵיהֶם, כָּל־שֶׁהוּא, שֶׁמַּצְנִיעִין אוֹתָן לְגָנְזָן.

ר' עובדיה מברטנורא

על הכתם. הגמלא בבגד ואין ידוע אם דם נדה הוא אם לאו, מעבירין עליו שבעה דברים לבדוק אותו בהם. ומכללם ארבעה סמנין הללו. ואין הלכה כרבי יהודה: (ו) **פלפלת בל שהוא.** דחזיא לריח הפה, ואין זה פלפל המלוי בעינינו: **עטרן בל שהוא.** שמרפאים בו מי שיש לו כאב חלי הראם: **מיני בשמים** כל שהן. לריח טוב: **מיני מתכות בל שהן.** שראוי לעשות מהן לרבן קטן: **מקק.** רקב הגופל מספרים או ממטפחות שבלו, לשון הגמק בשרו (וכריה י״ד): **שמצניעים אותו לגונזו.** שכל דבר קדש טעון גניזה.

יד אברהם

— רַבִּי יְהוּדָה אוֹמֵר: כְּדֵי לְהַעֲבִיר עַל הַכֶּתֶם. *R' Yehudah says: Enough to pass over a stain.*

Niddah 9:6,7 delineates the procedure for testing a stained garment to determine the source of the stain. Seven cleansing agents are applied to the stain in a given order. As each one is applied, the garment is rubbed against itself three times in an effort to remove the stain. If, after this process has been completed with each of the seven substances, the stain remains unchanged, then the stain is certainly not blood. If the stain disappears or its color changes it must be treated as menstrual blood which renders the garment *tamei*. Of the seven cleansing agents specified for this test, five are listed in our mishnah. The halachah regarding the Sabbath does not follow R' Yehudah (*Rav*).

[The mishnah printed in the *Gemara* reads לְהַעֲבִיר אֶת הַכֶּתֶם, *to remove the stain*, but the meaning remains the same (see *Shinuyai Nuschaos*).]

6.

פִּלְפֶּלֶת, — *Pepper*,

A certain species of pepper which was carried in the mouth as a breath sweetener (*Rav* from *Gem.* 90a; see also 6:5).

This is not the pepper commonly found in our area [Western Europe] (*Rav*; *Rashi*). The common pepper is called פִּלְפֵּל, *pilpel*, פִּלְפֶּלֶת, *pilpeles*, is a different species (*Tos. Yom Tov*).

That this is not the ordinary pepper is further attested to by the fact that this mishnah considers one liable for carrying out even the least amount of it. We therefore cannot identify this with the common pepper, which is included in mishnah 5 among condiments for which one is liable only if he takes out enough to season an egg (*Rash, Orlah* 2:10).

Tosefos Yom Tov questions this latter proof. Since the mishnah does not list the various condiments, it is possible that pepper is excluded from this list and is

R' Yehudah says: Enough to pass over a stain.

6. Pepper, any amount; tar, any amount; types of spices and types of metals, any amount; of the Altar stones, of the Altar earth, decay of old scrolls, or decay of their wraps, any amount, for we put them away to save them.

YAD AVRAHAM

an exception to the general rule of condiments.

כָּל־שֶׁהוּא — *any amount;*

Since even a small quantity of this spice is useful in combating halitosis, any amount is considered of value (*Rav* from *Gem.* 90a).

וְעִטְרָן, כָּל־שֶׁהוּא; — *tar, any amount;*

עִטְרָן, *tar,* is mentioned in 2:2 as one of the fuels unsuitable for the Sabbath lamp. It was used as a remedy for migraine [hemicrania] (*Rav, Rashi* from *Gem.* 90a).

מִינֵי בְשָׂמִים — *types of spices*

This mishnah here speaks of spices used for fragrance (*Rav; Rashi*). Mishnah 5, which speaks of spices used in seasoning food, gives a more lenient amount. If a particular spice serves both functions, it is judged according to its more common use. If it is commonly used as both a seasoning agent and as a scent, then the stricter rule is in effect (*Tos. Yom Tov;* see above 8:1).

וּמִינֵי מַתָּכוֹת, כָּל־שֶׁהֵן; — *and types of metals, any amount;*

A minute quantity of metal can be used to make the point of an ox-goad (*Rav.* from *Gem.* 90a).

The words כָּל־שֶׁהֵן, *any amount,* apply to both *spices* and *metals.* In some editions (see *Rav and Rashi*) this phrase appears after each item.

מֵאַבְנֵי הַמִּזְבֵּחַ, וּמֵעֲפַר הַמִּזְבֵּחַ, מֶקֶק סְפָרִים, וּמֶקֶק מִטְפְּחוֹתֵיהֶם, — *of the Altar stones, of the Altar earth, decay of old scrolls, or decay of their wraps,*

I.e., chips of stone which have come from the Altar, or bits of earth from the base of the Altar or decayed matter [that falls (*Meleches Shlomo*)] from scrolls or the cloths in which they are wrapped (*Rav*), due to age or bookworms (*Rashi*).

כָּל־שֶׁהוּא, — *any amount,*

[I.e., one is liable for any amount.]

שֶׁמַּצְנִיעִין אוֹתָן לְגָנְזָן. — *for we put them away to save* (lit. *to hide*) *them.*

This was not done to prevent anyone from seeing them. Rather, it was done to provide a respectable resting place for holy articles which could no longer be used. Such items may not be discarded in a disrespectful manner, as, for instance, by casting them on a garbage heap. They were, therefore, put away in special chambers which were eventually sealed (*Rav, Rashi*). [Such a storage area is called a גְּנִיזָה, *genizah.* Some of these old *genizos* have been discovered and have yielded old manuscripts of great value. Today, however, the custom is to bury such worn-out holy articles.] Since one is required by the Torah to save even the smallest pieces of such articles, they are considered of value (*Shenos Eliyahu*).

שבת ט/ז

רַבִּי יְהוּדָה אוֹמֵר: אַף הַמּוֹצִיא מִמְּשַׁמְּשֵׁי עֲבוֹדַת כּוֹכָבִים, כָּל־שֶׁהוּא, שֶׁנֶּאֱמַר: "וְלֹא־יִדְבַּק בְּיָדְךָ מְאוּמָה מִן־הַחֵרֶם."

[ז] **הַמּוֹצִיא קֻפַּת** הָרוֹכְלִין, אַף־עַל־פִּי שֶׁיֵּשׁ בָּהּ מִינִין הַרְבֵּה, אֵינוֹ חַיָּב אֶלָּא חַטָּאת אֶחָת.

זֵרְעוֹנֵי גִנָּה, פָּחוֹת מִכִּגְרוֹגֶרֶת. רַבִּי יְהוּדָה בֶן בְּתֵירָא אוֹמֵר: חֲמִשָּׁה.

זֶרַע קִשּׁוּאִין, שְׁנַיִם; זֶרַע דְּלוּעִין, שְׁנַיִם; זֶרַע פּוֹל הַמִּצְרִי, שְׁנַיִם; חָגָב חַי טָהוֹר, כָּל־שֶׁהוּא; מֵת,

ר׳ עובדיה מברטנורא

מאומה. אלמא אתחשביה קרא לאסורים. ותקון גדול הוא עושה כשמוליא ט"ז מביתו. ואין הלכה כרבי יהודה: (ז) **הרוכלין.** מוכרי בשמים לקשוטי נשים, ויש להם קופות קטנות לגרורות הבשמים: **אינו חייב אלא חטאת אחת.** דכולן חדא הולאה היא: **פחות מכגרוגרת.** אף על גב דכל האוכלין שיעורן כגרוגרת, הני כיון דלזריעה קיימי אפילו בפחות מכגרוגרת נמי מחייב. ואין הלכה כרבי יהודה בן בתירא שאומר חמשה: **זרע קשואין.** חשוב משאר זרעוני גינה, וכן זרע דלועין, וזרע פול המלרי, והוא שקורין לו פאסול"י בלע"ז: **חגב חי כל שהוא.** שמלניעין אותו לקטן לשחק בו:

יד אברהם

רַבִּי יְהוּדָה אוֹמֵר: אַף הַמּוֹצִיא מִמְּשַׁמְּשֵׁי עֲבוֹדַת כּוֹכָבִים, כָּל־שֶׁהוּא, — *R' Yehudah says: Also, one who takes out accessories of [objects of] idolatry, any amount,*

[This refers to any articles used in conjunction with idol worship.]

שֶׁנֶּאֱמַר: וְלֹא־יִדְבַּק בְּיָדְךָ מְאוּמָה מִן־הַחֵרֶם. — *For it is stated: "Nothing of that which is banned shall cleave to your hand" (Deuteronomy 13:18).*

Hence, the Torah imparts significance, albeit a negative one, to even a minute of accessory of idol worship (*Rashi*). One who removes such an article from his home improves its (spiritual) quality. He is consequently engaged in productive labor and may therefore be held liable for carrying on the Sabbath.

This opinion of R' Yehudah is in dispute with the rule stated in mishnah 7:3, which exempts objects used in idol worship from liability, since they must be burnt (*Rashi*) [see comm. to 7:3]. The halachah is not in accord with R' Yehudah (*Rav*) but rather in accord with mishnah 7:3 (*Maggid Mishneh, Hil. Shabbos* 8:22).

7.

הַמּוֹצִיא קֻפַּת הָרוֹכְלִין, — *One who takes out a peddler's basket,*

Cosmetic peddlers carried small baskets in which they kept phials of perfume (*Rav; Rashi*).

אַף־עַל־פִּי שֶׁיֵּשׁ בָּהּ מִינִין הַרְבֵּה, — *though*

[236]

9
7

R' Yehudah says: Also, one who takes out accessories of [objects of] idolatry, any amount, for it is stated: *Nothing of that which is banned shall cleave to your hand* (*Deuteronomy* 13:18).

7. One who takes out a peddler's basket, though it contains many sorts, is liable for but one sin offering.

Garden seeds, less than the equivalent of a dried fig. R' Yehudah ben Beseira says: Five.

Cucmber seeds, two; gourd seeds, two; Egyptian bean seeds, two; a live kosher locust, any size; [a] dead

YAD AVRAHAM

t contains many sorts,
[I.e., though it contains a variety of cosmetics and perfumes.]

אֵינוֹ חַיָּב אֶלָּא חַטָּאת אֶחָת — *is liable for but one sin offering.*
This is regarded as but one transfer (*Rav; Rashi*). See below 10:2.

זֵרְעוֹנֵי גִנָּה, פָּחוֹת מִכִּגְרוֹגֶרֶת. — *Garden seeds, less than the equivalent of a dried fig.*
Rav and *Rashi* understand the mishnah to refer to edible seeds. Although liability for carrying out a food is normally incurred only for a volume equivalent to a dried fig, edible seeds which may also be used for sowing have a smaller minimum for liability. *Meiri* and *Rambam* (*Comm.* and *Hil. Shabbos* 8:6), however, explain that the mishnah speaks of inedible seeds.

Since the mishnah does not specify how much less than the volume of a dried fig the minimum is, we assume that it is only slightly less (*Tos. Yom Tov*). This indeed is the view of *Rambam* in his Commentary. Others, however, speculate that it is the equivalent of an olive (*Sefer HaLikutim* from *Mayim Chaim, Rambam*, ed. *Frankel*).

רַבִּי יְהוּדָה בֶּן בְּתֵירָא אוֹמֵר: חֲמִשָּׁה. — *R' Yehudah ben Beseira says: Five.*
I.e., if one carried out even five garden seeds, he is liable (*Rambam; Tos. Yom Tov*).

The halachah is not in accordance with R' Yehudah ben Beseira (*Rav*).

זֶרַע קִשּׁוּאִין, שְׁנַיִם; זֶרַע דְּלוּעִין, שְׁנַיִם; זֶרַע פּוֹל הַמִּצְרִי, שְׁנַיִם; — *Cucumber seeds, two; gourd seeds, two; Egyptian bean seeds, two;*
The seeds of these three vegetables are more valuable than those of other garden vegetables and are therefore assigned a smaller minimum (*Rav*).

This ruling is not part of R' Yehudah ben Beseira's statement, but a unanimous one (*Rambam; Tos. Yom Tov*).

חָגָב חַי טָהוֹר, — *a live kosher locust,*
Leviticus describes certain species of locust that are exceptions to the general prohibitions against eating insects. Although טָהוֹר, *tahor*, usually means pure, i.e., uncontaminated, in

שבת
ט/ז

כִּגְרוֹגֶרֶת; צִפֹּרֶת כְּרָמִים, בֵּין חַיָּה בֵּין מֵתָה, כָּל־שֶׁהִיא, שֶׁמַּצְנִיעִין אוֹתָהּ לִרְפוּאָה.

רַבִּי יְהוּדָה אוֹמֵר: אַף הַמּוֹצִיא חָגָב חַי טָמֵא, כָּל־שֶׁהוּא, שֶׁמַּצְנִיעִין אוֹתוֹ לְקָטָן לְשַׂחֶק־בּוֹ.

ר' עובדיה מברטנורא

מת כגרוגרת. כדין שאר אוכלין: צפורת כרמים. עוף שמלוי בין הדקלין הבחורים: בין חיה בין מתה כל שהוא. שעושים ממנו רפואה לפקח ולהחכים: חגב חי טמא כל שהוא. ותנא קמא סבר טמא אין מלניעין אותו לתינוק, דלמא מיית ואכיל ליה. ואין הלכה כרבי יהודה:

יד אברהם

this case we cannot render it in this manner, since all insects are *tahor* in that sense. Insects are not affected by *tumah* contamination.

Although *Chullin* 3:7 delineates four signs which indicate that a locust is kosher, R' Yose adds a fifth, namely, that it be a member of the family called חָגָב, *chagav*. Since the halachah follows R' Yose, and as *Rashi* (*Lev.* 11:21) points out, we no longer can distinguish this species, we do not eat locusts today.

כָּל־שֶׁהוּא — *any size;*

Small children often kept live locusts as pets [regardless of the locust's size] (*Rav; Rashi*).

מֵת, כִּגְרוֹגֶרֶת; — [*a*] *dead* [*one*], *the size of a dried fig;*

A dead kosher locust falls into the category of food, whose minimum is the equivalent of a dried fig (*Rav; Rashi*). Kosher locusts are like fish and do not require ritual slaughter.

Parents should allow their children to keep only kosher species of locusts as pets. This is to prevent the children from eating a non-kosher locust, if, as often happened, the locust died while the child was playing with it. There-

9 7 [one], the size of a dried fig; a bird of the vineyards, whether alive or dead, any size, for they store it for medicinal purposes.

R' Yehudah says: Also, one who takes out a live non-kosher locust [is liable for] any size, since they store it for a child to play with.

YAD AVRAHAM

fore, liability for even the smallest locust is restricted to the kosher varieties only (*Rav, Tos. Yom Tov.* from *Gem.* 90b).

צִפֹּרֶת כְּרָמִים — *a bird of the vineyards,*

A variety of bird that was known to frequent young palms (*Rav*). *Meiri* specifies that it was a non-kosher bird.

Others identify it as a kosher locust (*Aruch; Rabbeinu Chananel*).

בֵּין חַיָּה בֵּין מֵתָה, כָּל־שֶׁהִיא, שֶׁמַּצְנִיעִין אוֹתָהּ לִרְפוּאָה. — *whether alive or dead, any size, for they store it for medicinal purposes.*

It was used to increase one's mental capacity (*Rav* from *Gem.* 90b).

[According to *Meiri*, who claims that it was a non-kosher bird, it may have been applied externally.]

Anything stored for medicinal purposes bears liability for any amount as in 10:1.

רַבִּי יְהוּדָה אוֹמֵר: אַף הַמּוֹצִיא חָגָב חַי טָמֵא, כָּל־שֶׁהוּא, שֶׁמַּצְנִיעִין אוֹתוֹ לְקָטָן לְשַׂחֶק־בּוֹ. — *R' Yehudah says: Also, one who takes out a live non-kosher locust [is liable for] any size, since they store it for a child to play with.*

In contrast to the first *Tanna* who prohibits the practice of giving a non-kosher locust to a child, lest it die and be eaten by the child, R' Yehudah holds that one may give a non-kosher locust to a child as a pet. It is his opinion that children do not eat their dead pets, but, rather, lament their death and eulogize them (*Gem.* ibid).

The halachah is not in accordance with R' Yehudah (*Rav*).

פרק עשירי
Chapter Ten

שבת
י/א

[א] **הַמַּצְנִיעַ** לְזֶרַע, וּלְדֻגְמָא, וְלִרְפוּאָה, וְהוֹצִיאוֹ בַּשַּׁבָּת, חַיָּב בְּכָל־שֶׁהוּא. וְכָל אָדָם אֵין חַיָּב עָלָיו אֶלָּא כְשִׁעוּרוֹ. חָזַר וְהִכְנִיסוֹ, אֵינוֹ חַיָּב אֶלָּא כְשִׁעוּרוֹ.

---- ר' עובדיה מברטנורא ----

פרק עשירי – **המצניע.** (א) **המצניע.** קודם השבת: **לזרע ולדוגמא.** להראות שיש לו סממנים ויקנו ממנו: **ולרפואה.** ושכח בשבת למה הצניע, והוציאו סתם, חייב טלוי בכל שהוא, שעל דעת הראשונה הוציאו והא מחשביה: **אלא כשיעורו.** כל אחד שיעור המפורש בו: **חזר והכניסו.** זה שהצניע פחות מכשיעור והוציאו, אם נמלך בו שלא לזרעו וחזר והכניסו: **אינו חייב.** בהכנסה זו אלא אם כן יש בו שיעור שלם, דכיון דנמלך שלא לזרעו בטלה מחשבתו והרי הוא ככל אדם:

---- יד אברהם ----

1.

Inadvertent transgression of the labor of *transferring objects from one domain to another* entails the bringing of a sin offering only if a set minimum of the particular substance or item was carried. These minimums were the subject of the preceding chapters. The mishnah now delineates circumstances under which these minimums are waived, so that even lesser amounts render one liable for a sin offering (*Tif. Yis.*).

הַמַּצְנִיעַ — *One who stored [a seed]*
   Before the Sabbath (*Rav*) one stored; i.e., set aside for safekeeping, less than the prescribed minimum of a particular substance, with the intention of using it for a specific purpose, as delineated below (*Tif. Yis.*). [Although the mishnah speaks of a seed, the same rule applies to any object or substance.]

לְזֶרַע, וּלְדֻגְמָא, וְלִרְפוּאָה, — *[to be used] for sowing, or as a sample, or for medicine* (lit., *cure*),
   His initial intention in setting aside a minute amount of seeds was that they later be used for sowing, or to show prospective customers, or for a small dose of medicine. Subsequently, however, his original purpose escaped him (*Rav* from *Gem.* 90b).

וְהוֹצִיאוֹ בַּשַּׁבָּת, — *and took it out on the Sabbath,*
   I.e., forgetting his reason for storing it, he carried the item out on the Sabbath with no special purpose in mind (*Rav* from *Gem.* 90b, 91a), but only with the intention to transfer the seeds from one place to another (*Rashi* 90b).

חַיָּב בְּכָל־שֶׁהוּא. — *is liable for any amount.*
   By having set aside a small quantity for a specific purpose, he indicated that this amount is important to him. Even when his purpose has subsequently been forgotten, this small quantity remains important (vis-à-vis him) and renders him liable for a sin offering (*Rav* from *Gem.* 91a).
   This rule is to be interpreted literally — even if only one tiny seed is involved (*Tos. Yom Tov* from *Gem.* 91a).

וְכָל אָדָם אֵין חַיָּב עָלָיו אֶלָּא כְשִׁעוּרוֹ. — *Other people, however, are not liable except for its prescribed amount.*

1. One who stored [a seed to be used] for sowing, or as a sample, or for medicine, and took it out on the Sabbath, is liable for any amount. Other people, however, are not liable except for its prescribed amount. If he changed his mind and brought it in, he is not liable except for its prescribed amount.

YAD AVRAHAM

[Someone other than the one who set aside this minute quantity is not liable for a sin offering even if he carried out these seeds.] We do not judge him according to the whims of one individual, but rather according to the minimums set forth in the preceding two chapters. These minimums represent the smallest amounts *commonly* used in the various endeavors listed. Barring any indications to the contrary, one is presumed to share the prejudices of the common person (*Rav*).

The *Gemara* (90b) points out that one who carries out one seed in order to plant it is liable even though he has not previously stored it. By actually carrying it out to plant he has attached at least as much importance to it as by storing it with intent to plant. The mishnah discusses the case of one who stored it, to teach that in such a case, even though the carrying was not for the purpose of using the seed but merely to transfer the seed from one place of safekeeping to another, one is, nevertheless, liable if he personally had previously stored it (*Gem.* 90b; *Rashi* ad loc.).

This mishnah echoes 7:3 which states: *Or [people] do not store [it in] such a quantity, and one carried it out on the Sabbath, the only one liable is the one who stores it.* Nevertheless, the *Tanna* occasionally repeats brief selections mentioned elsewhere in the mishnah (*Tos. Yom Tov*).

חָזַר וְהִכְנִיסוֹ, — *If he changed his mind and brought it in,*

If the one who stored it and carried it out reminded himself of his original intention, changed his mind and decided not to use the seeds for sowing [or as a sample or a medicine], and *then* brought them from the public domain into a private one (*Rav; Rashi*).

אֵינוֹ חַיָּב אֶלָּא כְּשִׁעוּרוֹ. — *he is not liable except for its prescribed amount.*

He is not liable for *transferring the seed from the public domain to the private, unless he carried the prescribed amount. Since he decided against planting the seed, it has no more importance to him than it has to the general public (*Rav; Rashi; Rambam*).

2.

One is liable for *transferring from one domain to another* only if he picks up an article (*akirah*) in one domain and deposits it (*hanachah*) in the other domain [see prefatory remarks to 1:1 and General Introduction, p. 12]. Here the mishnah teaches us that if in the process of transferring an article from one domain to another he first places it in a *karmelis*, a semipublic domain [see General Introduction, p. 13], and then picks it up from there to deposit in the second domain, he is exempt.

שבת [ב] **הַמּוֹצִיא** אֲכָלִין וּנְתָנָן עַל הָאִסְקֻפָּה, בֵּין
י/ב שֶׁחָזַר וְהוֹצִיאָן בֵּין שֶׁהוֹצִיאָן
אַחֵר, פָּטוּר, מִפְּנֵי שֶׁלֹּא עָשָׂה מְלַאכְתּוֹ בְּבַת אַחַת.
קֻפָּה שֶׁהִיא מְלֵאָה פֵּרוֹת וּנְתָנָהּ עַל הָאִסְקֻפָּה
הַחִיצוֹנָה, אַף־עַל־פִּי שֶׁרֹב הַפֵּרוֹת מִבַּחוּץ,

ר' עובדיה מברטנורא

(ב) **על האסקופה.** שהיא כרמלית, כגון שגבוהה משלשה ועד תשעה ורחבה ארבעה: **שלא עשה מלאכתו בבת אחת.** לא עשה עקירה מרשות היחיד והנחה ברשות הרבים שהם מקום חיוב, דבהכי הויא מלאכה גמורה. אלא עקר ממקום חיוב והניח בכרמלית שהוא פטור באותה הנחה, והדר עקר לה מכרמלית שאינו מקום חיוב והניח ברשות הרבים, ונמצא שלא נעשית עקירה ממקום חיוב והנחה במקום חיוב בפעם אחת: **אסקופה החיצונה.** אלטבא שלפני פתח הבית לצד רשות הרבים:

יד אברהם

In addition to this, the mishnah teaches us that partially transferring a filled container from one domain to another, even when most of the contents of that container are transferred in the process, does not render one liable for a sin offering. One is liable only if he transferred the entire container.

הַמּוֹצִיא אֲכָלִין וּנְתָנָן עַל הָאִסְקֻפָּה, — One who took out foodstuffs and placed them on the threshold,

I.e., one took foodstuffs out of his house towards the public domain but did not deposit them in the public domain. Rather, he placed them on the threshold which is situated between his house and the public domain.

The mishnah speaks of a threshold which is a *karmelis*, i.e., at least four handbreadths square and elevated from the ground at least three handbreadths but less than nine handbreadths (*Rav; Rashi;* from *Gem.* 91b).

Should the threshold be elevated ten or more handbreadths it would be a private domain. Between nine and ten handbreadths would render it a part of the public domain since passers-by could conceivably use it as a rest for adjusting burdens carried on their shoulders. An elevation of less than three handbreadths would also render it part of the public domain (*Rashi* 91b).

Although the mishnah says וּנְתָנָן, *and he placed them*, on the threshold, the same is true even if he did not put them down but just stopped a moment to rest while carrying them. The *Tanna* mentions *placing them* to underscore his rejection of Ben Azzai's view מְהַלֵּךְ כְּעוֹמֵד, *walking is tantamount to standing*. According to this view, one who carries an object from a private domain through a *karmelis* is not liable because it is considered as if one put the object down in the *karmelis*. The *Tanna* therefore emphasizes that only where one actually places the object in the *karmelis* is he exempt.

בֵּין שֶׁחָזַר וְהוֹצִיאָן בֵּין שֶׁהוֹצִיאָן אַחֵר, — *whether he* [himself] *subsequently returned and took them out or whether someone else took them out,*

[After placing them on the threshold, the foodstuffs were again picked up and carried out to the public domain, where they were placed. Regardless of whether this was done by the one who first placed them on the threshold or someone else . . .]

2. One who took out foodstuffs and placed them on the threshold, whether he [himself] subsequently returned and took them out or whether someone else took them out, he is exempt, since he did not perform his work at one time.

[One who took out] a basket which was full of produce, and placed it on the outer threshold, even though the greater portion of the produce is outside,

YAD AVRAHAM

פָּטוּר, — *he is exempt,*
[Both the one who placed the foodstuffs on the threshold originally and the one who moved them from there to the public domain (even if it is the same person) are exempt from a sin offering. From this rule, it is clear that the mishnah must be referring to a threshold which is a *karmelis*. If the threshold was a public domain the one who placed the foodstuffs on it would be liable; and if it was a private domain, placing the food there would not only be exempt but even permissible, while the one taking the food from the threshold to the public domain would be liable.]

מִפְּנֵי שֶׁלֹּא עָשָׂה מְלַאכְתּוֹ בְּבַת אַחַת. — *since he did not perform his work at one time.*
[In order to be liable for the *melachah* of *transferring between domains, one must not only make an *akirah* (see prefatory note) in either a private or public domain and a *hanachah* in the opposite domain, but must do so as a single transfer. By first placing the object in a *karmelis* before moving it to the opposite domain, one has made two separate transfers; namely, (a) from the private domain to the *karmelis*, and (b) from the *karmelis* to the public domain. Transferring an object from a public or private domain to a *karmelis* or vice versa is also prohibited, but it does not entail a sin offering since the prohibition is only Rabbinical.]

קֻפָּה שֶׁהִיא מְלֵאָה פֵּרוֹת, — [*One who took out*] *a basket which was full of produce,*
[The word הַמּוֹצִיא, *one who took out*, at the beginning of this mishnah refers to this case, too.]

וּנְתָנָהּ עַל הָאִסְקֻפָּה הַחִיצוֹנָה, — *and placed it on the outer threshold,*
I.e., one took a basket of produce from his house (private domain) and placed it on the outermost step leading to the public domain (*Rav*). The mishnah here speaks of a threshold or step less than three handbreadths above the ground. Being that low, it is not sufficiently separated from the public domain to be considered a domain (*karmelis*) by itself. Since it is not enclosed by walls and it abuts the public domain, it is viewed as part of the public domain to which it is adjacent (*Tos. Yom Tov*).

אַף־עַל־פִּי שֶׁרֹב הַפֵּרוֹת מִבַּחוּץ, — *even though the greater portion of the produce is outside,*
[I.e., the basket was so placed that only a small part of it was still within the private domain (e.g., a fence encircling the house divided the threshold) while the majority of produce was set in the public domain.]

שבת י/ג

פָּטוּר עַד שֶׁיּוֹצִיא אֶת כָּל הַקֻּפָּה.

[ג] **הַמּוֹצִיא**, בֵּין בִּימִינוֹ בֵּין בִּשְׂמֹאלוֹ, בְּתוֹךְ חֵיקוֹ, אוֹ עַל כְּתֵפוֹ, חַיָּב, שֶׁכֵּן מַשָּׂא בְּנֵי קְהָת.

ר' עובדיה מברטנורא

עד שיוציא. כלומר אלא אם כן הוציא בראשונה כל הקופה. ולא שנו אלא בקופה מלאה קשואין ודלועין שהן ארוכין ועדיין יש מהם לפנים, אבל מלאה חרדל שהרי יש הרבה ממנו כולו מבחוץ, נעשה כמי שהוציאה את כל הקופה וחייב: (ג) **שכן משא בני קהת.** בכתף ישאו, וימין ושמאל וחיק אורחא דארעא: **מרפקו.** הפרק האמצעי שבזרוע, ובערבי כך שמו מרפ"ק:

יד אברהם

— פָּטוּר עַד שֶׁיּוֹצִיא אֶת כָּל הַקֻּפָּה. — he is exempt until he takes out the entire basket.

He is not liable for a sin offering unless he takes the entire basket out at once. Putting the basket down after it has been only partially taken out exempts him even if he subsequently moves the rest of it out, too [in this respect it is the same as the first case of this mishnah] (*Rashi; Rav* as explained by *Tos. R' Akiva* from *Maggid Mishnah, Hil. Shabbos* 12:11).

The reason for this exemption is that an object cannot be said to have been transported from one domain to another unless it has been removed entirely from the one and been placed entirely in the other. Since part of this basket still rests in its original domain, no liability for *transferring from one domain to another can be imposed.

The question, however, arises as to the produce inside the basket. Since several individual units of produce may be resting in their entirety outside their original domain, why should one not be held liable for *transferring these foodstuffs, even if he cannot be held liable for *transferring the basket?

The *Gemara* (91b) offers two divergent opinions. Chizkiah is of the opinion that this mishnah refers only to a basket containing units of long produce such as cucumbers or gourds whose lengths reach across the entire interior of the basket. Therefore, as long as part of the basket remains within its original domain, so necessarily does a part of each unit of produce contained within that basket. If, however, the basket contains small units of produce such as mustard seeds (the example cited by the *Gemara*) so that the protrusion of the basket inevitably results in the complete removal of some units of that produce from their original domain, one is then liable for having transported those units of produce from one domain to another. This, despite the fact that one is not liable for having transported the basket itself.

According to this view, when the mishnah says, *though the greater portion of the produce is outside*, it refers to the greater portion of each individual unit.

R' Yochanan, however, maintains that the rule of the mishnah applies to all instances, regardless of the type of produce contained in the basket. According to him, this mishnah states the following new rule: אֶגֶד כְּלִי שְׁמֵהּ אֶגֶד, *the bond of a vessel is regarded as a*

10
3

he is exempt until he takes out the entire basket.

3. One who takes out, either with his right hand or with his left hand, in his bosom, or on his shoulder, is liable, for such was the [method of] carrying used by the sons of Kehath.

YAD AVRAHAM

bond. Rambam (*Hil. Shabbos* 12:11) interprets this as meaning that all the various units contained in a vessel are considered as if (legally) bound together (by that vessel) and are therefore viewed by the law as one unit. Accordingly, unless the basket has been removed entirely from its original domain, even the individual units contained within that basket, since they are "bound together" by the basket, are viewed by the halachah as being still partially in the original domain. This, despite the fact that several of these units may physically be entirely removed from their original domain. *Rambam* (ibid.) rules in accordance with this latter view. *Rav*, however, explains the mishnah according to the former.[1]

3.

The next mishnah teaches us that one is not liable for carrying from one domain to another unless he carries in a normal manner. If he carries in an unusual manner, however, he is exempt both from capital punishment if the sin is intentional, and from a sin offering if the sin is unintentional.

[Since clothing, in olden times, did not have pockets, various methods were employed to transport small items. The mishnah delineates which of these were considered usual and which were considered unusual.]

הַמוֹצִיא, — *One who takes out,*
[I.e., one who carries out an item from one domain to another.]

בֵּין בִּימִינוֹ בֵּין בִּשְׂמֹאלוֹ, בְּתוֹךְ חֵיקוֹ, אוֹ עַל כְּתֵפוֹ, חַיָּב — *either with his right hand or with his left hand, in his bosom, or on his shoulder, is liable,*

Since objects are commonly carried with either hand or tucked into the bosom, no Scriptural support is needed in categorizing such carrying as the usual manner. However, the less common method of transporting objects, by carrying them on the shoulder, might be classed as an unusual manner of carrying. The *Tanna*, therefore, cites a Scriptural reference [see below] to prove that such carrying is normal and thus culpable (*Rav; Rashi*).

שֶׁכֵּן מַשָּׂא בְּנֵי קְהָת. — *for such was the [method of] carrying used by the sons of Kehath.*

During the Israelites' travels through the wilderness, the *Mishkan* (Tabernacle) was taken down each time they broke camp and was re-erected at the

---

1. R' Chananel explains אֶגֶד כְּלִי differently. According to him it should read *the retention of a vessel is considered a retention.* He seems to learn that the pieces are not viewed as one unit but rather that the pieces are not totally removed from the first domain since they are in a vessel which is still in that domain and can thus be drawn back into that domain. *Rashi* apparently concurs with R' Chananel.

שבת י/ג

כִּלְאַחַר יָדוֹ: בְּרַגְלוֹ, בְּפִיו, וּבְמַרְפְּקוֹ, בְּאָזְנוֹ, וּבִשְׂעָרוֹ, וּבִפֻנְדָּתוֹ וּפִיהָ לְמַטָּה, בֵּין פֻּנְדָּתוֹ לַחֲלוּקוֹ, וּבִשְׂפַת חֲלוּקוֹ, בְּמִנְעָלוֹ, בְּסַנְדָּלוֹ,

---
ר' עובדיה מברטנורא

באפונדתו. אזור חלול: **פיה למטה.** אין דרך הוצאה בכך. אבל פיה למעלה דרך הוצאה בכך. פירוש אחר, אפונדתו בגד שלובש סמוך לבשרו לקבל הזיעה, ורגילין לעשות בו כעין כיסין, וכשמהפכים אותו מלמטה למעלה נמלא פי הכיס למטה: **שפת חלוקו.** השפה התחתונה של חלוק:

יד אברהם

new encampment. Transporting the Mishkan was the responsibility of the three Levite families, with the most sacred objects — the Ark, Table, Menorah and two Altars — being entrusted to the family of Kehath. Although other parts of the *Mishkan* (e.g., the walls and coverings) were carried on wagons, these objects of extreme sanctity were, by Divine decree, to be borne on the shoulders only (*Rav; Rashi* from *Numbers* 7:9).

Furthermore, the Torah describes the duties of the family of Kehath with the words: כִּי־עֲבֹדַת הַקֹּדֶשׁ עֲלֵהֶם בַּכָּתֵף יִשָּׂאוּ, *For the work of the Sanctuary is upon them, with the shoulder shall they carry* (*Numbers* 7:9), clearly identifying such carrying as עֲבוֹדָה, *work* (*Rambam, Comm.*). [It is, therefore, to be considered proper work in regard to all matters including the laws of Sabbath.]

An alternative reason is given for the singling out of these four body parts: *And the charge of Elazar the son of Aaron the Kohen was* וּקְטֹרֶת, *oil of lighting;* שֶׁמֶן הַמָּאוֹר, וּמִנְחַת הַתָּמִיד, *the incense of spices;* הַסַּמִּים, *the daily meal offering;* וְשֶׁמֶן הַמִּשְׁחָה, *and the oil of anointment* (*Numbers* 4:16). During the Israelites' travels through the wilderness Elazar would carry these four items on his person; the two types of oil in his two hands, the incense in his bosom, and the meal offering on his shoulder

(*Rashi* citing *R' Yitzchok bar Yehudah* quoting *R' Hai Gaon's* version of *Yerushalmi*. *R' Chananel* and *Meiri* cite a slightly different version, while extant editions of *Yerushalmi* have still a third reading).

כִּלְאַחַר יָדוֹ: — [*If he carried*] *backhandedly*:

According to our reading, כִּלְאַחַר יָדוֹ *backhandedly*, is not meant as a specific example of carrying in an unusual manner. Rather it is the general term used for anything done in an unusual way. Thus the mishnah means, *if he carried backhandedly, e.g., with his foot, in his mouth . . .* (*Tos.* 92a).

Rambam and *Tosafos* read לְאַחַר יָדוֹ, *on the back of his hand.* Accordingly, this phrase is a specific example of carrying in an unusual manner and the mishnah is punctuated, *if he carried on the back of his hand, with his foot, in his mouth, . . .* (*Tos.*). This reading is also found in 12:5 which lists unusual manners of holding a pen for writing (*Tos. Yom Tov*).

בְּרַגְלוֹ, בְּפִיו, — *with his foot, in his mouth,*

The latter refers to non-foods. However, if one carries food in his mouth on the Sabbath, he is liable since it is not unusual to carry out food in such a manner (*Tos.*; *Tif. Yis.* from *Gem.* 102a).

10
3   [If he carried] backhandedly: with his foot, in his mouth, with his elbow, in his ear, in his hair, in his moneybelt with its opening [hanging] downward, between his moneybelt and his shirt, in the hem of his shirt, in his shoe, or in his sandal,

YAD AVRAHAM

וּבְמַרְפְּקוֹ, — *with his elbow,*
I.e., carrying out an object in the crook of one's arm (the inside of the elbow). In this position, an object can be inserted in the bend and transported. Since it is unusual to carry in this manner, one is not liable for doing so.

A basket or other container suspended from the elbow, however, is commonly used for carrying. One who carries in such manner is liable (*Tif. Yis.; Tos. Yom Tov,* from *Tos., Menachos* 37).

Our translation follows *Tosafos* who renders קוּדָא [*coude,* French for elbow]. *Rashi* has אייש׳לא [*aisselle,* armpit].

בְּאָזְנוֹ, וּבִשְׂעָרוֹ, וּבְפֻנְדָּתוֹ וּפִיהָ לְמַטָּה, — *in his ear, in his hair, in his moneybelt with its opening* [*hanging*] *downward,*
Rashi describes פֻנְדָּתוֹ as a *hollow belt. Meiri* and *Chidushei HaRan* add that money was placed into the belt which was then knotted. As an additional security measure the knotted end was not usually permitted to hang down because of the tendency of the knot to become undone, thus causing the money to fall out. Instead, that end was fastened to his waist. If he did not wear the belt in this usual manner, but allowed the knotted end to hang freely, he is not liable for carrying out what is in the belt.

Alternatively, פֻנְדָּתוֹ is a tight-fitting *undershirt* worn mainly to absorb perspiration, but having pockets sewn to its hem. If the garment is worn upside down, the openings of the pockets will face downwards. Lightweight objects may, however, still be held fast by the tightness of the garment. It is, nevertheless, an unusual manner of carrying (*Rav; Rambam*).

בֵּין פֻּנְדָּתוֹ לַחֲלוּקוֹ, — *between his moneybelt and his shirt,*
I.e., draped over the moneybelt, partly between the belt and the shirt and partly over the outside of the belt. An object transported in this manner is insecure since its weight often shifts, thereby unbalancing the object. People, therefore, do not usually carry in this manner (*Meiri; Chidushei HaRan*).

וּבִשְׂפַת חֲלוּקוֹ, — *in the hem of his shirt,*
Our translation follows *Rashi, Ramban* and *Rav.*

Meiri and *Chidushei HaRan* apparently understand חֲלוּקוֹ as a long tunic extending down to the ankles. They explain that since the lower hem of the garment is not close to his hand, it is not easy to tap the hem to see whether his articles are secure. Furthermore, the garment sometimes drags or snags, causing the stitches of the bottom hem to become undone. It was therefore not customary for people to transport items in these hems.

Others read וּבְחֵפֶת חֲלוּקוֹ also denoting a hem (*Aruch*).

בְּמִנְעָלוֹ, בְּסַנְדָּלוֹ, — *in his shoe, or in his sandal,*
A מִנְעָל is made of soft leather, a סַנְדָּל of hard leather (*Tif. Yis.*).

שבת
י/ד

פָּטוּר, שֶׁלֹּא הוֹצִיא כְּדֶרֶךְ הַמּוֹצִיאִין.

[ד] **הַמִּתְכַּוֵּן** לְהוֹצִיא לְפָנָיו, וּבָא לוֹ לְאַחֲרָיו, פָּטוּר; לְאַחֲרָיו, וּבָא לוֹ לְפָנָיו, חַיָּב.

בֶּאֱמֶת אָמְרוּ: הָאִשָּׁה הַחוֹגֶרֶת בְּסִינָר, בֵּין מִלְּפָנֶיהָ וּבֵין מִלְּאַחֲרֶיהָ, חַיֶּבֶת, שֶׁכֵּן רָאוּי לִהְיוֹת חוֹזֵר.

ר' עובדיה מברטנורא

(ד) **לפניו ובא לו לאחריו פטור.** דנתכוון לשמירה מעולה ועלתה בידו שמירה פחותה: **לאחריו ובא לו לפניו חייב.** דנתכוון לשמירה פחותה, ועלתה בידו שמירה מעולה: **סינר.** כעין מכנסיים קטנים חוגרות אותן לגניבות. ואם תלתה בהן שום דבר להוליך ובא לו לצד אחר חייבת: **שכן ראוי להיות חוזר.** דרכו להיות חוזר וסובב סביבותיה, ומתחילה ידעה שסופו להתהפך:

יד אברהם

פָּטוּר, שֶׁלֹּא הוֹצִיא כְּדֶרֶךְ הַמּוֹצִיאִין — *he is exempt, because he did not carry out in a manner of those who carry things out.*

[I.e., in all the cases listed above, he is exempt, since he carries in an unusual manner.]

4.

The following mishnah deals with one who intended to do prohibited work in a certain manner, but due to happenstance, did it in a different manner. Implicit in the mishnah is this rule regarding his liability: If the manner in which it was done is superior to the one intended, he is liable. If it is inferior, he is not liable.

הַמִּתְכַּוֵּן לְהוֹצִיא לְפָנָיו — *One who intended to take out [an object] in front of him,*

For example, if one tied money in his cloak in such a manner that it would hang in front of him, thus enabling him to guard it closely (Rav; Rashi).

וּבָא לוֹ לְאַחֲרָיו — *and it slipped* (lit., *and it came*) *behind him,*

I.e., instead of staying in front of him, where he could exert a strong vigilance over it, the article shifted to the back, where he could exert only a weak vigilance over it (Rav from Gem. 92b).

פָּטוּר; — *is exempt;*

Since the act which actually took place is inferior to the one he intended and he is presumably dissatisfied with it, his intent is regarded as not being fulfilled. He is therefore exempt. This case is similar to מִתְעַסֵּק, *one who commits a sin absent-mindedly* (Rashi). The origin of both those rules is from מְלֶאכֶת מַחֲשֶׁבֶת אָסְרָה תּוֹרָה, *only a purposeful labor was prohibited by the Torah* (see General Introduction, p. 6). Among other things, this implies that a person cannot be held liable unless his intention is actually fulfilled.

לְאַחֲרָיו — *behind him,*

The words *One who intended to take out [an object]* stated at the beginning of the mishnah are understood to apply to this case, too. The meaning is

משניות / שבת – פרק י: המצניע לזרע [250]

he is exempt, because he did not carry out in a manner of those who carry things out.

4. One who intended to take out [an object] in front of him, and it slipped behind him, is exempt; behind him, and it shifted to the front of him, is liable.

Indeed, they said: A woman girded with an apron, whether in front of her or behind her, is liable, for it is common [for it] to shift around.

YAD AVRAHAM

therefore: *One who intended to take out an object behind him ...*

וּבָא לוֹ לְפָנָיו, — *and it shifted to the front of him* (lit. *and it came to him before him*),

His original intention would only allow him to exert a weak vigilance, whereas the unexpected shift of position afforded him a stronger vigilance (*Rav* from *Gem.* 92b).

חַיָּב. — *is liable.*

Since the act which actually took place was superior to his origin intention, we assume that he is satisfied with it, and his intention may therefore be regarded as fulfilled (*Rav*; *Tif. Yis.*).

בֶּאֱמֶת אָמְרוּ: — *Indeed, they said:*

This expression connotes a statement of either Biblical or Rabbinic origin handed down from previous generations, whose authority was so great as to be indisputable (*Rav*, *Terumos* 2:1) (see also comm. above 1:3).

הָאִשָּׁה הַחוֹגֶרֶת בְּסִינָר, — *A woman girded with an apron,*

In translating the word סִינָר, *apron,*

we have followed *Tiferes Yisrael*. This view is by no means unanimous.

Meiri describes an apronlike cloth, worn for the sake of modesty, to prevent the exposure of the lower abdomen. *Rashi* and *Rav* render *drawers* [see *Bava Kamma* 82a] while *Rambam* (*Comm.*) renders *belt* or *girdle*.

According to all of the above, the mishnah is discussing the case of someone who hung an object from the front upper part of the garment but which subsequently shifted to the back.[1]

בֵּין מִלְּפָנֶיהָ וּבֵין מִלְאַחֲרֶיהָ, חַיֶּבֶת, — *whether in front of her or behind her, (she) is liable,*

[I.e., whether the apron or the object placed there shifted from in front of her to behind her or vice versa, she is liable.]

שֶׁכֵּן רָאוּי לִהְיוֹת חוֹזֵר. — *for it is common [for it] to shift around.*

Since it is likely to shift its position, she knew in advance that it might possibly slip behind her. From the outset, therefore, her intent must have been to carry it either way (*Rav*; *Rashi*).

---

1. *Maaseh Rokeach* follows *Rashi* in translating *drawers*. However, he describes them as being fastened tightly around the leg or thigh at the bottom. The mishnah is then discussing a woman who placed an article in one of these legs. Although the object will not fall out, it will shift position.

שבת
י/ה

רַבִּי יְהוּדָה אוֹמֵר: אַף מְקַבְּלֵי פִתְקִין.

[ה] הַמּוֹצִיא כִכָּר לִרְשׁוּת הָרַבִּים חַיָּב; הוֹצִיאוּהוּ שְׁנַיִם, פְּטוּרִין. לֹא יָכוֹל אֶחָד לְהוֹצִיאוֹ וְהוֹצִיאוּהוּ שְׁנַיִם, חַיָּבִים. וְרַבִּי שִׁמְעוֹן פּוֹטֵר.

──────── ר' עובדיה מברטנורא ────────

רבי יהודה אומר אף מקבלי פתקין. של מלך. הרצים הנושאים אגרות נותנים מותס בעלים חלולים כדמות קנים ותולים בצוארם, ודרך אותו קנה להיות חוזר וסובב מלפניו ומאחריו סביב לצוארו יודע היה שסופו להתהפך. ואין הלכה כרבי יהודה: (ה) הוציאוהו שנים פטורים. כדילפינן (ויקרא ד) בעשותה אחת מכל מצות ה', העושה את כולה ולא העושה מקצתה: ורבי שמעון פוטר. דסבר אפילו כשאין יחיד יכול לעשותה אם עשאוה שנים פטורים. ואין הלכה כרבי שמעון:

──────── יד אברהם ────────

— רַבִּי יְהוּדָה אוֹמֵר: אַף מְקַבְּלֵי פִתְקִין. R' Yehudah says: Also letter carriers.

Mailmen (*Meiri*), couriers (*Rambam; Rav*), or court officials (*Tos.*) would hang pouches or tubes from their belts or from a loop around their necks to carry messages or documents. As they walked or ran these containers would shift from front to back.

Since the rule of the letter carriers is cited in the name of R' Yehudah, most commentators assume that the first *Tanna* disagrees. Though the tubes do shift, they do so less frequently than does the object carried on the apron discussed previously. The first *Tanna* considers this occasional shift somewhat an unusual occurrence, and therefore not necessarily expected or accepted by the carrier, while R' Yehudah classes it as usual. It is therefore expected and thus inherently part of his intent (*Tos.* as explained by *Tos. Yom Tov*).

Both *Rambam* and *Rav* state that the halachah does not follow R' Yehudah.

Meiri, however, writes that the first *Tanna* and R' Yehudah are not in disagreement. R' Yehudah merely amplifies the original statement.

5.

הַמּוֹצִיא כִכָּר לִרְשׁוּת הָרַבִּים חַיָּב; — One who takes a loaf of bread out to a public domain is liable;

[This ruling is obvious and is stated only as an introduction to the following case.]

הוֹצִיאוּהוּ שְׁנַיִם, פְּטוּרִין. — If two [people] took it out, they are [both] exempt.

Since no assistance is required to carry out a loaf of bread, the assistance of the second person serves merely to detract from the amount of labor being done by the first. Both are therefore exempt. This rule is derived from the verse (*Lev.* 4:27): וְאִם־נֶפֶשׁ אַחַת תֶּחֱטָא בִשְׁגָגָה ... בַּעֲשֹׂתָהּ אַחַת מִמִּצְוֹת ה' אֲשֶׁר לֹא־תֵעָשֶׂינָה וְאָשֵׁם, *And should one person (lit., soul) sin inadvertently ... by his doing one of the commandments of* HASHEM *which may not be done and [so] be guilty.* (This is the first verse of a section describing the obligation and rules of a personal sin offering.) By

משניות / שבת – פרק י׳ – המצניע לזרע [252]

10
5

R' Yehudah says: Also letter carriers.

5. One who takes a loaf of bread out to a public domain is liable; if two [people] took it out, they are [both] exempt. If one could not take it out [by himself] and two took it out, they are [both] liable. R' Shimon, however, exempts [them].

YAD AVRAHAM

stating *by his doing*, the Torah implies that in order to be liable for a sin offering, a person must do the entire act, to the extent of which he himself is capable, himself.[1]

לֹא יָכוֹל אֶחָד לְהוֹצִיאוֹ — *If one could not take it out [by himself]*

For example, two people carried out a beam too heavy for either of them to carry alone (*Rambam, Hil. Shabbos* 1:16).

וְהוֹצִיאוּהוּ שְׁנַיִם, חַיָּבִים. — *and two took it out, they are [both] liable.*

Since neither one was capable of doing the work himself, the assistance of the one does not detract from the level of work of the other; on the contrary, it makes it possible. Since the act requires the concerted efforts of both, each can be said to be doing a full act; i.e., that part of the act of which he alone is capable. They are, therefore, both liable (*Ramban; Ritva* 93a).[2]

וְרַבִּי שִׁמְעוֹן פּוֹטֵר. — *R' Shimon, however, exempts [them].*

The *Gemara* 93a explains that in the verse cited above, there appear three singular expressions which indicate that liability is incurred only when one person sinned by himself: (a) ... נֶפֶשׁ תֶּחֱטָא, *should "a" person sin;* (b) אַחַת תֶּחֱטָא, *should "one" sin;* and (c) בַּעֲשֹׂתָהּ,

1. [The *Baraisa* quoted on 92b seems to derive this from the word בַּעֲשֹׂתָהּ, *by his doing*. The *Gemara* on 93a states that there are three words in this verse to be used as derivations. The *Gemara* cites the three *halachos* derived but does not state which word applies to which halachah. *Toras Kohanim* on this verse seems to derive this from the word אַחַת, *one*. This is the derivation followed by *Malbim* in his commentary to the *Sifra* on this verse in *Leviticus*. *Tosafos* (3a) seems to assume the former derivation, though from *Tosafos* on 93a this is not apparent. It may possibly be that the three derivational words are used in toto as a source for three *halachos* without any necessity of specifying which applies to which. (See commentary of Rabbi S.R. Hirsch on this verse.) This would fit the language of the *Gemara* on 93a and the wording of *Tosafos'* question there.]

2. *Rashi* (93a) offers a different explanation. As explained above, this verse excludes one who performs less than the full act of sin. It is reasonable, however, to presume that the Torah meant to exclude only that instance in which either one is capable of performing it himself since it is then not customary for two people to do it together. If, however, the act cannot be performed without the efforts of two people, that becomes the normal manner of its performance and, it is reasonable to presume, they should both be held liable. According to the general principles of derivations, wherever there is a logical distinction to be made, a single derivation may be applied only to the case it most logically fits. [For this reason numerous derivations are often required to cover all possible cases of a single topic.] The rule limiting liability for a sin offering to one who performs the entire forbidden act himself can, therefore, be applied only to the former case.

שבת י/ה

הַמּוֹצִיא אֳכָלִין פָּחוֹת מִכַּשִּׁעוּר בִּכְלִי, פָּטוּר אַף עַל הַכְּלִי, שֶׁהַכְּלִי טְפֵלָה לוֹ; אֶת הַחַי בְּמִטָּה, פָּטוּר אַף עַל הַמִּטָּה, שֶׁהַמִּטָּה טְפֵלָה לוֹ;

ר' עובדיה מברטנורא

את החי במטה. על החי לא מחייב בהולאתו אם אינו כפות, לפי שהוא נושא את עצמו. והכ"מ אדם אבל בהמה חיה ועוף לא, דכמאן דכפותין דמו:

יד אברהם

by "his" (lit., its) doing. Thus, three times the Torah excludes a sin committed by more than one person from liability for a sin offering. This repetition indicates that three cases are excluded. One of these is the case of each person doing only a part of the forbidden labor, i.e., one makes an *akirah* and the other a *hanachah* as explained in 1:1. Another is the case of a forbidden labor which either person can do alone yet is performed by two together, e.g., a loaf of bread carried by two people. The third exclusion is the subject of a disagreement between R' Yehudah [who is identified as the first *Tanna* of our mishnah (*Gem.* 93a)] and R' Shimon. R' Shimon says that this is to exclude even two people performing a labor that neither could do himself. R' Yehudah says that this is to exclude one who committed a sin which results from a mistaken ruling of the Sanhedrin. [It may therefore be viewed as not being *his* sin — i.e., his responsibility] (See *Horayos* 1:1).

The *Gemara* (93a) further explains that if two people carried out an object together which one of them (by virtue of his greater strength) could have carried himself but which the other (due to his lesser strength) could not, only the one who could have done it himself is liable. The weaker person is exempt because his contribution, being unnecessary, accomplished nothing.

הַמּוֹצִיא אֳכָלִין פָּחוֹת מִכַּשִּׁעוּר בִּכְלִי — One who takes out foodstuffs less than the prescribed amount in a vessel

[To render one liable to a sin offering, at least the equivalent of a dried fig must be carried out (see 7:4).]

פָּטוּר אַף עַל הַכְּלִי — is exempt even for the vessel,

Even a vessel for which one is normally liable for carrying out is in this instance exempted.

שֶׁהַכְּלִי טְפֵלָה לוֹ — because the vessel is secondary to it;

Since he did not carry out the vessel for its own sake but rather as a container for the foodstuffs, the vessel, relative to this act of carrying, has no inherent importance but is merely an accessory. It is therefore deemed subordinate to the foodstuffs. Since there can be no liability for carrying out the major part (the foodstuffs), there can, in consequence, be no liability for taking out the subordinate minor part (the vessel).

However, if he needed the vessel as well in the place to which it was carried, he is liable (*Gem.* 93b).

אֶת הַחַי בְּמִטָּה, — a live person on a bed,

[The words *one who takes out* which prefaced the previous case are understood to apply also to both this case and the next. The mishnah should be read thus: One who takes out: (a) foodstuffs ... in a vessel; (b) a live person on a bed ...; or (c) a corpse on a bed ...

10
5
One who takes out foodstuffs less than the prescribed amount in a vessel is exempt even for the vessel, because the vessel is secondary to it; a live person on a bed, he is exempt even for the bed, for the bed is secondary to him;

YAD AVRAHAM

The question common to all of these cases is the determination of liability for carrying out objects which are accessories of other objects.]

פָּטוּר — *he is exempt*

The *melachah* of carrying objects from one domain to another on the Sabbath does not include the carriage of live people who are capable of such movement by their own power. [This exemption is only from liability. It is, however, Rabbinically prohibited (*Shulchan Aruch* 308:41; *Mishnah Berurah* 308:154).] This exception is based on the principle חַי נוֹשֵׂא אֶת־עַצְמוֹ, *a living creature carries itself.*

Tosafos, citing *R' Yitzchak,* explain the basis of this rule in the following manner. We have previously explained [General Introduction, p. 3] that the forbidden labors of the Sabbath are those labors which were performed in the construction of the *Mishkan*. At no time during the building of the *Mishkan* were live creatures carried. Only three animals were needed; rams, *techashim* [whose hides were used for the topmost coverings (*Exodus* 26:14) and the carrying cases of the vessels (*Numbers* 4:6-14)], and the *chilazon* fish [whose blood was the basis of the תְּכֵלֶת, *techeiles,* a blue dye used for the curtains and covers of the *Mishkan*]. The first two walked on their own and had only to be carried after their slaughter. The *chilazon* was punctured immediately upon being removed from the water, for any delay would affect the quality of the dye. Thus, in the Torah there is no source to prohibit the carrying of a living creature (*Tos.* 94a).

Korban Nesanel, followed by *Tiferes Yisrael,* finds difficulty with *Tosafos'* conclusion, according to which no distinction should be drawn between man and beast. Yet the *Gemara* (94a) clearly teaches that the Sages apply the principle "a living creature carries himself" only to man and not to animals. (This is, however, disputed by R' Nassan who holds that even the carrying of animals is exempted.)

Korban Nesanel (in note 6 to this chapter) answers that since derivatives from the construction of the *Mishkan* need not be precisely as they were in the *Mishkan* (see prefatory note to Chap. 7), the lack of a clear source for carrying out a living creature is not definitive unless there is also a logical reason to differentiate. The obvious distinguishing characteristic of the transportation of a live person is that he aids in his own transportation by holding on and by tensing his muscles so as to distribute his weight equally. [This is most clearly seen from the fact that a person can lift a child of a given weight though he would find great difficulty in lifting an inanimate object of equal "dead" weight.] This, however, is not true of an animal, which resists being held. Therefore, logic dictates that only the carrying of a person may be exempted by the lack of a clear source for it in the construction of the *Mishkan*. The carrying of an animal, however, should be equated with the carrying of inanimate objects.

אַף עַל הַמִּטָּה, שֶׁהַמִּטָּה טְפֵלָה לוֹ; — *even for the bed, for the bed is secondary to him;*

He is exempt for carrying the bed

שבת
י/ו

אֶת הַמֵּת בְּמִטָּה, חַיָּב. וְכֵן כְּזַיִת מִן הַמֵּת, וּכְזַיִת מִן הַנְּבֵלָה, וְכָעֲדָשָׁה מִן הַשֶּׁרֶץ, חַיָּב. וְרַבִּי שִׁמְעוֹן פּוֹטֵר.

[ו] **הַנּוֹטֵל** צִפָּרְנָיו זוֹ בָּזוֹ, אוֹ בְשִׁנָּיו; וְכֵן שְׂעָרוֹ, וְכֵן שְׂפָמוֹ, וְכֵן זְקָנוֹ; וְכֵן הַגּוֹדֶלֶת, וְכֵן הַכּוֹחֶלֶת, וְכֵן הַפּוֹקֶסֶת, רַבִּי אֱלִיעֶזֶר מְחַיֵּב. וַחֲכָמִים אוֹסְרִין מִשּׁוּם שְׁבוּת.

─────── ר׳ עובדיה מברטנורא ───────

וכן כזית מן המת. חייב אם הוליאו, דהואיל ומטמא, הולאה חשובה היא להליל עלמו מן הטומאה. **וכן כזית מן הנבלה וכעדשה מן השרץ, דהכי הוי שיעורן לטומאה: ורבי שמעון פוטר.** אפילו במת שלם, דהוי מלאכה שאינה לריכה לגופה, דכל שאינו אלא לסלקו מעליו הויא מלאכה שאינה לריכה לגופה ולאו מלאכת מחשבת היא. ואין הלכה כרבי שמעון: (ו) **ובן שערו.** התולש שער ראשו בידו: **ובן הגודלת.** שער ראשה וקולעת אותו, תרגום עבות (שמות כח) גדיל: **הבוחלת.** נותנת כחול בעיניה: **הפוקסת.** מחלקת שער שבאמלע הראש מכאן ומכאן אלל הלדעים: **רבי אליעזר מחייב חטאת.** כוחלת משום כותבת, גודלת ופוקסת משום בונה: **וחכמים אוסרים משום שבות.** דסברי אין דרך כתיבה בכך ואין דרך בנין בכך, והלכה כחכמים. ודוקא הנוטל

─────── יד אברהם ───────

since it is not carried out for itself but as a means of carrying the person. Since he is exempt for carrying the person, he cannot be liable for carrying the bed which is only an accessory to that person. This is the same exemption as that of the vessel containing the foodstuffs, explained above.

אֶת הַמֵּת בְּמִטָּה, חַיָּב. — *a corpse on a bed, he is liable.*

[If one carries out a corpse on a bed, he is liable, since the principle "a living creature carries itself" obviously does not apply.]

וְכֵן כְּזַיִת מִן הַמֵּת, וּכְזַיִת מִן הַנְּבֵלָה, וְכָעֲדָשָׁה מִן הַשֶּׁרֶץ, חַיָּב. — *And similarly,* [one *who takes out a part*] *of a corpse the size of an olive, or* [*a piece*] *of an animal's carcass the size of an olive, or* [*a piece*] *of a dead sheretz the size of a lentil, he is liable.*

Sheretz refers to certain species of creeping animals. See 14:1.

The amounts listed in our mishnah are the minimums of each object that convey *tumah-*contamination. Their transfer, for the purpose of removing *tumah*, is therefore considered significant enough to render one liable for a sin offering (*Rav; Rashi*).

[As delineated by *Toras Kohanim*, quoted by *Rashi* in *Lev.* 22:5, the minimum amount of a corpse or an animal carcass that can convey *tumah* is the equivalent of an olive's bulk. The minimum of a dead rodent is the equivalent of a lentil's bulk.]

וְרַבִּי שִׁמְעוֹן פּוֹטֵר. — *R' Shimon, however, exempts* [*him*].

R' Shimon exempts even the one who carries out a corpse, since this is a מְלָאכָה שֶׁאֵינָהּ צְרִיכָה לְגוּפָהּ, *labor not done for its defined purpose* [see below and General Introduction, p. 9] (*Rav; Rashi*).

a corpse on a bed, he is liable. And similarly, [one who takes out a part] of a corpse the size of an olive, or [a piece] of an animal's carcass the size of an olive, or [a piece] of a dead *sheretz* the size of a lentil, he is liable. R' Shimon, however, exempts [him].

6. One who removes his fingernails one with the other, or with his teeth, and similarly, [one who removes] his hair, his moustache, or his beard [in such a manner]; and one who braids [her hair], or paints [her eyes], or parts [her hair], R' Eliezer declares liable. But the Sages prohibit [them] as Rabbinical enactments.

YAD AVRAHAM

6.

Although Chapters 10 and 11 deal with the labor of transferring from one domain to another, mishnah 6, which deals with *tolados* of various *avos*, is added here because it, too, speaks of מְלָאכָה שֶׁאֵינָהּ צְרִיכָה לְגוּפָהּ, labor not performed for its defined purpose.

הַנּוֹטֵל צִפָּרְנָיו זוֹ בְזוֹ, אוֹ בְשִׁנָּיו; — One who removes his fingernails one with the other, or with his teeth;

[A person used the edge of one of his fingernails as a blade to remove the others, or he bit his nails.]

וְכֵן שְׂעָרוֹ, וְכֵן שְׂפָמוֹ, וְכֵן זְקָנוֹ; — and similarly, [one who removes] his hair, his moustache, or his beard [in such a manner];

I.e., he plucked his hair, moustache, or beard with his hands (*Rav; Tif. Yis.*).

Cutting either the hair or the fingernails is a *toladah* of *shearing (Tos. Yom Tov).

וְכֵן הַגּוֹדֶלֶת, וְכֵן הַכּוֹחֶלֶת, וְכֵן הַפּוֹקֶסֶת, — and one who braids [her hair], or paints [her eyes], or parts [her hair],

The translation *parts her hair* follows *Rashi's* first interpretation. Others explain this as a woman who smears dough on her face so that when she removes it her face should become reddened (*Rashi* quoting his teachers).

Braiding and parting the hair are *tolados* of *building. Painting the eyes is a *toladah* of *writing (*Rav* from Gem. 94b), since using a brush to apply her make-up is tantamount to writing with a pen (*Rashi*). This latter classification follows the first opinion stated in the *Gemara*. The *Gemara's* conclusion, however, is that by painting her eyes she is liable for *dyeing (Tos. Yom Tov; Tif. Yis.).

רַבִּי אֱלִיעֶזֶר מְחַיֵּב. וַחֲכָמִים אוֹסְרִין מִשּׁוּם שְׁבוּת. — R' Eliezer declares liable. But the Sages prohibit [them] as Rabbinical enactments.

The Sages exempt all the acts mentioned above because they are not

שבת י/ו

הַתּוֹלֵשׁ מֵעָצִיץ נָקוּב, חַיָּב; וְשֶׁאֵינוֹ נָקוּב, פָּטוּר. וְרַבִּי שִׁמְעוֹן פּוֹטֵר בָּזֶה וּבָזֶה.

ר' עובדיה מברטנורא

לפרניו וסטרו בידיו, הוו דפטרי רבנן מחטאת ומסקילה, אבל הנוטל שערו בכלי מודים חכמים דחייב חטאת. ומכי נטל שתי שערות חייב, והנוטל שער לבן מתוך שחורות אפילו אחת חייב. ולפורן שפרשה רובה או שער שנתלש רובו ומלער אותו, מותר ליטלו ביד לכתחלה: **התולש מעציץ נקוב חייב.** דהוי כמחובר, דיונק מן הקרקע ט"י הנקב שמריח לחלוחית הקרקע, ואפילו הנקב בצדו. ושיעור הנקב כדי שרש קטן: **ורבי שמעון פוטר בזה ובזה.** דלא חשיב ליה כמחובר לחייבו סקילה. ואין הלכה כרבי שמעון:

יד אברהם

done in the usual manner of that particular labor (see General Introduction, p. 11 and mishnah 3 of this chapter) (*Rav; Tif. Yis.* from *Gem.* 94b). However, since they do in some way resemble these labors the Sages prohibit them by dint of Rabbinic enactment (*Meiri*). [This sort of Sabbath prohibition is called שְׁבוּת, literally *rest*.]

If the hair or nails are cut with a tool usually used for that purpose, e.g., a scissors, then the perpetrator may be liable even according to the Sages.

In order to be liable for cutting hair, he must cut at least two hairs or a single white hair growing among dark hairs (*Rav; Tif. Yis.* from *Gem.* 94b). Furthermore, he must have a need for the nails or the hair which he cuts off. Otherwise, his act is *a labor not performed for its designated purpose* and is exempt (*Tos.* 94b).

⥤§ Perforated Flowerpots

The Torah, relative to many *halachos*, distinguishes between a plant growing in a perforated flowerpot and one growing in an unperforated flowerpot. The former is considered attached to the ground, since it can draw some sustenance by absorption through the hole. The latter is not considered attached to the ground. Furthermore, all laws regarding growing (e.g., *terumah, maaser, sheviis*) do not apply to plants growing out of soil in a pot or any other container, but only to soil still connected to the ground. Therefore, these laws apply to plants growing in a perforated pot (as explained above) but not to plants growing in an unperforated pot.

In regard to the laws of Sabbath, this distinction is important with regard to the *melachah* of *reaping. Since liability for this labor extends only to detaching plants which are in some fashion connected to the ground (e.g., through a

10. 6 One who detaches [a plant] from a perforated flowerpot is liable; [from] an unperforated one, is exempt. R' Shimon, however, exempts in both cases.

YAD AVRAHAM

stalk or a tree), it applies to plants in a flowerpot only if that pot is perforated.[1]

Detaching a plant from an unperforated pot is, nevertheless, Rabbinically prohibited (*Shulchan Aruch* 336:7).

הַתּוֹלֵשׁ מֵעָצִיץ נָקוּב, חַיָּב; — *One who detaches [a plant] from a perforated flowerpot is liable;*

Since the flowerpot is perforated, the plant growing in it is regarded as growing from the ground. Anyone who pulls it out is therefore liable for performing a *toladah* of *reaping*. This applies even if the hole is on the side of the flowerpot as long as it is large enough for a small root to fit through it (*Rav* from *Gem.* 95b; *Rashi; Rambam, Hil. Shabbos* 8:3).

If it is only cracked, however, there is no liability for pulling out the plant, since it is still considered unperforated (*Tif. Yis.*).

וְשֶׁאֵינוֹ נָקוּב, פָּטוּר. — *[from] an unperforated one, is exempt.*

Since the flowerpot is not perforated, the plant cannot derive its nourishment from the ground. It is therefore not regarded as attached to the earth. One who pulls up such a plant is, therefore, exempt from a sin offering. Nevertheless, this is still Rabbinically prohibited (*Beis Yosef* 336, *Shulchan Aruch* 336:7).

וְרַבִּי שִׁמְעוֹן פּוֹטֵר בָּזֶה וּבָזֶה. — *R' Shimon, however, exempts in both cases.*

R' Shimon does not regard a perforated flowerpot as attached to the earth, and it therefore bears no liability. The halachah is in accordance with the first opinion (*Rav*).

---

1. There is one type of pot which does not require perforation (*Gem.* 84b). Its identity, however, is subject to a difference of opinion. *Rashi* (*Gittin* 7b) states that an earthenware pot, even without a hole, is dealt with as a perforated pot. Accordingly, our mishnah, which differentiates between perforated and unperforated pots, is discussing either wooden or metal pots. *Tosafos* (ibid. and in *Menachos* 85a) identify the exception as being wooden, *not* earthenware, pots. According to this explanation, our mishnah is discussing either an earthenware or metal pot. (There is a third opinion, quoted in the name of *Rabbeinu Tam*, which states that a wooden pot, even if it is perforated, is dealt with as an unperforated pot.) *Shulchan Aruch* (336:8) states that we adopt the stringencies of both opinions.

פרק אחד עשר
Chapter Eleven

As explained in the General Introduction (p. 12), there are four *domains* delineated by the Torah and the Rabbis in regard to the *melachah* of *transferring from one domain to another:* רְשׁוּת הַיָּחִיד, *a private domain,* רְשׁוּת הָרַבִּים, *a public domain;* מְקוֹם פְּטוּר, *an exempt area;* and כַּרְמְלִית, *karmelis,* i.e., a semipublic domain. Only transfers from a private domain to a public one, and vice versa, or carrying four cubits within a public domain are Biblically prohibited. Transferring from one private domain to another, even if they are owned by different people, is not Biblically prohibited. There is, however, one exception to this rule which will be explained in this chapter.

In the previous chapters the *Tanna* delineated the laws governing *transferring by carrying. He proceeds now to delineate the laws of transfer by throwing and handing over. These are *tolados* of the former (*Tif. Yis.*).

שבת [א] **הַזּוֹרֵק** מֵרְשׁוּת הַיָּחִיד לִרְשׁוּת הָרַבִּים,
יא/א מֵרְשׁוּת הָרַבִּים לִרְשׁוּת הַיָּחִיד, חַיָּב.
מֵרְשׁוּת הַיָּחִיד לִרְשׁוּת הַיָּחִיד וּרְשׁוּת הָרַבִּים
בָּאֶמְצַע, רַבִּי עֲקִיבָא מְחַיֵּב, וַחֲכָמִים פּוֹטְרִין.

ר' עובדיה מברטנורא

פרק אחד עשר – הזורק. (א) הזורק מרשות היחיד לרשות הרבים. רשות היחיד הוא מקום שהוקף ארבע מחיצות גבוהות עשרה טפחים ובינייהן ד' טפחים על ד' טפחים או יותר, על כן אפילו יש בו כמה מילין, אם הוקף לדירה כגון מדינה שמוקפת חומה ודלתותיה נעולות בלילה. ומבואות שיש להן ג', וכתלין ולחי ברוח רביעית. וכן תל גבוה עשרה ורחב ד', או חריץ שהוא עמוק עשרה ורחב ד'. ואפילו כלים, כגון ספינה ומגדל של עץ וכיוצא בהם, אם יש בהם ד' על ד' בגובה עשרה כל אלו רשות היחיד הן. ואויר רשות היחיד כרשות היחיד עד לרקיע. וטובי הכתלים של רשות היחיד נדון כרשות היחיד. ורשות הרבים הוא כגון השווקים והרחובות, המדברות והדרכים המפולשים להם, והוא שיהיה רוחב הדרך ט"ז אמה ולא יהיה עליו תקרה, ואיכא למאן דאמר שצריך נמי שיהיו בוקעים בהם שש מאות אלף בכל יום כדגלי מדבר. ואויר רשות הרבים אינו כרשות הרבים אלא עד עשרה טפחים, ולמעלה מי' ברשות הרבים מקום פטור הוא. ומקום שאין בו ד' על ד', וגבוה מג' טפחים ולמעלה הוא מקום פטור, אפילו קוצים וברקנים וגללין ברשות הרבים גבוהים משלשה ולמעלה ואין בהם ד' על ד' הרי הן מקום פטור, וכן מקום המוקף מחיצות ואין בו ד' על ד', או חריץ שאין בו ד' על ד' או יותר. ומקום שהוקף ד' מחיצות גובהן מג' ועד עשרה ויש בו ד' על ד' או יותר, או תל שיש בו ארבעה על ארבעה או יותר גבוה מג' ועד עשרה, או חריץ שיש בו ד' על ד' עמוק מג' ועד עשרה, ומבוי סתום ממלא רוחותיו שאין לו לחי או קורה ברוח רביעית, והים, והבקעה, כל אלו כרמלית הן. ופירוש כרמלית, כארמלית, כלומר כמו אלמנה שאינה בתולה ולא נשואה לבעל, כך רשות זו אינה לא רשות היחיד ולא רשות הרבים. ואויר כרמלית עד עשרה, ומעשרה ולמעלה בכרמלית הוי מקום פטור. והמוליך מרשות היחיד לרשות הרבים, או המכניס מרשות הרבים לרשות היחיד, חייב חטאת. מרשות היחיד לכרמלית, או מרשות הרבים לכרמלית, וכרמלית לשתיהן פטור אבל אסור. מרשות היחיד או מרשות הרבים למקום פטור או ממקום פטור לשניהן, מותר לכתחלה. ואינו צריך לומר מכרמלית למקום פטור, או ממקום פטור לכרמלית, שהוא מותר. והמעביר מתחלת ד"א לסוף ד"א ברשות הרבים, חייב חטאת. בכרמלית, פטור אבל אסור. ברשות היחיד ובמקום פטור, מותר לכתחלה לטלטל ולהעביר בכל הרשות כולו ואפילו הוא כמה מילין: **רבי עקיבא מחייב.** דס"ל מכי עבר החפץ באויר רשות הרבים

יד אברהם

1.

הַזּוֹרֵק מֵרְשׁוּת הַיָּחִיד לִרְשׁוּת הָרַבִּים, — מֵרְשׁוּת הָרַבִּים לִרְשׁוּת הַיָּחִיד, חַיָּב. — *One who throws from a private domain to a public domain, [or] from a public domain to a private domain, is liable.*

Since זוֹרֵק, *throwing*, is a *toladah* of *transferring, throwing from a private domain to a public one is tantamount to carrying out. It is, nevertheless, considered a *toladah* since in the construction of the *Mishkan*, things were either carried or handed over but never thrown (*Meiri*).

מֵרְשׁוּת הַיָּחִיד לִרְשׁוּת הַיָּחִיד וּרְשׁוּת הָרַבִּים בָּאֶמְצַע, — *[One who throws] from one private domain to another private*

1. One who throws from a private domain to a public domain, [or] from a public domain to a private domain, is liable.

[One who throws] from one private domain to another private domain, and a public domain [lies] in between, R' Akiva holds [him] liable. The Sages, however, exempt [him].

YAD AVRAHAM

domain and a public domain [lies] in between,

[As will be explained below, this refers to an object traversing the airspace of the public domain at a height of less than ten handbreadths.]

רַבִּי עֲקִיבָא מְחַיֵּב, — *R' Akiva holds [him] liable.*

R' Akiva bases his ruling on the legal principle of *kelutah* [קְלוּטָה כְּמִי שֶׁהֻנְּחָה, *something encompassed is considered at rest*], i.e., when an object enters the airspace of the public domain, it is encompassed by that domain and "caught" in it. It is, accordingly, legally regarded as having come to rest there. The one who threw it is, therefore, guilty of throwing into the public domain.[1] This is true only if the object thrown traversed the public domain within ten handbreadths of the ground, since, as has been explained in the General Introduction, the public domain extends only to that height. If, however, the object traversed the public domain at a height greater than ten handbreadths, he is exempt, since the air above ten handbreadths is regarded as an exempt region. In this domain, even R' Akiva agrees the principle of *kelutah* does not apply (*Rav* from *Gem.* 97a; *Rashi* on *Gem.* 4b).

וַחֲכָמִים פּוֹטְרִין. — *The Sages, however, exempt [him].*

The Sages do not subscribe to the principle of *kelutah*. Consequently,

---

1. Theoretically, one should be liable twice, since the article "came to rest" in the public domain and then was again transferred from that public domain to the second private domain. There is, however, another factor to consider. The *Gemara* (*Shabbos* 4a) quotes various tannaic opinions as to whether the *akirah* and *hanachah*, involved in the *melachah* of *transferring from one domain to another*, have to be from a surface of at least four handbreadths by four handbreadths in order for one to be liable. [It is, however, at least Rabbinically prohibited from a surface of any size.]

Since R' Akiva renders one liable for throwing through a public domain, by dint of the principle of *kelutah* he obviously does not require that the *hanachah* be on such a surface. The principle of *kelutah* merely views a flying object as a stationary one; it does not render the air in which the object is considered "resting" as a surface of four handbreadths square. The *Gemara*, however, states that perhaps R' Akiva nevertheless requires such a surface for *akirah*; i.e., although one may be liable for carrying without setting the object down on a surface of less than four handbreadths square, he is not liable unless he originally lifted that object from a surface of at least four handbreadths square. *Rashi*, taking this to be a definite assertion that R' Akiva does require such a surface for *akirah*, cites as its source the fact that R' Akiva does not, in our mishnah, consider him liable twice. According to *Rashi* the reason for this is that the second transfer, i.e., from the theoretical place of rest in the airspace of the

שבת
יא/ב

[ב] **בֵּיצַד?** שְׁתֵּי גְזוּזְטְרָאוֹת זוֹ כְּנֶגֶד זוֹ

―― ר' עובדיה מברטנורא ――

בְּתוֹךְ עֲשָׂרָה הֲרֵי הוּא כְּאִלּוּ נָח. וְרַבָּנָן סָבְרֵי קְלוּטָה בְּתוֹךְ עֲשָׂרָה בַּאֲוִיר רְשׁוּת הָרַבִּים לָאו כְּמִי שֶׁהוּנְחָה דָּמֵי. אֲבָל לְמַעְלָה מֵעֲשָׂרָה שֶׁהוּא מְקוֹם פְּטוּר כּוּלֵי עָלְמָא לֹא פְּלִיגֵי דִּפְטוּר. וַהֲלָכָה כַּחֲכָמִים: (ב) **בֵּיצַד.** רַבָּנָן קָאָמְרֵי לֵיהּ: שְׁתֵּי גְזוּזְטְרָאוֹת. וְהֵן נְסָרִים יוֹצְאִים מִכּוֹתֶל הָעֲלִיָּה וְלַחוּץ

יד אברהם

the article is not regarded as having come to rest in the public domain. Since the object never came to rest in the public domain, the only transfer occurring was from one private domain to another, for which there is no liability. The halachah is in accordance with the Sages (*Rav*).

If the article passes through the public domain within three handbreadths of the ground, there is a difference of opinion in the *Gemara* (97a) as to whether the Sages agree in regarding it as having come to rest on the ground; i.e., that within three handbreadths of the ground the Sages agree to the principle of *kelutah*, disputing only its application to heights greater than three handbreadths. (See *Rashba* ad loc. that the dispute quoted in the *Gemara* is over this point, too.) *Rambam, Comm.,* and *Maggid Mishneh* (Hil. Shabbos 13:16) point out the opinion of Rava quoted on 100a disputes any agreement on the part of the Sages.[1] (This is also the opinion of *Rashi* and *Tos.* on 100a. Cf. *Ma'aracha* 2 of *Derush Ve-Chidush R' Akiva Eiger* which deals extensively with this point.)

2.

During Israel's travels through the wilderness, the *Mishkan* was repeatedly dismantled, transported and subsequently re-erected at a new site. The boards which formed the walls of the *Mishkan* were transported on wagons. Four wag-

public domain to the surface of the second private domain, does not result from an *akirah* from a surface of four handbreadths by four handbreadths. Consequently, he can be held liable only for the first transfer, i.e. from the surface of the first private domain from which he picked up the object prior to throwing it, to the theoretical "resting place" in the air space of the public domain. Though here too we lack a *hanachah*, setting down on a surface of four handbreadths square, this does not exempt him since, in the opinion of R' Akiva, *hanachah* need not be on such a surface, this requirement being restricted to *akirah* (*Rashi* 4b).

Tosafos there, however, state that the *Gemara* only considers the possibility that R' Akiva distinguishes between the surfaces required for *akirah* and *hanachah* without making any definitive statement in that regard. Consequently, it is possible that R' Akiva does not require a four handbreadths-square surface even for *akirah*. Though this would seemingly necessitate a double liability in our mishnah (a) it is possible that according to R' Akiva he actually is liable twice (the fact that the mishnah does not say so clearly is not necessarily proof to the contrary, as *Tosafos* shows from other places); (b) even if the mishnah does mean that he is obligated to bring but one sin offering this may be due to the fact that he committed two transgressions of the same category (see 7:1). *Ran* agrees with this second alternative. [Cf. *Tos. R' Akiva* to this mishnah for *Rashi's* reasons for rejecting *Tos.* objections.]

1. However, even according to this latter opinion, if the object rested, even momentarily, on any surface whatsoever (even less than four handbreadths by four handbreadths; see previous footnote) he is liable (*Gem.* 100a; Rambam, Hil. Shabbos 13:16). [Within three handbreadths of the ground, a resting object is considered to be resting on the ground itself, thus supplying the legal requirement of a surface of four handbreadths square.]

משניות / שבת – פרק יא: הזורק [264]

2. In what manner? Two balconies, one opposite the

YAD AVRAHAM

ons lined up in two pairs, one pair behind the other in the public domain outside the *Mishkan*. Boards were hoisted from the ground to each of the front wagons and were then passed from the front wagons to the wagons behind them until they were full. Each of these wagons had walls ten handbreadths high and was therefore a private domain. Thus, we find in the *Mishkan* an instance in which objects were handed over from one private domain (the front wagon) to another (the rear wagon) over a public domain (the gap between the front and rear wagons). This transfer, however, took place only along the length of the public domain (from front to rear wagon) but never across its width (from one front wagon to the other). Furthermore, the boards were handed over, never thrown.

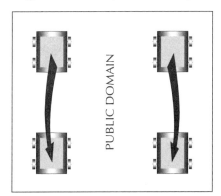

According to *Chidushei HaRan* and *Midrash Lekach Tov* the boards were not stacked on individual wagons but were supported by two wagons, one at each end.

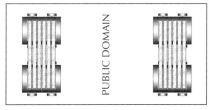

כֵּיצַד — *In what manner?*

I.e., in what manner of transferring from one private domain to another via a public domain do the Sages (quoted in the precious mishnah) exempt him? (*Rashi; Rav*).

[The necessity of posing this question is because there are instances when even the Sages agree that one is liable for *transferring from one private domain to another via a public one. Although, as will be explained below, this is true only in the handing over of objects but not in the throwing of them, the mishnah, nevertheless, poses this question to emphasize this distinction.]

Tosefos Yom Tov questions this attribution of the question, *In what*

manner, solely to the opinion of the Sages. As explained in the previous mishnah, the dispute between R' Akiva and the Sages relates only to throwing within ten handbreadths of the ground; throwing above ten handbreadths is exempted even by R' Akiva. It follows consequently that the question of liability for this sort of transference is equally pertinent to R' Akiva's view. Moreover, since the second mishnah discusses a case completely different from that of the first mishnah, i.e., an object traversing the public domain above a height of ten handbreadths rather than below, the word כֵּיצַד, *In what manner*, does not apply. Indeed, *Tosafos* quotes the *Yerushalmi* as deleting the word

שבת יא/ב

בִּרְשׁוּת הָרַבִּים, הַמּוֹשִׁיט וְהַזּוֹרֵק מִזּוֹ לָזוֹ פָּטוּר. הָיוּ שְׁתֵּיהֶן בִּדְיוּטָא אַחַת, הַמּוֹשִׁיט חַיָּב, וְהַזּוֹרֵק פָּטוּר. שֶׁכָּךְ הָיְתָה עֲבוֹדַת הַלְוִיִּם:

ר' עובדיה מברטנורא

על רשות הרבים, והגזוזטראות שלהן הן רשות היחיד, וכשהן זו כנגד זו בשני צדי רשות הרבים המושיט והזורק מזו לזו פטור, שלא מלינו זריקה והושטה במלאכת המשכן מרשות היחיד לרשות היחיד ורחב רשות הרבים מפסיק ביניהן: **היו שתיהן בדיוטא אחת**. כלומר בעליה אחת בארוך רשות הרבים, ויש הפסק רשות הרבים ביניהן: **הזורק פטור**. הואיל ולמעלה מעשרה הוא, ולא מלינו זריקה מרשות היחיד לרשות היחיד דרך רשות הרבים במשכן, והמושיט חייב, ואף על פי שמושיט למעלה מעשרה, שמלינו הושטה כיולא בה במשכן מרשות היחיד לרשות היחיד וארוך רשות הרבים מפסיק ביניהן: **שכך היתה עבודת הלוים**. מושיטים מזה לזה למעלה מעשרה וארוך רשות הרבים באחמלט, כיצד [שתי] עגלות זו אחר זו ברשות הרבים ופורקי המשכן היו מושיטין לחותם שעל הטעלות שאללן הן סמוכות וקרובות והן מושיטין לאלו שלפניהם, וכל אחת מהטעלות רשות היחיד הן:

יד אברהם

כֵּיצַד,[1] explaining the second mishnah as the unanimous ruling of both R' Akiva and the Sages.

Tiferes Yisrael points out that mishnah 2, by not specifying that it is referring to above ten handbreadths only, appears to be discussing both above and below an altitude of ten handbreadths. Thus, in distinguishing between handing over (which in some instances is liable) and throwing (which is never liable), the mishnah is clearly stating that one who throws an object from one private domain to another via the airspace of a public domain below the height of ten handbreadths is exempt. This is true only according to the Sages in mishnah 1, since according to R' Akiva one would still be liable, by dint of the principle of *kelutah*. *Rav* states, therefore, that this mishnah expresses the view of the Sages and not R' Akiva.

שְׁתֵּי גְזוּזְטְרָאוֹת — *Two balconies*,

These are actually just boards which protrude from the wall of a house over the public domain. They are both made in such a fashion as to constitute private domains (*Rav*; *Rashi*).

זוֹ כְנֶגֶד זוֹ בִּרְשׁוּת הָרַבִּים, — *one opposite the other in a public domain*,

I.e., on opposite sides of the street facing each other across the width of the street (*Rashi*).

---

1. The *Yerushalmi* states that the word כֵּיצַד is added only according to an alternate explanation of the mishnah, which explains the dispute of R' Akiva and the Sages as related to throwing above ten handbreadths, rather than below. According to this explanation, throwing below ten handbreadths is liable even according to the Sages who agree to the principle of *kelutah*. Above ten handbreadths, however, where, as explained above, the principle of *kelutah* does not apply, there is a dispute whether to equate the rule of throwing with that of handing over for which there is liability even in such a case (see below). Though our mishnah does differentiate between throwing with that of handing over (see below), this (according to *Yerushalmi*) reflects the view of the Sages only. R' Akiva disputes it. Our Talmud, however (4b and 97a), considers and rejects this alternate explanation.

11 2 other, in a public domain, one who hands over or throws from one to the other is exempt. If both were in one row, one who hands over is liable, [whereas] one who throws is exempt. For such was the work of the Levites:

YAD AVRAHAM

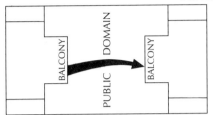

הַמּוֹשִׁיט וְהַזּוֹרֵק מִזּוֹ לָזוֹ — *one who hands over or throws from one to the other* [Across the public domain.]

פָּטוּר. — *is exempt.*

Since, in the transportation of the *Mishkan* boards, we find no instance of throwing or handing over from one private domain to another across the *width* of a public domain, derivation for liability in this type of transfer is restricted to transferring along the *length* of the public domain, the way it occurred in the *Mishkan* (*Rav; Rashi; Meiri*).

הָיוּ שְׁתֵּיהֶן בִּדְיוֹטָא אַחַת, — *If both were in one row,*

I.e., if both of them were along the same side of the public domain, with a strip of the public domain between them, e.g., two balconies protruding from the same wall of a building and perched above the public domain (*Rav; Ramban; Rashi*).

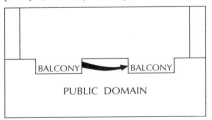

הַמּוֹשִׁיט חַיָּב, — *one who hands over is liable,*

I.e., one who hands an object over from one balcony to another, even if he hands over the article above ten handbreadths he is liable, since that was done by the Levites in transporting the boards of the *Mishkan* (*Tif. Yis.*).

וְהַזּוֹרֵק פָּטוּר. — *[whereas] one who throws is exempt.*

Since this is higher than ten handbreadths, and we do not find any instance of throwing from one private domain to another over the public domain in the *Mishkan*, he is exempt. If one hands something over, however, he is liable, since we do find the Levites handing over boards from one wagon to the wagon in front of them, over the public domain (*Rav; Rashi*).

[We mentioned above that even if one throws an article from one private domain to another over the public domain, even below ten handbreadths, the Sages exempt him, since they do not subscribe to the principle of *kelutah*.]

שֶׁכָּךְ הָיְתָה עֲבוֹדַת הַלְוִיִּם: — *For such was the work of the Levites:*

I.e., the Levites of the House of Merari whose special province was the transportation of the boards [see Numbers 4:31] would hand over the boards from the wagon closer to the *Mishkan* to the wagon further from the *Mishkan* along the length of the public domain (*Rav*).

שבת יא/ב

שְׁתֵּי עֲגָלוֹת זוֹ אַחַר זוֹ בִּרְשׁוּת הָרַבִּים, מוֹשִׁיטִין הַקְּרָשִׁים מִזּוֹ לְזוֹ, אֲבָל לֹא זוֹרְקִין. חֻלְיַת הַבּוֹר וְהַסֶּלַע שֶׁהֵן גְּבוֹהִין עֲשָׂרָה וְרָחְבָּן אַרְבָּעָה, הַנּוֹטֵל מֵהֶן וְהַנּוֹתֵן עַל גַּבָּן

ר' עובדיה מברטנורא

אבל לא זורקים. שאין הקרשים נזרקין מפני כובדן: **חוליית הבור.** עפר שמוליאין מחפירת הבור רגילין ליתן סביבות פי הבור כמין חומה להיקף, ואשמעינן דבור וחולייתו מצטרפין לעשרה, ותני בור לעמקו ותני סלע לגבהה: **הנוטל מהן.** ומניח ברשות הרבים, או הנוטל מרשות הרבים ונותן על גבן, חייב:

יד אברהם

שְׁתֵּי עֲגָלוֹת זוֹ אַחַר זוֹ בִּרְשׁוּת הָרַבִּים — [There were] two wagons one behind the other in a public domain,

As explained above, four wagons lined up in two pairs, one pair behind the other, in the public domain outside the Mishkan (Rav).

[Though there were actually two sets of wagons involved, no one board traveled through more than two wagons. The mishnah therefore restricts itself to discussing just one set.]

Since the wagons had walls ten handbreadths high, they had the status of private domains (Tif. Yis.).

מוֹשִׁיטִין הַקְּרָשִׁים מִזּוֹ לְזוֹ — they would hand over the boards from one to the other,

The boards were handed over from the front wagon to the wagon directly behind it. They were not passed either in the front row or in the back row from side to side. Therefore, the melachah of handing over from one private domain to another over an intervening public domain, derived from this Mishkan activity, is restricted to handing over along the length of the public domain, corresponding to passing the boards from the front to back wagons. Handing across the width of the public domain, which corresponds to passing the boards from one front wagon to the other or from one rear wagon to the other, cannot be derived, since no such activity occurred in the Mishkan. This latter case is not only exempted but under certain conditions may even be permissible (see Shulchan Aruch 353:1).

Though other melachos need not correspond so precisely to the Mishkan activity for them to be considered tolados (see General Introduction, p. 3 and 7:2), *transferring from one private domain to another is an exception. Since one is generally exempt for a transfer from one private domain to another, any instance in which one is liable is exceptional. Consequently, the parameters of this liability extended beyond the absolute minimum dictated by the derivation (Rambam, Comm.).

Tos. (2a, quoted here by Tos. Yom Tov) extends this idea to include the entire melachah of *transferring from one domain to another. Only in this melachah do we find that qualitatively slight variations in activity differentiate between liability and permissibility: e.g., carrying four cubits in a public domain is liable while doing precisely the same thing in a private domain is permissible; carrying from a

11
2

[There were] two wagons one behind the other in a public domain, they would hand over the boards from one to the other, but they would not throw [them].

The bank of a cistern and a rock that are ten [handbreadths] high and four [handbreadths] wide, one who takes [an article] from them or places [an article] upon

YAD AVRAHAM

private domain to a public one is liable while doing so from one private domain to another is Biblically permissible. Since such relatively minor differences are the source of major legal distinctions, all rules derived from this *melachah* must adhere very closely to the source of that derivation.

אֲבָל לֹא זוֹרְקִין — *but they would not throw [them].*

They would not throw the boards because of their weight (*Rav; Rashi; Meiri*).

Alternatively, they would not throw the boards because of their sanctity (*Tif. Yis.* from anonymous sources).

Since this activity did not take place in the *Mishkan*, no such *melachah* may be derived.

חֻלְיַת הַבּוֹר וְהַסֶּלַע — *The bank of a cistern and a rock.*

When a cistern was constructed, the earth dug out was placed around it as a wall, enclosing it (*Rav; Rashi*).

[Both of these are in a public domain, a *karmelis*, or an exempt area adjoining a public domain.]

שֶׁהֵן גְּבוֹהִין עֲשָׂרָה וְרָחְבָּן אַרְבָּעָה, — *that are ten [handbreadths] high and four [handbreadths] wide,*

These are the minimum dimensions of a private domain. Though this rule is obvious, the mishnah teaches us that the height of the bank and the depth of the cistern may be counted together to provide the necessary minimum height of ten handbreadths (*Rav*).

According to this, only the interior of the enclosure is considered a private domain. The top of the bank, being separated from the public domain adjoining it by less than a height of ten handbreadths, is not considered a private domain. The mishnah, however, in stating *or places upon them is liable*, seemingly refers to the top of the bank, too, declaring it a private domain. For this reason, *Tosafos* (99a) object to this explanation of this mishnah, though the halachah is certainly true (see *Eruvin* 10:7). Instead, *Tosafos* explain that the mishnah is discussing a case in which the height of the bank itself is ten handbreadths. The lesson of the mishnah is that the minimum width of four handbreadths may include the width of the banks on either side of the cistern plus the width of the cistern itself. The reason for this is that a plank may be placed across the entire width forming a usable surface of four handbreadths. Though one has not actually done so, the top is still considered a usable surface of four handbreadths (*Tos.* from *Eruvin* 78b).

הַנּוֹטֵל מֵהֶן — *one who takes [an article] from them*

And then places it in the public domain (*Rav; Meiri*).

וְהַנּוֹתֵן עַל גַּבָּן — *or places [an article] upon them*

Having previously picked it up from a public domain (*Rav*).

שבת יא/ג

חַיָּב; פָּחוֹת מִכֵּן, פָּטוּר.

[ג] **הַזּוֹרֵק** אַרְבַּע אַמּוֹת בַּכֹּתֶל, לְמַעְלָה מֵעֲשָׂרָה טְפָחִים, כְּזוֹרֵק בָּאֲוִיר; לְמַטָּה מֵעֲשָׂרָה טְפָחִים, כְּזוֹרֵק בָּאָרֶץ.

ר' עובדיה מברטנורא

(ג) **הזורק ארבע אמות בכותל.** מתחלת ד' לסוף ד' ונח בכותל הסמוך לרשות הרבים, למעלה מעשרה טפחים, כגון שהיתה דבלה שמנה ונדבקה בכותל למעלה מעשרה באויר רשות הרבים, פטור, דכל למעלה מעשרה ברשות הרבים מקום פטור הוא: **למטה מעשרה כזורק בארץ.** מתחלת ארבע לסוף ארבע ברשות הרבים, וחייב אף על פי שאין מקום עקירת החפץ לכותל אלא ארבע אמות מלומלמות לא אמרינן דטובי הדבלה ממעט בד"ח ואין כאן מתחלת ד' לסוף ד', דכיון שאינו מבטל את הדבילה בכותל אין עוביה ממעט כלום.

יד אברהם

חַיָּב; — *is liable;*
Since they constitute a private domain (*Tif. Yis.*).

פָּחוֹת מִכֵּן, — *less than these [dimensions],*
[I.e., if they are less than ten handbreadths high or less than four handbreadths square.]

פָּטוּר. — *he is exempt.*
As explained in the General Introduction, an area four handbreadths square whose height or depth is less than ten handbreadths constitutes a *karmelis*. Hence, one is not liable for *transferring from it to a public domain, or vice versa. It is, nevertheless, prohibited by Rabbinic decree.

If the area is less than four handbreadths square, it is an exempt area and it is even permissible to transfer to and from it.

If the height or depth is less than three handbreadths, it is regarded as subordinate to and part of the public domain.

3.

Just as one is liable for carrying or throwing anything from a private domain to a public domain or vice versa, so is one liable for carrying or throwing a distance of four cubits in a public domain. There is no Scriptural reference or allusion to this prohibition. It is a part of the oral tradition known as הֲלָכָה לְמשֶׁה מִסִּינַי, *a halachah to Moses from Sinai*, i.e., laws told by God to Moshe on Sinai concurrently with the Scriptural laws but which were neither written nor alluded to in the Torah. These laws were reserved for the oral tradition (*Gem.* 96b). Though this activity takes place entirely within the public domain, it is a *toladah* of *transferring from one domain to another.

The rationale offered for this Sinaitic decree is that the area of four cubits around a person is regarded as under his control and, therefore, momentarily his private domain. This concept finds application when an ownerless object comes within four cubits of a person. The Rabbis, viewing these four cubits as his "private" domain, grant him ownership of that object. Although this latter application is a Rabbinical institution (*Bava Basra* 10a; Rambam, *Hil. Gezeilah VaAveidah* 17:9), the concept illustrates the rationale for this Sinaitic decree (*HaMaor HaKatan* to 96b).

them is liable; less than these [dimensions], he is exempt.

3. One who throws [an article a distance of] four cubits against a wall, above ten handbreadths [from the ground], it is as though he is throwing in the air; below ten handbreadths [from the ground], it as though he is throwing on the ground.

YAD AVRAHAM

הַזּוֹרֵק אַרְבַּע אַמּוֹת בְּכֹתֶל, — *One who throws [an article a distance of] four cubits against a wall,*

I.e., one who, standing in a public domain, throws an object a distance of four cubits which then attaches itself to a wall abutting the public domain. This is possible in the case of a sticky object, such as a thick ripe fig (*Rav* from *Gem.* 100a).

לְמַעְלָה מֵעֲשָׂרָה טְפָחִים, — *above ten handbreadths [from the ground],*

If it adheres to the wall at a point more than ten handbreadths from the ground (*Rav*).

כְּזוֹרֵק בָּאֲוִיר; — *it is as though he is throwing in the air;*

It is as though it came to rest in the air of a public domain above ten handbreadths, which is an exempt area. Consequently, he is exempt (*Rav*).

לְמַטָּה מֵעֲשָׂרָה טְפָחִים, — *below ten handbreadths [from the ground],*

If it adheres to the wall at a point less than ten handbreadths from the ground (*Rav*).

כְּזוֹרֵק בָּאָרֶץ. — *it is as though he is throwing on the ground.*

I.e., it is as though it came to rest on the ground of the public domain, since the airspace of a public domain is regarded as a public domain up to a height of ten handbreadths.

Although any object between three and ten handbreadths high constitutes either a *karmelis* or an exempt area, depending on whether it is four handbreadths square or not (see General Introduction), this is true only for a functional surface, such as the top of a post or low wall. The side of a wall, not being a functional surface, is regarded merely as the airspace of the public domain, to which these rules do not apply (*Tos. R' Akiva* quoting *Rashi:* 7a).[1]

Even though when one throws a fig exactly four cubits the bulk of the fig is within the four cubits, he is nevertheless liable. Since he does not intend to leave the fig permanently stuck to the wall, its bulk does not detract from

---

1. There is, however, a dispute as to whether the wall to which the fig adheres must be four handbreadths wide in order to incur liability. (See first footnote of this chapter.) According to *Rabbeinu Tam*, if the fig adheres to the wall above three handbreadths, the side of the wall must be at least four handbreadths wide. According to *Riva*, however, as long as nothing comes between it and the ground of the public domain, it is regarded as lying on the ground, which is itself four handbreadths by four handbreadths (*Tos. Rabbi Akiva* from *Tos.* 7a).

[*Rashi* and *Rav* apparently understand the halachah to mean that if one throws an article to the end of four cubits, he is liable. If he intends to leave it stuck to the wall, however, it becomes part of the wall, thereby detracting from the four cubits.]

שבת יא/ג

הַזּוֹרֵק בָּאָרֶץ אַרְבַּע אַמּוֹת חַיָּב. זָרַק לְתוֹךְ אַרְבַּע אַמּוֹת, וְנִתְגַּלְגֵּל חוּץ לְאַרְבַּע אַמּוֹת, פָּטוּר; חוּץ לְאַרְבַּע אַמּוֹת, וְנִתְגַּלְגֵּל לְתוֹךְ אַרְבַּע אַמּוֹת, חַיָּב.

ר' עובדיה מברטנורא

ונתגלגל חוץ לארבע אמות פטור. שהרי לא נתכוין לזריקה של חיוב: **ונתגלגל לתוך ארבע אמות חייב.** והוא דנח משהו חוץ לד"א קודם שנתגלגל לפנים:

יד אברהם

the four cubits (*Rav*). This is also the opinion of *Rashi* (99b). *Tosafos*, however, understand the *Gemara* to mean that it traveled four cubits plus the thickness of the fig.

הַזּוֹרֵק בָּאָרֶץ אַרְבַּע אַמּוֹת חַיָּב — *One who throws [an article a distance of] four cubits on the ground is liable.*

If one throws a distance of four cubits and it does indeed land on the ground of a public domain, he is liable.

זָרַק לְתוֹךְ אַרְבַּע אַמּוֹת, — *[If] one threw [to a point] within four cubits,*

I.e., if one threw an article with the intention that it come to rest within four cubits, thus not intending to perform an act involving liability (*Rav*).

וְנִתְגַּלְגֵּל חוּץ לְאַרְבַּע אַמּוֹת, — *but it rolled beyond four cubits,*

[I.e., it carried to a point beyond four cubits. The thrower has, in consequence, unwittingly performed an act for which one is liable on the Sabbath.]

פָּטוּר; — *he is exempt;*

Since he had no intention of performing this act, he is exempt (*Rav; Rambam, Comm.*).

[Although all liability for sin offering is for desecrating the Sabbath inadvertently, the meaning is that he intends to perform the act, but is unaware that it is prohibited, either because he forgot that this is a *melachah,* or that the day is the Sabbath. If he performed the act unintentionally as in our case where he had no intention of throwing the article over a distance of four cubits, he is exempt.]

Others explain this mishnah as having nothing to do with one's lack of intent. Rather, the mishnah discusses the case of one who threw an object, with no specific destination in mind, i.e., he wanted the object to land in a certain general area but did not care about the precise spot. The object came to rest, momentarily, within four cubits and then rolled to beyond four cubits. Having come to rest within four cubits, his act of throwing had ended without the object having traveled the minimum four cubits. There is, consequently, no liability (*Rashba; Meiri;* implied by *Tos.*).

חוּץ לְאַרְבַּע אַמּוֹת, — *[if he threw] beyond four cubits,*

[According to the first explanation cited in the previous paragraph, this would mean that he threw the object with the intent that it carry beyond four cubits, which it did, only to roll back to a point within four cubits. According to the second explanation, his intent was again only for a general area. According to both explanations, the object momentarily rested at a spot beyond four cubits.]

וְנִתְגַּלְגֵּל לְתוֹךְ אַרְבַּע אַמּוֹת, חַיָּב. — *but it [then] rolled [back] to within four cubits, he is liable.*

Having momentarily rested beyond

11 **One who throws** [an article a distance of] **four**
3 **cubits on the ground is liable.** [If] **one threw** [to a point] **within four cubits, but it rolled beyond four cubits, he is exempt;** [if he threw] **beyond four cubits, but it** [then] **rolled** [back] **to within four cubits, he is liable.**

YAD AVRAHAM

four cubits, liability has been incurred. The subsequent retrogression to within four cubits can no longer undo that liability.

If it did not rest at all, however, he is exempt. According to *Rashi* (100a), even if the wind momentarily held it in place in the air and then blew it back, he is liable. According to *Rambam* (*Hil. Shabbos* 13:16), however, he is liable only if it rests on a surface, though it need not have any specific dimensions. If it is held in the air, however, he is exempt (*Tif. Yis.*).

4.

✥ The Status of the Sea as a Karmelis

Much has been written to account for the sea's status as a *karmelis*, and why it is neither a private domain — although it is surrounded by banks or shorelines with a depth of more than ten handbreadths — nor a public domain — although it is the concourse for marine traffic.

As to the first question, *Magen Avraham* 345:14 cites the rule stated in the *Gemara* 100a that a gradual slope reaching a height of ten handbreadths is considered an enclosing wall only if it reaches that height within a span of four cubits or less. If the slope is less steep than that, it is viewed as part of the general terrain and not as a wall. Based on this, he explains that, since most shorelines are not that steep, their slopes cannot be considered as walls enclosing the water. If, however, there is a river with such steep banks, or a declivity in the sea with this configuration, it would indeed be Biblically considered a private domain, though Rabbinically a *karmelis*.[1] [See footnote below, s.v., פָּחוֹת מֵעֲשָׂרָה טְפָחִים, *less than ten handbreadths.*]

This is the opinion quoted by most authorities. *Aruch HaShulchan* (345:38), however, states that even if its banks *are* sufficiently steep, an area as vast as a sea cannot be considered enclosed. [He seems to follow the opinion of *Ritva* in the name of *Ramban* in *Eruvin* 22b (quoted by *Shaar HaTziyun* 363:94) that the limit of an enclosure is an area sufficiently small for a person to realize that he is in an enclosure. Once the area enclosed becomes so vast that he no longer perceives himself as being enclosed, it loses its status as a private domain.] Accordingly, a river might still be considered (Biblically) a private domain if its banks are steep enough. [A third opinion, offered by *Ohr Samayach*, is quoted in the footnote below.]

---

1. As to whether this Rabbinic decree of *karmelis* applies to it only if it is at least 70⅔ cubits squared or even less, see the dispute between *Pri Megadim* and *Machatzis HaShekel*, ibid.

שבת יא/ד

[ד] **הַזּוֹרֵק** בַּיָּם אַרְבַּע אַמּוֹת פָּטוּר. אִם הָיָה רְקַק מַיִם וּרְשׁוּת הָרַבִּים מְהַלֶּכֶת בּוֹ, הַזּוֹרֵק לְתוֹכוֹ אַרְבַּע אַמּוֹת חַיָּב. וְכַמָּה הוּא רְקַק מַיִם? פָּחוֹת מֵעֲשָׂרָה טְפָחִים.

ר' עובדיה מברטנורא

(ד) **הזורק בים.** מתחלת ד' לסוף ד' פטור, דכרמלית הוא: **רקק מים.** שאינם גבוהים מן הארץ ויש בהם רפש וטיט נקראים רקק: **ורשות הרבים מהלכת בו.** שרבים מהלכים בו: **ובמה הוא רקק.** כמה הוא עומקו דניחא אכתי רשות הרבים הוא ולא נעשה כרמלית:

יד אברהם

Granting that the shorelines of the sea do not constitute enclosing walls, the question becomes why the sea is not considered a public domain, since it is the concourse for marine traffic. *Magen Avraham* (ibid.) states that since travel on it is difficult in comparison to a road, it cannot be considered a public domain no matter how many people travel it. [This is based on the discussion in *Eruvin* 22b.] *Tosafos Shabbos* 345:41 says that since it is not similar to the encampment in the wilderness — from which all the rules of *transferring from domain to domain* are derived — it cannot be considered a public domain.

הַזּוֹרֵק בַּיָּם אַרְבַּע אַמּוֹת פָּטוּר. — *One who throws [a distance of] four cubits in the sea is exempt.*

Since the sea is a *karmelis*, there is no liability involved (*Rav* from *Gem.* 6a).

The same law applies to a river. The *Tanna* chooses to state this law as regards a sea, since a sea is invariably ten handbreadths deep. Rivers, on the other hand, may be shallower, in which case they would have the status of the domain through which they run (*Tif. Yis.*).

אִם הָיָה רְקַק מַיִם — *If there was a shallow pool of muddy water*

Though this rule is true for any type of water, the *Tanna* refers to a pool of muddy water because that is its normal condition when found in the middle of a street (*Tif. Yis.*).

וּרְשׁוּת הָרַבִּים מְהַלֶּכֶת בּוֹ, — *with a public domain passing through it,*

I.e., that people, while traveling through the public domain, go through this pool (*Rav; Rambam, Comm.; Rashi* 8b and 100b).

הַזּוֹרֵק לְתוֹכוֹ אַרְבַּע אַמּוֹת חַיָּב. — *one who throws [a distance of] four cubits in it is liable.*

Since the pool does not interrupt the flow of traffic, it too is regarded as part of the public domain (*Gem.* 100b).

וְכַמָּה הוּא רְקַק מַיִם? — *How much is a shallow pool?*

I.e., to what maximum depth does this shallow pool retain its status as a public domain and not become a *karmelis*? (*Rav; Rashi*).

פָּחוֹת מֵעֲשָׂרָה טְפָחִים. — *Less than ten handbreadths.*

Only if the pool is less than ten handbreadths deep is it considered a public domain. If, however, the water is ten handbreadths deep, it is a *karmelis* like a sea and there is no *liability* for throwing a distance of four cubits in it (*Rambam, Hil. Shabbos* 14:24).

4. One who throws [a distance of] four cubits in the sea is exempt.

If there was a shallow pool of muddy water with a public domain passing through it, one who throws [a distance of] four cubits in it is liable. How much is a shallow pool? Less than ten handbreadths.

YAD AVRAHAM

Although a pit between three and ten handbreadths deep is usually regarded as a *karmelis* (if it is at least four handbreadths wide) or as an exempt area (if it is less), this rule applies only if the traffic of the public domain does not actually pass through this declivity. If the traffic does travel through it, however, it is regarded as part of a public domain (*Gem.* 100b, see *Rashi*). If the pit is ten handbreadths deep or more, even though the traffic passes through it, it can no longer be considered part of the public domain, since it has proper walls. It is therefore regarded as a *karmelis*[1] (*Rambam, Hil. Shabbos* 14:24). [If traffic does not pass through it, it is a private domain (ibid. 23).]

1. As explained in the General Introduction (p. 13), the restrictions of a *karmelis* are a Rabbinic institution. Generally speaking, a *karmelis* has Biblically the same rules as an exempt area, since it is neither a private domain (lacking walls) nor a public one (lacking a sufficient volume of traffic). For this reason, transferring from a *karmelis* to either a private or public domain entails no liability for a sin offering; since it is Biblically permissible and only Rabbinically prohibited there can be no sin offering, which is for Biblical transgressions only. However, there are certain instances of private domains which are also Rabbinically deemed a *karmelis* (such as an enclosure not enclosed for residential purposes; see General Introduction, p. 13). Though in regard to carrying in them they are deemed a *karmelis*, i.e., one is not permitted to carry in them a distance of four cubits, nevertheless, they are regarded Biblically as a private domain with the consequence that one who carries into them from a public domain is liable for a sin offering. The question here, therefore, arises as to whether this pit is Biblically a private domain — by virtue of its being four handbreadths wide and having a depth of ten handbreadths — and only Rabbinically a *karmelis* — or whether it is even Biblically not a private domain. Though the *Rambam* compares this to a sea, which is even Biblically not a private domain, this is not conclusive since most of the reasons given for a sea not being a private domain are not applicable to this case (see next footnote). Indeed, *Pri Megadim* in *Aishel Avraham* 345:11 rules that this pit, despite the passage of traffic through it, is Biblically a private domain. Even its Rabbinical status as a *karmelis* is only in cases of muddy water, where the depth of the walls is not apparent. A pool of clear water, on the other hand, would even Rabbinically retain its status as a private domain. As has been explained above, our mishnah deals with a pool of muddy water. There may also be a difference as to whether the depth of this pit resulted from the natural contours of the terrain or from human activity. See *Tosafos* to *Eruvin* 22b whose opinion *Pri Megadim* follows (*Shaar HaTziyun* 363:94). *Ohr Samayach* to *Rambam, Hil. Shabbos* 14:24, however, states that a flowing pool, e.g., a brook, is even Biblically not a private domain, though it has banks ten handbreadths high. This type of pool, according to him, is the subject of our mishnah. A still-water pool, however, would Biblically be considered a private domain. [From the discussions cited in the next mishnah as to why a sea is not a private domain, it would appear that this latter opinion is a minority one.]

Though the rules of *karmelis* do not apply above the height of ten handbreadths, the

שבת יא/ה

רְקַק מַיִם וּרְשׁוּת הָרַבִּים מְהַלֶּכֶת בּוֹ, הַזּוֹרֵק בְּתוֹכוֹ אַרְבַּע אַמּוֹת חַיָּב.

[ה] הַזּוֹרֵק מִן הַיָּם לַיַּבָּשָׁה, וּמִן הַיַּבָּשָׁה לַיָּם, וּמִן הַיָּם לַסְּפִינָה, וּמִן הַסְּפִינָה לַיָּם, וּמִן הַסְּפִינָה לַחֲבֶרְתָּהּ, פָּטוּר.

ר׳ עובדיה מברטנורא

ורקק מים ורשות הרבים מהלבת בו. האי דכפליה תנא למלתיה, לאשמועינן דאפילו רקק רחב ארבעה הואיל והוא פחות מעשרה נדון כרשות הרבים. וכפל נמי ורשות הרבים מהלכת בו, לאשמעינן דאף על גב דאין מהלכים בו רבים אלא על ידי הדחק, הלוך על ידי הדחק שמיה הלוך:
(ה) **מן הים ליבשה.** מכרמלית לרשות הרבים: **מן הים לספינה.** מכרמלית לרשות היחיד:

יד אברהם

רְקַק מַיִם וּרְשׁוּת הָרַבִּים מְהַלֶּכֶת בּוֹ, הַזּוֹרֵק בְּתוֹכוֹ אַרְבַּע אַמּוֹת חַיָּב. — A shallow pool with a public domain passing through it, one who throws [a distance of] four cubits in it is liable.

Although this sentence is identical to the one stated at the beginning of the mishnah, the *Gemara* (100b) explains that the repetition is added to teach one of the following lessons:

— This pool is deemed a public domain both in the summer and in the winter. Since in the summer people are less likely to avoid the water since it cools them off whereas in the winter wet clothing chills them, it is necessary to state even in the winter that the pool is considered a public domain, i.e., fit for traffic. On the other hand, since in the winter when their clothing is mud spattered anyway (old roads not being paved), there is less resistance to going through a muddy area, whereas in the summer when the roads are dry and people wish to avoid needlessly soiling their clothes, they are more reluctant to do so, it is necessary to state that it is then too considered a thoroughfare and therefore a public domain.

— Even if the pool is wider than four cubits, making travel through it more cumbersome than around it, it is nevertheless still considered a part of the public domain, since people do travel through it.

— If the pool is narrow, causing many people to skip over it rather than walk through it, it is still a public domain since some people do walk through it.

According to *Rambam* 14:24 even if most people skip over it, it is still a public domain. According to *Magen Avraham* 345:11, *Rashi's* opinion is that the majority of travelers must actually walk through it in order for it to be a public domain. *Eliyah Rabbah* (ibid. 20), however, states that *Rashi* agrees with *Rambam* that only a minority need actually walk through it.

[Though the *Gemara* offers these three explanations as alternative interpretations, all are actually true; namely, that the pool is a public domain re-

karmelis of a river, sea, or pool is measured from its surface rather than its bed (*Tos. Yom Tov* from *Gem.* 100b). In conjunction with the rules of *karmelis*, however, the pool must be at least four handbreadths wide to be considered a *karmelis* (*Rambam*, ibid.).

11
5

A shallow pool with a public domain passing through it, one who throws [a distance of] four cubits in it is liable.

5. One who throws from the sea to the dry land, from the dry land to the sea, from the sea to the ship, from the ship to the sea, or from one ship to another, is exempt.

YAD AVRAHAM

gardless of season or width. See *Rambam, Hil. Shabbos* 14:24 and *Maggid Mishneh* there.]

Although the redundancy in this mishnah is added to teach the above lessons, the mishnah could still have stated the repetition more simply by stating *a shallow pool of water with a public domain in it.* The repetition of the phrase *passing through it* is to emphasize yet another point: that only the passage of traffic through such unsuitable terrain renders it part of the public domain. Any other use, even in conjunction with its use as a public thoroughfare, does not render it a public domain, since it is not really suited for such use (*Gem.* 100b).[1]

5.

הַזּוֹרֵק מִן הַיָּם לַיַּבָּשָׁה, — *One who throws from the sea to the dry land,*

I.e., from the sea, which is a *karmelis*, to a dry land which is a public domain (*Rav; Rashi*).

וּמִן הַיַּבָּשָׁה לַיָּם, — *from the dry land to the sea,*

Which constitutes throwing from a public domain to a *karmelis* (*Meiri*).

וּמִן הַיָּם לַסְּפִינָה, — *from the sea to the ship,*

I.e., from a *karmelis* to a private domain (*Rav; Rashi*).

The mishnah refers to a case where the person is within ten handbreadths of the surface of the water, and the walls of the ship are at least ten handbreadths high. Thus he is throwing something into a private domain from a *karmelis*. If the walls are lower than ten handbreadths, the ship, too, is a *karmelis*, just like the sea. One may, therefore, move articles from the sea to the ship, as long as the total distance moved is less than four cubits (*Tif. Yis.*).

וּמִן הַסְּפִינָה לַיָּם, — *from the ship to the sea,*

Constituting from a private domain to a *karmelis* (*Meiri*).

וּמִן הַסְּפִינָה לַחֲבֶרְתָּהּ, — *or from one ship to another,*

Constituting from one private domain to another via a *karmelis*, i.e., over the water between the two ships (*Meiri*).

פָּטוּר. — *is exempt.*

Since there is no transfer between a private domain and a public domain,

---

1. In a form suited for such use, however, adjuncts to the public domain are also considered a public domain. An example of this is a post nine handbreadths high in a public domain. Though strictly speaking it should be considered a *karmelis*, since it is the right height to serve as a place for people to rearrange their loads it serves as an adjunct to the public domain and is therefore considered part of it (*Gem.* 8b).

שבת יא/ו

סְפִינוֹת קְשׁוּרוֹת זוֹ בָזוֹ, מְטַלְטְלִין מִזּוֹ לָזוֹ. אִם אֵינָן קְשׁוּרוֹת, אַף־עַל־פִּי שֶׁמֻּקָּפוֹת, אֵין מְטַלְטְלִין מִזּוֹ לָזוֹ.

[ו] **הַזּוֹרֵק**, וְנִזְכַּר לְאַחַר שֶׁיָּצְתָה מִיָּדוֹ; קְלָטָהּ אַחֵר; קְלָטָהּ כֶּלֶב; אוֹ

ר' עובדיה מברטנורא

מטלטלין מזו לזו. אם הן של שני בני אדם מטלטלים על ידי עירוב דהוי להו כשתי חצירות: **מוקפות.** סמוכות זו לזו, כמו אין מקיפין בבוטי: **אין מטלטלין מזו לזו.** דכי מפרשי מהדדי, כרמלית מפסקת ביניהן ובטל העירוב: (ו) **הזורק.** בשבת בשוגג, ונזכר שהוא שבת לאחר שיצתה האבן מתחת ידו קודם שתנוח, אפילו לא קלטה אחר אלא שנחה כדרכה פטור, דהכי תנן לקמן עד שתהא תחלתן וסופן בשגגה, והאי תחלתו בשגגה וסופו מזיד, הואיל ונזכר שהוא שבת קודם שתנוח. ומתניתין הכי מיפרשא הזורק ונזכר לאחר שיצאה מתחת ידו, אי נמי לא נזכר אלא שקלטה אחר וכו' פטור, דהוה ליה שנים שעשאוה פטורים, הא נחה חייב חטאת, במה דברים אמורים כשחזר ושכח, אבל לא חזר ושכח פטור שכל חייבי וכו':

יד אברהם

there is no violation of Torah law. Hence there is neither capital punishment for intentional transgression, nor obligation to bring a sin offering for unintentional transgression. All these acts are, however, prohibited by Rabbinic decree lest one confuse a *karmelis* with a public domain (*Rambam, Hil. Shabbos* 14:11).

סְפִינוֹת קְשׁוּרוֹת זוֹ בָזוֹ, — *If the ships are tied together,*

I.e., if they are tied together without any gap between them (*Meiri*).

מְטַלְטְלִין מִזּוֹ לָזוֹ. — *we may move [things] from one to the other.*

Even if the two ships belong to two people, they may carry from one to the other by making an *eruv chatzeiros* [see General Introduction p. 13, for explanation of, necessity for, and mechanism of *eruv chatzeiros*].

Though *eruv chatzeiros* generally helps for all combinations of private domains, the *Tanna* feels it necessary to teach us that even two private domains not permanently established in one place may be combined through an *eruv chatzeiros* (*Tos.* 10lb).

אִם אֵינָן קְשׁוּרוֹת, אַף־עַל־פִּי שֶׁמֻּקָּפוֹת, אֵין מְטַלְטְלִין מִזּוֹ לָזוֹ. — *If they are not tied [together], even though they are close to each other, we may not move [things] from one to the other.*

An *eruv chatzeiros* is valid only if the two private domains "combined" are contiguous to each other with a doorway or window between them or connected by some passageway which is itself a private domain (*Shulchan Aruch,* 372:4). If they are separated by any other domain, they cannot be combined by an *eruv* even for the purposes of passing or throwing from one to another. If the ships are not bound together, they are apt to spread apart, creating a gap of a *karmelis* between them and thereby invalidating the *eruv.* The Rabbis therefore forbade making an *eruv* between ships not tied together (*Rav* from *Gem.* 10b).

11
6

If ships are tied together, we may move [things] from one to the other. If they are not tied [together], even though they are close to each other, we may not move [things] from one to the other.

6. One who threw [something], and reminded himself after it had left his hand; [or] another [person] caught it; [or] a dog caught it; [or]

YAD AVRAHAM

6.

As has been discussed in Ch. 7, one is required to bring a sin offering only for an unintentional violation of the Sabbath. If this violation was in any way intentional, however, one is not afforded the privilege of attaining atonement through a sin offering. The following mishnah elaborates on this principle.

הַזּוֹרֵק, — *One who threw [something]*,

I.e., if one forgot that it was the Sabbath, and threw something from one domain to another (*Rav; Rashi*).

This phrase is a preface to all the following cases (*Rav*).

וְנִזְכַּר — *and reminded himself*

I.e., he reminded himself that it was the Sabbath (*Rav*).

לְאַחַר שֶׁיָּצְתָה מִיָּדוֹ; — *after it had left his hand;*

As the mishnah explains further on, for one to be liable to a sin offering he must perform the entire *melachah* inadvertently. Since in this case, at the conclusion of the *melachah* its perpetrator is aware that it is the Sabbath, even though he can no longer retract the object, he is, nevertheless, exempt from a sin offering (*Rav*).

This follows the explanation of the mishnah given in the *Gemara* (102a) by *Rava*. Rav Ashi explains the mishnah differently. His explanation will be discussed at the end of this mishnah.

קְלָטָה אַחֵר; — *[or] another [person] caught it;*

[This case is unrelated with the previous case of remembering before the completion of the *melachah*. The mishnah lists several possible exemptions for the act of throwing, all based on some flaw in the landing.]

I.e., if someone else moved to the spot where the object was flying and intercepted it, the one who threw it is exempt since the one who intercepted it completed the *melachah* thus making it a *melachah* performed by two people, for which both are exempt [see above 10:5 for explanation of this principle] (*Tos. Yom Tov; Tif. Yis.* from *Rashi*).

קְלָטָה כֶלֶב; — *[or] a dog caught it;*

Since the dog's mouth does not accommodate an area of four handbreadths square, the one who threw the article is not liable for such a *hanachah* (*Tos. Yom Tov; Tif. Yis.* from *Rashi*). See mishnah 1.

Hence, even if the dog stood in its place and the object landed in its mouth there is no liability (*Tif. Yis.*).

If, however, the one who threw the object intended to throw it into the dog's mouth, his intention to have it there imparts to it a status equivalent

שבת
יא/ו

שֶׁנִּשְׂרְפָה; פָּטוּר. זָרַק לַעֲשׂוֹת חַבּוּרָה בֵּין בְּאָדָם וּבֵין בִּבְהֵמָה, וְנִזְכַּר עַד שֶׁלֹּא נַעֲשָׂה חַבּוּרָה, פָּטוּר. זֶה הַכְּלָל: כָּל חַיָּבֵי חַטָּאוֹת אֵינָן חַיָּבִין עַד שֶׁתְּהֵא תְחִלָּתָן וְסוֹפָן שְׁגָגָה. תְּחִלָּתָן שְׁגָגָה וְסוֹפָן זָדוֹן, תְּחִלָּתָן זָדוֹן וְסוֹפָן שְׁגָגָה, פְּטוּרִין, עַד שֶׁתְּהֵא תְחִלָּתָן וְסוֹפָן שְׁגָגָה.

ר' עובדיה מברטנורא

זה הכלל. לאתויי נמי מעביר חפץ ממקום למקום, שאם עקר בשגגה ונזכר שהוא שבת קודם שיניח, פטור:

יד אברהם

to an area four handbreadths square (Tos. Yom Tov from Gem. 102a).[1]

אוֹ שֶׁנִּשְׂרְפָה — [or] it was burnt [in flight];
I.e., it was burnt in the air before it landed. Hence, there was no hanachah[2] (Tif. Yis.).

פָּטוּר — he is exempt.
[I.e., if any of the above-mentioned possibilities occurred he is exempt.]

זָרַק לַעֲשׂוֹת חַבּוּרָה בֵּין בְּאָדָם וּבֵין בִּבְהֵמָה — [If] one threw [a stone] with the intention of inflicting a wound upon either a man or a beast,
[Similarly, if one forgot that it was the Sabbath and threw a stone with the intention of inflicting a wound either on a man or on a beast, which is a violation of the Sabbath, (see 14:1) . . .]

וְנִזְכַּר עַד שֶׁלֹּא נַעֲשָׂה חַבּוּרָה — and he reminded himself when the wound had not yet been inflicted,
[Hence, the melachah was not concluded in a state of unawareness.]

פָּטוּר — he is exempt.
[From a sin offering.]

זֶה הַכְּלָל: כָּל־חַיָּבֵי חַטָּאוֹת אֵינָן חַיָּבִין עַד שֶׁתְּהֵא תְחִלָּתָן וְסוֹפָן שְׁגָגָה — This is the rule: All who are liable for sin offerings are not liable unless the beginning and the end of their acts are [both] inadvertent.

This comes to add the case of one who carries a distance of four cubits in the public domain and, while carrying, reminds himself of the Sabbath, yet continues to carry to the end of four cubits. He is exempt from a sin offering because the conclusion of the melachah was done intentionally (Rav; Tif. Yis.).

תְּחִלָּתָן שְׁגָגָה וְסוֹפָן זָדוֹן, תְּחִלָּתָן זָדוֹן וְסוֹפָן שְׁגָגָה, פְּטוּרִין, עַד שֶׁתְּהֵא תְחִלָּתָן וְסוֹפָן שְׁגָגָה — [If] their beginning was inadvertent but their end was intentional, [or if] their beginning was intentional

---
1. If he threw towards a person and it landed in his hand, even if he did not specifically intend for it to land there he is liable, since a person's hand always has the status of an area of four handbreadths square. Therefore, in the previous case he is exempt only if the second person moved to intercept the object (Tos. Yom Tov from Rashi).

2. If the object either momentarily landed on even a minimal surface or was momentarily held up in the air within three handbreadths of the ground before being burnt, he is liable as explained above in mishnah 1 (see especially footnote there) (Tif. Yis.).

11 it was burnt [in flight]; he is exempt.

6 [If] one threw [a stone] with the intention of inflicting a wound upon either a man or a beast, and he reminded himself when the wound had not yet been inflicted, he is exempt.

This is the rule: All who are liable for sin offerings are not liable unless the beginning and the end of their acts are [both] inadvertent. [If] their beginning was inadvertent but their end was intentional, [or if] their beginning was intentional but their end was inadvertent, they are exempt, unless their beginning and their end are inadvertent.

YAD AVRAHAM

but their end was inadvertent, they are exempt, unless (lit. *until*) *their beginning and their end are inadvertent.*

The repetition of this phrase is for its implication, viz., that only the beginning and end of the act need be inadvertent. The middle, however, even if it occurs with awareness of the transgression, does not exempt one from a sin offering. For example: One threw an object a distance of six cubits inadvertently but, after the object had traveled the first two cubits, he became aware of the prohibition. After the object had traveled the second two of those cubits he subsequently forgot again, causing the last two cubits of flight to be accomplished during a second period of unawareness. Since both the beginning and the end of this act occurred during periods in which he was unaware of commission of a transgression, and the distances traversed by the object during those periods of unawareness add up to the four cubits necessary for liability, he is liable despite his passing realization during the middle of the act[1] (*Tos. Yom Tov; Shenos Eliyahu; Tif. Yis.*).

1. The *Gemara* discusses also the explanation of Rav Ashi, who interprets even the beginning of the mishnah as referring to one who threw an object while unaware of the violation, and who, in midflight, realized his error and then again forgot before the object landed. Accordingly, he is exempt only if it was either intercepted, landed in a dog's mouth or was burnt. The beginning of the mishnah is not, however, listing a separate exemption for one whose act ends in awareness; this is dealt with only in the end of the mishnah.

Tosefos Yom Tov points out, however, that this last phrase of the mishnah even according to Rava is referring to Rav Ashi's ruling. This seems strongly indicated from *Shenos Eliyahu* and *Tif. Yis.*, too. Accordingly, the only dispute between Rava and Rav Ashi is whether only the end of the mishnah refers to this case or whether the beginning of the mishnah, too, refers to this. According to Rava the beginning of the mishnah deals with a list of different exemptions, i.e., one who remembered before the object landed and is exempt for that reason *or* one who is exempt by reason of the object not having had a proper landing because it was either intercepted, or landed in a dog's mouth or was burnt while in flight. The end of the mishnah, however, expresses liability by implication for an act whose beginning and end were both during periods of unawareness, despite there having been an awareness in the middle.

There is some ambiguity in the explanations of *Rambam* and *Rav*. For this reason we have omitted them. [See *Tos. Yom Tov*, *Meleches Shlomo* and *Beis David*.]

פרק שנים עשר
Chapter Twelve

שבת יב/א

[א] הַבּוֹנֶה, כַּמָּה יִבְנֶה וִיהֵא חַיָּב? הַבּוֹנֶה כָּל־שֶׁהוּא; וְהַמְסַתֵּת, וְהַמַּכֶּה בְּפַטִּישׁ וּבְמַעֲצָד, הַקּוֹדֵחַ, כָּל־שֶׁהוּא, חַיָּב.

ר׳ עובדיה מברטנורא

פרק שנים עשר — הבונה. (א) הבונה. שאמרו באבות מלאכות: **כמה יבנה ויהיה חייב. כל שהוא: מסתת.** מרבע את האבן או מחליקה ומתקנה, הכל לפי מנהג המקום. והיא תולדה דמכה בפטיש: **והמכה בפטיש.** היא גמר מלאכה של חולבי אבן, לאחר שחלב האבן מן ההר סביב והבדילה מכה עליה מכה גדולה והיא מתפרקת ונופלת. וכל הגומר מלאכה בשבת תולדה דמכה בפטיש היא: **מעצד.** קופיץ קטן: **והקודח.** הנוקב: **כל שהוא.** אכולהו קאי, אמסתת ואמכה בפטיש ובמעצד, והקודח:

יד אברהם

1.

After delineating in detail the laws of the *melachah* of *transferring from one domain to another*, the mishnah proceeds to delineate the laws of the other *avos* and their *tolados*.

The mishnah begins with the *av* of *building*, for the following reason:

Having just dealt with the *melachah* of *transferring from one domain to another*, which is the last of the thirty-nine *avos* enumerated in the mishnah (see 7:2), the *Tanna* wishes to continue by discussing the *melachah* immediately preceding it, namely, *striking the final blow* (the thirty-eighth on the list). Since, however, this *melachah* is inherently related to the *melachah* of *building*, and since *building* is a far more common *melachah*, the *Tanna* begins by discussing *building* (Tos. Yom Tov).

הַבּוֹנֶה, — *One who builds*,

I.e., the one who engages in the activity of building mentioned above (7:2) as one of the *avos melachos* (*Rav; Rashi*).

כַּמָּה יִבְנֶה וִיהֵא חַיָּב? — *how much must he build to be liable?*

I.e., what is the minimum one must build on the Sabbath to be liable to capital punishment in cases of willful transgression, or to a sin offering in cases of inadvertent transgressions? [We have previously seen (7:3) that though one is forbidden to do a *melachah* in any amount, one is not liable for punishment unless he engages in a certain minimum amount of that activity. Each *melachah* has its own minimum requirements for liability.]

הַבּוֹנֶה כָּל־שֶׁהוּא; — *One who builds any amount;*

The conclusion of this statement is to be found at the end of the sentence. Thus we understand the sentence to read: *One who builds any amount; one who chisels a stone ... is liable*. This follows the reading in all standard editions of Mishnah, Talmud, and *Rif*.[1]

Building any amount includes fill-

---

1. Meiri and Meoros, however, delete the word הַבּוֹנֶה, *if one builds* (from the second sentence), thus rendering the mishnah, *One who builds — how much must he build to be liable? Any amount*. The statement, *One who chisels a stone*, then begins a new thought and is not an explanation of the first statement.

משניות / שבת — פרק יב: הבונה [284]

12 **1.** One who builds, how much must he build to be liable? One who builds any amount; one who chisels [a stone], strikes with a hammer or with an adz, [or] drills, any amount, is liable.

YAD AVRAHAM

ing up a hole in the wall of a house. This type of building was found in the construction of the *Mishkan*. If a woodworm had bored into the boards of the *Mishkan*, the hole would be filled with molten lead (*Tos. Yom Tov* from *Gem.* 102b).

וְהַמְסַתֵּת, — *one who chisels [a stone],*
I.e., if one cuts the stone into a square, or smooths it, or in any other way prepares it for building according to local custom. This is a *toladah* of *striking the final blow (Rav; Rashi; Rambam).* As an example, *Rashi* adds that in Germany it was customary to make grooves in building stones. Consequently, this process, too, would constitute a *toladah* of *striking the final blow.*

וְהַמַּכֶּה בְּפַטִּישׁ — *strikes with a hammer*
This is the final step performed in quarrying. After the stone has been hewn on all sides and has been almost entirely separated from the mountain, the quarrier deals it one final blow with a hammer thus separating it completely from the mountain. Similarly, anyone who puts the finishing touches on any article is guilty of a *toladah* of *striking the final blow (Rav; Rashi).*

Tosafos explain this to mean the final hammer blow dealt to any metal utensil upon its completion.

Tosafos object to *Rashi's* interpretation on the ground that no quarrying was involved in the construction of the *Mishkan* (which was not a stone structure). It would, therefore, be inappropriate for the *Tanna* to select quarrying as an example of *striking the final blow.* Rather, he should have selected some activity which did in fact take place in the construction of the *Mishkan* as an example.

Tosefos Yom Tov reconciles this difficulty by explaining that though the criterion of what is called an *av* is dependent on its having been used in the construction of the *Mishkan*, the *Tanna* nevertheless selects activities of everyday life as examples of the *avos.* [We find a similar case in 7:2, where the mishnah enumerates *baking rather than *cooking, though it was *cooking that was actually done in the *Mishkan* in the manufacture of dyes. Here too, the *Tanna* chooses a more common example of the completion of labor — namely, the final hammer blow of the quarrier, rather than the one found in the construction of the *Mishkan*.

Beis David questions the assumption that quarrying stones is more common than putting the finishing touches on metal utensils.

Rashash, too, questions *Tosefos Yom Tov's* reconciliation for other reasons. He understands *Tosafos'* question to mean that according to *Rashi*, the final hammer blow struck by the quarrier is an *av*, whereas in reality it is only a *toladah*, since it was not performed in the construction of the *Mishkan*.

וּבְמַעֲצָד, — *or with an adz,*
This follows *Rav*, who describes a small axe. *Rashi*, however, interprets this as a sledgehammer. In *Bava Kamma* 10:10 and in *Makkos* 3:5, it is explained as a wood plane (*Tos. Yom Tov*).

הַקּוֹדֵחַ — [*or] drills,*
I.e., if one bores a hole (*Rav; Rashi; Rambam*).

This, too, is a *toladah* of *striking the final blow (Rambam).*

See *Lechem Mishneh, Hil. Shabbos*

שבת יב/א

זֶה הַכְּלָל: כָּל הָעוֹשֶׂה מְלָאכָה, וּמְלַאכְתּוֹ מִתְקַיֶּמֶת, בַּשַּׁבָּת חַיָּב.
רַבָּן שִׁמְעוֹן בֶּן גַּמְלִיאֵל אוֹמֵר: אַף הַמַּכֶּה בְקֻרְנָס עַל הַסַּדָּן בִּשְׁעַת מְלָאכָה חַיָּב, מִפְּנֵי שֶׁהוּא כִּמְתַקֵּן מְלָאכָה.

ר' עובדיה מברטנורא

ומלאכתו מתקיימת. שאין צריך להוסיף עליה: **קורנס.** מרטי"ל: **סדן.** אנקודי"נא בלט"ז: **מפני שהוא כמתקן מלאכה.** אף על פי שאינו מכה על המלאכה אלא על הסדן, מתקן הוא, שכן מרדדי טסי משכן היו עושין, מכין על הטס שלש הכאות ועל הסדן הכאה אחת להחליק הקורנס שלא יבקע הטס שהוא דק. ואין הלכה כרבי שמעון בן גמליאל:

יד אברהם

10:14, that according to *Rambam* he is liable in this case for both *building and *striking the final blow.[1]

כָּל-שֶׁהוּא, חַיָּב. — *any amount, is liable.*

This applies to all the aforementioned labors, viz., chiseling a stone, striking with a hammer or an adz, and drilling. Liability for each of these is for any amount (*Rav; Rash*).

זֶה הַכְּלָל: כָּל הָעוֹשֶׂה מְלָאכָה, וּמְלַאכְתּוֹ מִתְקַיֶּמֶת, בַּשַּׁבָּת חַיָּב. — *This is the rule: Anyone who works, and his work endures, on the Sabbath is liable.*

This sentence is in inverted order. The intent is: Anyone who works on the Sabbath and whose work endures is liable (*Rashi; Ran*).

Although the phrase, *on the Sabbath,* is superfluous, the *Tanna* occasionally adds such expressions (as in 17:1) (*Beis David*).

[Although the mishnah has stated that one is liable for *building even the least amount, the mishnah qualifies that with the stipulation that the work must be of an enduring nature. The minimum required for liability in any *melachah* is derived from an evaluation of the smallest amount of an activity considered to be significant. *Building is considered significant even in the smallest amount, but only where the work done is useful in its present form, i.e., it need not be expanded. If the work done is only the start of some larger process, however, and must be expanded before being useful, it cannot be considered significant in its own right. One is, therefore, not liable for having performed a *melachah.*]

With regard to the laws of Sabbath, work is considered enduring in cases where *some* people would retain the object for use in its present form (without enhancement). In such instances, however, even one who intends to expand the work is also liable for that part already done since the work can be considered enduring with regard to certain people. An example of this is if one carves a hole the

---

1. This double liability, though, applies only to drilling in a structure. For drilling in a utensil, however, one is liable only for *striking the final blow (Machatzis HaShekel 314:3).

This is the rule: Anyone who works, and his work endures, on the Sabbath is liable.

Rabban Shimon ben Gamliel says; Also one who strikes with a sledge hammer on the anvil while working is liable, since he is as one who improves the work.

YAD AVRAHAM

size of three quarts in a block of wood which is large enough to accommodate a hole the size of six quarts. Since some people use it in this smaller size, even one who intends to enlarge the hole is liable for what he has already done (*Tos. Yom Tov* from *Ran; Rashi; Gem.* 103a).

Others explain the sentence in the order it appears, thus *anyone who works and his work endures on the Sabbath* — i.e., on the Sabbath his work has reached its permanent status, and he does not intend to add to it — is liable (*Pri Chadash*). This is diametrically opposed to the previous interpretation.

Still others, also explaining the sentence in the order it appears, interpret as follows: *Anyone who works and his work endures on the Sabbath is liable.* I.e., if his work remains so on the Sabbath, even though he plans to complete it after the Sabbath, he is, nevertheless, liable. According to this, in the example cited above, one who notched a cavity in a block of wood even if he plans to enlarge the cavity after the Sabbath, and even if others would not leave it like this, is still liable since it will remain as is throughout the Sabbath. The fact that he uses it in this stage throughout the Sabbath gives it the significance of a *melachah* (*Shenos Eliyahu*).[1]

רַבָּן שִׁמְעוֹן בֶּן גַּמְלִיאֵל אוֹמֵר: אַף הַמַּכֶּה בְּקֻרְנָס עַל הַסַּדָּן — *Rabban Shimon ben Gamliel says: Also one who strikes with a sledge hammer on the anvil*

I.e., even when the smith is not striking the utensil upon which he is working but rather the anvil, if he does so during his work on the utensil, he is liable for that blow alone (*Rav; Rashi*).

בִּשְׁעַת מְלָאכָה — *while working* (lit. *during the work*)

It was the custom of the metal workers in the construction of the *Mishkan* to strike the metal being beaten into sheets three times and the anvil once (to flatten any jagged edges which may have formed on the hammer-head while pounding on the metal plate) (*Rav*; from *Gem.* 103a, *Rashi*).

חַיָּב, — *is liable,*

Although this blow is not dealt on the metal upon which he is working, nevertheless, he is liable (*Rav; Rashi*).

מִפְּנֵי שֶׁהוּא כִמְתַקֵּן מְלָאכָה. — *since he is as one who improves the work.*

I.e., by smoothing his hammer to prevent it from becoming jagged (and puncturing the thin sheets of gold) he is improving the ultimate quality of the work (*Rav*).

The *Tanna Kamma* does not dis-

---

1. This seems to have been the way *Rambam* understood the mishnah as well. He adds that if the work will fade before the end of the Sabbath it is considered impermanent and he is not liable (*Hil. Shabbos* 9:13 as explained by *Maggid Mishneh* there).

שבת
יב/ב

[ב] **הַחוֹרֵשׁ** כָּל־שֶׁהוּא; הַמְנַכֵּשׁ, וְהַמְקַרְסֵם, וְהַמְזָרֵד, כָּל־שֶׁהוּא, חַיָּב.

────────── ר' עובדיה מברטנורא ──────────

(ב) **המנכש.** תולש עשבים רעים מתוך טובים. פ"א חופר סביב עקרי הצמחים והיא מלאכה מעין חרישה: **מקרסם**. קוצץ ענפים יבשים מן האילן לתקנו: **מזרד.** זרדים לחים חדשים של שנה זו, ופעמים שהן מרובים ומתגדלים ומכחישים כח האילן וקוצצין אותן ממנו.

יד אברהם

pute the fact that the smiths struck the anvil with their hammers when beating the sheets of gold for the *Mishkan*. This was common practice in even later times, as attested to by *Rashi* and *Rambam* in their descriptions of the work customs of their times. He disagrees, however, with regard to counting it as a separate *melachah* involving its own liability (*Tos. Yam Tov*).

The halachah is not in keeping with Rabban Shimon ben Gamliel (*Rav; Rambam*).

2.

The mishnah now deals primarily with the *melachah* of *plowing. Although according to the order established in the preceding mishnah, delineating the *melachos* in reverse of the order in which they appeared in 7:2, the next *melachah* discussed should be *writing, the *Tanna* nevertheless chooses to delineate first the *melachah* of *plowing since it is the reverse of *building (which was discussed in the preceding mishnah). *Building consists generally of filling up holes or augmenting a structure, whereas *plowing consists of digging holes or diminishing that which is already there (*Tos. Yom Tov*).

Alternatively, *plowing and *building are very similar, because in both of these *melachos*, holes are dug and filled. In fact, removing a hillock from the dirt floor of a house is a *toladah* of *building. Also, both are liable for any amount (*Tif. Yis.*).

הַחוֹרֵשׁ — *One who plows*
[I.e., the one who performs the labor of *plowing listed above (7:2).]

כָּל־שֶׁהוּא; — *any amount;*
One is liable for *plowing any amount since even the smallest area plowed is fit for planting a pumpkin seed. Similarly, in the *Mishkan* the smallest area was fit for planting one stalk of a dye-producing herb (*Tos. Yom Tov from Gem.* 103a).

Even though with regard to *transferring from one domain to another we learned (9:7) that one is not liable for carrying fewer than two pumpkin seeds, that is because one would not ordinarily take the trouble to carry out just one seed to plant. With regard to *plowing, however, each hole must in any case be dug individually and the digging of each hole is therefore regarded as a significant activity (*Tos. Yom Tov from Rashi* ibid.).[1]

1. Even though one plows an entire furrow at one time, too, and not just one hole at a time this is considered to be a sequence of separate acts (i.e., digging hole one, hole two, hole three, etc.) since the two acts occur consecutively rather than simultaneously.

2. One who plows any amount; one who weeds, or prunes dry branches, or prunes young shoots, in any amount, is liable.

YAD AVRAHAM

הַמְנַכֵּשׁ, — *one who weeds,*

I.e., if one pulls out weeds from between the plants (*Rav; Tif. Yis.*).

Alternatively, this refers to digging around the base of trees or plants, performing labor very similar to *plowing (Rav; Rambam, Comm.*). According to *Kesef Mishneh* (*Hil. Shabbos* 8:2), pulling out weeds from between the plants, since it stimulates their growth, is a *toladah* of *sowing. Digging around the roots, however, since it improves the soil, is a *toladah* of *plowing.

וְהַמְקַרְסֵם, — *or prunes dry branches,*

I.e., if one cuts dead branches from a tree in order to improve the tree (*Rav; Rashi; Tif. Yis.*).

Since he cuts off the branches to stimulate the tree's growth, he is in effect planting the extra growth of the tree. He is, therefore, liable for *sowing (*Tos. Yom Tov* from *Rambam*).

Rambam translates this as one who cuts off wild plants or grasses which have sprouted in a field (in preparation for planting the field with some other species). This then constitutes a *toladah* of *plowing (*Hil. Shabbos* 8:1).

Rambam explains both מְקַרְסֵם and מְזָרֵד as being to improve the arability of the soil. He therefore considers them to be *tolados* of *plowing. *Rashi* and *Rav* however explain them to be types of pruning for the purpose of improving the tree and consequently to be *tolados* of *sowing.

וְהַמְזָרֵד, — *or prunes young shoots,*

I.e., one who prunes the excess young shoots which, due to their abundance, diminish the strength of the tree (*Rav*).

Alternatively, one who cuts off branches to improve the arability of the ground beneath them (*Rambam, Hil. Shabbos* 8:1).

כָּל־שֶׁהוּא, חַיָּב. — *in any amount, is liable.*

[I.e., one is liable for any of the above types of work in any amount.]

◆§ The Role of Intent in Classifying Tolados

As we have seen before (see commentary to וְהַמְזָרֵד), the determination of an act as being a *toladah* of one *melachah* or another often depends upon the intent of the one who performs the act. An act may at times be considered a *toladah* of one *melachah* while the identical act will at other times be considered a *toladah* of another *melachah*. This occurs where an act achieves two ends, e.g., cutting off of branches from a tree whereby (a) the tree is strengthened and (b) wood is collected. The determination as to which *melachah* this case belongs is therefore based on the cutter's intent. Where his intent is to prune, his act is categorized as a *toladah* of *sowing. If his intent is to collect wood, his act is categorized as a *toladah* of *reaping. If his intent is for both purposes, his act is categorized as a *toladah* of both (*Gem.* 73b).

שבת יב/ב

הַמְלַקֵּט עֵצִים, אִם לְתַקֵּן, כָּל־שֶׁהֵן; אִם לְהֶסֵּק, כְּדֵי לְבַשֵּׁל בֵּיצָה קַלָּה. הַמְלַקֵּט עֲשָׂבִים, אִם לְתַקֵּן, כָּל־שֶׁהוּא; אִם

ר׳ עובדיה מברטנורא

אם לתקן. את האילן או את הקרקע, וקלטו מן המחובר: **ביצה קלה.** כגרוגרת מביצת תרנגולת, שהיא קלה להתבשל יותר משאר ביצים:

יד אברהם

הַמְלַקֵּט עֵצִים, — *One who gathers wood,*

I.e., by cutting branches off a tree (*Meiri; Rashi; Rav*).

אִם לְתַקֵּן, — *if [his intent is] to effect an improvement,*

I.e., if he intends to effect an improvement in either the tree or arability of the ground (*Rav; Meiri*).

כָּל־שֶׁהֵן; — *[he is liable for] any amount;*

If his intent is to improve the soil, he is liable for *plowing;* if his intent is to improve the tree, he is liable for *sowing.* In either case, the liability is for any amount (*Meiri*).

אִם לְהֶסֵּק, — *if [his intent is] for kindling,*

[I.e., if his intent is to collect firewood.]

כְּדֵי לְבַשֵּׁל בֵּיצָה קַלָּה. — *[he is liable] for the amount [of wood] required to cook an easily cooked egg.*

As explained above (8:5) this does not mean the amount necessary to cook an entire egg but rather the amount necessary to cook an egg equal in volume to a dried fig. [*Rambam, Hil. Shabbos* [8:5] states that this equals one third the size of a medium egg; for further clarification see above 8:5.]

For this measurement, a chicken egg is used, since it is the most *easily cooked* (i.e., requiring the least amount of heat) of all eggs. Therefore, one is liable for cutting off the amount of wood sufficient to cook that part of a chicken egg, even though it would be insufficient to cook an equal part of a duck or goose egg.

The liability here is apparently for the *melachah* of *reaping,* the same as for cutting down any growing plant. This follows the explanation of *Rashi, Meiri* and *Rav* who explain the mishnah as dealing with gathering wood from a growing tree (by cutting off its branches).

Even if his intent is to collect wood, he may also be liable for having improved the tree (since, whatever his intent, the tree was actually pruned and thereby improved). This follows the well-known rule of פְּסִיק רֵישֵׁיהּ, the unintended but inevitable performance of a *melachah* while engaged in another act. (For further clarification of this rule see General Introduction, p. 8.) Following the stipulations of this rule, if the unintended but inevitable consequence of an act is the performance of a *melachah*, and if the one who performs this act benefits from that consequence, too, he is liable for the performance of that consequence as if he had intentionally performed it. Accordingly, if one cuts wood for kindling from his own tree (and thereby benefits from the pruning aspect of the act), he is liable for a *toladah* of *sowing* in addition to the *melachah* of *reaping.* This, however, cannot be the case of our *mishnah;* since it would then follow that he would be liable for *any* amount no matter what his intent (the liability for *sowing* being for any amount rather than the larger amount required for liability under the *melachah* of *reaping*). Therefore, we must conclude that our *mishnah* is referring

12 2 One who gathers wood, if [his intent is] to effect an improvement, [he is liable for] any amount if [his intent is] for kindling, [he is liable] for the amount [of wood] required to cook an easily cooked egg. One who gathers grasses, if [his intent is] to effect an improvement, [he is liable for] any amount; if

YAD AVRAHAM

to a case of cutting the branches from someone else's tree. Since he is not the owner, he derives no incidental benefit from the pruning of the tree and therefore is not liable for *sowing*, since the pruning aspect was both unintended and of no consequence to him. [If he *intended* to prune also, he is liable for *pruning*, too, whether or not he derives benefit from it (*Tos. R' Akiva* similar to *Gem.* 103a).]

Where, however, his intent is only to prune (rather than to gather wood) he is liable only for *sowing* and not for *reaping*. This despite the fact that he has also inevitably "reaped" (and thereby collected) the wood. This is because wood is not usually a harvested crop. Therefore the concept of *reaping* does not of itself apply to the activity of cutting wood unless one specifically applies it [through his intent] (*Tos. Shabbos* 73b).[1]

Rambam, however, states that the liability is for the *melachah* of **gathering into sheaves*, which, as explained in 7:2, means gathering uprooted or detached plants into one pile. It is therefore apparent that *Rambam* explains the mishnah as dealing with gathering wood previously detached from the tree (and now lying on the ground). This, indeed, is the explanation given by *Tiferes Yisrael*. Accordingly, the phrase אִם לְתַקֵּן, *if [his intent is] to effect an improvement*, refers not to improving the tree but rather to improving the arability of the ground beneath the tree — in which case he is liable for the *melachah* of **plowing* — or improving the growth of any plants upon which the branches are lying — in which case he is liable for the *melachah* of **planting* (*Tif. Yis.*).

The same minimum is necessary for liability for the *melachah* of **gathering into sheaves* as is necessary for liability for the *melachah* of **reaping* (*Rambam, Hil. Shabbos* 8:3,5).

הַמְלַקֵּט עֲשָׂבִים, — *One who gathers grasses*,

I.e., if one uproots growing grass (*Meiri*).

As explained above, *Rambam* (followed by *Tif. Yis.*) explains this in reference to one gathering grass that has already been uprooted.

אִם לְתַקֵּן, — *if [his intent is] to effect an improvement*,

I.e., if he intends to effect an improvement in the arability of the soil (*Meiri*).

כָּל־שֶׁהוּא; — *[he is liable for] any amount;*

[As explained above, the liability is for **plowing*.]

---

1. In earlier times, trees were not planted and harvested as a regular crop. When wood was needed it was taken from fallen branches or trees or at least dead ones. Even today, when *trees* are regularly harvested in large numbers, it might still be accurate to say that *branches* of trees are not usually "harvested" for use as wood.

שבת
יב/ג

לִבְהֵמָה, כִּמְלֹא פִי הַגְּדִי.

[ג] **הַכּוֹתֵב** שְׁתֵּי אוֹתִיּוֹת, בֵּין בִּימִינוֹ בֵּין בִּשְׂמֹאלוֹ; בֵּין מִשֵּׁם אֶחָד בֵּין מִשְּׁנֵי שֵׁמוֹת; בֵּין מִשְּׁנֵי סַמָּנִיּוֹת;

ר׳ עובדיה מברטנורא

(ג) **בין בימינו בין בשמאלו.** באדם שהוא שולט בשתי ידיו, דאילו בשאר כל אדם כתיבת שמאל אינה כתיבה: **בין משם אחד.** שתיהן אלפי״ן: **משני שמות.** אל״ף בי״ת. **משני סממניות.** אחד בדיו ואחד בסיקרא. ואית ספרים דגרסי משני סמניות כלומר משני סימנים, כגון שכותבים א׳ לסימן אחד וב׳ לסימן שנים:

יד אברהם

אִם לִבְהֵמָה — *if [his intent is] for animal [fodder],*

[I.e., if he gathers the grass with the intention of feeding it to animals.]

כִּמְלֹא פִי הַגְּדִי — *[he is liable] for as much as a kid's mouthful.*

As mentioned above, according to *Rav* and *Meiri*, the liability is for **reaping* since they explain the mishnah in reference to uprooting growing grass. According to *Rambam*, however, the mishnah refers to grass which has already been uprooted. Accordingly, the liability is for the *melachah* of **gathering into sheaves.*

[The measure is set as a *kid's mouthful* because a kid is the smallest animal to which one regularly feeds grass. Therefore, a kid's mouthful is the smallest amount considered significant. See above 7:4.]

3.

Mishnayos 3-6 deal with the melachah of **writing two letters.*

The *Tanna* is now reverting back to the order established in mishnah 1 of dealing with the *melachos* enumerated in 7:2 in reverse order. (See prefatory note to mishnah 2.)

הַכּוֹתֵב שְׁתֵּי אוֹתִיּוֹת, — *One who writes two letters,*

[I.e., the one who performs the labor of **writing two letters* listed above (7:2). This includes letters, numbers, or other symbols.]

בֵּין בִּימִינוֹ בֵּין בִּשְׂמֹאלוֹ; — *whether with his right hand or with his left;*

This applies only to one who is ambidextrous. A right-handed person, however, is liable only for writing with his right hand. Writing with his left hand is not viewed as a normal form of writing and he is therefore not liable (see General Introduction p. 11), although it is still Rabbinically prohibited (*Rav* from *Gem.* 103a). Similarly, a left-handed person is liable only for writing with his left hand but not for writing with his right hand. An ambidextrous person is liable for writing with either hand (*Gem. Shabbos* 103a).

בֵּין מִשֵּׁם אֶחָד — *whether of one character* (lit. *name*)

I.e., if one wrote the same letter twice, e.g., אא (*Rav, Rashi*).

12 3 [his intent is] for animal [fodder], [he is liable] for as much as a kid's mouthful.

3. One who writes two letters, whether with his right hand or his left; whether of one character or of two characters; whether with two inks;

YAD AVRAHAM

Rambam rules that if one writes the same letter twice so that the result is a complete word — as דַּד (breast), תֵּת (giving), גַּג (roof), יָי (drips), שֵׁשׁ (six), סָס (moth), חָח (nose ring) — he is liable (*Hil. Shabbos* 11:10). It is apparent from this that if one writes the same letter twice and does not form a word thereby, e.g., אא, he is not liable. This is in accordance with the opinion of R' Yehudah in the name of Rabban Gamliel, mentioned in the *Gemara* (103b). The *Tanna* of this mishnah, however, makes a general statement, that if one writes two letters of one character, he is liable, without qualifying that it applies only where he thereby forms a word (*Tif. Yis.*).

בֵּין מִשְׁנֵי שֵׁמוֹת — *or of two characters*; E.g., אב (*Rav; Rashi; Tif. Yis.*)

בֵּין מִשְׁנֵי סַמָּנִיּוֹת — *whether with two inks*;
I.e., if he wrote one letter with ink and one with vermilion (*Rav; Rashi*).

Other editions read: סִמָּנִיּוֹת, *symbols* (*Rambam*). I.e., if one writes א as a symbol of 1 and ב as a symbol of 2 (*Rav; Rambam*).

Although we already learned in the beginning of the mishnah that one is liable for writing two letters of two different characters, the *Tanna* found it, nevertheless, necessary to teach us that if he wrote the letters as numerical symbols he is also liable. Otherwise, we might think that one is liable for **writing two letters*, where together they form a single word, but not for writing two numerical symbols which are read independently of one another. The *Tanna* therefore informs us that in this case, too, one is liable. Alternatively, we might possibly think that only if one writes letters as parts of a word, must he write two letters in order to be liable. Where, however, he uses a letter as a numeral, he should be liable for writing even one letter (since it represents an entire idea by itself). The *Tanna*, therefore, teaches us that even in this case, he is not liable unless he writes two letters.

Another explanation is that the *Tanna* is not referring to Hebrew letters at all, but rather to other symbols, such as Arabic numerals. [The commentators chose א and ב merely as examples of numeric symbols] (*Tos. Yom Tov*).

Maggid Mishneh (*Hil. Shabbos* 11:10) quotes *Rav Hai Gaon* who explains that the letters mentioned here are representative neither of language nor of numbers but are used merely as markers (to indicate the end of a paragraph, for example). Such a usage is found even in the Torah where two inverted נ's are used to set *Numbers* 10:35-36 apart from the rest of the text.

Rashba favors *Rambam's* reading (סִמָּנִיּוֹת, *symbols*) over *Rashi's* (סַמָּנִיּוֹת, *inks*). Since the different types of ink are discussed in the fourth mishnah and the types of letters are discussed in the third

[293] THE MISHNAH/SHABBOS — Chapter Twelve: *Haboneh*

שבת יב/ג

בְּכָל לָשׁוֹן, חַיָּב.
אָמַר רַבִּי יוֹסֵי: לֹא חִיְּבוּ שְׁתֵּי אוֹתִיּוֹת אֶלָּא מִשּׁוּם רֹשֶׁם, שֶׁכָּךְ הָיוּ כוֹתְבִין עַל קַרְשֵׁי הַמִּשְׁכָּן, לֵידַע אֵיזוֹ בֶּן זוּגוֹ.

ר׳ עובדיה מברטנורא

בכל לשון. וכתב של כל אומה ואומה: **משום רושם.** סימן שהיו טושין בקרשי המשכן, מפני שמפרקים אותן ולכשיקימוהו לא יחליפו סדר הקרשים. ואתא רבי יוסי למימר דאפילו לא כתב אלא שרשם שני רשימות בעלמא לסימן, חייב. ואין הלכה כרבי יוסי:

יד אברהם

mishnah it is more likely that in the third mishnah the *Tanna* is referring to letters, or symbols, rather than to types of ink used.

Moreover, once the *Tanna* teaches us that one is liable for writing two letters with two different types of ink, it follows that one is certainly liable for writing both letters with the same type of ink. Mishnah 4, which enumerates the various types of ink, would, accordingly, be superfluous (*Lechem Shamayim*).

בְּכָל לָשׁוֹן, — *in any language,*

I.e., in the script used by any nation (*Rav; Rashi; Rambam, Comm.*).

Others maintain that, aside from the Assyrian script (in which Hebrew is written), one is only liable for *writing in Greek script. All other scripts, including Latin, are proscribed only by Rabbinic enactment (*Or Zarua,* quoting *Rabbeinu Yoel bar Yitzchak HaLevi*).

חַיָּב. — *he is liable.*

[I.e., he is liable for a sin offering if he wrote without realizing it was the Sabbath day or without knowing that writing is proscribed on the Sabbath. However, even those cases exempted from liability are still forbidden Rabbinically.]

אָמַר רַבִּי יוֹסֵי: לֹא חִיְּבוּ שְׁתֵּי אוֹתִיּוֹת אֶלָּא מִשּׁוּם רֹשֶׁם, שֶׁכָּךְ הָיוּ כוֹתְבִין עַל קַרְשֵׁי הַמִּשְׁכָּן, לֵידַע אֵיזוֹ בֶּן זוּגוֹ. — *R' Yose says: They declared [writing] two letters liable only* (lit. *they did not declare liability for two letters except*) *because of marking, for thus would they write on the boards of the Mishkan to know which ones were mates* (lit. *which was its mate*).

R' Yose maintains that the Sages declared liability for *writing two letters only because one is thereby making a mark or a sign, i.e., that the essence of the *melachah* of *writing is the making of symbols whether or not they are representative of any formal language. The letters served this purpose in the construction of the *Mishkan*, where letters were written on the boards of the *Mishkan* so that when the boards were reassembled after traveling, the identifying letters on the boards would enable them to reassemble the boards in their original order.[1]

---

1. The necessity for preserving the order of the boards was because of their varying degrees of sanctity, the sanctity of the boards being a function of their proximity to the holy utensils of the *Mishkan*. The boards used for the north side were not as holy as those used for the south side (where the *Menorah* stood). Similarly, the boards nearer to the east were not as holy as those nearer the west (where the Holy of Holies stood) (*Tif. Yis.; Ran*

12
3 in any language, he is liable.

R' Yose says: They declared [writing] two letters liable only because of marking, for thus would they write on the boards of the *Mishkan*, to know which ones were mates.

YAD AVRAHAM

R' Yose, therefore, reasons that since the letters used in the *Mishkan* had no linguistic content but were used merely as signs, there should be no special significance attached to the use of letters more than to any other symbols.[1]

Consequently, one who writes any two symbols is just as liable as one who writes two letters (*Rav; Rashi; Rambam, Comm.*).

According to this explanation, R' Yose differs from the *Tanna Kamma* (first opinion) in the following respect: The *Tanna Kamma* considers one liable only for using written characters which are part of the conventionally accepted symbol system of some language or nation (e.g., alphabet, hieroglyphic, or mathematical symbol) but not for making arbitrary signs which hold no generally accepted meaning (e.g., the scratches or chalk marks made by workmen to mark various points on their work); whereas R' Yose considers one equally liable for even these latter marks (*Rav; Tif. Yis.*).

Rambam, however, explains that R' Yose considers רוֹשֵׁם, *marking*, to be a *melachah*, distinct from כּוֹתֵב, *writing*. Furthermore, writing just two letters falls within the category of *marking* rather than *writing*. Two letters which are not part of a larger piece of writing are not viewed as a significant amount of writing and have, therefore, no greater importance than just ordinary markings — according to R' Yose. Since in the *Mishkan* the boards were numbered from א through כ we have a basis for considering *marking* to be a *melachah* in its own right.[2]

The halachah is in accordance with the *Tanna Kamma* (*Rav; Rambam*). Making a sign or a drawing is, then, a *toladah* of *writing* (*Rambam, Hil. Shabbos* 11:17).

from *Yerushalmi* 12:3).

As a derivation from this practice, many Jews mark the boards of the *sukkah* to assure them their same position in subsequent years (*Maharil*).

Also, it is customary to sew a strip of silk or other fabric onto the upper side of the *tallis* to assure the front fringes their honored position (*Magen Avraham* 8:6).

1. Some explain that R' Yose means to describe the event in the *Mishkan*; that is to say, that the marks made on the boards of the *Mishkan* were not letters at all, but scratches. Therefore, making marks of any kind is an *av melachah* (*Meiri; Aruch HaShulchan* 340:18).

2. The practical difference according to this explanation between R' Yose and the *Tanna Kamma* is where one writes a long piece and subsequently writes just two letters within the same period of forgetfulness (i.e., without having realized in between the two acts that it was Shabbos; for further clarification of this rule, see 7:1, 12:6). According to the *Tanna Kamma*, he has transgressed only one category of *melachah* and is therefore obligated to bring only one sin offering. According to R' Yose, however, he has transgressed two categories of *melachah* and is obligated to bring two sin offerings (*Rambam, Comm.* as explained by *Meleches Shlomo*).

שבת
יב/ד

אָמַר רַבִּי: מָצִינוּ שֵׁם קָטָן מִשֵּׁם גָּדוֹל, שֵׁם מִשִּׁמְעוֹן וּשְׁמוּאֵל, נֹחַ מִנָּחוֹר, דָּן מִדָּנִיֵּאל, גָּד מִגַּדִּיאֵל.

[ד] הַכּוֹתֵב שְׁתֵּי אוֹתִיּוֹת בְּהֶעְלֵם אֶחָד חַיָּב. כָּתַב בִּדְיוֹ, בְּסַם, בְּסִקְרָא, בְּקוֹמוֹס,

---
ר' עובדיה מברטנורא

מצינו שם קטן. כלומר אף על פי שלא נגמר מלאכתו, שנתכוין לכתוב תיבה גדולה וכתב מקלתה, הואיל ואותו מקלת הוויא תיבה ומתקיימת במקום אחר חייב, וכן הלכה: (ד) בסם. אורפימנ"ט בלע"ז: בסיקרא. מין אבן שצובעת אדום: בקומוס. מין עפר ולבטו שחור. פ"א שרף אילן גומא בלע"ז:

יד אברהם

אָמַר רַבִּי: — Rabbi [Yehudah HaNassi] said:

[Rabbi Yehudah HaNassi (Rabbi Judah the Prince) is known throughout the Talmud simply as Rebbi.] This is the version found in the current editions of the Mishnah. Earlier editions of the Mishnah read: R' Yehudah (referring to R' Yehudah ben R' Elai). Since this latter version is found in both Talmudim, also Rif, Rosh, Rambam, Ran, and other early works, our version is most likely erroneous (Rishon LeTzion).

מָצִינוּ שֵׁם קָטָן מִשֵּׁם גָּדוֹל, — We find a short name which is part of a long name,

I.e., if one intended to write a long word, but after writing two letters of it he reminded himself that it was the Sabbath and stopped writing. If the letters he wrote comprise a short name by themselves, he is liable even though he did not complete the word he intended to write (Rav; Rashi).

This is analogous to one who intends to weave a garment twenty cubits long and stops after just two threads. It is untenable to assume that he is not liable just because he did not do as much as he had intended. Similarly for all melachos, one is liable for having done the minimum amount of any melachah whether or not one has done the full amount he set out to do (Rambam, Comm.). [This is the ruling according to the halachah. R' Yehudah, however, diverges slightly from this point of view, as will be explained below.]

שֵׁם מִשִּׁמְעוֹן וּשְׁמוּאֵל, נֹחַ מִנָּחוֹר, דָּן מִדָּנִיֵּאל, גָּד מִגַּדִּיאֵל. — SHeM from SHiMon or SHMuel, NoaCH from NaCHor, DaN from DaNiel, GaD from GaDiel.

The Tanna lists examples of short names included in long names. Since the short name is in itself a complete word, if one writes it while intending to write the longer name, he is liable.

It appears that R' Yehudah declares one liable only if he writes two different letters. If he repeats the same letter, however, he is exempt. In this, he disagrees with the first Tanna of the mishnah. The Gemara attributes this view to Rabban Gamliel, whom R' Yehudah is only quoting. R' Yehudah

12
4
Rabbi [Yehudah HaNassi] said: We find a short name which is part of a long name, SHeM from SHiMon, or SHMuel, NoaCH from NaCHor, DaN from DaNiel, GaD from GaDiel.

4. One who writes two letters in one period of forgetfulness is liable. [Whether] he wrote with ink, with orpiment, with vermilion, with gum,

YAD AVRAHAM

himself rules that one is liable even for repeating the same letter (*Gem.* 103b).

It is furthermore evident that R' Yehudah declares one liable for *writing two letters only if they form a complete word. The halachah is, however, that if one writes two different letters, he is liable even if they do not form a word (*Meiri*).

4.

הַכּוֹתֵב שְׁתֵּי אוֹתִיּוֹת בְּהֶעְלֵם אֶחָד — *One who writes two letters in one period of forgetfulness*

I.e., if one forgot that it was the Sabbath, and did not remind himself until after he had written two letters. This halachah is indeed superfluous, since we have already learned above (11:6) that one is not liable for a sin offering unless both the beginning and the end of the labor have been performed inadvertently (i.e., without realizing at the time that one was transgressing the prohibition).

The mishnah repeats this here merely as an introduction to mishnah 6 (*Tos. Yom Tov*).

חַיָּב. — *is liable.*

[I.e., he is liable for a sin offering.]

כָּתַב בִּדְיוֹ, — *[Whether] he wrote with ink,*

I.e., with black ink that maintains its color on parchment (*Tif. Yis.* to *Megillah* 2:2).

Nowadays, it is customary to make ink for Torah scrolls from a combination of ferrous sulphate, gallnuts and gum arabic, which form a stable thick black compound (*Mishnah Berurah* 32:8).

בְּסַם, — *with orpiment,*

This follows *Rav* and *Rashi*. Orpiment is yellow arsenic. *Rambam*, however, renders it as an ink derived from a grass root (*Rambam, Comm.*).

בְּסִקְרָא, — *with vermilion,*

Rashi interprets this as a red dye. *Rav* and *Rambam* (*Comm.*) interpret this as red chalk. According to *Kaffich*, *Rambam* interprets this a a type of red mud from which red dye is obtained.

בְּקוֹמוֹס — *with gum,*

Rashi, *Rav*, and *Tiferes Yisrael* render this as gum arabic, which is used in the manufacture of ink. Alternatively, it is a type of black earth (*Rav*; *Rambam, Comm.*).

According to *Rambam* (*Comm. Megillah* 2:2), it is a type of yellow

שבת יב/ד

וּבְקַנְקַנְתּוֹם, וּבְכָל דָּבָר שֶׁהוּא רוֹשֵׁם; עַל שְׁנֵי כָתְלֵי זָוִיוֹת, וְעַל שְׁנֵי לוּחֵי פִנְקָס, וְהֵן נֶהְגִּין זֶה עִם זֶה, חַיָּב.

הַכּוֹתֵב עַל בְּשָׂרוֹ חַיָּב.

הַמְסָרֵט עַל בְּשָׂרוֹ, רַבִּי אֱלִיעֶזֶר מְחַיֵּב חַטָּאת, וְרַבִּי יְהוֹשֻׁעַ פּוֹטֵר.

ר' עובדיה מברטנורא

בקנקנתום. זא"ג בערבי, ובלע"ז ודריא"לי: לחתוי מיס עשרו בהס עפליס, גאלי"ש בלע"ז, שהוא רושם שרשומו מתקיים: **על ב' כותלי זויות.** אחת במזרח ואחת בלפון, סמוכות זו לזו במקצוע: **על ב' לוחי פנקס.** ספר שהחנווני כותב בו חשבונותיו, ואף על גב דלחו על לוח א' הס, אם נהגין ונקראין זה עס זה כגון שכותבין על שני שפתי הלוחין הסמוכין זה לזה, חייב: **הכותב על בשרו:** בצדיו: **והמשרט על בשרו.** בבדזל טושה לורת מותיות בבשרו: **רבי יהושע פוטר.** ואפילו הוליא דס, לפי שאין דרך כתיבה בכך. והלכה כרבי יהושע:

יד אברהם

earth. Kaffich explains this and the following as kinds of yellow or green salts that fade with age. They become black on contact with gall-nuts.

וּבְקַנְקַנְתּוֹם, — *with ferrous sulphate*,

This is also know as copperas or vitriol (*Rav*).

The *Gemara* describes it as "the blacking used by shoemakers."

וּבְכָל דָּבָר שֶׁהוּא רוֹשֵׁם; — *or with anything that marks;*

I.e., with anything that makes a permanent mark (*Rambam, Comm.*).

This includes water in which gall-nuts have been soaked (*Rav; Gem.* 104b).

Among other materials that produce a mark, the *Gemara* mentions lead.

עַל שְׁנֵי כָתְלֵי זָוִיוֹת, — *on two walls forming a corner*,

E.g., if one wrote one letter on the east wall and one letter on the north wall of a room, both close to the northeast corner (*Rav; Rashi*).

וְעַל שְׁנֵי לוּחֵי פִנְקָס, — *or on two pages of a ledger*,

I.e., if one wrote one letter on each two facing pages of a book (*Tif. Yis.*).

Alternatively, it refers to a book used by merchants which consisted of tablets coated with wax, upon which they could write with a stylus (*Rashi*).

וְהֵן נֶהְגִּין זֶה עִם זֶה, חַיָּב. — *that can be read together, he is liable.*

I.e., where one wrote two letters on two adjacent walls or on two facing pages of a ledger, in such a manner that they are near enough to one another to be read together, he is liable (*Rav; Rashi; Tif. Yis.*).

If they were written on different levels, he is exempt [since they are not read together] (*Shoshanim LeDavid*).

Though we learned in mishnah 3

12 4 with ferrous sulphate, or with anything that marks; on two walls forming a corner, or on two pages of a ledger, that can be read together, he is liable.

One who writes on his skin is liable.

One who scratches on his skin, R' Eliezer holds him liable for a sin offering. But R' Yehoshua exempts [him].

YAD AVRAHAM

that, according to many opinions, one is liable even where the two letters do not form a word, nevertheless, the two letters must at least have the potential for forming a word — namely, the possibility of being read together. In this case, they can then be made into a meaningful word by adding other letters to them. Where, however, they cannot be read together, they can never become part of a meaningful word and therefore have no significance at all. Consequently, one is not liable for writing them [though it is still forbidden to do so] (from *Gem.* 103b).

הַכּוֹתֵב עַל בְּשָׂרוֹ חַיָּב. — *One who writes on his skin is liable.*

Although the body's heat will cause the script to disappear after a while, he is still liable. This is analogous to one who writes something that will later be erased (*Rambam, Hil. Shabbos* 11:16). [One is liable because the script does not dissolve by itself but is dissolved by some external force (e.g., the eraser or the body heat).]

הַמְסָרֵט עַל בְּשָׂרוֹ, — *One who scratches on his skin,*

I.e., if one scratches letters into his flesh with a stylus or with lime (*Rashi*).

רַבִּי אֱלִיעֶזֶר מְחַיֵּב חַטָּאת, — *R' Eliezer holds him liable for a sin offering.*

[He regards this as *writing].

וְרַבִּי יהוֹשֻׁעַ פּוֹטֵר. — *But R' Yehoshua exempts [him].*

[The text found in *Talmud Bavli* as well as in *Rosh* and *Hagahos Maimonios* (*Hil. Shabbos* 11:16) reads: וַחֲכָמִים פּוֹטְרִין, *and the Sages exempt. Rif, Rambam, Yerushalmi, Maggid Mishneh,* and others conform to our reading. See *Meleches Shlomo.*]

Even where one draws blood by scratching letters on his body, he is exempt, since this is not the customary method of *writing (*Rambam; Rav*).

Not only is he exempt from a sin offering for the *melachah* of *writing, but he is likewise exempt from a sin offering for the secondary *melachah* of drawing blood (see 14:1). *Tiferes Yisrael* considers this a פְּסִיק רֵישֵׁיהּ דְּלֹא נִיחָא לֵיהּ, *an inevitable result not desired by its performer.* [See General Introduction, p. 8.]

Alternatively, since he does not derive use from the blood, his action is considered destructive and there is no liability, as in 13:3 (*Tos Yom Tov*).

The halachah is in accordance with R' Yehoshua (*Rav; Rambam, Comm. and Hil. Shabbos* 11:16).

שבת
יב/ה

[ה] **כָּתַב** בְּמַשְׁקִין, בְּמֵי פֵרוֹת, בַּאֲבַק דְּרָכִים, בַּאֲבַק הַסּוֹפְרִים, וּבְכָל דָּבָר שֶׁאֵינוֹ מִתְקַיֵּם, פָּטוּר. לְאַחַר יָדוֹ, בְּרַגְלוֹ, בְּפִיו, וּבְמַרְפֵּקוֹ; כָּתַב אוֹת אַחַת סָמוּךְ לִכְתָב; כָּתַב עַל-גַּבֵּי כְתָב;

ר' עובדיה מברטנורא

(ה) **במשקין.** שמשחירין, כמו מי תותים וכיוצא בהן: **במי פירות.** של כל שאר פירות: **באבק דרכים.** כגון ששרט באצבעו צורת אותיות על החול והאבק שבדרכים: **באבק סופרים.** עפרורית של קסת הסופר: **לאחר ידו.** על גב ידו, שאחז הקולמוס באצבעותיו והפך ידו וכתב: **ובמרפקו.** הפרק האמצעי שבזרוע: **אות אחת סמוך לכתב.** אצל אות כתובה זיווג לה אחת והשלימה לשתים: **כתב על גבי כתב.** העביר קולמוס על אותיות הכתובים כבר וחדשם:

יד אברהם

5.

בְּמַשְׁקִין, — [If] *one wrote with liquids,*

I.e., if one wrote with mulberry juice or some other liquid substance which produces a black effect (*Rav; Rashi*).

Others explain this as one who dips his finger into a liquid which has spilled on a table and forms letters on the table (*Or Zarua*, vol. 2, p. 32; see *Beis Yosef* 340 and *Perishah* ad loc.).

בְּמֵי פֵרוֹת, — *with fruit juices,*

I.e., if he wrote with juices of other fruits *Rav; Rashi*).

Tiferes Yisrael explains that *liquids* refers to extracts of fruits whose juices are usually extracted (such as grapes) whereas *fruit juices* refers to the extracts of fruits not normally made into juice (such as strawberries).

בַּאֲבַק דְּרָכִים, — *in road dust,*

I.e., if one formed letters in the dust of the road (*Rav; Rashi*), or on some other surface upon which the dust had settled (*Tif. Yis.*).

Others explain that he wrote *with* road dust, i.e., with road dust that became wet and formed mud (*Rashi*).

בַּאֲבַק הַסּוֹפְרִים, — *in scribes' dust,*

I.e., in the dry residue found at the bottom of the inkwell (*Rav; Rashi*).

Alternatively, when a scribe makes ink, he pulverizes the ingredients and while doing so, dust flies and settles on the parchment he is using. If someone forms letters in this dust, he is exempt from a sin offering (*Aruch*).

Shenos Eliyahu explains the entire mishnah as referring to the materials with which one writes, not the object upon which one writes. Thus the explanation here would be to forming letters *with* scribes' powder (rather than *in* scribes' powder).

וּבְכָל דָּבָר שֶׁאֵינוֹ מִתְקַיֵּם, — *or with anything that does not endure,*

Similarly, if one wrote with ink on something upon which the ink cannot endure, e.g., on vegetables and the like, he is exempt. One is liable only for *writing with an enduring ink on an enduring object (*Meiri; Rambam, Hil. Shabbos* 11:16, from *Yerushalmi* 12:4).

5. [If] one wrote with liquids, with fruit juices, in road dust, in scribes' dust, or with anything that does not endure, he is exempt.

[If one wrote] with the back of his hand, with his foot, with his mouth, or with his elbow; [if] one wrote one letter alongside a written letter; [if] one wrote over [other] writing;

YAD AVRAHAM

פָּטוּר. — *he is exempt.*
I.e., he is exempt from a sin offering. It is, however, Rabbinically prohibited to write with one's finger in liquids spilled on the table or in ashes (*Shulchan Aruch* 340:4).
To form imaginary letters in the air or on a dry table is permissible, however, since no mark is made (*Turei Zahav*, ibid. 3).

◆§ Writing in an Unusual Manner

We have previously learned (10:3) that if one carries an object from one domain to another in an unusual manner (different from the manner in which it is usually done) he is exempt from a sin offering (though it is still prohibited Rabbinically). The same ruling applies to all other types of work. The mishnah proceeds to delineate some unusual manners of writing which are exempted on the Sabbath.

לְאַחַר יָדוֹ, — [*If one wrote*] *with the back of his hand,*
I.e., if one held the pen with the point toward him, and then turned his hand around and wrote (*Rav; Rashi; Tif. Yis.*).

בְּרַגְלוֹ, בְּפִיו, וּבְמַרְפְּקוֹ; — *with his foot, with his mouth, or with his elbow;*
[I.e., if one held the pen with his toes, or in his mouth, or with his elbow and wrote.]

כָּתַב אוֹת אַחַת סָמוּךְ לִכְתָב; — [*if*] *one wrote one letter alongside a written letter;*
If a letter had been written before the Sabbath, and one wrote a second letter alongside it on the Sabbath, thereby completing a word (*Tif. Yis.*).
Despite the fact that his writing resulted in a complete word, he is exempt because he did not perform on the Sabbath itself the minimum amount of writing required for liability.
[This mishnah does not conform to the opinion of R' Eliezer stated later (13:1) who holds that one is liable for the completion of a task even where one did not perform the usually required minimum amount of activity (*Gem.* 104b). The halachah is in accordance with the view of our mishnah.]

כָּתַב עַל-גַּבֵּי כְתָב, — [*if*] *one wrote over* [*other*] *writing;*
I.e., if one wrote two letters, superimposing them over two letters that were already there, thereby reinforcing them (*Rav; Rashi; Tif. Yis.*).
[Since he did not add anything with his writing, this is not considered *writing.*]

שבת
יב/ה

נִתְכַּוֵּן לִכְתּוֹב חֵי"ת וְכָתַב שְׁנֵי זַיְינִ"ן; אֶחָד בָּאָרֶץ וְאֶחָד בַּקּוֹרָה; כָּתַב עַל שְׁנֵי כָתְלֵי הַבַּיִת, עַל שְׁנֵי דַפֵּי פִנְקָס, וְאֵין נֶהְגִּין זֶה עִם זֶה, פָּטוּר.

כָּתַב אוֹת אַחַת נוֹטָרִיקוֹן, רַבִּי יְהוֹשֻׁעַ

ר' עובדיה מברטנורא

וכתב שני זייני"ן. שלא נראה לגג של חי"ת אלא שני הרגלים נראה כאילו הס שני זייני"ן: **על שני כותלי הבית.** שאינן במקצוע. **על שני דפי פנקס.** שעשויין עמודים עמודים, כתב אות אחת בעמוד זה ואות אחת בעמוד זה, ואינו יכול לקרבן אלא אם כן יחתוך מה שמפסיק ביניהן. ותנא ברישא כותלי הבית המרוחקים זה מזה והדר תני דפי פנקס, ולא זו אף זו קתני: **אות אחת על שם נוטריקון.** שעושה סימן נקודה עליה ומבינים מאותה האות תיבה שלימה כגון קו"ף קרבן, מ"ס מעשר, תי"ו תרומה:

יד אברהם

נִתְכַּוֵּן לִכְתּוֹב חֵי"ת — [if] one intended to write a ח,

A ח written in the Assyrian[1] script (the script used in *sifrei Torah, tefillin,* and *mezuzos*) is composed of two ז's joined on the top by a pointy roof. The mishnah speaks of one who intended to write a ח, i.e., to write two ז's and to connect them.

וְכָתַב שְׁנֵי זַיְינִ"ן — but wrote two ז's;

I.e., he failed to complete the roof that joins the two ז's into a ח (*Rav; Rashi; Tif. Yis.*).

[Thus unintentionally writing two letters while intending to write only one. For this reason he is exempt.]

אֶחָד בָּאָרֶץ וְאֶחָד בַּקּוֹרָה — [if one wrote] one [letter] on the ground and one [letter] on a beam;

I.e., if he wrote one letter on the floor and one letter on a beam of the ceiling, making it impossible to read them together (*Tif. Yis.*).

כָּתַב עַל שְׁנֵי כָתְלֵי הַבַּיִת, — [or if] one wrote on two walls of the house,

I.e., if one wrote on two walls that are not adjoining each other (*Rav;*

---

1. כְּתָב אַשּׁוּרִי, *Asshuri script,* refers to Hebrew written in Assyrian characters. The Torah was originally written in ancient Hebrew script like that found on ancient monuments and coins. In the time of King Belshazzar of Babylon, a hand wrote on the wall in a script which no one present could read (*Daniel* 5:7, 8). By conveying his prophecy in this manner, God indicated that there was to be a new holy script to be used for writing Scripture. Ezra wrote the Torah in this new script and called it כְּתָב הַנִּשְׁתְּוָן, *the script that was changed* (*Ezra* 4:7). This script is used to this very day for Torah scrolls, Prophets, Megillos, *tefillin,* and *mezuzos* (*Rashi* to *Sanhedrin* 22a).

An alternative explanation of the name of this script is that כְּתָב אַשּׁוּרִי, *Asshuri script,* means that script that is the most מְאוּשָׁר, *praiseworthy,* of all scripts; additionally, it was brought to *Eretz Yisrael* via Assyria (*Yerushalmi*). According to *Piskei HaTosafos* (23) this honor of calling the Torah script אַשּׁוּרִי, *Asshuri,* was accorded Asshur when he went forth from the land of Shinar and left his children behind, for they were rebelling against God by following Nimrod (see *Rashi* to *Gen.* 10:11).

12
5
[if] one intended to write a ח, but wrote two ז's; [if one wrote] one [letter] on the ground and one [letter] on a beam; [or if] one wrote on two walls of the house, or on two pages of a ledger, that cannot be read together, he is exempt.

[If] one wrote one letter as an abbreviation, R'

YAD AVRAHAM

Rashi; Tif. Yis.).

This may also include writing on two outside walls of a house even where the walls adjoin. Since the two walls face away from each other the two letters cannot be read together (Shenos Eliyahu).

עַל שְׁנֵי דַפֵּי פִנְקָס, — or on two pages of a ledger,

The mishnah refers here to a ledger arranged in columns in such fashion that a letter written in the middle of one column cannot be read together with a letter written in the middle of another column. Since they cannot be read together, one is not liable (as was explained in mishnah 4).

[Where the two letters can be brought together (and therefore read together) one is liable, even without actually juxtaposing them (Gem. 104b). According to Rashi this is so only when they can be brought together without altering the surface upon which they are written (e.g., where the two letters are written on two separate pieces of paper). Where one must alter the surface in order to bring the two letters together (e.g., where the two letters are not on one piece of paper and one must either cut away the intervening space or fold the page), one is not liable. Maggid Mishneh explains that Rambam (Hil. Shabbos 11:12) holds liable even where one must fold the paper in order to bring together the two letters. If, however, the surface cannot be folded and the letters can only be brought together by first cutting out the letters, then Rambam agrees with Rashi that he is not liable. (See

Shaar HaTziyun 340:42).]

וְאֵין נֶהְגִּין זֶה עִם זֶה, — that cannot be read together,

[As explained above, since they are written in two columns, they cannot be read together.]

פָּטוּר. — he is exempt.

[In all the preceding cases, he is exempt, in each case for its own particular reason.]

כָּתַב אוֹת אַחַת נוֹטָרִיקוֹן, — [If] one wrote one letter as an abbreviation,

I.e., he wrote one letter followed by a period or an apostrophe to indicate that it stands for an entire word (Rashi; Rav). [It was customary to mark vessels to indicate the halachic status of their contents or of the vessels themselves. A vessel could be marked 'ת for תְּרוּמָה, terumah, 'מ for מַעֲשֵׂר, maaser, or 'ד for דְּמַאי, demai [see 2:7]. When gentile rulers prohibited the observance of mitzvos, vessels were marked with the initials of these words to conceal the fact that Jews were observing the mitzvos. Similarly, abbreviations were used by the inhabitants of other places, too, for various reasons (Rav).]

The word נוֹטָרִיקוֹן, according to Aruch, denotes initials. According to Tishbi, however, it denotes any short form of writing, such as shorthand. It is derived from the Latin, notarius, a secretary. See Raglei Mevasser. According to Tos. Yom Tov, the two opinions coincide.

[303] THE MISHNAH/SHABBOS — Chapter Twelve: Haboneh

שבת יב/ו

בֶּן בְּתֵירָא מְחַיֵּב, וַחֲכָמִים פּוֹטְרִין.

[ו] **הַכּוֹתֵב** שְׁתֵּי אוֹתִיּוֹת בִּשְׁתֵּי הֶעְלֵמוֹת, אַחַת שַׁחֲרִית וְאַחַת בֵּין הָעַרְבַּיִם,

---
ר' עובדיה מברטנורא

רבי יהושע בן בתירא אומר חייב. כיון שהכל מבינים מאותה האות תיבה שלימה, כאילו כתב אותיות של כל התיבה. **וחכמים פוטרין.** שהרי לא כתב שתי אותיות. והלכה כחכמים: (ו) **בשתי העלמות.** לאחר שכתב אות אחת בשוגג נודע לו שטעה, וחזר ונתעלם ממנו ושגג וכתב אות שניה בלבד: **אחת בשחרית ואחת בין הערבים.** כיון דהוי ליה שהות בינתיים כדי לידע הוה ליה כשתי העלמות:

יד אברהם

וַחֲכָמִים פּוֹטְרִין — But the Sages exempt [him].

Although a complete word is understood from this initial, he nevertheless wrote but one letter. The halachah is in accordance with the Sages (Rav).

רַבִּי יְהוֹשֻׁעַ בֶּן בְּתֵירָא מְחַיֵּב, — R' Yehoshua ben Beseira holds [him] liable.

Since a complete word is understood from this initial, it is as though he wrote a complete word (Rav; Tif. Yis.).

6.

~§ Forgetting, Transgressing, Becoming Aware

We have learned many times throughout this tractate that if someone desecrates the Sabbath inadvertently, either because he forgot that it was the Sabbath day or because he forgot that a particular type of word was prohibited, he is required to bring a sin offering to atone for his transgression. If one inadvertently transgresses one of the Sabbath work prohibitions several times without realizing that he has sinned, although he is liable for each individual transgression, he is obligated to bring only one sin offering upon becoming aware of his mistake (see 7:1). This is because the actual obligation to bring a sin offering is not incurred at the time one transgresses the sin but rather at the time that one becomes *aware* of his transgression. Each transgression may make one liable for a sin offering but that liability is only a *potential* obligation. The *actual* obligation takes place at the moment of awareness. Consequently, one sin offering may atone for several transgressions (and liabilities) as long as those transgressions all took place before the legal *obligation* to bring a sin offering was incurred.

It therefore follows that there are three steps to becoming obligated to bring a sin offering:

(a) *Forgetting* (either the Sabbath day or the specific prohibition), this makes the ensuing transgression *inadvertent*;

(b) *Transgressing*, this establishes *liability* for a sin offering, no actual legal obligation, however, exists at this point;

(c) *Becoming aware*, this creates the actual *obligation* to bring a sin offering. Several *liabilities* may be included in one sin offering as long as the *obligation* for all of them is incurred at on time.

Once the obligation is incurred, any new liabilities (if one forgot a sec-

12 6 Yehoshua ben Beseira holds [him] liable. But the Sages exempt [him].

6. One who writes two letters in two periods of forgetfulness, one in the morning and one in the after-

YAD AVRAHAM

ond time and thereby committed further transgressions) necessitate a second sin offering. The obligation for this second sin offering will take effect the moment that he becomes aware of his second lapse of memory and will include all liabilities incurred during this second period of forgetfulness. In this manner, one may actually be obligated to bring several sin offerings depending on and equal to the number of times one forgot, transgressed and remembered.

A practical application of this rule is if one forgets that it is the Sabbath and writes an entire essay. Though he may have written many hundreds of letters, he is liable for only one sin offering, since they were written as a result of one lapse of memory. One, however, who writes just two letters and then remembers that it is the Sabbath, and then forgetting a second time writes another two letters, is liable for two sin offerings. Though he has written a total of only four letters, he must bring two sin offerings since the second writing occurs after he has already incurred the obligation for the first sin offering. This ruling is universally accepted.

If one committed a partial transgression, however, reminded himself of his transgression, subsequently forgot again and committed the second part of the transgression, that awareness in between did not obligate him to bring a sin offering since he had committed but a partial transgression. We therefore find a dispute between the *Tannaim* whether such awareness divides the *melachah* into two halves, which are not combined to make him liable for a sin offering, or whether this awareness has no bearing whatsoever.

הַכּוֹתֵב שְׁתֵּי אוֹתִיּוֹת בִּשְׁתֵּי הֶעְלֵמוֹת, — *One who writes two letters in two periods of forgetfulness,*

I.e., if after writing one letter, one became aware of his sin and subsequently forgot again and wrote a second letter alongside the first (*Rav*; *Tif. Yis.*).

[As explained above (mishnah 4) the minimum amount of *writing required for liability is two letters.]

אַחַת שַׁחֲרִית וְאַחַת בֵּין הָעַרְבַּיִם, — *one in the morning and one in the afternoon,*

I.e., one letter was written in the morning during one period of forgetfulness, and a second letter was written in the afternoon during a second period of forgetfulness [i.e., having realized his mistake after writing the first letter, he subsequently forgot a second time and then wrote a second letter]. This phrase not only illustrates the first clause of the mishnah (*one who writes two letters in two periods of forgetfulness*) but also adds the idea that though the two acts of *writing were separated by a lapse of several hours, they nevertheless combine to make one liable, according to Rabban Gamliel (*Tos. Yom Tov* from *Tos.* 105a).

Rashi and *Rav* explain this phrase as expressing a new case and not as an illustration of the first clause. The

[305] THE MISHNAH/SHABBOS — Chapter Twelve: *Haboneh*

שבת
יב/ו

רַבָּן גַּמְלִיאֵל מְחַיֵּב, וַחֲכָמִים פּוֹטְרִין.

ר' עובדיה מברטנורא

רבן גמליאל מחייב. דסבר אין ידיעה לחצי שיעור לחלק שלא יצטרף עמו החצי האחר: **וחכמים פוטרין.** דסברי הידיעה שבין שני חצאי שיעור מחלקת ביניהם ולא נעשה כאילו היו שני חצאי שיעור בהעלם אחת. והלכה כחכמים:

יד אברהם

Tanna teaches us here that even if one is not cognizant of having realized his mistake between the writing of the first and second letters, if an interval of time long enough for a person to have learned of his mistake elapsed before writing the second letter, the halachah presumes that he had, in fact, realized his mistake in the interim. (See above 7:1, s.v. חַיָּב עַל־כָּל שַׁבָּת וְשַׁבָּת for fuller explanation of this rule.)

[Since in the case described in this mishnah this idea makes no practical difference according to Rabban Gamliel[1] (who holds that one is in any case liable for writing one letter in each of two periods of forgetfulness), this phrase is added to the mishnah to elucidate the opinion of the Sages. This is in contrast to the explanation of *Tosafos*, according to whom the phrase is added to elucidate the opinion of Rabban Gamliel.]

[*Tosafos* questions *Rashi's* explanation on the grounds that the *Tanna* should have specified the minimum time required for this presumption of realization (of one's mistake) to take effect, since this is the entire point of this phrase of the mishnah.

Furthermore, *Tosafos* quotes the *Gemara* (104b) as saying that a person may be liable even for writing one letter in each of two cities. Presumably, this would necessitate a lapse of several hours. Since, according to *Rashi*, the Sages consider him exempt where there has been a substantial lapse between the time he wrote the first letter and the time he wrote the second, and since the halachah is according to the view of the Sages, the *Gemara* should not declare him liable.]

Maginei Shlomo answers on behalf of *Rashi* that we do not consider the inadvertent transgressor as having become aware unless so much time has elapsed that he must surely have become aware of it. This presumption can only safely be made if he wrote one letter in the morning and one letter in the afternoon. Thus, the mishnah is actually giving the time limit necessary for

---

1. This ruling does have practical difference even according to the view of Rabban Gamliel, where one performs two complete *melachos*, one in the morning and one in the afternoon. Here, Rabban Gamliel would agree that the two liabilities cannot be atoned for by one sin offering due to the presumption of realization. (See prefatory note to this mishnah.) This, however, is not the case of our mishnah. The addition of this phrase, within the context of our mishnah, must therefore be for the purpose of elucidating the opinion of the Sages.

noon, Rabban Gamliel holds [him] liable. But the Sages exempt [him].

YAD AVRAHAM

this presumption to be made. [For further discussion of this dispute see *Tos. Yom Tov* and *Maginei Shlomo*.]

Tosefos Yom Tov, too, questions *Rashi's* understanding of the mishnah. He questions whether the mishnah deals with one who was aware that it was the Sabbath but forgot that *writing is proscribed, or with one who was aware that *writing is proscribed on the Sabbath but was unaware that it was the Sabbath. If he forgot that *writing is proscribed on the Sabbath, how are we sure that he reminded himself during the interval between morning and afternoon? We learned above (7:1) that even if a whole week elapsed, we are not assured that he became aware that he sinned unless he studied the laws of the Sabbath. If he was unaware that it was the Sabbath, we are sure that he became aware of it only after six days, again as is implied by that mishnah. After the short lapse of time from morning to evening, there is no assurance that he discovered that it was the Sabbath.

Maginei Shlomo replies that the mishnah deals with one who knew that it was the Sabbath, but forgot that *writing is proscribed. Since he once knew of this prohibition, we are certain that he will remind himself during the lapse of time from morning to afternoon. The above mishnah (7:1), however, deals with one who never knew that *writing is forbidden on the Sabbath. We have, therefore, no assurance that he will become cognizant of this restriction unless he studies the laws of the Sabbath.

רַבָּן גַּמְלִיאֵל מְחַיֵּב. — *Rabban Gamliel holds [him] liable.*

Rabban Gamliel holds that becoming aware that one has committed less than the minimum amount of work required for a sin offering is not considered a true *awareness*, and does not, therefore, prevent the two half measures from combining to create one liability (as explained in prefatory note) (*Rav* from *Gem*.).

Rabban Gamliel bases his view on the verse (*Lev*. 4:28): אוֹ הוֹדַע אֵלָיו חַטָּאתוֹ, *Or his sin became known to him*, which Rabban Gamliel explains to mean, *if his sin offering became known to him* [the word חַטָּאת in the Torah is used to describe both the sin and the sin offering], denoting that only knowledge which makes one liable for a sin offering is considered significant. Knowledge of a half measure of a sin, however, since it in any case does not create liability, is not regarded as significant. It therefore does not prevent the two halves from combining to form a complete *melachah* and liability (*Tos. Yom Tov* from *Tos*.).

וַחֲכָמִים פּוֹטְרִין. — *But the Sages exempt [him].*

The Sages maintain that his awareness between the two half measures separates them and does not allow them to be counted as one liability, as explained in the prefatory note (*Rav* from *Gem*.).

פרק שלשה עשר
Chapter Thirteen

As mentioned above, the *Tanna*, from mishnah 7:2 and on, elaborates upon the *melachos* enumerated in 7:2 but in inverted order. Since the preceding chapter deals with *writing, we would expect this chapter to deal with the *melachos* involved in the preparation of the parchment for writing, which commence with *trapping a deer and terminate with *cutting the hide (25-31). Instead, it commences with *weaving and other *melachos* involved in the weaving process (13-19). *Tosefos Yom Tov* accounts for this deviation from the obvious order, in the following manner: The *Tanna* juxtaposes *weaving with *writing because of the striking similarity between the prescribed measurements of both *melachos*, viz. *writing two letters and *weaving two threads. Even R' Eliezer who requires weaving three threads for liability concurs with the *Tanna Kamma* in certain instances. He declares one liable for weaving two threads if they are thick, and therefore noticeable. According to others, R' Eliezer concurs in the case of thin threads since they adhere to one another and will not become separated.

Although *setting two heddles precedes *weaving, both in the process and in the mishnah (7:2), it is discussed here after *weaving. Since there is a dispute concerning the prescribed measurement of *weaving, and there is no dispute concerning the prescribed measurements of *setting two heddles, the latter is juxtaposed with *sewing and *tearing, whose measurements are similarly undisputed (*Tos. Yom Tov*).[1]

---

1. [For a more complete description of the weaving process as discussed in the Mishnah and Talmud see *The Melachos Pertaining to the Weaving Process* by Rabbi P. Bodner, and *Maaseh Oreg* by Dayan I. Gukovitzki.]

שבת
יג/א-ב

[א] **רַבִּי אֱלִיעֶזֶר** אוֹמֵר: הָאוֹרֵג שְׁלֹשָׁה חוּטִין בַּתְּחִלָּה, וְאֶחָד עַל הָאָרִיג, חַיָּב. וַחֲכָמִים אוֹמְרִים: בֵּין בַּתְּחִלָּה בֵּין בַּסּוֹף, שִׁעוּרוֹ שְׁנֵי חוּטִין.

[ב] **הָעוֹשֶׂה** שְׁנֵי בָתֵּי נִירִין בְּנִירִין, בְּקֵירוֹס;

ר׳ עובדיה מברטנורא

פרק שלשה עשר – רבי אליעזר אומר. (א) רבי אליעזר אומר האורג שלשה חוטין בתחלה. אם זו תחלת אריגתו של בגד אינו חייב עד שיארוג ג׳ חוטין, ואם מוסיף הוא על האריג שיעורו באחד דמלתרף עם השאר. ואין הלכה כרבי אליעזר: **(ב) שתי בתי נירין.** שנקח שני חוטין של שתי בניר שקורין ליל״ש: **בנירין.** מפרש בגמ׳ שמרכיב שני פעמים [כל] חוט של שתי בניר ובפעם השלישית מרכיבו על חוט המורכב על הקנה: **בקירוס.** יריעה ארוגה מסיב של דקל

יד אברהם

1.

רַבִּי אֱלִיעֶזֶר אוֹמֵר: הָאוֹרֵג שְׁלֹשָׁה חוּטִין בַּתְּחִלָּה, — *R' Eliezer says: One who weaves three threads at the beginning,*

I.e., if one commences to weave a new fabric on the Sabbath he is liable for weaving three threads (*Rav; Rashi*).

וְאֶחָד עַל הָאָרִיג, חַיָּב. — *or [adds] one thread to woven fabric, is liable.*

I.e., if one adds even one thread to a previously woven material he is liable (*Rav; Rambam, Comm.; Rashi*).

Since this thread is combined with already woven material it is of greater significance, and the one who wove it is therefore liable to a sin offering (*Rashi*).

It should be noted that 12:5, which *exempts* one for writing one letter alongside one already written, a case analogous to adding one thread to woven fabric, does not follow R' Eliezer's ruling here (*Tos. Yom Tov* from *Gem.* 104b).

וַחֲכָמִים אוֹמְרִים: בֵּין בַּתְּחִלָּה בֵּין בַּסּוֹף, שִׁעוּרוֹ שְׁנֵי חוּטִין. — *But the Sages say: Whether at the beginning or at the end, its amount is two threads.*

I.e., whether one starts to weave a new fabric or whether he adds to an already woven fabric, he is not liable unless he weaves two threads. The expression, "at the end," is not meant to denote the completion of the garment, for if he completes the garment he is liable for weaving even one thread. This is similar to completing a book by writing one letter, for which one is liable, as explained above (12:5) (*Tos. R' Akiva* from *Tos.* 105a).

The halachah is not in accordance with R' Eliezer (*Rav; Rambam, Comm., and Hil. Shabbos* 9:18).

2.

The next mishnah delineates the *melachah* of *setting two heddles*. This *melachah* is part of the weaving process. Its precise definition is, however, the

13
1-2

1. R' Eliezer says: One who weaves three threads at the beginning, or [adds] one thread to woven fabric, is liable. But the Sages say: Whether at the beginning or at the end, its amount is two threads.

2. One who sets two heddles of a home loom, [or] of a commercial loom; [and one who

YAD AVRAHAM

subject of very divergent views. [The translation *setting two heddles* follows *Rashi's* interpretation only.] This is further complicated by the fact that the act takes different forms in the different weaving processes described in this mishnah. To facilitate understanding, the commentary will first explain the entire mishnah according to *Rashi's* view, adding only those opinions which share *Rashi's* general explanation while differing in certain details. Then *Rambam's* explanation will be given.

הָעוֹשֶׂה שְׁנֵי בָתֵּי נִירִין בְּנִירִין, — *One who sets two heddles of a home loom*,

As explained in 7:2 (see "The Process of Weaving") the warp threads are inserted through two frames, known as harnesses. These harnesses consist of heddles, i.e., threads with rings or loops in their middle. All the odd threads are threaded first through rings or loops of the first harness, allowing them to be raised or lowered as the harness is raised or lowered. Then they pass between the threads of the second harness. The even threads are first drawn between the threads of the first harness frame and subsequently, through the rings or loops of the second harness frame. Then they go through a comblike tool, known as a reed. Its purpose is to press the woven fabric together after the weft has gone through it. The mishnah states that if one introduces two warp threads through the two frames and the reed he is liable (*Rashi* 105a according to emendation of *Chazon Ish* in *Keilim* section 26, no. 3).

Others explain that the mishnah is not discussing the threading of the rings but rather the making of the rings themselves on the heddles. Thus, the mishnah reads, *If one makes two rings in the heddles* (*Tif. Yis.* from *Lechem Mishneh*, *Hil. Shabbos* 9:16; see also *Kalkalas Shabbos* 18).

בְּקֵירוֹס; — *[or] of a commercial loom;*

The difference between this case and the previous one is that נִירִין refers to a housewife's loom, in which the two heddles were manipulated by hand whereas this case refers to a commercial loom, in which the two heddles were manipulated by pedals. *Tiferes Yisrael* explains this latter case as inserting the threads through the reed. (According to him, the former case refers to making the rings of the heddles, as explained above.)

Rav, though following *Rashi* in the translation of נִירִין, does not distinguish between home and commercial looms. He translates קֵירוֹס in the same manner as *Rambam*. See below.

שבת
יג/ג

בְּנָפָה, בִּכְבָרָה, וּבְסַל, חַיָּב. וְהַתּוֹפֵר שְׁתֵּי תְפִירוֹת, וְהַקּוֹרֵעַ עַל מְנָת לִתְפֹּר שְׁתֵּי תְפִירוֹת.

[ג] הַקּוֹרֵעַ בַּחֲמָתוֹ, וְעַל מֵתוֹ, וְכָל הַמְקַלְקְלִין, פְּטוּרִין. וְהַמְקַלְקֵל

ר' עובדיה מברטנורא

(ג) הקורע על מתו וכו'. במת שאינו חייב לקרוע עליו הוא דהוי מקלקל ופטור, אבל על מת שחייב לקרוע עליו, מתקן הוא וחייב: ובחמתו וכל המקלקלים פטורין. הא מתניתין אדחיא לה, והלכה שהקורע בחמתו חייב, שאף על פי שמקלקל הוא אצל הבגד, מתקן הוא אצל יצרו ודעתו מתישבת עליו בכך:

יד אברהם

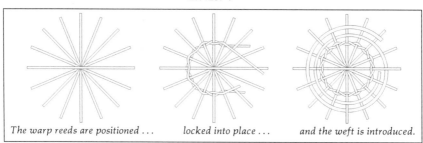

The warp reeds are positioned ...   locked into place ...   and the weft is introduced.

בְּנָפָה, בִּכְבָרָה, וּבְסַל, — [and one who positions the warp reeds of] a sifter, a sieve, or a basket,

Rashi explains how the melachah of *setting two heddles is applicable to reed sifters, sieves and baskets. After the warp reeds are laid out to form the "skeleton" of the object to be woven, the weaver loops two reeds around each reed of the warp, thus locking that reed into position [see diagram above].

Since the function of this looping is to position the warp reeds for weaving, twisting the loops serves a purpose similar to inserting the warp threads into the heddles. He is, therefore, liable for performing a toladah of *setting two heddles (Rashi).

חַיָּב. — is liable.

[I.e., in all those cases he is liable to a sin offering for performing a toladah of *setting two heddles.]

וְהַתּוֹפֵר שְׁתֵּי תְפִירוֹת, וְהַקּוֹרֵעַ עַל מְנָת לִתְפֹּר שְׁתֵּי תְפִירוֹת. — One who sews two stitches, and one who tears in order to sew two stitches.

[I.e., is liable.]

Though these two melachos have already been listed above (7:2), they are repeated here in order to introduce the following mishnah, which states instances in which one is exempt for tearing (Tos. Yom Tov from Gem. 105a).

⋅⋅§ **The Mishnah According to Rambam**

[Though there are several opinions as to the proper interpretation of Rambam's view, we follow here the one given by Mirkeves HaMishneh on Rambam, Hil. Shabbos 9:16.]

13
3 positions the warp reeds of] a sifter, a sieve, or a basket, is liable. One who sews two stitches, and one who tears in order to sew two stitches.

3. One who tears in his anger, or for his dead, and all who act destructively, are exempt. But one

YAD AVRAHAM

הָעוֹשֶׂה שְׁנֵי בָתֵּי נִירִין בְּנִירִין, — *One who makes two boxes in a netting,*

This *melachah* refers to the weaving of lace or net-type materials. Unlike woven material, which is woven without spaces between the threads, lace and netting are created by weaving individual boxes or spaces in the fabric. These boxes are the בָתֵּי נִירִין referred to by the mishnah. If one makes two such boxes, he is liable.

Rambam considers weaving of net-like material so different from ordinary weaving that it cannot be considered אֲרִיגָה. Since making nets was required for the construction of the *Mishkan* (for catching the *chilazon* fish to make the *techeiles* dye), it is a separate *melachah*. Each box of the net is called a בַּיִת, literally *a house,* made of

נִירִין, *string,* hence the name בָתֵּי נִירִין.

בְּקִירוֹס, — *or [two weft threads] in a cloth made of palm fiber,*

Fabric of palm fiber was used for sifting. It was woven in the manner in which sieves and baskets are woven (see diagram, p. 296).

בְּנָפָה, בִּכְבָרָה, וּבְסַל, — *a sifter, a sieve or a basket,*

This type of weaving is similar to weaving nets and lace since there are spaces between the weave. It is, therefore, regarded as a *toladah* of making two boxes in a netting.

חַיָּב. — *is liable.*

[I.e. in all these cases, he is liable to a sin offering for performing a *toladah* of making two boxes in a netting.]

3.

הַקּוֹרֵעַ בַּחֲמָתוֹ, — *One who tears in his anger,*

I.e., if one tears his garments in a fit of rage (*Rambam, Comm.* and *Hil. Shabbos* 10:10).

Others explain the mishnah as referring to one who tears his garments in order to instill fear in the members of his household (*Rashi, Tos.* according to conclusion of *Gem.*).

וְעַל מֵתוֹ, — *or for his dead,*

I.e., if one rends his garments as a sign of mourning for his dead, he is exempt from a sin offering since this is considered destructive.

וְכָל הַמְקַלְקְלִין, — *and all who act destructively,*

[I.e., all persons who perform labor on the Sabbath with the sole intention of destroying an object without at the same time effecting any improvement in it.]

פְּטוּרִין. — *are exempt.*

I.e., they are exempt from a sin offering (see General Introduction, p. 9).

Though tearing in anger is an objectively destructive act, it does offer the concomitant benefit of soothing the person's anger. Whether one may be held liable for the concomitantly

שבת
יג/ג

עַל־מְנָת לְתַקֵּן, שִׁעוּרוֹ כִּמְתַקֵּן.

יד אברהם

constructive aspect of his act depends on the issue of *a labor not done for its defined purpose* [see General Introduction, p. 9]. According to R' Yehudah, who considers one liable for such an act, though it fulfills only a purpose other than its designated one and one not of benefit to the object of that activity (see examples in General Introduction), one would be liable here, too, since the secondary benefit of soothing anger is a constructive one. This causes us to view the act, taken as a whole, as constructive. Consequently, the exemption of the mishnah is in disagreement with the opinion of R' Yehudah and must be seen as expressing the view of R' Shimon, who exempts *a labor not done for its defined purpose* (*Rambam, Comm.*). Those who rule in accord with R' Yehudah's opinion therefore rule that one who tears in anger is liable, in contrast to the view of the mishnah. This is the ruling of *Rav* and *Rambam* (*Hil. Shabbos* 10:10). However, as pointed out in 2:5, the great majority of authorities rule in accord with R' Shimon. Therefore, according to most opinions, the exemption expressed in this mishnah is indeed the halachah (*Tos. R' Akiva*). [Even according to these opinions, tearing is still Rabbinically prohibited.]

As explained above, the exemption for rending one's garments in mourning is also because the act is a destructive one. However, even if the act were deemed constructive, it would still seem to qualify as a *labor not performed for its defined purpose*. Liability for this act would again depend on one's opinion in that controversy, as in the case of one who tears in anger. There are, therefore, two possible sources of exemption for rending in mourning.

The *Gemara* 105b states that rending in mourning is deemed a destructive act, however, only for a relative *other* than those enumerated in *Lev.* 21:23 (viz., wife, father, mother, son, daughter, brother, and sister), for whom even a *Kohen* is required to contaminate himself and to participate in their burial. For these relatives, however, there are mandated mourning observances and rending of garments (see *Moed Katan* 3:7). Since the rending of garments for these relatives is obligatory, doing so on the Sabbath is regarded as doing constructive work. Liability for this act is therefore dependent solely on the issue of a *labor not performed for its defined purpose* [this will be further explained below] (*Rav* from *Gem.*).

This applies as well to rending the garments in mourning for a Torah scholar, a very pious person or for anyone at whose demise one is present, since one is obligated to rend his garments for these people (*Gem.*, ibid.). [As to the rules and customs pertaining to this, see *Shulchan Aruch, Yoreh Deah* 340:5-7 and commentaries there.]

Rambam (*Comm.* and *Hil. Shabbos* 10:10) adds that rending the garments for one at whose death he is required to do so relieves his mind and eases his anguish. The fact that his anguish is diminished as a result of this action makes it a constructive action, and he is accordingly liable.[1]

Whether this act is considered construc-

---

1. *Tos. Yom Tov* questions that if the reason for liability is the fact that he soothes his anger, why is he liable only for tearing his clothes for those upon whose death he is obliged to tear his clothes, and not for those for whom he is not obliged to do so? He replies that the Rabbis perceived that a person does not harbor strong feelings except on the

**13 who destroys in order to repair, his [minimum] mea-
3   sure [for liability] is the same as for repairs.**

YAD AVRAHAM

tive by reason of fulfillment of a Rabbinic obligation or of relief of one's anguish it would still nevertheless, as explained above, seem to be a *labor not performed for its defined purpose* since the rending of the garment is of no improvement to the garment itself. According to R' Shimon, one is therefore exempt, no matter for which relative one is rending his garments. Indeed, *Rashi* (105b) states that the mishnah exempts the rending of garments for all relatives from liability and here too follows only the opinion of R' Shimon.

Tosafos 105b, however, contends that since a mourner may not wear an untorn garment, tearing the garment is indeed an improvement to the garment itself, since it renders it Rabbinically fit to be worn.[1]

Accordingly, the mishnah, according to all opinions, must be referring to a death for which one is not obligated to rend his garments. Though the previous case of the mishnah follows only the opinion of R' Shimon, this case so qualified is true according to all opinions.

[Since this improvement is accomplished only by rending when it is obligatory, one is exempt in all other cases, even if he is responsible for the burial of the deceased.]

וְהַמְקַלְקֵל עַל־מְנָת לְתַקֵן, — *But one who destroys in order to repair,*

Such as erasing in order to write something else in the same space (*Tif. Yis.*).

שִׁעוּרוֹ כִּמְתַקֵן. — *his [minimum] measure [for liability] is the same as for repairs.*

I.e., he is liable for erasing enough script to make space to write two letters (the minimum for liability for *writing*) (*Tif. Yis.*).

[The same is true in the case of tearing. If one tears in order to be able to restitch the garment, he is liable for making a tear long enough to require two stitches.]

4.

The *Tanna* proceeds to delineate the minimum amount required for the remaining *melachos* performed in the preparation of wool. They are listed above (7:2) as *whitening, *combing, *dyeing, and *spinning. He then returns to the details of *weaving. Although he has previously been discussing *weaving, he interrupts with the other *melachos*, because of the similarity of their minimum; namely, double that of *weaving (*Tos. Yom Tov*).

demise of the seven kinsmen enumerated in Scripture.

He also points out that the fulfillment of a legal obligation, in *Rambam's* opinion, is an insufficient reason to consider a basically destructive act as a constructive one. Only if the destructive act has practical constructive characteristics, such as relieving his anguish, can it be considered a constructive act.

1. [This is according to the reading of *Maharshal*. According to *Tosefos Yom Tov's* reading, *Tosafos'* reasoning is that since wearing a rent garment diminishes a mourner's anguish, the rending of the garment improves its quality vis-à-vis the mourner. There is further discussion of the correct reading of the *Tosafos* by *Beis David* and *Shoshanim LeDavid.*]

שבת
יג/ד-ה

[ד] **שִׁעוּר** הַמְלַבֵּן, וְהַמְנַפֵּץ, וְהַצּוֹבֵעַ, וְהַטּוֹוֶה, כִּמְלֹא רֹחַב הַסִּיט כָּפוּל. וְהָאוֹרֵג שְׁנֵי חוּטִין, שִׁעוּרוֹ כִּמְלֹא הַסִּיט.

[ה] **רַבִּי יְהוּדָה** אוֹמֵר: הַצָּד צִפּוֹר לַמִּגְדָּל, וּצְבִי לַבַּיִת,

---

ר' עובדיה מברטנורא

(ד) **המלבן**. את הצמר, והמנפצו והצובעו והטווהו ממנו, שהן כולן אבות מלאכות, שיעורן כדי שיטוה מטווהו הצמר חוט ארוך כמלא רוחב הסיט כפול. והסיט הוא כדי הפסק שיש בין אמה לאצבע כל מה שיוכל אדם להרחיבו, וכשיעור הריוח הזה שתי פעמים הוא הסיט כפול. וריוח שבין גודל לאצבע פעם אחת הוא ג"כ כמלא רוחב הסיט כפול, מפני שיש בו כפלים כמותו שיש בין אמה לאצבע: **האורג שני חוטין**. שיעורן ברוחב הבגד כמלא הסיט, שאף על פי שלא ארגן על פני כל רוחב הבגד חייב: (ה) **הצד צפור**. עד שהכניסו למגדל של עץ, ארמריא"ו בלע"ז, חייב, שזו הוא צידתו, אבל אם הכניסו לבית אינו נצוד בכך: **וצבי**. נצוד משהכניסו לבית ונעל בפניו, אבל אם הכניסו לגינה או לחצר אין זו צידה:

יד אברהם

שִׁעוּר הַמְלַבֵּן, וְהַמְנַפֵּץ, וְהַצּוֹבֵעַ, וְהַטּוֹוֶה, — *The [minimum] measure [for liability] of one who whitens, combs, dyes, or spins,*

I.e., the prescribed minimum amount required for liability for one who performs one of these previously listed (7:2) *melachos* (*Rav*; *Rashi*).

כִּמְלֹא רֹחַב הַסִּיט כָּפוּל. — *is double the width of a* sit.

A *sit* is the maximum space between the index finger and the middle finger when they are stretched apart. Double this space is equal to the space between the thumb and the index finger. If one whitens, combs, dyes, or spins enough wool for a thread of this length, he is liable for a sin offering (*Rav*; *Rashi*).

Rambam (*Comm.*) differentiates between a *sit* and the "width of a *sit*," explaining the width of a *sit* as the maximum space between the thumb and the index finger (double *Rashi's* amount) and a *sit* as the space between the index finger and the middle finger when open but not stretched. This is half the stretched size (and therefore one-half *Rashi's* amount) (see *Maggid Mishneh, Hil. Shabbos* 9:7). *Rambam* additionally equates double the width of a *sit* with four handbreadths (*Hil. Shabbos* 9:12).

וְהָאוֹרֵג שְׁנֵי חוּטִין, — *And one who weaves two threads,*

I.e., if he inserts two weft threads into the warp (*Tif. Yis.*).

שִׁעוּרוֹ כִּמְלֹא הַסִּיט. — *his [minimum] measure [for liability] is a full* sit.

I.e., he is liable for *weaving these two weft threads through the warp for the length of a *sit*, whatever the width of the fabric (*Rav*; *Rashi*). As explained above, *Rashi* and *Rav* do not distinguish between the phrases *a full sit*, and *the width of a sit*, whereas *Rambam* considers the former to be one fourth the size of the latter. In *Hilchos Shabbos* 9:18 he gives the value of a full *sit* as the thickness of two fingers.

4. The [minimum] measure [for liability] of one who whitens, combs, dyes, or spins, is double the width of a *sit*. And one who weaves two threads, his [minimum] measure [for liability] is a full *sit*.

5. R' Yehudah says: One who traps a bird [by driving it] into a closet, or a deer into a house, is liable. But the Sages say: [One is liable for driving] a bird into a closet, or a deer into a house,

YAD AVRAHAM

5.

The *Tanna* now delineates the laws of **trapping* on the Sabbath.

As explained in the preface to this chapter, the *melachos* required for the preparation of the skins should have followed the *melachah* of **writing* dealt with in the previous chapter. For the reasons mentioned there, the *Tanna* deviated from this order to elaborate on the *melachah* of **weaving*. Now that he has completed the laws of **weaving* and its related *melachos*, he returns to the previous order and elaborates on the *melachah* of **trapping*, before going on to elaborate on **tying* and **untying* (*Tos. Yom Tov*).

רַבִּי יְהוּדָה אוֹמֵר: הַצָּד צִפּוֹר לְמִגְדָּל, — *R' Yehudah says: One who traps a bird [by driving it] into a closet*,

The halachic definition of *trapped* means, as explained at the end of the mishnah, that the animal's freedom of movement has been reduced to the extent where it is accessible to a person who wishes to use it with little or no further effort. Obviously, the precise confines in which this limit is reached differ from species to species. Following this general rule, a bird in a closet is considered trapped. A bird in a house, however, where it has room to maneuver, is not considered trapped (*Rav; Rashi*).

The *Gemara* (106b) qualifies the mishnah as referring to a very small bird such as a sparrow (*Tif. Yis.*) which is adept at flitting from corner to corner (*Rashi* ibid.) to avoid people.[1]

וּצְבִי לְבַיִת, — *or a deer into a house*,

A deer is considered trapped when it is driven into a house and the door is closed. If it is driven into a garden or into a courtyard, it is not considered trapped (*Rav; Rashi*).

---

1. Others explain that a bird is not regarded as trapped when it is locked in a house because it can escape through the windows (*Rashi* on the mishnah) or cracks (*Meiri*). [According to *Rashi*, the mishnah is referring to a house whose windows are open.]

Since any bird can escape through a window, this seems to be inconsistent with the *Gemara*, which explains the mishnah as referring to a sparrow only (*Rashash*; cf. *Taz* 316:1 who deals with this question, and comments of *Pri Megadim* in *Mishbetzos Zahav*).

שבת
יג/ו

חַיָּב. וַחֲכָמִים אוֹמְרִים: צִפּוֹר לְמִגְדָּל, וּצְבִי לְבַיִת, וְלֶחָצֵר, וְלַבִּיבָרִין.
רַבָּן שִׁמְעוֹן בֶּן גַּמְלִיאֵל אוֹמֵר: לֹא כָל הַבִּיבָרִין שָׁוִין. זֶה הַכְּלָל: מְחֻסַּר צִידָה, פָּטוּר; וְשֶׁאֵינוֹ מְחֻסַּר צִידָה, חַיָּב.

[ו] **צְבִי** שֶׁנִּכְנַס לְבַיִת וְנָעַל אֶחָד בְּפָנָיו, חַיָּב. נָעֲלוּ שְׁנַיִם, פְּטוּרִין. לֹא יָכֹל אֶחָד לִנְעֹל, וְנָעֲלוּ שְׁנַיִם, חַיָּבִין. וְרַבִּי שִׁמְעוֹן פּוֹטֵר.

ר' עובדיה מברטנורא

ולביברין. קרפיפות המוקפים חומה שמכניסין שם חיות ונשמרים שם: **כל המחוסר צידה.** שקשה לתפשו שם, כגון שאינו מגיע לו בשחיה אחת שעוה לתפשו, והלכה כרשב"ג [דמפרש] למלתייהו דרבנן: (ו) **צבי שנכנס.** מלאוי לבית ונעל אחד בפניו, זו היא לידתו: **נעלו שנים פטורים.** דהוו להו שנים שעשאוה: **לא יבול אחד לנעול.** אורחיה הוא לנועלו בשנים והרי לכל אחד מלאכה דבלאו איהו לא מתעבדה: **ורבי שמעון פוטר.** ואין הלכה כרבי שמעון:

יד אברהם

חַיָּב. — *is liable.*
[I.e., he is liable for a sin offering for *trapping on the Sabbath.]*

וַחֲכָמִים אוֹמְרִים: צִפּוֹר לְמִגְדָּל — *But the Sages say: [One is liable for driving] a bird into a closet,*

[On this point there is no disagreement between the Sages and R' Yehudah.]

וּצְבִי לְבַיִת, וְלֶחָצֵר, וְלַבִּיבָרִין — *or a deer into a house, a courtyard, or a vivarium.*

[The Sages regard a deer as trapped if it is driven into a garden or a court, and the door is locked. They dispute R' Yehudah in the degree to which an animal must be immobilized to be considered trapped.]

In the mishnah appearing with the Gemara and in *Yerushalmi*: לְגִנָּה, *into a garden,* is substituted for לְבַיִת, *into a house.*

Others read: לְבַיִת, לְגִנָּה, וְלֶחָצֵר, *into a house, a garden, a courtyard (Rif; Rosh; Rambam).*

רַבָּן שִׁמְעוֹן בֶּן גַּמְלִיאֵל אוֹמֵר: לֹא כָל הַבִּיבָרִין שָׁוִין. — *Rabban Shimon ben Gamliel says: Not all vivaria are alike.*

[I.e., there are some large vivaria in which an animal is not considered trapped.]

זֶה הַכְּלָל: מְחֻסַּר צִידָה — *This is the rule: [If] it requires [further] trapping,*

I.e., if the enclosure is so large that the deer cannot be caught with a single lunge (*Rav* from *Gem.* 106b).

פָּטוּר — *one is exempt;*

[Since the animal requires further trapping, it cannot, at present, be regarded as trapped.]

וְשֶׁאֵינוֹ מְחֻסַּר צִידָה — *[if] it does not require [further] trapping,*

I.e., if the enclosure is so small that the animal can be caught with one lunge (*Rav* from *Gem.* 106b).

13
6

a courtyard, or a vivarium.

Rabban Shimon ben Gamliel says: Not all vivaria are alike. This is the rule: [If] it requires [further] trapping, one is exempt; [if] it does not require [further] trapping, one is liable.

6. If a deer entered a house and one locked [the door] in front of it, he is liable. If two [people] locked [the door], they are exempt. If one [person alone] could not lock [the door], and two locked it, they are [both] liable. R' Shimon, however, exempts [them].

YAD AVRAHAM

חַיָּב. — *one is liable.*

For *trapping. The halachah is in accordance with Rabban Shimon Ben Gamliel, since he does not differ with the Sages, but is merely explaining their statement[1] (*Rav; Rambam, Comm.*).

6.

צְבִי שֶׁנִּכְנַס לְבַיִת — *If a deer entered a house*

I.e., if it entered by itself (*Rav; Rashi*).

וְנָעַל אֶחָד בְּפָנָיו, חַיָּב. — *and one locked [the door] in front of it, he is liable.*

[I.e., after it entered, one locked the door, thus preventing the deer from escaping.]

Although he has not directly trapped it, he is regarded as having trapped it since by locking the door he prevents its escape (*Rav; Rashi*).

נָעֲלוּ שְׁנַיִם, — *If two [people] locked [the door],*

[I.e., if two locked the door when it was possible for one to do it alone.]

פְּטוּרִין. — *they are exempt.*

[The exemption of two people performing a labor that it is possible for one to perform has already been discussed above, 10:5.] It is, nevertheless, Rabbinically prohibited.

לֹא יָכֹל אֶחָד לִנְעֹל, וְנָעֲלוּ שְׁנַיִם, — *If one [person alone] could not lock [the door], and two locked it,*

[I.e., if the door was too heavy for one person to close without assistance.]

חַיָּבִין. — *they are [both] liable.*

Since it is normal for two people to lock such a door, it is considered as though each person performed the *melachah*, since without him it could not have been accomplished (*Rav; Rashi*).

וְרַבִּי שִׁמְעוֹן פּוֹטֵר. — *R' Shimon, however, exempts [them].*

R' Shimon exempts from liability any labor done by two people together even when two are necessary for that labor, as explained above 10:5 (*Rashi*). The halachah is not in accordance with R' Shimon (*Rav*).

Although this dispute has been

---

1. Although the language would indicate that he disagrees, there are numerous other instances of this sort, as discussed in *Bikkurim* 3:6 (*Tos. Yom Tov*).

שבת
יג/ז

[ז] יָשַׁב הָאֶחָד עַל הַפֶּתַח וְלֹא מִלְּאָהוּ, יָשַׁב הַשֵּׁנִי וּמִלְּאָהוּ, הַשֵּׁנִי חַיָּב. יָשַׁב הָרִאשׁוֹן עַל הַפֶּתַח וּמִלְּאָהוּ, וּבָא הַשֵּׁנִי וְיָשַׁב בְּצִדּוֹ, אַף־עַל־פִּי שֶׁעָמַד הָרִאשׁוֹן וְהָלַךְ לוֹ, הָרִאשׁוֹן חַיָּב וְהַשֵּׁנִי פָּטוּר. הָא לְמַה זֶּה דּוֹמֶה?

────────── ר' עובדיה מברטנורא ──────────

(ז) **השני חייב.** שהוא לד מותו: **הא למה זה דומה.** מאחר שנעוד ט"י ראשון:

יד אברהם

stated above with regard to *transferring* a loaf of bread from one domain to another, it is nevertheless repeated here as an introduction to the following mishnah. This also occurred in mishnah 2 of this chapter (*Tos. Yom Tov*).

Alternatively, the above mishnah teaches us that even though the loaf of bread could have been divided between the two perpetrators, with each of them carrying out the minimum amount required for liability, R' Shimon, nevertheless, exempts them. On the other hand, this mishnah teaches us that even though neither of the two could accomplish the *melachah* by himself, the Sages, nevertheless, declare them liable (*Tif. Yis.*; cf. *Melechas Shlomo* and *Shoshanim LeDavid* for other explanations).

7.

יָשַׁב הָאֶחָד עַל הַפֶּתַח — **If one [person] sat in the doorway**

[I.e., if after the deer entered the house one person sat down in the doorway.]

וְלֹא מִלְּאָהוּ, — **but did not [fully] block it,**

I.e., there was sufficient room left for the deer to escape (*Chidushei HaRan*).

יָשַׁב הַשֵּׁנִי וּמִלְּאָהוּ, — **[and then] a second [person] sat down and blocked it,**

[I.e., a second person sat down alongside the first and, by occupying the remaining space, blocked the doorway completely, thus preventing the deer from escaping.]

הַשֵּׁנִי חַיָּב. — **the second one is liable.**

The second one is liable because he effected the capture (*Rav; Rashi*). Were it not for him, the deer could still have escaped. Even though the first one assisted him in the capture by remaining in place, he is, nevertheless, exempt, since at the moment of capture his participation was completely passive (*Chidushei HaRan*).

יָשַׁב הָרִאשׁוֹן עַל הַפֶּתַח וּמִלְּאָהוּ, — **[If] the first [person] sat in the doorway and blocked it [completely],**

[Thereby capturing the deer without any assistance.]

וּבָא הַשֵּׁנִי וְיָשַׁב בְּצִדּוֹ, — **[then] the second [person] came and sat down alongside him,**

I.e., the second [person] sat in the doorway in such a way that he too blocked the passageway completely; e.g., the first person sat in the doorway facing the interior of the house, and then the second [person] sat down back to back with the first one, facing out. The second person, too, is thus completely blocking the doorway

משניות / שבת – פרק יג: רבי אליעזר

7. If one [person] sat in the doorway but did not [fully] block it, [and then] a second [person] sat down and blocked it, the second one is liable. [If] the first [person] sat in the doorway and blocked it [completely], then the second [person] came and sat down alongside him, even though the first [person] stood up and went away, the first [person] is liable and the second [person] is exempt. To what is this [case] analogous?

YAD AVRAHAM

(*Chemed Moshe* 316:3, according to *Tos. Yom Tov*).

אַף־עַל־פִּי שֶׁעָמַד הָרִאשׁוֹן וְהָלַךְ לוֹ, — *even though the first [person] stood up and went away,*

Thereby leaving the second one guarding the deer alone (*Tos. Yom Tov*).

הָרִאשׁוֹן חַיָּב — *the first [person] is liable*

[He is liable for effecting the original capture.]

וְהַשֵּׁנִי פָּטוּר. — *and the second [person] is exempt.*

Since when he sat down in the doorway the deer had already been trapped by the first one, he merely added to the security of the trap without, however, in any way participating in the act of *trapping itself. When the first one leaves, the second person, who is merely sitting still, is again not engaging in any act of *trapping. He is thus exempt (*Rav*). Furthermore, under these conditions the second person is *permitted* to sit there and to remain sitting after the departure of the first person, even if his intent is to prevent the escape of the deer (*Mishnah Berurah* 316:25). This is one of the three instances in this tractate where the mishnah states that one is exempt and means that it is permissible. Aside from these three, all exemptions stated in this tractate imply that the act is still Rabbinically prohibited (*Gem.* 107a).

This law applies only when the first one walks toward the interior of the house, thus not necessitating any movement on the part of the second one. If, however, the second person must make room for the first to get through, thus momentarily leaving space for the deer to escape, the second person, upon returning to his former position, is, in effect, trapping the deer and is therefore liable (*Tos. Yom* Tov).[1]

הָא לְמָה זֶה דוֹמֶה? — *To what is this [case] analogous?*

I.e., to what is this act of the second person, which intensified the security around an already trapped creature, analogous (*Rashi*).

---

1. Others contend that, since the deer was once trapped, it is considered as being in captivity, and one is no longer liable for trapping it. It is analogous to trapping beasts and birds in one's private domain, which 14:1 permits (*Magen Avraham* 316:11; *Beis David*).

Shoshanim LeDavid rebuts that 14:1 applies only to taking in hand a beast or bird already kept in an enclosure. In our case, however, when the second person moves over to allow the first one out, he is, in effect, releasing the deer. Thus, the second one is recapturing it. This is the view of most authorities (*Mishnah Berurah* 316:25; see also *Beur Halachah* there).

שבת
יג/ז

לְנוֹעֵל אֶת בֵּיתוֹ לְשָׁמְרוֹ, וְנִמְצָא צְבִי שָׁמוּר בְּתוֹכוֹ.

ר' עובדיה מברטנורא

לנועל את ביתו לשמרו. ולא לצוד: ונמצא צבי. שהוא ניצוד כבר שמור בתוכו, כך זה אף על פי שעמד ראשון אין זה אלא כשומרו לצבי שהיה לו מאתמול. והשני פטור האמור במתניתין, פטור ומותר:

יד אברהם

לְנוֹעֵל אֶת בֵּיתוֹ לְשָׁמְרוֹ, — *To one who locks his house to safeguard it,*

I.e., to one who locks his house to safeguard it from thieves, not to trap animals (*Rav; Rashi*).

וְנִמְצָא צְבִי שָׁמוּר בְּתוֹכוֹ. — *and a deer is found to be guarded therein.*

I.e., a deer that had already been trapped is found guarded in the house (*Rav; Rashi*).

This refers to a case where a deer is either bound inside the house or trapped behind a closed door and someone then locks the door, too. Since

13. To one who locks his house to safeguard it, and a
7 deer is found to be guarded therein.

YAD AVRAHAM

the deer, at the time the person locks the door, is in any case trapped, locking the door merely increases the security of that trap but is not in itself an act of trapping. Therefore, even if the deer escapes the original trap (e.g., the deer tears the rope binding or the door originally enclosing the deer comes open), and the deer is thereby found to be trapped only by virtue of the subsequently added lock, the person who locked the door is neither liable nor required to release the lock. Since at the moment of locking the door no act of trapping was performed, subsequent events cannot retroactively cause that act to be viewed as an act of trapping. Similarly, in our case, when the second person sits down, the deer is already trapped. Hence, the second person does not effect the capture and is not required to leave the doorway to allow the deer to escape (*Tos. Yom Tov* from *Ran*).

פרק ארבעה עשר
Chapter Fourteen

שבת
יד/א

[א] **שְׁמֹנָה** שְׁרָצִים הָאֲמוּרִים בַּתּוֹרָה, הַצָּדָן וְהַחוֹבֵל בָּהֶן חַיָּב. וּשְׁאָר שְׁקָצִים וּרְמָשִׂים, הַחוֹבֵל בָּהֶן פָּטוּר; הַצָּדָן לְצֹרֶךְ חַיָּב,

---
ר' עובדיה מברטנורא

פרק ארבעה עשר — שמנה. (א) שמונה. החולד והעכבר וכו'. המנויין בפרשת ויהי ביום השמיני: הצדן חייב. שיש במינן גלוד: והחובל בהן חייב. דיש להן עור והויא לה חבורה שאינה חוזרת, וחייב משום מפרק שהיא תולדה דדש. אי נמי כיון דיש להן עור נצבע העור בדם הנגרר בו וחייב משום צובע: ושאר שקצים ורמשים. כגון תולעים וחלזונות ועקרבים, החובל בהם פטור, דאין להם עור:

יד אברהם

1.

The mishnah proceeds to elaborate on the *melachah* of *trapping, discussed in the preceding chapter. Also discussed is the liability involved in wounding any living creature.

שְׁמֹנָה שְׁרָצִים הָאֲמוּרִים בַּתּוֹרָה — *The eight sheratzim mentioned in the Torah,*

The mishnah refers to the eight creeping creatures listed in *Lev.* 11:29,30 (*Rav*). [Although the identification of these *sheratzim* is by no means unanimously agreed upon, the following commonly used translations are offered as an indication of the type of creatures in this classification: הַחֹלֶד, *the weasel;* הָעַכְבָּר, *the mouse;* הַצָּב, *the toad* or *the turtle;* הָאֲנָקָה, *the hedgehog;* הַכֹּחַ, *the chameleon;* הַלְּטָאָה, *the lizard;* הַחֹמֶט, *the snail;* הַתִּנְשֶׁמֶת, *the mole.* These are all small animals whose carcasses convey *tumah*-contamination. Since this group includes reptiles, rodents, amphibians, and mollusks, we have left the word שְׁרָצִים, *sheratzim,* untranslated.]

הַצָּדָן — *one who traps them*

One who traps them is liable since these species are customarily hunted (*Rav; Rashi*) for their hides (*Ran*).

וְהַחוֹבֵל בָּהֶן חַיָּב. — *and one who bruises them is liable.*

Since the skins of these animals are tougher than the flesh beneath them, any bruise mark visible in them is of such severity that the blood of that bruise can no longer be reabsorbed by the body, and it is only the thickness of the skin which prevents the blood from flowing out (*Rambam*). One who bruises them, therefore, is liable. The exact *melachah* for which one is liable is the subject of differing opinions. Some rule that he is liable for מְפָרֵק, *unloading,* i.e., separating the blood from the flesh. This is a *toladah* of *threshing,* which consists of separating the kernels of grain from the chaff (*Rav; Rambam*).[1]

Others maintain that since these creatures have skins, which become colored by the blood coming to the surface, the perpetrator is liable for

---

1. Although *threshing* bears liability only when performed on things that grow from the earth, since animals derive their sustenance from the earth, they, too, are regarded as such (*Rav; Rambam, Hil. Shabbos* 8:7).

14
1

1. The eight *sheratzim* mentioned in the Torah, one who traps them and one who bruises them is liable. But other vermin and crawling things, one who bruises them is exempt; one who traps them because he needs them is liable,

YAD AVRAHAM

*dyeing (*Rav*; *Rashi*).

Still another reason given is that in wounding these animals the blood flows from the wounded area and it is regarded as though one took the life from this area. Consequently, this is a *toladah* of *slaughtering (*Rashi*; *Tos.*). This is the opinion accepted by most *poskim* (*Magen Avraham* 316:9).[1]

The special status of these eight species is with regard to bruising rather than wounding; i.e., where the blood remains trapped beneath the skin in contrast to where the skin is pierced and the blood flows out. However, one who actually causes an animal to bleed is liable for any species, for one of the above reasons (*Gem.* 107b; *Shulchan Aruch* 316:8).

Rambam (*Comm.* and *Hil. Shabbos* 8:9) seems to dispute this. He holds that one who causes any of the other creeping things to bleed is exempt. [See *Maggid Mishneh* there for a discussion of the difficulties involved with this opinion.]

וּשְׁאָר שְׁקָצִים וּרְמָשִׂים, — *But other vermin and crawling things,*

Such as worms, *chilazons,* and scorpions (*Rav*), and snakes (*Rashi*). [According to those exegetes who identify the *chilazon* with the snail (*Aruch*), the *chilazon* is included among the eight mentioned above. *Rav* obviously identifies the *chilazon* as a fish, as do *Rambam* (*Hil. Shabbos* 2:2) and *Tosafos* (3b).]

הַחוֹבֵל בָּהֶן פָּטוּר; — *one who bruises them is exempt;*

Since their skin is soft, the blood rushes easily to the surface if the bruise is not severe. If the severity of the wound were sufficient to prevent the blood from being reabsorbed by the body, the blood would have immediately flowed through the soft skin of these animals (*Rambam*). Since it will eventually be reabsorbed by the body, one is exempt. This is true of any instance where the skin becomes only temporarily suffused with blood (e.g., a slap to a human being) (*Tif. Yis.; Mishnah Berurah* 316:32). As explained above, if one actually causes the animal to bleed, he is liable for any species.

הַצָּדָן לְצֹרֶךְ חַיָּב, — *one who traps them because he needs them is liable,*

The mishnah specifies that one is

1. There are several practical differences to this controversy. According to the first opinion (*Rambam*), one would not be liable unless (a) he needed the blood for some use, and (b) he drew at least the volume of blood equivalent of a fig (*Rambam, Hil. Shabbos* 8:7; *Ravad* gives a slightly different measure). According to the second opinion (*Rashi*), he would be liable only if he needed the skin dyed and only in the measure necessary for dying skins (*Rashba*). According to the third opinion (*Tos.*), he would be liable for any amount of blood drawn and even if he did not need the blood, as long as there was constructive purpose to his wounding the animal [e.g., for medical reasons] (*Magen Avraham* 316:9). For a full discussion of these differences see *Beur Halachah* 316:8.

שבת יד/ב

שֶׁלֹּא לְצֹרֶךְ פָּטוּר. חַיָּה וָעוֹף שֶׁבִּרְשׁוּתוֹ, הַצָּדָן פָּטוּר, וְהַחוֹבֵל בָּהֶן חַיָּב.

[ב] **אֵין עוֹשִׁין** הִילְמִי בַשַּׁבָּת, אֲבָל עוֹשֶׂה

ר' עובדיה מברטנורא

שלא לצורך פטור. דאין במינן נלוד: **חיה ועוף שברשותו, הצדן פטור.** שהרי נלודים ועומדים הן: **והחובל בהן חייב.** דיש להן עור, ואין החובל חייב בכל הני דתנינן במתניתין אלא בצריך לדם, אבל אם לא חבל אלא להזיק, הא קיי"ל כל המקלקלים פטורים: **(ב) אין עושין הילמי.** מי מלח מרובים שנותנים לתוך ירקות שכובשין אותן להתקיים: **אבל עושין.** מי מלח מועטים כדי לטבל בהן פתו או לתוך התבשיל:

יד אברהם
---

liable only if he needs the creature, because these other creatures are generally not needed and are therefore usually captured only to be rid of them. If, however, one captured one of them for some use, he is indeed liable. The eight creatures of the first case, however, because they are usually trapped for their skins, one is liable for their capture, without any qualification (*Tos.* 107a).

שֶׁלֹּא לְצֹרֶךְ, פָּטוּר. — *if he does not need them, he is exempt.*

This mishnah follows the opinion of R' Shimon who rules that *a labor not performed for its defined purpose is exempt* (*Gem.* 107b).

Rashi, followed by *Rav*, adds that he is exempt because these species are not customarily hunted.

Tosafos (107a) questions this addition, since the *Gem.* 106b states that there is no liability for a species not generally hunted even when one captures it to use. *Tosafos* therefore states that the mishnah refers to a species which is generally trapped and the exemption is strictly because it is not being captured to be used.

Rashi, it seems, understands that the exemption for a species not customarily hunted is for the very reason that its capture is not for its use. Species which are used are generally hunted or trapped. Accordingly, the exemption for trapping a species not customarily hunted is not universal but merely general, i.e., one is generally exempt for trapping such a species unless he specifically intends to use it. On the other hand, species customarily hunted or trapped are generally subject to liability for their capture, unless specifically not intended for use (*Maginei Shlomo*).

חַיָּה וָעוֹף שֶׁבִּרְשׁוּתוֹ, הַצָּדָן פָּטוּר, — *Beasts and birds that are in one's domain, one who traps them is exempt,*

Since they are already trapped in his domain, the prohibition for catching them does not apply (*Rav; Rashi*).

[See above 13:7 for a full discussion of the details of this rule.]

וְהַחוֹבֵל בָּהֶן חַיָּב. — *but one who bruises them is liable.*

Since they have hide, one is liable for bruising them, just as one is liable for bruising the eight *sheratzim* mentioned in the Torah. This is true only if the one who inflicts the wound is drawing the blood for use. If the wound is inflicted to harm the beast, it is considered a destructive act and is exempted as are *all those who destroy* (See above 13:3; *Rav* from *Gem.* 106a.)

Tosefos Yom Tov questions how this is consistent with the ruling mentioned above, that one is liable for bruising a creature even though the blood does not flow out. Since the *Gemara* (106a) states that one is liable only when he needs the blood, this

14 if he does not need them, he is exempt. Beasts and
2 birds that are in one's domain, one who traps them is exempt, but one who bruises them is liable.

2. We may not make pickling brine on the Sabbath,

YAD AVRAHAM

precludes any liability for bruising, unless the blood actually comes out.

The resolution of this problem is different for each of the three explanations offered above for the *melachah* involved in bruising. *Tosefos Yom Tov* explains that according to the second explanation, that one is liable for **dyeing* the skin, the Gemara means only to state one of several possible reasons for liability, viz., that he needs the blood; however, the same is true if he wounds in order to dye the skin, since this, too, is a constructive use of the blood. Therefore, one is liable even though the blood has not come out. If the blood does come out and one needs the blood for some other purpose, he would be liable for one of the other reasons.

According to *Rambam*, who holds that one is liable for *unloading*, i.e., a *toladah* of **threshing*, the blood from the flesh, even though his intention here to extract blood was not completed, he is, nevertheless, liable. This is akin to one who intends to write ''SHiMon,'' and writes only ''SHeM,'' who is liable, as explained above in 12:3 (*Tos. Yom Tov*).

Lechem Shamayim, Tosefos R' Akiva, and *Tiferes Yisrael* question this analogy. Whereas one who writes ''SHeM'' has completed a *melachah*, since he has written two letters, he may be held liable for the *melachah* he has already performed though he intended to write a longer word. In our case, however, since when one wounds an animal without extracting its blood one is performing a destructive act for which there is normally no liability, it does not follow that there should be liability for this act merely because it is part of an intended *melachah*.

Lechem Shamayim suggests that whether the liability is for **threshing*, **dyeing*, or **slaughtering*, he is liable even though the blood did not flow out. Since it has now converged in the bruised area, under the skin, it is available for use by removing the skin. The fact that another step is necessary does not make him any less liable.

2.

The following mishnah deals with the Rabbinical prohibition of making pickling brine on the Sabbath. Since this activity resembles those involved in **tanning* hides, which follows **slaughtering* (7:2), it is included here after laws of **trapping* and bruising animals (*Tif. Yis.*).

אֵין עוֹשִׂין הִילְמֵי בַשַּׁבָּת, — *We may not make pickling brine on the Sabbath,*

Pickling brine consists of a mixture of water, oil, and salt. Salt was placed in a container to which water was added, producing a strong solution of salt water. To this a small quantity of oil was added for taste. The Rabbis prohibited preparing this on the Sabbath because one appears to be pickling foods to preserve them. It follows, obviously, that actually pickling the foods is certainly forbidden. Even though there is no Biblical prohibition against pickling foods on the Sabbath, the Rabbis prohibited it because of its similarity to **tanning* hides (*Meri*).

This prohibition applies only to preparing large quantities of pickling brine, used in pickling vegetables (*Rav* from *Gem.* 108b).

[329]   THE MISHNAH/SHABBOS — Chapter Fourteen: *Shemoneh Sheratzim*

שבת יד/ב

הוּא אֶת מֵי הַמֶּלַח וְטוֹבֵל בָּהֶן פִּתּוֹ, וְנוֹתֵן לְתוֹךְ הַתַּבְשִׁיל.

אָמַר רַבִּי יוֹסֵי: וַהֲלֹא הוּא הִילְמִי בֵּין מְרֻבֶּה וּבֵין מֻעָט? וְאֵלּוּ הֵן מֵי מֶלַח הַמֻּתָּרִין: נוֹתֵן שֶׁמֶן בַּתְּחִלָּה לְתוֹךְ הַמַּיִם אוֹ לְתוֹךְ הַמֶּלַח.

ר' עובדיה מברטנורא

והלא היא הילמי. בין מרובה בין מועט כלומר אם המרובים אסורים אף המועטים אסורים, דיאמרו מלאכה מרובה אסורה ומלאכה. מועטת מותרת, אלא אלו ואלו אסורים מפני שהוא כמעבד ומתקן את האוכל הניתן בתוכו כדי שיתקיים: **ואלו הן המותרים.** נותן שמן בתוך המים בתחלה, קודם שיתן המלח, או נותן שמן בתחלה לתוך המלח, קודם שיתן את המים דהשמן מעכבו שאין המלח מתערב יפה עם המים ומתיש את כחו. אבל לא יתן מים ומלח בתחלה ואחר כך את השמן, דמשעה שנותן מים ומלח יחד הוא נראה כמעבד. ואין הלכה כרבי יוסי:

יד אברהם

אֲבָל עוֹשֶׂה הוּא אֶת מֵי הַמֶּלַח — *but one may make salt water*

I.e., one may make small quantities of salt water (*Rav*; *Rambam, Comm. from Gem.* ibid.).

וְטוֹבֵל בָּהֶן פִּתּוֹ, וְנוֹתֵן לְתוֹךְ הַתַּבְשִׁיל. — *and dip his bread in it, or add it to cooked food.*

I.e., one may make a small quantity in order to dip his bread in it while eating or to mix into a cooked dish (*Rav; Tif. Yis.*).

If the solution consists of two parts salt and one part water, it is forbidden even in small quantities (*Tif. Yis.* from *Gem.* 108b). Such a solution is so strong that an egg will float in it (*Gem.* ibid.).

אָמַר רַבִּי יוֹסֵי: וַהֲלֹא הוּא הִילְמִי בֵּין מְרֻבֶּה וּבֵין מֻעָט? — *Said R' Yose: But is this not pickling brine whether it is a large or a small quantity?*

If a large quantity is prohibited, why should a small quantity be permitted? To distinguish on a solely quantitative basis might cause people to say that only work involving large quantities is forbidden on the Sabbath, while work involving small quantities is permissible. Therefore, since there is no qualitative distinction between them, both large and small quantities must be prohibited because of their resemblance to the *tanning process (*Rav* from *Gem.* ibid.).

וְאֵלּוּ הֵן מֵי מֶלַח הַמֻּתָּרִין: נוֹתֵן שֶׁמֶן בַּתְּחִלָּה לְתוֹךְ הַמַּיִם — *[Rather] these are the permissible [ways to make] salt water: One first adds oil to the water*

I.e., R' Yose does not dispute the Tanna Kamma that the Sages who prohibited the making of salt water did not forbid all forms of salt water. However, the permissible form of salt water must be qualitatively different from the prohibited kind. This is accomplished by first adding oil to the water and then adding the salt ... (*Rav*).

אוֹ לְתוֹךְ הַמֶּלַח. — *or to the salt.*

... or first adding the oil to the salt and then adding the water. In both these cases the oil hinders the proper mixing of the salt with the water, thus resulting in a weak solution unfit for *tanning. He may not mix the salt and the water before adding the oil since

14
2

but one may make salt water and dip his bread in it, or add it to cooked food.

Said R' Yose: But is this not pickling brine whether it is a large or a small quantity? [Rather] these are the permissible [ways to make] salt water: One first adds oil to the water or to the salt.

YAD AVRAHAM

in the initial stages the solution would appear like *tanning (Rav; Rashi).

The halachah is not in accordance with R' Yose (Rav).

The Sages, who disagree with R' Yose, and whose view is accepted as halachah, differentiate between large quantities of salt water — which may be used for preserving foods — and small quantities sufficient only for table use. The former resembles *tanning, whereas the latter, being of such small amounts, bears no similarity to it (Tos. Yom Tov from Tur 321). As stated above, a solution of two or more parts salt to one part water is forbidden in any quantity.

Rambam (Hil. Shabbos 22:10) explains that making large quantities of salt water resembles one of the processes involved in *cooking. [Thus, he appears to be preparing to cook.] He rejects the reason that the prohibition is due to its resemblance to *tanning because the prohibition of *tanning does not apply to foodstuffs (Hil. Shabbos 11:5).

Consequently, though there is a Rabbinic prohibition against pickling (Shulchan Aruch 321:3-6; see also Mishnah Berurah there for the various reasons for this prohibition), to prohibit making salt water because it appears as if one is preparing to pickle foods is a sort of גְּזֵרָה לִגְזֵרָה, double safeguard, which the Sages do not decree.

Yerushalmi explains the distinction between pickling brine and salt water in a different way. Pickling brine must be compounded according to a specific recipe, to insure the proper proportion of its ingredients. It therefore requires a professional to prepare it and one who does this appears to be preparing to cook. Salt water, used for dipping bread while eating meals, requires no such exactitude and can be prepared by anybody (Yerushalmi as explained by Pnei Moshe).

Another view is that pickling brine contains so much salt that it does not dissolve. In salt water, however, it does dissolve. Others maintain that if an egg sinks to the bottom, the liquid is known as salt water and may be prepared. If the egg floats, however, the solution is very strong, and it may not be prepared on the Sabbath (Yerushalmi 14:2).

3.

The next two mishnayos deal with the use of medicines on the Sabbath. The general rules governing this matter are as follows: (a) A person whose life is threatened may perform even labors prohibited by the Torah, as stated in Yoma 8:6; (b) a sick person whose life is not in danger may use medication if he is so ill that he must go to bed (Ran; Maggid Mishneh, Hil. Shabbos 2:10; Shulchan Aruch 328:17, 37); (c) a healthy person, who suffers from a pain or an ailment but is not confined to bed, is not permitted to use medication. The Rabbis

שבת
יד/ג

[ג] **אֵין אוֹכְלִין** אֵזוֹב יָוָן בַּשַּׁבָּת, לְפִי שֶׁאֵינוֹ מַאֲכַל בְּרִיאִים; אֲבָל אוֹכֵל הוּא אֶת יוֹעֶזֶר, וְשׁוֹתֶה אַבּוּבְרוֹעֶה. כָּל הָאֳכָלִין אוֹכֵל אָדָם לִרְפוּאָה; וְכָל הַמַּשְׁקִין שׁוֹתֶה, חוּץ מִמֵּי דְקָלִים וְכוֹס עִקָּרִים,

---
ר' עובדיה מברטנורא

(ג) אזוב יון. מין אזוב שגדל בין הקולים וממית התולעים שבמעים: **שאינו מאכל בריאים.** ומוכחא מלתא דלרפואה אכיל ליה, ואסור לאוכלו בשבת גזירה שמא ישחוק סממנים, דהוי תולדה דטוחן: **אבל אוכל הוא את יועזר.** הרבה אוכלין אותו כשהן בריאים. יועזר, פולי"ו בלע"ז והוא מכלה התולעים שבכבד: **אבוב רועה.** עץ שגדל יחידי ואין לו ענפים, וקורין אותו בערבי עולא"ל רט"י, והוא טוב למי שניזק על שתה מים מגולים: **כל האוכלים אוכל אדם לרפואה.** כל דבר שהוא אוכל והבריאים אוכלים אותו, יכול אדם לאוכלו בשבת אף על פי שהוא מתכוין לרפואה: **חוץ ממי דקלים.** הם שני אילנות ממיני הדקלים שהיו בארץ ישראל וביניהם מעין מים, והשותה מהם כוס ראשון מרפה הזבל שבמעיו, וכוס שני משלשל, וכוס שלישי מנקה את בני מעים עד שאדם מוציאם צלולים כדרך שהכניסם: **וכוס של עיקרין.** לוקחין שרף אילן שקורין לו בערבי זא"ג אלכסנדרי"א, וטסב שקורין לו עשב"א אלסדו"ר, פירוט עשב של שמחה, וכרכוס, וכותשין אותן ונותנין את עפרן ביין. והאשה זה שתשתה מהן ג' כוסות תרפא:

יד אברהם
---

prohibited this in order that one not come to crush herbs on the Sabbath (medicines generally being prepared from crushed herbs). To do so would be to perform a *toladah* of *grinding.

These rules are cited here because they resemble the previous case of salt water in that they are items which are ingested but which are not, properly speaking, foods (Tos. Yom Tov).

אֵין אוֹכְלִין אֵזוֹב יָוָן בַּשַּׁבָּת — We may not eat Greek hyssop on the Sabbath,

In the *Gemara* this appears as one word, אֵיזוֹבְיוֹן. It is a type of hyssop that grows among thorns and is used medicinally to kill intestinal worms (*Rav* from *Gem.* 109b). [According to these versions, the word is not related to יָוָן, Greece.] It is, in any case, a species of hyssop, related to that mentioned in the Torah to be used for cleansing the *metzora* (*Lev.* 14:1-6) and in the preparation of the ashes of the פָּרָה אֲדֻמָּה, red cow, used for cleansing those contracting *tumah* from a human corpse (*Num.* 119:6).

Rambam (*Comm.*) identifies it with lavender (*Kaffich*; *Aruch HaShalem*).

לְפִי שֶׁאֵינוֹ מַאֲכַל בְּרִיאִים — because it is not food for healthy people;

Since it is not eaten by healthy people, the one who eats it is obviously doing so for medicinal purposes. This is prohibited by Rabbinic decree, lest one crush the herbs used in medicines. To do so would be to perform a *toladah* of *grinding (Rav).

אֲבָל אוֹכֵל הוּא אֶת יוֹעֶזֶר — but one may eat pennyroyal,

Although this plant is used medicinally to kill worms in the liver, it may,

14
3

3. We may not eat Greek hyssop on the Sabbath, because it is not food for healthy people; but one may eat pennyroyal, or drink knotgrass water. A person may eat any foods for healing; and he may drink any beverages, except for the water of palm trees or a potion of roots,

YAD AVRAHAM

nevertheless, be eaten on the Sabbath, since many healthy people eat it as well. Since it is not *apparent* that one is eating it for its medicinal properties, the Rabbis did not prohibit it.

וְשׁוֹתֶה אֲבוּבְרוֹעֶה — *or drink knotgrass water* (lit. *the shepherd's staff*).

This refers to a species of branchless tree that grows singly. It was an antidote used by one who had drunk uncovered water which may have been poisoned by a snake (*Rav* from *Gem.* 109b).

כָּל הָאֳכָלִין אוֹכֵל אָדָם לִרְפוּאָה; — *A person may eat any foods for healing;*

I.e., any food eaten by healthy people may be eaten on the Sabbath, even if one's intent is to eat it solely for its medicinal properties (*Rav*).

Though this rule is seemingly apparent from the previous cases of the mishnah, it is added to teach that even foods whose consumption causes certain inimical side effects — and is therefore usually eaten only by sick people requiring its beneficial effects — are permissible, if they are occasionally eaten by healthy people, too. Specifically this refers to eating spleen, which is beneficial for the teeth but bad for the intestines, or vetch, which is beneficial for the intestines but bad for the teeth. Since they are only occasionally eaten by healthy people, we might think that one who eats them for their beneficial effects indicates his intent to eat them for purely therapeutic purposes, and it should, therefore, be prohibited. The mishnah, therefore, emphasizes that *all* foods, even those only occasionally eaten by healthy people, may be eaten, even for therapeutic reasons, on the Sabbath (*Tos. Yom Tov* from *Gem.* 110a).

וְכָל הַמַּשְׁקִין שׁוֹתֶה, — *and he may drink any beverages,*

This includes vinegar added to water in which capers have been soaked (*Gem.* ibid.). Since healthy people only occasionally drink such a concoction, its primary use being to relieve toothaches, it might be thought to be forbidden. The mishnah, therefore, adds the statement that *any* beverage may be drunk on the Sabbath.

חוּץ מִמֵּי דְקָלִים — *except for the water of palm trees*

This refers to water obtained from a certain well in *Eretz Yisrael* situated between two trees of the palm family. This water was noted for its purgative properties (*Rav* from *Gem.* 110).

וְכוֹס עִקָּרִים, — *or a potion of roots,*

The translation follows *Rashi* to 109b.

A three-part mixture, each the weight of a *zuz*, of Alexandrian gum, liquid alum (*Rashi*; *Rav* has variety of grass) and garden crocus. These were crushed and the powder was then mixed with beer and drunk as a remedy for jaundice. It was also used, mixed with wine rather than beer, to cure a woman experiencing an unusually long menstrual flow (*Rav*).

שבת יד/ד

מִפְּנֵי שֶׁהֵן לִירוֹקָה. אֲבָל שׁוֹתֶה הוּא מֵי דְקָלִים לִצְמָאוֹ, וְסָךְ שֶׁמֶן עִקָּרִין שֶׁלֹּא לִרְפוּאָה.

[ד] הַחוֹשֵׁשׁ בְּשִׁנָּיו לֹא יִגְמַע בָּהֶן אֶת הַחֹמֶץ, אֲבָל מְטַבֵּל הוּא כְּדַרְכּוֹ, וְאִם נִתְרַפֵּא, נִתְרַפֵּא.

ר' עובדיה מברטנורא

מפני שהן לירוקה. בעל חולי הנקרא ירקון, אם ישתה מהן ירפא מחולי הירקון אבל ישאר עקר ולא יוליד, ולכך נקרא כוס עיקרין: **לצמאו.** אם אינו חולה: (ד) **לא יגמע את החומץ.** ויפלוט, דמוכחא מלתא דלרפואה הוא. ואם מגמע ובולע שפיר דמי: **לא יסוך בהם יין וחומץ.** דאין

יד אברהם

מִפְּנֵי שֶׁהֵן לִירוֹקָה — *because they are [cures] for jaundice.*

The *Gemara* specifies that as a cure for jaundice, it was necessary to use only two of the aforementioned ingredients and to mix them with beer. However, mixed in this manner, though effective against jaundice, it caused sterility, hence the name כּוֹס עֲקָרִים, which can also be derived from the word עָקָר, *a sterile person (Rav from Gem.* 110a). A woman drinking a potion composed of all three ingredients mixed with wine, the cure for an unusually heavy flow, does not become sterile. It is, nevertheless, even in this form called the cup of sterility to warn people of its undesirable side effect (*Tos. Yom Tov*).

The *Gemara* 110b questions the permissibility of taking a potion that causes sterility, apart from any Sabbatical considerations. The *Gemara's* conclusion is that only a woman may avail herself of this remedy since the commandment to be *fruitful and multiply* is obligatory only on men, not women. A man, however, may not drink this potion, since he is forbidden to cause himself to become sterile. Even an old man is forbidden to do so (*Gem.* 111a).

This mishnah presents a number of difficulties: (a) Why does the mishnah give the reason for the prohibition of the potion of roots and omit the reason for the prohibition of the water of palm trees? Though the expression *since "they" are [cures] for jaundice* indicates that water of palm trees, too, is a cure for jaundice, the *Gemara* states only that it is a cure for constipation. Only the potion of roots is referred to as a cure for jaundice. (b) Why does the mishnah refer to the potion of roots only as a cure for jaundice and not as a cure for an unusually heavy menstrual flow as well?

The answer is that the mishnah is not telling us the medicinal uses of these two beverages. They were well known at that time. However, since the *Tanna* uses the ambiguous term, כּוֹס עֲקָרִים, which could mean *potion of roots* or *potion of sterility*, intimating that drinking this potion causes sterility, he must account for people using this potion. For this reason the *Tanna* adds *since they are for jaundice*, i.e., mixed in the manner in which it causes sterility it is effective in curing jaundice. It is just in this proportion that it causes sterility. However, in the proportion used for curing an unusually heavy flow, it is also prohibited, since it is used only as a remedy (*Shoshanim Le-David*).

אֲבָל שׁוֹתֶה הוּא מֵי דְקָלִים לִצְמָאוֹ, — *How-*

because they are [cures] for jaundice. However, one may drink the water of palm trees to quench his thirst, and he may anoint himself with root oil [if it is] not for healing.

4. One whose teeth pain him may not sip vinegar through them, but he may dip [his bread] in vinegar in his usual manner, and if he is [thus] cured, he is cured.

YAD AVRAHAM

ever, one may drink the water of palm trees to quench his thirst,
I.e., if he does not suffer from any ailment (Rav; Tif. Yis. from Magen Avraham 328:43).

Others, however, state that even a sick person may drink it, as long as he is doing so to quench his thirst and not as a cure (Shenos Eliyahu; Halachah 328:37).

וְסָךְ שֶׁמֶן עִקָּרִין שֶׁלֹּא לִרְפוּאָה. — and he may anoint himself with root oil [if it is] not for healing.
I.e., with oil to which has been added extracts from the roots of spices and herbs (Tos. Yom Tov).

[Anointing was a common practice, used to keep the skin soft. Various types of oils (in liquid form) were used.]

4.

הַחוֹשֵׁשׁ בְּשִׁנָּיו לֹא־יִגְמַע בָּהֶן אֶת־הַחֹמֶץ, — One whose teeth pain him may not sip vinegar through them,

Rinsing one's mouth with vinegar relieves toothaches. One, however, who has no toothache would not rinse his mouth with vinegar.

Accordingly, one may not rinse his mouth with vinegar for a toothache and eject it, since it is obvious that he is doing so for therapeutic reasons. One may, however, sip vinegar and swallow it (Rav from Gem. ibid.). Even so he may not hold it in his mouth before swallowing, since this again makes it obvious that he is drinking the vinegar for its therapeutic benefits (Mishnah Berurah 328:102).

אֲבָל מְטַבֵּל הוּא כְדַרְכּוֹ, — but he may dip [his bread] in vinegar in his usual manner,

Eating bread dipped in vinegar was a common practice. As mentioned above, one may also sip the vinegar and swallow it. The mishnah however mentions dipping bread because this was the more common practice (Tos. Yom Tov from Tos.).

Alternatively, the mishnah does not state the alternative of swallowing vinegar, because it is unhealthy to swallow vinegar in its pure state. [See ArtScroll Yoma 8:3.] Moreover, one who eats bread dipped in vinegar can hold it between his teeth longer, since he must chew it, thus producing more beneficial results than if he were to swallow it (Lechem Shamayim).

וְאִם נִתְרַפֵּא, נִתְרַפֵּא. — and if he is [thus] cured, he is cured.
I.e., it is permissible to effect a cure in this manner.

שבת יד/ד

הַחוֹשֵׁשׁ בְּמָתְנָיו לֹא יָסוּךְ יַיִן וְחֹמֶץ. אֲבָל סָךְ הוּא אֶת הַשֶּׁמֶן, וְלֹא שֶׁמֶן וֶרֶד. בְּנֵי מְלָכִים סָכִין שֶׁמֶן וֶרֶד עַל מַכּוֹתֵיהֶן, שֶׁכֵּן דַּרְכָּם לָסוּךְ בַּחֹל. רַבִּי שִׁמְעוֹן אוֹמֵר: כָּל יִשְׂרָאֵל בְּנֵי מְלָכִים הֵם.

ר' עובדיה מברטנורא

אדם סך מהן אלא לרפואה: אבל לא שמן ורד. לפי שדמיו יקרים ומוכחא מלתא דלרפואה קעביד: שכן דרכן לסוך. בלא מכה: רבי שמעון אומר בו'. ואין הלכה כרבי שמעון:

יד אברהם

This mishnah applies to an ordinary toothache. One, however, who experiences pain so excruciating that it weakens his entire body may use any medicines (*Tif. Yis.* from *Turei Zahav* 328:24). He may also tell a non-Jew to extract the tooth (*Rama* 328:24).

Obviously, where the threat of a spreading infection poses a life-threatening danger, even a Jewish dentist may treat it (*Shulchan Aruch* 328:3). [Gum *infections* (rather than just pains) are often considered life threatening (see *Mishnah Berurah* 328:8).]

הַחוֹשֵׁשׁ בְּמָתְנָיו לֹא יָסוּךְ יַיִן וְחֹמֶץ. — *One whose loins pain him may not anoint himself with wine or vinegar.*

Since no one anoints himself with these liquids except for therapeutic purposes, his intention is obvious (*Rav; Rashi*).

אֲבָל סָךְ הוּא אֶת הַשֶּׁמֶן. — *He may, however, anoint himself with oil,*

14. One whose loins pain him may not anoint himself with wine or vinegar. He may, however, anoint himself with oil, but not [with] rose oil. Princes may rub rose oil on their wounds, for such is their custom to anoint [themselves] on weekdays. R' Shimon says: All Israel are princes.

YAD AVRAHAM

I.e., he may even anoint a wound with oil since healthy people too anoint themselves with it (Tif. Yis.).

וְלֹא שֶׁמֶן וֶרֶד — *but not [with] rose oil.*

Since rose oil is expensive, healthy people do not anoint themselves with it except for therapeutic purposes (Rav; Rashi).

בְּנֵי מְלָכִים סָכִין שֶׁמֶן וֶרֶד עַל מַכּוֹתֵיהֶן, שֶׁכֵּן דַּרְכָּם לָסוּךְ בַּחֹל. — *Princes may rub rose oil on their wounds, for such is their custom to anoint [themselves] on weekdays.*

Since, owing to their wealth, even on weekdays they use rose oil to anoint themselves, applying it to a wound on the Sabbath does not indicate that it is being done for therapeutic reasons (Rav; Rashi; Tif. Yis.).

רַבִּי שִׁמְעוֹן אוֹמֵר: כָּל יִשְׂרָאֵל בְּנֵי מְלָכִים הֵם. — *R' Shimon says: All Israel are princes.*

Therefore, anything permitted for royalty is permitted for all Jews.

The halachah is not in accordance with R' Shimon (Rav). However, where rose oil is inexpensive and therefore commonly used, one may use it to rub on his wounds (Tos. Yom Tov from Gem. 111b).

◆§ פרק חמשה עשר
Chapter Fifteen

The following two mishnayos deal with the *melachos* of קוֹשֵׁר, *tying*, and מַתִּיר, *untying*, listed in Ch. 7:2.

The mishnah lists three categories of knots. One category entails liability, the second is exempted but Rabbinically forbidden, while the third is permissible. Though the mishnah lists several examples of each category, the general rule to be derived from these examples is subject to two different interpretations. The opinion of *Rif* and *Rambam* (*Comm.* and *Hil. Shabbos* 10:1) is that two conditions must be met for liability. The first is that the knot must be a professional knot, i.e., a knot requiring special training to tie, such as a sailor's knot.[1] The second is that it must be a permanent knot, i.e., a knot tied with the intention that it be left tied indefinitely. Any person tying a knot on the Sabbath which meets these two conditions is liable. A person tying a knot meeting only one of these two conditions, i.e., either a professional knot which one ties with the intention of undoing it at a specific future date, or a permanent knot which is, however, an ordinary, non-professional knot, is exempt. To tie such a knot is, however, Rabbinically prohibited. A knot meeting neither of these conditions, i.e., an ordinary, non-professional knot tied with the intention of undoing it at or by a specific date, may be tied on the Sabbath.

Rashi and *Rosh*, however, delineate the three categories differently. In their opinion, the only significant factor is the duration for which the knot was tied. A permanent knot entails liability regardless of its type. A temporary knot which, however, one intends to leave for at least several days before untying is exempt but, nevertheless, Rabbinically prohibited. A knot tied to be undone within the same day is permissible from the start[2] (*Rama* 317:1). Some give the time limit of the permissible category as seven days rather than one (*Tur; Mordechai*, quoted by *Rama*, ibid.). This latter dispute is relevant only to the view of *Rashi* and *Rosh*.

---

1. *Taz* (317:1) understands the significance of a professional knot to be its strength. According to him, any very strong knot, regardless of its actual status among professionals, is in the category of a professional knot. *Beur Halachah*, however, questions this.

2. *Taz* states that the status of the knot is determined solely by the duration intended by the one who tied it. This seems to be the view of *Pri Megadim* in *Aishel Avraham* 317:6, too. However, *Beur Halachah* to 317:1 states that the determining factor is the intention most people have when tying such a knot, rather than the intention of the individual. For example, one who ties *tzitzis* to his *tallis* would be liable, according to *Beur Halachah*, even if his intention was to remove the *tzitzis* after the Sabbath. Since most people tie the *tzitzis* knots intending to leave them indefinitely, the individual's intention to untie it after the Shabbos does not alter the status of this knot. It should be pointed out that even the first opinion, which follows the individual's intentions, agrees that it is at least Rabbinically forbidden to tie such a knot, since he may forget or change his mind about untying the knot after the Sabbath.

The question, however, does not arise according to the view of *Rif* and *Rambam*, since according to their opinion there are but two time distinctions — permanent or temporary, not three.

The knots prohibited by Rabbinic injunction were prohibited only for their resemblance to the Biblically prohibited one. According to *Rambam*, therefore, any knot meeting *either* of the two conditions requisite for liability, and therefore in that respect similar to the Biblically prohibited knot, was prohibited by the Rabbis. A knot, however, meeting neither of these conditions, and thus not to be confused with the Biblically prohibited knot, was not banned. According to *Rashi's* view, that the sole distinguishing characteristic of the Biblically prohibited knot is its degree of permanence, any knot made for a long duration, and therefore possibly misconstrued by some as being a permanent knot, was Rabbinically banned. A knot, however, made for but one day, or, according to *Tur*, for one week, cannot possibly be mistaken for a permanent knot. It was therefore not banned by the Sages (*Rav; Rashi*).

Mishnah 1 discusses those knots for which there is liability; mishnah 2 begins by discussing those knots which do not entail liability, but which are, nevertheless, Rabbinically prohibited. It concludes with those that are actually permissible.

שבת
טו/א

[א] **אֵלּוּ קְשָׁרִים** שֶׁחַיָּבִין עֲלֵיהֶן: קֶשֶׁר הַגַּמָּלִין וְקֶשֶׁר הַסַּפָּנִין. וּכְשֵׁם שֶׁהוּא חַיָּב עַל קִשּׁוּרָן, כָּךְ הוּא חַיָּב עַל הֶתֵּרָן.

רַבִּי מֵאִיר אוֹמֵר: כָּל קֶשֶׁר שֶׁהוּא יָכֹל לְהַתִּירוֹ בְּאַחַת מִיָּדָיו, אֵין חַיָּבִין עָלָיו.

ר' עובדיה מברטנורא

פרק חמשה עשר – אלו קשרים. (א) **אלו קשרים. קשר הגמלים.** שנוקבים לגמל בחוטמו ונותנין בו רצועה וקושרים אותה קשר עולם. וכמו כן נוקבים בראש הספינה נקב ונותנין בו חבל וקושרין אותו קשר של קיימא מתירו לעולם, והוי דומיא דקושרי חוטי יריעות הנפסקים במשכן. **וקשר של קיימא ואינו מעשה אומן, או מעשה אומן ואינו של קיימא** פטור אבל אסור, ואינו חייב עד שיהא של קיימא ומעשה אומן. ושאינו של קיימא ולא מעשה אומן מותר לכתחלה: **ובשם שחייב על קשרן כך חייב על התירן.** שכן ליידי חלזון היו נזקקין לפרקים להתיר קשרי רשתות הקיימים כדי לקצרן או להרחיבן: **שיכול להתירו.** דלא הדקיה: **אין חייבין עליו.** ואפילו עשאו לקיימא. ואין הלכה כרבי מאיר:

יד אברהם

1.

אֵלּוּ קְשָׁרִים שֶׁחַיָּבִין עֲלֵיהֶן — *These are the knots for which we are liable:*

I.e., these are the knots referred to above (7:2), where *tying a knot* and *untying a knot* are enumerated among the principal categories of *melachah*. Only knots bearing similarity to those used for tying together any torn threads in the curtains of the *Mishkan*, or the nets of those who fished for the *chilazon*, entail liability (*Rashi; Rav; Tos. R' Akiva* from *Gem.* 74b). As mentioned in the prefatory note to this chapter, some authorities rule that only professional knots tied to remain permanently entail liability (*Rav; Rambam, Comm. and Hil. Shabbos* 10:1; *Rif*). Others rule that any knot tied to remain indefinitely, whether professional or otherwise, entails liability (*Rashi; Rosh*).

קֶשֶׁר הַגַּמָּלִין — *the camel drivers' knot.*

The septum of the camel's nose was punctured and a leather thong was inserted in the hole. The ends of the thong were then knotted permanently to form a ring to which ropes or reins could be fashioned (*Rav*).

וְקֶשֶׁר הַסַּפָּנִין. — *and the sailors' knot.*

The prow of the ship was punctured so that a rope could be inserted and knotted to form a ring. To this could be fastened the long ropes used to tie the ship in place while in dock (*Rashi*). The knot closing this ring was tied by the sailors to remain permanently (*Rav*).[1]

וּכְשֵׁם שֶׁהוּא חַיָּב עַל קִשּׁוּרָן, כָּךְ הוּא חַיָּב עַל

---

1. The mishnah, by referring to this as *the camel drivers' knot* and *the sailors' knot* rather than *the camel's knot* and *the ship's knot*, seems to intimate that one is liable only if he

1. These are the knots for which we are liable: the camel drivers' knot and the sailors' knot. And just as one is liable for tying them, so, too, is one liable for untying them.

R' Meir says: Any knot which one can untie with one hand, we are not liable for.

YAD AVRAHAM

הֶתֵּרָן — *And just as one is liable for tying them, so, too, is one liable for untying them.*

[I.e., for the same knots for which one is liable for *tying, he is also liable for *untying.]

Those who would hunt the *chilazon*, the fish (or snail) whose blood was utilized for תְּכֵלֶת [*techeiles*], blue dye, would sometimes untie the knots in their nets to readjust them (*Rav; Rashi* from *Gem.* 74b).

Accordingly, one is liable for *untying a knot if he does so for a constructive purpose. If he does so destructively, however, he is exempt (see above 13:3; *Perush Kadmon MiMitzraim; Rambam, Hil. Shabbos* 10:7).

Tosafos (73a) goes further by stating that one is not liable unless he unties a knot specifically in order to be able to retie it. Many authorities, however, disagree with *Tosafos*, declaring any constructive function sufficient for liability (*Beur Halachah* to 317:2).

רַבִּי מֵאִיר אוֹמֵר: כָּל קֶשֶׁר שֶׁהוּא יָכֹל לְהַתִּירוֹ בְּאַחַת מִיָּדָיו, אֵין חַיָּבִין עָלָיו. — R' *Meir says: Any knot that one can untie with one hand, we are not liable for.*

I.e., any knot made loosely enough that one can untie it with one hand, even if it was tied to remain indefinitely, does not entail liability (*Rav; Rashi*).

The halachah is not in accordance with R' Meir (*Rav; Rambam, Comm.*). Therefore, one is liable for tying a permanent knot even if it can be untied with one hand.[1]

ties the professional knot of the camel drivers or sailors. Should one, however, tie an amateur knot in the camel's nose, even though he intends it to remain indefinitely, he would be exempt (footnotes of *Shenos Eliyahu* from *Beur HaGra* 317:2 cited in proof of opinion of *Rif* and *Rambam*). [Although the word גַּמָּלִין could also be read as גְּמָלִין, *camels*, this is not true for סַפָּנִין since the word for *ships* would be סְפִינוֹת — a completely different spelling.]

1. According to *Rambam* and *Rif*, who rule that one is liable only for tying a professional knot, this ruling creates a difficulty. As explained in footnote 1, *Taz* rules that a *professional knot* implies a strong knot. How, then, is it possible for one not to be liable for tying a knot that can be untied with one hand, yet only be liable for tying a professional, i.e., strong, knot?

This may be reconciled in the following manner: A strong knot refers to one that cannot either be pulled open (*Mirkeves HaMishneh*) or become untied by itself (*Beur Halachah* to 317:1). The fact that one can untie it with one hand does not diminish its status as a strong, and therefore professional, knot.

[ב] יֵשׁ לְךָ קְשָׁרִים שֶׁאֵין חַיָּבִין עֲלֵיהֶן כְּקֶשֶׁר הַגַּמָּלִין וּכְקֶשֶׁר הַסַּפָּנִין. קוֹשֶׁרֶת אִשָּׁה מִפְתַּח חֲלוּקָהּ; וְחוּטֵי סְבָכָה, וְשֶׁל פְּסִיקְיָא; וּרְצוּעוֹת מִנְעָל וְסַנְדָּל; וְנוֹדוֹת יַיִן וְשֶׁמֶן;

ר׳ עובדיה מברטנורא

(ב) יש לך קשרים שאין חייבין עליהם. חטאת כמו שחייבים על קשר גמלים וקשר של ספנים, אלא פטור אבל אסור ולא נזכרו קשרים הללו במשנה. ובגמרא מפרש כגון רצועה ארוכה שקושרים בטבעת שבחוטם הגאמה, וכמו כן חבל ארוך שקושרים בחבל העשוי כמין טבעת התלוי בנקב שבראש הספינה, ופעמים מניחה שם שבוע ושבועיים ומתירה. וכן כל קשר שקושרים אותו לעמוד כך זמן ידוע, לא שיהיה קיים לעולם, אין חייבין עליו: קושרת אשה מפתחי חלוקה. כעין לשונות לכאן ולכאן וקושרים של ימין בכתף שמאל ושל שמאל בכתף ימין, דכיון דכל יומא שרי ליה לא דמי לקשר של קיימא ומותר לכתחלה: סבכה. מגבעת שעל הראש עשויה כעין רשת: פסיקיא. אזור רחב וחוטין תלוין בראשו לקושרו בהן: ונודות יין. של עור שכופפין פיהם וקושרין אותן. אף על גב דאית לה תרתי איסרי, ולא אמרינן חד מינייהו בטולי מבטל לה והוי קשר של קיימא:

יד אברהם

2.

יֵשׁ לְךָ קְשָׁרִים שֶׁאֵין חַיָּבִין עֲלֵיהֶן כְּקֶשֶׁר הַגַּמָּלִין וּכְקֶשֶׁר הַסַּפָּנִין — *There are knots for which we are not liable as [we are for] the camel drivers' knot and the sailors' knot.*

Though there is no liability for these knots, they are, nevertheless, Rabbinically prohibited.

After making this general statement, the mishnah does not go on to enumerate the knots in this category.

The *Gemara* explains them to be the knot by which the reins are tied to the nose ring of the camel[1] and the knot by which the rope is tied to the ship's ring. These are sometimes left tied for a week or two at a time, and then untied. Similarly, any knot made to remain tied for only a definite period of time does not entail liability (*Rav*; *Rashi* on *Gem*. 112a).

[As explained in the prefatory note to

---

1. *Rambam* (*Hil. Shabbos* 10:2) states that if he tied a halter to an animal, he is exempt, as are all similar knots which are the work of amateurs and are generally tied to remain permanently. This is in accord with the previously stated opinion of *Rambam* and *Rif* that the tying of either a permanent knot which is not a professional one, or a temporarily tied professional knot, is exempt. Tying a knot which is neither permanent nor professional is permissible. *Rambam* is therefore forced to explain this knot as being either permanent, or an amateur knot, and therefore exempt. Yet the *Gemara* states explicitly that these knots are not permanent. Hence, in order to be prohibited according to *Rambam*, the *Gemara* must be referring to professional knots. This, however, directly contradicts *Rambam's* statement. To reconcile this difficulty, we must say either that *Rambam* understood the *Gemara* to be using the term *temporary knots* as an expression for all non-professional knots even if they are permanent, or that the reins or halter referred to by *Rambam* are not the same as those referred to by the *Gemara*. While *Rambam* discusses reins tied permanently to the animal in an amateur fashion, the *Gemara* discusses reins tied professionally to the animal but for only a fixed period of time (*Lechem Mishneh*, ad loc.).

15 2 2. There are knots for which we are not liable as [we are for] the camel drivers' knot and the sailor' knot. A woman may tie the opening of her chemise; strings of a hair net or of a girdle; straps of a shoe or a sandal; [leather] canteens of wine or oil;

YAD AVRAHAM

this chapter, there is a difference of opinion whether the boundary of permissibility is set at one day or at seven days. Furthermore, according to *Rif* and *Rambam*, any temporary knot, even if tied for more than seven days, is permissible if it is also a nonprofessional one.]

קוֹשֶׁרֶת אִשָּׁה מִפְתַּח חֲלוּקָהּ — *A woman may tie the opening of her chemise;*

[The mishnah begins to describe the knots that are permissible.]

This garment was open in the front. From the top of each corner extended a strap which was tied across the opposite shoulder, thereby closing the garment. Since the woman unties this knot daily [and since it is not a master knot (*Rambam, Hil. Shabbos* 10:3)] it is permissible.

This particular example is chosen because there is reason for prohibiting it. Since by undoing one strap the woman can remove the chemise by slipping it over her head, it is possible that she will not trouble to undo the second one, leaving it as a permanent knot. Since we do not know which one she will leave, they should both be prohibited. The mishnah therefore teaches us that we need not concern ourselves with this possibility (*Rambam, Comm.; Tos. Yom Tov* from *Gem.* 112a).

וְחוּטֵי סְבָכָה — *strings of a hair net,*

A netlike hat worn on the head (*Rav*).

Since a woman is particular about her hair, she will not slip the net off, even where possible, without first untying the strings holding the net to her hair for fear of pulling out some of her hair. It is therefore a knot which is undone every day (*Tos. Yom Tov* from *Gem.* 112a).

וְשֶׁל פְּסִיקְיָא — *or of a girdle;*

This was a wide belt with laces tied at its end (*Rav; Rashi*).

Although it is possible to remove the girdle by slipping it down over the feet and allowing the laces to remain tied permanently, it is not customary for a woman to do so because it is a breach of modesty (*Tos. Yom Tov* from *Rashi* 112a).

וּרְצוּעוֹת מִנְעָל וְסַנְדָּל — *(we may tie) straps of a shoe or a sandal;*

Shoe refers to one made of soft leather while *sandal* refers to one made of hard leather. (See *Yevamos* 12:1.)

The *Gemara* differentiates between various knots on a shoe or sandal, e.g., the knot fastening the bottom of the strap to the shoe or sandal, and the knot which one fastens each day upon putting on the shoe. *Rambam* explains that the permitted knots are those that are tied when the shoes are put on each morning, for they are neither professional nor permanent knots (*Tos. Yom Tov* from *Rambam* 10:3).

וְנוֹדוֹת יַיִן וְשֶׁמֶן — *[leather] canteens of wine or oil;*

The openings of these canteens were flaps which were tied together. Even a canteen with two openings may be tied. Although it is possible to

שבת טו/ב

וּקְדֵרָה שֶׁל בָּשָׂר.
רַבִּי אֱלִיעֶזֶר בֶּן יַעֲקֹב אוֹמֵר: קוֹשְׁרִין לִפְנֵי הַבְּהֵמָה בִּשְׁבִיל שֶׁלֹּא תֵצֵא.
קוֹשְׁרִין דְּלִי בִּפְסִיקְיָא, אֲבָל לֹא בְחֶבֶל. רַבִּי יְהוּדָה מַתִּיר.
כְּלָל אָמַר רַבִּי יְהוּדָה: כָּל קֶשֶׁר שֶׁאֵינוֹ שֶׁל

ר׳ עובדיה מברטנורא

וקדירה של בשר. פעמים שקושר בה בגד סביב לפיה. ואף על פי שיש לה דדין שיכולין להוציא המרק מהן בלא היתר הקשר אפילו הכי לא הוי קשר: **קושרין לפני בהמה.** חבל ברוחב הפתח לנטול בפניה שלא תצא. וכן הלכה: **קושרין דלי בפסיקיא.** על פי הבור שיהיה קשור ותלוי שם, דפסיקיא לא מבטל ליה התם. **אבל לא בחבל.** דמבטל ליה התם והוי קשר של קיימא: **רבי יהודה מתיר.** לא התיר רבי יהודה אלא בחבל של גרדי שגריך לו למלאכתו ולא מבטל ליה התם, ורבנן סברי אי שרית ליה חבל של גרדי יקשור נמי בשאר חבלים דחבל בחבל מיחלף. והלכה כחכמים:

יד אברהם

pour the wine or oil through one opening, thus leaving the second one permanently closed, this was not customarily done, since it would then be difficult to pour out a large amount at once. Consequently, we need not be concerned about the permanence of these knots (*Rav; Tos. Yom Tov* from *Gem.* 112b).

וּקְדֵרָה שֶׁל בָּשָׂר. — *or a pot of meat.*

Occasionally, a piece of cloth was tied over the top of a pot, and removed when the pot was emptied. Since the knot fastening the cloth to the top of the pot is a temporary one, it may be tied on the Sabbath. Even a pot having spigots, through which soup may be removed without untying the cloth, may be tied. Since it is not customary for the pot to be emptied in this manner, the knots are regarded as temporary (*Rav* from *Gem.* 112b).

רַבִּי אֱלִיעֶזֶר בֶּן־יַעֲקֹב אוֹמֵר: קוֹשְׁרִין לִפְנֵי הַבְּהֵמָה בִּשְׁבִיל שֶׁלֹּא תֵצֵא. — *R' Eliezer ben Yaakov says: We may tie [a rope] in front of an animal in order that it not go out.*

I.e., we may tie a rope across the opening of a cattle stall in order that the animal not leave the stall (*Rav; Rashi*).

Even where there are two cords, one above the other, and it is possible to release the animal by untying one cord, thereby leaving the second cord permanently tied, we do not assume that he will do so, since it is easier to remove the animal by untying both.

Alternatively, even if there is one cord which one ties to either side of the entrance, we have no fear that he will leave one end tied permanently and release the animal by untying only the second end. Since a stall usually has a door, this rope is obviously hung only temporarily, until a door can be installed (*Tos. Yom Tov* from *Rashi, Gem.* 112b, as explained by *Aruch HaShulchan* 317:28).

The halachah is in accordance with R' Eliezer ben Yaakov since the *Tanna Kamma* concurs with him (*Tos. Yom Tov* from *Gem.* 113a).

קוֹשְׁרִין דְּלִי בִּפְסִיקְיָא, אֲבָל לֹא בְחֶבֶל. — *We may tie a pail with a belt but not with a rope.*

15
2

or a pot of meat.

R' Eliezer ben Yaakov says: We may tie [a rope] in front of an animal in order that it not go out. We may tie a pail with a belt but not with a rope. [But] R' Yehudah permits [it].

R' Yehudah stated a general rule: Any knot which

YAD AVRAHAM

I.e., one may suspend a pail from the top of a well by tying a belt to the pail and to the top of the well.

Since one needs the belt, he will surely not leave it tied permanently to the pail. Consequently, there is no danger of the knot becoming permanent. One who ties a rope to a pail, however, will probably leave it there permanently. It is therefore prohibited (*Rav*).

רַבִּי יְהוּדָה מַתִּיר. — *[But] R' Yehudah permits [it].*

The *Gemara* explains that even R' Yehudah does not permit tying an ordinary rope to a pail, since this will doubtlessly become a permanent knot. He permits tying only a weaver's rope, since the weaver, requiring the rope for his work, will not leave it tied permanently to the pail. The *Tanna Kamma*, however, prohibits its use, since one might in consequence use an ordinary rope for this purpose, not realizing that there is a difference between a weaver's rope and an ordinary rope. A belt, however, cannot be confused with a rope (*Rav; Tif. Yis.* from *Gem.* 113a).

The halachah is in accordance with the Sages (*Rav; Rambam, Comm.; Shulchan Aruch* 317:4).

According to *Rif* and *Rambam*, who rule that there is no liability unless one ties a permanent knot that is also a professional knot, there is a difficulty involved in the Sages' view. Since the dispute between R' Yehudah and the Sages must obviously be whether one may tie a weaver's rope to a pail with a non-professional knot, a professional knot being Rabbinically prohibited according to all *Tannaim*, we have only to fear that one will tie an ordinary rope in this same manner. However, to do so even with an ordinary rope would constitute only a Rabbinic infraction. This would, consequently, amount to a גְּזֵרָה לִגְזֵרָה, *double safeguard*, which the Rabbis do not decree.

This can be reconciled according to *Rambam* (see footnote to 4:1, above) who states that at the time of one enactment, another can be promulgated even though its purpose is to safeguard the first one. The only time the Rabbis do not enact a double safeguard is if they have to convene a second time to enact a safeguard to protect their first enactment. Therefore, the dispute between R' Yehudah and the Sages is whether or not the second decree of tying a weaver's rope to a pail was enacted simultaneously with the original decree against tying permanent non-professional knots [*ed.*].

It is noteworthy that the mishnah deals only with a pail which one attaches to the well. It is, however, permissible to tie even a regular rope to a pail that is not fastened to the well, since he will then surely untie it within a short time (*Rashba; Ritva,* quoting *Tos., Maggid Mishneh* 10:34; *Shulchan Aruch* 317:4; see also *Beur Halachah*, there).

כְּלָל אָמַר רַבִּי יְהוּדָה: כָּל קֶשֶׁר שֶׁאֵינוֹ שֶׁל קַיָּמָא, אֵין חַיָּבִין עָלָיו. — *R' Yehudah stated a general rule: Any knot which is not permanent, we are not liable for.*

This statement does not seem relevant to R' Yehudah's previous ruling

שבת טו/ג

קַיָּמָא, אֵין חַיָּבִין עָלָיו.

[ג] מְקַפְּלִין אֶת הַכֵּלִים אֲפִלּוּ אַרְבָּעָה וַחֲמִשָּׁה פְעָמִים. וּמַצִּיעִין אֶת הַמִּטּוֹת מִלֵּילֵי שַׁבָּת לַשַּׁבָּת, אֲבָל

ר' עובדיה מברטנורא

(ג) **מקפלין את הכלים.** בגדים שפושטן מקפלן אפילו ארבעה וחמשה פעמים כדי לחזור וללבשם בו ביום. ולא שנו אלא באדם אחד אבל בשני בני אדם לא, שנראים כמתקנין. ובאדם אחד נמי לא אמרן אלא בבגדים חדשים שהם קשים ואינן ממהרים לקמוט, אבל ישנים קפולן מתקן טפי ומיחזי כמתקן. ובחדשים נמי לא אמרן אלא בלבנים, אבל לצבועים לא, שהצבועים קפולן מתקן ביותר. ובלבנים נמי לא אמרן אלא בגדים לו שאין לו בגדים אחרים להחליף, אבל יש לו בגדים אחרים להחליף לכבוד שבת אסור לקפל:

יד אברהם

in which he permits tying a pail with a weaver's rope since the latter statement merely exempts the perpetrator from liability but does not permit the act. It seems, therefore, that this statement of R' Yehudah is not made in reference to his previous statement but in regard to some other point.

One interpretation is that R' Yehudah means to emphasize that any knot which is not permanent entails no liability. If it is permanent, however, even a bow, though not strictly a knot, entails liability. According to this interpretation, he disagrees with the Rabbis quoted in the *Gemara* (113a) who distinguish between a bow and a knot and permit making even a permanent bow on the Sabbath.

Alternatively, R' Yehudah disputes R' Meir, who exempts one who ties a knot that can be untied with one hand. R' Yehudah maintains that the criterion is not whether one can untie it with one hand, but whether it is a permanent knot (*Tos. Yom Tov* quoting *Tos.* 113a, as explained by *Maharsha* and *Shabbos Shel Mi*). (Cf. *Shenos Eliyahu* and the footnotes to it for a different explanation.)

3.

Since the preceding mishnah deals with various forms of adjusting garments having to do with tying knots, such as tying the opening of a chemise and the strings of a girdle, the *Tanna* proceeds to enumerate other rules regarding the adjustment of clothing on the Sabbath, though these are not specifically relevant to the *melachah* of *tying a knot (Tos. Yom Tov).

מְקַפְּלִין אֶת הַכֵּלִים — **We may fold garments**

One who takes off his clothes on the Sabbath may fold them to wear them later on the same day.

Though one is only folding the garment to prevent any future wrinkles, it may nevertheless be prohibited if he appears to be pressing out any wrinkles which may have already formed. The Rabbis, therefore, prohibited many instances of folding. They are as follows: (a) Two people may not fold a garment together; this is forbidden, for

---
משניות / שבת – פרק טו: אלו קשרים [346]

3. We may fold garments even four or five times. We may make the beds on the night of the Sabbath for the Sabbath, but is not permanent, we are not liable for.

YAD AVRAHAM

since they stretch the garment between them, thus flattening the wrinkles completely, they *appear* to be making major adjustments in the garment; (b) even one person may fold only new garments, which are stiff and not easily wrinkled, and for which, therefore, folding is of only minor benefit and therefore permissible; old clothes, however, may not be folded since folding achieves a major improvement in their looks; (c) new garments may not be folded unless they are white; if they are colored, they may not be folded since folding substantially improves their appearance (*Rashi; Rav*). [*Rambam* explains that on the contrary, the Rabbis permitted folding only new white garments because they are so easily wrinkled and soiled (*Hil. Shabbos* 22:22).] (d) even if all the above conditions are met, the Rabbis permitted folding only if one has no other garments to wear on the Sabbath; if he has other garments, however, he may not fold this one (*Rav* from *Gem.* 113a and *Rashi*).

Tosafos and other *Rishonim* deduce that even if all the above conditions have been met, one may not fold his *tallis* after the Sabbath morning services, since one does not intend to use it again on that day (*Tos.* 113a; *Magen Avraham* 302:6).

Some permit folding the garment if it is not folded along its previous folds (*Shulchan Aruch* 302:3, from *Mordechai*).

Others permit all folding of garments unless it is done with professional exactitude (*Kol Bo*). The reasons for these views will be discussed below. *Aruch HaShulchan* notes that in his time, it was common practice for people to fold the *tallis* after services. He assumes, therefore, that the ruling of *Kol Bo* is accepted procedure. *Mishnah Berurah* and others, however, do not mention this leniency.

Some explain the ruling of the mishnah as referring to folding garments with a press. (This was made of two flat boards which could be clamped together. The garment was inserted between the boards and thus folded and pressed.) Accordingly, folding by hand is not included in the prohibition of the mishnah (*Chidushei HaRan*). This, too, is not quoted by later authorities.

אֲפִלּוּ אַרְבָּעָה וַחֲמִשָּׁה פְּעָמִים — *even four or five times.*

I.e., one may make whatever number of folds is necessary (*Meiri; Tif. Yis.*).

Rashi apparently explains this to mean that he may fold and refold the garment as many times during the day as necessary, as long as he still needs it for use on the Sabbath.

וּמַצִּיעִין אֶת הַמִּטּוֹת מִלֵּילֵי שַׁבָּת לַשַּׁבָּת, — *We may make the beds on the night of the Sabbath for the Sabbath,*

I.e., we may prepare the beds on the night of the Sabbath for sleeping on them anytime during the Sabbath (*Tos. Yom Tov* quoting *Rambam*, *Comm.*).

In Kaffich's version of *Rambam's Commentary*, the words, "for sleeping," are absent. In those days, it was customary to recline on beds while dining.

שבת
טו/ג

לֹא מְשַׁבַּת לְמוֹצָאֵי שַׁבָּת.
רַבִּי יִשְׁמָעֵאל אוֹמֵר: מְקַפְּלִין אֶת הַכֵּלִים וּמַצִּיעִין אֶת הַמִּטּוֹת מִיּוֹם הַכִּפּוּרִים לַשַּׁבָּת; וְחֶלְבֵי שַׁבָּת קְרֵבִין בְּיוֹם הַכִּפּוּרִים.
רַבִּי עֲקִיבָא אוֹמֵר: לֹא שֶׁל שַׁבָּת קְרֵבִין בְּיוֹם הַכִּפּוּרִים, וְלֹא שֶׁל יוֹם הַכִּפּוּרִים קְרֵבִין בַּשַּׁבָּת.

ר' עובדיה מברטנורא

מיום הכפורים לשבת. כשחל יום הכפורים להיות בערב שבת, לפי ששבת חמור מיום כפור: ושל יום הכפורים אינן קריבין בשבת. דהוי כטולה חול בשבת: רבי עקיבא אומר. שוין הן ואין קרבנו של אחד מהן קרב בחבירו. והלכה כרבי עקיבא:

יד אברהם

but not on the Sabbath for the night after the Sabbath. — אֲבָל לֹא מְשַׁבַּת לְמוֹצָאֵי שַׁבָּת.

Since this, too, is a form, albeit a minor one, of adjusting an article (the bed) for use, it was permitted only when necessary for use on the Sabbath (*Rambam, Hil. Shabbos* 13:7; cf. *Rambam's* explanation of folding a new white garment, quoted above). *Ravad* (ad loc.), however, explains that to make the bed for use after the Sabbath is forbidden under the general prohibition of preparing on the Sabbath for weekdays.

Aruch HaShulchan (302:11) explains that *Rambam's* view is that preparing for a weekday is prohibited only if some improvement is effected in the article. Otherwise, there is no prohibition even if it involves toil.

Our custom follows the opinion that all forms of preparation for weekdays, or even for *Yom Tov*, are prohibited on the Sabbath. See *Magen Avraham* 667:3 (quoting *Maharil*) regarding adjusting a Torah scroll on the Sabbath for the festival reading.

If, however, one's intention in making the bed is that the room be neat for the rest of the Sabbath, it is permissible (*Magen Avraham* 302:6; cf. *Aruch HaShulchan* 302:13).

רַבִּי יִשְׁמָעֵאל אוֹמֵר: מְקַפְּלִין אֶת הַכֵּלִים וּמַצִּיעִין אֶת הַמִּטּוֹת מִיּוֹם הַכִּפּוּרִים לַשַּׁבָּת. — **R' Yishmael says: We may fold garments and make beds on Yom Kippur for the Sabbath;**

This applies only if Yom Kippur falls on Friday [an impossibility with our present fixed calendar; see ArtScroll *Megillah* 1:2, *Rosh Hashanah* 1:2]. Since the Sabbath is more stringent than Yom Kippur [the former

15 3 not on the Sabbath for the night after the Sabbath.

R' Yishmael says: We may fold garments and make beds on Yom Kippur for the Sabbath; and fats of the Sabbath [sacrifices] may be offered on Yom Kippur.

R' Akiva says: Neither those of the Sabbath may be offered on Yom Kippur, nor may those of Yom Kippur be offered on the Sabbath.

YAD AVRAHAM

bearing capital punishment for willful transgression in contradistinction with the latter, which bears the penalty of *kares*], preparation may be made on Yom Kippur for the Sabbath (*Rav*).

וְחֶלְבֵי שַׁבָּת קְרֵבִין בְּיוֹם הַכִּפּוּרִים. — *and fats of the Sabbath [sacrifices] may be offered on Yom Kippur.*

I.e., if Yom Kippur falls on Sunday, the fats of any Sabbath-day sacrifices not yet consumed by the conclusion of the Sabbath may be offered that night, even though it is Yom Kippur. Since the Sabbath is more stringent than Yom Kippur, its needs may be fulfilled on Yom Kippur. If Yom Kippur falls on Friday, however, the fats of Yom Kippur sacrifices may not be offered on the Sabbath, since the sanctity of the Sabbath is greater than that of Yom Kippur (*Rav*).

רַבִּי עֲקִיבָא אוֹמֵר: לֹא שֶׁל שַׁבָּת קְרֵבִין בְּיוֹם הַכִּפּוּרִים, וְלֹא שֶׁל יוֹם הַכִּפּוּרִים קְרֵבִין בַּשַּׁבָּת. — *R' Akiva says: Neither those of the Sabbath may be offered on Yom Kippur, nor may those of Yom Kippur be offered on the Sabbath.*

R' Akiva regards the sanctities of both days as equal, and we may therefore not prepare from one day to the next. The halachah is in accordance with R' Akiva (*Rav*).

There is no doubt that R' Akiva agrees that the sanctity of the Sabbath is greater than that of Yom Kippur. However, he shows from certain Biblical verses that with respect to burning the sacrifices of one on the other they are regarded as equal (*Tos. Yom Tov*).

Just as R' Akiva prohibits offering the fats of Sabbath sacrifices on Yom Kippur and vice versa, he also prohibits folding garments and making beds on Yom Kippur for the Sabbath.

[We have already mentioned that these cases could come about only in Talmudic times, when the Sanhedrin would declare the New Moon after witnesses testified that they saw its first phase. According to our present fixed calendar, however, Yom Kippur can only fall on Monday, Wednesday, Thursday or the Sabbath.]

פרק ששה עשר
Chapter Sixteen

This chapter deals with what one may or may not do if a fire breaks out on the Sabbath. The first several mishnayos deal with what, how and to where a person may remove his possessions from a house which has caught fire. The remaining mishnayos discuss what one may do about the fire. [Obviously, this chapter pertains to fires that threaten only property, not human life, e.g., where there is no one in the building at the time of the fire, or if one is sure that all the occupants can be safely evacuated without resorting to *extinguishing the fire. Where lives may be lost, however, one is obligated to extinguish the fire. Though one may not violate the Sabbath laws to save property, one is obligated to violate them to save lives.] Since a person becomes panicky over the fact of his property in a burning building, he is liable to extinguish the fire while trying to rescue his possessions. To do so would violate the *melachah* of *extinguishing a fire.*[1] The Rabbis, therefore, limited what a person may rescue in order that the owner realize that he must abandon hope of saving all his property. Knowing this, he will not come to extinguish the fire in an attempt to salvage all his possessions (*Gem.* 117b; *Rambam, Hil. Shabbos* 23:20).

This rule applies only to rescuing items found in a house or yard which the fire has reached. Items found in houses that the fire has not yet reached are not included in this prohibition. Since the tenants of those dwellings are not yet panicky, they may rescue all their possessions (*Tos.* 115a; *Shulchan Aruch* 334:1).

---

1. Extinguishing a fire to save one's belongings is a *work not done for its defined purpose*, viz., making charcoal (see above 2:5). According to the halachah, one who performs such work on the Sabbath is exempt from a sin offering since he has not infracted a Torah prohibition. Consequently, enacting a safeguard lest one extinguish the fire is a גְּזֵרָה לִגְזֵרָה, *a double safeguard*, which the Rabbis do not enact. *Meiri* explains, therefore, that this is not a decree lest one extinguish the fire, but a positive fact that one will extinguish the fire if he is not limited. *Pri Megadim, Aishel Avraham* 334:2 states that the *Gemara* follows R' Yehudah who declares one liable for performing *work not done for its defined purpose*. According to R' Shimon who exempts him, the limits were enacted to prevent one from carrying things out into a public domain.

שבת
טז/א

[א] **כָּל כִּתְבֵי** הַקֹּדֶשׁ מַצִּילִין אוֹתָן מִפְּנֵי הַדְּלֵקָה, בֵּין שֶׁקּוֹרִין בָּהֶן וּבֵין שֶׁאֵין קוֹרִין בָּהֶן. וְאַף־עַל־פִּי שֶׁכְּתוּבִים בְּכָל לָשׁוֹן, טְעוּנִים גְּנִיזָה.

ר' עובדיה מברטנורא

פרק ששה עשר – כל כתבי. (א) **כל כתבי הקדש.** אפילו נביאים וכתובים, מצילין אותן מחצר שנפלה בו הדליקה לחצר אחרת שבאותו מבוי, אף על פי שלא ערבו. והוא שיהיו כתובים בכתב אשורי ובלשון הקודש: **בין שקורין בהן.** כגון נביאים שמפטירין בהן בשבת בבית הכנסת: **בין שאין קורין בהן.** כגון כתובים דאף יחידים אין קורין בהן בשבת מפני ביטול בית המדרש כדלקמן, שהיו דורשים לעם בשבת ומורים להן הלכות איסור והיתר, לפי שכל ימות החול הם עסוקים במלאכתן, ואסרו לקרות בכתובים בשבת בשעת בית המדרש משום דמשכי לבא ואתו לאמנועי מלשמוע הדרשה: **ואף על פי שכתובים בכל לשון.** ואיכא למאן דאמר דלא נתנו לקרות בהן ואין מצילין אותן, אפילו הכי טעונים גניזה ואסור להניחן במקום הפקר:

יד אברהם

1.

The mishnah commences with the rescue of books of Holy Scripture and other sacred articles, and continues with the laws of rescuing foodstuffs and utensils.

כָּל כִּתְבֵי הַקֹּדֶשׁ — *All [books of] Holy Scripture*

These include תּוֹרָה, *Torah*, i.e., Pentateuch, נְבִיאִים [*Neviim*], *Prophets*, and כְּתוּבִים, [*Kesuvim*], *the Holy Writings (Hagiographa), if they are written in the original Hebrew with the Assyrian script* (see footnote to 12:4; *Rav* from *Gem.* 115a).

מַצִּילִין אוֹתָן מִפְּנֵי הַדְּלֵקָה — *may be saved from the fire,*

I.e., they may be removed from a house or courtyard where a fire has broken out, as long as they themselves have not caught fire (*Meiri*).

בֵּין שֶׁקּוֹרִין בָּהֶן — *whether we read from them*

E.g., Torah scrolls, which are read regularly in the synagogue, and scrolls of *Neviim*, Prophets, used to read the *haftarah* (*Rav; Rashi; Rambam, Comm.; Tif. Yis.* from *Gem.* 115a).

וּבֵין שֶׁאֵין קוֹרִין בָּהֶן — *or whether we do not read from them.*

Viz., the books of *Kesuvim*, Hagiographa, which were not read even privately on the Sabbath, as will be explained below (*Rav; Rashi; Rambam, Comm.;* from *Gem.* ll5a).

וְאַף־עַל־פִּי שֶׁכְּתוּבִים בְּכָל לָשׁוֹן, טְעוּנִים גְּנִיזָה. — *Even though they are written in any [foreign] language, they warrant being hidden away.*

The mishnah is to be understood as follows: All books of Scripture, whether read on the Sabbath or not, are to be saved from a fire on the Sabbath, *if they are written in Hebrew.* If they are written in a foreign language, *though they may not be saved from a fire on the Sabbath,* they must, at other times, be put away in a repository for holy objects when they become worn out (*Rav* from *Gem.* 115a). [The italicized phrases are assumed by the mishnah to be understood, and

1. All [books of] Holy Scripture may be saved from the fire, whether we read from them or whether we do not read from them. Even though they are written in any [foreign] language, they warrant being hidden away.

YAD AVRAHAM

therefore not stated.]

According to the view of Rabban Shimon ben Gamliel, which our mishnah follows, books of Scripture were not permitted to be written in any language other than Hebrew or, in the case of the Pentateuch, Greek (*Megillah* 1:8). One was therefore not permitted to read foreign-language versions of them, either on the Sabbath or any other day of the week. Consequently, one was not permitted to save these books of foreign-language Scripture from a fire. [This is in contrast to the books of *Kesuvim* which, though not to be read on the Sabbath, may be read during the week and even on part of the Sabbath and are therefore to be saved from a fire on the Sabbath.] The mishnah, however, states that although they lack the sanctity to warrant saving them from a fire on the Sabbath, they may not, at other times, be discarded if they are worn out, but must be put away in a repository for holy objects. [This was a room or vault were holy objects no longer fit for use were placed. The place was eventually sealed when it became filled.]

Rashi cites the opinion of his teachers who state that the prohibition against writing Scripture in foreign languages applies only to *Kesuvim*. *Neviim*, however, having already been translated by Yonasan ben Uziel (a pupil of the *Tanna* Hillel) into Aramaic, could be written in other languages too. *Rashi* himself, however, maintains that even though Yonasan ben Uziel translated *Neviim*, he did not commit his translation to writing, but recited it orally. There is therefore no precedent for assuming the permissibility of writing foreign-language translations of *Neviim*.

During the Tannaic and Amoraic periods, the Rabbis realized that the Torah was becoming forgotten by the people. They therefore permitted the Oral Law to be committed to writing. This originally included books of *Mishnah* only. Subsequently, *Aggadah*, *Siddur*, *Gemara*, and other holy books were also written. They permitted also the writing of the Holy Scriptures in foreign languages for the benefit of the untutored. Additionally, they permitted the Scripture to be written in any script, with any type of ink. Since today all these books may be written, they, too, are to be rescued from fire on the Sabbath (*Tos.* from *Gittin* 60a; *Shulchan Aruch* 334:12).

In this context, printed books are regarded as written ones (*Magen Avraham* 334:17, 284; *Turei Zahav* 284:2).

This should not be misconstrued as a blanket sanction to override prohibitions whenever deemed beneficial. Writing the Oral Law was permitted only because there was a threat that the entire body of Jewish Law would be forgotten, posing a threat to Jewish life in general. Even this was permitted

שבת טז/א

וּמִפְּנֵי מָה אֵין קוֹרִין בָּהֶם? מִפְּנֵי בִּטוּל בֵּית הַמִּדְרָשׁ. מַצִּילִין תִּיק הַסֵּפֶר עִם הַסֵּפֶר, וְתִיק הַתְּפִלִּין עִם הַתְּפִלִּין, וְאַף־עַל־פִּי שֶׁיֵּשׁ בְּתוֹכָן מָעוֹת. וּלְהֵיכָן מַצִּילִין אוֹתָן? לְמָבוֹי שֶׁאֵינוֹ מְפֻלָּשׁ.

ר' עובדיה מברטנורא

למבוי שאינו מפולש. שיש לו שלש מחיצות ולחי אחד ברוח רביעית, זה מבוי שאינו מפולש האמור כאן. שלש מחיצות בלא לחי, זהו מבוי מפולש. והכי מפרש לה בגמרא. ואין הלכה כבן בתירא:

יד אברהם

only after much deliberation and hesitation. First, only the Mishnah was written (see *Igeres Rav Sherira Gaon*). Later, various components of the explanations of the Mishnah, e.g., *Gemara*, *Aggadah*, prayers, *Targum*, were gradually committed to writing (see *Gittin* 60a).

וּמִפְּנֵי מָה אֵין קוֹרִין בָּהֶם? — *Now why do we not read from them?*

I.e., why may we not read from the *Kesuvim* on the Sabbath?

מִפְּנֵי בִּטוּל בֵּית הַמִּדְרָשׁ. — *Because of the neglect of the lecture hall.*

In Talmudic times it was customary to lecture for the general population on the Sabbath. In these lectures were included discourses on the various laws of Halachah. This could not be done during the week when most people were occupied with earning a livelihood. In order to insure attendance, the Rabbis prohibited the reading of *Kesuvim* on the Sabbath during the lecture hours (i.e., before the noonday meal), since people would become engrossed in them and fail to attend the lecture. Since the lecture pertained to daily observances, it was more beneficial for the public to attend the lectures than to study *Kesuvim*. After the noonday meal, it was permissible to read from the *Kesuvim* (Rashi; Rav from Gem. 116b).

[*Kesuvim* was regarded as the most interesting part of Scripture, as evidenced by the fact that its books were read to the *Kohen Gadol* on the night of Yom Kippur to keep him awake. See *Yoma* 7:1.]

Nowadays, in places where it has become common for everyone to attend Sabbath lectures, all holy books may be read. They may certainly be read in those places where no lecture at all is held (*Tif. Yis.* from *HaMaor HaKatan*; see *Meiri*, who explains *HaMaor HaKatan* slightly differently).

מַצִּילִין תִּיק הַסֵּפֶר עִם הַסֵּפֶר, וְתִיק הַתְּפִלִּין עִם הַתְּפִלִּין, — *We may save the case of the scroll with the scroll, and the case of the tefillin with the tefillin,*

[When saving a Torah scroll or a pair of *tefillin* from a fire on the Sabbath, their cases may be saved along with them.]

וְאַף־עַל־פִּי שֶׁיֵּשׁ בְּתוֹכָן מָעוֹת. — *even though there is money in them.*

Even though in addition to the Torah scroll or *tefillin* these cases also contain money, they may still be rescued on the Sabbath (*Tif. Yis.*).

[Money is regarded as *muktzeh*,

16 Now why do we not read from them? Because of
1 the neglect of the lecture hall.

We may save the case of the scroll with the scroll, and the case of the *tefillin* with the *tefillin*, even though there is money in them. To where may we take them for safety? To a blind alley.

YAD AVRAHAM

something set aside from use on the Sabbath, and therefore normally forbidden to be moved on the Sabbath (*Shulchan Aruch* 309:4, 310:7). The laws of *muktzeh* are explained in Chapters 3 and 17.]

וּלְהֵיכָן מַצִּילִין אוֹתָן? — *To where may we take them for safety?*

[I.e., where may we take the books of Scripture or *tefillin* (either with or without any money in them). The removal of items from a burning building in addition to concerning itself with the special Rabbinic decrees regarding fires must also concern itself with the general laws governing the transfer of objects from one domain to another. Needless to say, no transfer from a private domain to a public one is permitted. Since this involves violation of a Torah law, it can be done only to save lives, not property. However, removal to certain Rabbinically prohibited domains is permissible. It is to the question of which of these domains one may remove these objects that the mishnah addresses itself.]

לְמָבוֹי שֶׁאֵינוֹ מְפֻלָּשׁ. — *To a blind alley.*

In this context, *a blind alley* refers to an alley enclosed on three sides, with a post at the open end. An open alley is one enclosed on three sides, without a post at the open end (*Rav* from *Gem.* 117b).

An alley enclosed on three sides and completely open on the fourth side is a domain in which, according to Biblical law,[1] one is permitted to carry. Additionally, one is permitted to carry from a private domain into this alley. Carrying either in or into this alley was, however, Rabbinically prohibited because, lacking any enclosure on the fourth side, it resembles a public domain (*Rashi* to *Eruvin* 2a). The Rabbis, however, did not require a full enclosure for the fourth side. Rather, they declared it sufficient to close the fourth side with a minimal, symbolic enclosure, since such would suffice to indicate to people the distinction between an open alley and a public domain.[2] The mishnah in *Eruvin* (1:2) states that there is a dispute as to precisely what form of minimal enclosure the Rabbis required for the fourth side. Beis Shammai require both a post at least ten handbreadths high at the open end (and placed at the mouth of the alley

---

1. The exact nature of this domain according to Biblical law is the subject of a dispute between *Rambam* (*Hil. Shabbos* 17:2) who regards it as an exempt area and the majority of other *Rishonim* who regard it as a private domain. See General Introduction, p. 12, for a fuller discussion of this point and its implications.

2. According to *Rambam* (see previous footnote), the post has Biblical significance, too, altering the status of the alley from an exempt area to a private domain.

שבת
טז/ב

בֶּן בְּתֵירָא אוֹמֵר: אַף לִמְפֻלָּשׁ.

[ב] **מַצִּילִין** מְזוֹן שָׁלֹשׁ סְעוּדוֹת; הָרָאוּי לְאָדָם לְאָדָם, הָרָאוּי לִבְהֵמָה לִבְהֵמָה. כֵּיצַד? נָפְלָה דְלֵקָה בְּלֵילֵי שַׁבָּת, מַצִּילִין מְזוֹן שָׁלֹשׁ סְעוּדוֹת; בַּשַּׁחֲרִית, מַצִּילִין מְזוֹן שְׁתֵּי סְעוּדוֹת;

ר' עובדיה מברטנורא

(ב) **מצילין מזון שלש סעודות.** ואף על גב דבהתירא קא טרח דהא לא שרו ליה לאצולי אלא לחצר המעורבת בלבד, אפילו הכי לא שרו ליה לאצולי טפי, מפני שאדם בהול על ממונו ואי שרית ליה אתי לכבויי: **נפלה דליקה בלילי שבת.** קודם אכילה: **שחרית.** קודם סעודה:

יד אברהם

near one of the two side walls) plus a crossbar spanning the entire mouth of the alley: Beis Hillel require only one of these two devices; i.e., either a post or a crossbar. R' Eliezer requires two side posts, one on either side of the mouth of the alley. [There is a question in the Gemara there (11b) as to whether or not he requires a crossbar as well.]

The mishnah here follows the opinion of R' Eliezer that an alley with three walls requires two side posts on the fourth side if it is to satisfy the Rabbinic requirements for carrying in it or into it from a private domain. This requirement, however, is only for usual, optional carrying. For the purpose of saving Scripture or *tefillin*, R' Eliezer permits carrying even into an alley with only one post at its mouth (*Rav* from *Gem.* 117b).

Furthermore, it is permissible to remove these objects even to an alley which lacks the *eruv chatzeiros* (see General Introduction, p. 15) normally required before one may carry into it (*Tos. Yom Tov*). [This point will be more fully discussed at the end of mishnah 3.]

בֶּן בְּתֵירָא אוֹמֵר: אַף לִמְפֻלָּשׁ. — **Ben Beseira says: Even to an open one.**

I.e., R' Eliezer permits removal of a Torah scroll to an alley without any post at all affixed to its open end (*Rav* from *Gem.*). The halachah is not in accordance with Ben Beseira (*Rav*).

2.

מַצִּילִין מְזוֹן שָׁלֹשׁ סְעוּדוֹת; — **We may save [enough] food for three meals;**

I.e., one may save enough food to fulfill his obligation of eating three meals on the Sabbath [i.e., Friday evening, Shabbos morning and Shabbos afternoon] (*Tos. Yom Tov*).[1]

In contrast to books of Scripture and *tefillin*, foodstuffs may be removed only to an area into which one is otherwise permitted to carry, i.e., a yard properly enclosed on its fourth side and incorporated by an *eruv chatzeiros* (*Rav*). [See the end of mishnah 3.]

---

1. In instructing Israel concerning the eating of the portion of *manna* reserved for the Sabbath, Moses used the word הַיּוֹם, *this day*, three times in the same verse (*Exodus* 16:25). From this the *Gemara* (117b) derives the obligation to eat three meals in honor of the Sabbath.

16 Ben Beseira says: Even to an open one.
2

2. **W**e may save [enough] food for three meals; what is fit for people [may be saved] for people, what is fit for animals [may be saved] for animals. How so? If a fire broke out on the Sabbath eve, we may save [only enough] food for three meals; if during the morning, we may save [only enough] food for two meals;

YAD AVRAHAM

Even though he is transferring the foodstuffs to a yard into which he is otherwise permitted to carry, the Rabbis nevertheless restricted removing any more than these minimum food requirements. They did so for fear that in his haste to save his property he might extinguish the fire (*Rav* from *Gem.* 117b). By limiting the amount of food he can remove to that needed for the Sabbath, they removed the element of haste from his salvage efforts, thereby making it unlikely that he forget the prohibition of *extinguishing (*Tos. Yom Tov*).

הָרָאוּי לְאָדָם לְאָדָם, — *what is fit for people [may be saved] for people,*
[I.e., three meals of food fit for human consumption may be saved for every person who requires it.]

הָרָאוּי לִבְהֵמָה לִבְהֵמָה. — *what is fit for animals [may be saved] for animals.*
I.e., three feedings of animal fodder may be saved for each animal. Obviously, there is no obligation to feed one's cattle with three Sabbath meals. However, since the Talmud (*Berachos* 40a) requires a person to feed his animals before he himself sits down to eat, in order to partake of the three Sabbath meals, he must have sufficient fodder for three feedings for his livestock (*Tif. Yis.*).

כֵּיצַד? — *How so?*
[I.e., under what circumstances may one save enough food for three meals?]

נָפְלָה דְלֵקָה בְּלֵילֵי שַׁבָּת, — *If a fire broke out on the Sabbath eve,*
I.e., if one's house caught fire on Friday night before he ate (*Rav; Rashi*).

מַצִּילִין מְזוֹן שָׁלֹשׁ סְעוּדוֹת; — *we may save [only enough] food for three meals;*
[I.e., we may save enough for the three Sabbath meals. Only in this circumstance did the Rabbis permit saving food for three meals.]

בְּשַׁחֲרִית, — *if during the morning,*
I.e., if the fire broke out before the morning meal (*Rav; Rashi*).

מַצִּילִין מְזוֹן שְׁתֵּי סְעוּדוֹת; — *we may save [only enough] food for two meals;*
[Since only two meals remain to be eaten on this Sabbath.[1]

---

1. Peculiarly, in the case of the fire breaking out at night, *Rav* and *Rashi* state, "before he ate," whereas concerning the fire breaking out in the morning, they state, "before the meal." One reason given for this change is as follows: Since the evening meal may be eaten anytime during the night, even though the usual suppertime has passed, one may save food for three meals, as long as he has not yet eaten. In the daytime, however, if one has not eaten until the afternoon, he can no longer fulfill his obligation to eat the morning meal. *Rashi*, therefore, states, "before the meal," to intimate that he may save food for two meals only if the usual mealtime has not yet passed. If it has passed, even though he himself

בְּמִנְחָה, מְזוֹן סְעוּדָה אֶחָת. רַבִּי יוֹסֵי אוֹמֵר: לְעוֹלָם מַצִּילִין מְזוֹן שָׁלֹשׁ סְעוּדוֹת.

[ג] **מַצִּילִין** סַל מָלֵא כִּכָּרוֹת — וְאַף־עַל־פִּי שֶׁיֵּשׁ בּוֹ מֵאָה סְעוּדוֹת — וְעִגּוּל שֶׁל דְּבֵלָה, וְחָבִית שֶׁל יַיִן. וְאוֹמֵר לַאֲחֵרִים: ״בֹּאוּ וְהַצִּילוּ לָכֶם.״

―――― ר' עובדיה מברטנורא ――――

רבי יוסי אומר לעולם הוא מציל. הואיל ויומא בר הכי הוא ובהתירא טרח. ואין הלכה כרבי יוסי: (ג) **מצילין סל מלא בככרות.** הואיל ובבת אחת הוא מציל מה לי פורתא מה לי טובא: **ועגול של דבילה.** אף על פי שהוא גדול ויש בו סעודות הרבה:

יד אברהם

בְּמִנְחָה, מְזוֹן סְעוּדָה אֶחָת — *if in the afternoon, [we may save only enough] food for one meal.*

[I.e., if the fire broke out in the afternoon, before the third meal, we may save only enough food for one meal.]

רַבִּי יוֹסֵי אוֹמֵר: לְעוֹלָם מַצִּילִין מְזוֹן שָׁלֹשׁ סְעוּדוֹת. — *R' Yose says: We may always save [enough] food for three meals.*

Since the day requires the partaking of three meals, the Rabbis did not differentiate between the various times of the day. Rather, they made a general rule permitting the removal of enough food for three meals (*Rav; Rashi; Tif. Yis.*). Since, as explained above, he is permitted to carry the food only to an area into which he is otherwise permitted to carry, there was no reason for the Rabbis to vary their limitations according to the time of day. Whatever reduction of haste is achieved by the three-meal limitation is achieved equally well whether applied on a Friday evening or Shabbos afternoon (*Rashi*).

The halachah is not in accordance with R' Yose.

One may, however, remove as much beverage as he may use during the rest of the day, even if he has already eaten all his meals (*Beur Halachah* to 334:1 from *Tos. Shabbos*).

3.

מַצִּילִין — *We may save*

[I.e., we may save from fire on the Sabbath.]

סַל מָלֵא כִּכָּרוֹת — *a basket full of loaves* —

has not yet eaten, he may save only enough food for one meal (*Bach* 334).

Others disagree and explain this differently. In view of the *Baraisa* quoted in the *Gemara* (118a), that one may wash the dishes after the morning meal for the noon meal, and after the noon meal for the late afternoon meal, it appears that it was customary for them to eat a light breakfast in the morning, and then to eat the regular Sabbath meal at noon, followed by another meal in the late afternoon. *Rashi*, therefore, by stating "before the meal" indicates that even if one has eaten breakfast, as long as one has not yet eaten the regular Sabbath meal, he may still save food for two meals since it was customary to eat this much (*Pri Megadim, Mishbetzos Zahav* 334:1).

if in the afternoon, [we may save only enough] food for one meal. R' Yose says: We may always save [enough] food for three meals.

3. **We** may save a basket full of loaves — even though there is [enough] in it for one hundred meals — or a round cake of pressed figs, or a barrel of wine. And one may say to others, "Come and save for yourselves."

YAD AVRAHAM

Since he is removing but one basket from the house, which he must in any case be permitted to remove since it contains the loaves necessary for his three meals, there can be no objection to any additional loaves contained in that basket (*Rav*).

וְאַף-עַל-פִּי שֶׁיֵּשׁ בּוֹ מֵאָה סְעוּדוֹת — *even though there is [enough] in it for one hundred meals* —

[I.e., even though it contains much more than is needed for the three Sabbath meals.]

וְעָגוּל שֶׁל דְּבֵלָה, — *or a round cake of pressed figs*,

Dried figs were customarily pressed into large round cakes. This, too, contained much more than was needed for three meals (*Rav*).

וְחָבִית שֶׁל יַיִן. — *or a barrel of wine*.

[This, too, contained much more wine than was required for the three Sabbath meals.]

וְאוֹמֵר לַאֲחֵרִים: ״בֹּאוּ וְהַצִּילוּ לָכֶם.״ — *And one may say to others, "Come and save for yourselves."*

By announcing that they may save for themselves, he relinquishes his title to the property, and it becomes הֶפְקֵר, *ownerless*. Accordingly, others may retrieve it for themselves (*Rashi, Gem.* 120a).

Ran questions the necessity of a formal renunciation of title. He contends that since the property is irretrievably lost to its owner (because the halachah forbids him to save it), it is automatically regarded as ownerless. *Ran* cites as proof of this principle the rule that an object swept out to sea, being irretrievably lost to its owner, may be salvaged and kept by any passing boat. According to *Ran*, the point of the mishnah is quite the reverse; namely, that even though he is telling them to salvage what they can in the hope that they will return it to him, they are still permitted to do so, since legally it is ownerless and therefore theirs to keep.

R' Yitzchak Abohab, siding with *Rashi*, draws a distinction between something physically irretrievable — which is thereby deemed ownerless — and something which is physically retrievable but which the halachah prevents one from retrieving — which is not in consequence regarded as ownerless. *Beis Yosef* 334 sides with *Ran* and finds this distinction unsatisfactory.

Others reconcile *Rashi* in the following manner: Since the householder is permitted to announce before non-Jews, "Anyone who extinguishes the fire will not lose" (*Gem.* 121a), thus hinting to the non-Jewish populace that they will be rewarded for their services, the food is regarded as retrievable. It is, therefore, not automatically

שבת טז/ג

וְאִם הָיוּ פִּקְחִין, עוֹשִׂין עִמּוֹ חֶשְׁבּוֹן אַחַר הַשַּׁבָּת. לְהֵיכָן מַצִּילִין אוֹתָן? לֶחָצֵר הַמְעֹרֶבֶת. בֶּן בְּתֵירָא אוֹמֵר: אַף לְשֶׁאֵינָהּ מְעֹרֶבֶת.

ר' עובדיה מברטנורא

ואם היו פקחים. ויודעים שאם ישאלו שכר כפועלים לאו שכר שבת שקלי, כיון דמעיקרא לאו אדעתא דשכר פעולה באו, עושין עמו חשבון לאחר שבת. ובגירסא שמיס עסקינן, דאף על גב דמהפקירא קא זכי ומה שהציל דידיה הוי, מכל מקום לא ניחא ליה דליתהני מאחרים מידע דעל כרחיה אפקריה, ובהנס נמי לא ניחא ליה דלטרח, הילכך שקיל אגריה.

יד אברהם

ownerless unless he announces, "Come and save for yourselves" (*Bach* 334).

Magen Avraham (334:11) adds that since it is possible for him to find even Jews who are well disposed towards him and who would rescue the food and return it to him (which, as will be explained below, is their prerogative), it does not automatically become ownerless unless he formally renounces his ownership.

As regards the amount others may save, many authorities rule that they may save no more than the owner, i.e. sufficient food for the three Sabbath meals for each of them, or the contents of one large vessel (*Rambam, Hil. Shabbos* 23:24; *Tur* 334).

Others, however, maintain that only the owner, who is likely to panic and extinguish the fire in order to save his possessions, is limited to the above maximum. Strangers, who are not losing anything and who therefore have no reason to panic and extinguish the fire, are not limited and may therefore salvage as much as they can. Furthermore, since if the fire were to be extinguished they would lose their privilege of acquiring any property from that house (because the owner would no longer be enjoined from saving his property), it is, therefore, not to their advantage to extinguish the fire. Consequently, no decrees are necessary to prevent them from forgetfully extinguishing the fire (*Tif. Yis.,* quoting *Ran* from *Rabbeinu Yeshayah of Trani*).

וְאִם הָיוּ פִקְחִין — *If they were discerning,*

I.e., if they were sophisticated in their knowledge of the Sabbath laws.

עוֹשִׂין עִמּוֹ חֶשְׁבּוֹן אַחַר הַשַּׁבָּת. — *they would make a reckoning with him after the Sabbath.*

I.e., they may accept wages for effecting the rescue. Generally, wages may neither be paid nor accepted for work done on the Sabbath, even if that work is permissible. For example, one may not pay someone for watching his field or his child on the Sabbath, though such work in no way violates the Sabbath laws (*Bava Metzia* 58a; *Shulchan Aruch* 306:4,5). Only if one is being paid a weekly, monthly, or yearly rate, may the Sabbath work be included (ibid.). In the case of this mishnah, however, their efforts to save the food were not made for the purpose of earning wages on the Sabbath because the food rescued was actually ownerless and therefore rightfully the property of the rescuers. It is therefore their prerogative to exchange the food for the worth of their labor (*Rav; Rashi*).

The mishnah deals here with God-fearing people, who, knowing that the householder relinquished title to the food under duress, refuse to take advantage of the situation, though they

16 3 If they were discerning, they would make a reckoning with him after the Sabbath.

To where may they take them for safety? To a courtyard provided with an *eruv*. Ben Beseira says: Even to one not provided with an *eruv*.

YAD AVRAHAM

are legally entitled to do so. On the other hand, they are not that pious that they would rescue the food completely gratis. They may, therefore, make a reckoning after the Sabbath (*Rav*). Truly pious people, however, would not accept any money so as not to benefit financially from anything even resembling tainted money, i.e., money earned for Sabbath work (*Rav, Rashi* from *Gem.* 120a).

לְהֵיכָן מַצִּילִין אוֹתָן? — *To where may they take them for safety?*

I.e., where may he take food and drink?

לְחָצֵר הַמְעוֹרֶבֶת. — *To a courtyard provided with an eruv.*

[I.e., in contrast to the rescue of Scripture and *tefillin*, no leniency is granted for the removal of food on the Sabbath. Foodstuffs may be carried only to and in places where carrying is otherwise permitted. The requirements include:

(a) A properly enclosed fourth side, i.e., the mouth of the alley, if not actually enclosed, must have either a crossbar or a post.[1]

(b) A courtyard, into which two or more Jewish-owned houses open, may not be carried in by Rabbinic decree. The mechanism established by the Rabbis to enable one to carry there is known as an *eruv chatzeiros*. [The reasons for this decree and the rationale of the *eruv* have been explained in the General Introduction, p. 15.] Thus, one may not remove the food to a courtyard unless it has been incorporated by an *eruv chatzeiros*.

(c) Similarly, a properly enclosed alley, into which several courtyards open, is forbidden by Rabbinic decree to be carried in unless it, too, has been incorporated by a merger of the alleys. This is a procedure similar to an *eruv chatzeiros* and accomplishes for the courtyards what the *eruv chatzeiros* does for the dwellings. Those rules and mechanisms are discussed in tractate *Eruvin*, Chap. 6.

בֶּן בְּתֵירָא אוֹמֵר: אַף לְשֶׁאֵינָהּ מְעֹרֶבֶת — *Ben Beseira says: Even to one not provided with an eruv.*

[Ben Beseira maintains that leniency is granted even for the removal of foodstuffs, to the extent that they be removed to a courtyard lacking an *eruv chatzeiros*. In contrast, however, to his ruling in mishnah 2 permitting the removal of books of Scripture and *tefillin* to even a courtyard without any enclosure whatever on its fourth side, he agrees that foodstuffs may be removed only to a courtyard properly enclosed on its fourth side.] The halachah follows the first opinion (*Tif. Yis.*).

---

1. [Although mishnah 1 indicated that to be properly enclosed the open side must have two posts, that is because mishnah 1 follows the ruling of R' Eliezer, as explained there. The halachah, however, is in *accordance* with Beis Hillel who require only one post (*Shulchan Aruch* 363:3).]

[ד] **וּלְשָׁם** מוֹצִיא כָּל כְּלֵי תַשְׁמִישׁוֹ, וְלוֹבֵשׁ כָּל מַה שֶּׁיָּכוֹל לִלְבֹּשׁ, וְעוֹטֵף כָּל מַה שֶּׁיָּכוֹל לַעֲטֹף. רַבִּי יוֹסֵי אוֹמֵר: שְׁמוֹנָה עָשָׂר כֵּלִים. וְחוֹזֵר וְלוֹבֵשׁ וּמוֹצִיא.

---- ר' עובדיה מברטנורא ----

(ד) **ולשם הוא מוציא.** לחצר קמא לחצר המעורבת, ולבן בתירא אפילו לחצר שאינה מעורבת: **כלי תשמישו.** שצריכים לו לאותו היום לסעודה: **שמונה עשר כלים.** שהוא רגיל ללבוש בחול בבת אחת ותו לא. ואלו הן, הסרבל העליון, ומלבוש שממלאין אותו מוך וצמר גפן בין תפירה לתפירה שקורין בערבי מחש"א, וחגור רחב שחוגר ממעל למדיו, ובגד לר וקלר שקורין בלע"ז גוג"א, וחלוק שלובש על בשרו שקורין קמי"א, וחגור שחוגרים עליה, וכובע שבראשו, ומגנפת ושני מנעלים שברגליו, ושני בתי שוקים, ושני בתי ידים שמלבישים אותם על הידים ומכסין בהן הזרועות עד האצילים, ושני רדידים שמתנגב בהן, וטלית קטן שמכסה בו ראשו וכתפיו, וסודר שבצוארו ותלויין שני ראשיו לפניו וקורין לו בערבי שי"ד: **בואו והצילו עמי.** שכשם שהוא מטיל כך הם מטילים.

---- יד אברהם ----

4.

וּלְשָׁם — *And to there*

I.e., to whatever area foodstuffs may be removed, so, too, may those other items be removed. As seen in the previous mishnah, the removal of items to a courtyard lacking an *eruv chatzeiros* is the subject of a dispute between the *Tanna Kamma* and Ben Beseira (*Rav*).

מוֹצִיא כָּל כְּלֵי תַשְׁמִישׁוֹ — *he may take out all the utensils required for his use,*

I.e., he may carry out all utensils required for serving meals on that Sabbath (*Rav; Rashi*).

וְלוֹבֵשׁ כָּל מַה שֶּׁיָּכוֹל לִלְבֹּשׁ — *and he may don all that he can wear,*

I.e., he may dress himself in various garments for the purpose of removing them from the burning house.

Some authorities maintain that just as one may not carry his utensils into any domain other than a courtyard provided with an *eruv*, so too, he may not don any clothing for the purpose of saving it from the fire except to go out to such a domain. Thus, this is a continuation of the preceding sentence (*Rambam, Hil. Shabbos* 2.3:20; *Ran;*

Shulchan Aruch 334:10).

Others, however, rule that since the clothing is being worn rather than carried, it may be worn even to a courtyard not provided with an *eruv*. Since one may, under ordinary circumstances, wear whatever garments he wishes when going out to a courtyard incorporated by an *eruv*, to allow him to do so even in case of a fire does not amount to any special leniency. According to these authorities, this phrase is not a continuation of the previous section of the mishnah but marks the beginning of a new section (*Mordechai; Sefer HaTerumah* Ch. 245, quoted by *Semag; Rama* 334:10).

According to this latter opinion, some conjecture that it is even permissible to do so even when escaping via a public domain. Since this, too, is permissible under ordinary circumstances it is permissible even in cases of a fire (*Tos. R' Akiva; Mishnah Berurah* 334:26).

וְעוֹטֵף כָּל מַה שֶּׁיָּכוֹל לַעֲטֹף — *and wrap himself in all that he can wrap himself.*

[Certain garments, such as turbans and shawls, were not made to be put on and fastened but were merely wrapped around the body.]

4. And to there he may take out all the utensils required for his use, and he may don all that he can wear, and wrap himself in all that he can wrap himself. R' Yose says: [He may don only] eighteen articles [of apparel]. And he may return and don [other garments] and take [them] out.

YAD AVRAHAM

רַבִּי יוֹסֵי אוֹמֵר: שְׁמוֹנָה עָשָׂר כֵּלִים. — *R' Yose says:* [He may don only] *eighteen articles* [of apparel].

I.e., only the eighteen articles of clothing commonly worn on weekdays, viz. (1) a cloak, (2) a quilted coat [similar to a down jacket or a coat lining], (3) a hollow belt worn over the outer garments, (4) a linen tunic, (5) an undershirt, (6) a shawl wrapped around the body, (7) a turban, (8,9) two belts, (10,11) a pair of shoes, (12,13) a pair of stockings, (14,15) leggings, (16) a belt worn on the undershirt, (17) a hat, (18) and a scarf (*Rashi*).

Others list them as follows: (1) a cloak, (2) quilted coat, (3) a wide belt worn over the garments, (4) a vest, (5) an undershirt, (6) a belt worn on the undershirt, (7) a hat, (8) a cap, (9,10) a pair of shoes, (11,12) a pair of leggings, (13,14) a pair of gloves that cover the arms as far as the elbows, (15,16) two kerchiefs (worn but used to dry oneself), (17) a small shawl that covers the head and shoulders, (18) a scarf (*Rav*). *Rambam* (*Comm.*) offers yet a third list.

R' Yose rules that only these eighteen commonly worn garments may be worn for the purpose of removing them from a burning house. Any other garments worn in addition to these, being superfluous, would constitute a burden were one to wear them in a public domain. Therefore, one may not wear them to remove them from the scene of the fire, even if his intention is to wear them out to a courtyard in which he may normally carry, for fear that in his state of turmoil he will forget and continue wearing them out to a public domain (*Tos. Yom Tov* from *Ran*). [The *Tanna Kamma*, however, places no limit on the number of garments one may remove by dressing in them.]

It is possible that even the *Tanna Kamma* concurs with R' Yose that no more than these eighteen garments may be worn when going out to a public domain. He differs only insofar as he does not fear that the householder will forget and go into a public domain wearing the additional garments after removing them from the fire (*Ran*, quoted by *Tos. R' Akiva*).

According to this, therefore, one may not go out into a public domain wearing garments not usually worn together (*Ran* quoted by *Tos. R' Akiva*; *Shibolei Haleket*, Ch. 107).

[Obviously, those who explain that the *Tanna Kamma* permits wearing an unlimited number of garments in a public domain (see above) explain that the *Tanna Kamma* and R' Yose differ on the fundamental law of the Torah, as to whether wearing a combination of garments not usually worn together is considered carrying.]

The practical application of this mishnah is discussed in *Shulchan Aruch* 301:36-37. See *Mishnah Berurah* there.

וְחוֹזֵר וְלוֹבֵשׁ וּמוֹצִיא. — *And he may return and don* [other garments] *and take* [them] *out.*

I.e., after reaching a haven, he may remove the garments, return to the

שבת טז/ה

וְאוֹמֵר לַאֲחֵרִים: "בּוֹאוּ וְהַצִּילוּ עִמִּי."

[ה] **רַבִּי** שִׁמְעוֹן בֶּן נַנָּס אוֹמֵר: פּוֹרְסִין עוֹר שֶׁל גְּדִי עַל גַּבֵּי שִׂדָּה, תֵּיבָה, וּמִגְדָּל שֶׁאָחַז בָּהֶן אֶת הָאוּר, מִפְּנֵי שֶׁהוּא מְחָרֵךְ. וְעוֹשִׂין מְחִצָּה בְּכָל הַכֵּלִים, בֵּין מְלֵאִים בֵּין רֵיקָנִים,

---

ר' עובדיה מברטנורא

אֲבָל לְטַיֵּל אָמַר בּוֹאוּ וְהַצִּילוּ לָכֶם, שֶׁפְּעָמִים שֶׁהוּא מַצִּיל יוֹתֵר מִמָּה שֶׁהֵם יְכוֹלִים לְהַצִּיל, כְּגוֹן שֶׁהוּא לֹא סָעַד וְהֵן סָעֲדוּ, אוֹ אִיפְּכָא: (ה) **שִׂדָּה.** עֲשׂוּיָה כְּמִין אָרוֹן: **תֵּיבָה.** קְטַנָּה שֶׁל שֻׁלְחָנִים: **וּמִגְדָּל.** אַרְמַארִי"א בְּלַעַ"ז, וּבַעֲרָבִי מִנְשָׁ"ר, וְשֻׁלְחָנָן שֶׁל עֵץ: **מִפְּנֵי שֶׁהוּא מְחָרֵךְ.** וְאֵין הָאוּר נֶאֱחֶזֶת בּוֹ וּמַצִּיל עַל כְּלִי עֵץ שֶׁלֹּא יִשָּׂרֵף: **בֵּין מְלֵאִים.** מַיִם:

יד אברהם

house and put on another set of garments.

In rescuing foodstuffs, the Rabbis did not permit returning to carry out the allotted amount a second time. Since the owner is carrying out the food in the usual manner, there is the danger that he will forget the prohibition of extinguishing fire on the Sabbath and inadvertently do so. In rescuing clothing, however, since he is permitted to remove garments only by wearing them, his mind is kept focused on the laws of the Sabbath. The Rabbis, therefore, permitted him to return for a second set of garments.

There is some question as to whether the permission to return for more clothing expresses the view of the *Tanna Kamma*, R' Yose, or both. *Rashi* and *Rosh* seem to say that this is the view of the *Tanna Kamma* only. Just as he places no limit on the number of garments one may don to remove from the scene of a fire, so too, he does not place any limit on the number of times one may avail himself of this method. R' Yose, however, who limits the number of items one may remove at one time, also limits the number of times one may do so to one.[1]

וְאוֹמֵר לַאֲחֵרִים: "בּוֹאוּ וְהַצִּילוּ עִמִּי." — *And he may say to others, "Come and save with me."*

The phrasing here is notable for its contrast to that of mishnah 3. Whereas in regard to saving food the mishnah states there that he says to others, "Come and save for yourselves," here, in regard to saving clothing the mishnah states that he says, "Come and save with me." Since the amount of food one may save is contingent upon the number of meals that individual has already eaten (as explained in mishnah 3), and since at the outbreak of the fire it is possible that either the

---

1. This follows the opinion of *Maharsha* and *Korban Nesanel*. *Tosefos Yom Tov*, however, has a different reading of *Rosh*. According to him the mishnah expresses the view of both the *Tanna Kamma* and R' Yose. (See *Tiferes Shmuel* on *Rashi*.)

Rambam (*Hil. Shabbos* 23:25), as explained by *Kesef Mishneh* there, understands this leniency to be the opinion of R' Yose only. The *Tanna Kamma*, however, forbids returning for more. He therefore rules that one may *not* return for a second set of clothing in accord with his interpretation of the view of the *Tanna Kamma*.

משניות / שבת — פרק טז: כל-כתבי [364]

16 5   And he may say to others, "Come and save with me."

5. R' **Shimon ben Nannas says: We may spread a kid's hide over a chest, a box, or a closet that has caught fire, because it singes. Likewise, we may make a partition with any vessels, whether full or empty,**

YAD AVRAHAM

owner or the bystander has already eaten a meal while the other has not, the amounts that each may remove are not necessarily equal. Therefore, it would be imprecise for the mishnah to phrase the owner's appeal as *come save with me*, implying the same amount. Rather, it is more correct to phrase that appeal as *come save for yourselves*, i.e., each according to what he is permitted to save. Since with regard to clothing, however, there are no limitations, the mishnah phrases the appeal as *come save with me*, i.e., as much as I do (*Rav*).

Alternatively, since with regard to foodstuffs anything in excess of three meals is considered irretrievable, and, as explained above, accordingly *hefker*, ownerless, he must, therefore, tell the bystanders to rescue for themselves. In the case of clothing, however, since he himself may return to put on more clothing, it is still regarded as retrievable. He therefore tells the bystanders to save with me, i.e., for me, since that is what they are doing (*Tos. R' Akiva*).

As for the practical application of these rules to current circumstances see *Beis Yosef* 334, *Rama* 334:26, and *Eliyah Rabbah* 334:25.

5.

The following mishnah deals with the methods one may employ on the Sabbath to prevent a fire from spreading.

רַבִּי שִׁמְעוֹן בֶּן נַנָּס אוֹמֵר: פּוֹרְסִין עוֹר שֶׁל גְּדִי — *R' Shimon ben Nannas says: We may spread a kid's hide*

I.e., a raw hide which is still moist [and therefore more fire resistant].

עַל גַּבֵּי שִׂדָה, תֵּיבָה, וּמִגְדָּל — *over a chest, a box, or a closet*

All of them made of wood (*Rav*).

שֶׁאָחַז בָּהֶן אֶת הָאוּר, — *that has caught fire,*

[I.e., that the fire has just gotten to them but they have not yet burst into flame.]

מִפְּנֵי שֶׁהוּא מְחָרֵךְ. — *because it singes.*

Because a hide singes and does not burn. Thus, it protects the wooden boxes from burning (*Rav; Rashi*). The mishnah is not giving the reason one is permitted to spread a kid's hide over burning boxes, but the reason one should want to do it (*Rambam, Comm.*).

וְעוֹשִׂין מְחִצָּה בְּכָל הַכֵּלִים, — *Likewise, we may make a partition with any vessels,*

I.e., we may erect a partition in the path of the fire (*Tif. Yis.*).

בֵּין מְלֵאִים בֵּין רֵיקָנִים, — *whether full or empty,*

I.e., whether they contain water or are empty (*Rav; Rashi*).

[365]   THE MISHNAH/SHABBOS — Chapter Sixteen: *Kol-Kisvei*

שבת טז/ו

בִּשְׁבִיל שֶׁלֹּא תַעֲבֹר הַדְּלֵקָה. רַבִּי יוֹסֵי אוֹסֵר בִּכְלֵי חֶרֶס חֲדָשִׁים מְלֵאִין מַיִם, לְפִי שֶׁאֵין יְכוֹלִין לְקַבֵּל אֶת הָאוּר, וְהֵן מִתְבַּקְעִין וּמְכַבִּין אֶת הַדְּלֵקָה.

[ו] **עוֹבֵד כּוֹכָבִים** שֶׁבָּא לְכַבּוֹת, אֵין אוֹמְרִים לוֹ: "כַּבֵּה,"

ר' עובדיה מברטנורא

שאין יכולין לקבל את האור. מפני שחדשים הס, וסבר רבי יוסי גרס כבוי אסור אפילו במקום הפסד ממון. ואין הלכה כרבי יוסי: (ו) אין אומרים לו כבה. דאמירה לנכרי שבות: ואל תכבה. אין צריך למחות בידו, אלא יניחנו ויכבה מפני שאין שביתת הנכרי עליהס, דישראל אינו מוזהר על שביתת הנכרי כשאינו עבדו:

יד אברהם

בִּשְׁבִיל שֶׁלֹּא תַעֲבֹר הַדְּלֵקָה — *so that the fire not spread.*

Even if the heat will burst the vessels, thereby releasing the water and quenching the fire, this is still permissible. This fits into the category of גְּרַם כִּבּוּי, *indirectly causing a fire to be extinguished*, rather than extinguishing it by direct effort. The causation (rather than direct performance) of a *melachah* is generally Rabbinically prohibited. However, in a case of financial loss the Rabbis did not prohibit it (*Shulchan Aruch* and *Rama* 334:22).

[The precise delineation of what is considered a direct performance of *melachah* and what is only a causation of *melachah* are very abstruse and cannot be properly explained within the parameters of this volume. Suffice it to say that here, as well as in all practical situations regarding Torah law, one should not draw halachic conclusions based on his own study of the Mishnah. In addition to the Mishnah, halachic decisions must take into consideration the *Gemara*, as well as the works of the *Geonim*, *Rishonim* and later *Poskim*. Such decisions can only be rendered by qualified Rabbinic authorities.]

רַבִּי יוֹסֵי אוֹסֵר בִּכְלֵי חֶרֶס חֲדָשִׁים מְלֵאִין מַיִם, לְפִי שֶׁאֵין יְכוֹלִין לְקַבֵּל אֶת הָאוּר, — *R' Yose prohibits [making a partition] with new earthenware vessels filled with water, because they cannot endure the fire,*

This refers to new earthenware vessels that have not hardened sufficiently to be able to endure the heat of a fire (*Rav*).

וְהֵן מִתְבַּקְעִין וּמְכַבִּין אֶת הַדְּלֵקָה. — *and they crack and [thereby] extinguish the fire.*

R' Yose rules that causing a fire to be extinguished is also prohibited even in cases involving financial loss. The halachah is not in accordance with R' Yose (*Rav*; *Rambam, Comm.*) but rather with the *Tanna Kamma* who rules that in order to prevent loss of property, fire may be extinguished by indirect causation (*Shulchan Aruch* 334:22).

משניות / שבת – פרק טז: כל-כתבי [366]

so that the fire not spread. R' Yose prohibits [making a partition] with new earthenware vessels filled with water, because they cannot endure the fire, and they crack and [thereby] extinguish the fire.

6. If a gentile came to extinguish, they may not say to him, "Extinguish," nor [must they say

YAD AVRAHAM

Similarly, if a garment has caught fire, one may spread it out or put it on, though the fire will thereby be quenched. He may not run and jump while wearing it, however, since this is considered directly extinguishing the fire (*Magen Avraham*, 334:25).

Similarly, a *sefer Torah* which has caught fire may be unwound to be read from, and the fire thereby indirectly extinguished (*Gem.* 120a).

6.

This mishnah deals with one's reactions to others who set about extinguishing the fire for him. Obviously, one may not permit another Jew to desecrate the Sabbath. The mishnah, however, discusses whether one may permit a non-Jew or a child to do so.

עוֹבֵד כּוֹכָבִים שֶׁבָּא לְכַבּוֹת — *If a gentile (lit. a gentile who) came to extinguish,*

[I.e., if a gentile came on the Sabbath to extinguish a fire that had broken out in a Jew's home.]

אֵין אוֹמְרִים לוֹ: ,,כַּבֵּה,'' — *they may not say to him, "Extinguish,"*

I.e., one may not ask the non-Jew to extinguish the fire. To do so violates the Rabbinic injunction against telling a non-Jew to perform any work on the Sabbath for a Jew which the Jew is himself forbidden to perform. [Whether this interdict applies to prohibitions other than those of the Sabbath as well is discussed in *Bava Metzia* 90.] This injunction was decreed in order "that the Sabbath not be trivial in their (Jewish) eyes, and they come to perform prohibited work themselves" (*Rambam, Hil. Shabbos* 6:1). *Mechilta* (*Ex.* 12:16) finds Biblical support for this Rabbinic decree from the verse כָּל־מְלָאכָה לֹא יֵעָשֶׂה בָהֶם, *no work shall be done thereon,* which, by its phrasing of the prohibition in terms of the work not being done rather than the people not doing the work, indicates that it shall not even be done for you by a person who may otherwise do it for himself, i.e., by a non-Jew.[1]

1. Extinguishing a fire for the purpose of preventing its spread is a מְלָאכָה שֶׁאֵינָהּ צְרִיכָה לְגוּפָהּ, *labor not performed for its defined purpose* — the proper function of extinguishing being to make charcoal — which in the opinion of R' Shimon is only Rabbinically prohibited (see above 2:5). According to *Shulchan Aruch* (307:5), therefore, who rules that one may tell a non-Jew to engage in an activity which is only Rabbinically prohibited in order to prevent great financial loss (*Mishnah Berurah* 307:22 and 334:8), the question arises as to why it is forbidden to tell a non-Jew to extinguish the fire. *Mishnah Berurah* (334:68) answers that to allow one to tell a non-Jew directly might cause him, in his anxiety, to join in the effort of extinguishing the fire (see *Shaar HaTziyun* 307:57).

שבת טז/ז

וְ"אַל תְּכַבֶּה," מִפְּנֵי שֶׁאֵין שְׁבִיתָתוֹ עֲלֵיהֶן. אֲבָל קָטָן שֶׁבָּא לְכַבּוֹת, אֵין שׁוֹמְעִין לוֹ, מִפְּנֵי שֶׁשְּׁבִיתָתוֹ עֲלֵיהֶן.

[ז] **כּוֹפִין** קְעָרָה עַל-גַּבֵּי הַנֵּר בִּשְׁבִיל שֶׁלֹּא תֶאֱחֹז בַּקּוֹרָה; וְעַל

ר' עובדיה מברטנורא

(ז) **כופין קערה.** של חרס על גבי הנר ובלבד שלא יכבה. ואף על פי שנוטל כלי להצלת קורה שאינה ניטלת בשבת, הא אותיבנא מינה לרבי יצחק דאמר אין כלי ניטל אלא לצורך דבר הניטל,

---

יד אברהם

וְ"אַל תְּכַבֶּה," — *nor [must they say to him], "Do not extinguish,"*

I.e., neither is one obligated to object to the gentile's extinguishing the fire on their behalf (Rav; Rashi).

מִפְּנֵי שֶׁאֵין שְׁבִיתָתוֹ עֲלֵיהֶן. — *because his resting is not their responsibility.*

I.e., unless the gentile is our slave, we are not responsible to see that he rests on the Sabbath (Rav; Rashi).

This expression is somewhat misleading, since a gentile has no obligation whatsoever to rest on the Sabbath. On the contrary, even a gentile who adheres to the seven Noachide laws is not allowed to observe a day of rest (see *Sanhedrin* 58b). The mishnah uses this expression, however, in order to contrast the gentile coming to extinguish the fire with the minor (see below) coming to extinguish the fire, in reference to whom this expression is applicable (*Beis David* from *Ramaz*).

Even if the gentile is aware that the householder will be pleased with his extinguishing the fire, he is not regarded as the Jew's agent, since he quenches the fire for his own benefit, i.e., to gain compensation for his act (*Tif. Yis.* from *Gem.* 121a).

The householder may even announce, "Anyone who quenches will not lose," since he is not ordering him to quench the fire, and the gentile is doing so for his own benefit (*Rashi; Gem.* 121a).

This lenient ruling applies as well to any sudden catastrophe, such as a flood or a crack in a vat of wine, through which the wine is leaking (*Rosh; Shulchan Aruch* 334:26).

If no non-Jews are present, one may be called to the scene, although it is certain that upon seeing the fire, he will extinguish it (*Rosh; Shulchan Aruch*, ibid.).

Similarly, one may summon a non-Jew and then say to him, "Anyone who quenches will not lose," although it resembles ordering the individual to perform labor on the Sabbath (*Beis Yosef* quoting *R' Yitzchak Abohab; Mishnah Berurah* 334:71).

To phrase the statement, "If *you* quench, you will not lose," is prohibited. This phrasing, by referring the appeal specifically to this individual, is tantamount to ordering him to quench the fire. This ruling is, however, not definite (*Tos. R' Akiva.* See also *Mishnah Berurah* 334:67).

Similarly, announcing, "Anyone who wishes should quench the fire," is forbidden since it is construed as making the one who quenches the fire his agent (*Tif. Yis.*).

The Rabbis balanced very carefully the leniencies granted in the event of a fire. They did not permit directly ordering a non-Jew to extinguish the flames, for fear that the Jew would join in doing so himself. They permitted this only to save holy books from being disgraced. On the other

to him], "Do not extinguish," because his resting is not their responsibility. But if a minor comes to extinguish, they may not allow him [to do so], because his resting is their responsibility.

7. We may invert a bowl over a lamp in order that it not set fire to a beam; or

YAD AVRAHAM

hand, they permitted hinting to non-Jews to extinguish the fire, lest the householder lose himself completely and and do so himself (*Mishnah Berurah* 334:68,69).

אֲבָל קָטָן שֶׁבָּא לְכַבּוֹת, — *But if a minor comes to extinguish,*

[I.e., if a Jewish boy under thirteen or a girl under twelve comes to extinguish the fire.]

אֵין שׁוֹמְעִין לוֹ, — *they may not allow him [to do so],*

[I.e., even if the child is attempting to do so of his own initiative the adult is required to prevent him from extinguishing the fire.]

מִפְּנֵי שֶׁשְּׁבִיתָתוֹ עֲלֵיהֶן. — *because his resting is their responsibility.*

I.e., because the Torah enjoins us to rest with our son and daughter. This is derived from the verse: לֹא־תַעֲשֶׂה כָל־מְלָאכָה אַתָּה וּבִנְךָ וּבִתֶּךָ, *you shall do no work, [neither] you nor your son nor your daughter* (*Exodus* 20:10). This cannot refer to sons and daughters who are of age because they are responsible in their own right to observe the Sabbath, as they are all *mitzvos*. Therefore, this must refer to children who are not of age, who have no personal responsibility to observe the Sabbath (*Rashi*, to *Exodus* 20:10). This verse is then to be understood as stating that our observance of the Sabbath must be even through our children; meaning, that we may not allow them to violate the Sabbath on our behalf (*Ramban*, *Exodus* 20:9).

Although there is, generally speaking, no requirement to prevent a minor from violating any of the Torah commandments, that is so only where the minor is doing so for his own benefit or pleasure, e.g., if he eats non-kosher food. If he does so on behalf of an adult, however, the adult is obligated to make him refrain. Similarly, an adult may not feed a minor non-kosher food, or put it into his hand. Neither may he tell him to engage in forbidden activities (*Shulchan Aruch* 343:1).

This entire discussion applies only to a child not sufficiently mature to be educated in the performance of *mitzvos*. When the child has reached that age, however, his father is obligated to make him refrain from violating any commandments, as part of his general obligation to train his child in the performance of *mitzvos* (*Tos.* 121a; *Mishnah Berurah* 334:64).

7.

כּוֹפִין קְעָרָה עַל־גַּבֵּי הַנֵּר — *We may invert a bowl over a lamp*

We may do so only as long as we do not thereby extinguish the lamp (*Rav; Rashi*).

בִּשְׁבִיל שֶׁלֹּא תֶאֱחֹז בַּקּוֹרָה; — *in order that it not set fire to a beam;*

I.e., in order to prevent the lamp

[369] THE MISHNAH/SHABBOS — Chapter Sixteen: *Kol-Kisvei*

שבת
טז/ז

צוֹאָה שֶׁל קָטָן; וְעַל עַקְרָב שֶׁלֹּא תִשֹּׁךְ. אָמַר רַבִּי יְהוּדָה: מַעֲשֶׂה בָא לִפְנֵי רַבָּן יוֹחָנָן בֶּן זַכַּאי בַּעֲרָב, וְאָמַר: "חוֹשְׁשַׁנִי לוֹ מֵחַטָּאת."

ר' עובדיה מברטנורא

ושני לה בצריך למקומו של כלי, דשרי לטלטלו לצורך מקומו: ועל צואה של קטן. לאו צואה של נער קטן קאמר, דהא גרף של רעי הוא ומותר לטלטלו ולהוציאו לאשפה, אלא הכי קאמר ועל צואה של תרנגולים, מפני הקטן שלא יטפח ויתלכלך בה. וכגון שצואה זו מונחת באשפה שבתוך דלא רמיא קמיה ולאו גרף של רעי הוא, הילכך אין מותר לטלטלה ולהוציאה, אבל כופין עליה קערה בשביל הקטן שלא יתלכלך: מעשה בא. כפיית כלי על עקרב: בערב. שם מקום: חושש אני לו מחטאת. דכיון שלא היה עקרב רץ אחריו חושש אני שמא חטאת חייב משום צידה. ולעניין פסק ההלכה בעלי הארם שנושכין וממיתין ודאי, כגון הנחשים השרפים וכלב שוטה, מותר להרגן מיד כשיראה אותו ואפילו שאין רצים אחריו. ואותן שאינן נושכים וממיתין ודאי אלא פעמים ממיתין ופעמים אין ממיתין, אם רצים אחריו מותר להרגן, ואם אין רצים אחריו כופה עליהם כלי, ואם דרסן והרגן לפי תומו מותר. ולגוד נחש מפני שרוחה לנשוך בו, אסור:

יד אברהם

flame from setting fire to the beam under which it is situated.

The Gemara in Chapter 2 (43a) asks that this mishnah contradicts a ruling put forth by the Amora R' Yitzchak, that even a utensil that is not *muktzeh* may be moved only for the sake of something that may itself be moved. Our mishnah, however, permits moving a utensil to protect a beam of a house (which may not be moved on the Sabbath). The Gemara there answers that R' Yitzchak explains our mishnah as referring to where one needed to move the utensil in any case to make use of its place. Since he is permitted to move the utensil for this purpose, he may tailor its movement to protect the beam as well (*Rav*).

וְעַל צוֹאָה שֶׁל קָטָן; — *or over feces [because] of a child*;

The mishnah literally reads *over the feces of a child*. This would, however, imply that one may only cover it with a bowl but not remove it, since it is *muktzeh* [see preface to Chapter 17]. This implication would, however, be erroneous. Since the waste of a child is generally found in a place frequented by people, one is permitted to remove it under the special exemption to the ban of *muktzeh* accorded for the removal of repulsive objects. The mishnah, therefore, must be read as *over feces [because] of a child*, and is referring to the feces of a bird, which is generally found only in trash heaps. Since these places are not frequented by people who would find it repulsive, it may not be moved away. Since children have a predeliction for playing there, however, the droppings may be covered with a bowl to prevent the children from becoming soiled (*Rav*, as explained by *Tos. Yom Tov*).

Accordingly, there is no legal difference between human wastes and those of fowl. Both may be moved if they are lying in places frequented by people, and both may be covered if lying in places unfrequented by people, to prevent the children from dirtying themselves. The only difference is one of general location, i.e., that a child's waste is often found in the yard, whereas bird droppings are usually found in the trash heaps. This follows

16 over feces [because] of a child; or over a scorpion so
7 that it not sting. R' Yehudah said: An incident came before Rabban Yochanan ben Zakkai in Arab, and he said, "I fear for him [that he is liable] for a sin offering."

YAD AVRAHAM

the reading of *Rif* and *Rosh*.

According to *Rashi's* reading of the Gemara, however, human wastes may be moved no matter where they are found, since they are fit for dog food. Bird droppings, not being fit for that purpose, may be moved only if they are lying in a yard frequented by people. Otherwise, they may be covered up to prevent children from becoming soiled by playing with them (*Tos. Yom Tov*).

וְעַל עַקְרָב — *or over a scorpion*
[I.e., we may invert a bowl over a scorpion.]

שֶׁלֹּא תִשּׁךְ — *so that it not sting* (lit. *bite*).
Although one thereby traps the scorpion, violating the *melachah* of *trapping (7:2), one may nevertheless do so because a scorpion sting is a threat to human life. Some qualify this ruling to refer only to places where the scorpions are known to sting (*Ramaz*).

Others qualify this as referring to a scorpion pursuing a person, and thus likely to bite him (*Hon Ashir*).

אָמַר רַבִּי יְהוּדָה: מַעֲשֶׂה בָּא לִפְנֵי רַבָּן יוֹחָנָן בֶּן זַכַּאי בַּעֲרָב — *R' Yehudah said: An incident came before Rabban Yochanan ben Zakkai in Arab,*
I.e., an incident once occurred concerning one who inverted a bowl over a scorpion, in the city of Arab, a Galilean city where Rabban Yochanan ben Zakkai lived for eighteen years (*Meleches Shlomo* from *Yerushalmi*).[1]

וְאָמַר: ״חוֹשְׁשַׁנִי לוֹ מֵחַטָּאת״. — *and he said, "I fear for him [that he is liable] for a sin offering."*

An incident is usually cited in support of a previously mentioned ruling. In this instance, however, R' Yehudah cites Rabban Yochanan ben Zakkai's decision in contradiction to the previous ruling of the *Tanna Kamma*. In order to avoid this contradiction, the commentators offer the following explanations:

The *Tanna Kamma* refers to a type of scorpion that usually stings. It is therefore permissible to trap it because it endangers human life. R' Yehudah, however, cites Rabban Yochanan ben Zakkai's ruling regarding a scorpion that does not usually sting (*Ramaz*).

Others explain that the *Tanna Kamma* refers to trapping a scorpion that is chasing a person, whereas R' Yehudah's incident involved one that was not chasing anyone. It was, therefore, not deemed dangerous (*Rashi,* according to *Hon Ashir*).

The halachah is that any creature whose bite or sting is known to be fatal, such as a poisonous snake or a rabid dog, may be killed on sight on the Sabbath even if it poses no immediate danger. Creatures whose bites are painful but not fatal may not be killed unless they are chasing or attempting to bite a person. The Rabbi further permitted

---

1. During the eighteen years that Rabban Yochanan ben Zakkai lived in Arab, he was asked only two questions in halachah, this one and the one in 2:3. He became incensed at their unconcern about the laws of the Torah and declared, "Galilee, O Galilee, how you hate the Torah! You will eventually become olive pickers," i.e., you will remain farmers and no Torah scholars will spring from you (*Yerushalmi* according to *P'nei Moshe*). Others render: You will eventually be overrun by bandits (*Korban HaEdah*).

שבת
טז/ח

[ח] **עוֹבֵד כּוֹכָבִים** שֶׁהִדְלִיק אֶת הַנֵּר, מִשְׁתַּמֵּשׁ לְאוֹרוֹ יִשְׂרָאֵל; וְאִם בִּשְׁבִיל יִשְׂרָאֵל, אָסוּר. מִלֵּא מַיִם לְהַשְׁקוֹת בְּהֶמְתּוֹ, מַשְׁקֶה אַחֲרָיו יִשְׂרָאֵל;

────────── ר' עובדיה מברטנורא ──────────

(ח) מילא מים. מבור ברשות הרבים:

────────── יד אברהם ──────────

killing even those creatures in an inconspicuous manner; i.e., by stepping on them (even intentionally) while walking, as long as one does not make it obvious that this is his intention.

Although killing an animal violates a *melachah* (see 7:2), since one is doing so only to avoid injury, rather than for the purpose of using its meat or hide, it is *a melachah not performed for its defined purpose*. As has been explained several times before, such a labor is the subject of a dispute between R' Yehudah and R' Shimon, and most authorities rule in accord with R' Shimon's view that it is only Rabbinically prohibited. Therefore, in cases involving pain the Rabbis did not apply their prohibition, permitting one to kill an animal to prevent any injury. If, however, the non-lethal creature is not obviously threatening him, they permitted him only to step on it, while walking (*Shulchan Aruch* 316:10 as explained by *Mishnah Berurah* 316:46). Furthermore, one may also invert a bowl over it, even though this traps it (*Mishnah Berurah* 316:4). To trap them by inverting a bowl over them is an unusual method of trapping, in addition to being *a labor performed for its defined purpose*. For both these reasons, it is only Rabbinically prohibited. Therefore, wherever one is permitted to kill them, he is certainly permitted to trap them under a bowl.

As stated above, this ruling follows the opinion of the majority authorities who rule (in accord with R' Shimon's view) that *a labor not performed for its defined purpose* is only Rabbinically prohibited. *Rambam* and *Rav*, however, follow the opinion of R' Yehudah who holds that such labor is Biblically prohibited. Accordingly, it is not within the power of the Rabbis to allow any leniencies not accorded by the Torah. According to them, therefore, an animal may be killed only if its bite is generally fatal. A creature whose bite is never fatal, though it may be painful, may not be killed, since to do so, in their opinion, violates a Torah prohibition. This may not be done to prevent injury which poses no threat to life. Creatures whose bites are only rarely fatal may be killed only if they are pursuing a person or otherwise attempting to attack him. Otherwise, one may kill them only by stepping on them in passing, as explained above. Similarly, he may invert a bowl over them, thereby trapping them. This is permitted because it is an unusual method of trapping and therefore only Rabbinically prohibited. Consequently, the Rabbis permitted it to avoid injury.

Alternatively, since it may bite many people, it is regarded as a threat to life, for which even a Torah prohibition may be violated (*Maggid Mishneh* 10:17). [Perhaps *Maggid Mishneh* means that although the danger of fatality is rare, if it bites many people, the odds in favor of fatality are greatly increased.]

Others explain that if the perpetrator does not need the object involved in the *melachah* at all, even R' Yehudah declares him exempt. Therefore, since the one who traps the snake has no use for it whatsoever, merely wishing to rid himself of its bite, he is exempt even according to R' Yehudah. Because of the danger involved, the Rabbis even permitted him to do so (*Sefer HaBattim*, added to *Maggid Mishneh* ibid.; *Avnei Nezer* 189, 16, quoted in *Sefer HaLikutim*, Frankel ed. of *Rambam, Hil. Shabbos* 10:25).

8. If a gentile lit a lamp, a Jew may use its light; but if [he did so] for a Jew, he may not [use it]. If [a gentile] drew water to water his own animal, a Jew may water [his animal] after him;

YAD AVRAHAM

8.

The following mishnah teaches us that if a non-Jew performs any labor for a Jew on the Sabbath, no Jew is permitted to derive any benefit from that labor on the Sabbath. This is true even if the Jew did not instruct the gentile to do it. If, however, the non-Jew does this labor for himself we may derive benefit from it (*Rambam, Hil. Shabbos* 6:2).

עוֹבֵד כּוֹכָבִים שֶׁהִדְלִיק אֶת הַנֵּר, — *If a gentile* (lit. *a gentile who*) *lit a lamp,*

I.e., for his own use (*Tif. Yis.*).

מִשְׁתַּמֵּשׁ לְאוֹרוֹ יִשְׂרָאֵל; — *a Jew may use its light;*

Since it was lit for the gentile's own use, not for the Jew's, a Jew may make use of its light on the Sabbath (*Meiri*).

We do not fear that by permitting the Jew to derive benefit from the light, he may forget himself and light a lamp (*Tos.* 122a).

וְאִם בִּשְׁבִיל יִשְׂרָאֵל, — *but if [he did so] for a Jew,*

I.e., even if he did so on his own initiative (*Rambam, Comm.*).

אָסוּר. — *he may not [use it].*

The Rabbis prohibited him to make use of the light. Even another Jew, for whom it was not lit, may not make use of a light lit on the Sabbath for a Jew. The Rabbis feared that should people be permitted to use the light they might be tempted to ask the gentile to light the lamp for them.[1]

Furthermore, in order not to benefit from the work done on the Sabbath, one must wait even after the Sabbath the time it would take to do such work before being able to derive benefit from that work (*Rambam, Hil. Shabbos* 6:2).

In mishnah 7 we learned that one may even hint to a gentile to extinguish a fire as long as we do not order him to do so. Since the gentile does so in expectation of a reward, he is considered to be working in his own behalf and not for the benefit of the Jew. Since the benefit to both parties is strictly financial — the Jew having his property saved and the gentile earning a reward — the act of the gentile is judged as having been done primarily for his own benefit. However, in a case in which the Jew benefits from the act personally (e.g., by being able to use the light of the candle) while the gentile benefits only financially, the act cannot be judged as having been performed primarily for the benefit of the gentile, i.e., the personal benefit of the Jew is considered more significant than, and therefore outweighs, the purely financial benefit of the gentile (*Tos.* 122a).

מִלֵּא מַיִם לְהַשְׁקוֹת בְּהֶמְתּוֹ, — *If [a gentile] drew water to water his own animal,*

[Since the well itself is a private domain (being 10 handbreadths deep), and the animal is in a public domain, the animal cannot be watered without transferring the water from one domain to the other.]

מַשְׁקֶה אַחֲרָיו יִשְׂרָאֵל; — *a Jew may water [his animal] after him;*

---

1. See footnote to prefatory note to 4:1 for an explanation of why this is not considered גְּזֵרָה לִגְזֵרָה, *a double safeguard.*

שבת
טז/ח

וְאִם בִּשְׁבִיל יִשְׂרָאֵל, אָסוּר. עָשָׂה עוֹבֵד כּוֹכָבִים כֶּבֶשׁ לֵירֵד בּוֹ, יוֹרֵד אַחֲרָיו יִשְׂרָאֵל; וְאִם בִּשְׁבִיל יִשְׂרָאֵל, אָסוּר. מַעֲשֶׂה בְרַבָּן גַּמְלִיאֵל וּזְקֵנִים שֶׁהָיוּ בָאִין בִּסְפִינָה,

---
ר' עובדיה מברטנורא

כבש. עושין בספינה גדולה לירד בו מן הספינה ליבשה. ואיצטריך תנא לאשמעינן נר ומים, דאי תנא נר הוה אמינא נר הוא דשרי דליכא למיגזר שמא ירבה בשביל ישראל דנר לאחד נר למאה, אבל מים דאיכא למיגזר אסור. ואי אשמעינן מים הוה אמינא מים הוא דבשביל ישראל אסור, אבל נר אף על גב דבשביל ישראל כיון דאיהו נמי צריך ליה שרי, דנר לאחד נר למאה, צריכא. וכבש אף על גב דדמי לנר, דככב לאחד כבש למאה, משום מעשה דרבן גמליאל וזקנים תנא ליה, דמעשה רב:

יד אברהם

The mishnah teaches us that we need not fear that the gentile will draw extra water for the Jew's animal.

This is true only if the Jew is a stranger to the gentile. If he knows the Jew, however, the water may not be used, since we do indeed fear that the gentile will draw more water than he needs in order to water the livestock belonging to his Jewish acquaintance (*Tif. Yis.* from *Gem.* 122a).

וְאִם בִּשְׁבִיל יִשְׂרָאֵל, — *but if [he did so] for a Jew,*

[I.e. if the gentile drew the water expressly for a Jew.]

אָסוּר. — *he may not [use it].*

I.e., he may not water his animal with this water. As mentioned above, the Rabbis enacted this prohibition as a precautionary measure lest the Jew *ask* the gentile to draw water for him, thus violating the Rabbinic injunction against telling a gentile to perform labor on the Sabbath (*Tos.*).

Since the *Tanna* states that a Jew may not water his animal with water drawn for that animal by a gentile, many authorities deduce that if the water was drawn by the gentile for the Jew himself rather than his animal, he may indeed drink it. The distinction is that since one cannot water his animal without drawing water from the well or cistern, a private domain, and carrying it out into a public domain, the Jew by giving it to his animal is benefiting from the labor performed by the gentile. He himself, however, can climb down into the well and drink the water there without first transferring it to the public domain. Consequently, though the gentile has made it easier for the Jew to drink, he has provided him with no real benefit since the Jew could have had it even on his own (*Tos.* quoting *Rabbeinu Tam* and *Rabbeinu Eliyahu*; *Rama* 325:10).

Others dispute this. They contend that being able to drink the water while remaining in place is also regarded as benefiting from a labor performed on the Sabbath. According to these opinions, the reason the *Tanna* chooses to depict the halachah in terms of water drawn for animals rather than for people is as follows: Were he not to tell us that the Jew may water his animal, we would be inclined to believe that this would be prohibited in all cases. Since animals drink copious amounts of water, if there is sufficient water left for the Jew's animal, too, it should lead us to be concerned that the gentile has drawn extra water specifically for the Jew's animal. If, however, the gentile has drawn water for his personal drinking there would be no such concern, since for human drinking one bucketful easily suffices for two people. The *Tanna* therefore chooses the case of water drawn for animals to inform us that even there we need not, barring evidence to the contrary, concern ourselves.

16
8
but if [he did so] for a Jew, he may not [use it]. If a gentile made a gangway upon which to disembark, a Jew may disembark after him; but if [he did so] for a Jew, he may not [use it]. It once happened that Rabban Gamliel and the elders were arriving on a ship,

YAD AVRAHAM

Others explain that the *Tanna* chooses to discuss the instance of water drawn for animals because it was common for Jews and gentiles to be found together in the place where the animals were watered (*Tos. Yom Tov* from *Ran*).

עָשָׂה עוֹבֵד כּוֹכָבִים כֶּבֶשׁ לֵירֵד בּוֹ, — *If a gentile* (lit. *a gentile who*) *made a gangway upon which to disembark,*

I.e., a ramp without steps (*Tos. Yom Tov* from *Rambam, Comm.*).

[The *Tosefta* (14:13) substitutes the word סִיקְלָא, or אַסְקַלְיָא, defined by *Aruch* as a long board, in which grooves are carved out, upon which to place the feet. They would extend it from the ship to the dry land and go up and down on it. *Rabbeinu Gershom* (*Bava Basra* 73a) also defines it as a ladder used for disembarking from a ship. Hence כֶּבֶשׁ, too, is a ladder with steps.]

יוֹרֵד אַחֲרָיו יִשְׂרָאֵל; — *a Jew may disembark after him;*

Since he did not make it for the Jew, it may be used on the Sabbath.

Since the principle of all three cases is identical, the inclusion of all three would appear to be redundant. The *Gemara* accounts for their inclusion as follows: Were the *Tanna* to teach us the law in the case of the lamp, we would not extend it to the other cases. Since the light of a lamp sufficient for one person is equally sufficient for a hundred persons, there need not be any concern that the gentile had added anything for the Jew. In the case of drawing water, however, we would be inclined to consider the water prohibited out of concern that the gentile has indeed drawn for the Jew. The *Tanna* must, therefore, inform us of the rule in regard to water (*Gem.* 122a).

Conversely, were the *Tanna* to teach us the rule only in terms of drawing water, we might think that the water drawn for the Jew is prohibited only because the gentile himself derives no use from it. In the case of the lamp, however, even if the gentile has lit it for the Jew's use, since he too derives benefit from it, we might think that its use is permitted. Therefore the *Tanna* states the ruling in terms of the lamp, too. The case of the gangway, though indeed similar to that of the lamp, is added because of the precedent set by Rabban Gamliel in this context. This is in keeping with the maxim, מַעֲשֶׂה רַב, *an incident* (in which a ruling has actually been applied) *is a teacher* (*Rav*).

וְאִם בִּשְׁבִיל יִשְׂרָאֵל, — *but if [he did so] for a Jew,*

[I.e., if he made the gangway specifically for a Jew.]

אָסוּר. — *he may not [use it].*

[I.e., a Jew may not use the gangway until sufficient time after the Sabbath has elapsed for a gangway to be prepared.]

מַעֲשֶׂה בְּרַבָּן גַּמְלִיאֵל וּזְקֵנִים שֶׁהָיוּ בָּאִין בִּסְפִינָה, — *It once happened that Rabban Gamliel and the elders were arriving on a ship,*

I.e., the ship landed on the Sabbath.

וְעָשָׂה עוֹבֵד כּוֹכָבִים כֶּבֶשׁ לֵירֵד בּוֹ, וְיָרְדוּ בוֹ רַבָּן גַּמְלִיאֵל וּזְקֵנִים.

יד אברהם

Although it is usually prohibited to disembark on the Sabbath, it is permitted where the ship was within two thousand cubits of the shore before the onset of the Sabbath. Rabban Gamliel determined this by looking through a telescope calibrated to resolve images up to a distance of two thousand cubits. [This telescope was a hollow tube which operated on the same principle which enables one to resolve a distant image by looking through a small hole] (*Tosefta* 14:13).

16 8 and a gentile made a gangway by which to disembark, and Rabban Gamliel and the elders disembarked by it.

YAD AVRAHAM

וְעָשָׂה עוֹבֵד כּוֹכָבִים כֶּבֶשׁ לֵירֵד בּוֹ, — *and a gentile made a gangway by which to disembark,*

[I.e., he made it for himself.]

וְיָרְדוּ בּוֹ רַבָּן גַּמְלִיאֵל וּזְקֵנִים. — *and Rabban Gamliel and the elders disembarked by it.*

Since the gentile had made it for himself, they too used it. *Rif* reads: וְיָרְדוּ אַחֲרָיו, *disembarked after him,* indicating clearly that the gentile had made it for his own use.

פרק שבעה עשר
Chapter Seventeen

Objects which in the normal course of events do not stand to be used on the Sabbath are defined as מֻקְצֶה [*muktzeh*], *set apart*. The legal status of these objects was set by the Rabbis (in the era of Nehemiah the son of Hachaliah), who decreed that such things may not be נִטָּלִין, *taken or picked up*, i.e., they may neither be handled nor moved about on the Sabbath (*Gem.* 123b). *Rambam* gives three reasons for this enactment:

(a) If the prophet admonished us (*Isaiah* 58:13): *If you restrain, because of the Sabbath, your feet . . . from seeking your personal* [*mundane*] *needs* [i.e., those forbidden on the Sabbath] or *discussing the forbidden* [that is, not to walk or talk on the Sabbath in the same manner as we do on the weekdays]; then, how surely ought we to refrain from moving about articles on the Sabbath in the manner we move them about on weekdays. This serves as a precaution that we not regard the Sabbath the same as a weekday and come to lift and rearrange articles from one part of the house to another . . . or to put stones out of the way. Being at leisure and at home, one might look for something with which to occupy himself and, as a result, not rest at all.

(b) If it were permitted to handle utensils normally used for doing *melachos*, one might inadvertently commit a *melachah* on Shabbos.

(c) People who have no trade or craft . . . who do not work all week . . . would not be discerned as resting on the Sabbath, thus the added prohibition of *muktzeh* (*Rambam, Hil. Shabbos* 24:12,13).[1]

Ravad comments that the laws of *muktzeh* were promulgated for the purpose of preventing people from inadvertently carrying on the Sabbath. Originally, this decree included *all* utensils. Later, it was modified to permit handling utensils used for permissible work (*Gem.* 123b, see below).

The *Gemara* (123b) states as follows:

Originally they used to say [i.e. the original enactment prohibiting the handling of *muktzeh* stated]: Only three utensils may be handled on the Sabbath — the knife used to cut a cake of pressed figs; the spoon used to skim off the foam of a pot; and the small knife which is [found] on the table (used for cutting bread, meat and other foods). These were permitted because their use was constantly necessary (*Rashi*). [Subsequently] they permitted and then again permitted and yet again permitted. [I.e., at three subsequent times parts of the original enactment were repealed, resulting in a progressively more lenient law of *muktzeh*.] Until they

---

1. *Aruch HaShulchan* (308) interprets *Rambam* to mean that the Torah's command to rest on the Sabbath proscribes the handling of *muktzeh*. As *Rambam* states, without this prohibition, there could be no Sabbath rest. When the general populace became lax in their Sabbath observance in Nehemiah's time, the Rabbis deemed it necessary to enact more stringent regulations. These were eventually repealed, reverting to the restrictions imposed by the Torah.

said [in the final version of the law] all utensils may be handled with the exception of the large saw and the colter [i.e., all other utensils may be handled either at will or at least under certain specific conditions, with the exception of these two — and any others which conform to the same principles as these — which may never be handled on the Sabbath. These categories will be explained below].

The *Gemara* later states: In the days of Nehemiah son of Hachaliah this mishnah [i.e., the original enactment] was formulated. As it is written (Nehemiah 13:15): *In those days I saw in Judea [people] treading wine-presses on the Sabbath and hauling the sheaves [of grain]* . . . [i.e., the Rabbis of Nehemiah's time enacted the laws of *muktzeh* to counter the flagrant violations of the Sabbath which Nehemiah found on his arrival in Jerusalem]. The subsequent weakenings of the *muktzeh* laws resulted from the increased meticulousness with which the Sabbath laws were observed, thereby obviating the need for such stringent safeguards.

Tosafos (ibid.) point out that the original enactment, permitting the use of only three utensils, refers only to utensils which were not receptacles, i.e., tools and implements and the like. However, receptacles — i.e., utensils constructed to hold things — were never included in the original ban, since it is obvious that people were always permitted to use dishes and cups.

ᴥ§ The Categories of Muktzeh

The basic definition of *muktzeh* is any item which was not "prepared" for use before the Sabbath. This preparation, however, need not be active. Any object which in the normal course of events stands to be used is considered "prepared," and consequently is נִטָּל [*permitted to be*] *taken*, i.e., it may be handled and moved about. Only objects which, for one reason or another, do not stand to be used, are deemed *muktzeh*.

Since there are several reasons for which an object may be declared *muktzeh*, such objects are classified into various categories. *Beis Yosef* (308) classifies the various types of *muktzeh*:

(a) מֻקְצָה מֵחֲמַת חֶסְרוֹן כִּיס, *set aside for fear of monetary loss*. This category included any utensil whose general use is objected to by the owner for fear it will become damaged, e.g., a slaughterer's knife or a barber's razor. [Though the owner certainly uses these for their primary function, that function is prohibited on the Sabbath. Since these blades must be kept perfectly sharp, the owner objects to their being used for any secondary, permissible function (e.g., as a table knife) for fear of damaging the cutting edge.]

(b) כְּלִי שֶׁמְלַאכְתּוֹ לְאִסוּר, *a utensil used primarily for work prohibited on the Sabbath*. This includes any utensil (such as a hammer) whose primary use (building) is forbidden on the Sabbath but which is also occasionally used for permissible activities, such as cracking nuts. Since the items in this category are not easily damaged, the owner does not object to their being used for these secondary purposes.

(c) מֻקְצָה מֵחֲמַת גּוּפוֹ, *set aside because of its intrinsic properties*. This refers to anything which is neither a utensil nor a food edible to humans, or animals; e.g., stones, money, reeds, wood, beams, earth, sand, a corpse, living animals, figs and raisins in the process of being dried, and anything else not fit for use on the Sabbath.

(d) בָּסִיס לְדָבָר הָאָסוּר, *a base to a muktzeh object*. This group comprises all otherwise non-*muktzeh* articles upon which lies an item of *muktzeh*, e.g., a barrel upon which a stone is lying, or a pillow upon which money is lying. Even after the *muktzeh* has been removed (e.g., by a non-Jew), the base remains *muktzeh* until the end of that Sabbath. This rule applies only to utensils which served as a base to a *muktzeh* object at the onset of the Sabbath, i.e., at twilight.

(e) מְחֻבָּר וּמְחֻסַּר צִידָה, *attached [to the ground] or lacking capture*. Included in this category are any animal which was not trapped[1] and any growing item, such as a fruit, vegetable, or wood, which had not been reaped as of twilight on the eve of the Sabbath.

(f) מֻקְצֶה לְמִצְוָתוֹ, *set aside because of its mitzvah*. Such items as the wood of a *sukkah* and its ornaments fall into this classification.

There is yet a seventh category of *muktzeh* known as נוֹלָד (lit. *just born*). *Nolad* is any otherwise non-*muktzeh* object which has first achieved its presently useful state on this Sabbath. Since it was not in a usable state prior to the Sabbath, it cannot be said to have been "prepared" before the Sabbath. Consequently it is *muktzeh*. As with many of the categories of *muktzeh*, the limits of the law of *nolad* are subject to a dispute between R' Yehudah and R' Shimon. R' Shimon limits the prohibition of *nolad* to only those items whose present form and function is radically different from their pre-Sabbath one (*Tos. Beitzah* 2a, *Eruvin* 46a). R' Yehudah, however, prohibits even certain items whose function has changed on the Sabbath, though their form has not (*Gem.* 124b). [This will be discussed more fully in mishnah 5.]

Anything one is permitted to prepare on the Sabbath is not regarded as *nolad* since it is within one's power to ready it. For this reason, a pot left on the fire at the beginning of Shabbos, despite its being too hot to eat, is not *nolad* since one may at any time remove it from the fire, allow it to cool and thereby render it edible (*Beitzah* 26b).

According to many authorities, the halachah with regard to the laws of the Sabbath follows the opinion of R' Shimon. With regard to Yom Tov, it follows the opinion of R' Yehudah (*Shulchan Aruch* and *Rama*, 495:4; see *Mishnah Berurah* 495:17).

---

1. This is relevant primarily to *Yom Tov*, when animals may be slaughtered and their meat cooked, but when they may not be trapped.

שבת
יז/א

[א] **כָּל הַכֵּלִים** נִטָּלִין בַּשַּׁבָּת וְדַלְתוֹתֵיהֶן עִמָּהֶן, אַף־עַל־פִּי שֶׁנִּתְפָּרְקוּ בַשַּׁבָּת; שֶׁאֵינָן דּוֹמִין לְדַלְתוֹת הַבַּיִת, לְפִי שֶׁאֵינָן מִן הַמּוּכָן.

ר' עובדיה מברטנורא

פרק שבעה עשר – כל הכלים. (א) כל הכלים. יש להן דלתות: ניטלים בשבת ודלתותיהן עמהן. ואף על פי שנתפרקו הדלתות מן הכלים קודם השבת, ניטלים בשבת אגב הכלים: ואינן דומין לדלתות הבית. שאפילו נתפרקו בשבת אין ניטלין, לפי שדלתות הבית אינן מן המוכן, כלומר לא נעשו לטלטול:

יד אברהם

1.

כָּל הַכֵּלִים — *All utensils*

I.e., all utensils whose function is permissible on the Sabbath — namely, non-*muktzeh* utensils [those used primarily for prohibited work are discussed below in mishnah 4] (*Tos. Yom Tov from Ran; Tif. Yis.*).

נִטָּלִין בַּשַּׁבָּת וְדַלְתוֹתֵיהֶן עִמָּהֶן, — *may be taken on the Sabbath and their doors with them,*

I.e., any doors or lids to these utensils which have become detached may also be moved. Since these doors were originally part of a permissible utensil, and they stand to be reattached to that utensil after the Sabbath, even now they are deemed part of the original, still functional utensil, and in consequence not *muktzeh* (*Rav; Rashi*).

Since the doors are not deemed *muktzeh*, they may certainly be moved independently of the original utensil, too. The mishnah states that they may be moved with the utensil, to teach us that we need not fear that by carrying the utensil together with its detached door one will forgetfully reattach the door on the Sabbath (*Tif. Yis.*).

Alternatively, the mishnah states *with them* to point out the reason that they may by moved, i.e., because they are with them, meaning that they stand to be reattached to them. Therefore, they retain their status as utensils and do not fall into the category of inherently *muktzeh* (*Shoshanim LeDavid*).

In view of the fact that not all utensils may be moved about on the Sabbath, as will be explained in mishnah 4, some emend the mishnah to read: כָּל־הַכֵּלִים הַנִּטָּלִין בַּשַּׁבָּת דַּלְתוֹתֵיהֶן עִמָּהֶן, *all utensils which may be taken on the Sabbath, their doors [may be taken] with them* (*Tos.*).

אַף־עַל־פִּי שֶׁנִּתְפָּרְקוּ בַשַּׁבָּת; — *even though they were detached on the Sabbath;*

The *Gemara* explains that the phrase *on the Sabbath* refers back to the statement *may be taken*. Thus the mishnah is understood as: all utensils and their doors may be moved on the Sabbath. Even though the doors became detached (during the week), they may still be moved on the Sabbath (*Rav; Tos. Yom Tov*). [If they became detached on the Sabbath, they may certainly be moved since even at the onset of the Sabbath the doors were still part of the utensil.]

17 **1.** **A**ll utensils may be taken on the Sabbath and their
1 doors with them, even though they were detached on the Sabbath; for they are not like house doors, which are not prepared.

YAD AVRAHAM

However, if not for the fact they stand to be reattached, the fact of their detachment occurring on the Sabbath would not suffice to deem them a utensil. They would then fall into the category of broken utensils which, if not at all functional, are *muktzeh*, even if broken on the Sabbath (*Tos.* 122b).

שֶׁאֵינָן דּוֹמִין לְדַלְתוֹת הַבַּיִת, — *for they are not like house doors*,

I.e., the doors of utensils are not halachically akin to the doors of houses. The latter, upon becoming detached, may *not* be moved on the Sabbath regardless of when they have become detached (*Rav*).

לְפִי שֶׁאֵינָן מִן הַמּוּכָן. — *which* (lit. *because they*) *are not prepared*.

I.e., not prepared to be moved.

The doors of buildings are not designed to be moved about but rather to be swiveled on a hinge while remaining attached to the door-frame. They are, therefore, considered (part of) *a structure* rather than a *utensil*. Not being a utensil, they may not be moved upon becoming detached from the house.[1] The doors of utensils are, on the other hand, designed to be moved about together with the utensil to which they are attached. They are, therefore, considered "prepared" to be moved and are not *muktzeh* (*Rav; Rashi*). [Any object designed not to be moved is automatically *muktzeh*.]

2.

As explained in the prefatory note to this chapter, any utensil used primarily for an activity prohibited on the Sabbath is called כְּלִי שֶׁמְּלַאכְתּוֹ לְאִיסוּר, a *utensil used primarily for work prohibited on the Sabbath*, and is *muktzeh*. Its rules, however, differ greatly from those of the other categories. Whereas most categories of *muktzeh* may never be moved directly, a utensil whose primary use is for an activity prohibited on the Sabbath may be moved for one of two purposes: (a) לְצֹרֶךְ גּוּפוֹ, *to make use of it*, i.e., for any activity permissible on the Sabbath; (b) לְצֹרֶךְ מְקוֹמוֹ, *to make use of its place*, i.e., to remove it from where it is in order to make other use of that place. Its being *muktzeh* prohibits it only from being

---

1. *Rambam* (*Hil. Shabbos* 25:6) adds that doors which have become detached from buildings may not be moved on the Sabbath even if they are utensils because they are not prepared. *Beur Halachah* (308:10) explains that even doors which can function as utensils [e.g., as a tabletop] may not be moved because they are not prepared, i.e., because they stand to be reattached to the building rather than to be used as utensils. Therefore, even in their detached state they are viewed as relating to the building rather than as utensils (see below mishnah 8, s.v. נִטָּלִים בַּשַּׁבָּת).

As to whether the detached doors of utensils must also be usable in their detached form to be considered non-*muktzeh* or whether the mere intent to reattach them is in itself sufficient to classify them as such, see *Mishnah Berurah* 308:35 who adopts the latter position. Other authorities, however, dispute this, adopting the former position.

שבת
יז/ב

[ב] **נוטֵל** אָדָם קֻרְנָס לְפַצֵעַ בּוֹ אֶת הָאֱגוֹזִים; וְקַרְדֹּם לַחְתּוֹךְ אֶת הַדְּבֵלָה; מְגֵרָה לִגְרֹר בָּה אֶת הַגְּבִינָה; מַגְרֵפָה לִגְרֹף בָּה אֶת הַגְּרוֹגָרוֹת; אֶת הָרַחַת וְאֶת הַמַּזְלֵג לָתֵת עָלָיו לְקָטָן; אֶת הַכּוּשׁ וְאֶת הַכַּרְכַּר לִתְחֹב בּוֹ;

ר' עובדיה מברטנורא

(ב) **קורנס.** פטיש: **הדבלה.** לאחר שנטשאה עגול היא עבה וקשה וצריכה קרדום לחתכה: **מגרה.** כעין סכין ארוך ויש בו פגימות הרבה: **לגרור בו את הגבינה.** לחתכה ולחלקה לחלקים שעל ידי פגימותיו ממהר וחותך הדבר הטוב: **מגריפה.** לגרוף בה הגרוגרות מן החבית: **רחת.** לוח שיש לה בית יד ושתי דפנות וזורין בה את החטה: **ומזלג.** כלי שיש לו שלש שינים ומהפכים בו את הקש בגורן: **כוש.** פלך שטווות בו הנשים: **כרכר.** עץ של אורגים ודומה למחט של סקאין: **לתחוב בו.** לאכול בו תותים וכל מיני פרי רך:

יד אברהם

moved for its own sake, e.g., to prevent its being either damaged by the elements or stolen. This is known as מֵחַמָּה לְצֵל, lit. *from sun to shade.* [In the context of this idiom, the sun, which causes warping, is presumed to be more detrimental to the condition of the utensil than the shade.][1]

נוֹטֵל אָדָם קֻרְנָס — *A person may take a hammer*

I.e., even a goldsmith's hammer may be used. Although it may become damaged, it can be easily repaired by striking it upon an anvil. A spice hammer, however, may not be used because people are particular not to let it become soiled. [A soiled hammer will in turn soil and thereby damage the quality of the spices. For this reason spice-makers were careful never to use their instruments for anything but spices.] It falls consequently into the category of *muktzeh for fear of mone-* tary loss (*Rambam, Hil. Shabbos* 25:9; *Rif; Rosh; Shulchan Aruch* 308:1).

If one is not particular about soiling his spice hammer, he may use it for cracking nuts (*Magen Avraham* 308:2).

לְפַצֵעַ בּוֹ אֶת הָאֱגוֹזִים — *with which to crack nuts;*

[This, as well as all the other cases cited in the mishnah, are examples of *utensils used primarily for work prohibited on the Sabbath* being moved in order to make permissible use of them.]

וְקַרְדֹּם — *or a hatchet*

[A hatchet's primary use is for chop-

---

1. The leniencies accorded this category of *muktzeh* apply only to utensils. Since people occasionally use their utensils for functions other than their primary ones, a utensil used primarily for work prohibited on the Sabbath, though *set aside* from its primary use, still *stands* to be used for secondary permissible functions. The Sages, therefore, did not totally ban its being moved. An item which is not a utensil, such as a stone, although it may also occasionally be used for some specific purpose, does not, in the normal course of events, *stand* to be used on the Sabbath, i.e., there is no likelihood that a specific stone or piece of wood will come to be used on the Sabbath. The Sages, therefore, prohibited the entire category of *muktzeh because of its intrinsic properties* from being moved on the Sabbath for any reason.

משניות / שבת – פרק יז: כל-הכלים [384]

2. A person may take a hammer with which to crack nuts; or a hatchet [with which] to cut a cake of pressed figs; a saw with which to slice cheese; a shovel with which to scoop up dried figs; a winnowing shovel or a pitchfork on which to put [something] for a child; a spindle or a weaver's reed with which to spear [fruit];

YAD AVRAHAM

ping wood, a labor forbidden on the Sabbath.]

לַחְתּךְ אֶת הַדְּבֵלָה; — *[with which] to cut a cake of pressed figs;*

After the figs were dried, they were pressed into a circular cake. This cake was thick and hard, and required a hatchet to cut it (*Rav; Rashi*).

מְגֵרָה — *a saw*

[I.e., a saw generally used for sawing wood.]

לִגְרֹר בָּהּ אֶת הַגְּבִינָה; — *with which to slice* (lit. *to saw*) *cheese;*

I.e., to divide it into portions. Since a saw has a serrated edge, it cuts through the thick cheese quickly (*Rav*).

מַגְרֵפָה — *a shovel*

[This word sometimes denotes a scoop or a trowel.]

Tiferes Yisrael renders it *a rake.*

לִגְרֹף בָּהּ אֶת הַגְּרוֹגְרוֹת; — *with which to scoop up dried figs;*

I.e., to scoop out dried figs from a barrel (*Rav; Rashi*).

אֶת הָרַחַת — *a winnowing shovel*

This consists of a board with a frame on both sides, and a handle. It is used for *winnowing wheat, one of the thirty-nine principal categories of labor [see 7:2] (*Rav*).

וְאֶת הַמַּזְלֵג — *or a pitchfork*

A fork with three prongs used for turning over the straw on the threshing floor (*Rav*).

לָתֵת עָלָיו לְקָטָן; — *on which to put [something] for a child;*

I.e., to pass food to a child who is on the opposite side of a stream. An older person will usually cross the stream to obtain his food (*Tif. Yis.*).

Alternatively, this refers to one who has not washed his hands or whose hands are *tamei*[1] who wishes to feed *terumah* to a child who is a *Kohen*. Since he is not permitted to touch the *terumah* with his bare hands, he must pick it up and pass it to the child with one of these implements (*Meiri*, see *Chagigah* 2:5).

אֶת הַכּוּשׁ — *a spindle*

Used in spinning (*Rav*).

וְאֶת הַכַּרְכַּר — *or a weaver's reed*

This is used in the weaving process to arrange the threads one beside the other. It resembles a sackmaker's needle (*Rav; Tif. Yis.*). [Ancient looms did not use the comblike reed described in 7:2 (see "The Weaving Process," p. 184). A single reed was used to beat in the weft thread after it passed through the shed formed by the warp threads.]

לִתְחֹב בּוֹ; — *with which to spear [fruit];*

I.e., into mulberries, or any other

---

1. Such as one who has handled contaminated food (*Gem*, 14a). One whose entire body is *tamei* is not permitted to handle *terumah* even with an instrument.

שבת
יז/ג-ד

מַחַט שֶׁל יָד לִטֹּל בּוֹ אֶת הַקּוֹץ; וְשֶׁל סַקָּאִים לִפְתֹּחַ בּוֹ אֶת הַדֶּלֶת.

[ג] **קָנֶה** שֶׁל זֵיתִים, אִם יֵשׁ קֶשֶׁר בְּרֹאשׁוֹ, מְקַבֵּל טֻמְאָה; וְאִם לָאו, אֵין מְקַבֵּל טֻמְאָה. בֵּין כָּךְ וּבֵין כָּךְ נִטָּל בַּשַּׁבָּת.

[ד] **רַבִּי יוֹסֵי** אוֹמֵר: כָּל הַכֵּלִים נִטָּלִין חוּץ

ר' עובדיה מברטנורא

מחט של יד. מחט קטנה שתופרים בה בגדים: **ליטול בו את הקוץ.** שנכנס בבשרו, שמותר ליטלו בשבת כמו שמותר להפיס מורסא להוציא ממנה ליחה ובלבד שלא יתכוין לעשות לה פה: **ושל סקאים.** מחט גדול שתופרין בה שקין: **לפתוח בו את הדלת.** מי שאבדה לו מפתח: (ג) **קנה של זיתים.** קנה שעשוי לבדוק הזיתים שבמעטן אם נתאספו שמנן בתוכו והגיע רחויין לבית הבד: **אם יש קשר בראשו.** כעין פקק שבקנה, מקבל טומאה, לפי שעל ידי שהוא פקוק בקשר משתייר בו מן השמן הזב מן הזיתים ובודק בו אם הגיע לעשור והוא ליה בית קבול: **ואם לאו.** שאין בו קשר אף על פי שהוא חלול אין חללו עשוי לקבל כלום, הילכך הוה ליה פשוטי כלי עץ ואינו מקבל טומאה: **בין כך ובין כך ניטל בשבת.** דהא כלי הוא ועשוי להפוך בו את הזיתים:

יד אברהם
---

soft fruit, in order to eat it without soiling one's hands (Rav; Rashi; Tif. Yis.).

מַחַט שֶׁל יָד — *a hand needle*

I.e., a sewing needle (Rav; Rashi).

לִטֹּל בּוֹ אֶת הַקּוֹץ; — *with which to take [out] a thorn;*

I.e., a thorn or splinter embedded in one's skin. Although he may cause his skin to bleed, he may nevertheless remove the thorn on the Sabbath. Since he does not intend to make his skin bleed, the Rabbis permitted removing the thorn to alleviate his pain (Tos. R' Akiva). This is similar to the rule that one may lance a boil to remove the pus as long as he does not intend to make an opening for the air to enter (Rav; Tif. Yis.).

וְשֶׁל סַקָּאִים — *or [a] sackmakers' [needle]*

A large needle used in sewing sacks (Rav; Rashi).

לִפְתֹּחַ בּוֹ אֶת הַדֶּלֶת. — *with which to open a door.*

Someone who lost his key would use such a needle as a lock pick (Rav; Rashi).

3.

קָנֶה שֶׁל זֵיתִים, — *A cane for olives,*

A cane made for testing the olives in the vat, to ascertain whether they are ready to be pressed (Rav).

The cane is inserted into the olives and removed. The oil adhering to the end of the cane indicates whether the olives are ready to be pressed (Tif. Yis.).

Alternatively, this cane is used to knock the olives off the tree, and later to turn them over in the press (Rambam, Comm.).

17
3-4

a hand needle with which to take [out] a thorn; or [a] sackmakers' [needle] with which to open a door.

3. A cane for olives, if there is a knot at its end, it is susceptible to *tumah*-contamination; and if not, it is not susceptible to *tumah*-contamination. In either case it may be taken on the Sabbath.

4. R' Yose says: All utensils may be taken except

YAD AVRAHAM

אִם יֵשׁ קֶשֶׁר בְּרֹאשׁוֹ, — *if there is a knot at its end,*
I.e., if the hollow cane is enclosed at its tip by a natural knot (*Rav; Rashi*), or by a specially constructed bowl (*Rambam, Comm.; Tif. Yis.*).

מְקַבֵּל טֻמְאָה; — *it is susceptible to tumah-contamination;*
In order for a non-metallic utensil to be subject to the rules of *tumah*, it must also be a receptacle (*Rav*).
Since oil can be collected on the tip of the cane, it is deemed a receptacle and is in consequence susceptible to *tumah* (*Rav; Rambam, Comm.*).

וְאִם לָאו, — *and if not,*
I.e., if there is no knot or bowl at the end of the cane in which oil can be collected (*Rav*).

אֵין מְקַבֵּל טֻמְאָה. — *it is not susceptible to tumah-contamination.*
Even though the cane is hollow, without a knot at its end, any oil collected will spill as soon as the cane is turned over. It is therefore not a receptacle (*Rav; Meiri*).

בֵּין כָּךְ וּבֵין כָּךְ — *In either case*
[I.e., whether it has a knot or not.]

נִטָּל בַּשַּׁבָּת. — *it may be taken on the Sabbath.*
Even though it is not considered a utensil with regard to the laws of *tumah*, it is nevertheless considered a utensil with regard to the laws of *muktzeh* and may be moved on the Sabbath to be used for some permissible activity or to make use of its place (*Rambam, Hil. Shabbos* 25:7).
[It is regarded as *a utensil used primarily for work prohibited on the Sabbath* because it is used to extract oil from the olives, which is forbidden on the Sabbath. See 7:2 (s.v. דָּשׁ) and 22:1.]
Since the laws of *muktzeh* do not require that a utensil be a receptacle, the cane is deemed a utensil because it can be used to turn over the olives regardless of whether it can also hold oil. Since the laws of *tumah* do require a utensil to be a receptacle, the cane is deemed a proper utensil in regard to *tumah* only if it is capable of holding oil (*Tos. Yom Tov; Tif. Yis*).

4.

רַבִּי יוֹסֵי אוֹמֵר: כָּל הַכֵּלִים — *R' Yose says: All utensils*
I.e., even those used primarily for work prohibited on the Sabbath (*Meiri*).

נִטָּלִין — *may be taken*
On the Sabbath. Non-*muktzeh* utensils may be moved even for their own protection, while *utensils used*

שבת יז/ה מִן הַמַּסָּר הַגָּדוֹל וְיָתֵד שֶׁל מַחֲרֵשָׁה. כָּל הַכֵּלִים נִטָּלִין לְצֹרֶךְ וְשֶׁלֹּא לְצֹרֶךְ. רַבִּי נְחֶמְיָה אוֹמֵר: אֵין נִטָּלִין אֶלָּא לְצֹרֶךְ.

[ה] **כָּל הַכֵּלִים** הַנִּטָּלִין בַּשַּׁבָּת, שֶׁבְרֵיהֶן נִטָּלִין

────── ר' עובדיה מברטנורא ──────

(ד) **מסר הגדול.** מגרה גדולה שנוסרים בה קורות: **ויתד של מחרישה.** כלי גדול הטשוי כסכין שבו עושין חריץ של תלם המענה והנך קפיד עלייהו ומייחד להו מקום דלא חזו למלאכה אחריתי: **כל הכלים ניטלים לצורך ושלא לצורך.** הכי קאמר כל הכלים שמלאכתן להיתר כגון קערות וכוסות ניטלים לצורך גופו ולצורך מקומם של כלי, ושלא לצורך, אפילו שאינו צריך לגופו ולמקומו של כלי אלא לטלטלו ממחמה נגל או שלא יגנבוהו הגנבים שרי דבכלי שמלאכתו להיתר. וכלי שמלאכתו לאיסור כגון מדוכות ורחיים וכיוצא בהן, לצורך גופו ולצורך מקומו מותר, ממחמה נגל או מפני הגנבים אסור: **רבי נחמיה אומר אין ניטלים אלא לצורך.** מפרש בגמרא לצורך תשמיש המיוחד לו בלבד, ולא לצורך דבר אחר ואפילו לצורך גופו, כגון סכין לחתוך בו בלבד שרי ולא לסמוך בו את הקטרה. ואין הלכה כרבי נחמיה:

──────── יד אברהם ────────

primarily for work prohibited on the Sabbath may at least be moved to be used for permissible activities or to make other use of their place (*Meiri*).

חוּץ מִן הַמַּסָּר הַגָּדוֹל — *except for a large saw*

I.e., the type used for sawing beams (*Rav; Rashi*).

וְיָתֵד שֶׁל מַחֲרֵשָׁה. — *and a colter.*

This is the large knifelike part of a plow that cuts into the ground to make furrows.

Since people are careful not to use these implements for anything other than their designated purposes, they set them aside before the Sabbath (when their designated uses are forbidden). They are, therefore, *muktzeh*, and may not be moved even for a permissible use or for use of their place (*Rav; Rashi*).

As explained in the prefatory note this category of *muktzeh* includes all other implements that are set aside to be used strictly for their designated purpose, e.g., knives used for slaughtering, for circumcising, barbers' razors, knives used by scribes to fix their quills, spice hammers, and any utensils put away for sale (*Shulchan Aruch* 308:1).

Even if one changes their designation on the Sabbath, i.e., he decides to use these instruments henceforth for functions not requiring such sharp blades, or even for tasks permissible on the Sabbath, they remain *muktzeh* until the end of that Shabbos (glosses of R' Akiva Eger to *Shulchan Aruch* 308:1 from *Tos. Beitzah* 2b).

[The examples cited here are those given by *Shulchan Aruch* 308:1. The rule, however, applies to any delicate utensil, tool, instrument or appliance which one reserves from any secondary use for fear of its being damaged.]

כָּל הַכֵּלִים — *All utensils*

I.e., all utensils primarily used for permissible work, such as bowls and cups (*Rav* from *Gem.* 124a).

נִטָּלִין לְצֹרֶךְ — *may be taken either out of necessity*

17
5
for a large saw and a colter. All utensils may be taken either out of necessity or not out of necessity. R' Nechemiah says: They may not be taken except out of necessity.

5. All utensils which may be taken on the Sabbath, fragments of them may [also] be taken with

YAD AVRAHAM

I.e., if they are required either for use or for their place (*Rav* from *Gem.* ibid.).

וְשֶׁלֹּא לְצֹרֶךְ — *or not out of necessity.*
I.e., without a necessity for the utensil itself or its place. There must however be some purpose for the movement such as removing it either from the sun to the shade to prevent its deteriorating or to a safe place to prevent its being stolen or broken. One may not move even a permissible utensil for no purpose whatsoever. Books of Scripture and foods do not fall into this category and may be moved about even for no purpose whatsoever (*Shulchan Aruch* 308:4).

רַבִּי נְחֶמְיָה אוֹמֵר: אֵין נִטָּלִין אֶלָּא לְצֹרֶךְ —
R' Nechemiah says: They may not be taken except out of necessity.
I.e., they may be moved about only for their designated purpose, e.g., a knife may be moved to cut with but not to prop up a bowl (*Rav* from *Gem.* 146a).

Since even a utensil used for permissible work may be moved about only for its usual use it follows obviously that a utensil used for prohibited work may not be moved for any use at all, since its designated function is prohibited and no utensil may be moved, according to this opinion, for any secondary purpose. It may, however, be removed to make use of its place (*Tos. R' Akiva* from *Gem.* 124a; cf. *Tif. Yis.*).

The halachah is in accordance with the *Tanna Kamma*, not R' Nechemiah. Hence, a utensil used for prohibited work may be moved about if required either for permissible use or for use of its place. It may not, however, be moved to protect it from loss, such as from sun to shade, or to remove it to a safe place from where it will not be lost or stolen. A utensil primarily used for permissible work, on the other hand, may be moved even to protect it from loss (*Rav* from *Gem.* ibid.).

5.

The following mishnah deals with the laws of handling the fragments of broken utensils on the Sabbath.

כָּל הַכֵּלִים הַנִּטָּלִין בַּשַּׁבָּת, שִׁבְרֵיהֶן נִטָּלִין עִמָּהֶן — *All utensils which may be taken on the Sabbath, fragments of them may [also] be taken with them,*
I.e., if any of these utensils broke, their fragments may be moved about on the Sabbath, whether they broke on or before the Sabbath (*Tif. Yis.* from *Gem.* 124b).

[In some editions, the word עִמָּהֶן, *with them,* is omitted. See above, mishnah 1. Neither of the reasons cited there for including this word apply here. *Meleches Shlomo* approves of the omission.]

שבת יז/ה

עִמָּהֶן, וּבִלְבַד שֶׁיִּהְיוּ עוֹשִׂין מֵעֵין מְלָאכָה; שִׁבְרֵי עֲרֵבָה לְכַסּוֹת בָּהֶן אֶת פִּי הֶחָבִית, שִׁבְרֵי זְכוּכִית לְכַסּוֹת בָּהֶן אֶת פִּי הַפָּךְ.

רַבִּי יְהוּדָה אוֹמֵר: וּבִלְבַד שֶׁיִּהְיוּ עוֹשִׂין מֵעֵין מְלַאכְתָּן; שִׁבְרֵי עֲרֵבָה לָצוּק לְתוֹכָן מִקְפָּה, וְשֶׁל זְכוּכִית לָצוּק לְתוֹכָן שֶׁמֶן.

ר' עובדיה מברטנורא

(ה) מעין מלאכה. איזו מלאכה שתהיה, ואפילו אינה מעין מלאכתן הראשונה: **לצוק בתוכן מקפה.** עבה, דומיא דעיסה מעורבת במים. ולא פליגי אלא בנשברו בשבת, אבל נשברו מערב שבת כולי עלמא מודים דניטלים אפילו אין עושין מעין מלאכתן הראשונה. ואין הלכה כרבי יהודה:

יד אברהם

וּבִלְבַד שֶׁיִּהְיוּ עוֹשִׂין מֵעֵין מְלָאכָה — provided they can [still] be used to perform some sort of task;

I.e., any sort of task, even one not in any way related to the original function of the utensil. Since these fragments are still functional, they do not lose their designation as utensils. Consequently, they are not *muktzeh* (*Rav* from *Gem.* ibid.).

[Fragments of utensils that are no longer useful fit into the category of *muktzeh because of its intrinsic properties*. They may, therefore, not be moved for any purpose.]

שִׁבְרֵי עֲרֵבָה לְכַסּוֹת בָּהֶן אֶת פִּי הֶחָבִית, — [for example,] fragments of a mixing bowl with which to cover the mouth of a cask,

[The mishnah proceeds to illustrate the rule just stated. Shards of a mixing bowl (used to make dough), although no longer fit to hold dough, may be moved as long as they are large enough to cover the mouth of a cask. In mishnaic times, it was common to use pieces of broken utensils as covers for casks, jugs, jars and even pots. A shard fit for such use is, therefore, still functional.]

שִׁבְרֵי זְכוּכִית לְכַסּוֹת בָּהֶן אֶת פִּי הַפָּךְ. — [or] fragments of a glass with which to cover the mouth of a flask.

[A glass is generally used as a container. Shards of a broken glass which are no longer fit to contain anything may, nevertheless, be moved as long as they are large enough to be used as a cover of a jar or flask.]

רַבִּי יְהוּדָה אוֹמֵר: וּבִלְבַד שֶׁיִּהְיוּ עוֹשִׂין מֵעֵין מְלַאכְתָּן; — R' Yehudah says: Provided they can [still] perform in the nature of their [former] task;

The dispute between the *Tanna Kamma* and R' Yehudah is only in regard to utensils which have broken on the Sabbath. If the fragments cannot be used to perform something in the nature of the original function of the utensil, they are *muktzeh*. Since their continued designation as utensils could only derive from their use as something for which the original utensil was not used, they must be regarded as newly made utensils, which are considered נוֹלָד, *nolad* [see

משניות / שבת – פרק יז: כל־הכלים [390]

17
5
them, provided they can [still] be used to perform some sort of task; [for example,] fragments of a mixing bowl with which to cover the mouth of a cask, [or] fragments of a glass with which to cover the mouth of a flask.

R' Yehudah says: Provided they can [still] perform in the nature of their [former] task; [for example,] fragments of a mixing bowl into which to pour porridge, [or] fragments of a glass into which to pour oil.

YAD AVRAHAM

prefatory note]. R' Yehudah, therefore, requires that the fragments be capable of fulfilling something in the nature of their former function, in which case they can be regarded as a remnant of the old utensil, thereby maintaining their classification as utensils. The *Tanna Kamma* maintains that as long as the fragments are fit for any use at all, they may be considered as remnants of the original utensil, and may be moved about on the Sabbath.[1]

Even R' Yehudah agrees, however, that if they were broken before the Sabbath they may be moved as long as they serve some purpose. Since their new function had already been achieved before the Sabbath they are not *nolad* (*Rav* from *Gem.* ibid.).

שִׁבְרֵי עֲרֵבָה לָצוּק לְתוֹכָן מִקְפָּה, — [for example,] fragments of a mixing bowl into which to pour porridge,

The translation follows *Rashi* who describes a thick mixture similar to kneaded dough (*Rashi*).

וְשֶׁל זְכוּכִית לָצוּק לְתוֹכָן שֶׁמֶן. — or [fragments of] a glass into which to pour oil.

This too resembles the original use of the glass vessel. The halachah is not in accordance with R' Yehudah (*Rav; Rambam, Comm., Kaffich ed.; Rif; Rosh*).

6.

This mishnah teaches that if an object that is *muktzeh* is attached to an object that is not *muktzeh* and functions as part of that object, the *muktzeh* article may also be handled.

1. This explanation follows *Beur Halachah* to 308:6. *Magen Avraham* 308:15, on the other hand, explains that even the *Tanna Kamma* views this as *nolad*. However, he sides with R' Shimon's more limited definition of *nolad* and therefore permits it. The practical difference is in regard to *Yom Tov* where the halachah adopts the opinion of R' Yehudah (see prefatory note to this chapter). According to the first explanation, even on *Yom Tov* we would follow the opinion of the *Tanna Kamma*.

שבת [ו] **הָאֶבֶן** שֶׁבְּקֵרוּיָה, אִם מְמַלְאִין בָּהּ וְאֵינָהּ נוֹפֶלֶת, מְמַלְאִין בָּהּ; וְאִם לָאו, אֵין מְמַלְאִין בָּהּ.

זְמוֹרָה שֶׁהִיא קְשׁוּרָה בִּטְפִיחַ, מְמַלְאִין בָּהּ בַּשַּׁבָּת.

[ז] **פְּקַק** הַחַלּוֹן, רַבִּי אֱלִיעֶזֶר אוֹמֵר: בִּזְמַן שֶׁהוּא קָשׁוּר וְתָלוּי, פּוֹקְקִין בּוֹ;

ר׳ עובדיה מברטנורא

(ו) **האבן שבקרויה.** דלעת יבשה וממלאים בה מים, ומתוך שהיא קלה אינה שואבת אלא לפה ונותנין בה אבן להכבידה: **אם ממלאין.** בקרויה: **ואין האבן נופלת.** שהדקוה יפה בפי הקרויה הוה כלי: **ואם לאו.** הרי היא כשאר אבנים ואין מטלטלים את הקרויה, שנעשית בסיס לאבן שנעשתה: **זמורה שהיא קשורה לטפיח.** לפך קטן שואבין בו מים מן הבור או מן המעין ממלאים בו דשוויה להך זמורה כלי: (ז) **פקק החלון.** כגון לוח ומסך או שאר כל דבר שסותמים בו החלון: **ותלוי.** שאינו נגרר בארץ:

יד אברהם

הָאֶבֶן שֶׁבְּקֵרוּיָה, — *A stone that is in a gourd-shell,*

Dry gourd-shells, or dry pumpkin-shells, were used as buckets to draw water. Since the shell is light, it will not sink into the water unless a stone is placed in it to weigh it down (*Rav; Rashi*).

אִם מְמַלְאִין בָּהּ וְאֵינָהּ נוֹפֶלֶת, — *if water can be drawn with it without its falling out,*

I.e., if the gourd-shell can be used to draw water without the stone's falling out, indicating that the stone is securely attached to the gourd-shell (*Rav; Rashi*).

מְמַלְאִין בָּהּ; — *we may draw [water] with it;*

I.e., we need not refrain from using the gourd-shell because of any *muktzeh* considerations.

Since the stone is securely fastened to the gourd-shell, it is regarded as a part of the latter and is therefore deemed a utensil, not *muktzeh* (*Rav; Rashi*).

וְאִם לָאו, — *and if not,*

[I.e., if it is not fastened securely enough to the gourd-shell to prevent it from falling out when submerged.]

אֵין מְמַלְאִין בָּהּ. — *we may not draw [water] with it.*

We may not draw water with this gourd-shell. Since the stone is not considered part of the gourd-shell, it is *muktzeh*, as are all other stones. The gourd-shell, therefore, may also not be moved, since it serves as a בָּסִיס לְדָבָר הָאָסוּר, *a base for a prohibited object*, namely, the rock (*Rav; Rashi*).

זְמוֹרָה שֶׁהִיא קְשׁוּרָה בִּטְפִיחַ, — *A branch that is tied to a pitcher,*

This was used to draw water from a well or cistern (*Rav; Rashi*).

מְמַלְאִין בָּהּ בַּשַּׁבָּת. — *we may draw water with it on the Sabbath.*

By the branch being tied to the pitcher, it becomes a part of a utensil and may therefore be used on the Sabbath (*Rav; Rashi*).

If it was not tied to the pitcher be-

6. A stone that is in a gourd-shell, if water can be drawn with it without its falling out, we may draw [water] with it; and if not, we may not draw [water] with it.

A branch that is tied to a pitcher, we may draw water with it on the Sabbath.

7. A window shutter, R' Eliezer says: When it is fastened and suspended, we may shut [the window]

YAD AVRAHAM

fore the Sabbath, even though it was designated for that purpose, one may not use it to draw water on the Sabbath. Although temporarily tying the branch to the pitcher involves no prohibition of *tying a knot (see Chap. 13), it is nevertheless prohibited for fear that he will discover that the branch is too long and clip it off, thus fashioning it into a utensil on the Sabbath. This is a *toladah* of *striking the final blow (Tos. Yom Tov from Gem. 125b, Rashi ad loc.). For this reason, one may not hang a pitcher from a crook or fork in the branch and draw water (Rashi).

7.

Erecting a tent on the Sabbath is tantamount to *building, and is, therefore, prohibited. Erecting even a temporary tent is Rabbinically prohibited [because it might lead to the construction of a permanent one (Rambam, Hil. Shabbos 22:27)].[1] Making a temporary *addition* to a structure[2] is the subject of a dispute between the Sages (who permit it) and R' Eliezer (who forbids it). Making a permanent addition to a structure is Biblically prohibited.

The mishnah discusses inserting a shutter into a window. This constitutes a temporary addition to a permanent structure.

פְּקַק הַחַלוֹן, — *A window shutter,*
A board, curtain, or anything else used to close a window (Rav).

רַבִּי אֱלִיעֶזֶר אוֹמֵר: בִּזְמַן שֶׁהוּא קָשׁוּר וְתָלוּי, — *R' Eliezer says: When it is fastened and suspended,*
I.e., if the shutter is tied to the win-

dow by a rope so short that the shutter, when hanging from the rope, does not reach the ground (Rav; Rashi).

פּוֹקְקִין בּוֹ; — *we may shut [the window] with it;*
[Since it is attached to the window and never rests on the ground, it is

---

1. The prohibition of erecting even temporary tents applies only to roofs. One is, however, permitted to put up partitions (Ran in explanation of Rashi). Others prohibit erecting a partition where its purpose is to create a halachically significant barrier, such as: (a) to set up partitions around an open area to render it a private domain in which carrying is permitted, or (b) to complete a *sukkah* by adding a third wall, thus rendering it a valid *sukkah* (Tos. quoting R' Tam).

2. This is true even if one is making a temporary addition to a permanent structure.

שבת יז/ח

וְאִם לָאו, אֵין פּוֹקְקִין בּוֹ. וַחֲכָמִים אוֹמְרִים: בֵּין כָּךְ וּבֵין כָּךְ פּוֹקְקִין בּוֹ.

[ח] כָּל כִּסּוּי כֵּלִים שֶׁיֵּשׁ לָהֶם בֵּית אֲחִיזָה נִטָּלִים בַּשַּׁבָּת.

ר' עובדיה מברטנורא

ואם לאו אין פוקקין בו. שָׁאִם נִגְרַר עַל גַּבֵּי קַרְקַע כְּשֶׁהוּא שׁוֹמְטוֹ מֵעַל הָאָרֶץ לִסְתּוֹם בּוֹ, מִיחֲזֵי כְּמוֹסִיף עַל הַבִּנְיָן, וּסְבַר רַבִּי אֱלִיעֶזֶר אֵין מוֹסִיפִין עַל אֹהֶל עֲרָאִי בְּשַׁבָּת: **בֵּין כָּךְ וּבֵין כָּךְ.** בֵּין קָשׁוּר בֵּין אֵינוֹ קָשׁוּר פּוֹקְקִין בּוֹ, הוֹאִיל וְהָיָה מוּכָן וְהָיָה מֵאֶתְמוֹל לְכָךְ, דִּסְבָרֵי רַבָּנָן מוֹסִיפִין עַל אֹהֶל עֲרָאִי בְּשַׁבָּת. וַהֲלָכָה כַּחֲכָמִים:

יד אברהם

regarded as part of the building. Therefore, when one covers the window with the shutter he is not adding in any way to the building. A hinged shutter or window is, of course, also viewed in this manner.]

וְאִם לָאו — **and if not,**

I.e., if when hanging from the rope it is not suspended in the air, even though it is attached by a rope to the window ... (*Meiri*).

אֵין פּוֹקְקִין בּוֹ. — **we may not shut [the window] with it.**

Since it rests on the ground, when one picks it up to shut the window with it he appears to be adding to the building. Though one is making only a temporary addition to the building (since the shutter will later be removed), R' Eliezer rules that making even a temporary addition to a structure is prohibited. Therefore, anything which even *appears* to be a temporary addition is Rabbinically prohibited (*Rav; Rashi*).

וַחֲכָמִים אוֹמְרִים: בֵּין כָּךְ וּבֵין כָּךְ פּוֹקְקִין בּוֹ. — **But the Sages say: In either case we may shut [the window] with it.**

I.e., whether or not it is attached to the window one is permitted to shut the window with it. As explained above the Sages rule that making a temporary addition is permissible on the Sabbath. Therefore, it need not even be tied since one is, at worst, making only a temporary addition to the building.

One must, however, have prepared this board for such use prior to the Sabbath, or else it is *muktzeh*. However, no direct act of preparation is required. Rather, the mere intention of the person before the Sabbath to use this board as a shutter is sufficient (*Tos.*, ibid.).

8.

The final mishnah deals with removing and replacing the covers of fixtures or utensils built into the ground. In order to be allowed to handle the lid of any utensil, it must, of course, have the status of a utensil,[1] otherwise it is *intrinsically muktzeh*.

---

1. According to some authorities, it must be a utensil that can be used for purposes other than covering a vessel (*Rashi*). According to others, it is sufficient if it is fashioned for use as a lid (*Tos.* quoting *Rabbeinu Tam; Shulchan Aruch* 308:10).

17
8

with it; and if not, we may not shut [the window] with it. But the Sages say: In either case we may shut [the window] with it.

8. All utensil covers which have handles may be taken on the Sabbath.

YAD AVRAHAM

As long as it has the status of a utensil, there are no restrictions on its use. The cover of an opening in the ground, such as a well or a cistern, however, is additionally required to have a handle before it may be used on the Sabbath. This is because one who places a cover over a hole in the ground appears to be *building; i.e., permanently blocking up the hole. Conversely, one who removes the cover from such a hole appears to be *demolishing, i.e., opening a hole which had been previously sealed. If the cover possesses a handle, it may be opened and closed since it is then evident that this is a cover rather than a seal (Rashi; Meiri). Since placing a lid on a utensil does not appear as sealing the utensil, this requirement does not apply to the covers of utensils (Meiri). The following mishnah discusses whether the covers of utensils which have been connected to the ground must also possess handles before they may be used.

כָּל כִּסּוּי כֵּלִים שֶׁיֵּשׁ לָהֶם בֵּית אֲחִיזָה — *All utensils covers which have handles*

The Gemara (126b) explains this statement as referring to utensils which have been cemented or otherwise connected to the ground.

As explained above, the lids of movable utensils do not require handles. For this reason, some authorities delete the word כָּל, *all*, since the ruling of the mishnah does not apply to the lids of movable utensils (Maharshal; Kol HaRemez; Shoshanim LeDavid).

We, nevertheless, find this word in many early editions, e.g., Rif; Rosh; Rabbeinu Chananel; Maggid Mishneh, Hil. Shabbos 25:13.

Meiri explains the word *all* as referring even to those of movable utensils. As explained above, these must have the status of utensils. A flat piece of wood that has not been specifically designated as a lid prior to the Sabbath (see Mishnah Berurah 308:45) is not considered a utensil. If a handle has been attached to it, it is automatically considered a utensil. The mishnah is therefore saying that any cover or potential cover may be carried if it has a handle. This does not, however, preclude the permissibility of covers without handles, i.e., those that have been specifically designated as covers to movable utensils.

נִטָּלִים בַּשַּׁבָּת. — *may be taken on the Sabbath.*

Any cover possessing a handle may be used on the Sabbath since it is then evident that it is a lid, not a seal. One not possessing a handle may not be moved. Since permission to move the lid of a *utensil* connected to the ground may lead to the mistaken impression that even the lid of a cistern or well may be moved, the Rabbis, according to the Tanna Kamma,

שבת יז/ח

אָמַר רַבִּי יוֹסֵי: בַּמֶּה דְבָרִים אֲמוּרִים? בְּכִסּוּי קַרְקַע; אֲבָל בְּכִסּוּי כֵּלִים, בֵּין כָּךְ וּבֵין כָּךְ נִטָּלִים בַּשַּׁבָּת.

ר' עובדיה מברטנורא

(ח) **במה דברים אמורים בכסויי קרקעות**. בגמרא קאמר דבכסויי כלים כולי עלמא לא פליגי דשרי אף על גב דלית להו בית אחיזה, ובכסויי קרקעות כגון כסוי של בור ודות כולי עלמא לא פליגי דאסור אי לית להו בית אחיזה. כי פליגי בכסויי כלים המחוברים לקרקעות, מר סבר כקרקעות דמיין, ומר סבר לאו כקרקעות דמיין. והלכה כחכמים שהמחובר לקרקע הרי הוא כקרקע:

יד אברהם

applied the rules of the latter to the former; i.e. that it too must possess a handle.[1]

אָמַר רַבִּי יוֹסֵי: בַּמֶּה דְבָרִים אֲמוּרִים? — *Said R' Yose: When is this said?*

[I.e., when do we say that unless they have handles they may not be moved.]

בְּכִסּוּי קַרְקַע; — *Regarding a cover of [a hole in] the ground;*

I.e., only in the case of coverings over holes in the ground such as wells and cisterns (*Rav* from *Gem.* 126b).

If the lids do not have handles with which to remove and replace them, they appear to be part of the ground, and picking them up and replacing them resembles building and demolishing (*Rashi; Meiri*).

אֲבָל בְּכִסּוּי כֵּלִים, — *but regarding covers of utensils,*

I.e., even lids of utensils which are

---

1. Because the lid of a utensil connected to the ground may neither be removed nor replaced, it is viewed as part of this structure. Therefore, even if it was removed prior to the Sabbath and is a perfectly usable utensil (e.g., as a cover to a crate), it is nevertheless regarded as *muktzeh*, just as is a door which has been detached from a house [see mishnah 1] (*Magen Avraham* 308:23 from *Ran*, as explained by *Beur Halachah* 308:10).

17 8   Said R' Yose: When is this said? Regarding a cover of [a hole in] the ground; but regarding covers of utensils, in either case we may take them on the Sabbath.

YAD AVRAHAM

cemented to the ground (*Rav* from *Gem.* ibid.).

בֵּין כָּךְ וּבֵין כָּךְ נִטָּלִים בַּשַּׁבָּת — *in either case we may take them on the Sabbath.*

Whether or not they are equipped with handles, they may be moved about on the Sabbath (*Rav* from *Gem.*).

Some authorities rule that the halachah is in accordance with the *Tanna Kamma* who rules that even the covers of utensils connected to the ground must have handles to be moved (*Rav; Rambam, Comm.; Rif*).

This decision is seemingly contradicted by the *Gemara* (125a) that decides that we may move an oven lid on the Sabbath. [Quoted in the name of R' Eliezer ben Yaakov.] Since the ovens of that time were cemented to the ground [*Rashi* 126b cites ovens as an example of utensils cemented to the ground], and since the lids of the oven discussed did not have handles (*Rashi* 125a) it would seem that the opinions of R'

Eliezer ben Yaakov and R' Yose are identical and, by ruling that oven lids may be moved, the *Gemara* is, in effect, ruling with R' Yose, too. Some authorities, therefore, rule that the halachah is, indeed, in accordance with R' Yose, who permits removing the lids of utensils connected to the ground even if they are not equipped with handles (*Rosh*).

Others explain that our mishnah in dealing with utensils connected to the ground is referring only to those completely buried in the ground. Since these appear almost identical to cisterns, they are prohibited according to the *Tanna Kamma*. In this, the halachah follows the *Tanna Kamma*. R' Eliezer ben Yaakov, however, refers to ovens which are completely above ground. Since these are not so readily confused with cisterns, despite their being connected to the ground, even the *Tanna Kamma* agrees that their lids need not have handles for them to be moved on the Sabbath. This is apparently the view of *Rif, Rambam,* and *Rav* (*Ran; Maggid Mishneh, Hil. Shabbos* 25:13).

פרק שמונה עשר
Chapter Eighteen

In addition to the Torah prohibitions of *melachah* on the Sabbath, the Rabbis prohibited certain activities because they require excessive toil and are considered *weekday activities* (see General Introduction, p. 17). Under certain circumstances, these prohibitions were relaxed. They are activities that are necessary for: (a) performance of a *mitzvah*; (b) care of livestock; and (c) care of the ill, especially for the care of a new mother and her infant (*Meiri*). These three exemptions are discussed, respectively, in the mishnayos of this chapter.

שבת
יח/א

[א] **מְפַנִּין** אֲפִילוּ אַרְבַּע וְחָמֵשׁ קֻפּוֹת שֶׁל תֶּבֶן וְשֶׁל תְּבוּאָה מִפְּנֵי הָאוֹרְחִים וּמִפְּנֵי בִטּוּל בֵּית הַמִּדְרָשׁ, אֲבָל לֹא אֶת הָאוֹצָר.

— ר' עובדיה מברטנורא —

פרק שמונה עשר מפנין. (א) מפנין – מפנין. אם צריך למקומן להושיב שם אורחין להסב בסעודה או תלמידים לשמוע הדרשה, ודוקא לדבר מצוה שרי ולא חיישינן לטירחא דשבת: **ארבע וחמש**. לאו דוקא, דהי בעי אפילו טובא נמי: **אבל לא את האוצר**. כלומר ובלבד שלא יגמור את האוצר כולו עד שיגיע לקרקעיתו, דלמא אתי לאשווי גומות:

יד אברהם

1.

מְפַנִּין — *We may clear away*
I.e., if their place is needed, the objects mentioned below may be cleared on the Sabbath, although this involves excessive toil. As stated above, this is permissible only to facilitate the performance of a *mitzvah* (*Rav*).

אֲפִילוּ אַרְבַּע וְחָמֵשׁ — *even four or five*
[There is a difference of opinion in the *Gemara* (126b) between Shmuel and Rav Chisda as to whether the numbers four or five are to be taken literally or not. The mishnah will be explained first according to Shmuel's opinion that they are not meant literally, since this is the explanation adopted by *Rav* in his commentary. Rav Chisda's view, which takes them literally, will be given below, s.v. אֲבָל לֹא אֶת־הָאוֹצָר.]

❧ The Mishnah According to Shmuel

In reality, one may clear away any number of baskets (*Rav* from *Gem*. 127a). The *Tanna* avails himself of a common idiom to indicate that there is no fixed limit to how many he may clear if he needs the extra space (*Rashi* on *Gem*. ibid.). Alternatively, this is a specifically Tannaic idiom found throughout Mishnah (see above 15:3; for full list see *Tos. Yom Tov*). Although the intent, as explained above, is not to set an absolute limit, the *Tanna's* preference for these numbers derives from the Biblical statement (*Exodus* 21:37), *Five cattle shall he pay in lieu of the ox* [*which he has stolen*] *and four sheep in lieu of the sheep*. Although those numbers are specific, the Tanna uses them here to indicate a non-specific number.

קֻפּוֹת שֶׁל תֶּבֶן וְשֶׁל תְּבוּאָה — *baskets of straw or of produce*
These were large containers, each of which held three *se'ah* [a measure of volume equal to the displacement of 144 average-sized chicken eggs] (*Tos. Yom Tov, Tif. Yis.* from *Tos.*)

מִפְּנֵי הָאוֹרְחִים — [*to make room*] *for* (lit. *because of*) *the guests*
Hospitality to those who need a place to stay or eat is a *mitzvah*. However, inviting a friend who could just as easily eat in his own house to join him for a meal is not considered a *mitzvah*, and the lenient ruling of the mishnah does not apply (*Rama* 333:1 from *Terumas HaDeshen* 72).

וּמִפְּנֵי בִטּוּל בֵּית הַמִּדְרָשׁ — *or to avoid* (lit. *because of*) *curtailment of study* (lit. *the study hall*),
I.e., to make room for the pupils

[400] משניות / שבת – פרק יח: מפנין

18
1

1. We may clear away even four or five baskets of straw or of produce to make room for guests or to avoid curtailment of study, but not a storehouse.

YAD AVRAHAM

wishing to attend a Torah lecture (*Rav; Rashi*).

The *Tanna* states *guests* before *study* because hospitality to those who need it is considered an even greater *mitzvah* than welcoming the *Shechinah*. [This is derived from the fact that our Patriarch Abraham interrupted his conversation with God to serve the three strangers (not realizing that they were angels). See *Genesis* 18:1-3 (*Gem*. 127a).] The *Tanna* therefore teaches us that not only for the *mitzvah* of hospitality may we clear away baskets of straw or produce, but even for the *mitzvah* of the study of Torah we may do the same, although it involves excessive toil (*Tif. Yis.* based on *Gem*. 127a).

Additionally, the *Tanna* teaches us that for *mitzvos* we may clear away not only light containers (straw) but even heavy ones (produce). For other reasons, however, we may not even clear away light containers because even they involve too much toil to be carried on the Sabbath (*Tif. Yis.*), or because such removal is regarded as a weekday activity (*Bach* 333).

אֲבָל לֹא אֶת הָאוֹצָר. — *but not a storehouse*.

I.e., we may clear away baskets only as long as we do not thereby clear away the entire storehouse. The Rabbis prohibited this because they were concerned that once the floor was uncovered one might discover irregularities in the floor of the storehouse and, in a moment of forgetfulness, even clear out the floor. [This would constitute (*Gem*. 73b) building] (*Rav* from *Gem*. 127a).

This is true even if there are only three or four baskets in the storehouse (*Mishnah Berurah* 333:6 from *Eliyah Rabbah*).

◆§ The Mishnah According to Rav Chisda

We have, up to this point, explained the mishnah according to Shmuel, who, the *Gemara* (127a) states, interprets the mishnah according to R' Shimon, who, although accepting the basic law of *muktzeh*, has a much narrower definition of what constitutes *muktzeh* (*Gem*. 45a; *Tos., Beitzah* 2a). According to this definition, straw placed in storage before the Sabbath is not considered *muktzeh* despite the fact that one did not intend to use it on the Sabbath. Thus, he rules that although the storehouse was not even partially cleared before the Sabbath, and he had no intention of using the baskets, he may, nonetheless, clear them away in order to facilitate a *mitzvah*. Since no prohibition is involved here other than that of excessive toil or weekday activities, he may clear away as many baskets as necessary, provided he does not clear out the storehouse completely. Rav Chisda, however, interprets the mishnah according to R' Yehudah[1] who

---

1. It is because Rav Chisda understands the numbers *four or five* to be literal that he is forced to explain the mishnah according to R' Yehudah. Since one is normally permitted to clear five baskets, the only explanation for a limit of four can be where there are only five baskets to start off with. Therefore, the mishnah has already stated the principle of not completely clearing a storehouse. The phrase *but not a storehouse* is then

שבת
יח/א

מְפַנִּין תְּרוּמָה טְהוֹרָה; וּדְמַאי; וּמַעֲשֵׂר

───────────── ר' עובדיה מברטנורא ─────────────

מפנין תרומה טהורה. ואפילו ישראל דלא חזיא ליה יוכל לטלטלה ולפנותה, כיון דחזיא לכהן: **ודמאי.** דחזי לעניים, כדתנן מאכילין את העניים דמאי, ואי בעי הוה מפקיר לנכסיה והוי עני וחזי ליה, השתא נמי חזי ליה:

יד אברהם

has a much broader definition of *muktzeh* and considers any item placed in long-term storage as *muktzeh*. [This is because the person indicates his intention *not* to use it by placing it in storage.] Consequently, clearing any part of a storehouse should be prohibited because the stored matter is *muktzeh*. He therefore explains that the mishnah is speaking of a storehouse from which one had already begun using the straw before the Sabbath, thereby indicating his intention to use the straw rather than store it. Consequently, it is no longer *muktzeh*. He may not, however, clear away baskets in a storehouse in which none have been previously cleared.

He explains the mishnah as follows: *We may clear away four baskets* [in a small storehouse containing five baskets], because we may not completely clear a storehouse [as explained above], *or* [a maximum of] *five baskets* [in a larger storehouse. More than five are prohibited either due to excessive toil or because it is a weekday activity] *of straw or produce ... but not an* [untapped] *storehouse.*

The halachah is decided in favor of Rav Chisda, with regard to the number of baskets that may be cleared from a storehouse; i.e., one may clear only four out of a storehouse containing five baskets and a maximum of five out of any larger storehouse. However, with regard to whether one may clear a previously untapped storehouse, the halachah is decided in favor of Shmuel, since the halachah is generally in accordance with R' Shimon's narrower definition of *muktzeh*. As long as the straw and grain are fit for fodder, they may be moved on the Sabbath (*Shulchan Aruch* 333:1).[1]

מְפַנִּין תְּרוּמָה טְהוֹרָה; — *We may clear away terumah that is tahor;*

[See commentary to 2:6 for a description of *terumah* and other tithes mentioned below.]

The *Tanna* proceeds to delineate what we may clear away. The general rule is that we may clear away any food fit for consumption on the Sabbath. This includes not only ordinary produce, which all may eat, but even *terumah*, which only a *Kohen* may eat. Being fit for a *Kohen*, it is considered fit for consumption, and is not

---

redundant if one explains it to mean not to clear a storehouse completely. Consequently, we are forced to explain it as meaning *but not an* [untapped] *storehouse*, thus expressing the view of R' Yehudah that items in such a storehouse are *muktzeh* (*Gem.* 126b).

1. According to *Sh'iltos d'Rav Achai* 11, even Shmuel rules that no more than four or five barrels may be removed from the storehouse. See *Milchamos Hashem* ad loc., *Maggid Mishneh, Hil. Shabbos* 26:15.

18 1 We may clear away *terumah* that is *tahor; demai;*

YAD AVRAHAM

muktzeh (*Rav; Rashi* from *Gem.* 127b).

This ruling applies only to *terumah* that is *tahor*, however. As learned above (2:1), contaminated *terumah* may not be eaten even by a *Kohen*. It must be destroyed by being either burnt or fed to *a Kohen's* livestock. As was explained there, there is a prohibition against destroying *terumah* on either the Sabbath or *Yom Tov*. [Whether this prohibition is Biblical or Rabbinical has been discussed above. However, the ban on feeding it to one's livestock is certainly only Rabbinic.] Consequently, contaminated *terumah* is of no possible use on the Sabbath. This renders it *muktzeh*, and it may not be handled even to make room for the performance of a *mitzvah* (*Rashi*).

וּדְמָאי; — *demai;*

As explained above (2:7), *demai* is produce belonging to, or purchased from, עַמֵּי הָאָרֶץ [*ammei haaretz*], unlearned people. When the Rabbis discovered that many of them were lax in their observance of the laws of tithes, they decreed that any produce purchased from unlearned people must be tithed to remove all doubt. However, since the majority of even unlearned people did faithfully observe the tithe laws, there is no Biblical requirement to retithe *demai*. Consequently, when enacting this law, the Rabbis could be lenient in its application. They therefore chose not to impose this requirement on the poor. As a result, a poor man may purchase produce from an *am haaretz* and eat it without tithing.

It is Rabbinically forbidden to tithe produce on either the Sabbath or *Yom Tov* (above 2:7, *Beitzah* 1:6). Since *demai* must be tithed before being used, it should seemingly be unusable on the Sabbath and therefore *muktzeh* (as is any unusable item). However, since one has the right to renounce his property, thereby rendering himself impoverished, it is regarded as at least *possible* for anyone to be able to eat *demai*. Therefore, it is not *muktzeh* (*Rav* from *Gem.* 127b).

Tosafos point out that it was not really necessary for the *Gemara* to mention that the owner is himself theoretically able to use the *demai* by renouncing ownership of his property. The mere fact that it is fit for the poor makes it non-*muktzeh* even for the rich, just as *terumah*, which may be eaten only by a *Kohen*, is not *muktzeh* to a *non-Kohen*. *Tosafos* explain that since the reason mentioned in the *Gemara* renders it fit for the owner himself, the *Gemara* chooses to answer in this manner (*Tos. Yom Tov* from *Tos.* 127b).

Others say that *demai* differs from *terumah*. *Terumah*, although unfit for a non-*Kohen*, will eventually be given to a *Kohen* for whom it is fit. *Demai*, on the other hand, although fit for the poor, will probably never be given to the poor, but will be tithed and consumed by the owner. Since those to whom it is presently fit will probably never receive it, it cannot be regarded as a usable and therefore *non-muktzeh* item unless its present owner can himself use it. The *Gemara* must therefore explain that it is theoretically usable by its present owner because he is able to renounce his ownership of his property and thus render himself impoverished (*Tos. R' Akiva* from *Rashba; Lechem Shamayim*).

שבת יח/א

רִאשׁוֹן שֶׁנִּטְּלָה תְרוּמָתוֹ; וּמַעֲשֵׂר שֵׁנִי וְהֶקְדֵּשׁ שֶׁנִּפְדּוּ; וְהַתֻּרְמוֹס הַיָּבֵשׁ, מִפְּנֵי שֶׁהוּא מַאֲכָל לָעֲנִיִּים: אֲבָל לֹא אֶת הַטֶּבֶל; וְלֹא מַעֲשֵׂר רִאשׁוֹן שֶׁלֹּא נִטְּלָה תְרוּמָתוֹ; וְלֹא אֶת מַעֲשֵׂר שֵׁנִי וְהֶקְדֵּשׁ שֶׁלֹּא נִפְדּוּ;

ר׳ עובדיה מברטנורא

ומעשר ראשון שנטלה תרומתו. שנטלה ממנו תרומת מעשר ולא נטלה ממנו תרומה גדולה, כגון שהקדים בן לוי ולקח המעשר בשבלין, דעדיין לא חלה עליה חובת תרומה שאין הדגן חייב בתרומה גדולה עד שיתמרח בכרי, וזה שהקדים ולקח המעשר בשבלין אינו מפריש אלא תרומת מעשר בלבד, ומותר באכילה אף על פי שלא הפרישו ממנה תרומה גדולה: **ומעשר שני והקדש שנפדו.** שפדו אותן הבעלים ונתנו את הקרן ולא נתנו את החומש, וסמכינן מהכא שהם פדויין והחומש הוי מלוה גבי בעלים: **אבל לא את הטבל.** ואפילו טבל דרבנן, כגון הזרוע בעציץ שאינו נקוב: **ולא את מעשר ראשון שלא נטלה תרומתו.** אם הקדים בן לוי ולקח המעשר אחר שנתמרחה התבואה בכרי קודם שהפרישו ממנו תרומה גדולה, והפריש תרומת מעשר ולא הפריש תרומה גדולה זה, מעשר ראשון שלא נטלה תרומתו האמור כאן, שכיון שנתמרחה בכרי ונתחייבה בתרומה, כשלוקח המעשר ראשון אף על פי שמפריש ממנו תרומת מעשר כל זמן שלא הפריש ממנו תרומה גדולה הוי טבל ואסור לטלטלו בשבת: **ולא מעשר שני והקדש שלא נפדו.** כגון שנפדו אבל לא נפדו כהלכה, כגון שפדה המעשר שני על גרוטאות של כסף, ואין מעשר שני נפדה אלא במטבע שיש עליהם צורה דכתיב (דברים יד) וצרת הכסף בידך. והקדש אינו נפדה בקרקע דכתיב (ויקרא כז) ונתן את הערכך ביום ההוא דבר הניתן מיד ליד:

יד אברהם

וּמַעֲשֵׂר רִאשׁוֹן שֶׁנִּטְּלָה תְרוּמָתוֹ — *first tithe whose terumah has been separated from it;*

If this statement were taken literally it would be obvious; since *terumah* was separated one may eat it. The Gemara (127b), therefore, states that the mishnah is concerned with a situation in which only *its* (the first tithe's) *terumah*, i.e., "the tithe from the tithe" which the Levite gives the *Kohen* was separated, but not the regular *terumah* (תְּרוּמָה גְדוֹלָה). Under normal circumstances this would render the produce *tevel* (untithed) and forbidden, but the mishnah refers to a case in which the first tithe has been separated before the grain has been threshed — before threshing, the obligation to separate *terumah* and the other tithes is not yet in effect. Therefore the Levite who receives his first tithe is obligated to give the *Kohen* only the tithe of the tithe, and not the regular *terumah* (Rav).

וּמַעֲשֵׂר שֵׁנִי וְהֶקְדֵּשׁ שֶׁנִּפְדּוּ — *second tithe and consecrated property that have been redeemed;*

One may redeem his second tithe (מַעֲשֵׂר שֵׁנִי) or consecrated objects (הֶקְדֵּשׁ) with money.[1]

The redeemed produce loses its sacred status and may be consumed as ordinary, non-sanctified food. The redemption money assumes, in turn, the sacred status of the second tithe or consecrated substance. If the redeemer is

---

1. Not all consecrated objects can be redeemed. Animals fit for a sacrifice may not be redeemed unless they have become disqualified for sacrifice such as by a permanent major blemish.

18
1
first tithe whose *terumah* has been separated from it; second tithe and consecrated property that have been redeemed; and dry lupine, because it is food for the poor. But [we may] not [clear away] untithed produce; nor first tithe whose *terumah* has not been separated [from it]; nor second tithe nor consecrated property that have not been redeemed;

YAD AVRAHAM

the original owner, he must add a fifth to the value of the item being redeemed.

Since redeemed produce is considered ordinary food, it would seem obvious that it may be handled on the Sabbath. The *Gemara* explains that the mishnah speaks of a situation in which the fifth was not added, and instructs us that though adding the fifth is an obligation, failure to do so does not invalidate the redemption. Therefore, one may handle this produce on the Sabbath (*Rav* from *Gem.* 127b).

וְהַתֻּרְמוֹס הַיָּבֵשׁ, — *and dry lupine,*

Only dried lupines may be handled on the Sabbath. Fresh ones, however, are so bitter that they are completely inedible (*Tif. Yis.* from *Gem.* 127b).

מִפְּנֵי שֶׁהוּא מַאֲכָל לָעֲנִיִּים. — *because it is food for the poor.*

I.e., even dried ones are so bitter that ordinary people would not eat them until they were cooked seven times (see *R' Chananel* to *Beitzah* 25b; cf. *Tos. Yom Tov* to *Tevul Yom* 1:4). [Poor people, however, would eat them.]

In the mishnah printed with the *Gemara*, as well as in *Meiri*, we find: מִפְּנֵי שֶׁהוּא מַאֲכָל לָעִזִּים, *since it is food for goats.*

אֲבָל לֹא אֶת הַטֶּבֶל; — *But [we may] not [clear away] untithed produce;*

Ordinary טֶבֶל [*tevel*], *untithed produce,* because it may not be eaten [see

2:7], is obviously *muktzeh*. Our mishnah means to include even Rabbinically forbidden *tevel*, e.g., grain grown in an unperforated flowerpot [see 10:6]. By Scriptural law, such grain is not considered produce of the earth and need not be tithed, but the Sages imposed the tithe obligation on it (*Rav* from *Gem.* 128a).

וְלֹא מַעֲשֵׂר רִאשׁוֹן שֶׁלֹּא נִטְּלָה תְרוּמָתוֹ; — *nor first tithe whose terumah has not been separated [from it];*

The circumstances referred to in the mishnah includes even a situation in which he reversed the regular sequence and gave the first tithe to the Levite before separating the regular *terumah*. In this case, because the first tithe was taken off after threshing and storing, when the obligation to separate the regular *terumah* had taken effect, the Levite must separate both *terumah* and his own tithe, as opposed to the instance (above) in which the first tithe has been separated before the *terumah* obligation took effect.

וְלֹא אֶת מַעֲשֵׂר שֵׁנִי וְהֶקְדֵּשׁ שֶׁלֹּא נִפְדּוּ; — *nor second tithe nor consecrated property that have not been redeemed;*

Even if they were redeemed but that redemption was not performed properly, e.g., second tithe was redeemed with uncoined metal, or consecrated produce was redeemed with land (ibid.).

שבת
יח/ב

וְלֹא אֶת הַלּוּף; וְלֹא הַחַרְדָּל. רַבָּן שִׁמְעוֹן בֶּן גַּמְלִיאֵל מַתִּיר בַּלּוּף, מִפְּנֵי שֶׁהוּא מַאֲכַל עוֹרְבִין.

[ב] **חֲבִילֵי קַשׁ**, וַחֲבִילֵי עֵצִים, וַחֲבִילֵי זְרָדִים, אִם הִתְקִינָן לְמַאֲכַל בְּהֵמָה, מְטַלְטְלִין אוֹתָן; וְאִם לָאו, אֵין מְטַלְטְלִין אוֹתָן. כּוֹפִין אֶת הַסַּל לִפְנֵי הָאֶפְרוֹחִים כְּדֵי

ר׳ עובדיה מברטנורא

לוף. מין קטנית שאינו ראוי חי אפילו לבהמה. ורמב״ס פירש מין ממיני הבצלים: **לעורבין.** כגון עשירים שמגדלים עורבים לגדולה. ואין הלכה כרבן שמעון בן גמליאל: (ב) **חבילי. זרדים.** ענפי האילן לחים שמזרדין אותם למאכל בהמה: **כופין את הסל לפני האפרוחים.** ומבטל כלי

יד אברהם

וְלֹא אֶת הַלּוּף — *nor colocasia;*

The translation follows *Aruch Ha-Shulchan*. *Rav* describes a type of bean [or a species of onion (*Rambam*)] inedible even to cattle in its raw state (*Rav*).

וְלֹא הַחַרְדָּל — *nor mustard.*

This refers to green mustard, fit only for doves. The mishnah deals with a place where doves are not common. The mustard, therefore, is of no use and is consequently *muktzeh* (*Tif. Yis.* based on *Ran*).

רַבָּן שִׁמְעוֹן בֶּן גַּמְלִיאֵל מַתִּיר בַּלּוּף, מִפְּנֵי שֶׁהוּא מַאֲכַל עוֹרְבִין — *Rabban Shimon ben Gamliel permits colocasia, since it is food for ravens.*

Although only the wealthy raise ravens for pets, Rabban Shimon ben Gamliel rules that since all Israel are considered royal children, anything considered fit for royalty is considered fit for them, too. In this, his opinion is similar to R' Shimon's in 14:4 (*Tos. R' Akiva* from *Gem.* 128a).

The halachah is in accordance with the *Tanna Kamma*, who rules that only food fit for common beasts and fowl may be handled on the Sabbath (*Shulchan Aruch* 308:29).

The mishnah refers to the great majority of places, where ravens are uncommon. Where ravens are common, even the *Tanna Kamma* concurs that we may handle colocasia, since it is food for ravens, even though one does not own any (*Tif. Yis.* from *Shulchan Aruch* ibid.).

2.

חֲבִילֵי קַשׁ, וַחֲבִילֵי עֵצִים — *Bundles of straw, bundles of twigs,*

The mishnah is referring to bundles of tender twigs (*Mishnah Berurah* 308:117).

וַחֲבִילֵי זְרָדִים — *and bundles of green branches,*

These, too, are used for cattle fodder (*Rav; Rashi*).

In *Succah* (1:5) *Rav* translates *cane* used for cattle feed when fresh, and for firewood when dry.

משניות / שבת – פרק יח: מפנין [406]

nor colocasia; nor mustard. Rabban Shimon ben Gamliel permits colocasia, since it is food for ravens.

2. Bundles of straw, bundles of twigs, and bundles of green branches, if we prepared them for animal feed, we may handle them; and if not, we may not handle them.

We may invert a basket in front of chicks so that

YAD AVRAHAM

אִם הִתְקִינָן לְמַאֲכַל בְּהֵמָה, — *if we prepared them for animal feed*,

I.e., if they were set aside before the Sabbath for cattle feed (*Rashi on Gem.* 128a).

מְטַלְטְלִין אוֹתָן; — *we may handle them;*

[Since they are usable on the Sabbath, they are not *muktzeh*, and may be handled.]

וְאִם לָאו, — *and if not,*

[I.e., if they were not set aside for cattle feed.]

אֵין מְטַלְטְלִין אוֹתָן. — *we may not handle them.*

Since they are usually used as kindling, and, as such, do not stand to be used on the Sabbath, they are *muktzeh* unless they were expressly set aside for cattle feed (*Beis Yosef* 308).

כּוֹפִין אֶת הַסַּל לִפְנֵי הָאֶפְרוֹחִים — *We may invert a basket in front of chicks*

Although the chicks themselves may not be handled on the Sabbath (see preface to Chapter 17, p. 287) the basket may be handled for their benefit.[1]

We have learned above (3:6) that one may not nullify the usability of a utensil by causing it to become *muktzeh*, such as by placing a utensil under a lamp to catch the dripping oil. [Since the oil falling into this dish is *muktzeh*, the dish beneath it, serving as a base for this oil, is also *muktzeh*.] Since the chicks are *muktzeh*, the question arises as to how we may place a basket for chicks to climb on, since by climbing on it they will render the basket a *base to a prohibited article* and thus *muktzeh*. *Tosafos* answer that since the chicks do not stay on the basket (merely using it as a step up to their coop), the basket will not remain a *base to the muktzeh* for the entire Sabbath. Consequently, one has not made it unusable. The rule that something which became *muktzeh* as a *base* remains *muktzeh* even after the object resting on it has been removed applies only to something which was a *base to muktzeh* at the *onset* of the Sabbath. Something which first becomes a *base to muktzeh* in the middle of the Sabbath does not remain *muktzeh* once the object resting on it has been removed[2] (*Rav; Tif. Yis.* from *Tos.* who quote this in the name of *Ri*). [Accordingly, one may not place this basket in front of the chicks during twilight of Friday night (see *Gem.* 43a).]

1. R' Yitzchak, who rules that a utensil may be moved only for the benefit of something not *muktzeh*, interprets the mishnah as referring only to the case that one needs the place in which the basket is lying. Since he must, in any case, move the basket, he may place it where it will be accessible to the chicks (*Rav; Rashi* from *Gem.* 43a).

2. Although the use of the basket is still being nullified for the time the chicks are on it, this is not considered a nullification because they can easily be chased off the basket any time the owner desires to use it (*Tos.* ibid.).

שבת
יח/ב

שֶׁיַּעֲלוּ וְיֵרְדוּ.
תַּרְנְגֹלֶת שֶׁבָּרְחָה, דּוֹחִין אוֹתָהּ עַד שֶׁתִּכָּנֵס.
מְדַדִּין עֲגָלִין וּסְיָחִין בִּרְשׁוּת הָרַבִּים. אִשָּׁה
מְדַדָּה אֶת בְּנָהּ. אָמַר רַבִּי יְהוּדָה: אֵימָתַי? בִּזְמַן

ר׳ עובדיה מברטנורא

מהיכנו לא הוי, שאין האפרוחים עומדים עליו. והאומר אין כלי ניטל אלא לצורך דבר הניטל, מוקי למתניתין בצריך למקומו של כלי: **שברחה**. מן הבית: **דוחין אותה**. בידים: **עד שתכנס**. ודוקא דוחין אבל לא מדדין, לפי שהתרנגולת מגבהת עצמה מן הארץ ונמצא שהוא מטלטלה. אבל אווזין ושאר עופות מדדין: **מדדין עגלים**. אוחז בצוארו ובגלדדיו וגוררו ומסיטו ומניחנו לו רגליו: **והאשה מדדה את בנה**. אוחזתו בזרועתיו מאחוריו והוא מניע רגליו והולך:

יד אברהם

כְּדֵי שֶׁיַּעֲלוּ וְיֵרְדוּ. — so that they may [use it to] climb up and down.

[I.e., as a ladder to go to their coop or nest.]

תַּרְנְגֹלֶת שֶׁבָּרְחָה, — A hen that has run away,

From the house (Rav; Rashi). [It would seem unnecessary to tell us from where the hen ran. Perhaps Rashi (and Rav) follow the reading of the mishnah which omits the words בִּרְשׁוּת הָרַבִּים, in a public domain (see below). Accordingly, the leniency in permitting one to make calves and foals walk only exists within an enclosed courtyard. Even in this area, however, we may only push a hen but not help it to walk. Thus, Rashi explains that the mishnah refers to a hen that ran away, even if it only ran "from the house" into the courtyard. Nevertheless, we may not help her walk but we may push her.]

דּוֹחִין אוֹתָהּ עַד שֶׁתִּכָּנֵס. — we may push her until she enters.

I.e., we may push the hen from behind (Tif. Yis.) even with our hands, until it enters the house. We may not, however, help her walk by holding her wings, since chickens have a tendency to jump and one will then find himself in the position of carrying the chicken, which is *muktzeh*. [This prohibition, therefore, applies even in a properly enclosed yard, where one may normally carry (Gem. 128b). As will be explained below, in a public domain no animal may be made to walk.]

Other birds, such as geese, may be helped along, since they do not exhibit this tendency (Rav from Gem. 128b).

Although one is, in any case, moving part of the chicken by pushing it along, and movement of even part of a *muktzeh* object is also forbidden,[1] the Rabbis permitted it because of the principle making us responsible for בַּעֲלֵי חַיִּים, [prevention of] pain to animals, i.e., to assist the hen back to its place. For this reason, too, one is permitted to catch the hen, which should ordinarily be Rabbinically prohibited because it represents *trapping. [Since it is domesticated, trapping it is not

---

1. This is derived from 23:5, which states that one may not move even one limb of a corpse (Tif. Yis.).

18 2 they may [use it to] climb up and down.

A hen that has run away, we may push her until she enters.

We may make calves and foals walk in a public domain. A woman may make her child walk. Said R' Yehudah: When? At the time he

YAD AVRAHAM

Biblically prohibited.] Since the hen is lost, the Rabbis permitted trapping it in order to spare it any pain (*Tif. Yis.*). One is not, however, permitted to transgress a Biblical prohibition for this purpose.]

מְדַדִּין עֲגָלִין וּסְיָחִין — *We may make calves and foals walk*

I.e., we may hold them by their necks and sides, and move their legs (*Rav; Rashi*).

בִּרְשׁוּת הָרַבִּים. — *in a public domain.*

In the mishnah printed with the *Gemara*, these words are missing. Indeed, the *Gemara* seems to indicate that animals may not be made to walk in a public domain (out of concern that one will pick them up and carry them). This, in fact, is the halachah (*Shulchan Aruch* 308:40).

Ran, however, although agreeing that the words do not appear in the mishnah, understands this law as applying to a public domain. He qualifies it as applying only to large calves and foals, which walk well by themselves and can therefore be easily led. Consequently, there is no reason to be concerned that he will pick them up and carry them. Small ones, however, may not be made to walk in a public domain, because they are difficult to lead. Consequently, there is reason to be concerned that one will pick them up and carry them while in the public domain, thereby violating a Torah prohibition. They may, therefore, be led only in a yard, where no Torah prohibition can be violated. [Although one could still violate the Rabbinic injunction of *muktzeh* by carrying them, the Rabbis did not prohibit pushing them, since this would have amounted to a *safeguard to a safeguard*, which the Rabbis do not enact.] Even other fowl, such as geese, which may be made to walk, may be done so only in a yard, not in a public domain (*Tos. Yom Tov; Tif. Yis.*).

These *halachos* are based on the premise that the principle of *a living creature carries itself* does not apply to an animal. Therefore, if one carries a living animal in a public domain, he is liable to a sin offering. See above 10:5 (*Tif. Yis.*).

אִשָּׁה מְדַדָּה אֶת בְּנָהּ. — *A woman may make her child walk.*

I.e., she may walk in a public domain holding his arms from the rear so that he move his feet (*Rav; Rashi* from *Gem.* 128b).

In this case, we need not be concerned that she will carry him, since even if she does she is not liable to a sin offering. As mentioned above, in the case of human beings the principle of *a living creature carries itself* does apply, exempting one from any sin offering (*Tif. Yis.*).

אָמַר רַבִּי יְהוּדָה: אֵימָתַי? — *Said R' Yehudah: When?*

I.e., in what case did the *Tanna Kamma* permit a woman to make her child walk in a public domain? (*Rav; Rosh*).

שבת
יח/ג

שֶׁהוּא נוֹטֵל אַחַת וּמַנִּיחַ אַחַת; אֲבָל אִם הָיָה גּוֹרֵר, אָסוּר.

[ג] **אֵין מְיַלְּדִין** אֶת הַבְּהֵמָה בְּיוֹם טוֹב, אֲבָל מְסַעֲדִין. וּמְיַלְּדִין אֶת הָאִשָּׁה בַּשַּׁבָּת; וְקוֹרִין לָהּ חֲכָמָה מִמָּקוֹם לְמָקוֹם; וּמְחַלְּלִין עָלֶיהָ אֶת הַשַּׁבָּת;

ר' עובדיה מברטנורא

שנוטל אחת ומניח אחת. כשהתינוק מניע את רגליו מניח אחת ומגביה אחת: **אבל גורר אסור.** שנגוררתו. וכל מקום שאמר רבי יהודה אימתי במשנה לא בא לחלוק אלא לפרש דברי חכמים, הילכך הלכתא כוותיה: **(ג) אין מילדין.** אין מוטכין הולד מן הרחם ביום טוב, דאיכא טרחא יתירא: **אבל מסעדין.** אוחז את הולד שלא יפול לארץ: **חכמה.** מילדת בקיאה: **ממקום למקום.** ואין חוששין לאיסור תחומים: **ומחללין עליה את השבת.** משעה שהיא יושבת על המשבר ומתחיל הדם להיות שותת עד כל שלשה ימים אחר שילדה, בין אמרה צריכה אני בין לא

יד אברהם

בְּזְמַן שֶׁהוּא נוֹטֵל אַחַת וּמַנִּיחַ אַחַת — *At the time he raises one foot and puts down the other;*

I.e., the child can himself alternate movement of his feet, picking up one foot and putting down the other.

[In this manner, he is considered to be walking, albeit with help.]

אֲבָל אִם הָיָה גּוֹרֵר, אָסוּר — *but if he drags* (lit. *was dragging; his feet*), *it is prohibited.*

I.e., if he cannot move his own feet, but his mother must hold his hand and drag him, it is tantamount to carrying (*Rav; Rashi*). Since the child is so young that he cannot walk without dragging his feet, the principle of *a living creature carries itself* does not apply to him (*Ran*). This implies that the word אָסוּר, *prohibited*, actually involves liability, since the mother is, in effect, carrying a child who cannot walk through a public domain. [As mentioned in 10:5, *Tosafos* disputes this] (*Tos. Yom Tov*).

According to this, we may not walk with such a child even in a *karmelis*, since we would, in effect, be carrying him (*Magen Avraham* 308:71).

Beur Halachah (308:41) contends that *Ran*, although quoting *Rashi*, actually holds that walking with a child who drags his feet is not regarded as tantamount to carrying. It is prohibited only as a precaution against the chance that the mother will pick up the child and carry him on her shoulders. Consequently, this precaution would apply only in a public domain, where picking up the child would violate a Torah prohibition. In a *karmelis*, however, where even if she would actually carry the child she would be violating only a Rabbinic prohibition the Rabbis do not enact any additional precautions, since these would constitute a *safeguard to a safeguard*. Accordingly, *Ran* permits dragging the child through a *karmelis*. Actually carrying a child on one's shoulder in a *karmelis* is, however, definitely prohibited, *even if the child can walk.*

The halachah is in accordance with R' Yehudah, since he does not dispute the ruling of the *Tanna Kamma*, but merely qualifies it (*Rav; Rif; Rambam, Comm.*).

raises one foot and puts down the other; but if he drags [his feet], it is prohibited.

3. We may not assist an animal in delivering its young on *Yom Tov*, but we may support [it]. We may assist a woman in childbirth on the Sabbath; we may call a midwife from place to place for her; we may desecrate the Sabbath on her behalf;

YAD AVRAHAM
3.

אֵין מְיַלְּדִין אֶת הַבְּהֵמָה — *We may not assist an animal in delivering its young*

I.e., we may not draw the fetus from the uterus, since this is excessive toil (*Rav*).

בְּיוֹם טוֹב, — *on Yom Tov,*

I.e., even on a festival, and surely not on the Sabbath (*Meiri*).

אֲבָל מְסַעֲדִין. — *but we may support [it].*

We may catch the newborn animal so that it does not fall to the ground (*Rav*).

Rosh, quoting *Ri*, questions whether the previous phrase, *on a festival*, is added only in relation to not assisting an animal in delivering its young — but as far as the permission to support there is no distinction between the Sabbath and a festival, and we may, in fact, support the newborn animal even on the Sabbath — or whether the mishnah means that we may support the newborn animal only on a festival but not on the Sabbath.

Rashi, apparently, adopts the second interpretation. *Magen Avraham* 332:1, as well as many other authorities, adopts this stringent ruling. (See *Shaar HaTziyun* ibid. 2.)

וּמְיַלְּדִין אֶת הָאִשָּׁה בַּשַּׁבָּת; — *We may assist a woman in childbirth on the Sabbath;*

[I.e., even on the Sabbath we may draw the fetus from the uterus, and surely on a festival. It goes without saying that we may support the infant.]

וְקוֹרִין לָהּ חֲכָמָה מִמָּקוֹם לְמָקוֹם; — *(and) we may call a midwife* (lit. *a wise woman*) *from place to place for her;*

Even if there is a midwife here, but there is a more expert one elsewhere, the distant one may be summoned (*Tif. Yis.*), even from beyond the *Sabbath boundary* [see 2:7 and 23:3] (*Rav*).

Furthermore, we may summon one even from beyond twelve *mil*, from which point, according to *Rif* and *Rambam*, there is a Torah prohibition to travel (*Tos. Yom Tov; Tif. Yis.*).

וּמְחַלְּלִין עָלֶיהָ אֶת הַשַּׁבָּת; — *(and) we may desecrate the Sabbath on her behalf;*

I.e., to light a candle or to engage in any other necessity for the delivery. The *Gemara* (129a) questions the need for this last statement. This is the meaning of the previous statement, *we may assist a woman in childbirth on the Sabbath.* The *Gemara* (ibid.) explains that candles may be lit even for a blind woman in childbirth. Even if she does not benefit directly from the light, she nevertheless feels more at ease with the knowledge that there is adequate light for the

שבת
יח/ג

וְקוֹשְׁרִין אֶת הַטַּבּוּר. רַבִּי יוֹסֵי אוֹמֵר: אַף חוֹתְכִין. וְכָל צָרְכֵי מִילָה עוֹשִׂין בַּשַּׁבָּת.

ר' עובדיה מברטנורא

אמרה צריכה אני מחללין. משלשה ועד שבעה, אמרה צריכה אני מחללין, לא אמרה צריכה אני אין מחללין. משבעה ועד שלשים אפילו אמרה צריכה אני אין מחללין, אבל עושים על ידי נכרי מפני שהיא כחולה שאין בו סכנה, ודבר שאין בו סכנה עושין לצרכיו על ידי נכרי: **וקושרים הטבור**. של ולד שהוא ארוך, ואם לא יקשרוהו ויכרכוהו יצאו מעיו. אבל אין כורתין אותו בשבת לדברי תנא קמא: **רבי יוסי אומר אף חותכין**. והלכה כר"י שחותכין אותו ומנקים אותו ונותנין עליו אבק הדם וכיוצא בו: **וכל צרכי מילה עושין בשבת**. ולקמן באידך פירקא מפרש לצרכי מילה מאי ניהו:

יד אברהם

This ruling pertains from the time the woman goes into labor or begins to bleed[2] until three days after the delivery. During this time, if it is necessary, in our estimation, we may desecrate the Sabbath for her whether or not she feels that it is necessary.[3]

midwives to work by.[1]

[A woman at this time is *presumed* to be in a life-threatening situation. Therefore no *specific* indications of danger are necessary to allow us to do those things deemed essential for a woman giving birth.]

1. Thus the candles are lit as much for the mother's peace of mind as for actual necessity. Therefore, even if the midwives do not ask for a light, the room should nevertheless be properly illuminated (*Mishnah Berurah* 330:3).

2. This is true only for those things which can wait until the last minute. The midwife or doctor may be called as soon as contractions begin (*Mishnah Berurah* 330:9).

3. However, whatever can be done in an unusual manner (thereby avoiding a Biblical violation) should be done in that manner (*Shulchan Aruch* 330:1). Although this is not usually required in life-threatening situations, the threat to life involved in childbirth is not considered that great, under ordinary circumstances (*Mishnah Berurah* 330:5).

18 3 and we may tie the umbilical cord. R' Yose says: we may even cut [it].

And all requirements of circumcision may be performed on the Sabbath.

YAD AVRAHAM

וְקוֹשְׁרִין אֶת הַטַּבּוּר. — *and we may tie the umbilical cord.*

Tying the umbilical cord is permitted in order to prevent the infant's intestines from protruding through the open navel when he is picked up (*Rav; Rashi*).

This *Tanna*, however, permits only tying it, not cutting it off (*Rav*).

רַבִּי יוֹסֵי אוֹמֵר: אַף חוֹתְכִין. — *R' Yose says: We may even cut [it].*

R' Yose permits cutting off the umbilical cord, cleansing it, and applying the necessary medications, such as myrtle powder. The halachah is in accordance with R' Yose (*Rav; Rambam, Comm.*).

וְכָל צָרְכֵי מִילָה עוֹשִׂין בַּשַּׁבָּת. — *And all requirements of circumcision may be performed on the Sabbath.*

All these requirements are delineated in the following chapter (*Rav; Rambam, Comm*).

From then until the seventh day after birth, we desecrate the Sabbath only when the new mother states that it is absolutely necessary for her health. From then until the thirtieth day, even if she claims that it is necessary to her health to desecrate the Sabbath, we may not do so ourselves, but we may call a non-Jew to give her the necessary care. Her situation is then analogous to that of a sick person whose life is not in danger. For such a patient, a non-Jew may be summoned to perform any necessary treatment (*Rav* from *Gem.* ibid.). [This rule applies only to a woman who has no medical condition other than having delivered a baby. Where life-threatening complications arise from that delivery, she may obviously be treated even by Jews in any way necessary, since she is then no different than any other person whose life is threatened.]

פרק תשעה עשר
Chapter Nineteen

This chapter elaborates upon the various laws of circumcision as they relate to the Sabbath. The actual circumcision consists of cutting off the foreskin and afterwards, exposing the corona. This is followed by drawing some blood from, and then bandaging, the wound. Various antiseptics are usually applied to the wound prior to the bandaging. During the times of the mishnah, the common practice was to apply cumin and a mixture of wine with oil.

In order to perform the circumcision, one must be equipped with a knife or scalpel. Making this knife and transporting it to the location of the circumcision are not part of the circumcision itself, but are considered מַכְשִׁירֵי מִילָה, *preliminaries to the circumcision.*

The Torah teaches us that the *mitzvah* of circumcision, though it involves a *toladah* of the *melachah* of **slaughtering* (see 7:21), overrides the Sabbath but only when performed on the eighth day after birth. [If the circumcision has been postponed beyond the eighth day, it does not override the Sabbath and must therefore be postponed until the following day.] There is, however, a Tannaic dispute as to whether activities regarded as preliminaries to the circumcision also supersede the Sabbath, as will be discussed in the first mishnah of the present chapter.

[א] **רַבִּי אֱלִיעֶזֶר** אוֹמֵר: אִם לֹא הֵבִיא כְלִי מֵעֶרֶב שַׁבָּת, מְבִיאוֹ בַשַּׁבָּת מְגֻלֶּה; וּבַסַּכָּנָה, מְכַסֵּהוּ עַל־פִּי עֵדִים.

וְעוֹד אָמַר רַבִּי אֱלִיעֶזֶר: כּוֹרְתִין עֵצִים

ר׳ עובדיה מברטנורא

פרק תשעה עשר – רבי אליעזר. (א) רבי אליעזר אומר אם לא הביא כלי. איזמל למול את התינוק: **מביאו בשבת מגולה.** להודיע שחביבה מצוה זו שמחללים עליה את השבת: **ובסכנה.** שגזרו גזרה על המילה: מכסהו על פי עדים. שיעידו שאיזמל של מצוה הוא מביא, ולא יחשדוהו שהוא נושא שאר חפציו.

יד אברהם

1.

In the final mishnah of the preceding chapter we learned that all integral parts of the circumcision override the Sabbath. The mishnah now elaborates on this topic, commencing with a discussion concerning whether or not the preliminaries to circumcision also override the Sabbath (*Meiri*).

רַבִּי אֱלִיעֶזֶר אוֹמֵר: אִם לֹא הֵבִיא כְלִי מֵעֶרֶב שַׁבָּת, — *Rabbi Eliezer says: If one did not bring an instrument [for circumcision] before the Sabbath,*

I.e., before the Sabbath one did not bring the circumcision knife to the house where an infant is scheduled to be circumcised on the Sabbath (*Rav; Rashi*).

מְבִיאוֹ בַשַּׁבָּת — *he should bring it on the Sabbath*

R' Eliezer rules that in order to perform the *bris milah* on the Sabbath, it is permissible to engage even in activities which are only preliminaries to the circumcision, even when such preliminaries could have been prepared prior to the Sabbath.

It is unclear, however, why R' Eliezer permits carrying the knife through a public domain, rather than carrying the infant to the place where the knife is situated. The latter method should be preferable since it does not involve a Torah prohibition, due to the principle of חַי נוֹשֵׂא אֶת־עַצְמוֹ, *a living crea-*ture aids in its own carriage (see 18:2). One answer is that since the infant requires his mother's care after the circumcision, and she is unable to go to him since she has not yet recovered from the birth, the child will have to be carried back to his mother. Since the infant is considered ill after being circumcised, and is, therefore, not considered to be *aiding in his own carriage* (as explained in 18:2), carrying him back to his mother will in any case involve us in the same Torah prohibition as carrying the knife. Therefore, one is permitted to carry the knife to the child. [Furthermore, as explained above (18:2), in the opinion of *Ran*, any child, whether healthy or ill, who cannot yet walk is not regarded as *aiding in his own carriage*. Therefore, since the child must also be carried back, carrying the child involves two violations, whereas carrying the knife, which after the circumcision may be left where it is, involves only one.]

Another answer is that since it is easier to bring the knife to the child than to bring the child to the knife, it is preferable to carry the knife to the child since this would hasten the performance of the mitzvah (*Tos. Yom*

19
1

1. ר׳ Eliezer says: If one did not bring an instrument [for circumcision] before the Sabbath, he should bring it on the Sabbath exposed; and in [times of] danger, he should cover it in the presence of witnesses.

Furthermore, said R' Eliezer: We may fell trees

YAD AVRAHAM

Tov from *Tos.*). This is permitted, however, only because one must in any case violate the Sabbath for the actual circumcision (*Tos. R' Akiva* from *Rashba*).

Additionally, although a child who is capable of moving himself is considered *aiding in his own carriage*, it is, nevertheless, Rabbinically prohibited to carry him (*Aruch HaShulchan* 301:28 from *Gem.* 3a).

מְגֻלֶּה; — *exposed;*

He should carry it exposed in order to demonstrate the preciousness of this *mitzvah*, by showing that one is even permitted to violate the Sabbath in order to fulfill it (*Rav, Tif. Yis.* from *Gem.* 130a).

וּבַסַּכָּנָה, — *and in [times of] danger,*

At times when the gentiles prohibited the performance of circumcision upon pain of death (*Rav; Rashi*). This occurred specifically during the Roman occupation of Israel (see *Me'ilah* 17a; *Mechilta* 20:6), during the reign of Hadrian. It was one of the prime causes of the Bar Kochba uprising (*Doros HaRishonim* vol. 4 [of the reprinted edition, published in Jerusalem 1967] Chap. 27).

מְכַסֵּהוּ עַל־פִּי עֵדִים. — *he should cover it in the presence of* (lit. *upon the words of*) *witnesses.*

The purpose of this practice is to forestall the suspicion of the onlookers who, seeing him furtively carrying a circumcision knife on the Sabbath, might suspect him of carrying an ordinary knife for his personal use (*Rav*). These witnesses would be able to inform them that the knife he is carrying is a circumcision knife.

The witnesses do not actually have to follow him through the streets refuting the suspicions of any bystanders, [nor would it make sense for them to do so during a time of persecution]. Furthermore, one can easily conceal an object as small as a circumcision knife under his clothing without anyone suspecting him of carrying. Rather, the suspicion we wish to forestall is that, upon his arrival at the circumcision site, people, seeing him taking the knife out from under his clothing, will suspect him of carrying articles for his own personal use as well. Therefore, we require witnesses to testify that this man carried only a circumcision knife needed for the performance of the *mitzvah* (*Shoshannim LeDavid*). Alternatively, the witnesses are needed so that those who see him hide the knife under his clothes and carry it out should not think that he is doing so for his own purposes (*Tif. Yis.*).

וְעוֹד אָמַר רַבִּי אֱלִיעֶזֶר: — *Furthermore, said R' Eliezer:*

[I.e., in addition to permitting carrying a circumcision knife on the Sabbath.]

כּוֹרְתִין עֵצִים לַעֲשׂוֹת פֶּחָמִין — *We may fell trees in order to make charcoal*

If there is no knife available, they may even fell trees to make the charcoal necessary to forge iron in order to make a knife. R' Eliezer tells us here that even these remote preliminaries to the circumcision, which could have easily

שבת
יט/ב

לַעֲשׂוֹת פֶּחָמִין וְלַעֲשׂוֹת כְּלִי בַרְזֶל. כְּלָל אָמַר רַבִּי עֲקִיבָא: כָּל מְלָאכָה שֶׁאֶפְשָׁר לַעֲשׂוֹתָהּ מֵעֶרֶב שַׁבָּת אֵינָהּ דּוֹחָה אֶת הַשַּׁבָּת; וְשֶׁאִי אֶפְשָׁר לַעֲשׂוֹתָהּ מֵעֶרֶב שַׁבָּת, דּוֹחָה אֶת הַשַּׁבָּת.

[ב] **עוֹשִׂין** כָּל צָרְכֵי מִילָה בַּשַּׁבָּת: מוֹהֲלִין, וּפוֹרְעִין, וּמוֹצְצִין,

---
ר׳ עובדיה מברטנורא

ולעשות ברזל. כדי לעשות ממנו איזמל למילה: **כל מלאכה שאפשר לעשותה.** כגון מכשירי מילה הואיל ואפשר לעשותן מערב שבת אין דוחין את השבת, ופליג אדרבי אליעזר: **שאי אפשר לעשותה מערב שבת.** כגון מילה עצמה שאי אפשר לה ליעשות, דזמנה בשמיני דוחה שבת. והלכה כרבי עקיבא: (ב) **מוהלין.** חותך את הערלה: **ופורעין.** הטור המכסה ראש הגיד:

יד אברהם

been arranged before the Sabbath, also override the Sabbath (*Tif. Yis.*).

וְלַעֲשׂוֹת כְּלִי בַרְזֶל. — *and to form an iron instrument.*

I.e., a circumcision knife (*Rav*).

It is apparent from several commentators that the word כְּלִי, *an instrument*, did not appear in their editions of the mishnah. According to those editions, the text is, *to make iron*. The circumcision knife is simply referred to as a piece of iron (not as an iron *instrument*) to tell us that even according to this lenient opinion, it may not be fashioned into a finished instrument on the Sabbath, merely into a sharp piece of iron, since this suffices for the performance of the circumcision (*Tif. Yis.*).

כְּלָל אָמַר רַבִּי עֲקִיבָא: כָּל מְלָאכָה שֶׁאֶפְשָׁר לַעֲשׂוֹתָהּ מֵעֶרֶב שַׁבָּת אֵינָהּ דּוֹחָה אֶת

הַשַּׁבָּת; — [But] R' Akiva stated a rule: *Any work that can be done before the Sabbath does not override* (lit. *push aside*) *the Sabbath;*

R' Akiva differs with R' Eliezer, who permits preliminaries of circumcision on the Sabbath. His ruling is that inasmuch as work such as the preliminaries of circumcision can be done before the Sabbath, they may not be done on the Sabbath (*Rav; Rashi*).

וְשֶׁאִי אֶפְשָׁר לַעֲשׂוֹתָהּ מֵעֶרֶב שַׁבָּת, דּוֹחָה אֶת הַשַּׁבָּת. — *but [any work] that cannot be done before the Sabbath does override the Sabbath.*

Namely, the circumcision itself, which cannot be performed before the eighth day, overrides the Sabbath (*Rav; Rashi*).

The halachah is in accordance with Rabbi Akiva (*Rav*).

2.

The various components of the circumcision operation and the various medications applied afterwards are now discussed with regard to which ones may be performed on the Sabbath.

משניות / שבת – פרק יט: רבי אליעזר [418]

19
2

in order to make charcoal and to form an iron instrument.

[But] R' Akiva stated a rule: Any work that can be done before the Sabbath does not override the Sabbath; but [any work] that cannot be done before the Sabbath does override the Sabbath.

2. We may perform all the necessities of circumcision on the Sabbath: we may circumcise, uncover [the corona], draw [the blood],

YAD AVRAHAM

In order to understand this mishnah properly, one must familiarize himself with the various steps of the circumcision operation. Prior to the circumcision, the corona has two coverings. The outer covering is a thick layer of skin called the foreskin. Beneath it, a thin membrane covers the corona. The *mohel* first cuts off the foreskin. This act is called מִילָה, *circumcision*. He then tears the membrane and pulls it back, thereby exposing the corona. This is called פְּרִיעָה, *uncovering*. This is followed with מְצִיצָה, *drawing the blood*, and dressing the wound.

עוֹשִׂין כָּל צָרְכֵי מִילָה בַּשַּׁבָּת: — *We may perform all the necessities of circumcision on the Sabbath:*

This statement is not intended to be merely an introduction to the mishnah. Rather, it is meant to teach us that one, who, in performing a circumcision on the Sabbath, failed to remove some shreds of flesh whose presence do not invalidate the circumcision [as will be explained in mishnah 6], may, nevertheless, resume and remove them as long as he is still occupied with the circumcision (*Tos. Yom Tov* from *Gem.* 133b). This is indicated by the addition of the word *all* (*Rashi* ibid.).

Although this regulation has already been stated at the end of the preceding chapter, it is repeated here. In the previous chapter it is mentioned only incidentally because it, too, is a law concerning infants. In this chapter, however, which discusses the laws of circumcision, it is repeated because this is its proper place (*Tos.*

Yom Tov from *Tos.*).

מוֹהֲלִין, — *we may circumcise,*

I.e., cut off the foreskin (*Rav*; *Rashi*).

וּפוֹרְעִין, — *(and) uncover [the corona],*

By tearing and pulling back the thin membrane under the foreskin the corona is uncovered (*Rav*; *Rashi*).

According to one opinion the *mitzvah* of exposing the corona was given to Abraham when he was initially commanded to circumcise himself. According to most opinions, however, Abraham was commanded merely to remove the foreskin but he was not obliged to split the membrane and pull it back. He did so, however, just as he fulfilled all other commandments destined to be given to the children of Israel. This component of circumcision became mandatory when the Torah was given to Moshe at Mount Sinai. At that time, it was given orally as הֲלָכָה לְמשֶׁה מִסִּינַי, *a halachah given to Moshe at* (lit. *from*) *Sinai.* It was recorded in

שבת
יט/ב

וְנוֹתְנִין עָלֶיהָ אִסְפְּלָנִית וְכַמּוֹן. אִם לֹא שָׁחַק מֵעֶרֶב שַׁבָּת, לוֹעֵס בְּשִׁנָּיו וְנוֹתֵן. אִם לֹא טָרַף יַיִן וְשֶׁמֶן מֵעֶרֶב שַׁבָּת, יִנָּתֵן זֶה בְּעַצְמוֹ וְזֶה בְּעַצְמוֹ.

וְאֵין עוֹשִׂין לָהּ חָלוּק לְכַתְּחִלָּה, אֲבָל כּוֹרֵךְ עָלֶיהָ סְמַרְטוּט. אִם לֹא הִתְקִין מֵעֶרֶב שַׁבָּת, כּוֹרֵךְ עַל אֶצְבָּעוֹ וּמֵבִיא,

ר' עובדיה מברטנורא

ומוצצים. את הדם, ואף על פי שהוא עושה חבורה שאין הדם ניתק מחיבורו אלא על ידי מלילה: **אספלנית.** תחבושת: **לועס בשיניו:** דכל מה דאפשר לשנות משנה: **אם לא טרף יין ושמן.** רגילים היו שהיו טורפים בקערה יין ושמן ומערבין אותן יחד לרפואה על המילה כדרך שטורפים ביצים בקערה: **חלוק.** חתיכה של בגד נקובה, ומכניסין המילה באותו הנקב כדי שלא יחזור העור ויכסה את הגיד: **לא התקין: כורך על אצבעו.** דרך מלבוש לשנותו מדרך הולאה בחול:

יד אברהם

Scripture when Joshua implemented it in the mass circumcision performed when the Jews entered the Land of Israel as described in *Joshua* 5 (*Yevamos* 71b; *Rashi; Tos.;* see commentary to *Joshua* 5:2).

The law requiring the uncovering of the corona is mandatory. Therefore, if the circumciser fails to expose the corona, the infant is considered uncircumcised (see mishnah 6).

וּמוֹצְצִין — *draw [the blood]*,

The blood is drawn out of the wound to prevent it from coagulating under the skin and causing the penis to swell (*Tif. Yis.*).

Rambam (*Hil. Milah* 2:2) specifies that the blood must be drawn from even beyond the immediate area of the wound in order to avoid fatal danger to the circumcised.

Normally, one who causes blood to flow on the Sabbath (where it can be considered a constructive act), violates a *toladah* of *slaughtering. However, in this instance it is permissible since it is being done to prevent a potentially fatal condition from developing (*Rav; Rashi*).

Some authorities hold that aside from any medical considerations, drawing out the blood is an inherent part of the *mitzvah* of circumcision (see *Sefer HaBris*, pp. 185, 216-226).

וְנוֹתְנִין עָלֶיהָ אִסְפְּלָנִית וְכַמּוֹן — *and place a bandage and cumin upon it.*

[These are applied for therapeutic purposes. The cumin must be crushed to be effective, as is evident below.]

אִם לֹא שָׁחַק מֵעֶרֶב שַׁבָּת, לוֹעֵס בְּשִׁנָּיו וְנוֹתֵן. — *If he did not crush [the cumin] before the Sabbath, he may chew [it] with his teeth and apply [it].*

Crushing cumin on the Sabbath is prohibited [it is a *toladah* of *grinding]. Therefore, one must crush it in an unusual manner such as by chewing it, which even ordinarily is only Rabbinically prohibited, and is therefore permissible for the necessity of circumcision (*Rav; Rashi*).

19
2

and place a bandage and cumin upon it. If he did not crush [the cumin] before the Sabbath, he may chew [it] with his teeth and apply [it]. If he did not vigorously mix wine and oil before the Sabbth, each one should be added [to the bowl] by itself.

We may not fashion a shirtlike bandage for it, but one may wrap a piece of cloth around it. If he did not prepare [it] before the Sabbath, he may wrap [it] around his finger and bring [it],

YAD AVRAHAM

אִם לֹא טָרַף יַיִן וְשֶׁמֶן מֵעֶרֶב שַׁבָּת, — *If he did not vigorously mix wine and oil before the Sabbath*,

At the time of the mishnah it was customary to mix wine and oil by beating them in a bowl (as we do with eggs). This was then applied to the incision as a medication (*Rav; Rashi*).

Beating wine with oil on the Sabbath is prohibited by Rabbinic decree, as is beating eggs. The reason for this is that it appears as if one is preparing food for cooking. Though this is only a Rabbinic prohibition, it is, nevertheless, prohibited even when the mixture is needed for post-circumcision medication (*Tif. Yis.*).

יִנָּתֵן זֶה בְעַצְמוֹ וְזֶה בְעַצְמוֹ. — *each one should be added [to the bowl] by itself* (lit. *this one should be placed by itself and this one by itself*).

I.e., though one may not vigorously mix them, he may pour first the wine and then the oil (or vice versa) into the same bowl and stir them lightly (*Meiri; Tos. Rabbi Akiva*).

וְאֵין עוֹשִׂין לָהּ חָלוּק לְכַתְּחִלָּה, — *We may not fashion a shirtlike bandage for it*,

After applying medications to the circumcision wound, the wound is bandaged. During the mishnaic era, it was common to employ for this purpose a cloth shaped like a finger, with openings at either end. This bandage would be drawn over the corona, thereby preventing the skin from growing back over it (*Rav; Rashi*).

Fashioning such a bandage on the Sabbath is prohibited because it is considered forming a utensil. It may therefore only be placed over the circumcision if it has already been prepared before the Sabbath (*Meiri*).

אֲבָל כּוֹרֵךְ עָלֶיהָ סְמַרְטוּט. — *but one may wrap a piece of cloth around it.*

[If he did not prepare a shirtlike bandage, he may wrap an ordinary piece of cloth around it.]

אִם לֹא הִתְקִין מֵעֶרֶב שַׁבָּת, — *If he did not prepare [it] before the Sabbath,*

I.e., if before the Sabbath he did not even bring a piece of cloth to the site where the circumcision was to be performed (*Rav; Rashi; Meiri*).

כּוֹרֵךְ עַל־אֶצְבָּעוֹ וּמֵבִיא, — *he may wrap [it] around his finger and bring [it],*

He should wrap it around his finger [like a glove] and transport it in this irregular manner (*Rav; Rashi; Tif. Yis.*).

The prohibition of carrying on the Sabbath does not apply to the clothing one is wearing. However, this is true only of clothing worn in its normal mode. One may not "wear" an article

שבת
יט/ג

וַאֲפִלּוּ מֵחָצֵר אַחֶרֶת.

[ג] **מַרְחִיצִין** אֶת הַקָּטָן בֵּין לִפְנֵי הַמִּילָה

ר' עובדיה מברטנורא

אפילו מחצר אחרת. לא מיבעיא מבית לבית באותו חצר אף על פי שלא ערבו, אלא אפילו לחצר אחרת שאינה מעורבת עמהם: (ג) **מרחיצין את הקטן.** האי מרחיצין לאו כדרכו הוא, דתנא סיפא לפרושי רישא כיצד מרחיצין כגון לזלף ביד אבל בכלי אפילו לזלף אסור וכ"ש לרחוץ כדרכו: רבי אלעזר בן עזריה כו'. פליג אתנא קמא וסבר מרחיצין את הקטן כדרכו בין לפני המילה בין לאחר המילה, וביום השלישי למילה נמי בין בחמין שהוחמו בערב שבת בין בחמין שהוחמו בשבת עצמו דסכנת נפשות היא, והלכה כרבי אלעזר בן עזריה:

יד אברהם

which is not considered apparel. Hence, the bandage on one's finger permitted in our mishnah is limited to cases where it is done for the purpose of bandaging the circumcision wound. One may not, however, go into a public domain wearing a handkerchief wrapped around his wrist (*Tif. Yis.*). [One may, however, wear his handkerchief around his neck as he would wear his scarf (*Tif. Yis.; Kitzur Shulchan Aruch* 84:14; *Minchas Shabbos*).]

וַאֲפִלּוּ מֵחָצֵר אַחֶרֶת — *even from another courtyard.*

There is a Rabbinical enactment prohibiting the carrying of articles from the property of one person to that of another unless they have merged their properties by means of an *eruv chatzeiros* [explained at length in the General Introduction, p. 15]. The circumcision bandage, however, may be brought from another person's property in the above-mentioned manner even if they have not merged their properties by means of an *eruv chatzeiros* (*Rav*).

3.

In mishnaic times it was customary to bathe the infant with hot water twice, once prior to the circumcision to strengthen him to endure the circumcision, and again following the circumcision as a therapeutic measure. Failure to perform either of these washings was considered endangering the infant's life. The Rabbis, therefore, permitted bathing the infant on the Sabbath if he is to be circumcised then.

On the third day following the circumcision, the child is also considered critically ill, and is, therefore, in need of being bathed then, too. Consequently, if the third day occurs on the Sabbath, this bathing, too, is permitted.

Today, these washings are no longer considered necessary to safeguard the child's life (*Shulchan Aruch* 331:9), due to changes in the constitution of people over the course of centuries (*Mishnah Berurah* ibid.31).[1]

---
1. These changes may be the result of environmental or dietetic changes, which have been known to alter biochemical reactions. Whatever their cause, they have undoubtedly taken place. There are several common, easily observable biological phenomena described in the *Gemara* as being almost invariable, yet rarely found today. One of the most obvious examples of this is the statement (*Tur, Yoreh De'ah* 184, based on *Gem. Niddah* 9b) that

19. even from another courtyard.

3. We may bathe the infant both prior to the circum-

YAD AVRAHAM

מַרְחִיצִין אֶת הַקָּטָן — **We may bathe the infant**

I.e., with hot water on the day of his circumcision (*Tif. Yis.*).

There is a difference of opinion in the *Gemara* (134b) as to whether the mishnah means that the child may be washed in the normal manner (Rava) or [since whatever can be done in an unusual manner should be done in such a manner] only by sprinkling water on him (Rabbah bar Avuha). *Rav* and *Rambam* (*Comm.*) follow the latter explanation.

בֵּין לִפְנֵי הַמִּילָה — **both prior to the circumcision**

As explained in the prefatory note to this mishnah, this was done to build up the infant's strength to endure the operation[1] (*Tif. Yis.*).

Heating the water is a preliminary to circumcision which, in the opinion of R' Akiva, may not be done on the Sabbath. As explained in mishnah 1, the halachah is in accordance with this opinion. It follows, therefore, that the hot water discussed here has to have been heated before the Sabbath and kept warm until the circumcision.

If there is no hot water available, the circumcision is postponed, as is done when any of the preliminaries to circumcision are lacking. [Since prior to circumcision the child is not in danger, exemption granted to perform labor in life-threatening situations does not apply. Once the infant has been circumcised, however, if the hot water prepared before Shabbos should spill, even a Jew may heat water since the infant is now in danger (*Ran; Rambam, Hil. Milah* 2:8).]

There is a difference of opinion whether one may tell a non-Jew to heat water on the Sabbath in order to perform the circumcision.

Some hold that in cases involving the observance of a *mitzvah*, it is permissible to instruct a non-Jew to do work for him even if this work is proscribed by the Torah (*Ittur* vol. 2 p. 97, *Halachos Gedolos*).

Most authorities, however, maintain that this exemption is only with regard to Rabbinically ordained prohibitions (*Rif; Rambam, Hil. Milah* 2:9; *Rash; Tur* 331; *Ramah* 276:2). Other authorities add, however, that water heated by non-Jews for their own use or even that which was heated by Jews (transgressingly) on the Sabbath may also be used (*Rosh; Tur* 331).

the majority of women have a fixed period, i.e., that their cycle is always *exactly* the same number of days. From the commentaries it is clear that this was an overwhelming majority, with only rare exceptions. It is further clear from some of the later commentaries that this was still true as recently as two hundred years ago. Yet today the situation is reversed, with only a minority of women having fixed periods.

1. *Ran* explains that even though one is normally forbidden to bathe in hot water on the Sabbath even if it was heated before the Sabbath, it is nonetheless permissible to bathe the infant in this water. The reason is that this prohibition of bathing in hot water was enacted by the Rabbis at the time when bathhouse attendants were suspected of heating water on the Sabbath while claiming that it was heated beforehand. Since this suspicion is not applicable to cases involving *milah* (since only a small amount of water is necessary for bathing the infant) the prohibition was never instituted relative to *milah*.

וּבֵין לְאַחַר הַמִּילָה; וּמְזַלְּפִין עָלָיו בַּיָּד, אֲבָל לֹא בִכְלִי.

רַבִּי אֶלְעָזָר בֶּן עֲזַרְיָה אוֹמֵר: מַרְחִיצִין אֶת הַקָּטָן בַּיּוֹם הַשְּׁלִישִׁי שֶׁחָל לִהְיוֹת בַּשַּׁבָּת, שֶׁנֶּאֱמַר: "וַיְהִי בַיּוֹם הַשְּׁלִישִׁי בִּהְיוֹתָם כֹּאֲבִים".

יד אברהם

וּבֵין לְאַחַר הַמִּילָה; — *and following the circumcision;*

This was done for therapeutic purposes (*Tif. Yis.*).

וּמְזַלְּפִין עָלָיו בַּיָּד; — *and we may sprinkle [water] upon him by hand,*

This passage is an explanation of the initial passage, clarifying that bathing the infant prior to and following the circumcision is permissible only by sprinkling (*Rav; Rambam, Comm.*; following the interpretation of Rav Yehudah and Rabbah bar Avuha in the *Gem.* 134b).

אֲבָל לֹא בִכְלִי. — *but not with a utensil.*

Although sprinkling warm water by hand is permitted, sprinkling it from a utensil is prohibited (*Rav*).

רַבִּי אֶלְעָזָר בֶּן עֲזַרְיָה אוֹמֵר: מַרְחִיצִין אֶת הַקָּטָן בַּיּוֹם הַשְּׁלִישִׁי שֶׁחָל לִהְיוֹת בַּשַּׁבָּת, — *R' Elazar ben Azariah says: We may bathe the infant on the third day [following the circumcision] when it occurs on the Sabbath,*

R' Elazar ben Azariah differs with the *Tanna Kamma* on two counts: (a) He permits bathing the infant in the usual manner both before and after the circumcision, whereas the *Tanna Kamma* permits only sprinkling; (b) he also permits bathing the infant on the third day following the circumcision with hot water (*Rav*).

The halachah is in accordance with R' Elazar ben Azariah (*Rav*).

Others question *Rav's* assertion that R' Elazar ben Azariah permits bathing the infant before and after the circumcision in the normal manner. They contend that, just as the *Tanna Kamma* permits only sprinkling, so does R' Elazar. He differs only insofar as he permits sprinkling on the third day, whereas the *Tanna Kamma* prohibits it (*Maharsha on Rashi* 134b; *Tos. R' Akiva; Kesef Mishneh, Hil. Milah* 2:8 side with *Rav*).[1]

שֶׁנֶּאֱמַר: — *as it is said:*

[As it is said in connection with the people of Shechem, who circumcised themselves and were attacked on the third day thereafter by Shimon and Levi.]

1. According to the opinion mentioned above (s.v. מַרְחִיצִין), that the *Tanna Kamma*, too, permits bathing the infant in the usual manner both before and after the circumcision and, also, sprinkling on the third day, R' Elazar ben Azariah surely permits bathing him in the usual manner before and after the circumcision. They differ only insofar as the *Tanna Kamma* permits only sprinkling on the third day, whereas R' Elazar ben Azariah permits even bathing in the usual manner (*Ran*).

19
3

cision and following the circumcision; and we may sprinkle [water] upon him by hand, but not with a utensil.

R' Elazar ben Azariah says: We may bathe the infant on the third day [following the circumcision] when it occurs on the Sabbath, as it is said: *And it came to pass on the third day, when they were in pain (Genesis 34:25).*

YAD AVRAHAM

„וַיְהִי בַיּוֹם הַשְּׁלִישִׁי בִּהְיוֹתָם כֹּאֲבִים". — *And it came to pass on the third day, when they were in pain (Genesis 34:25).*

From this passage we see that on the third day following circumcision the pain is very acute. This proof is not, however, conclusive since this verse refers to adults who have been circumcised. Infants, however, heal much more rapidly (*Gem.* 134b).

Some authorities reason that if on the third day the pain is acute, it would certainly be so on the second day. The danger, therefore, exists on the second day, too (*Meiri*). Accordingly, R' Elazar ben Azariah, who permits bathing the child on the third day, certainly permits it on the second day. Others maintain that the danger increases on the third day. Accordingly, R' Elazar ben Azariah's lenient ruling applies only to the third day, not to the second (*Rav;* see *Tos. Yom Tov* 9:3).

Although, as explained in the prefatory note, the practice of bathing the infant is not common in our societies, these rulings are, nevertheless, pertinent. In some communities, a circumcision which has been postponed for health reasons is not performed on Thursdays. Since the child's life is in danger on the third day, they wish to avoid having the third day fall out on the Sabbath, in order to prevent possible violation of the Sabbath, should it be necessary. Another reason for this practice is not to cause the child to be in pain on the Sabbath. According to this custom, whether the circumcision may be performed on Friday is dependent upon the dispute quoted above. According to the view that danger exists on the second day, too, the child is not circumcised on Friday since the second day will then occur on the Sabbath. However, those who follow the view of *Rif* and *Ran* may perform the circumcision on Fridays since one need not suspect danger to the child's life on the second day (see *Shach, Yoreh Deah* 266:18, *Taz* 262:3). *Magen Avraham* (331:9), however, maintains that since it is not common practice to bathe the child following his circumcision, we should disregard these rulings and perform the circumcision on Thursday and Friday as well as on any other weekday. Besides heating water, which nowadays is unnecessary, other types of work are rarely required. *Shach* (*Yoreh Deah* 266:18) maintains that even in Talmudic times, the *mitzvah* was not delayed for fear of the necessity to violate the Sabbath.

שבת יט/ג

סָפֵק וְאַנְדְּרוֹגִינוֹס, אֵין מְחַלְּלִין עָלָיו אֶת הַשַּׁבָּת. וְרַבִּי יְהוּדָה מַתִּיר בְּאַנְדְּרוֹגִינוֹס.

────────── ר' עובדיה מברטנורא ──────────

סָפֵק. בֶּן שְׁמוֹנָה חֳדָשִׁים סָפֵק בֶּן תִּשְׁעָה. דְּאִי בֶּן שְׁמוֹנָה כְּאֶבֶן בְּעָלְמָא הוּא וְאֵין מִילָתוֹ דּוֹחָה שַׁבָּת: **וְרַבִּי יְהוּדָה מַתִּיר בָּאַנְדְּרוֹגִינוֹס.** מִדִּכְתִיב (בראשית י"ז) הִמּוֹל לָכֶם כָּל זָכָר לְרַבּוֹת אַנְדְּרוֹגִינוֹס. וְתַנָּא קַמָּא, עָרְלָתוֹ כְּתִיב, מִי שֶׁהוּא כּוּלוֹ עָרֵל, יָצָא זֶה שֶׁחֶצְיוֹ נְקֵבָה. וְאֵין הֲלָכָה כְּרַבִּי יְהוּדָה:

יד אברהם

סָפֵק — *A questionable one*

I.e., a baby possibly born during the eighth month of pregnancy (*Rav; Rashi*).

The ordinary incubation period for a child is nine months. Some babies mature earlier and are born during the seventh month after conception. However, a child born during the eighth month cannot live and is halachically not considered alive (the *Gemara*'s expression is *he is like a stone*).[1]

Accordingly, there is no obligation to circumcise him, and his circumcision certainly does not override the Sabbath. Consequently, if there is uncertainty as to whether or not a child was born during the eighth month of his incubation period, his circumcision also does not take place on the Sabbath. A "seven-month" child, however, is considered viable, and his circumcision does override the Sabbath (*Gem.* 135a). The *Gemara* (136a) explains that the circumcision of an "eighth-month" baby in itself does not involve any violation of the Sabbath. Since such a child is not considered a life, causing its blood to flow is not a *toladah* of *slaughtering, but rather like causing blood to flow from an animal which is no longer alive. Therefore, it should be permissible to circumcise even a child whose incubation period may have been eight months. This mishnah must, therefore, be understood as following the opinion of R' Eliezer, who, as explained in mishnah 1, holds that even preliminaries to the circumcision may be done on the Sabbath. Accordingly, the mishnah teaches us that if the cir-

1. The Talmud (*Yevamos* 80b) cites a Tannaic dispute regarding the halachic definition of an eighth-month baby. One Tanna accepts the term literally and includes all babies born during the eighth month after conception. Rabbi [Yehudah HaNassi] limits the rules governing an eighth-month baby to those born in the eighth month and having definite signs of immaturity, e.g., incomplete nails and hair. The Talmud explains that a baby born during the eighth month and exhibiting signs of maturity is actually a seventh-month baby which remained in the womb longer than necessary. [Since it could have been born in the seventh month and remain viable, such a baby is halachically regarded as a seventh-month baby.]

Rambam decides the halachah in accordance with the view of Rabbi [Yehudah HaNassi] and adds: If the eighth-month baby's nails and hair show definite immaturity of development, then the baby should have remained in its mother's womb for the full nine-month term. Having emerged before its time, the baby is not viable (*Rambam, Hil. Milah* 1:13). *Tosafos* (135a citing *Ri*) rules that even a baby of whose eighth-month status we can be perfectly sure [e.g., the mother only had coitus once and delivered during the eighth month following] may, nevertheless, be circumcised on the Sabbath, unless he shows signs of immature nail or hair formation.

19
3   A questionable one or an androgyne, we may not violate the Sabbath on his behalf. R' Yehudah, however, permits [it] in [the case of] an androgyne.

YAD AVRAHAM

cumcision requires certain preliminaries, they may not be done on the Sabbath for such a child.

Although a child born in the eighth month does not require circumcision, it is, nonetheless, customary to circumcise him, as well as any infants who die either before being circumcised, or are stillborn. (This, however, may not be done on the Sabbath.) It is also customary to name even these babies. The circumcision is performed before the burial but no benedictions are recited. Its purpose is to remove the stigma of remaining uncircumcised, and, also, to invoke divine mercy upon him so that he be resurrected together with the other dead of Israel (*Shulchan Aruch, Yoreh Deah* 263:5, *Be'er HaGolah*, also see *Magen Avraham* 526:20).

Meiri explains that the phrase *a questionable one* refers to a child born during the *bain hashmashos* (twilight) period of either Friday or Saturday evenings. As will be discussed in mishnah 5, circumcision cannot override the Sabbath unless one is certain that this Sabbath is the eighth day following the infant's birth. Since there is a halachic uncertainty as to whether *bain hashmashos* is considered the end of the preceding day or the beginning of the following night, the exact age of this child is doubtful, and, in consequence, his circumcision does not override the Sabbath.

וְאַנְדְּרוֹגִינוֹס, — *or an androgyne,*

An individual possessing both male and female organs (*Tif. Yis.*).

His sexual status (with regard to halachah) is doubtful (*Rashi* 135a), and the obligation to circumcise him is therefore in doubt.[1]

אֵין מְחַלְּלִין עָלָיו אֶת הַשַּׁבָּת. — *we may not violate the Sabbath on his behalf.*

[I.e. to perform circumcision. Since, in both cases, the obligation of circumcision is questionable, it may not be performed on the Sabbath. Although one is obligated to circumcise even a child whose requirement for circumcision is questionable, this can be done after the Sabbath, when it does involve any possibly unwarranted desecration of the Sabbath.]

וְרַבִּי יְהוּדָה מַתִּיר בְּאַנְדְּרוֹגִינוֹס. — *R' Yehudah, however, permits [it] in [the case of] an androgyne.*

The *Gemara* explains that R' Yehudah bases his view on the passage (*Gen.* 17:10) הִמּוֹל לָכֶם כָּל־זָכָר, *Every male among you shall be circumcised.* The word, כָּל, *every*, alludes to the androgyne [*every male* being interpreted as *every type of male*], teaching us that his obligation to be circumcised is definite. The *Tanna Kamma*, however, bases his ruling on the verse (*Lev.* 12:3) וּבַיּוֹם הַשְּׁמִינִי יִמּוֹל בְּשַׂר עָרְלָתוֹ, *And on the eighth day, the flesh of his foreskin shall be circumcised.* The words וּבַיּוֹם הַשְּׁמִינִי, *and on the eighth day,* imply that we shall perform the circumcision on the eighth day even if it should occur on the Sabbath. The term עָרְלָתוֹ, *his foreskin,* implies a foreskin which must definitely be circumcised and not to one whose obligation is doubtful. Accordingly, we deduce that only a definitely

---

1. *Rav,* unlike *Rashi,* explains that the androgyne is not a creature of doubtful status, but rather one of distinct status, i.e., half male and half female (*Beis David*).

שבת
יט/ד

[ד] **מִי שֶׁהָיוּ** לוֹ שְׁנֵי תִינוֹקוֹת, אֶחָד לָמוּל אַחַר הַשַּׁבָּת וְאֶחָד לָמוּל בַּשַּׁבָּת, וְשָׁכַח וּמָל אֶת שֶׁל אַחַר הַשַּׁבָּת בַּשַּׁבָּת, חַיָּב; אֶחָד לָמוּל בְּעֶרֶב שַׁבָּת וְאֶחָד לָמוּל בַּשַּׁבָּת, וְשָׁכַח וּמָל אֶת שֶׁל עֶרֶב שַׁבָּת בַּשַּׁבָּת,

---------- ר' עובדיה מברטנורא ----------

(ד) **מי שהיו לו שתי תינוקות וכו'**. פליגי אמוראי בגמרא בגרסת משנה זו, והגרסא שתפסו רבותי עיקר כך היא, מי שהיו לו שתי תינוקות אחד למול אחר שבת ואחד למול בשבת, ושכח ומל את של אחר שבת בשבת חייב. אחד למול בערב שבת ואחד למול בשבת, ושכח ומל את של ערב שבת בשבת, רבי אליעזר מחייב חטאת ורבי יהושע פוטר. והכי פירושה, שכח ומל את של אחר השבת בשבת חייב לדברי הכל, שהרי טעה בדבר מצוה ולא עשה מצוה כשהקדים ומל את של אחר השבת בשבת, ובהא אפילו רבי יהושע מודה: **אחד למול בשבת ואחד למול בערב שבת ושכח ומל את של ערב שבת בשבת, רבי אליעזר מחייב חטאת**. דמילה שלא בזמנה אינה דוחה שבת. ואף על גב דטעה בדבר מצוה שהיה טרוד בחותו של שבת ומתוך כך טעה בזה,

---------- יד אברהם ----------

obligatory circumcision overrides the Sabbath and not a doubtful one such as that of an androgyne (*Gem.* according to *Rashi's* commentary).

The halachah is in accordance with the *Tanna Kamma* (Rav).

4.

As seen in the preceding mishnayos, the performance of circumcision, although it involves violating the Torah injunction against making a wound on the Sabbath, overrides the Sabbath laws. This applies, however, only to a circumcision performed on the eighth day. If the circumcision had to be postponed beyond the eighth day [e.g., for health reasons], it may not be performed on the Sabbath. As mentioned in the commentary to the preceding mishnah, the halachah that circumcision overrides the Sabbath is derived from the verse (*Lev.* 12:3), *And on the eighth day . . .* , accordingly, only a circumcision performed on the eighth day overrides the Sabbath laws, not a circumcision performed on a later day. Needless to say, an invalid circumcision, such as one performed prior to the eighth day, does not override the Sabbath laws. The following mishnah deals with a מוֹהֵל [*mohel*], *circumciser*, who inadvertently circumcised a child on the Sabbath although it was not the eighth day.

מִי שֶׁהָיוּ לוֹ שְׁנֵי תִינוֹקוֹת, — *One who had two infants*,

[If a *mohel* was engaged to circumcise two infants.]

אֶחָד לָמוּל אַחַר הַשַּׁבָּת — *one to circumcise after the Sabbath*

[One was born on the preceding Sunday and is therefore to be circumcised on the following Sunday.]

וְאֶחָד לָמוּל בַּשַּׁבָּת, — *and one to circumcise on the Sabbath*,

[The other one was born on the previous Sabbath and is therefore to be circumcised on the Sabbath.]

משניות / שבת – פרק יט: רבי אליעזר [428]

4. One who had two infants, one to circumcise after the Sabbath and one to circumcise on the Sabbath, and he forgot and circumcised the one who was [to be circumcised] after the Sabbath on the Sabbath, he is liable; [if he had] one to circumcise before the Sabbath and one to circumcise on the Sabbath, and he forgot and circumcised the one who was [to be circumcised] before the Sabbath on the Sabbath,

YAD AVRAHAM

וְשָׁכַח וּמָל אֶת שֶׁל אַחַר הַשַּׁבָּת בַּשַּׁבָּת, — *and he forgot and circumcised the one who was [to be circumcised] after the Sabbath on the Sabbath,*

[He confused the two, and circumcised the child who was supposed to be circumcised on Sunday, on the Sabbath.]

חַיָּב; — *he is liable;*

This *mohel* is liable for a sin offering because he made a wound (a *toladah* of *slaughtering*).

The circumcision, having been performed prior to the eighth day, is invalid, and the *mohel* has, therefore, violated the Sabbath without fulfilling any *mitzvah*. Hence, according to all opinions, he is liable (*Rav* from *Gem.* 137a).

Although the circumcision is invalid because it was performed prematurely, it is, nevertheless, regarded as constructive, since there is no longer any necessity to remove the foreskin (*Tos. Yom Tov* quoting *Rambam, Comm.*). The Gemara (*Kerisus* 19b), however, identifies this mishnah with the *Tanna* who rules that one is liable for wounding even if it is destructive (*Tos.*

R' Akiva). [See *Gem.* 106a which explains that according to R' Shimon wounding and burning are exceptions to the general rule stated in 13:3) that there is no liability for destructive acts.[1]]

אֶחָד לָמוּל בְּעֶרֶב שַׁבָּת — *[if he had] one to circumcise before the Sabbath*

[I.e., one was born on Friday and should therefore have been circumcised before the Sabbath. However, for some reason he was not circumcised on that day. Since the Sabbath is not his eighth day, he may not be circumcised then, but must wait for Sunday.]

וְאֶחָד לָמוּל בַּשַּׁבָּת, — *and one to circumcise on the Sabbath,*

[The other one was born on the preceding Sabbath, and therefore his eighth day is on the Sabbath.]

וְשָׁכַח וּמָל אֶת שֶׁל עֶרֶב שַׁבָּת בַּשַּׁבָּת, — *and he forgot and circumcised the one who was [to be circumcised] before the Sabbath on the Sabbath,*

Since this is a postponed circumcision, its performance does not override the Sabbath (*Rav* from *Gem.* 137a).

---

1. *Tosafos* there add that even R' Shimon declares him liable only for destructive acts which have some constructive feature to them, although their overall effect is destructive. Acts which are totally destructive are exempted even according to R' Shimon. *Rashi* seems to dispute this.

שבת
יט/ה

רַבִּי אֱלִיעֶזֶר מְחַיֵּב חַטָּאת. וְרַבִּי יְהוֹשֻׁעַ פּוֹטֵר.

[ה] קָטָן נִמּוֹל לִשְׁמוֹנָה, לְתִשְׁעָה, וְלַעֲשָׂרָה, וּלְאַחַד עָשָׂר, וְלִשְׁנֵים עָשָׂר, לֹא פָחוֹת וְלֹא יוֹתֵר. הָא כֵּיצַד? כְּדַרְכּוֹ, לִשְׁמוֹנָה; נוֹלַד לְבֵין

ר' עובדיה מברטנורא

ואף בזה עשה מצוה שהרי ראוי הוא למול אלא שאינו דוחה שבת, סבירא ליה לרבי אליעזר טעה בדבר מצוה ועשה מצוה שאינה דוחה את השבת חייב: **ורבי יהושע פוטר.** דסבירא ליה טעה בדבר מצוה ועשה מצוה שאינה דוחה את השבת פטור, כיון דסבור היה שברשות בית דין הוא עושה. והלכה כרבי יהושע:

יד אברהם

רַבִּי אֱלִיעֶזֶר מְחַיֵּב חַטָּאת. — R' Eliezer declares [him] liable for a sin offering.

Although by circumcising a child who is already more than eight days old he has completed a *mitzvah*, he is nevertheless liable, since that *mitzvah* is not one which overrides the Sabbath (*Rav* from *Gem.* ibid.).

וְרַבִּי יְהוֹשֻׁעַ פּוֹטֵר. — But R' Yehoshua exempts [him].

Since he erred while attempting to perform a *mitzvah* (the circumcision of the child born on the preceding Sabbath), and the end result was that he did, in fact, fulfill a *mitzvah* (circumcising the child born Friday of the previous week, who is more than eight days old), albeit the wrong one, R' Yehoshua exempts him. R' Yehoshua considers one liable for inadvertent transgression of a *melachah* only when one engages in a discretionary activity and inadvertently transgresses. However, one who engages in a divinely ordained activity, such as circumcision, and inadvertently transgresses is exempted from the laws of liability. In the first case of this mishnah regarding a baby not yet eight days old, however, R' Yehoshua agrees that one is liable. Since a child less than eight days old is not yet eligible for circumcision, the *mohel* cannot be considered to be engaged in a divinely ordained activity (*Rav* from *Gem.* ibid.).

There is another version of this dispute quoted by the *Gemara* which states that even R' Eliezer agrees that if one has, in fact, fulfilled a *mitzvah* (by circumcising a child of more than eight days), he is exempt. The dispute is rather in the first case of the mishnah, in which one has not fulfilled a *mitzvah* (since he circumcised a child of less than eight days). R' Eliezer declares him liable for the reason explained above. R' Yehoshua, according to this version, exempts him because he was nevertheless *attempting* to perform a divinely ordained task (circumcising the child he thought to be eight days old). *Rav* rules according to the opinion of R' Yehoshua as found in our mishnah. *Rambam* (*Hil. Shabbos* 2:8) rules according to R' Yehoshua as expressed in the alternate version.

5.

In the preceding mishnayos we learned that circumcision may not be performed

19
5
R' Eliezer declares [him] liable for a sin offering. But R' Yehoshua exempts [him].

5. An infant may be circumcised [either] on the eight, ninth, tenth, eleventh, or twelfth [day], not earlier not later. How is this? In the normal course, [he is circumcised] on the eight; if he was born at

YAD AVRAHAM

on the Sabbath if: (a) it is not the eighth day after birth; or (b) the requirement of circumcision of the particular baby is in doubt. The mishnah now discusses cases in which there is doubt whether the Sabbath is the eighth day. In such instances the circumcision is postponed until after the Sabbath. The following mishnah delineates various instances in which the circumcision must be postponed until the ninth, tenth, eleventh, or twelfth day.

קָטָן נִמּוֹל לִשְׁמוֹנָה, לְתִשְׁעָה, וְלַעֲשָׂרָה, וּלְאַחַד עָשָׂר, וְלִשְׁנֵים עָשָׂר — *An infant may be circumcised [either] on the eighth, ninth, tenth, eleventh, or twelfth [day],*

[I.e., there are various circumstances as a result of which a child born at twilight, although perfectly healthy, must have his circumcision postponed until one of these days.]

לֹא פָחוֹת — *not earlier*

It can never be performed prior to the eighth day, even if the father knows that a *mohel* will not be available later (*Tif. Yis.*).

וְלֹא יוֹתֵר. — *nor later.*

The circumcision of a *healthy* child is never postponed beyond the twelfth day, on account of the child being born at twilight.[1]

הָא כֵּיצַד? כְּדַרְכּוֹ, לִשְׁמוֹנָה; — *How is this? In the normal course, [he is circumcised] on the eighth;*

[If the child was not born at twilight, he is circumcised on the eighth day following his birth. For this purpose, we consider the day of his birth as the first day. Even if he is born just before sunset, it is considered a full day.]

נוֹלַד לְבֵין הַשְּׁמָשׁוֹת, — *if he was born at twilight,*

[Halachically, twilight is the period of time between sunset and nightfall. There is a halachic question as to whether it is to be judged the end of the preceding day or the onset of the following night. Therefore, if a child was born Sunday between sunset and nightfall, we are uncertain if he is considered born on Sunday or Monday.] The length of twilight has been discussed above (2:7).

---

1. In cases where there are two children to be circumcised, and one of them is being circumcised on the eighth day whereas the other is a postponed circumcision, priority is given to the punctual one. An infant whose circumcision was delayed because he was born at twilight, however, is considered punctual and takes priority over one whose circumcision was postponed for other reasons (*Tif. Yis.*). There is, however, a view which maintains that a postponed circumcision always takes priority (*Sheilos Uteshuvos Dvar Avraham*, vol. 1, responsa 33, and vol. 2, responsum 1-4).

שבת יט/ה

הַשְּׁמָשׁוֹת, נִמּוֹל לְתִשְׁעָה; בֵּין הַשְּׁמָשׁוֹת שֶׁל עֶרֶב שַׁבָּת, נִמּוֹל לַעֲשָׂרָה; יוֹם טוֹב לְאַחַר הַשַּׁבָּת, נִמּוֹל לְאַחַד עָשָׂר; שְׁנֵי יָמִים טוֹבִים שֶׁל רֹאשׁ הַשָּׁנָה, נִמּוֹל לִשְׁנֵים עָשָׂר.

ר' עובדיה מברטנורא

(ה) **נולד בין השמשות נמול לתשיעי.** שהרי יום שמיני של מחר הוא נמול, ושמא בין השמשות יום הוא ונמול לתשיעי. היה היום ערב שבת אי אפשר למולו בשבת הבא דשמא תשיעי הוא והויא לה מילה שלא בזמנה ואינה דוחה שבת, וצריך להמתין עד לאחר השבת שהוא עשירי: **חל יום טוב להיות אחר השבת.** אין מילה שלא בזמנה דוחה אותו ונמול לאחד עשר: **שני ימים טובים של ראש השנה.** דקדושה אחת הן ואין מילה שלא בזמנה דוחה את יום טוב השני של ראש השנה, נימול לשנים עשר:

יד אברהם

נִמּוֹל לְתִשְׁעָה; — he is circumcised on the ninth;

Since the twilight period may actually be part of the incoming night, the child may not be circumcised until the eighth day from that night. Counting from the day preceding the twilight (of which the twilight may actually be a part), it is, however, reckoned the ninth day (Rav; Rashi).

בֵּין הַשְּׁמָשׁוֹת שֶׁל עֶרֶב שַׁבָּת, — [if he was born] at twilight on the eve of the Sabbath,

[If he was born at twilight of Friday evening, there is doubt whether his day of birth is Friday or Saturday. Hence, we are uncertain whether his circumcision should be performed on Friday or on the Sabbath.]

נִמּוֹל לַעֲשָׂרָה; — he is circumcised on the tenth;

I.e., he is circumcised on Sunday. He cannot be circumcised on Friday, since perhaps the time of his birth is judged to be Saturday and Friday's circumcision would be premature. Similarly, he cannot be circumcised on the Sabbath, since perhaps the time of his birth is judged to be Friday, and the Sabbath would be the ninth day, when a postponed circumcision may not take place. The circumcision must, therefore, be postponed until Sunday, which is the tenth day (Rav).

יוֹם טוֹב לְאַחַר הַשַּׁבָּת, — [if] a festival [falls] after the Sabbath,

[If Yom Tov falls on the Sunday upon which this child mentioned in the previous case is scheduled to be circumcised.]

נִמּוֹל לְאַחַד עָשָׂר; — he is circumcised on the eleventh;

Since his circumcision is a postponed one, it does not supersede Yom Tov either. It is, therefore, postponed until Monday (the day following Yom Tov), which is the eleventh day after birth (Rav; Rashi).

שְׁנֵי יָמִים טוֹבִים שֶׁל רֹאשׁ הַשָּׁנָה, — [in the case of] the two festival days of Rosh Hashanah,

I.e., if the two Yom Tov days of Rosh Hashanah occur on Sunday and Monday.

In the times of the mishnah, it was possible for Rosh Hashanah to fall on Sunday, since the months were proclaimed by the Sanhedrin upon the

19
5
twilight, he is circumcised on the ninth; [if he was born] at twilight on the eve of the Sabbath, he is circumcised on the tenth; [if] a festival [falls] after the Sabbath, he is circumcised on the eleventh; [in the case of] the two festival days of Rosh Hashanah, he is circumcised on the twelfth.

YAD AVRAHAM

testimony of witnesses who had observed the מוֹלָד, *appearance of the moon's first phase* (*Tif. Yis.*).

[Nowadays, however, we use a fixed calendar, formulated in 4118 (358 C.E.) by Hillel HaSheini. According to this calendar, Rosh Hashanah cannot fall on Sunday, Wednesday, or Friday. See ArtScroll *Rosh Hashanah*, p. 17.]

נִמּוֹל לִשְׁנֵים עָשָׂר. — *he is circumcised on the twelfth.*

[Since the circumcision was postponed, it may not be performed on Rosh Hashanah, but must be delayed until thereafter, which is the twelfth day after birth.]

The *Tanna's* mention of the two festival days of Rosh Hashanah, and his omission of the two-day *Yom Tov* of the Diaspora, leaves open the question of whether a delayed circumcision may be performed on the second day of any festival other than Rosh Hashanah. The reason for this possible distinction is that while the sanctity of the second day of Rosh Hashanah is regarded as (Rabbinically) certain, the sanctity of the second *Yom Tov* day of the Diaspora derives from an uncertainty. The two-day celebration of *Yom Tov* in the Diaspora is an outgrowth of the Torah-prescribed procedure of the *Beis Din* fixing Rosh Chodesh (the New Moon) upon the testimony of witnesses who have sighted the new moon. Once one knew which day had been designated as Rosh Chodesh, he was able to determine which day in a particular month was to be celebrated as *Yom Tov*. To inform the public, messengers were dispatched to the rest of the land as far as they could travel from Rosh Chodesh till the holiday that fell in that month. Ancient modes of transportation did not allow them to get very far. In Tishrei, since they could not travel on Rosh Hashanah, Yom Kippur, or on the Sabbath, they would generally have only ten days of travel before Succos. As a result, although the exact day of *Yom Tov* was known in *Eretz Yisrael*, the Diaspora would not know the exact day until the *Yom Tov* had already passed. Because Rosh Chodesh must be either the thirtieth or the thirty-first day from the previous Rosh Chodesh, the question of which day to observe as *Yom Tov* was limited to two days. Therefore, all places too far away from Jerusalem to be reached by the messengers before *Yom Tov* were obliged to observe both possible days as *Yom Tov*.

The origin of the two-day celebration of Rosh Hashanah is delineated in Rosh Hashanah (4:4): "Originally they accepted testimony regarding the new moon all day. Once the witnesses were delayed in arriving, and the Levites erred in the [daily] hymn. So they ordained that they [the *Beis Din*] accept [new moon testimony] only until the *Minchah*; *and* that if witnesses came from the *Minchah* onward — that day should be kept holy and the next day, too."

Thus, even in Jerusalem, where no uncertainty as to the proper day existed, Rosh Hashanah was observed for two days if the witnesses arrived after the *Minchah* of the first day.

Consequently, we find a distinction between these two-day observances. Whereas the two-day observance of Succos,

[433] **THE MISHNAH/SHABBOS** — Chapter Nineteen: *Rabbi Eliezer*

שבת
יט/ו

קָטָן הַחוֹלֶה, אֵין מוֹהֲלִין אוֹתוֹ עַד שֶׁיַּבְרִיא.

[ו] **אֵלּוּ הֵן** צִיצִין הַמְעַכְּבִין אֶת הַמִּילָה: בְּשַׂר הַחוֹפֶה אֶת רֹב הָעֲטָרָה. וְאֵינוֹ אוֹכֵל בִּתְרוּמָה.

ר' עובדיה מברטנורא

עד שיבריא. ויעברו עליו שבעה ימים שלמים מעת מעת מיום שהבריא, ואחר כך מלין אותו:
(ו) **ציצין.** כמין נימין של בשר שנשארו מן הערלה: **עטרה.** היא שפה גבוהה המקפת את הגיד סביב, וממנה משפע ויורד לראשו. ובשר החופה את רוב העטרה דקתני מתניתין, לא תימא רוב הקיפה אלא אפילו רוב גבהה במקום אחד: **אינו אוכל בתרומה.** אם כהן הוא, דכהן ערל אסור לאכול בתרומה. נאמר בפסח (שמות יב) תושב ושכיר לא יאכל בו ונאמר בתרומה (ויקרא כב) תושב כהן ושכיר לא יאכל בו, מה פסח אסור לערל אף תרומה אסורה לערל:

יד אברהם

Pesach, and Shavuos in the Diaspora is due to the doubt as to which day is really the festival, the two-day observance of Rosh Hashanah was instituted even where it was definitely established which day was Rosh Hashanah. The result of this is that the Rabbis designated the two festival days of the Diaspora as two separate degrees of sanctity, while the two days of Rosh Hashanah were together designated as one level of sanctity.

Rambam (*Comm.* and *Hil. Milah* 1:15) rules that a delayed circumcision does not override the second day of Rosh Hashanah, since it has the status of one sanctity, whereas it does override the second day of the two-day *Yom Tov* of the Diaspora, which is of lesser sanctity than the first. *Rosh*, however, does not distinguish between the two, and rules that a postponed circumcision never overrides *Yom Tov*, even the second day of the Diaspora observance. According to *Rosh* the reason the mishnah discusses Rosh Hashanah rather than other festivals is because the *Tanna*, being a resident of *Eretz Yisrael*, chooses to discuss the observance prevalent in his country, rather than one prevalent only in the Diaspora (*Rosh* responsa 26, quoted by *Beis Yosef; Tur Yoreh Deah* 266; *Tif. Yis.*). [See also ArtScroll *Rosh Hashanah*, pp. 109-111.]

קָטָן הַחוֹלֶה, אֵין מוֹהֲלִין אוֹתוֹ עַד שֶׁיַּבְרִיא. — *A sick infant, we may not circumcise him until he recovers.*

We must wait seven full days (i.e., 168 hours) after his recovery before circumcising him (*Rav, Tif. Yis.* from *Gem.*).

The regulation of waiting seven full days applies only to children who suffer illnesses which affect their whole body. However, an ailment which is limited to only one of his limbs does not require this waiting period, and the child should be circumcised as soon as he has recuperated from his sickness (*Shulchan Aruch, Yoreh Deah* 262:2).

6.

אֵלּוּ הֵן צִיצִין — *These are the shreds*

I.e., shreds of the foreskin which failed to be removed during circumcision (*Rav; Rashi*). [Not all these shreds invalidate the circumcision, although they are part of the foreskin. The mishnah now explains which are the ones which do invalidate the cir-

19. A sick infant, we may not circumcise him until he recovers.

6. These are the shreds that invalidate the circumcision: flesh that covers the larger part of the corona. And he may not eat of *terumah*.

YAD AVRAHAM

cumcision, pending their removal.]

הַמְעַכְּבִין אֶת הַמִּילָה: — *that invalidate the circumcision*:

If they are not removed, the circumcision is invalid, and the person is regarded as uncircumcised.

When performing the circumcision on a weekday, it is proper for the *mohel* to remove all shreds. Many authorities maintain that even if the *mohel* has already withdrawn his hands from the circumcision, he should, nevertheless, return to remove even those shreds which do not invalidate the circumcision. This is considered adorning the *mitzvah*, by making the person to appear properly circumcised. On the Sabbath, however, he may return to remove only those shreds of skin whose presence invalidate the circumcision. Those shreds which do not invalidate the circumcision may be removed only as long as the *mohel* is still occupied with the initial circumcision. After he withdraws his hands, he may not return to remove them (*Tif. Yis.* in accordance with the ruling of *Tur, Yoreh Deah* 264 based on *Gem.* 133b). [By removing his hands, the *mohel* has completed the initial act of circumcision. To return and remove any remaining shreds involves a second violation of the Sabbath which may only be done to fulfill the *mitzvah* of circumcision. Since the remaining shreds do not invalidate the circumcision, the *mitzvah* is regarded as already fulfilled. Therefore, no new violation of the Sabbath is permitted. If, however, the *mohel* is still engaged in the initial act of circumcision, for which the Sabbath rules have been waived, he is permitted to remove even those shreds which do not invalidate the circumcision.]

Rambam (Hil. Milah 2:4), however, rules that even on weekdays, once the *mohel* has withdrawn his hands from the circumcision, he is not obligated to return to remove those shreds whose presence do not invalidate the circumcision.

בָּשָׂר הַחוֹפֶה אֶת רֹב הָעֲטָרָה. — *flesh that covers the larger part of the corona.*

I.e., the ridge surrounding the membrum, from which it tapers to a point. If this ridge is still covered with flesh, either over the majority of its circumference, or over the majority of its height (even in just one spot), the person is regarded as uncircumcised (*Rav; Rashi; Ran.* cf. *Beis Yosef* on *Tur, Yoreh Deah* 264).

וְאֵינוֹ אוֹכֵל בִּתְרוּמָה. — *And he may not eat of* terumah.

A *Kohen* may not eat *terumah* unless he is circumcised. [Even if he is uncircumcised for a valid reason (e.g., he is a hemophiliac) he may not eat *terumah*.] Any shreds remaining on a *Kohen* which invalidate the circumcision disqualify that *Kohen* from the right to eat *terumah* (*Rav*).

[435]   THE MISHNAH/SHABBOS — Chapter Nineteen: *Rabbi Eliezer*

שבת
יט/ו

וְאִם הָיָה בַּעַל בָּשָׂר, מְתַקְּנוֹ מִפְּנֵי מַרְאִית הָעַיִן. מָל וְלֹא פָרַע אֶת הַמִּילָה, כְּאִלּוּ לֹא מָל.

ר' עובדיה מברטנורא

ואם היה בעל בשר. שהיה שמן ונראה בשר שלמעלה מערלתו לאחר שניטלה הערלה כולה כאילו אותו בשר חוזר וחופה את הגיד: **מתקנו.** ומשפט בחזמל מאותו צובי: **מפני מראית העין.** שלא יהא נראה כערל: ולא פרע. לא גילה: **כאילו לא מל.** וישוב ויפרע, ואפילו סלק ידו ממנה. וכל זמן שהוא מתעסק במילה בשבת חותך בין ציצין המעכבין בין ציצין שאין מעכבין. לאחר שסלק ידו, על ציצין המעכבין חוזר, על ציצין שאינן מעכבין אינו חוזר.

יד אברהם

וְאִם הָיָה בַּעַל בָּשָׂר, — *If he was fleshy,* I.e., if he was obese and as a result, even after the foreskin has been removed, the flesh above his foreskin hangs down and appears to cover the corona *(Rav; Rashi).*

מְתַקְּנוֹ מִפְּנֵי מַרְאִית הָעַיִן. — *he must rectify it for appearances' sake.*

He must trim this flesh diagonally, so that he will not appear uncircumcised *(Rav; Rashi).*

The *Gemara* states that if, when the membrum is erect, he appears circumcised, he need not be recircumcised. Otherwise, he requires recircumcision.

Terumas HaDeshen responsa 264 (see also *Bach* to *Yoreh Deah* 264) explains this last phrase of the mishnah as referring only to a *Kohen* who wishes to eat *terumah.* In this case, even if the corona is exposed during erection, since it is otherwise not exposed, it must be trimmed (for appearances' sake) in order to qualify him to eat *terumah.* An infant who is not a *Kohen* need not have anything done

19 6 If he was fleshy, he must rectify it for appearances' sake. If he circumcised but did not expose the circumcision, it is as if he did not circumcise.

YAD AVRAHAM

as long as he appears circumcised during erection.

Rambam (*Hil. Milah* 2:5), as explained by *Terumas HaDeshen* and *Bach*, however, explains this phrase to mean that the flesh must be tied back so that it will not cover the corona. No further cutting, however, is ever required. This ruling is accepted by *Rama* (*Yoreh Deah* 264:6).

The halachah is that if he appears circumcised when erect, no cutting is required. It should, however, be tied back. If tying is impossible or ineffective, nothing more need be done (*Tif. Yis.*; *Chochmas Adam* 149:16).

מָל וְלֹא פָרַע אֶת הַמִּילָה, — *If he circumcised but did not expose the circumcision,*

[If he removed the foreskin, but did not split the membrane underneath it and pull it back to expose the glans. See mishnah 2 of this chapter.]

כְּאִלּוּ לֹא מָל. — *it is as if he did not circumcise.*

He must, therefore, complete the operation, even if he has already withdrawn from it and is no longer engaged in the circumcision (*Rav*).

Additionally, the mishnah teaches us that if one cut off the foreskin on the Sabbath but neglected to expose the corona, he is regarded as a desecrator of the Sabbath, since he inflicted a wound without performing a *mitzvah* (*Meiri*).

[See above mishnah 2 of this chapter.]

פרק עשרים
Chapter Twenty

שבת
כ/א

[א] **רַבִּי אֱלִיעֶזֶר** אוֹמֵר: תּוֹלִין אֶת הַמְשַׁמֶּרֶת בְּיוֹם טוֹב, וְנוֹתְנִין לִתְלוּיָה בַּשַּׁבָּת. וַחֲכָמִים אוֹמְרִים: אֵין תּוֹלִין אֶת הַמְשַׁמֶּרֶת בְּיוֹם טוֹב, וְאֵין נוֹתְנִין לִתְלוּיָה בַּשַּׁבָּת, אֲבָל נוֹתְנִין לִתְלוּיָה בְּיוֹם טוֹב.

―――――― ר' עובדיה מברטנורא ――――――

פרק עשרים ― רבי אליעזר. (א) רבי אליעזר אומר תולין את המשמרת. שמסננין בה שמרי יין, ומותח את פיה לכל צד בעגול ונעשה כאהל על חלל הכלי. ואף על גב דעביד אהל שרי ביום טוב, דסבירא ליה לרבי אליעזר מכשירי אוכל נפש שאפשר לעשותן מערב יום טוב מותר לעשותן ביום טוב. אבל בשבת [תולה] לכתחלה לא, אבל אם תלויה היא נותנין לתוכה שמרים ומסננין, דאין דרך בורר בכך: **אין תולין את המשמרת.** דעביד אהל עראי ומחזי כמעשה חול: **ואין נותנים לתלויה בשבת.** דהוה תולדת בורר או מרקד. והלכה כחכמים:

――――― יד אברהם ―――――

1.

All *melachos* prohibited on the Sabbath are also prohibited on *Yom Tov* except those necessary for the preparation of food (*Beitzah* 5:2; *Megillah* 1:5). This exemption applies only to those activities *directly* involved in the preparation of the food itself. Activities only indirectly involved with the preparation of food, as for example, the fashioning of the utensils in which to prepare the food, are termed *preliminaries to the preparation of food*. Their permissibility is the subject of a dispute between R' Eliezer and the Sages. R' Eliezer permits performing a *melachah* while attending to *preliminaries* even if they could have been prepared before the festival. The Sages, however, permit only such preliminaries that could not have been prepared before the festival.

רַבִּי אֱלִיעֶזֶר אוֹמֵר: תּוֹלִין אֶת הַמְשַׁמֶּרֶת — **R' Eliezer says: We may suspend a strainer**

I.e., a strainer through which wine is poured to eliminate its dregs. It is attached to the opening of a container and stretched tightly over the entire opening (*Rav; Rashi*).

בְּיוֹם טוֹב, — **on Yom Tov,**

Stretching a strainer over the opening of a container constitutes making a temporary tent (see 17:7), an act normally Rabbinically prohibited even on *Yom Tov* (see below, s.v. וַחֲכָמִים אוֹמְרִים). R' Eliezer permits it, though, if it is required for the preparation of the wine to be drunk on *Yom Tov*. He rules not only that the preparation of preliminaries to the preparation of food are permitted on *Yom Tov*, but that they are permitted even if they could have been performed prior to the *Yom Tov*. On the Sabbath, however, when there is no special dispensation for the preparation of food, this is prohibited (*Rav* from *Gem*. 137b).

Even R' Eliezer applies this lenient ruling only to Rabbinically prohibited labors, such as constructing a temporary tent. Biblically prohibited labors are prohibited even if they are prelim-

1. **R′** Eliezer says: We may suspend a strainer on *Yom Tov*, and we may pour into a suspended one on the Sabbath. But the Sages say: We may not suspend a strainer on *Yom Tov*, nor may we pour into a suspended one on the Sabbath, but we may pour into a suspended one on *Yom Tov*.

YAD AVRAHAM

inaries to the preparation of food, unless they could not have been performed prior to the festival (*Tos.* 137b).

וְנוֹתְנִין לִתְלוּיָה בַּשַּׁבָּת. — *and we may pour into a suspended one on the Sabbath.*

Even according to R′ Eliezer, the strainer may not be suspended on the Sabbath when there is no special dispensation for the preparation of food. If, however, it was suspended before the Sabbath, wine may be poured through it. This is not prohibited as *sorting, because, in R′ Eliezer's view, this is not the usual manner of sorting (*Rav; Rashi*).

וַחֲכָמִים אוֹמְרִים: אֵין תּוֹלִין אֶת הַמְשַׁמֶּרֶת בְּיוֹם טוֹב, — *But the Sages say: We may not suspend a strainer on Yom Tov,*

This is prohibited Rabbinically since it involves constructing a temporary tent[1] (*Rav, Shulchan Aruch* 315:9).

וְאֵין נוֹתְנִין לִתְלוּיָה בַּשַּׁבָּת, — *nor may we pour into a suspended one on the Sabbath,*

The Sages regard this as a *toladah* of either *sorting or *sifting (*Rav* from *Gem.* 138a). This is a Torah prohibition, for which one is liable for a sin offering (*Gem.* ibid.).

The halachah is in accordance with the Sages (*Rav; Tif. Yis.; Rambam, Comm.*).

אֲבָל נוֹתְנִין לִתְלוּיָה בְּיוֹם טוֹב. — *but we may pour into a suspended one on Yom Tov.*

I.e., if the strainer was suspended prior to the festival, we may pour wine into it on the festival. Since the wine is to be consumed on that day, preparing that wine by straining it is a *direct* preparation of food, and is permissible. Suspending the strainer, however, is regarded as a *preliminary* to the preparation of food and is therefore prohibited.

---

1. The *Gemara* (138a) states that the prohibition is in order that a person not do on the Sabbath as he does during the week. *Rashi* (139b s.v. מערים) takes this to mean that it is prohibited because it is a *weekday activity* (see General Introduction, p. 17) and not because of constructing a temporary tent. *Ramban, Rashba, Ritva* and *Meiri,* however, explain that the prohibition is because it is a *temporary* tent. [*Meiri* explains that the *Gemara* means that though suspending a strainer does not actually constitute constructing a temporary tent, it is banned because it resembles that process; see also *Chiddushei HaRan.*] This seems to have been the opinion of *Tosafos* (138a) too, and this is the explanation adopted by *Shulchan Aruch.*

Rambam (Hil. *Shabbos* 21:17) explains that by allowing him to suspend a strainer he may forget and strain since he is involved in his weekday routine. This view is adopted by *Magen Avraham* 315:11. *Ritva* states that *Rashi's* opinion is identical to *Rambam's*.

שבת כ/ב

[ב] **נוֹתְנִין** מַיִם עַל־גַּבֵּי הַשְּׁמָרִים בִּשְׁבִיל שֶׁיִּצַּלּוּ; וּמְסַנְּנִין אֶת הַיַּיִן בְּסוּדָרִין

ר' עובדיה מברטנורא

(ב) **נותנים מים.** בשבת על גבי שמרים הנתונים במשמרת מבעוד יום כדי שילכו, שיהיו השמרים צלולים ויזוב כל יינם. פירוש אחר, על גבי שמרים שנשארו בחבית, וקולטין המים טעם היין ומוליאין אותן בשבת ושותים אותן ואין בזה משום בורר: **את היין.** מפני הקמחים לבנים שמתהוים בו: **בסודרין.** המיוחדין לכך. וליכא למיגזר דלמא סחיט לה, הואיל ועשויין למלאכה זו. והוא שלא יעשה בידו בסודר כמין גומא בפי הכלי כדי שירד היין במדרון, שלא יעשה כדרך שהוא עושה בחול ובכפיפה מצרית. סל העשוי מנוצרי הדקל. והוא שלא תהיה הכפיפה גבוהה מקרקעית הכלי התחתון טפח, שלא יעשה אהל עראי:

יד אברהם

2.

נוֹתְנִין מַיִם — *We may pour water*
I.e., even during the Sabbath (*Rav; Rashi*).

עַל־גַּבֵּי הַשְּׁמָרִים — *over wine-dregs*
I.e., over wine-dregs which have been placed in a strainer prior to the Sabbath (*Rav; Rashi*).

בִּשְׁבִיל שֶׁיִּצַּלּוּ; — *so that they become clear;*
I.e., so that the dregs be drained of the residue of wine in them (*Rav; Rashi*).
Some understand the mishnah to mean pouring water into dregs which are still in the bottom of the barrel. By soaking the dregs in water, whatever residue of wine that remains is absorbed by the water, giving it a wine flavor. It is then poured off and drunk on the Sabbath (*Rav*).
According to both versions, the point of the mishnah is that there is no *sorting involved.
Although by pouring water through the dregs which are in the strainer one is causing the water to mix with the dregs and then separate from them, this is not considered *sorting because the person pouring is not himself doing any *sorting. His act merely creates the mixture and the *sorting then takes place by itself. Furthermore, since the water and the dregs came together only in a situation where they could not remain together, i.e., in a strainer, they are never considered mixed.
According to the second version, when he pours off the water, he must stop as soon as it stops running freely and commences to drip. Otherwise, he is guilty of *sorting (*Shulchan Aruch* 319:14, *Magen Avraham* 319:15). If he wishes to drink it immediately, then he may pour off all the liquid.

וּמְסַנְּנִין אֶת הַיַּיִן — *and we may filter wine*
I.e., we may filter the wine to eliminate the white flourlike particles that collect there (*Rashi; Rav*).
This refers to clear wine, from which the lees have already been removed. Since it is already drinkable as is, the filtering does not render it potable. For this reason, it is not prohibited as *sorting. Liquid containing matter which renders it undrinkable may not be filtered since this is indeed considered *sorting (*Gem.* 139b as explained by *Ran*).

בְּסוּדָרִין — *through cloths*
According to some opinions this is

2. We may pour water over wine-dregs so that they become clear; and we may filter wine through cloths

YAD AVRAHAM

permitted only with cloths especially designated for this purpose. One may not, however, use ordinary cloths since it is Rabbinically forbidden to wet fabrics on the Sabbath for fear one will wring them out [to do so is a *toladah* of either *whitening or *threshing[1]] (*Rav*).

If the cloths are designated for this purpose, however, we need not fear that one will wring them out since he does not object to their being wet. It is also unlikely that he will wring them merely to extract the few drops of wine absorbed by the cloth (*Tos.* 111a).

Others, however, permit using any cloths to filter wine. They reason that no matter what cloth one uses it is unlikely that he will subsequently wring out the wine remaining in them (*Beur Halachah* 319:10). However, water may not be filtered in cloths not especially designated for that (*Shulchan Aruch* 319:10).

When spreading the cloth over the mouth of the container, one may not form a hollow in the cloth. (A hollow is made to direct the flow of the wine into the center of the container, rather than have it drip from all points of the cloth.) This is forbidden because it is a *weekday activity*, i.e., in order that one's Sabbath activities be distinguished from his weekday activities. [The concept of *weekday*

activities is explained in the General Introduction, p. 17.] Rather, one must place the cloth flat over the mouth of the container (*Rav* from *Gem.* 139b). The hollow may, however, be allowed to form as a natural consequence of pouring the liquid through it (*Tur* 319). This is permissible only if the cloth has been spread out before the Sabbath. To spread it during the Sabbath constituted making a temporary tent (*Tif. Yis.*).

There is a difference of opinion whether one may use a strainer as well as a cloth. *Rambam* (*Hil. Shabbos* 8:14) rules that one may not use a strainer even for wine which most people never bother to strain. For this reason the mishnah specifies cloth. A strainer is prohibited apparently so that one may distinguish his Sabbath activities from his weekday ones (*Mishnah Berurah* 319:4; see General Introduction). Most authorities however permit one to strain such wine even with a strainer (ibid. 40). According to them the mishnah refers only to wine which although potable as is, most people prefer to strain. Since it can be drunk as is, there is no real *sorting involved. However, since most people prefer to filter it, the Rabbis required that one do so in an unusual fashion, i.e., by using a cloth rather than a strainer (*Ran*). If, however, the wine is so full of extraneous matter as to be undrinkable, one is not permitted to filter it even with a cloth. Since by filtering it one renders it potable, he is guilty of *sorting (*Ran*; *Shulchan Aruch* 319:10).

---

1. The determination of which *melachah* is involved depends on the nature of the liquid. If the liquid is a clear one, such as water, the removal of which cleans the fabric, one who wrings out the fabric is liable for *wringing*, which is a *toladah* of *whitening. If the liquid is of a color which stains the fabric, such as red wine, one is obviously not liable for *whitening but is liable for *pressing*, which is a *toladah* of *threshing. (This is the same *melachah* as is involved in the pressing of grapes to extract their juice.) This latter *melachah*, however, is only violated when it is done to use the liquid. Otherwise, it is a *melachah not performed for its defined purpose* (*Tos.* 111a).

שבת כ/ב

וּבִכְפִיפָה מִצְרִית; וְנוֹתְנִין בֵּיצָה בִּמְסַנֶּנֶת שֶׁל חַרְדָּל.

וְעוֹשִׂין אֲנוֹמְלִין בַּשַּׁבָּת. רַבִּי יְהוּדָה אוֹמֵר: בַּשַּׁבָּת; בְּכוֹס; בְּיוֹם טוֹב, בְּלָגִין; וּבַמּוֹעֵד, בְּחָבִית. רַבִּי צָדוֹק אוֹמֵר: הַכֹּל לְפִי הָאוֹרְחִין.

ר' עובדיה מברטנורא

ונותנין ביצה במסננת. שנתנו בה חרדל להסתנן, שרגילין ליתן ביצה טרופה בדברים העכורין והם מתלבנים ומזדככים על ידה: **ינומלין.** יין ודבש ופלפלין: **לגין.** גדול מכוס וקטן מחבית: **הכל לפי האורחים.** אם יש לו אורחין מרובין עושה הרבה, בין בשבת בין ביום טוב בין במועד. והלכה כתנא קמא שעושין ינומלין בשבת כפי מה שהן רגילים.

יד אברהם

וּבִכְפִיפָה מִצְרִית; — *or through a basket made of palm twigs;*

The translation follows *Rashi* and *Rav* who understand מִצְרִית as צוּרֵי הַדֶּקֶל, *palm twigs.* Alternatively, it is made of reed or willows (*Rama* 319:12).

The basket may be used only if it is *less* than a handbreadth above the floor of the container into which the wine is flowing (*Rav* from *Gem.* 139b).

Some explain that this is required to distinguish the Sabbath activity from the weekday one (*Ran* from *R' Yonah; Shulchan Aruch* 319:12). Others explain that this is required in order to avoid the construction of a temporary tent (see mishnah 1) since the basket is being inserted on the Sabbath (*Rav; Rashi; Rambam, Hil. Shabbos* 22:33).

וְנוֹתְנִין בֵּיצָה בִּמְסַנֶּנֶת שֶׁל חַרְדָּל. — *and we may put an egg into a mustard strainer.*

I.e., we may add a raw egg to a strainer in which mustard has been strained. The mustard itself, however, may not be strained on the Sabbath (*Gem.* 134a). The mishnah is referring only to mustard which is already lying at the bottom of a straining dish from before the Sabbath. It was customary to add an egg to dark foods to make them lighter (*Rav*).

Although the yolk goes through the strainer while the albumen remains above, putting the egg into the strainer is not forbidden under the *melachah* of *sorting*. This is because both parts of the egg are foods; i.e., neither one is considered refuse. Although separating one food from another falls under *sorting*, that is so only when he does so in order to be able to eat them separately. In the case of this mishnah, however, since he is separating them only to be able to use the yolk for coloring the mustard and the albumen is not actually refuse, it is not considered *sorting*. Accordingly, one may not strain the yolk from the albumen if he is doing so in order to eat only one of them (*Tur* 319, as explained by *Levush* and *Bach*).

Others, however, base this ruling on the concept that there is no sorting within one food type provided all the components are edible. [For this reason, one may sort the various pieces of one food type according to size (*Rama* 319:3).] Accordingly, though the yolk and albumen differ from each

20
2

or through a basket made of palm twigs; and we may put an egg into a mustard strainer.

We may make a honeyed wine on the Sabbath. R' Yehudah says: On the Sabbath [it may be made] in a cup; on *Yom Tov* [it may be made] in a bottle; and on [*Chol*] *HaMoed*, in a cask. [But] R' Tzaddok says: Everything depends on [the number of] the guests.

YAD AVRAHAM

other, they are both part of one food type — i.e., the egg. Separating them, therefore, does not involve *sorting. Therefore, one may do so even for the purpose of eating one of them apart from the other (*Tur* ibid., as explained by *Magen Avraham* 319:16).

וְעוֹשִׂין אֲנוֹמְלִין בַּשַׁבָּת. — *We may make a honeyed wine on the Sabbath.*

I.e., we may mix wine with honey and pepper in any quantity desired (*Rav* from *Gem.* 140a).

Though making this mixture involves a considerable amount of work, it is still permissible (*Tif. Yis.*).

רַבִּי יְהוּדָה אוֹמֵר: בַּשַׁבָּת, בְּכוֹס; — *Rabbi Yehudah says: On the Sabbath [it may be made] in a cup;*

I.e., on the Sabbath it may be made only one cupful at a time, because of the excessive toil involved in mixing large quantities (*Tif. Yis.*).

בְּיוֹם טוֹב, בְּלָגִין; — *on Yom Tov [it may be made] in a bottle;*

This is larger than a cup but smaller than a cask (*Rashi; Rav*).

וּבַמּוֹעֵד, בֶּחָבִית. — *and on [Chol] HaMoed, in a cask.*

During הַמּוֹעֵד (חוֹל) [(*Chol*) *Ha-Moed*], *the intermediate days of the festival*, though certain forms of labor are prohibited, one is permitted to toil more than on the festival itself (see tractate *Moed Katan*).

רַבִּי צָדוֹק אוֹמֵר: הַכֹּל לְפִי הָאוֹרְחִין. — *[But] R' Tzaddok says: Everything depends on [the number of] the guests.*

If one has many guests, he may prepare at one time even a large quantity of honeyed wine, whether on the Sabbath, festival, or the intermediate days of a festival (*Rav*). Others explain that R' Tzaddok differs with R' Yehudah only insofar as the festival is concerned. He agrees, however, as regards the Sabbath (*Rambam, Comm.*).

The halachah is in accordance with the *Tanna Kamma*, who permits making as much as one cares to make, even on the Sabbath (*Rav; Rambam, Comm.*).

3.

The following mishnah continues to enumerate acts that are prohibited because of their nature as weekday-type activities. As explained in the previous mishnah, the Rabbis prohibited certain ways of doing otherwise permissible acts in order that one's Sabbath activities be distinguished from his weekday ones.

שבת
כ/ג

[ג] אֵין שׁוֹרִין אֶת הַחִלְתִּית בְּפוֹשְׁרִין, אֲבָל נוֹתֵן לְתוֹךְ הַחֹמֶץ. וְאֵין שׁוֹרִין אֶת הַכַּרְשִׁינִין וְלֹא שָׁפִין אוֹתָן, אֲבָל נוֹתֵן לְתוֹךְ הַכְּבָרָה אוֹ לְתוֹךְ הַכַּלְכָּלָה. אֵין כּוֹבְרִין אֶת הַתֶּבֶן בִּכְבָרָה, וְלֹא יִתְּנֶנּוּ עַל־גַּבֵּי מָקוֹם גָּבוֹהַּ בִּשְׁבִיל שֶׁיֵּרֵד הַמּוֹץ;

ר' עובדיה מברטנורא

(ג) **חלתית.** כך שמה בערבי, והיא חמה ונוהגין לאכלה במקומות הקרים, ואין שורין אותה בשבת דמיחזי כמעשה חול: **את הכרשינין.** מליף עליהם מים בכלי לברור פסולתן, שהפסולת צף למעלה: **ולא שפין אותן.** ביד להשיר פסולתן, דהוה ליה בורר: אבל נותן בתוך הכברה, ואף על פי שפסולתן נופל לפטומיס דרך נקבי הכברה ונמלא מתברר מאליו: **התבן.** שהיו עושים מן הקש שמחתכין אותו במוריגים ונעשה כל זנב השבולין תבן: **מוץ.** הוא מזקן השבולת העליון, ואינו ראוי למאכל בהמה וכוברים אותו בכברה כי פול המוץ.

יד אברהם

אֵין שׁוֹרִין אֶת הַחִלְתִּית — *We may not soak asafetida*

[A gum resin having a bitter, acrid taste and obnoxious odor, obtained from the roots of several umbelliforous plants of the genus *Ferula*.]

This plant has a hot flavor and is for that reason popular in cold lands (*Rav; Rambam, comm.*).

Alternatively, this was used for therapeutic purposes (*Rashi*). Indeed, the *Gemara* 140a relates that this was used as a remedy for heaviness of the heart, a type of chest pain (*Meiri*). [This obviously refers to a noncritical condition, since in a life-threatening situation even Biblical prohibitions may be violated.]

Meiri and *Shulchan Aruch* 321:18 account for this prohibition as a precautionary measure lest one crush roots and herbs for medicinal purposes. The *Gemara* (140a), however, states that the reason is because it is reminiscent of a weekday activity. The *Gemara* adds this reason to explain that it is forbidden to soak it even for nonmedical uses, such as a beverage (*Beur Halachah* to *Shulchan Aruch* ibid.). [It is possible that it is for this very reason considered a weekday activity; i.e., because it appears that one is preparing a drug rather than a beverage. (See preface to Ch. 18.)]

בְּפוֹשְׁרִין — *in warm water,*

Soaking the roots in cold water however is permissible. [Since it is generally soaked in warm water, soaking it in cold water is not reminiscent of weekday activities.] The *Gemara* explains that the mishnah expresses the view of R' Yose. The Sages, however, prohibit soaking in cold water as well. The halachah is in accordance with the Sages (*Gem.* ibid.; *Rambam, Hil. Shabbos* 21:7).

אֲבָל נוֹתֵן לְתוֹךְ הַחֹמֶץ. — *but one may put [it] into vinegar.*

I.e., one may add asafetida to vinegar and dip his food into it (*Rashi*). Since healthy people partake of this concoction, it is not apparent that one's intention is for medicinal purposes. That being the case, the Rab-

3. We may not soak asafetida in warm water, but one may put [it] into vinegar. We may not soak vetches nor rub them, but one may put [them] into a sieve or into a basket. We may not sift straw with a sieve, nor put it on a high place so that the chaff will drop;

YAD AVRAHAM

binic injunction against the use of medicaments on the Sabbath does not apply. See above 14:3 (*Meiri; Tif. Yis.*). It is therefore permissible to do so even if one's intent is, indeed, for therapeutic purposes (*Beur Halachah* to 319:18).

Others explain that by soaking it in vinegar rather than water, he alters the preparation from its usual medicinal form. It is, therefore, not considered a weekday activity (*Mareh HaPenim, Yerushalmi* ad. loc.).

וְאֵין שׁוֹרִין אֶת הַכַּרְשִׁינִין — *We may not soak vetches*

This is a species of bean used for cattle fodder. Before feeding it to the cattle, it is soaked in water to soften it. See above 1:4 (*Meleches Shlomo*).

In some editions of the mishnah, the word appears as שׁוֹלִין, *to make float*. I.e., we may not pour water over them to make the refuse float to the top (*Rashi; Rav; Mishnah* as printed in the *Gemara*).

According to both versions this is done to separate the refuse from the food (by having it either float to the top or sink to the bottom). Doing so constitutes *sorting.

וְלֹא שָׁפִין אוֹתָן, — *nor rub them,*

I.e., one may not rub vetch with his hands to remove the refuse. This, too, is prohibited as *sorting (*Rav; Rashi*). [*Sorting is permitted only when one extracts the usable part while leaving behind the refuse, and even this, only if done by hand immediately before eating. To remove the refuse while leaving behind the usable part is forbidden even by hand. See 7:2.]

אֲבָל נוֹתֵן לְתוֹךְ הַכְּבָרָה אוֹ לְתוֹךְ הַכַּלְכָּלָה. — *but one may put [them] into a sieve or into a basket.*

I.e., one may put them into a sieve or basket for storage even though the refuse will sometimes fall through the holes of the sieve, thereby automatically sorting the food (*Rav; Rashi*). Since he has no intention of sorting them, and it is not inevitable that they will be sorted, it is permissible (*Mishnah Berurah* 319:30 and *Beur Halachah* there). [To put it into a sieve in order to sort it is obviously prohibited.]

אֵין כּוֹבְרִין אֶת הַתֶּבֶן בִּכְבָרָה, — *We may not sift straw with a sieve,*

I.e., straw that has been chopped up by means of a threshing-ledge (*Rav; Rashi*).

וְלֹא יִתְּנֶנּוּ עַל־גַּבֵּי מָקוֹם גָּבוֹהַּ בִּשְׁבִיל שֶׁיֵּרֵד הַמּוֹץ; — *nor put it on a high place so that the chaff will drop;*

I.e., one may not put the straw on a high place so that the inedible chaff blows away, leaving only the edible parts for the cattle (*Meiri*). This is probably a *toladah* of *winnowing.

Others explain that one may not place a sieve containing straw on a high place, so that the chaff falls through the holes, leaving clean straw for livestock. This constitutes *sifting (*Rambam, Hil. Shabbos* 21:32).

אֲבָל נוֹטֵל הוּא בִּכְבָרָה וְנוֹתֵן לְתוֹךְ הָאֵבוּס.

[ד] **גּוֹרְפִין** מִלִּפְנֵי הַפְּטָם, וּמְסַלְּקִין לַצְּדָדִין מִפְּנֵי הָרְעִי — דִּבְרֵי רַבִּי דוֹסָא. וַחֲכָמִים אוֹסְרִין.

נוֹטְלִין מִלִּפְנֵי בְהֵמָה זוֹ וְנוֹתְנִין לִפְנֵי בְהֵמָה זוֹ בַּשַּׁבָּת.

[ה] **הַקַּשׁ** שֶׁעַל-גַּבֵּי הַמִּטָּה, לֹא יְנַעְנְעוֹ

ר' עובדיה מברטנורא

אבל נוטל בכברה ונותן לתוך האבוס. ואף על פי שהמון נופל מאליו, דדבר שאינו מתכוין מותר כרבי שמעון: (ד) גורפין. בשבת אבוס שלפני השור שמפטמים אותו, שלא יתערב העפרורית שבאבוס בתבן ובשטורים שנותנים לפיו ויקוץ במאכלו, ומסלקין תבן שלפניו לצדדים כשהוא רב כדי שלא ידרסנו ברגליו ויתלכלך ברעי: וחכמים אוסרים. אתרוייהו קאי, אחד גריפת האבוס ואחד תבן שלפניו לא יסלקנו לצדדים. ולא נחלקו רבי דוסא וחכמים אלא באבוס של כלי, אבל באבוס של קרקע הכל מודים שאין גורפים, דלמא אתי לאשוויי גומות. ורבנן גזרו אבוס של כלי אטו אבוס של קרקע. והלכה כחכמים: נוטלים מלפני הבהמה זו ונותנים לפני זו. ולא אמרינן טלטול דלא חזי הוי, אלא ודאי חזי אין דאין בהמה קלה במאכל הגיעל מלפני חבירתה. ודוקא מלפני החמור ונותנין לפני השור וכיוצא בזה, אבל לא מלפני השור ונותנים לפני החמור, שמאכל השור מאוס בריריו היוצאים מפיו ואין החמור אוכל ממנו. סתמא להסקה ומוקצה הוא, ובא לשכב עליו

יד אברהם

אֲבָל נוֹטֵל הוּא בִּכְבָרָה וְנוֹתֵן לְתוֹךְ הָאֵבוּס. — *but one may take it up in a sieve and pour [it] into the feeding-trough.*

I.e., he may scoop the straw up with a sieve and pour it into the animal's feeding-trough. Although some chaff may thereby be eliminated by falling through the holes in the sieve, it is permissible since he does not intend to sort the straw. This fits into the category of דָּבָר שֶׁאֵינוֹ מִתְכַּוֵּן, *an unintended labor*, which is permissible according to R' Shimon where it is not inevitable (*Rav; Rashi; Rambam*, ibid.; see General Introduction, p. 8).

4.

גּוֹרְפִין מִלִּפְנֵי הַפְּטָם — *We may sweep out [the feeding-trough] from before a stall ox,*

I.e., we may clean out on the Sabbath the cinders and dirt from a manger so that they will not become mingled with the ox's food, thereby causing the food to be revolting to him (*Rav; Rashi*).

וּמְסַלְּקִין לַצְּדָדִין — *and we may move it to the sides*

When there is too much straw and fodder before the ox, we may move it aside (*Rav; Rashi*).

מִפְּנֵי הָרְעִי — *because of the excretum —*

I.e., lest the ox tread the fodder with his feet and dirty it with his excretum (*Rav; Rashi*).

20
4-5

but one may take it up in a sieve and pour [it] into the feeding-trough.

4. We may sweep out [the feeding-trough] from before a stall ox, and we may move it to the sides because of the excretum — [these are] the words of R' Dosa. But the Sages prohibit [it].

We may take [feed] from before one animal and place it before another animal on the Sabbath.

5. Straw that is on the bed, one may not move it

YAD AVRAHAM

Others explain this to mean that we may move the refuse aside for a pasture ox, who is not as particular as a stall ox (*Meiri*).

דִּבְרֵי רַבִּי דּוֹסָא. וַחֲכָמִים אוֹסְרִין. — [these are] the words of R' Dosa. But the Sages prohibit [it].

Both R' Dosa and the Sages agree that one may not sweep out a feeding-trough that has an earthen floor. This is prohibited for fear that while doing so one will flatten out any irregularities in the floor. [It was customary to do so in order that bits of feed not get stuck in the crevices of the manger (*Tos.* 140b).] To flatten out the floor of the trough violates the *melachah* of *building. For this same reason, one may not move aside the excess feed. The mishnah, however, is discussing a trough which is a utensil. Since it does not have an earthen floor, R' Dosa sees no reason to prohibit it. The Sages, however, prohibit it for fear people will fail to distinguish between a utensil and an earthen-floored trough (*Rav* from *Gem.* 140b).

נוֹטְלִין מִלִּפְנֵי בְהֵמָה זוֹ וְנוֹתְנִין לִפְנֵי בְהֵמָה זוֹ בַּשַּׁבָּת. — We may take [feed] from before one animal and place it before another animal on the Sabbath.

I.e., we may take away feed from before one animal and place it before another. Since one animal will eat the leftovers of another, moving the feed from one trough to another is a useful activity and therefore permissible. However, one may not take feed from an ox and give it to a donkey. Since an ox drools while eating, he makes the food repugnant to a donkey, who is more fastidious. Moving it is therefore unproductive and consequently prohibited (*Rav, Rashi* from *Gem.* ibid.).

5.

The following mishnah deals with *muktzeh* (see prefatory note to Chapter 17).

הַקַּשׁ שֶׁעַל־גַּבֵּי־הַמִּטָּה, — Straw that is on the bed,

Straw is usually used for kindling. Since it may not be used for that on the Sabbath, it is *muktzeh* (*Rav; Rashi*).

In this case, a person wishes to move straw in order to be able to lie down on the bed. *Rosh* (3:19) explains that he wishes to move the straw in order to make it comfortable to lie on. *Ran* (to *Gem.* 43b) explains that he wishes to remove the straw entirely.

שבת כ/ה

בְּיָדוֹ, אֶלָּא מְנַעְנְעוֹ בְּגוּפוֹ; וְאִם הָיָה מַאֲכַל בְּהֵמָה, אוֹ שֶׁהָיָה עָלָיו כַּר אוֹ סָדִין, מְנַעְנְעוֹ בְּיָדוֹ.

מַכְבֵּשׁ שֶׁל בַּעֲלֵי בָתִּים מַתִּירִין, אֲבָל לֹא כוֹבְשִׁין; וְשֶׁל כּוֹבְסִין, לֹא יִגַּע בּוֹ.

ר' עובדיה מברטנורא

ומנטנטו כדי שיהא רך וצף לשכב עליו: **לא ינענעו בידיו.** דמוקצה הוא, **אבל מנענעו בגופו** בכתפיו, דטלטול מן הצד הוא ולאו שמיה טלטול: **או שהיה עליו כר או סדין,** דגלי דעתיה דאקפייה לשכיבה מטמה תורת כלי עליו: **מכבש.** שני לוחות שמשימין ביניהן הבגדים לאחר כביסתן ומהדקין הלוח העליון על הבגדים המונחים בלוח התחתון כדי שיהא קיפולן נאה: **מתירין.** דהיינו לצורך שבת ליטול את הבגדים, אבל לא כובשים דהיינו צורך חול. **ושל כובסים לא יגע בו.** מפני שהוא עשוי לתקן בגדים ומהדק טפי והתרתו דומה לסתירה. ואין הלכה כרבי יהודה:

יד אברהם

לֹא יְנַעְנְעוֹ בְּיָדוֹ, — one may not move it with his hand,

Since it is *muktzeh*, one may not move it with his hand (*Rav; Rashi*).

אֶלָּא מְנַעְנְעוֹ בְּגוּפוֹ; — but he may move it with his body;

I.e., while lying down on the bed he may shift around the straw.

Since he moves the straw in an unusual fashion (with his body rather than his hands) it is regarded as an *indirect movement* of *muktzeh*, i.e., it is accorded the same rules as indirect movement of *muktzeh*, which is permissible.

Indirect movement of *muktzeh* is permitted only when it is done for the sake of a non-*muktzeh* object, i.e., to facilitate the use of a non-*muktzeh* object.[1] It is, how-

---

1. There are several opinions as to what the rule of *indirect movement of muktzeh* is. (See *Gem.* 43b and *Tos.* there.) The ruling given here expresses the opinion which the halachah follows. (See *Tos.* ibid., *Shulchan Aruch* 311:8.)

As explained, moving *muktzeh* in an unusual fashion (shifting the straw with one's body rather than with one's hands) is accorded the same rules as indirect movement of *muktzeh*. It should, therefore, be permissible only if one is moving the *muktzeh* (the straw) for the sake of a non-*muktzeh* object. According to *Ran* quoted above (s.v. הַקַּשׁ שֶׁעַל גַּבֵּי הַמִּטָּה) this presents no problem, since the straw is being pushed off the bed in order to be better able to use the bed (a non-*muktzeh* object). According to *Rosh*, however, who explains that the straw is being moved to make the straw itself into a more comfortable mattress, one is moving the *muktzeh* to better utilize the *muktzeh* object itself. This should, as explained above, be prohibited even through indirect movement.

As a result of this difficulty, *Rosh* (as explained by *Magen Avraham* and *Machtzis HaShekel* 311:24) concludes that moving *muktzeh* with one's body has even more lenient rules than indirect movement of *muktzeh*. Whereas the latter is permitted only for the sake of a non-*muktzeh* object, the former is permitted even for the sake of a *muktzeh* one. This opinion is adopted by *Shulchan Aruch* 311:8; see also *Rama* 308:3). This is the origin of the custom permitting the movement of *muktzeh* with one's foot (cf. notes of *R' Akiva Eiger* on *Magen Avraham* 279:9 who places certain restrictons on this rule). However this interpretation of *Rosh* is not universally accepted (*Chazon Ish* 47:13,14).

20
5

with his hand, but he may move it with his body; and if it was fodder for animals, or if a pillow or a sheet was over it, he may move it with his hand.

A householder's clothes-press we may undo, but we may not press down. A launderer's [press, however], one may not touch.

YAD AVRAHAM

ever, prohibited to move a *muktzeh* object even indirectly *for the sake of the muktzeh object itself,* i.e., to utilize or protect the *muktzeh* object. (See 21:2 for a full explanation of this.)

וְאִם הָיָה מַאֲכַל בְּהֵמָה, — *and if it was fodder for animals,*

I.e., if the straw had been reserved prior to the Sabbath for use as animal fodder, it is not *muktzeh.*

אוֹ שֶׁהָיָה עָלָיו כַּר אוֹ סָדִין, — *or if a pillow or a sheet was over it,*

By placing a pillow or a sheet over the straw, he indicates his intention to use it as a bed. Thus, it is no longer set aside for kindling but acquires the status of a utensil (bed) (*Rav; Rashi*).

מְנַעְנְעוֹ בְּיָדוֹ. — *he may move it with his hand.*

Since it is not *muktzeh.* This special designation is required only in places where straw is usually used for kindling. In our countries, however, straw is usually used for fodder. It is, therefore, not *muktzeh* even if it was not specifically designated for either of these (*Magen Avraham* 308:53).

מַכְבֵּשׁ שֶׁל בַּעֲלֵי בָתִּים — *A householder's clothes-press*

This was composed of two long, heavy boards. Garments were laid out on the lower one and the upper one was then lowered upon them to press them. Four posts were set in the four corners of the lower board. Corresponding to these four posts were four holes in the upper board, through which the posts passed. The upper board would move up or down along these posts. When the upper board was pressed down sufficiently, pegs were inserted into specially placed holes in the posts, thereby holding the upper board in place (*Rashi; Tos. Yom Tov*). [Since the pressing was achieved through pressure rather than heat, the board had to be held in place for some length of time.]

מַתִּירִין, — *we may undo,*

I.e., we may undo the press to remove the garments for Sabbath wear (*Rav; Rashi*).

אֲבָל לֹא כּוֹבְשִׁין. — *but we may not press down.*

Pressing the garments prepares them for use after the Sabbath (*Rav; Rashi*) [for they would not be ready for use on the Sabbath].

וְשֶׁל כּוֹבְסִין, לֹא יִגַּע בּוֹ. — *A launderer's [press, however,] one may not touch.*

I.e., one may not undo it. Since it is made to shape clothing, it is pressed together very tightly. Undoing it is therefore (Rabbinically) considered akin to *demolishing (Rav; Rashi).

Others rule that even if it is already undone, one may not handle it. Since it is used for professional work, and

שבת כ/ה

רַבִּי יְהוּדָה אוֹמֵר: אִם הָיָה מַתָּר מֵעֶרֶב שַׁבָּת, מַתִּיר אֶת כֻּלּוֹ וְשׁוֹמְטוֹ.

יד אברהם

may be damaged by using it for other purposes, it is regarded as *muktzeh* due to fear of monetary loss (*Rambam, Hil. Shabbos* 26:12; see prefatory note to Chapter 17.)

רַבִּי יְהוּדָה אוֹמֵר: אִם הָיָה מַתָּר מֵעֶרֶב שַׁבָּת, מַתִּיר אֶת כֻּלּוֹ — *R' Yehudah says: If it was undone from before the Sabbath, one may undo it completely*

I.e., if it was partially undone before the Sabbath, even though it was still partially fastened one may undo it completely (*Tif. Yis.*).

וְשׁוֹמְטוֹ. — *and remove it.*

I.e., he may remove his garment (*Meleches Shlomo*).

Other editions read: מַתִּיר אֶת־כֵּלָיו וְשׁוֹמְטָן, *He may release his garments and remove them* (*Rif* according to printed version). [In effect, this means the same as our editions.] Still others read: מַכִּיר אֶת כֵּלָיו וְשׁוֹמְטָן, *if he recognizes his garments, he may remove them.* The meaning is that if the press is *completely* open, one may remove his garments from among the garments of all the other customers of the launderer (*Meleches Shlomo; Bach, Tur* 302).

There is a question whether R' Yehudah is in dispute with the *Tanna Kamma* or not. According to *Rambam*, who explains that the *Tanna Kamma* regards the launderer's press as *muktzeh*, R' Yehudah obviously differs with the *Tanna Kamma*, since there

20
5 R' Yehudah says: If it was undone from before the Sabbath, one may undo it completely and remove it.

YAD AVRAHAM

is no reason to permit opening *muktzeh* just because it is already partially open. *Rambam*, therefore, rejects R' Yehudah's view in his *Commentary*, as well as in *Hilchos Shabbos* 26:12.

If, however, the press is completely open and the garments may be removed without moving the press at all, even the *Tanna Kamma* concurs that one is permitted to remove them (*R' Akiva Eiger* 302).

According to *Rashi*, however, who prohibits removing the garments because opening the press is akin to *demolishing, it is possible to assume that R' Yehudah and the *Tanna Kamma* do not differ. Since the press is already partially open it is possible that opening it completely is not viewed as resembling demolition. Indeed, many authorities rule that even the *Tanna Kamma* permits opening the press and removing the garments in concurrence with R' Yehudah (*Rabbeinu Yerucham* 12:13; *Eliyah Rabba* 302:11). Others, however, rule that the *Tanna Kamma* and R' Yehudah disagree on this issue, and that the *Tanna Kamma* prohibits opening the press completely even though it is already partially opened. This is as a precaution lest one infer that he may open it even if it is completely closed (*Maggid Mishneh, Hil. Shabbos* 26:12).

As mentioned above, *Tur* explains R' Yehudah as referring to the case in which the press was completely opened before the Sabbath. According to him, there is definitely no dispute between the *Tanna Kamma* and R' Yehudah (*R' Akiva Eiger*, ibid.).

פרק עשרים ואחד
Chapter Twenty-One

This chapter deals with exceptions to the ban on moving *muktzeh* (*Meiri*). In the course of this, various items deemed intrinsically *muktzeh* are discussed [see preface to Ch. 17 (c)].

Specifically discussed are stones, which are *muktzeh* because they are neither fashioned into utensils nor designated for any particular use, and therefore do not stand to be used on the Sabbath. Money, too, although a medium of exchange, is not regarded as a utensil because no actual use is made of the coin itself.

Terumah, which has contracted *tumah*-contamination, may not be eaten, but may be used for kindling. Since its use for kindling is forbidden on the Sabbath, it is therefore also regarded as *muktzeh* (see 18:1).

A permissible article upon which a *muktzeh* article is placed before the Sabbath to remain there on the Sabbath becomes a בָּסִיס לְדָבָר הָאָסוּר, *a base for a prohibited article*, and, it, too, is *muktzeh*. One exception is if an object is a base to both *muktzeh* and non-*muktzeh*. Its status depends on which of these is more important. If the non-*muktzeh* is the more important of the two, the base is considered to be supporting primarily the non-*muktzeh* and is therefore itself non-*muktzeh*. If, however, the *muktzeh* is more important, the base is considered to be primarily supporting the *muktzeh* and is, in consequence, also *muktzeh*.

Also explained in this chapter are the rules of indirect movement of *muktzeh* (see prefatory note to mishnah 2).

The first mishnah illustrates instances in which *muktzeh* articles may be moved together with non-*muktzeh* articles.

שבת כא/א

[א] **נוֹטֵל אָדָם** אֶת בְּנוֹ וְהָאֶבֶן בְּיָדוֹ, וְכַלְכָּלָה וְהָאֶבֶן בְּתוֹכָהּ. וּמְטַלְטְלִין תְּרוּמָה טְמֵאָה עִם הַטְּהוֹרָה

ר' עובדיה מברטנורא

פרק עשרים ואחד – נוטל אדם. (א) נוטל אדם את בנו. בחצר והאבן בידו ולא אמרינן דמטלטל לאבן. **סל: בכלכלה.** והוא שיהיו פירות בסל, שאם אין בו פירות נעשה בסיס לדבר האסור ואסור לטלטלו. וצריך נמי שיהיו בתוכו פירות שאם ישליכם בארץ ימאסו, כגון תותים וענבים וכיוצא בהם, אבל אם היו בו פירות כגון אגוזים ושקדים מנער את הפירות והם נופלים. ופירות הנמאסים נמי כגון תותים וענבים אם אפשר לסלקם לצדי הכלכלה ולנער האבן לבדה ולהשליכה אסור לטלטלה עם האבן. ומתניתין איירי כגון שנפתח מלמטה הכלכלה או שוליה והאבן דופן לה שאי אפשר להשתמש בכלכלה בלא האבן: **תרומה טמאה עם הטהורה ועם החולין.** אגב הטהורה ואגב החולין. אבל טמאה באנפי נפשה לאו בת טלטול היא: אף מעלין את המדומע באחד ומאה. סאה של תרומה שנפלה במאה סאים של חולין, מותר להעלותה לסאה של תרומה מהן בשבת ויהיו כולן חולין ומותרין לזרים, ולא אמרינן מתקן הוא, דתרומה שנפלה בחולין חשבינן לה כאילו מונחת לבדה ואינה מעורבת, וכשיעלה סאה ומאה באחד והתרומה עצמה שנפלה עולה הילכך לאו מתקן הוא. ואין הלכה כרבי יהודה:

יד אברהם

1.

נוֹטֵל אָדָם אֶת בְּנוֹ — *A man may pick up his son*

I.e., he may pick him up in [a house or in] a yard in which one is permitted to carry on the Sabbath (*Rav; Rashi; Tif. Yis.*).

וְהָאֶבֶן בְּיָדוֹ, — *[although] there is a stone in his hand,*

Although the child is holding a stone which he refuses to drop, and even though the stone is *muktzeh*, the father is permitted to pick up the child, and is not regarded as handling the stone itself (*Rav; Tif. Yis.*).

The *Gemara* (141b) qualifies the mishnah as referring only to a child who is so attached to his father that if his father does not pick him up, he may become ill. Even though the child's life is not endangered, the Rabbis permitted the father to pick him up since he is not handling the stone directly (*Rashi*).

The Rabbis did not require the father to force the child to drop the rock, since this would add to the child's distress (*Tos.* 142a).

Others rule that, although there is no danger that the child will become ill, since parting with his father causes him anguish, the Rabbis permitted the father to pick him up despite the stone in his hand (*Meiri*).

This dispensation was granted only if the child was holding a stone. Should he be holding a coin, however, no leniency was granted because the Rabbis feared that the child might drop the coin and the father would then be tempted to pick it up (*Gem* 142a). Consequently, even if the child walks with the coin in his hand, the father may not hold his hand, lest he drop the coin and the father be tempted to pick it up (*Rashi on Gem.* ibid.).

Others, however, assert that the *Gemara* means only to prohibit carrying a child with a coin in his hand. Walking with him, though, is permitted (*Ran from Ramban*).

1.

A man may pick up his son [although] there is a stone in his hand, or a basket [although] there is a stone in it. [Similarly,] we may move contaminated *terumah* together with uncontaminated *terumah*

YAD AVRAHAM

They explain that just as we do not ordinarily prohibit someone to stand next to a child who is holding a coin, so too, we do not prohibit his walking next to him. Only if permitted to carry the coin indirectly (by carrying the child) did the Rabbis fear that he might extend this leniency to carrying the coin directly.

וְכַלְכָּלָה וְהָאֶבֶן בְּתוֹכָהּ. — *or a basket [although] there is a stone in it.*

The *Gemara* explains that the stone is being used to fill a hole in the basket; consequently, the stone becomes part of the structure of the basket and is no longer *muktzeh* (*Tos. Yom Tov; Tif. Yis.* from *Gem.* 142a). [This is similar to the rule stated in 17:6.]

Others explain this mishnah as referring to a basket that has both a stone and fruit in it. In this way, the basket is a base to both a prohibited object (stone) and a permissible object (fruit). Should it contain only the stone, however, the basket would be a בָּסִיס לְדָבָר הָאָסוּר, *base for a prohibited object,* and would itself be regarded as *muktzeh*. In addition to this condition, two other conditions are required for permissibility to pick up the basket: (a) The fruit must be of a variety that is damaged when dumped out of the basket, such as mulberries, grapes or wet fruit which will become soiled; and (b) the situation must be such that the fruit cannot be pushed aside in the basket while the stone itself is being shaken out. If the basket contains a variety not damaged or soiled when dumped (such as nuts), so that they can be dumped from the basket together with the stone and then replaced by themselves, or if the fruit can be moved aside while the stone itself is shaken out, the basket may not be carried while the stone is still in it[1] (*Rambam, Hil. Shabbos* 26:16 as explained by *Maggid Mishneh*. This is based on a variant text in the *Gemara*).[2]

Both of these explanations are accepted as halachah (*Shulchan Aruch* 309:2,3).

וּמְטַלְטְלִין תְּרוּמָה טְמֵאָה עִם הַטְּהוֹרָה — *[Similarly] we may move contaminated terumah together with uncontaminated terumah*

Terumah which is *tamei* (contaminated) may not be eaten even by a *Kohen*. Since the only other thing for which it may be used is kindling —

---

1. All these requirements are necessary only if the basket is being moved for the purpose of using the fruit or the basket itself. If, however, one moves the basket because he needs the place occupied by the basket, he need not dump the contents of the basket even when this is feasible. Since the stone would merely replace the basket in preventing the use of the space, this procedure would accomplish nothing.

2. *Rav*, following *Rambam* in his commentary, has a different explanation of the mishnah, which seems to have been based on an alternate text in the *Gemara*. It poses, however, many difficulties, as pointed out by *Beis Yosef* 309 and *Tos. Yom Tov*. (See *Meiri* to this mishnah who answers some of these problems.) Indeed, *Rambam* himself in *Hilchos Shabbos* seems to have retracted that explanation (*Beis Yosef* ibid.). For this reason, it has been omitted.

שבת
כא/א

וְעִם הַחֻלִּין.
רַבִּי יְהוּדָה אוֹמֵר: אַף מַעֲלִין אֶת הַמְדֻמָּע בְּאֶחָד וּמֵאָה.

יד אברהם

which is forbidden on the Sabbath — it is obviously completely unusable on the Sabbath. Consequently, it is deemed *muktzeh* (*Meiri; Rashi; Rav*).

The mishnah, however, discusses a case in which both the contaminated and uncontaminated *terumah* are together in one container. This container is a base to both *muktzeh* (contaminated *terumah*) and non-*muktzeh* (uncontaminated *terumah*). Since the uncontaminated *terumah* is more valuable than the contaminated *terumah*, the base may be moved.

The *Gemara* (142a) qualifies the mishnah as referring to the case in which the contaminated *terumah* lies atop the uncontaminated *terumah*. Otherwise, the uncontaminated *terumah* could be removed and carried[1] while leaving the contaminated *terumah* in its place. Furthermore, even if the contaminated *terumah* lies atop the uncontaminated *terumah*, the basket may not be moved with the contaminated *terumah* in it unless it contains juicy fruit which will be soiled if shaken out. Otherwise, the contaminated *terumah* can be removed by dumping everything out of the basket and then replacing the uncontaminated *terumah*.[2]

וְעִם הַחֻלִּין. — *or with ordinary food.*

[The requirements mentioned above, in reference to moving contaminated *terumah* with uncontaminated *terumah*, apply equally to moving contaminated *terumah* with ordinary (i.e., unsanctified) food.]

רַבִּי יְהוּדָה אוֹמֵר: אַף מַעֲלִין אֶת הַמְדֻמָּע בְּאֶחָד וּמֵאָה. — *R' Yehudah says: We may also remove one part of terumah from a mixture with a hundred parts of ordinary food.*

If *terumah* becomes mixed with ordinary food, the entire mixture receives the stringency of *terumah*, i.e., it may be eaten only by a *Kohen*. If one-part *terumah* becomes mixed with one hundred parts of ordinary food, however, the *terumah* becomes nullified and the mixture may be eaten by anyone. Although it no longer has any sanctity, one part must be removed to avoid depriving the *Kohanim* of their due (*Terumos* 4:7).[3]

Should one possess such a mixture

---

1. As above, all these qualifications are required if one needs the *terumah* or the basket. If one needs the place which the basket is occupying, however, he may move the basket as is.

2. *Tosafos* add that this requirement applies only when the uncontaminated *terumah* is in an individual small basket within the large basket. If it is lying loose in the large basket, however, the basket may be carried as is, since without it he has no container in which to hold the uncontaminated *terumah*.

3. This method does not help if the mixture is one-part *terumah* to less than 100-parts ordinary food. Since there is no guarantee or even likelihood that the one part being removed is the original *terumah*, that *terumah* still possesses the rules of sanctity; namely, that it be eaten by a *Kohen* only. Therefore, even after removing one part, the *terumah* may still possibly be in the mixture. Consequently, a non-*Kohen* may not eat any part of

21
1
or with ordinary food.

R' Yehudah says: We may also remove one part of *terumah* from a mixture with a hundred parts of ordinary food.

YAD AVRAHAM

on the Sabbath, the *Tanna Kamma* rules that he may not remove the *terumah*, since this act renders the mixture permissible. It is, therefore, regarded as making it fit, or improving it, and is forbidden on the Sabbath (see above 2:7). R' Yehudah, however, maintains that the mixture can be rendered fit without any overt act by merely deciding which pieces he intends to remove for the *Kohen* and then eating produce from the other side of the pile. Therefore, removing it physically is not the factor that renders the mixture fit. Since the thought process involved in deciding which fruit to give to the *Kohen* is not apparent to the onlooker, one does not *appear* to be fixing (*Tif. Yis.* from *Gem.* 142). [The *Tanna Kamma* apparently holds that the mixture can be rendered fit only by removing one part. Hence, he appears to be fixing the mixture.]

Rav, following *Rambam's commentary*, explains that R' Yehudah's leniency is based on a different principle. Since the *terumah* has lost its rules of sanctity and the only necessity to remove one part is to protect the *Kohen's* property rights, the law *presumes* that the one part removed is, in fact, the original part of *terumah* which became mixed in. Although no statistical basis exists for this presumption, it is nevertheless employed in instances where the *terumah* is only of Rabbinic origin. By extension, R' Yehudah applies it to where the obligation to remove one part is also only Rabbinic. Since the part removed is *presumed* to be the original *terumah*, even before it is removed the mixture is not regarded as a true mixture but rather as two distinct piles of produce — one *terumah* and one ordinary food. Consequently, the ordinary food was never actually forbidden and the removal of the *terumah* from it, therefore, did not in any way affect it.

Tiferes Yisrael points out that this interpretation, although initially considered, is not the one finally adopted by the *Gemara*.

The halachah is not in accordance with R' Yehudah (*Rav; Rambam, Comm.*).

2.

◆§ Indirect Movement of Muktzeh

The mishnah discusses the rules of *indirect movement of muktzeh*. This refers to moving the *muktzeh* without direct contact with it but through the medium of another object. This may occur when the *muktzeh* is inside or atop of a non-*muktzeh* object which one wishes to move. By moving the non-*muktzeh* object one moves the *muktzeh* object as well, without, however, direct contact with the *muktzeh*. This is permitted under the following conditions:

(a) The purpose of this movement must be to facilitate the use of a non-

the mixture for fear of eating the forbidden (to him) *terumah*. Only when the *terumah* has become nullified by becoming mixed with one hundred or more parts of ordinary food, and its sanctity has thus been lost, can one rectify the situation by arbitrarily removing one part. Since the only consideration remaining is to protect the property rights of the *Kohen*, any one part suffices.

שבת כא/ב

[ב] **הָאֶבֶן** שֶׁעַל־פִּי הֶחָבִית, מַטָּהּ עַל צִדָּהּ וְהִיא נוֹפֶלֶת. הָיְתָה בֵּין הֶחָבִיּוֹת, מַגְבִּיהָהּ וּמַטָּהּ עַל צִדָּהּ וְהִיא נוֹפֶלֶת. מָעוֹת שֶׁעַל הַכַּר, נוֹעֵר אֶת הַכַּר וְהֵן נוֹפְלוֹת. הָיְתָה עָלָיו לִשְׁלֶשֶׁת, מְקַנְּחָהּ בִּסְמַרְטוּט.

ר' עובדיה מברטנורא

(ב) **מטה על צדה.** מטה החבית על צדה אם צריך ליטול מן היין והאבן נופלת ולא יטול אותה בידיה: **היתה בין החביות.** ומתירא שלא תפול האבן על החביות ותשברם מגביהה לחבית כולה ומסלקה מבין החביות ושם מטה אותה על צדה: **נוער את הכר והן נופלות.** כשהוא צריך לכר ואינו צריך למקום הכר, אבל אם צריך למקומו מגביה הכר עם המעות שעליו. ולא אמרן אלא כשלא שכחם המעות על הכר מערב שבת, אבל הניחן שם במתכוין נעשה הכר בסיס לדבר האסור ואסור לטלטלו ולא לנער המעות שעליו: **לשלשת.** דבר של טנוף כגון רוק או רעי או צואה: **מקנחה בסמרטוט.** ולא יתן עליה מים, דסתם כר של בגד הוא, ובגד שרייתו במים זהו כבוסו:

יד אברהם

muktzeh object, i.e., if as part of one's use of a non-*muktzeh* object, or as a prelude to its use, one must *indirectly* move the *muktzeh*, too, it is permitted. One may not, however, move *muktzeh* indirectly for the benefit of the *muktzeh*, e.g., to put it in a safe place.

(b) One must first try to remove the *muktzeh* by tilting the non-*muktzeh* object so that the *muktzeh* slides off. Although this, too, is an *indirect movement of muktzeh*, when feasible, it is preferable to actually carrying the non-*muktzeh* with the *muktzeh* on it.

(c) The *muktzeh* should not have been left on the non-*muktzeh* with the intention that it remain on it for the Sabbath. This may occur when one forgets to remove the *muktzeh* before the Sabbath or when the *muktzeh* falls on the non-*muktzeh*. If, however, one leaves the *muktzeh* in or atop the non-*muktzeh* with the intent that it remain there for the Sabbath,[1] the non-*muktzeh* itself becomes a *base to the muktzeh* and it too is deemed *muktzeh* (even if the *muktzeh* should somehow be removed on the Sabbath).

הָאֶבֶן שֶׁעַל־פִּי הֶחָבִית, — *A stone which is on the opening of a cask,*

I.e., if a stone is covering the mouth of a cask from which one wishes to draw wine. Since the stone is *muktzeh*, he may not remove it directly (*Rav*; *Rashi*). Instead, he may ...

מַטָּהּ עַל צִדָּהּ וְהִיא נוֹפֶלֶת — *one may tilt it* [i.e., the cask] *on its side so that it* [i.e., the stone] *falls off.*

[This is a form of indirect movement of *muktzeh*, since one is not directly handling the stone but rather moving it via the cask. Since it is done

---

1. The authorities differ whether this means the intent to leave it there for the entire Sabbath (*Tos.* 51a, 123a) or whether it means the intent to leave it there only for the onset of the Sabbath (*Rashi* 51a). *Mishnah Berurah* (309:21) rules that one should follow the more stringent (i.e., *Rashi's*) opinion. However, in cases of financial loss one may rely on the more lenient opinion.

2. A stone which is on the opening of a cask, one may tilt on its side so that it falls off. [If] it was among the [other] casks, one may lift it and [then] tilt it on its side so that it falls off.

Money which is on a pillow, one may shake the pillow so that it falls off. [If] there was filth on it, he may wipe it off with a rag.

YAD AVRAHAM

to enable one to draw wine from the cask, it is permissible.]

הָיְתָה בֵּין הֶחָבִיּוֹת — *[If] it* [i.e., the cask upon which the stone is lying] *was among the [other] casks,*

By causing the stone to fall off there is danger of breaking the other casks (*Rav; Rashi*).

מַגְבִּיהָהּ — *one may lift it*

I.e., one may remove the cask he wishes to use (with the stone still on it) to a safe area (*Rav; Rashi*). [This, too, is an indirect movement of *muktzeh*, since he is in direct contact only with the cask.]

וּמַטָּהּ עַל־צִדָּהּ וְהִיא נוֹפֶלֶת — *and [then] tilt it on its side so that it falls off.*

I.e., upon reaching an area where he can slide the stone off the cask without causing any damage, he must do so (*Rav; Rashi*). [He may not continue to carry the cask any further without first removing the stone, since such movement is unnecessary.]

מָעוֹת שֶׁעַל הַכַּר — *Money which is on a pillow,*

[I.e., if money, which is *muktzeh*, is lying on a pillow, and one wishes to use that pillow.]

נוֹעֵר אֶת הַכַּר וְהֵן נוֹפְלוֹת — *one may shake the pillow so that it falls off.*

[Just as in the previous case of the stone on the cask.]

This restriction applies only if he wishes to use the pillow. If, however, he wishes to use the place being occupied by the pillow, he may pick up the pillow with the money still on it and carry it away (*Rav* from *Gem.* 142b). [Since shaking the money off the pillow onto the bed will in any case prevent him from using the space, the Rabbis permitted him to carry everything away (via the pillow) since this is an indirect movement of *muktzeh*.] This ruling applies as well to the case of the cask upon which the stone is lying (*Tur* 309; *Tos. Yom Tov*).

These two cases refer only to a *muktzeh* article *forgotten* atop a permissible article. Should one *intentionally* leave the *muktzeh* article there, the permissible article becomes a *base for a muktzeh article*, thus becoming *muktzeh* in its own right. This being the case, tilting the cask or shaking the pillow would be tantamount to handling the stone or money itself (*Rav* from *Gem.* ibid.).

הָיְתָה עָלָיו לִשְׁלֶשֶׁת — *[If] there was filth on it,*

I.e., if there was filth, such as spittle, excretum (*Rav; Rashi*), or bird droppings (*Aruch*) on the pillow.

מְקַנְּחָהּ בִּסְמַרְטוּט — *he may wipe it off with a rag.*

He may not apply water, however, since the pillow is made of cloth. Soaking cloth in water is tantamount

שבת כא/ג

הָיְתָה שֶׁל עוֹר, נוֹתְנִין עָלֶיהָ מַיִם עַד שֶׁתִּכְלֶה.

[ג] **בֵּית שַׁמַּאי** אוֹמְרִים: מַגְבִּיהִין מִן הַשֻּׁלְחָן עֲצָמוֹת וּקְלִפִּין. וּבֵית הִלֵּל אוֹמְרִים: נוֹטֵל אֶת הַטַּבְלָה כֻלָּהּ וּמְנַעֲרָהּ.

ר' עובדיה מברטנורא

הָיְתָה. עַל כַּר. דְּלָאו בַּר כִּבּוּס הוּא: נוֹתֵן עָלֶיהָ מַיִם. עַד שֶׁתִּכְלֶה וְתֵלֵךְ הַלְּכְלֶשֶׁת. אֲבָל כִּבּוּס מַמָּשׁ לֹא, דְּהוֹאִיל וּסְתָם כָּרִים וּכְסָתוֹת כָּרִים רַכִּים מִינַיְהוּ שַׁיָּיךְ בְּהוּ כִּבּוּס בִּתְעוּרוֹת רַכּוֹת, וּמֵימָיו שְׁרִיתָן לֹא זֶהוּ כִּבּוּסָן: (ג) בֵּית שַׁמַּאי אוֹמְרִים מַגְבִּיהִין מֵעַל הַשֻּׁלְחָן עֲצָמוֹת וּקְלִפִּין. בַּגְּמָרָא קָאָמַר שֶׁאֵין אָנוּ סוֹמְכִים עַל מִשְׁנָתֵנוּ כְּמוֹת שֶׁהִיא שְׁנוּיָה, אֶלָּא מוּחְלֶפֶת הַשִּׁיטָה, שְׁבֵית הִלֵּל אוֹמְרִים מַגְבִּיהֵיהֶן מֵעַל הַשֻּׁלְחָן טַלְמוֹת וּקְלִפִּין, וּב"ש אוֹמְרִים מְסַלֵּק אֶת הַטַּבְלָה שֶׁיֵּשׁ עָלֶיהָ תּוֹרַת כְּלִי אֲבָל לֹא יְטַלְטֵל הָעֲצָמוֹת וְהַקְּלִפִּין בְּיָדָיו, דְּבֵית הִלֵּל כְּרַבִּי שִׁמְעוֹן וּבֵית שַׁמַּאי כְּרַבִּי יְהוּדָה. וּמֵימָיו לֹא שָׁרוּ בֵּית הִלֵּל אֶלָּא בְּטַלְמוֹת וּקְלִפִּין דַּחֲזוּ לְמַאֲכָל בְּהֵמָה אַף עַל גַּב דְּלֹא חֲזוּ לְמַאֲכָל אָדָם, אֲבָל כִּי לֹא חֲזוּ אַף לְמַאֲכָל בְּהֵמָה מוֹדוּ ב"ה דַּאֲסוּרִים לְטַלְטֵל, דִּבְכַה"ג אֲפִילוּ רַבִּי שִׁמְעוֹן מוֹדֶה:

יד אברהם

to washing it [an act prohibited on the Sabbath as a *toladah* of *whitening* (see 7:2)] (*Rav; Rashi*).

When wiping it with a damp rag, one must be careful to do so gently, so as not to wring out any water from the rag (*Tif. Yis.*). [See below, mishnah 3.]

הָיְתָה שֶׁל עוֹר — [If] it was [made] of leather,

I.e., if the filth was on a pillow made of leather (*Rav; Rashi*).

נוֹתְנִין עָלֶיהָ מַיִם עַד שֶׁתִּכְלֶה — we may pour water on it until it disappears.

The ruling that soaking is tantamount to washing applies only to cloth [which absorbs water], not to leather. Since pillows are made of soft leather, however, one may not actually scrub it [to remove the stain] since the *melachah* of washing is applicable to soft leather, too. Pouring water over it [to remove surface dirt] is permitted because the leather will not absorb the water. [Removal of surface dirt is not considered washing or *whitening* the pillow because the surface dirt was never absorbed by the leather and thus never became "part" of the leather. If, however, water is absorbed — as in the case of a fabric — this is automatically considered washing.]

3.

בֵּית שַׁמַּאי אוֹמְרִים: מַגְבִּיהִין מִן הַשֻׁלְחָן עֲצָמוֹת וּקְלִפִּין — *Beis Shammai say: We may pick up bones and husks from the table.*

I.e., bones fit for a dog or husks fit for cattle fodder may be removed from the table by hand. Since these bones and husks still qualify as animal food, they are not *muktzeh*. Bones and shells not fit for animals, and thus useless, are intrinsically *muktzeh* (like stones) (*Rav; Tos.; Rif; Rambam*).

וּבֵית הִלֵּל אוֹמְרִים: נוֹטֵל אֶת הַטַּבְלָה כֻלָּהּ וּמְנַעֲרָהּ — *But Beis Hillel say: One*

21 3 [If] it was [made] of leather, we may pour water on it until it disappears.

3. Beis Shammai say: We may pick up bones and husks from the table. But Beis Hillel say: One must pick up the entire table board and shake it.

YAD AVRAHAM

must pick up the entire table board and shake it.

According to *Rambam* (*Comm.*), this is a large board placed under a small table to catch the crumbs.

Alternatively, this is a bread board placed on the table (*Mishnah Berurah* 308:115).

Beis Hillel rule that the bones and husks may not be handled because they are *muktzeh*, under the category of *nolad* (see prefatory note to Chap. 17). Since before the Sabbath they were still part of the meat or produce, and thus deemed human food, and they have now become animal food, their change of status is sufficient to deem them *nolad*, i.e., in a newly created state (*Magen Avraham* 495:7, *Mishnah Berurah*, ibid.:17). [Beis Shammai, however, consider such a change insufficient for the article to be deemed *nolad*.]

The table or board, however, is not *muktzeh* because it is a utensil and may therefore be lifted on the Sabbath (*Rav; Rashi*).

[Although by lifting and shaking the board one is also moving the *muktzeh* (bones and husks), this is permitted because it is an *indirect* movement of *muktzeh* (as in the previous mishnah).]

The *Gemara* (143a) states that the proper reading of the mishnah should be in the reverse; viz., that it is Beis Shammai's view that the bones and husks not be directly handled while Beis Hillel permit this. This revised reading of the mishnah is substantiated by the *Tosefta* (17:4), as well as by the mishnah in *Eduyos* (5:1-5), in which the instances that Beis Hillel's rulings are more stringent than those of Beis Shammai are enumerated. Our mishnah is conspicuously absent, implying that here, too, Beis Hillel rule leniently regarding *muktzeh* while Beis Shammai rule stringently, as is true in the vast majority of cases (see *Tosafos*).

[The importance of this revision is that the halachah, with few exceptions, follows the opinion of Beis Hillel over Beis Shammai.]

Although Beis Hillel rule leniently regarding *muktzeh*, they nevertheless require that the scraps be fit for animal fodder. Otherwise, according to all opinions, they are *muktzeh*. Consequently, Beis Hillel permit picking up only soft bones, fit to be fed to dogs, and only such husks fit for cattle fodder. Hard bones, unfit for dogs, and nutshells, unfit for cattle, may not be picked up from the table, even according to Beis Hillel.

This is borne out by the mishnah's ruling regarding pods of chickpeas and pods of lentils. Their permissibility is stated by the mishnah to be based on their status as animal fodder. The *Gemara* attributes this ruling to R' Shimon, who is always viewed by the *Gemara* as being the most lenient of all *Tannaic* opinions with regard to the laws of *muktzeh*. This indicates, then, that

שבת
כא/ג

מַעֲבִירִין מִלִּפְנֵי הַשֻּׁלְחָן פֵּרוּרִין פָּחוֹת מִכַּזַּיִת, וְשֵׂעָר שֶׁל אֲפוּנִין וְשֵׂעָר שֶׁל עֲדָשִׁים, מִפְּנֵי שֶׁהוּא מַאֲכַל בְּהֵמָה. סְפוֹג, אִם יֵשׁ לוֹ עוֹר בֵּית אֲחִיזָה, מְקַנְּחִין בּוֹ; וְאִם לָאו, אֵין מְקַנְּחִין בּוֹ. וַחֲכָמִים אוֹמְרִים: בֵּין כָּךְ וּבֵין כָּךְ,

ר' עובדיה מברטנורא

מעבירין מעל השלחן פרורים פחות מכזית. אפילו פחות מכזית וטעמא כדמפרש בסמוך שהן ראויין למאכל בהמה: **ושער של פולין**. שרביטיס שהקטנית גדל בהן: **עור בית אחיזה.** בית אחיזה של עור שיאחזנו בו: **אין מקנחין בו.** שכשאוחזו נסחט בין אצבעותיו והוי פסיק רישיה ולא ימות דמודה ביה רבי שמעון. **בין כך ובין כך.** בין יש לו בית אחיזה בין אין לו בית אחיזה ניטל בשבת כשהוא נגוב:

יד אברהם

even according to R' Shimon, things unfit for cattle fodder are indeed *muktzeh* (*Tos.* 143a, s.v. עֲצָמוֹת). This view is shared by *Rambam* (*Comm.*; *Hil. Shabbos* 26:16), *Rif* and *Rav*.[1]

The halachah is that one may directly remove any bones or husks which are fit for animal consumption. Those which are not may be removed only by lifting the table board (or tablecloth) and shaking them off[2] (*Shulchan Aruch* 308:27). One may also remove them by scraping them off with a knife or other utensil, as long as one does not touch them directly. This constitutes an *indirect movement of muktzeh* to facilitate the use of a non-*muktzeh* object [the table] (*Taz* 308:18; *Mishnah Berurah* ibid.:115).[3]

Furthermore, if there is an accumulation of bones or nutshells whose presence is disturbing one may remove them even by hand since they constitute a repulsive item (see *Mishnah Berurah* ibid.; see above 16:7).

מַעֲבִירִין מִלִּפְנֵי הַשֻּׁלְחָן — **We may remove from the table** (lit. *from before the table*)

Other editions read: מַעֲבִירִין מֵעַל הַשֻּׁלְחָן, *we may remove from upon the table* (*Rav*; *Rashi*; *Rif*; *Rosh*).

פֵּרוּרִין פָּחוֹת מִכַּזַּיִת, — [*even*] *crumbs less than the size of an olive*,

Although people do not generally eat such small crumbs, these are still not *muktzeh* because they are animal fodder, as the mishnah goes on to explain (*Rav*).

וְשֵׂעָר שֶׁל אֲפוּנִין וְשֵׂעָר שֶׁל עֲדָשִׁים, מִפְּנֵי שֶׁהוּא מַאֲכַל בְּהֵמָה. — *as well as the*

---

1. *Rashi*, however, interprets the mishnah as referring to hard bones, unfit for dogs, and nutshells, unfit for cattle fodder. See *Maginei Shlomo* who explains *Rashi's* view.

2. Whether one may only shake it off in its place or may carry it to the garbage and shake it off there is the subject of a dispute. *Shulchan Aruch* (308:27) seems to adopt the former opinion. (See *Beur Halachah* there.)

3. See *Chazon Ish* 47:14 who disputes this last option.

21
3

We may remove from the table [even] crumbs less than the size of an olive, as well as the pods of chickpeas and the pods of lentils, because they are animal fodder.

A sponge, if it has a leather handle, we may wipe with it; if not, we may not wipe with it. The Sages, however, say: In either case,

YAD AVRAHAM

pods of chickpeas and the pods of lentils, because they are (lit. *it is*) *animal fodder.*

As mentioned above, this ruling follows the view of R' Shimon (and Beis Hillel according to the revised text), who does not consider such a change in status (from human fare to animal fodder) to be *nolad*. According to R' Yehudah (and Beis Shammai in the revised text), however, since prior to the Sabbath these pods were part of the food and were not yet designated for animal fodder, they are *nolad* and therefore *muktzeh* (*Rashi* on *Gem.* 143a).

Wringing water out of a wet cloth is a *toladah* of **whitening* (see 7:2). The same applies to wiping a table with a wet sponge if one thereby squeezes the water out of the sponge.

סְפוֹג, — *A sponge,*

It was customary to dip the sponge in water and to wipe the table (*Meiri*).

אִם יֵשׁ לוֹ עוֹר בֵּית אֲחִיזָה, מְקַנְּחִין בּוֹ; — *if it has a leather handle, we may wipe with it;*

Since it is possible to wipe the table board without squeezing the water out of the sponge, it may be used. This fits into the category of אֵינוֹ מִתְכַּוֵּן, *an unintentional act.* The mishnah follows R' Shimon, who permits performing a permissible act, even though it may unintentionally lead to a prohibited one (*Gem.* 143a; see General Introduction, p. 8).

וְאִם לָאו, אֵין מְקַנְּחִין בּוֹ. — *if not, we may not wipe with it.*

I.e., if the sponge does not have a leather handle, when one takes it into his hand he will inevitably squeeze out some of the water. In this case, even R' Shimon prohibits performing the permissible act (*Rashi; Rambam, Hil. Shabbos* 22:15).

Ravad objects to this explanation on the grounds that, although when one picks up the sponge with a handle the water will not necessarily be squeezed out, when he wipes the table with it, some water will inevitably be squeezed out. It should therefore be just as prohibited with a handle as without.

He explains that a sponge that has a handle is viewed as the equivalent of a bottle of water [since it, too, has been made into a utensil designed to hold water] from which one may empty the contents. A sponge without a handle is, however, viewed as the equivalent of a garment, which may not be wrung out on the Sabbath.

וַחֲכָמִים אוֹמְרִים: בֵּין כָּךְ וּבֵין כָּךְ, — *The Sages, however, say: In either case,*

[I.e., whether or not the sponge has a leather handle.]

שבת כא/ג

נִטָּל בַּשַּׁבָּת, וְאֵינוֹ מְקַבֵּל טֻמְאָה.

ר' עובדיה מברטנורא

ואינו מקבל טומאה. דאינו לא כלי עץ ולא בגד ולא שק ולא מתכת:

יד אברהם

נִטָּל בַּשַּׁבָּת, — *it may be moved about on the Sabbath,*

Since it is a utensil, it may be moved about on the Sabbath when it is dry (and no problem of squeezing exists) (*Rav; Rashi*).

Some editions omit: וַחֲכָמִים אוֹמְרִים, *The Sages, however, say*, thus making it a continuation of the aforegoing, stating that although we may not wipe with a wet sponge unless it has a handle, we may move about a dry

21 3 it may be moved about on the Sabbath, and it is not susceptible to *tumah*-contamination.

YAD AVRAHAM

sponge without a handle since it is a utensil (*Rashi; Tosafos;* and *Rif,* according to *Bach;* our edition of *Rif,* however, does include these words). *Rambam* (*Comm.*) and *Rosh* read as does our edition of the mishnayos.

וְאֵינוּ מְקַבֵּל טֻמְאָה. — *and is not susceptible to tumah-contamination.*

Tumah-contamination of utensils is limited by the Torah to garments, metal utensils, leather goods, and wooden utensils (*Numbers* 31:20). Since a sponge does not fit into any of these categories, it is not susceptible (*Rav; Rashi*).

Alternatively, since the sponge is derived from marine life, it is not susceptible to *tumah,* as in *Kelim* 17:13.

פרק עשרים ושתים
Chapter Twenty-Two

[א] **חָבִית** שֶׁנִּשְׁבְּרָה, מַצִּילִין הֵימֶנָּה מְזוֹן שָׁלֹשׁ סְעוּדוֹת. וְאוֹמֵר לַאֲחֵרִים: "בֹּאוּ וְהַצִּילוּ לָכֶם," וּבִלְבַד שֶׁלֹּא יִסְפֹּג.
אֵין סוֹחֲטִין אֶת הַפֵּרוֹת לְהוֹצִיא מֵהֶן מַשְׁקִין;

ר' עובדיה מברטנורא

פרק עשרים ושתים – מצילין מזון. (א) **מצילין מזון שלש סעודות.** ואפילו בכלים הרבה, דאילו בכלי אחד אמרו בפרק כל כתבי דכמה דבעי מציל: **לכם.** כל אחד מזון ג' סעודות: **ובלבד שלא יספוג.** שלא ישים ספוג לשאוב היין ולחזור ולהטיף, ואף על פי שיש לספוג בית אחיזה דליכא חשש סחיטה, שלא יעשה כדרך שהוא עושה בחול. ואפילו ליקח שמן ודבש שהן עבים ונדבקים ולקנח ידו בשפת הכלי אסור, שלא יעשה כמעשה חול: **אין סוחטין את הפירות.** דה"ל מפרק תולדה דדש:

יד אברהם

1.

חָבִית שֶׁנִּשְׁבְּרָה — *A cask which has broken,*

[I.e., a cask of wine or the like.]

מַצִּילִין הֵימֶנָּה מְזוֹן שָׁלֹשׁ סְעוּדוֹת — *we may save from it [enough] food for three meals.*

This applies only if the cask broke in the evening before the first Sabbath meal. If, however, it broke after the first meal, one may save only enough for the two remaining meals (*Meiri; Rambam, Hil. Shabbos* 22:16).

[See above 16:2, where we learned that the Rabbis — fearing that one would, in his panic, extinguish a fire on the Sabbath in order to salvage his property — set down rules limiting the amount of property one may save.

Thus, these limitations are forceful reminders of the prohibition of *extinguishing a fire.* As far as foodstuffs are concerned, the Rabbis allowed one to salvage only the amount required for the three Sabbath meals. Similarly here, the Rabbis — fearing that one would, in his distress over the loss of his wine, forget and carry containers through a public domain in order to salvage as much of his wine as possible — set down rules limiting the amount he is permitted to save (*Gem.* 117b).

Alternatively, they feared one would repair the broken cask on the Sabbath, in order to salvage the remaining wine (*Rama* 335:1).[1]

Above (16:3), we learned that, "we

---

1. The *Gemara* does not mention this reason, since in those days, the casks were usually earthenware, a material virtually irreparable. *Rama*, however, mentions this reason since in his time casks were made of wood. On the other hand, *Rama* omits the reason mentioned by the *Gemara*, since in his time a public domain, with all the qualifications expounded upon at the beginning of this tractate, was rare. He therefore gives the reason that one may repair the cask, to indicate that the regulation pertains even in such times (*Machatzis HaShekel* 335:1, quoting *Tosefos Shabbos* and *Chemed Moshe*).

22
1

1. A cask which has broken, we may save from it [enough] food for three meals. And one may say to others, "Come and save for yourselves," however, he may not soak [it] up with a sponge.

We may not press fruits to extract juice from them;

YAD AVRAHAM

may save one basket full of loaves, even if it contains enough for a hundred meals." That ruling applies here, as well. Hence, as long as one catches the wine in one large container, he may salvage even enough for a hundred meals. If, however, he requires more than one utensil, he may salvage only enough for the number of Sabbath meals he has not yet eaten (*Rav; Rashi; Shulchan Aruch* 335:1).

If the cask is not broken but merely cracked, so that its contents are slowly seeping out, he may save as much as possible. Since the owner does not panic over a slow leak, there is no reason to fear that he may profane the Sabbath in order to save his wine. There are, therefore, no restrictions (*Tos. R' Akiva* from *Tos.* 117b; *Rama* 335:1).

וְאוֹמֵר לַאֲחֵרִים: ,,בֹּאוּ וְהַצִּילוּ לָכֶם,'' — *And one may say to others, "Come and save for yourselves,"*

Thus, each one may save the requirements for those of the three meals he has not yet eaten [see 16:2] (*Tif. Yis.*).

וּבִלְבַד שֶׁלֹּא יִסְפֹּג. — *however, he may not soak [it] up with a sponge.*

Although the mishnah (21:3) states that one may wipe a table board with a sponge provided with a leather handle, here he may not absorb the wine with such a sponge and let it drip into a container, since this is reminiscent of weekday activity (*Rav* from *Tosafos,*

according to *Gem*). [This is probably considered a *weekday activity* because it may lead to pressing out the sponge. See General Introduction, p. 17.]

Similarly, one may not gather the oil or honey in his hand and wipe them off on a container. This, too, constitutes weekday activity (*Rav* from *Gemara*).

אֵין סוֹחֲטִין אֶת הַפֵּרוֹת — *We may not press fruits*

Literally the mishnah reads, "we may not press *the* fruits." The definite article alludes to the fruits customarily designated for pressing, viz., olives and grapes. As will be explained below, pressing these fruits on the Sabbath is forbidden by the Torah (*Gem*. 145a). Pressing other fruits is Rabbinically prohibited (*Kol Ha-Sofer*).

לְהוֹצִיא מֵהֶן מַשְׁקִין; — *to extract juice from them;*

Squeezing juice out of a fruit is prohibited on the Sabbath under the prohibition of מְפָרֵק, *extraction*, or, as *Rashi* (95a) explains it, *unloading*. (He unloads the food from the place in which it was concealed.) This is a *toladah* of *threshing* (*Rav; Rashi*).

Just as one threshes to extract the grains that lie hidden within the husk, so one presses fruit in order to extract the juice within it (*Aruch Ha-Shulchan* 320:3).

שבת כב/א

וְאִם יָצְאוּ מֵעַצְמָן, אֲסוּרִין. רַבִּי יְהוּדָה אוֹמֵר: אִם לָאֳכָלִין, הַיּוֹצֵא מֵהֶן מֻתָּר; וְאִם לְמַשְׁקִין, הַיּוֹצֵא מֵהֶן אָסוּר.

ר' עובדיה מברטנורא

אסורין. גזירה שמא יסחוט לכתחלה: ר"י אומר אם לאוכלין. היו אותן פירות מכונסים, היולא מהן מותר, דלא ניחא ליה במה שזבו וליכא למגזר בהו שמא יסחוט: **ואם למשקין.** היו מכונסין דניחא ליה במאי דנפק מנייהו, היולא מהן אסור, גזירה שמא יסחוט. ובזיתים וענבים מודה ר"י לחכמים דאף על גב דכנסן לאוכלים היולא מהן אסור, כיון דדרכן לסחיטה קיימי כי אתו לידי משקה יהיב דעתיה בהכי. ובשאר מיני פירות חכמים מודים לר"י, כיון דלאו דרכן לסחיטה. לא נחלקו אלא בתותים ורמונים, דרבי יהודה מדמה להו לשאר פירות וחכמים מדמו להו לזיתים וענבים. והלכה כר"י.

יד אברהם

וְאִם יָצְאוּ מֵעַצְמָן, — *and [even] if they flowed out by themselves,*

I.e., if some juice flowed out on the Sabbath even without the fruit being pressed.

אֲסוּרִין — *they are prohibited.*

I.e., one is prohibited to drink the juice on the Sabbath. This is a Rabbinic precaution against squeezing fruits on the Sabbath in order to obtain their juice (*Rav*; *Rashi*).

רַבִּי יְהוּדָה אוֹמֵר: אִם לָאֳכָלִין, — *R' Yehudah says: If [they were intended] for food,*

I.e., if the owner intended to eat these fruits rather than to extract their juice (*Rav*).

הַיּוֹצֵא מֵהֶן מֻתָּר; — *[the juice] that flows* (lit. *goes out*) *from them is permitted;*

I.e., one may drink the juice that flowed out by itself on the Sabbath. Since the fruits are stored to be eaten, one does not want the juice to flow out of them. There is, therefore, no reason to fear that one will forget and press them (*Rav*; *Rashi*).

וְאִם לְמַשְׁקִין, — *but if [they were intended] for juice,*

I.e., if the owner intends to extract their juice (*Rav*; *Rashi*).

הַיּוֹצֵא מֵהֶן אָסוּר. — *what flows* (lit. *goes out*) *from them is prohibited.*

I.e., one may not drink even the juice that flowed on its own on the Sabbath.

Since these fruits are intended for juice, one is pleased that the juice has flowed from them. We fear, therefore, that he may come to squeeze them on the Sabbath. To prevent this, the Rabbis prohibited their consumption on the Sabbath (*Rav*; *Rashi*).

The *Gemara* (143b) explains that the olive oil and grape juice are forbidden even if one has set aside the olives and grapes for eating rather than for pressing. Since the primary value of olives and grapes is their juice, the owner is satisfied with their flow, despite his original intention to eat the fruit. Consequently, this precautionary injunction is needed even according to R' Yehudah. The dispute between R' Yehudah and the Sages is over mulberries and pomegranates, the examples cited by the *Gemara*, which were only occasionally used for their juice. R' Yehudah's view is that

**22
1** and [even] if they flowed out by themselves, they are prohibited. R' Yehudah says: If [they were intended] for food, [the juice] that flows from them is permitted; but if [they were intended] for juice, what flows from them is prohibited.

YAD AVRAHAM

since these are not primarily valued for their juice, if one has gathered them to eat, he will certainly not be content to have the juice ooze from them. Therefore, we need not fear that he will come to press them. The Sages, however, hold that since these fruits are also occasionally used for their juice the owner may in the end be content to use them for that purpose. However, concerning fruits which are rarely pressed for their juice, such as plums, quinces and sorb-apples, even the Sages agree that any juice which flows from them may be used (*Rav*).

As explained above, the leniency of R' Yehudah is only in regard to juice which has flowed on its own without having been pressed. One may not, however, actually press mulberries or pomegranates. This is a Rabbinical prohibition. The Biblical prohibition to press fruits applies only to olives and grapes. Any other fruits which are customarily pressed for their juice are considered like mulberries and pomegranates and are Rabbinically prohibited (*Rama* 320:1). Even if they are only used as a juice in specific areas, it is, nevertheless, forbidden everywhere to press them for their juice on the Sabbath (*Magen Avraham* ibid.).

However, fruits which are not ordinarily made into juice may be pressed on the Sabbath by an individual who desires to drink their juice (*Gem.* ibid. as understood by *Rambam, Hil. Shabbos* 22:12; *Rif; Rosh; Semag; Semak*; though there are dissenting opinions, this ruling is accepted by *Shulchan Aruch* 320:1).

The examples used by the *Gemara* of fruits occasionally pressed and never pressed are descriptive of the customs and tastes of those times. These rules must be applied in each age and area in accord with the prevailing usages of that time and place. At one time pear juice was very popular and was therefore prohibited to be pressed (*Magen Avraham* ibid.). Lemons, in our times, may not be pressed, though the author of *Shulchan Aruch*, in his time [late 15th century], permitted it (*Mishnah Berurah* 320:22).

The *Gemara* (144b) states that one may squeeze any fruit, even olives and grapes, directly into food. Since the juice is being used as part of a solid food and not as a liquid, the juice itself is regarded as a food, rather than a liquid. The prohibition of *pressing* being a *toladah* of **threshing* applies only to juice being used as a liquid, since only then is it similar to **threshing*; i.e., just as threshing removes the useful kernel from within the non-useful shell, so too does pressing remove the useful liquid from the non-useful (in terms of a liquid) pulp. Where one uses the extract as a food rather than as a liquid this perspective does not apply. Rather, this is akin to cutting off a piece from a fruit, which is certainly permissible. For this reason, one may squeeze a lemon into sugar, even though it will later be used for tea. However, this is permitted only when one squeezes the juice directly into the food. One may not squeeze the juice into a bowl, even with the intention of subsequently mixing it into his food, since the juice, in the interim, has achieved the status of a liquid (*Tif. Yis; Mishnah Berurah* 320:22).

שבת
כב/ב

חַלּוֹת דְּבַשׁ שֶׁרִסְּקָן מֵעֶרֶב שַׁבָּת, וְיָצְאוּ מֵעַצְמָן, אֲסוּרִים. וְרַבִּי אֶלְעָזָר מַתִּיר.

[ב] **כָּל שֶׁבָּא** בְּחַמִּין מֵעֶרֶב שַׁבָּת שׁוֹרִין אוֹתוֹ בְּחַמִּין בַּשַּׁבָּת; וְכָל שֶׁלֹּא בָא בְּחַמִּין מֵעֶרֶב שַׁבָּת מְדִיחִין אוֹתוֹ בְּחַמִּין בַּשַּׁבָּת,

---- ר' עובדיה מברטנורא ----

חלות דבש. כשהן מרוסקים זה הדבש מטלמו מתוך הטפוח ואין דרך לסחטו, הילכך רבי אליעזר מתיר, וחכמים אוסרים גזרו אטו שאין מרוסקין. והלכה כרבי אלעזר: **(ב)** כל שבא בחמין. שנתבשל: **מדיחין.** דהדחתו אינה כשולו אבל לא שורין:

---- יד אברהם ----

חַלּוֹת דְּבַשׁ שֶׁרִסְּקָן מֵעֶרֶב שַׁבָּת, — Honeycombs which one crushed before the Sabbath,

To allow the honey to flow from them (Rav).

וְיָצְאוּ מֵעַצְמָן, — and [the honey] then flowed out by itself,

And the honey came out by itself on the Sabbath without being squeezed (Rav).

אֲסוּרִים. — are prohibited.

[I.e., one may not use the honey on that Sabbath.]

Although no squeezing was necessary to extract the honey from crushed honeycombs, the *Tanna Kamma* prohibits the honey lest one crush the honeycombs on the Sabbath (*Rav; Rashi*).

וְרַבִּי אֶלְעָזָר מַתִּיר. — R' Elazar, however, permits [them].

The proper reading is R' Elazar (ben Shamua), not R' Eliezer (ben Hyrcanos), as appears in most editions of the Mishnayos (*Tos. R' Akiva*).

Since one does not customarily press honeycombs to extract honey, the initial crushing being sufficient for the task, we need not fear that one will actually come to squeeze the honeycombs (*Rashi; Rav*). R' Elazar, however, agrees that one may not actually press honeycombs on the Sabbath (*Tif. Yis.* from *Magen Avraham* 320:16).

The halachah is in accordance with R' Elazar (*Rav; Rambam, Comm.* and *Hil. Shabbos* 21:15).

2.

The following mishnah is based on the principle of אֵין בִּשּׁוּל אַחַר בִּשּׁוּל, *there is no* **cooking after cooking*, i.e. once a food has been thoroughly cooked, there is no Torah prohibition on recooking it. For this reason, although one is not normally permitted to place food in a כְּלִי רִאשׁוֹן [*kli rishon*], primary vessel (a pot that has been standing on the fire and is still hot, although it is no longer on the fire; see above 3:5), food which has been completely cooked before the Sabbath may be soaked in a *kli rishon*. [However, one may not place it directly on the fire because this gives the *appearance* of cooking on the Sabbath. As explained above (3:1), even a pot which is boiling hot may not be placed on the fire on the Sabbath if it was removed before the

22 2 Honeycombs which one crushed before the Sabbath, and [the honey] then flowed out by itself, are prohibited. R' Elazar, however, permits [them].

2. Anything that was put in hot water before the Sabbath may be soaked in hot water on the Sabbath; but anything that was not put in hot water before the Sabbath may be rinsed in hot water on the Sabbath,

YAD AVRAHAM

Sabbath.] According to most authorities, this applies only to a dry food. If the food contains liquid, however, recooking it is prohibited (*Shulchan Aruch* 318:4).

כֹּל — *Anything*
I.e., any dry food (*Shulchan Aruch* 318:4).

שֶׁבָּא בְּחַמִּין מֵעֶרֶב שַׁבָּת — *that was put in hot water before the Sabbath*
I.e., it was cooked before the Sabbath (*Rav; Rashi*).

Others add: that it was completely cooked before the Sabbath (*Meiri*).

Rambam (*Hil. Shabbos* 22:8), however, states, "Anything that was cooked before the Sabbath or soaked in hot water before the Sabbath..." This implies that even a food which was not cooked before the Sabbath, but merely soaked in the hot water of a *kli rishon*, may again be soaked in hot water on the Sabbath.

Pri Megadim (*Eishel Avraham* 318:14) states that even those who permit resoaking (in hot water) a foodstuff that was only soaked in a *kli rishon* before the Sabbath do so only as regards foodstuffs that are easily cooked by simply soaking in a *kli rishon*. Other foods, i.e., those that require thorough cooking, may not be soaked in hot water on the Sabbath unless they were thoroughly cooked before the Sabbath (*Mishnah Berurah*, ibid. 31).

שׁוֹרִין אוֹתוֹ בְּחַמִּין בַּשַּׁבָּת — *may be soaked in hot water on the Sabbath;*

I.e., it may be soaked a second time even in a *kli rishon* since it has already been cooked before the Sabbath (*Tif. Yis.* from *Magen Avraham* 318:14).

וְכָל־שֶׁלֹּא בָא בְּחַמִּין מֵעֶרֶב שַׁבָּת — *but anything that was not put in hot water before the Sabbath*
E.g., dry meat, which can be eaten raw in case of emergency (*Rashi*).

מְדִיחִין אוֹתוֹ בְּחַמִּין בַּשַּׁבָּת, — *may be rinsed in hot water on the Sabbath,*
I.e., we may pour hot water onto it from a *secondary vessel*, i.e., a vessel which was not itself on the fire but into which hot water has been poured from a *kli rishon*. Soaking in a *secondary vessel* is, however, Rabbinically prohibited, since it appears like *cooking (Magen Avraham* 318:15).

Although, as explained above (3:5), there is no Biblical prohibition against warming most foods in a *secondary vessel*, the Rabbis prohibited placing uncooked food in such a utensil because it gives the appearance of *cooking. They, did, however, permit adding spices to a *secondary vessel* (above 3:5) because it is obvious that one is merely trying to flavor the food, not cook the spices. Consequently, there are no misleading appearances with which to be concerned (*Magen Abraham*, ibid.).

שבת
כב/ג

חוּץ מִן הַמָּלִיחַ הַיָּשָׁן, וְדָגִים מְלוּחִים קְטַנִּים, וְקוּלְיָס הָאִסְפָּנִין, שֶׁהֲדָחָתָן זוֹ הִיא גְּמַר מְלַאכְתָּן.

[ג] **שׁוֹבֵר** אָדָם אֶת הֶחָבִית לֶאֱכֹל הֵימֶנָּה גְרוֹגְרוֹת, וּבִלְבַד שֶׁלֹּא יִתְכַּוֵּן

ר' עובדיה מברטנורא

חוץ מן המליח הישן. דג מליח שעברה עליו שנה משנמלח: **וקוליס האספנין.** דג שקליפתו דקה והדחתו בחמין הוא גמר בשולו: **(ג) שובר אדם את החבית.** מפני שהוא מקלקל:

יד אברהם

חוּץ מִן הַמָּלִיחַ הַיָּשָׁן, — except an old salted fish,

I.e., fish that was salted a year before (*Rav; Rashi*). *Rambam* (*Comm.*) also interprets this as salted fish. *Rashi* in *Sefer HaPardes*, however, explains it as highly salted meat.

Tiferes Yisrael and others explain this as herring. This will be discussed below.

וְדָגִים מְלוּחִים קְטַנִּים, — small salted fish,

In many editions, these words are omitted (*Rif; Rosh*).

וְקוּלְיָס הָאִסְפָּנִין, — or a Spanish mackerel,

A type of tuna of the *Scombridae* family (*Rashi* 39a). Since its skin is thin, it becomes cooked by merely rinsing it with hot water (*Rav; Tif. Yis.*).

Alternatively, it becomes almost edible by salting alone and all that is needed to complete it is to soak it in hot water (*Rashi*).

שֶׁהֲדָחָתָן — because their rinsing [I.e., in hot water.]

זוֹ הִיא גְּמַר מְלַאכְתָּן. — completes their preparation.

[I.e., since even the low degree of heat available in a secondary vessel suffices to make them edible, this too is considered cooking.]

Some authorities (*Magen Avraham*) rule that this applies solely to those foods which can only be rendered edible by being rinsed in hot water. It does not apply to those foods that can be rendered edible by being rinsed even in cold water. These latter foods may be rinsed even with hot water, since the heat itself accomplishes nothing in the preparation of the food.

Others rule that, although soaking or rinsing with cold water will also render the food edible, one who rinses it with hot water is still liable for *cooking (*Turei Zahav*, ibid. 5; *Shulchan Atzei Shitim* 3:4; *Chayei Adam* 20:6).

Some authorities go so far as to prohibit soaking such foods even in cold water since it renders them edible. They regard this a *toladah* of *striking the final blow, since this completes the preparation of the foodstuff (*Chayei Adam*, ibid.; *Pri Megadim, Eishel Avraham* 318:16; *Levush HaChur* 318:4). *Beur Halachah*, however, rejects this view and permits soaking or rinsing food in cold water even if such rinsing renders the food edible.

3.

שׁוֹבֵר אָדָם אֶת הֶחָבִית לֶאֱכֹל הֵימֶנָּה גְרוֹגְרוֹת, — A person may break [open] a cask to eat dried figs from it,

Although one is demolishing the barrel, since this is a destructive act, it is permissible (*Rav; Rashi*).

except an old salted fish, small salted fish, or a Spanish mackerel, because their rinsing completes their preparation.

3. A person may break [open] a cask to eat dried figs from it, provided that he does not intend

YAD AVRAHAM

Ran objects to this on the grounds that the mishnah (13:3) states that *those who destroy are exempt.* According to the rule stated by the *Gemara* (3a), that wherever the mishnah in this tractate declares some activity *exempt* it means *exempt* from a sin offering, but Rabbinically prohibited, destructive acts are at least Rabbinically prohibited on the Sabbath. He therefore explains that although destructive acts are usually Rabbinically prohibited on the Sabbath, where they are necessary for the Sabbath, as, for example, to reach food, the Rabbis permitted them (*Tos. Yom Tov* from *Ran*).

As is evident from *Eruvin* 3:3, not all containers may be broken even for the purpose of removing food from within them. *Ran* qualifies this mishnah by saying that it refers only to small casks. Large ones, however, may not be broken. *Tosafos* and *Rosh* rule that this mishnah refers only to casks previously broken and glued back together. A perfectly good cask may not be broken open for fear that one will take care while doing so to form a proper opening for the barrel. (This is forbidden, as will be explained below.)

The basis for these qualifications is that this mishnah seems to be contradicted by *Eruvin* 3:3. There the mishnah discusses the placing of the food of *eruv techumin.* [This is the mechanism by which one is permitted to travel on the Sabbath beyond the normally allotted two thousand cubits from city limits. By placing one's food prior to the Sabbath at a point two thousand cubits away from one's actual dwelling, the Rabbis permit one to view the place of the food as one's campsite, thus allowing him to travel two thousand cubits in any direction from that campsite. This enables one to walk a total of four thousand cubits (two thousand until the campsite and two thousand more beyond it) from the place where one is actually staying.] In order for this mechanism to be operative, one must be able to retrieve and eat the food at the campsite. In consequence of this stipulation, the mishnah states that if one locked the food in a locker at the campsite and then lost the key, the *eruv* is invalid. According to the ruling of our mishnah, however, the *eruv* should still be valid, since one is permitted to retrieve the food by breaking open the locker.

In order to resolve this contradiction, the ruling of our mishnah must be qualified. *Ran* states that our mishnah permits breaking open a cask only if it is a small utensil. A large utensil, however, may not be broken open. The locker discussed in *Eruvin* 3:3 refers to a large locker. (The delineation of large and small is whether the utensil can hold at least forty *se'ah*, which is the equivalent of a volume of three cubic cubits (*Beis Yosef* 314 and *Rama*). [*Depending upon various halachic opinions regarding the conversion of cubits to feet, this would be between ten and twenty-four cubit feet.*]

The basis of this distinction is the statement by the *Gemara* (122b) that the *melachos* of *building and *demolishing do not apply to utensils to the same degree that they apply to structures. (Anything built into or otherwise attached to the ground is

שבת כב/ג

לַעֲשׂוֹת כְּלִי. וְאֵין נוֹקְבִים מְגוּפָה שֶׁל חָבִית – דִּבְרֵי רַבִּי יְהוּדָה. וַחֲכָמִים מַתִּירִין. וְלֹא יִקֳּבֶנָּה מִצִּדָּהּ. וְאִם הָיְתָה נְקוּבָה, לֹא יִתֵּן עָלֶיהָ שַׁעֲוָה, מִפְּנֵי שֶׁהוּא מְמָרֵחַ.

ר׳ עובדיה מברטנורא

ובלבד שלא יתכוין לעשותה כלי. לעשות לה פה נאה: אין נוקבים מגופה. הדבוקה בפי חבית אלא נוטל את כולה דכי נקיב לה מתקן פתחא הוא: רבי יוסי מתיר. דאין דרך פתח חבית בכך. והלכה כרבי יוסי: ולא יקבנה מצדה. כלומר הא דשרי רבי יוסי לנקוב את המגופה, לא שרי אלא למעלה בראש המגופה דלאו אורחא למעבד פתחא התם אלא נוטל את כל המגופה. אבל מלדה, זימנין דעביד ליה לנקב בלד המגופה משום פתחא ואינו רולה לפתחה למעלה שלא יפלו לדרורות או עפר בייןn: ממרח. ויש כאן משום ממחק: בערב. שם מקום:

יד אברהם

Rama 314:1, adopting the stringencies of both Ran and Rosh, permits breaking open a container only when it is both "small" and "inferior" (i.e., previously broken and fixed).

This, however, applies only to making a hole in the body of the cask. Breaking off the bung (a clay stopper used on the cask) from the body of the cask is permissible even on a good cask. Since the bung is not considered an integral part of the cask, one is not making a new opening in the cask but merely uncovering the old one (Mishnah Berurah 314:23).

Making a hole in the bung will be discussed below.

וּבִלְבַד שֶׁלֹּא יִתְכַּוֵּן לַעֲשׂוֹת כְּלִי. — provided that he does not intend to make a vessel.

I.e., provided he does not aim to make a proper opening for the cask (Rav; Rashi). Meiri adds: He should not make the hole with a measure, so that it should be like a utensil.

וְאֵין נוֹקְבִים מְגוּפָה שֶׁל חָבִית – דִּבְרֵי רַבִּי יְהוּדָה. — We may not perforate the bung of a cask — [these are] the

automatically considered a structure.) Whereas adding even the smallest refinements to a permanent structure violates the melachah of *demolishing, with regard to utensils the minimum is set at a complete utensil (Tos. and Ran 102b). (Though these activities do not violate a melachah, they are, nevertheless, Rabbinically prohibited lest one fix a utensil in such a fashion that it involves the melachah of *striking the final blow.) Therefore, for purposes necessary to the Sabbath, one may break open a small vessel since the rules of *building and *demolishing do not apply to it. A large vessel, however, is considered, in regard to this rule, a structure. Breaking it open therefore violates the melachah of *demolishing.

Rosh and Tosafos 146a, however, do not differentiate between large and small utensils. Rather, they explain that our mishnah refers specifically to a cask previously broken and glued back together. Since it is an inferior container, we need not fear that he will break it open in such a way as to fashion a proper opening to the cask. One may not, however, break open a good utensil for fear that one will in the process intend to fashion a proper opening. This, as the mishnah will soon explain, is forbidden. According to this explanation, Eruvin 3:3 refers to a previously unbroken locker.

22
3

to make a vessel.

We may not perforate the bung of a cask — [these are] the words of R' Yehudah. The Sages, however, permit [it]. [But] one may not perforate it in its side.

If it was perforated, one may not place wax upon it, because he smooths [it].

YAD AVRAHAM

words of R' Yehudah.

I.e., we may not perforate the bung (a clay stopper molded to the top of the cask) at the mouth of the cask. We must instead remove the entire bung. By perforating the bung, one would be guilty of making a proper opening (*Rav; Rashi*).

וַחֲכָמִים מַתִּירִין. — *The Sages, however, permit [it].*

The version is that of *Rashi, Rosh, Maggid Mishneh* (Hil. Shabbos 23:2), *Meiri* (in his text), and most editions of the mishnah and Talmud. *Rav*, and apparently *Rambam*, read: וְרַבִּי יוֹסֵי מַתִּיר, *R' Yose, however, permits [it].* Rif reads: דִּבְרֵי רַבִּי יוֹסֵי וַחֲכָמִים מַתִּירִין, *[These are] the words of R' Yose. The Sages, however, permit [it].*

Since it is not customary to make a hole in the top of the bung [so that dust and pebbles not fall in (Tif. Yis.)], one who does so is obviously not intending to fashion a proper opening for the cask. Since it is not considered fashioning a utensil, the Sages permit it.

וְלֹא יְקָבֶנָּה מִצִּדָּהּ. — *[But] one may not perforate it in its side.*

I.e., even the Sages [or R' Yose, according to *Rav* and *Rambam*] permit perforating the bung only on its top, since, as explained before, it is unusual to perforate it there. [When it is necessary to open the top, the entire bung is removed.] To perforate the bung on its side, however, *is* customary. It is, therefore, regarded as fashioning a utensil, which even the Sages prohibit, as a *toladah* of *striking the final blow (Rav from Gem.* 146a; *Rambam, Hil. Shabbos* 23:1,2).

The halachah is in accordance with the Sages (*Rav; Rambam, Comm.* and *Hil. Shabbos* ibid.).

We have explained the dispute between R' Yehudah and the Sages as Rav Huna explains it in the *Gemara.* Rav Chisda, however, explains that everyone permits making a hole on top of the bung, since it is not customary to make an opening there. The dispute is only regarding making a hole in the side of the bung, which R' Yehudah prohibits and the Sages permit. The mishnah's statement: And one may not perforate it from side to side, is to be interpreted as: One may not perforate the cask itself from the side. That is definitely prohibited, since it is regarded as fashioning a proper opening for the cask. In this case, even the Sages concur with R' Yehudah (*Gem.* ibid.).

וְאִם הָיְתָה נְקוּבָה, לֹא יִתֵּן עָלֶיהָ שַׁעֲוָה, — *If it was perforated, one may not place wax upon it,*

[I.e., if the cask was previously perforated, one may not place wax over the hole to close it on the Sabbath.]

מִפְּנֵי שֶׁהוּא מְמָרֵחַ. — *because he smooths [it].*

[I.e., in order to make it fill the hole and adhere properly to the cask, one must smooth the wax.]

שבת כב/ד

אָמַר רַבִּי יְהוּדָה: מַעֲשֶׂה בָּא לִפְנֵי רַבָּן יוֹחָנָן בֶּן זַכַּאי בַּעֲרָב, וְאָמַר: "חוֹשְׁשַׁנִי לוֹ מֵחַטָּאת."

[ד] **נוֹתְנִין** תַּבְשִׁיל לְתוֹךְ הַבּוֹר בִּשְׁבִיל שֶׁיְּהֵא שָׁמוּר; וְאֶת הַמַּיִם הַיָּפִים בָּרָעִים בִּשְׁבִיל שֶׁיִּצַּנּוּ; וְאֶת הַצּוֹנֵן בַּחַמָּה בִּשְׁבִיל שֶׁיֵּחַמּוּ. מִי שֶׁנָּשְׁרוּ כֵּלָיו בַּדֶּרֶךְ בַּמַּיִם מְהַלֵּךְ בָּהֶן

ר' עובדיה מברטנורא

חוששני לו מחטאת. אם מירח השעווה לדובקה בדופני הכלי סביב הנקב: (ד) **לתוך הבור.** שאין בו מים: **שיהא שמור.** שלא יסריח מחמת החום. והא קמ"ל דלא חיישינן דלמא אתי לאשוויי גומות שבקרקעית הבור כדי שיהא שוה להושיב שם הקדרה: **ואת המים היפים.** הרווחיים לשתיה: **ברעים.** בתוך מקוה מים רעים שאינן ראויין לשתיה. ומילתא דפשיטא היא ומשום סיפא נקט לה, דתנן ואת הצוננים [בחמה] בשביל שיחמו, מהו דתימא גזור דלמא אתי לאטמוני ברמץ, קמ"ל: **מי שנשרו כליו.** שנפלו במים בשבת: מהלך בהן ואינו חושש. שמא יחשדו אותו שכבסן:

יד אברהם

מְמָרֵחַ, smoothing, is a toladah of *smoothing hides (Rav; Rashi; Tif. Yis.; Rambam, Hil. Shabbos 23:11).

אָמַר רַבִּי יְהוּדָה: מַעֲשֶׂה בָּא לִפְנֵי רַבָּן יוֹחָנָן בֶּן זַכַּאי בַּעֲרָב, — Said R' Yehudah: An incident came before Rabban Yochanan ben Zakkai in Arab,

[I.e., when Rabban Yochanan ben Zakkai was in Arab, a case came before him of a person who had placed wax over a hole in the cask. See above 16:7.]

וְאָמַר: "חוֹשְׁשַׁנִי לוֹ מֵחַטָּאת." — and he said, "I fear on his account that he may be liable for a sin offering."

R' Yochanan ben Zakkai said he feared that perhaps the person had smoothed out the wax and was liable to a sin offering (Rav; Rashi; Ran; Rambam Comm.; Meiri).

This ruling applies as well to all materials that are customarily smoothed. One may not stop up a hole with any material usually smoothed over a hole even if he does not actually smooth it, for fear that he will smooth it and thereby violate a Torah prohibition. One may stop up a hole with dough, however, since it is not usually smoothed out, and there is consequently no fear that he will smooth it (Magen Avraham 318:22). Turei Zahav (318:10), however, rules that one may use dough only if he is not particular to stop up the hole thoroughly. Otherwise, even with dough we fear he may smooth it (Tif. Yis.).

4.

נוֹתְנִין תַּבְשִׁיל לְתוֹךְ הַבּוֹר בִּשְׁבִיל שֶׁיְּהֵא שָׁמוּר; — We may place a cooked dish in a pit in order that it be preserved;

I.e., we may place a cooked dish in a cool dry pit to prevent its spoiling from the heat (Rav; Rashi; Meiri).

The mishnah teaches us that we need not fear that one would smooth out the depressions at the bottom of the pit in order to place the dish on level ground (Rav; Tif. Yis. from Gem. 146b). [This is in contrast to 20:4.]

Said R' Yehudah: An incident came before Rabban Yochanan ben Zakkai in Arab, and he said, "I fear on his account that he may be liable for a sin offering."

4. We may place a cooked dish in a pit in order that it be preserved; good water in stale water in order that it cool off; and cold water in the sun in order that it become warm.

One whose garments fell into the water while traveling may [continue to] walk in them, and he

YAD AVRAHAM

וְאֶת הַמַּיִם הַיָּפִים — *good water*
I.e., a bottle of potable water (*Rav; Rashi*).

בְּרָעִים — *in stale water*
I.e., in a pool of stale water (*Rav; Rashi*).

בִּשְׁבִיל שֶׁיִּצַּנּוּ; — *in order that it cool off;*
In order to prevent it from becoming warm (*Rashi; Tif. Yis.*).

Meiri explains that they would take clear warm water from the rivers and submerge it in pits of cold stale or salt water to cool it off. He quotes other authorities who omit these words. They explain that the water in the pits is warm, and the potable water is submerged therein during the winter to prevent it from becoming too cold.

This ruling is, in fact, obvious, since there is no reason to believe that it should be prohibited. It is stated in the mishnah as a prelude to the following statement, that we may place cold water in the sun in order to warm it. This statement is not obvious, as will be explained below (*Rav* from *Gem.* 146b).

וְאֶת הַצּוֹנֵן בַּחַמָּה — *and cold water in the sun*
Some editions read: וְאֶת הַצּוֹנֵן בְּחַמִּין, *and cold water in hot water* (*Rif; Ran; Rosh; Rav's* first edition).

This is permissible if the hot water is in a *secondary vessel*, whether he mixes them or places a bottle of cold water into a container (*Mishneh Berurah* 318:86). In the latter case, he must be careful not to submerge the bottle completely, in which case it would constitute *hatmanah* [see preface to Ch. 4] (*Turei Zahav* 318:19).

בִּשְׁבִיל שֶׁיֵּחַמּוּ. — *in order that it become warm.*

The mishnah teaches us this so that we not think that it is forbidden because it might lead to burying it in hot ashes, which is prohibited on the Sabbath [see above 3:3] (*Rav* from *Gemara*).

מִי שֶׁנָּשְׁרוּ כֵלָיו בַּדֶּרֶךְ בַּמַּיִם — *One whose garments fell into the water while traveling* (lit. *on the road*)

I.e. while walking on the Sabbath, one's garments fell into the water (*Rav; Rashi*).

The correct vowelization of the word is: נָשְׁרוּ, meaning, *fell*, rather than נִשְׁרוּ, *were soaked*. See *Beitzah* 35b (*Tosafos; Tif. Yis.*).

מְהַלֵּךְ בָּהֶן, — *may [continue to] walk in them,*
[I.e., he need not shed his wet clothing.]

וְאֵינוֹ חוֹשֵׁשׁ. הִגִּיעַ לֶחָצֵר הַחִיצוֹנָה, שׁוֹטְחָן בַּחַמָּה, אֲבָל לֹא כְּנֶגֶד הָעָם.

[ה] הָרוֹחֵץ בְּמֵי מְעָרָה וּבְמֵי טְבֶרְיָא

ר' עובדיה מברטנורא

הגיע לחצר החיצונה. הסמוכה למבוי העיר שהוא מקום המשתמר: **שוטחן בחמה.** ליבשן: **אבל לא כנגד העם.** שיחשדוהו שכבסן. ומשנה זו דחויה היא, שהלכה בידינו כל דבר שאסרו חכמים מפני מראית העין אפילו בחדרי חדרים אסור, הילכך אסור לשטחן אפילו שלא כנגד העם:

יד אברהם

וְאֵינוֹ חוֹשֵׁשׁ — *and he need not fear.*

I.e., he need not fear that people will suspect him of washing his clothes on the Sabbath (*Rav, Rashi*).

Alternatively, he need not fear that he will come to wring the water out of them. This is in contrast to the following mishnah which states that one may not carry a wet towel in his hand because he may come to wring out the water (*Rambam, Hil. Shabbos* 2:20; *Tur* 301; *Kol Bo* quoted by *Beis Yosef*). In this case, however, out of respect for human dignity, the Rabbis did not require a person to go without his clothing or even to shed one item of his apparel (*Tos. Yom Tov*).

Although he may continue to wear his clothes, he may not shake the water out of them. This is tantamount to wringing them a *toladah* of *whitening (*Tif. Yis.*).

הִגִּיעַ לֶחָצֵר הַחִיצוֹנָה — *When he arrives at the outer courtyard,*

I.e., when he arrives at the first courtyard in which he may safely leave his garments (*Rav; Rashi*).

שׁוֹטְחָן בַּחַמָּה — *he may spread them out in the sun,*

In order to dry them (*Rav; Rashi*).

אֲבָל לֹא כְּנֶגֶד הָעָם — *but not in front of the people.*

I.e. he may not spread out his clothes in a public place lest people suspect him of having laundered them on the Sabbath. This mishnah is not the accepted halachah. The accepted halachah is in accordance with R' Eliezer and R' Shimon (quoted by *Gem.* 146b) who rule that one may not spread out the clothing even where it is not visible to the public. The rule is: "Anything that the Rabbis prohibited for appearance's sake (i.e., because it looks to people as if one is doing something wrong) is forbidden even in the innermost chambers" (*Rav; Rambam, Hil. Shabbos* 22:20; *Shulchan Aruch* 301:45).

5.

The mishnah now discusses bathing and drying oneself on the Sabbath. The Rabbis prohibited bathing in hot water on the Sabbath even if it was heated before the Sabbath. This was prohibited because the bathhouse attendants would heat the water on the Sabbath and claim that it had been heated before the Sabbath. Subsequently, the Rabbis prohibited even entering a bathhouse in order to perspire (this was akin to the saunas of today), since people would enter the bathhouse to bathe under the pretext of entering merely to perspire (*Gem.* 40a).

Initially, even bathing in the water of thermal springs was prohibited. When

need not fear. When he arrives at the outer courtyard, he may spread them out in the sun, but not in front of the people.

5. One who bathes in the water of a cave or in the water of Tiberias and

YAD AVRAHAM

the Rabbis saw that the people could not endure a total ban on hot-water bathing they lifted the ban on bathing in thermal springs (*Gem.* 40a; see above 3:4).

הָרוֹחֵץ — *One who bathes*

Seemingly, the mishnah should begin by stating רוֹחֵץ, *one may bathe*, rather than הָרוֹחֵץ, *one who bathes*. By phrasing the case as *one who bathes*, the mishnah implies that the bathing itself is prohibited and that we are dealing only with the aftermath of an act which should not have taken place. The mishnah must therefore be discussing the case of one who bathed in hot water. This is further indicated by the juxtaposition of cave water and thermal springs (see below), again indicating that the water being discussed is of the same general variety as that of the thermal spring; namely, hot water (*Gem.* 147a). The framing of the phrase in such a manner as to imply disapproval of the act of bathing on the Sabbath is, however, done only in reference to the case of the cave water. Bathing in the waters of Tiberias (i.e., the thermal springs) is permitted (*Tos.*; *Rosh*; *Ran*).

בְּמֵי מְעָרָה — *in the water of a cave*

I.e., from the start, one may not bathe in cave water that has been heated by fire (*Rosh*; *Ran* from *Ramban* and *R' Yonah*).

Others explain this as the water of thermal springs, such as those of Tiberias (*Rif*; *Rambam*; *Rashi*). Although one is generally permitted to bathe in the water of thermal springs, as will be explained below, one may do so, according to those latter authorities, only when the spring is not in an enclosed area, such as a cave. Since in an enclosed area the heat cannot dissipate, the enclosure becomes a sauna. Anyone entering to bathe will automatically perspire there too. As explained above, to enter a sauna in order to perspire is banned apart from the prohibition of bathing. Therefore, the rule permitting bathing in the water of thermal springs can apply only to those in an open area.

The first explanation rejects this view. According to those authorities, just as the Rabbis differentiate between bathing in water heated by fire and water heated by a thermal spring, so too did they differentiate between perspiring in a sauna heated by fire and one heated by thermal springs, permitting the latter. Accordingly, they explain the mishnah as referring only to water heated by fire.

וּבְמֵי טְבֶרְיָא — *or in the water of Tiberias*

I.e., in water of the thermal springs of Tiberias. In contrast to the previous case, such bathing is permissible. It is mentioned here only to indicate that the mishnah is discussing bathing in hot water and that the cave water mentioned is, therefore, also hot water. The *ban* against bathing in hot water, however, applies only to cave water (*Tos. Yom Tov* from *Gem.*).

שבת כב/ו

וְנִסְתַּפֵּג אֲפִלּוּ בְּעֶשֶׂר אֲלֻנְטִיאוֹת לֹא יְבִיאֵם בְּיָדוֹ; אֲבָל עֲשָׂרָה בְּנֵי אָדָם מִסְתַּפְּגִין בַּאֲלֻנְטִית אַחַת — פְּנֵיהֶם יְדֵיהֶם וְרַגְלֵיהֶם — וּמְבִיאִין אוֹתָהּ בְּיָדָן.

[ו] **סָכִין** וּמְמַשְׁמְשִׁין בִּבְנֵי מֵעַיִם, אֲבָל לֹא

ר' עובדיה מברטנורא

(ה) **ונסתפג. וקנח: אפילו בעשר אלונטיות.** סדינים שמקנחים בהן, ונסתפג בהן זה אחר זה אף על גב דלא נפישי מיא בכל חד וחד אפילו הכי לא יביאם בידו לתוך ביתו, אפילו על ידי עירוב, שאין כאן חיסור הולאה, אלא גזרה שמא ישכח ויסחוט בבואו: **אבל עשרה בני אדם.** הואיל ומרובין הם מדכרי אהדדי. ואפילו חדא אלונטית לעשרה בני אדם דהשתא נפישי בה מיא אפילו הכי מביאין אותה בידם ולא גזרינן שמא יסחטוה, הואיל ומרובים הן: **פניהם ידיהם ורגליהם.** אורחא דמלתא נקט וה"ה לכל גופן. ואין הלכה כמשנה זו אלא אחד מביא בידו אלונטית שנסתפג בה ולא חיישינן שמא יסחוט: (ו) **סבין.** שמן בשבת: **וממשמשין.** ביד על כל הגוף להנאה:

יד אברהם

וְנִסְתַּפֵּג — *and dried himself*

Although the word is used in the past tense, it is not meant to imply that one is not permitted to dry himself in the first place. On the contrary, since the mishnah will explicitly state below that ten people may dry themselves with one towel it follows that one person may certainly do so. (The mishnah distinguishes between one person and many persons only in regard to carrying the towels, not in regard to drying oneself.) Moreover, the *Gemara* states explicitly that one may dry himself with a towel on the Sabbath.

As explained in the previous mishnah, there are two reasons for the general prohibition of wetting fabrics on the Sabbath: (a) for fear he will wring them out, and (b) because soaking a fabric is tantamount to washing it. As far as the first consideration is concerned, since it is only Rabbinic, the Rabbis did not forbid it in this case, because they felt that such a measure could not endure. Since it was necessary to permit some bathing (see introduction to this mishnah), and it is customary for all bathers to dry themselves, no one would heed such a Rabbinic prohibition (*Tos. Yom Tov* from *Ran*).

As regards the second consideration, soaking a fabric is not regarded as tantamount to washing it unless it was originally soiled. Therefore, one may dry himself with a clean towel and thus avoid this prohibition (*Tos. Yom Tov*). Many early authorities, however, prohibit soaking even a clean garment. In this case, however, one may dry himself with a towel since he is soiling the towel, rather than washing it (*Tos.* 11b.).

אֲפִלּוּ בְּעֶשֶׂר אֲלֻנְטִיאוֹת — *with even ten towels*

I.e., even though he dried himself with ten towels, thus barely wetting any of them (*Rav; Rashi*).

לֹא יְבִיאֵם בְּיָדוֹ; — *may not carry them in his hand;*

I.e., even in a locale where one is permitted to carry, one may not carry the towels home in his hand, for fear that he will forget and wring them out on his way home (*Rav; Rashi*).

dried himself with even ten towels may not carry them in his hand; but ten people may dry themselves with one towel — their faces, their hands and their feet — and they may carry it in their hands.

6. We may anoint and massage the stomach, but

YAD AVRAHAM

By forbidding him to bring the towel home, we insure that he will not wring the towel even in its place, since he will not benefit from such an action (*Ramban, Comm.; Tos. Yom Tov*).

[Since the ban on bringing the towel home does not prevent people from bathing, the Rabbis were able to institute it.]

אֲבָל עֲשָׂרָה בְּנֵי אָדָם מִסְתַּפְּגִין בַּאֲלוּנְטִית — אַחַת — פְּנֵיהֶם יְדֵיהֶם וְרַגְלֵיהֶם — *but ten people may dry themselves with one towel — their faces, their hands and their feet —*

They may even dry their whole bodies with the same towel. The mishnah mentions faces, hands and feet, only because it is more usual for many people to use a common towel for their faces, hands and feet, than for their whole bodies (*Rav; Rashi*).

וּמְבִיאִין אוֹתָהּ בְּיָדָן. — *and they may carry it in their hands.*

Since many people are involved together, if one of them forgets that the towel may not be wrung out on the Sabbath, he will undoubtedly be reminded by the others. The ban against carrying the towel, therefore, does not apply (*Rav; Rashi*).

The *Gemara* (147b) quotes the opinion of R' Shimon who disputes the ruling of this mishnah and permits even an individual to carry home his towel. The *Amoraim* (Rabbis of the *Gemara*) rule in accord with this latter opinion, and this is the halachah (*Rav; Rif; Rosh; Rambam, Comm.; Shulchan Aruch* 301:48).

Although wet clothing may not, in general, be handled (*Rama* 301:46), since the Rabbis of necessity permitted one to dry himself, they also permitted him to carry home his towel (*Magen Avraham* 301:58). Accordingly, once reaching home, he is no longer permitted to handle the towel. *Eliyah Rabbah*, however, quotes *Sefer HaTerumah*, who maintains that the reason they permitted him to carry home his towel is because used towels are usually only slightly wet. According to this, even after the towel has been brought home, it may still be handled (*Mishnah Berurah*, ibid. 175).

6.

סָכִין — *We may anoint*

I.e., we may anoint with oil on the Sabbath (*Rav; Rashi*).

[It was the common practice, in those days, to rub olive oil into the skin to keep it soft and prevent its drying out.]

וּמְמַשְׁמְשִׁין בִּבְנֵי מֵעַיִם, — *and massage the stomach,*

I.e., we may massage the entire body gently for pleasure (*Rav; Rashi*).

Apparently the edition of the mishnah used by *Rav* and *Rashi* did not contain the words, בִּבְנֵי מֵעַיִם, *the stomach*. Neither did *Rif* and *Rosh* have these words in their mishnah. According to the version which

שבת כב/ו

מִתְעַמְּלִין וְלֹא מִתְגָּרְדִין. אֵין יוֹרְדִין לְקוֹרְדִּימָה; וְאֵין עוֹשִׂין אַפִּיקְטְוִיזִין; וְאֵין מְעַצְּבִין אֶת הַקָּטָן; וְאֵין מַחֲזִירִין אֶת הַשֶּׁבֶר. מִי שֶׁנִּפְרְקָה יָדוֹ וְרַגְלוֹ,

ר' עובדיה מברטנורא

אבל לא מתעמלין. לשפשף בכח: **ולא מתגרדין.** במגרדת, ודומה לו (איוב ב) ויקח לו חרש להתגרד בו, משום דהוי כעובדא דחול: **אין יורדין לפולימא.** בקעה מלאה מים ותחתיה טיט כמו דבק, ויש בה מקומות שיטבע הרוחץ שם באותו טיט וידבק בו ואינו יכול לעלות עד שיתקבצו בני אדם ויעלוהו בקושי גדול ובדוחק. פ"א בקעה שטיט שלה מחליק והרוחץ שם נופל ובגדיו נשורים במים ואתי לידי סחיטה: **אפיקטויזין.** להקיא. ופירושו אפיק טוי זיין, כלומר להוציא המזון ממקום בשולו שהיא האצטומכא. אפיק, מוציא. טוי, מתבשל. גלי לשון מתרגמינן טוי גור. זיין, מזון. ודוקא לשתות משקה שמביאו להקיא בשבת הוא שאסור אבל להכניס אצבעו לתוך פיו כדי להקיא מותר. והיכא דחייש ליה לצערא ואם יקיא יתרפא מותר אפילו על ידי משקה: **ואין מעצבין את הקטן.** לתקנו וליישב עצמותיו וחוליות שדרתו משום דמיחזי כבונה. ולא אמרן אלא לאחר זמן אבל ביום לידה שרי. מעצבין, לשון ידיך עצבוני ויעשוני (שם י'): **ואין מחזירין את השבר.** עצם שנשבר. ואין הלכה כמשנה זו, אלא הלכה מחזירין את השבר בשבת: **שנפרקה ידו.** שיצא העצם מן הפרק שלו

יד אברהם

does add "the stomach," it was customary to anoint the stomach specifically with oil and to massage it. Either it was first anointed and then massaged, or it was first massaged and then anointed. In order to avoid performing a *weekday activity* on the Sabbath, one is required to anoint and massage simultaneously (*Rambam, Hil. Shabbos* 21:28).

אֲבָל לֹא מִתְעַמְּלִין — *but we may neither knead*

I.e., we may not massage vigorously (*Rav; Rashi; Tif. Yis.*).

This is prohibited because it is a weekday-type activity (*Tos. Yom Tov; Tif. Yis.*).

Another explanation is that we may not pummel one's body with force until one grows tired and perspires, or to walk until one becomes tired and perspires. This is forbidden as part of the general ban of the use of curatives on the Sabbath (*Rambam, Hil. Shabbos* 21:28; *Meiri; Tos. Yom Tov; Tif. Yis.*).

וְלֹא מִתְגָּרְדִין — *nor scrape [the skin].*

I.e., we may not scrape the skin with a strigil (an instrument of metal, ivory or horn used, in olden times, to scrape the skin at the bath), since this, too, is a weekday activity (*Rav; Rashi; Rambam, Hil. Shabbos* 21:30).

אֵין יוֹרְדִין לְקוֹרְדִּימָה; — *We may not go down to Kordima;*

I.e., we may not go down to the Kordima river (*Rashi*).

The banks of this river abounded with very slippery spots where one was likely to fall and soak his clothes. He would, therefore, be placing himself in a position in which he would be likely to wring out his drenched garments (*Rashi on Gem.* 147b).

Rav reads לְפוּלִימָא, which he explains in one version similarly to *Rashi*, except that he renders it a valley rather than a river. In another version, he explains it as a valley filled with water under which there is treacherous quicksand. One who falls there is in danger of sinking in the quicksand and being unable to extricate himself until

22
6 we may neither knead nor scrape [the skin]. We may not go down to Kordima; nor take an emetic; nor straighten an infant['s limbs]; nor set a fracture. If one's hand or foot became dislocated,

YAD AVRAHAM

people gather there and pull him out. This explanation is offered by *Rif*, too. He offers a second explanation that it is a place where bathers become chilled and where the water causes diarrhea. *Rambam* (*Hil. Shabbos* 21:29) alludes to these two explanations. Since these cause discomfort, one may not subject himself to them on the Sabbath, for Scripture says (*Is.* 58:13) וְקָרָאתָ לַשַּׁבָּת עֹנֶג, *You shall call the Sabbath a delight* (*Rambam*, ibid.).

Rambam (*Comm.*) explains it as a cave full of water. Since the cave is closed, it is warm, and bathers perspire from the heat as in a sauna. As mentioned above, it is prohibited to induce perspiration on the Sabbath.

וְאֵין עוֹשִׂין אַפִּיקְטְוִיזִין; — *nor take* (lit. *make*) *an emetic;*

The term אַפִּיקְטְוִיזִין is a combination of three Aramaic words: אַפִּיק, *take out;* טְוֵי, *cooked*, or *digested;* זִין, *food*, i.e., to remove the food from the stomach, where it is becoming digested (*Rav*).

Others interpret it as a combination of: אַפִּיק, *take out;* טְפֵי, *extra;* זִין, *food*, i.e., take out the excess food causing discomfort (*Aruch*).

It is prohibited to induce vomiting by ingesting an emetic, since this resembles taking medicine, which is forbidden on the Sabbath (see above 14:3) (*Rashi*). If one needs to vomit, however, he may thrust his finger into his throat. If he is in great pain, he may even take medicine to induce vomiting (*Rav*).

וְאֵין מְעַצְּבִין אֶת הַקָּטָן; — *nor straighten an infant['s limbs];*

I.e., if one of the vertebrae becomes dislocated, it may not be reset, since this appears like *building (*Rav; Tif. Yis.* from *Gem.* 147b).

Should the infant suffer intense pain, however, it is permissible to reset the vertebrae through a non-Jew (*Tif. Yis.*).

These restrictions do not apply to the day of birth, when the limbs may be straightened (*Rav; Tif. Yis.; Shulchan Aruch* 330:9; see *Magen Avraham* 18; *Turei Zahav* 6).

וְאֵין מַחֲזִירִין אֶת הַשֶּׁבֶר. — *nor set a fracture.*

The *Gemara* reports an alternate reading of the mishnah that omits the word *nor* (*Rashi*). The halachah follows this reading. Accordingly, we may set a fracture on the Sabbath (*Rav; Tif. Yis.* from *Gem.* 148a).

Should the joint be dislocated, *Shulchan Aruch* (328:47) permits resetting it if it is completely dislocated (*Shulchan Atzei Shittim*, quoted by *Mishnah Berurah*, ibid. 145). *Magen Avraham* (ibid. 51), however, rules that only a broken bone may be reset on the Sabbath, but not a dislocated one. [It may, however, be reset by a non-Jew (*Mishnah Berurah*, ibid.).] Should a physician state that the limb is endangered by neglecting to set the bone, even *Magen Avraham* concurs that the bone may be set (ibid.).

מִי שֶׁנִּפְרְקָה יָדוֹ וְרַגְלוֹ, — *If one's hand or foot became dislocated,*

According to *Shulchan Aruch* and

[487] THE MISHNAH/SHABBOS — Chapter Twenty-Two: *Chavis*

שבת כב/ו

לֹא יְטָרְפֵם בְּצוֹנֵן, אֲבָל רוֹחֵץ הוּא כְּדַרְכּוֹ, וְאִם נִתְרַפֵּא, נִתְרַפֵּא.

ר' עובדיה מברטנורא

לא יטרפם. לשון בילים טרופות בקערה, שמשתתף [בצונן] על מקום השבר, דמיחזי דלרפואה קעביד:

יד אברהם

Shulchan Atzei Shittim mentioned above, this refers to a case in which the joint is not completely dislocated (*Mishnah Berurah* 328:148).

לֹא יְטָרְפֵם בְּצוֹנֵן — *he may not massage them with cold water,*

I.e., he may not rub vigorously with cold water (*Tur* 328), since this is obviously being done for therapeutic purposes (*Rav*).

22 6 he may not massage them with cold water, but he may bathe according to his usual manner, and if he is healed, he is healed.

YAD AVRAHAM

אֲבָל רוֹחֵץ הוּא כְּדַרְכּוֹ, — *but he may bathe according to his usual manner,*

[I.e., he may bathe his hands and feet with cold water in the usual manner.]

Others explain the mishnah as: He may not bathe the affected limbs alone, since it is then an obviously therapeutic measure, but he may bathe his entire body, thereby bathing the affected limbs as well (*Meiri*).

וְאִם נִתְרַפֵּא, נִתְרַפֵּא. — *and if he is healed, he is healed.*

[Since it is not apparent that he is bathing the limbs to reset them, it is permissible. See above 14:4.]

פרק עשרים ושלש
Chapter Twenty-Three

The prophet Isaiah proclaims (*Isaiah* 58:13-14): *If you restrain, because of the Sabbath, your feet, refrain from accomplishing your mundane needs on My holy day . . . and you honor it by not doing your ways,* מִמְּצוֹא חֶפְצְךָ, *from seeking your personal wants,* וְדַבֵּר דָּבָר, *and discussing the forbidden. Then you shall be granted pleasure with* HASHEM . . .

To insure compliance with words מִמְּצוֹא חֶפְצְךָ, *from seeking your personal wants*, the Rabbis banned commercial transactions on the Sabbath (*Rashi, Beitzah* 36a).

They also banned all activities related to such transactions, such as weighing, measuring or counting out precise amounts of produce or other merchandise (*Rambam, Lev.* 23:24). The reading of documents was also included in this ban (mishnah 2), as was making otherwise permissible arrangements or preparations for activities prohibited on the Sabbath (see mishnah 3).

To fulfill the words וְדַבֵּר דָּבָר, *or discussing the forbidden*, the Rabbis banned discussing one's plans to perform after the Sabbath any act forbidden on the Sabbath. Similarly, issuing instructions even to a non-Jew to engage in any activity prohibited on the Sabbath (whether Biblically or Rabbinically) was prohibited, even if those instructions pertain to work to be done after the Sabbath.

Rambam points out that according to strict Torah law, it would be possible for one to engage in commerce on the Sabbath to such an extent that it would no longer be recognizable as a holy day or day of rest. In a city enclosed by a wall, one is permitted to carry. He would, therefore, be able to load his goods on his animals (the use of pack animals on the Sabbath within an enclosure being only Rabbinically prohibited), haul it to the market, sell, buy, plan his week's activities, and review his records. All this, without violating any of the thirty-nine *melachos*. To preserve the special character and spirit of the Sabbath, the Rabbis, heeding the admonition of Isaiah, enacted a broad range of prohibitions designed to prevent the Sabbath from appearing as a workday (*Rambam, Lev.* 23:24; see also *Rambam, Hil. Shabbos* 21:1 as explained by *Maggid Mishneh*).

[א] **שׁוֹאֵל** אָדָם מֵחֲבֵרוֹ כַּדֵּי יַיִן וְכַדֵּי שֶׁמֶן, וּבִלְבַד שֶׁלֹּא יֹאמַר לוֹ: "הַלְוֵנִי."
וְכֵן, הָאִשָּׁה מֵחֲבֶרְתָּהּ, כִּכָּרוֹת.
וְאִם אֵינוֹ מַאֲמִינוֹ, מַנִּיחַ טַלִּיתוֹ אֶצְלוֹ וְעוֹשֶׂה עִמּוֹ חֶשְׁבּוֹן לְאַחַר שַׁבָּת. וְכֵן, עֶרֶב

ר' עובדיה מברטנורא

פרק עשרים ושלש - שואל. (א) **שואל.** ובלבד שלא יאמר הלוני. דהלואה לזמן מרובה משמע וקיי"ל סתם הלואה שלשים יום הלכך אתי מלוה לכתוב על פנקסו כך וכך הלויתי לפלוני כדי שלא ישכח: **מניח טליתו אצלו.** אם אינו מאמינו ולוקח מותו ומקדישו בשבת, דחובות שקבוע להן זמן יכולין להקדיש בשבת:

יד אברהם

1.

שׁוֹאֵל אָדָם מֵחֲבֵרוֹ כַּדֵּי יַיִן וְכַדֵּי שֶׁמֶן — *A person may borrow pitchers of wine or pitchers of oil from his friend,*

[I.e., on the Sabbath.]

וּבִלְבַד שֶׁלֹּא יֹאמַר לוֹ: "הַלְוֵנִי." — *provided he does not say to him: "Lend me."*

I.e., when asking for these items he may not use the term הַלְוֵנִי, because the Rabbis feared the lender might come to write up a note of this loan.

In Hebrew, there are two verbs meaning to borrow, לִשְׁאֹל and לִלְוֹת. The former refers to the loan of items which are *returned*, such as household utensils. The latter refers to the loan of items which are *replaced* or *repaid* rather than returned, such as food or money. (One does not return the same cup of sugar or dollar bill he has borrowed; rather, he replaces it with another.)

The halachah, too, differentiates between the two. A הַלְוָאָה, *loan*, such as money, is for a period of thirty days, unless otherwise specified at the time of the loan. During these 30 days, the lender cannot demand repayment. A שְׁאֵלָה, loan of an object meant to be returned intact, may be reclaimed by the lender at any time. Since the use of the verb לִלְוֹת connotes a loan for a period of thirty days, the Rabbis feared that a lender, responding to a request of הַלְוֵנִי, would make a note of this loan so as not to forget about it. They therefore required the borrower to state הַשְׁאִילֵנִי, which does not imply a loan of any specific duration. Since the lender can reclaim it at any time, he feels no necessity to make any note of it (*Rav; Rashi*). Although the term הַשְׁאִילֵנִי does not strictly apply to wine and oil (since the borrower intends to consume and then replace them), its use is the equivalent of stipulating that the lender may request repayment at any time (*Tos. R' Akiva from Rashba*).

Tosafos (148a) question the assertion that a loan made under the term הַשְׁאִילֵנִי may be reclaimed at any time. They therefore explain that the reason one generally makes note of a הַלְוָאָה is because the object lent is not itself returned but replaced. [It is therefore more likely to be forgotten.] A שְׁאֵלָה, however, does not need the reminder of a note, since the object itself attests

23
1

1. A person may borrow pitchers of wine or pitchers of oil from his friend, provided he does not say to him: "Lend me." In the same manner, a woman [may borrow] loaves [of bread] from her friend.

If he does not trust him, he may leave his cloak with him and make a reckoning with him after the Sabbath.

YAD AVRAHAM

to the loan. Though the wine and oil borrowed will not actually be returned, the imprecise use of this verb serves to remind the lender not to write a note on the Sabbath.

Obviously, these differences in expression apply only in Hebrew. In languages in which both types of borrowing are expressed in the same way, the only way one may ask to borrow any commodities on the Sabbath is to say, "Give me" (*Tif. Yis.* from *Shulchan Aruch* 307:11).

וְכֵן, הָאִשָּׁה מֵחֲבֶרְתָּהּ כִּכָּרוֹת. — *In the same manner, a woman [may borrow] loaves [of bread] from her friend.*

[I.e., the same regulations apply to a woman who wishes to borrow loaves of bread from a friend.]

The mishnah adds this case to teach us that although women do not usually write down the debts owed them, the Rabbis, nevertheless, included them in the prohibition of lending with the expression of הַלְוָאָה (*Shoshanim LeDavid*).

The *Gemara* seeks to reconcile this mishnah with the ruling of Hillel (*Bava Metzia* 5:9) that a woman may not lend a loaf of bread to a friend without first establishing its monetary value. This must be done to avoid the possibility of violating the prohibition against taking interest on a loan, in case the price of wheat should rise between the time of the loan and its repayment. By establishing the price at the time of the loan, we can insure that the *value* of the loaf repaid does not exceed the *value* of the one borrowed. I.e., if the *value* of a loaf increases, the borrower will repay a smaller loaf than the one borrowed. Our mishnah, however, implies, that aside from certain Sabbath considerations this type of loan is unrestricted.

The *Gemara* resolves this by explaining that our mishnah refers to a locale in which the price of a loaf of bread is well established and which, therefore, need not be determined. Hillel, on the other hand, refers to places where the prices tend to vary; hence, the need to fix its value at the time of the loan.

וְאִם אֵינוֹ מַאֲמִינוֹ — *If he does not trust him,*

[If the lender does not trust him to repay the wine or oil.]

מַנִּיחַ טַלִּיתוֹ אֶצְלוֹ — *he may leave his cloak with him*

I.e., as security for the loan. Since the mishnah does not state, "he may give him his cloak as security," we infer that one is not permitted to explicitly state, "Here is security." Such a statement, indicative as it is of a commercial transaction, represents weekday activity (*Rama*, 307:11, *Tif. Yis.*). [This, however, may not be done on the Sabbath itself.]

וְעוֹשֶׂה עִמּוֹ חֶשְׁבּוֹן לְאַחַר שַׁבָּת. — *and make a reckoning with him after the Sabbath.*

After the Sabbath they may reckon the precise amount owed (*Tif. Yis.*). [This, however, may not be done on the Sabbath itself.]

שבת כג/ב

פֶּסַח בִּירוּשָׁלַיִם שֶׁחָל לִהְיוֹת בַּשַּׁבָּת, מַנִּיחַ טַלִּיתוֹ אֶצְלוֹ, וְנוֹטֵל אֶת פִּסְחוֹ, וְעוֹשֶׂה עִמּוֹ חֶשְׁבּוֹן לְאַחַר יוֹם טוֹב.

[ב] **מוֹנֶה** אָדָם אֶת אוֹרְחָיו וְאֶת פַּרְפְּרוֹתָיו מִפִּיו, אֲבָל לֹא מִן הַכְּתָב. וּמֵפִיס

ר' עובדיה מברטנורא

(ב) **פרפרותיו.** מיני מטעמים: **אבל לא מן הכתב.** אם כתב מערב שבת כך וכך אורחים כדי שלא ישכחם, לא יקרא באותו כתב בשבת, גזירה שמא ימחוק. ח"נ שמא יקרא בשטרי הדיוטות, ואין מותר לקרות בשבת אלא בתורה שבכתב, ובתורה שבעל פה לאחר שכתבוה, ובפירושיהן, אבל בשאר דברים או בספרי חכמות, שאינו מדברי נבואה או מפירושיהן, אסורים: **מפיס.** מטיל גורל לחלק למי יגיע כל מנה ומנה:

יד אברהם

וְכֵן, עֶרֶב פֶּסַח בִּירוּשָׁלַיִם שֶׁחָל לִהְיוֹת בַּשַּׁבָּת, — So too, in Jerusalem, [when] the day before Passover falls out on the Sabbath,

I.e., if the first night of Passover falls out on Saturday night, in which case the *pesach* offering is brought on the Sabbath, one who forgot to acquire a lamb before the Sabbath is forced to acquire it on the Sabbath (*Rashi; Ran; Tos. Yom Tov*).

מַנִּיחַ טַלִּיתוֹ אֶצְלוֹ, וְנוֹטֵל אֶת פִּסְחוֹ, — he may leave his cloak with him, take his *pesach* offering,

If the seller does not trust him, the buyer may leave his cloak with the seller, as in the previous case (*Rav*).

וְעוֹשֶׂה עִמּוֹ חֶשְׁבּוֹן לְאַחַר יוֹם טוֹב. — and make a reckoning with him after Yom Tov.

[Just as one may not make a reckoning on the Sabbath, he may not do so on *Yom Tov*. Therefore, he must wait until after the first day of Passover (until the first day of the intermediate days) to make a reckoning for the animal.]

Before offering any animal as a sacrifice, one must first hallow it. This is done by the owner stating that he is designating this animal for whichever type of sacrifice he intends to offer. Upon so doing, the animal becomes designated for that sacrifice and all the laws pertaining to hallowed animals pertain to it.

Ordinarily, it is Rabbinically forbidden to *hallow* items on either the Sabbath or *Yom Tov* (*Beitzah* 5:2), because it resembles a commercial transaction (*Beitzah* 37a), by virtue of the fact that the ownership of the item changes from that of the hallower to that of the holy estate (*Rashi* there).

The *pesach* offering, however, is an exception. Since it is an obligatory offering which must be offered at a set time, the Rabbis permitted that it be hallowed on the Sabbath when no other time is possible (*Rav* from *Gem*. 148b).

Obligatory offerings which do not have a set time for their sacrifice may not be hallowed on either *Yom Tov* or the Sabbath (*Tos. Yom Tov* from *Gem*. ibid.).

So too, in Jerusalem, [when] the day before Passover falls out on the Sabbath, he may leave his cloak with him, take his *pesach* offering, and make a reckoning with him after Yom Tov.

2. A person may count his guests and desserts orally, but not from a written note. And

YAD AVRAHAM
2.

As mentioned in the prefatory note to this chapter, included in the prohibition stemming from the injunction of מִמְּצוֹא חֶפְצְךָ, *from seeking your personal wants*, is the reading of שְׁטָרֵי הֶדְיוֹטוֹת, *secular documents* (*Bach* 307). According to *Rashi* (*Shabbos* 116b), this includes both documents relating to matters of business and personal letters. *Tosafos*, differing with *Rashi's* ruling against reading personal letters on the Sabbath, justify the custom of reading them. *Rambam* (*Comm.*) includes all books of a secular and even scientific nature, since the Sabbath should be devoted solely to the study of Torah. *Ramban* and *Rashba*, however, permit reading scientific works (*Shulchan Aruch* 307:65). According to *Rama* (397:16), this applies only to those books written in languages other than Hebrew. Hebrew books, however, may be read, since the language itself possesses sanctity. Moreover, Biblical verses are usually quoted. This ruling is contested by many later authorities (see *Magen Avraham; Taz; Mishnah Berurah*).

מוֹנֶה אָדָם אֶת אוֹרְחָיו — *A person may count his guests*
I.e., he may count the number of guests he wishes to invite for the Sabbath in order to know how many loaves of bread he will need (*Meiri*).

וְאֶת פַּרְפְּרוֹתָיו — *and desserts*
I.e., he may count the number of portions of dessert he must serve to his guests (*Tif. Yis.*).

מִפִּיו, אֲבָל לֹא מִן הַכְּתָב — *orally, but not from a written note.*
I.e., from memory, but not from a guest list prepared before the Sabbath (*Rav; Rashi*).

The *Gemara* (149a) cites two explanations for the reason for this prohibition. One is that this is a precaution against the erasure of some of the names; i.e., the possibility that upon realizing that he has inadequate food for so large a number of guests, he will decide to invite fewer people and erase the names of those to be left out (*Tos. Yom Tov* from *Rashi* on *Gemara* 149a). Others give the reason as a precaution against reading secular documents on the Sabbath. This, in order to insure that any reading on the Sabbath be devoted solely to the reading of Torah topics; viz. the Bible, the Mishnah and Talmud, and their commentaries (*Rav, Rambam, Comm.* from *Gem.* ibid.).

שבת כג/ב

עִם בָּנָיו וְעִם בְּנֵי בֵיתוֹ עַל הַשֻּׁלְחָן, וּבִלְבַד שֶׁלֹּא יִתְכַּוֵּן לַעֲשׂוֹת מָנָה גְדוֹלָה כְּנֶגֶד קְטַנָּה, מִשּׁוּם קֻבְיָא. וּמַטִּילִין חֲלָשִׁים עַל הַקֳּדָשִׁים בְּיוֹם טוֹב, אֲבָל לֹא עַל הַמָּנוֹת.

ר' עובדיה מברטנורא

עם בניו ועם בני ביתו. שהן סמוכים על שולחנו שאין כאן קפידא. אבל עם אחר לא, דבני חבורה המקפידים זה על זה שאינן מוחלין ואינן מוותרים זה לזה עוברים משום מדה ומשום משקל ומשום מנין ומשום לווין ופורעין דגזרו בהו רבנן שמא יכתבו: **ובלבד שלא יתבוין וכו'.** מתניתין חסורי מחסרא והכי קתני, מפיס אדם עם בניו ועם בני ביתו על השלחן, ואפילו מנה גדולה כנגד מנה קטנה, ודוקא עם בניו ועם בני ביתו אבל עם אחר לא, ובלבד שלא יתכוין לעשות מנה גדולה כנגד מנה קטנה, ואז הוא דביום טוב אסור ובחול שרי, אבל אם נתכוין לעשות מנה גדולה כנגד מנה קטנה אפילו בחול אסור משום קוביא, דגול הוא ואסמכתא לא קניא, והאי אסמכתא היא דסמיך על הגורל אם יפול לו הגורל על המנה הגדולה יזכה בה, ולפיכך תלה עצמו אף לגורל הקטנה על הספק, ואילו ידע מתחילה שכן, לא היה מתרצה: **גורלות. חלשים**, כמו חולש על גוים (ישעיה יד, יב): **על הקדשים ביו"ט.** שנשחטו ביום טוב, לחלק אותם בין הכהנים. אבל לא על המנות. של קדשים של אתמול:

יד אברהם

וּמֵפִיס עִם־בָּנָיו וְעִם בְּנֵי בֵיתוֹ עַל הַשֻּׁלְחָן, — *And he may cast lots with his children and the members of his household [for portions] at the table,*

This refers to children who are dependents. Since one's dependents are not paying for their food, they are not overly particular about how large a portion each one gets. Consequently, we need not be concerned that this will lead to first measuring, weighing, or counting out exact portions on the Sabbath. With others, however, casting lots for portions is prohibited, since in their concern not to be cheated, they measure, weigh, or count out exact portions, as they are normally accustomed to doing. In so doing, they would be violating the Rabbinic injunctions prohibiting these activities on the Sabbath (*Tos. Yom Tov* from *Tos.*). Furthermore, they may violate the injunction against borrowing portions using the term *halveni*, which, as explained in mishnah 1, is prohibited (*Rav* from *Gem.* 149b).

וּבִלְבַד שֶׁלֹּא יִתְכַּוֵּן לַעֲשׂוֹת מָנָה גְדוֹלָה כְּנֶגֶד קְטַנָּה, — *provided he does not wager a large portion against a small portion,*

The *Gemara* (149b) explains that there is a phrase missing from the mishnah, and the mishnah should be understood as follows: *One may cast lots with his children and members of his household [for portions] at the table even if some portions are larger than others. With others (i.e., nondependents), however, he may not cast lots even for equal portions. If he casts lots for unequal portions, it is forbidden even during the week.* The phrase in our mishnah *provided he does not wager . . .* is to be understood as referring only to those not of one household. Its meaning is that the Sabbath prohibition against casting lots refers only to equal portions; casting lots for unequal portions is prohibited quite apart from any Sabbath consider-

23 2 he may cast lots with his children and the members of his household [for portions] at the table, provided he does not intend to wager a large portion against a small portion, because of [the prohibition of] gambling. And [*Kohanim*] may cast lots for sacrifices on *Yom Tov*, but not for portions.

YAD AVRAHAM

ations, since it constitutes gambling (*Rav; Rashi*).

מִשּׁוּם קֻבְיָא. — *because of [the prohibition of] gambling* (lit. *dice*).

Dice is a general term used for all forms of gambling.

Gambling is prohibited because the loser does not willingly part with his money. He agreed to the bet because he expected to win. Had he known that he would lose, he would not have entered into the bet. Taking his money is, therefore, Rabbinically considered akin to stealing (*Rav; Rashi*). [One who purchases an item or a service, however, receives something definite in return. He is, consequently, not merely giving away his money but exchanging it. His parting with the money is, therefore, considered a willing one.]

The consideration of gambling does not apply to casting lots for unequal portions with one's dependents because all the portions belong to the head of the house. Those drawing lots are not losing anything that was theirs (*Rashi*).

וּמְטִילִין חֲלָשִׁים עַל הַקֳּדָשִׁים בְּיוֹם טוֹב, — *And [Kohanim] may cast lots for sacrifices on Yom Tov,*

I.e., for the portions to be eaten by the *Kohanim* from sacrifices offered on the festival (*Rav from Gem.* 149b).

Since the *Kohen* fulfills a *mitzvah* when he eats those parts of the sacrifice designated for him, obtaining a large portion evidences his love and appreciation of this *mitzvah* (*Rambam, Hil. Yom Tov* 4:20). Therefore, eagerness on the part of *Kohanim* to eat from the sacrifices and to obtain a large portion is commendable. Consequently, the Rabbis permitted the casting of lots, as an expression of that sentiment (*Rav; Rambam Comm.*).

אֲבָל לֹא עַל הַמָּנוֹת. — *but not for portions.*

I.e., not for portions of sacrifices that were offered up on the weekday preceding the festival (*Rav from Gem.* 149b according to *Rashi; Ravad,* glosses on *Rambam, Hil. Yom Tov* 4:20). Since it was possible to cast lots for these portions before the festival, the Rabbis did not permit doing so on the festival (*Rav; Tos. Yom Tov*).

Rambam (*Comm.* and *Hil. Yom Tov* 4:20) does not differentiate between sacrifices offered up on the festival and those offered up prior to it. *Rambam* explains the mishnah's prohibition as referring to nonsacrificial portions. This view is shared by *Shenos Eliyahu*. He prefers this interpretation, since it makes the contrast between *sacrifices* and *portions* more understandable, whereas according to *Rashi* and *Ravad* both terms refer to portions of sacrifices (footnotes to *Shenos Eliyahu*).

Since the mishnah mentions above that

[ג] לֹא יִשְׂכֹּר אָדָם פּוֹעֲלִים בַּשַּׁבָּת, וְלֹא יֹאמַר אָדָם לַחֲבֵרוֹ לִשְׂכֹּר לוֹ פּוֹעֲלִים. אֵין מַחְשִׁיכִין עַל הַתְּחוּם לִשְׂכֹּר פּוֹעֲלִים וּלְהָבִיא פֵּרוֹת,

ר' עובדיה מברטנורא

(ג) **לא ישכור אדם פועלים.** דכתיב (ישעיה נח) ממצוא חפצך ודבר דבר: **ולא יאמר אדם לחבירו כו'.** לדיוקא נקטיה, לא יאמר לחבירו שכור לנו פועלים, אבל אומר לו הנראה שתעמוד עמי לערב, כלומר עכשיו נראה אם תבא אלי לכשתחשך, ואף על פי שהעיטס יודעים שעל מנת לשכרו לפעולתו הוא מזהירו, כיון דלא מפרש ליה שכירות בהדיא שרי, דקי"ל דבור אסור הרהור מותר: **אין מחשיכין על התחום.** לקרב עצמו בשבת עד סוף התחום ולהחשיך שם שיהא קרוב למקום הפועלים או לפרדס להביא פירות, דכל דבר שאסור לעשותו בשבת אסור להחשיך עליו, אבל מחשיך הוא להיות קרוב לצאת ולשמור פירותיו, דזה דבר המותר בשבת לשמור פירותיו:

יד אברהם

one may cast lots only with his children or household members, the ruling prohibiting *Kohanim* to do so (for their nonsacrificial portions) seems superfluous (*Lechem Mishneh* ad loc.). It is possible, however, that, since *Kohanim* were often quarrelsome,[1] the Rabbis would permit apportioning even their ordinary foods by lot, in order to avoid quarrels. Therefore, the mishnah tells us that even *Kohanim* may not cast lots on a festival for ordinary food (footnotes to *Shenos Eliyahu*).

3.

לֹא יִשְׂכֹּר אָדָם פּוֹעֲלִים בַּשַּׁבָּת, — *A person may not hire workers on the Sabbath,*

This too is based on the verse מִמְּצוֹא חֶפְצְךָ וְדַבֵּר דָּבָר, *from seeking your personal wants or discussing the forbidden* (*Rav*; *Rashi*). Hiring workers on the Sabbath even for work to be done after the Sabbath is considered attending to his everyday affairs (*Shulchan Aruch* 307:2, *Mishnah Berurah* 307:7,9).

One may also not say on the Sabbath, "Tomorrow I will do such and such a thing," if that activity is something one is prohibited to do on the Sabbath itself. This violates *discussing the forbidden* (*Rosh* 23:6; *Shulchan Aruch* 307:1,8). If a *mitzvah* is involved, some authorities permit it. If the *mitzvah* matter may come to be neglected, it is certainly permissible to mention it on the Sabbath (*Mishneh Berurah*).

וְלֹא יֹאמַר אָדָם לַחֲבֵרוֹ לִשְׂכֹּר לוֹ פּוֹעֲלִים. — *nor may a person tell his friend to hire workers for him.*

This ruling is obvious. Since his friend is himself a Jew, and is also forbidden to hire workers on the Sabbath, one may not cause him to commit a sin by telling him to do so. Rather, the lesson of this mishnah is its inference, that the prohibition is only to explicitly tell another to hire workers. He may, however, say to his friend, "Let us see whether you will join me in the evening." Although it is

---

1. See *Hosea* 4:4: וְעַמְּךָ כִּמְרִיבֵי כֹהֵן, *And your people are like quarrelsome Kohanim*. This follows the explanation of this verse adopted by the *Gemara* 149b as explained by *Rashi* there. *Rashi* in *Hosea* (ibid.) and other commentaries there explain the verse differently.

3. A person may not hire workers on the Sabbath, nor may a person tell his friend to hire workers for him. We may not [go to] await nightfall at the [Sabbath] boundary for the purpose of hiring workers or bringing produce,

YAD AVRAHAM

thereby understood that he wishes to hire him, this is permissible, since Scripture prohibits only speech, not thought. Since he merely intimates that he wishes to hire him, this is regarded, with respect to this halachah, as thought, not speech (*Rav* from *Gem.* 150a).

אֵין מַחְשִׁיכִין עַל הַתְּחוּם — *We may not [go to] await nightfall at the [Sabbath] boundary*

[As explained above (2:7), the Rabbis limited the distance a person may travel on the Sabbath. One may not go farther than two thousand cubits from the place he camps or from the edge of the city in which he resides on the Sabbath. This limit is known as תְּחוּם שַׁבָּת, *the Sabbath boundary*.]

Thus, the mishnah means that a person may not go on the Sabbath to the Sabbath boundary, i.e. to just within the limit of two thousand cubits, to await nightfall (*Kehati*).

לִשְׂכֹּר פּוֹעֲלִים וּלְהָבִיא פֵרוֹת, — *for the purpose of hiring workers or bringing produce,*

I.e., in order to reach the people he wishes to hire as soon after the Sabbath as possible, or to reach the field or orchard from which he wishes to take produce as soon after the Sabbath as possible. Since hiring workers and gathering produce are prohibited on the Sabbath, they fall into the category of the *wants* which one is prohibited from seeking on the Sabbath. Attending to the preliminaries necessary for the accomplishment of these objectives, i.e., by traveling toward their place on the Sabbath, constitutes *seeking your personal wants* (*Tos. Yom Tov* from *Rambam, Hil. Shabbos* 24:2).

The mishnah deals only with produce still attached to the ground or picked produce that is for some reason *muktzeh* (see preface to Chapter 17). Since one is forbidden to pick the produce or to move it on the Sabbath, his awaiting nightfall for that purpose is also prohibited.

If the produce is within the boundary, one may go to it on the Sabbath in order to pick it after nightfall. Since he does not go to the limits of the Sabbath boundary, it is not apparent that his traveling is for picking produce. It was therefore not banned (*Tif. Yis.* from *Shulchan Aruch* 307:9).

However, if the produce he wishes to bring in is both picked and non-*muktzeh* one is permitted to await nightfall at the boundary. This is because the hauling of such produce is only *circumstantially*, not *intrinsically*, prohibited, i.e., the act of transporting picked non-*muktzeh* produce is permissible under certain circumstances. An example is when there is a wall or an *eruv* enclosing the entire area between the field and the place to which one wishes to bring the produce. This would remove both the problem of carrying through a public domain or *karmelis* and the problem of traveling outside the *techum*. Therefore, even when the area is unenclosed, and one is consequently prohibited from transporting the produce,

שבת כג/ג

אֲבָל מַחְשִׁיךְ הוּא לִשְׁמֹר, וּמֵבִיא פֵרוֹת בְּיָדוֹ.
כְּלָל אָמַר אַבָּא שָׁאוּל: כָּל שֶׁאֲנִי זַכַּאי בַּאֲמִירָתוֹ, רַשַּׁאי אֲנִי לְהַחְשִׁיךְ עָלָיו.

ר' עובדיה מברטנורא

ומביא פירות בידו. הואיל ועיקר מחשבתו לא היתה לכך: **בלל אמר אבא שאול.** אתנא קמא פליג, דאסר כל החשכה ולא מפליג בין החשכה של מצוה להחשכה של רשות, ואתא איהו ואמר דהחשכה של מצוה שריא, שכשם שמותר לומר לחבירו בשבת תהיה מזומן לילך לאחר חשיכה להביא ארון ותכריכים למת, כך מותר להחשיך על התחום כדי שיהיה מזומן לאחר חשיכה להביא ארון ותכריכים. וסיפא דתנן מחשיכים על התחום [לפקח] על עסקי כלה ועל עסקי המת, אבא שאול היא. והלכה כמותו:

יד אברהם

that prohibition is not *intrinsic* to the act of hauling but is rather a product of circumstances; namely, the lack of an enclosure. Since the activity is not intrinsically prohibited, it cannot be defined *as seeking your wants*, which refers only to wants which are in themselves incompatible with Sabbath behavior. One is, however, prohibited from awaiting nightfall for produce still growing or *muktzeh* because no conceivable circumstances exist which would permit one to pick or transport that produce on the Sabbath. This rule applies as well to any other activity for which conceivable circumstances can be imagined which would enable one to engage in that activity on the Sabbath. While circumstances may prohibit one from actually engaging in that activity, one is permitted to travel to the boundary to await nightfall in order to engage in it. Similarly, one is permitted to discuss performing such an act as long as one does not say that he intends to do so in a prohibited manner. For example, one may say that he intends to bring his produce in from the field after the Sabbath as long as he does not specify that he will carry it through a public domain (*Gem.* 105b).

אֲבָל מַחְשִׁיךְ הוּא לִשְׁמֹר, — **but one may await nightfall [to enable him] to watch,**

I.e., he may await nightfall at the boundary in order to reach his field soon after the Sabbath to guard the produce at night. Since one may watch his produce on the Sabbath, he may await nightfall at the boundary for that purpose.

Though he is awaiting nightfall in order to pass beyond the Sabbath boundary, this, as explained above, is permissible, provided the activity for which he is traveling is in itself permissible.

וּמֵבִיא פֵרוֹת בְּיָדוֹ. — **and bring produce in his hand.**

I.e., one who awaited the nightfall at the Sabbath boundary to be able to guard his produce through the night, may, upon returning home, bring produce back with him. Since his intent is primarily to guard his produce, not to pick it, his awaiting nightfall is permissible despite the fact that some produce will also be picked (*Rav; Rashi*). He may bring only a small amount of produce lest it appear that his intention was to haul a wagon load, not to watch his produce (*Shoshanim LeDavid*).

כְּלָל אָמַר אַבָּא שָׁאוּל: — **Abba Shaul stated a general rule:**

23
3

but one may await nightfall [to enable him] to watch, and bring produce in his hand.

Abba Shaul stated a general rule: Whatever I am permitted to instruct [on the Sabbath], I am permitted to await nightfall for it.

YAD AVRAHAM

[I.e., a general principle regarding awaiting nightfall at the boundary.]

כָּל שֶׁאֲנִי זַכַּאי בַּאֲמִירָתוֹ, — *Whatever I am permitted to instruct [on the Sabbath],*

I.e., whatever I may instruct someone on the Sabbath to do either after the Sabbath (such as to bring a coffin and shrouds for the dead, see following mishnah) or on the Sabbath itself (such as to watch produce within his boundary) (*Rav; Rashi; Tos.* on *Gem.* 151a).

רַשַּׁאי אֲנִי לְהַחְשִׁיךְ עָלָיו. — *I am permitted to await nightfall for it.*

Whereas the *Tanna Kamma* permits awaiting nightfall at the Sabbath boundary only for acts permissible on the Sabbath, be those acts optional or *mitzvah* related, Abba Shaul's rule permits awaiting nightfall for matters of *mitzvah* (such as attending to the needs of the deceased), under all circumstances, i.e., even though they may not actually be attending to on the Sabbath. According to Abba Shaul, the regulations governing awaiting nightfall at the boundary are not stricter than those governing the instructions one may issue on the Sabbath. Since all agree that for the purposes of a *mitzvah* one is permitted to issue instructions even for acts one may not actually perform until after the Sabbath, Abba Shaul asserts that one may similarly await nightfall at the Sabbath boundary for those purposes. Abba Shaul's reasoning is that since Scripture prohibits only *seeking your personal wants*, the implication is that the wants of Heaven, i.e., *mitzvah* matters, may be sought on the Sabbath. We may, therefore, await nightfall at the boundary for such purposes (*Tos. Yom Tov* from *Gem.* 105a). The *Tanna Kamma*, however, restricts awaiting the nightfall more than issuing instructions, i.e., even for purposes of a *mitzvah*. Accordingly, the following mishnah, which permits awaiting the nightfall at the boundary to attend to the affairs of a bride or the affairs of the deceased, accords with Abba Shaul, not the *Tanna Kamma* and so too does the halachah (*Rav; Rashi; Tos.* on *Gem.* 151a).[1]

4.

As explained at the end of the previous mishnah, one is permitted to seek the affairs of heaven even where he is forbidden to do so for his own. This mishnah illustrates that ruling.

---

1. *Meiri* adopts the view that the *Tanna Kamma* concurs with Abba Shaul. Abba Shaul's insertion is merely for the purpose of clearly formulating the rule governing the matter.

שבת כג/ד

[ד] **מַחְשִׁיכִין** עַל הַתְּחוּם לְפַקֵּחַ עַל עִסְקֵי כַלָּה; וְעַל עִסְקֵי הַמֵּת, לְהָבִיא לוֹ אָרוֹן וְתַכְרִיכִין. נָכְרִי שֶׁהֵבִיא חֲלִילִין בַּשַּׁבָּת, לֹא יִסְפֹּד בָּהֶן יִשְׂרָאֵל, אֶלָּא אִם־כֵּן בָּאוּ מִמָּקוֹם קָרוֹב. עָשׂוּ לוֹ אָרוֹן וְחָפְרוּ לוֹ קֶבֶר, יִקָּבֵר בּוֹ יִשְׂרָאֵל;

ר' עובדיה מברטנורא

(ד) **לפקח על עסקי כלה.** לעיין ולחקור בצרכי הכלה: **חלילין.** כלי נגון חלולין מעורך הבכי: **לא יספוד בהן ישראל.** קנסא הוא משום דמוכחא מילתא שבשביל ישראל הובאו: **אלא אם כן באו ממקום קרוב.** אלא אם כן נודע לנו בבירור שבאו ממקום שבתוך התחום ולא הביאם מחוץ לתחום: **ארון.** לעצמו שיקבר בו נכרי, או למכור.

יד אברהם

מַחְשִׁיכִין עַל הַתְּחוּם — *We may await nightfall at the [Sabbath] boundary.*
[See previous mishnah.]

לְפַקֵּחַ עַל עִסְקֵי כַלָּה; — *to attend to the affairs of a bride;*
I.e., to ascertain what is necessary for her forthcoming nuptials (*Rav*).

וְעַל עִסְקֵי הַמֵּת, — *or to the affairs of the deceased,*
[I.e., for the necessities of the funeral.]

לְהָבִיא לוֹ אָרוֹן וְתַכְרִיכִין. — *[viz.,] to bring a coffin and shrouds for him.*
Even if the coffin and shrouds are not yet made, so that there is *melachah* involved in their preparation, one may nevertheless await nightfall on the boundary to arrange for it, since it is a *mitzvah* matter.
If they were already made, one would be permitted to await nightfall even apart from any considerations of *mitzvah*, as explained in the previous mishnah with regard to picked and non-*muktzeh* produce (*Tos. R' Akiva* from *Gem.* 150b).

נָכְרִי שֶׁהֵבִיא חֲלִילִין בַּשַּׁבָּת, — *If a gentile brought flutes on the Sabbath,*
It was the custom in those days to follow the coffin with flutes playing melancholy music invoking wailing (*Rav*; *Tif. Yis.*).
If a gentile brought flutes for a Jewish funeral and one is in doubt as to whether the flutes were brought from beyond the Sabbath boundary (*Tif. Yis.*).

לֹא יִסְפֹּד בָּהֶן יִשְׂרָאֵל, — *a Jew may not bewail with them,*
[This phrase is ambiguous. It may also be translated: *one may not bewail a Jew with them.*]
Some read לֹא יִסָּפֵד בָּהֶן, *a Jew may not be bewailed with them* (*Meleches Shlomo*).
Since it is obvious that the flutes were expressly brought for the funeral, these instruments not being used for any other purpose, the Rabbis penalized those involved by forever banning their use for *any* Jewish funeral (*Rashi*).
Most authorities, however, explain the ban as lasting only as long as would be required to obtain new ones after the Sabbath. After that time, one no longer benefits from the desecration of the Sabbath, since he could, in any case, have obtained new ones. There is, therefore, no reason to prohibit the use of those brought on the

4. **We** may await nightfall at the [Sabbath] boundary to attend to the affairs of a bride; or to the affairs of the deceased, [viz.,] to bring a coffin and shrouds for him. If a gentile brought flutes on the Sabbath, a Jew may not bewail with them, unless they came from a nearby place. If they made a coffin for him or dug a grave for him, a Jew may be interred in it;

YAD AVRAHAM

Sabbath (Tos., Rambam, Hil. Shabbos 6:6, Ran).

אֶלָּא אִם־כֵּן בָּאוּ מִמָּקוֹם קָרוֹב. — *unless they came from a nearby place.*

I.e., unless we are certain that they came from a place within the Sabbath boundary (Rav). This follows the explanation in the Gemara 151a of Rav (the Amora). Shmuel, however, explains the mishnah as permitting the use of any flutes which may have been brought from within the Sabbath boundary, while prohibiting the use of only those known to have been brought from outside the boundary (Rashi).

Other Rishonim explain the dispute of Rav and Shmuel as being whether it is sufficient to ascertain where the flutes came from on the Sabbath day, then accept the probability that they had already been in that place prior to the onset of Sabbath, or whether one must also ascertain where they had been prior to the onset of the Sabbath. According to this explanation, Shmuel is the stricter opinion, which the halachah follows (Rif as explained by Ran; Rambam, Hil. Shabbos 6:6 as explained by Maggid Mishneh).

If the flutes were brought from within the boundary, they may be used immediately, even though they were carried through a public domain. Tosafos account for this by stating that since they were brought from nearby, one saves very little time and therefore derives little benefit from their having been brought on the Sabbath. The Rabbis therefore did not require him to wait even that amount of time before using them after the Sabbath. Other authorities, however, rule that if they were carried through a public domain, they may not be used until the time when they could have been brought from that place after nightfall (Tos. Yom Tov from Ran, Rambam and Tur 325).

עָשׂוּ לוֹ אָרוֹן וְחָפְרוּ לוֹ קֶבֶר, — *If they made a coffin for him* (i.e., the gentile) *or (they) dug a grave for him,*

I.e., if a gentile had a coffin constructed or a grave dug on the Sabbath for his own purposes, either to bury another gentile or to sell (Rav; Rashi).

יִקָּבֵר בּוֹ יִשְׂרָאֵל; — *a Jew may be interred in it;*

According to Rashi, this is so only if the grave was dug in a public thoroughfare, or the coffin was placed on such a grave. In this case, it is obvious that the preparations were made for a gentile, since Jews do not customarily inter in such places. It is, furthermore, unnecessary to wait, before using this grave or coffin, the amount of time necessary for a grave to be dug or for a coffin to be constructed (Tos. Yom Tov).

According to Rambam and Ran, however, as long as it is known that the coffin or the grave was made for a gentile, a Jew may be buried in it (ibid.). This is indeed the decision of the Shulchan Aruch 325:14.

שבת
כג/ה

וְאִם בִּשְׁבִיל יִשְׂרָאֵל, לֹא יִקָּבֵר בּוֹ עוֹלָמִית.

[ה] **עוֹשִׂין** כָּל צָרְכֵי הַמֵּת: סָכִין וּמְדִיחִין אוֹתוֹ, וּבִלְבַד שֶׁלֹּא יָזִיזוּ בּוֹ אֵבֶר; שׁוֹמְטִין אֶת הַכַּר מִתַּחְתָּיו וּמַטִּילִין אוֹתוֹ עַל הַחוֹל.

ר' עובדיה מברטנורא

(ה) **סכין**. בשמן: **ומדיחין**. במים. ופוקקין נקביו, סותמין נקביו העליונים והתחתונים בבגד או בשום דבר כדי שלא תכנס בהם הרוח ויתפח: **ובלבד שלא יזיז בו אבר**. שלא יטלטל ויגביה לא ידו ולא רגלו ולא ריסי עיניו, שאסור לטלטל המת או חבר מאבריו, אף על פי שמותר ליגע בו. וכן כל מוקצה מותר בנגיעה ואסור בטלטול. ובזיה שנולדה בשבת או ביום טוב אסורה אפילו בנגיעה, שמפני כדוריתה נגיעתה זהו טלטולה: **ושומטים את הכר מתחתיו**. ונמצא מוטל על החול, אבל לא מטלטלין להניחו על החול, דהא תנא רישא ובלבד שלא יזיז בו אבר:

יד אברהם

וְאִם בִּשְׁבִיל יִשְׂרָאֵל, — *but if [it was done] for a Jew,*

[I.e., if the gentiles constructed the coffin or dug the grave on the Sabbath expressly for a Jew.]

לֹא יִקָּבֵר בּוֹ עוֹלָמִית. — *he may never be interred in it.*

I.e., the Jew for whom the coffin was made or for whom the grave was dug may never be buried in it.

The authorities differ as to whether another Jew may be buried in that grave or coffin (see *Ran*). The halachah is in accordance with the lenient view, that other Jews may be buried in it after enough time has elapsed to have dug the grave or built the coffin after the Sabbath (*Shulchan Aruch* 325:14).

We mentioned above that according to the majority of halachic authorities, if a gentile brought flutes on the Sabbath, they may be used to bewail a Jew after sufficient time has elapsed after the Sabbath to bring them from beyond the boundary. Yet in the case of a coffin or grave, the Jew for whom it was made may never be buried in it. The reason for this distinction, *Tosafos* point out, is that flutes are usually brought for several funerals, not just one. Since they were not brought expressly for one particular deceased, they may be used even for the first funeral for which they were brought, after sufficient time has elapsed to bring them after the Sabbath. Graves and coffins, on the other hand, are made for one specific individual. According to this, if the flutes were known to have been brought for one particular individual, they may never be used for him (*Tos. Yom Tov*).

Ran differentiates in a different manner. According to the generally accepted interpretation of the *Gemara* 151a, the mishnah refers to a grave being dug in an open place or a coffin lying on it. Hence, the labor was performed in flagrant desecration of the Sabbath. The Rabbis, therefore, banned their use permanently. Bringing flutes, however, is not so conspicuous an act. The Rabbis, therefore, did not prohibit their use after the required lapse of time. It follows, then, that if the grave was dug in a secluded place or the flutes were brought conspicuously, the reverse is true (*Tos. Yom Tov*).

Some authorities rule that this is true whenever the Sabbath has been flagrantly desecrated on behalf of a Jew (*Magen Avraham* 325:31 quoting *Rambam*). Others state that this ruling applies only to the case of burial, since it is a disgrace for a Jew to lie in a grave known to have been dug on

23
5   but if [it was done] for a Jew, he may never be interred in it.

5. We may attend to all the necessities of the deceased: We may anoint and rinse him, provided we do not move any of his limbs; we may pull the pillow from under him and lay him on the sand

YAD AVRAHAM

the Sabbath (*Taz* ibid.:13, quoting *Ran*). Since many authorities concur with this view, it may be followed in cases of necessity (*Mishneh Berurah* ibid. :73).

5.

The following mishnah delineates the procedure for attending to the dead on the Sabbath.

עוֹשִׂין כָּל צָרְכֵי הַמֵּת: — *We may attend to all the necessities of the deceased:*
[I.e., all that is necessary to retard the body's decomposition before the funeral, or to prevent its lying in an undignified state.]

סָכִין — *We may anoint*
I.e., with oil (*Rav*; *Rashi*).
Tiferes Yisrael specifies that the body is anointed with balsamum oil to mask the odor of decomposition.

וּמְדִיחִין אוֹתוֹ, — *and rinse him,*
The corpse may be rinsed with water (*Rav*; *Rashi*). [One may not, however, wet a cloth for this purpose.]
Also, the upper and lower orifices may be stopped with a cloth or the like, to prevent air from entering the body and causing it to bloat (*Rav* from *Gem.* 151b).

וּבִלְבַד שֶׁלֹּא יָזִיזוּ בוֹ אֵבֶר; — *provided we* (lit. *they*) *do not move any of his limbs;*
One may not lift a hand, a foot, or even an eyelid, since a corpse, or any part of it, is *muktzeh*. The prohibition against moving *muktzeh* applies to moving even a part of it. A corpse, as well as any other *muktzeh*, may be touched on the Sabbath, as long as it is not moved.
Ran (to mishnah 18:2) calls attention to the mishnah above which permits pushing along a hen even though we surely move a limb. He qualifies that mishnah as referring only to the case in which the hen would suffer by not being returned to its nest. To prevent unnecessary pain to an animal, the Rabbis were lenient and permitted partial movement of *muktzeh* (*Tos. Yom Tov*).

שׁוֹמְטִין אֶת־הַכַּר מִתַּחְתָּיו וּמַטִּילִין אוֹתוֹ עַל הַחוֹל — *we may pull the pillow from under him and lay him on the sand*
I.e., the pillow or mattress upon which the deceased is lying may be pulled out from under him, thereby laying him on the cool sand or dirt near his bed. He may not be picked up to be laid on the sand, however, since the mishnah states above that not even one limb of the deceased may be moved (*Rav*).

שבת כג/ה

בִּשְׁבִיל שֶׁיַּמְתִּין; קוֹשְׁרִים אֶת הַלֶּחִי, לֹא שֶׁיַּעֲלֶה, אֶלָּא שֶׁלֹּא יוֹסִיף.

וְכֵן, קוֹרָה שֶׁנִּשְׁבְּרָה, סוֹמְכִין אוֹתָהּ בְּסַפְסָל אוֹ בַּאֲרוּכוֹת הַמִּטָּה, לֹא שֶׁתַּעֲלֶה, אֶלָּא שֶׁלֹּא תּוֹסִיף.

אֵין מְעַמְּצִין אֶת הַמֵּת בַּשַּׁבָּת, וְלֹא בַחֹל עִם יְצִיאַת נֶפֶשׁ, וְהַמְעַמֵּץ עִם יְצִיאַת נֶפֶשׁ, הֲרֵי זֶה שׁוֹפֵךְ דָּמִים.

ר' עובדיה מברטנורא

בשביל שימתין. שלא יסריח מחמת חום הסדינים והכרים: **קושרים את הלחי.** של מת שהיה פיו הולך ונפתח: **ולא שיעלה.** להסגר מה שנפתח דהיינו מזיז אבר, אלא שלא יוסיף להפתח: **סומכים אותה בספסל.** שהרי תורת כלי עליו. ולא שתעלה. דהוה ליה בונה: **אין מעמצין** את עיניו בשבת אפילו לאחר יציאת נפש, דהוה ליה מזיז אבר: **שופך דמים.** שבדבר מועט מקרב מיתתו:

יד אברהם

בִּשְׁבִיל שֶׁיַּמְתִּין — *in order that [his body] keep;*

[*Aruch* renders: *In order that he remain fresh* (*Tos. Yom Tov; Tif. Yis.*).]

A body kept in a warm place begins decomposing more rapidly than one in a cool place. Since the pillows and mattress keep the body warmer, the body must be moved to the relatively cooler dirt floor to retard the rate of decomposition (*Rav; Rashi*).

קוֹשְׁרִים אֶת הַלֶּחִי — *we may bind up the jaw,*

I.e., if the mouth had begun to sag open as a result of the relaxing of the muscles, the jaw may be bound up (*Rav; Rashi*).

לֹא שֶׁיַּעֲלֶה — *not that it should close* (lit. *ascend*),

I.e., not to close the part that has already opened, since, as stated above, no limb may be moved (*Rav; Tif. Yis.*).

אֶלָּא שֶׁלֹּא יוֹסִיף — *but that it should not [open any] further.*

[I.e., one may tie a strip of cloth around the head and jaw sufficiently tight to prevent any further sagging of the jaw but not so tight as to force it closed.]

וְכֵן, קוֹרָה שֶׁנִּשְׁבְּרָה, סוֹמְכִין אוֹתָהּ בְּסַפְסָל — *So, too, [with] a beam that broke, we may support it with a bench*

One may move only a non-*muktzeh* item to support it. Therefore a bench may be used since, being a utensil, it is not *muktzeh* (*Rav*).

אוֹ בַּאֲרוּכוֹת הַמִּטָּה — *or with the side-pieces of a bed,*

23
5
in order that [his body] keep; we may bind up the jaw, not that it should close, but that it should not [open any] further.

So, too, [with] a beam that broke, we may support it with a bench or with the side-pieces of a bed, not that it should be raised, but that it should not [sag any] further.

We may not close the eyes of the dead on the Sabbath, nor [may we do so] on a weekday at the moment of death, [for] whoever closes the eyes [of a dying person] at the moment of death is a murderer.

YAD AVRAHAM

These too are regarded as utensils (Tif. Yis.).

לֹא שֶׁתַּעֲלֶה, — not that it should be raised,

I.e., we may not wedge it in such a manner as to raise it towards its original position, since that is akin to building (Rav; Rashi).

אֶלָּא שֶׁלֹּא תוֹסִיף. — but that it should not [sag any] further.

[The support may be inserted only to the level where it prevents the beam from sagging any lower.]

אֵין מְעַמְּצִין אֶת־הַמֵּת בַּשַּׁבָּת, — We may not close the eyes of the dead on the Sabbath,

Moving the eyelid is regarded as the equivalent of moving the limb of a corpse, which is prohibited because of muktzeh.

וְלֹא בַחֹל — nor [may we do so] on a weekday

[I.e., nor may they close the eyes on a weekday.]

עִם יְצִיאַת נֶפֶשׁ, — at the moment of death (lit. with the departure of the soul),

This is prohibited because we fear that he may not be quite dead yet but in a deep coma. In such a state, even the slightest movement can hasten his death (Rav; Rashi). One is obligated, therefore, to wait a while after the presumed moment of death before moving the body (Tif. Yis. from Rambam, Hil. Eivel 4:5, Shulchan Aruch, Yoreh Deah 339:1).

Not only may we not close the eyes, but we may not move any part of the body. The mishnah mentions closing the eyes because it is customary to do so for the dead (Tif. Yis.).

וְהַמְעַמֵּץ עִם יְצִיאַת נֶפֶשׁ, הֲרֵי־זֶה שׁוֹפֵךְ דָּמִים. — [for] whoever closes the eyes [of a dying person] at the moment of death is a murderer.

He is considered a murderer because causing someone to die even a moment earlier than necessary is considered murder (Rav; Rashi).

The Gemara compares this to a lamp that is flickering and about to go out. One who places his finger upon it extinguishes it immediately (151b).

פרק עשרים וארבעה
Chapter Twenty-Four

שבת כד/א

[א] **מִי** שֶׁהֶחְשִׁיךְ בַּדֶּרֶךְ, נוֹתֵן כִּיסוֹ לְנָכְרִי, וְאִם אֵין עִמּוֹ נָכְרִי, מַנִּיחוֹ עַל הַחֲמוֹר.

ר' עובדיה מברטנורא

פרק עשרים וארבעה — מי שהחשיך. (א) מי שהחשיך. נותן כיסו לנכרי. מבעוד יום. ואף על גב דשלוחו של ישראל הוא לישא את כיסו בשבת, קים להו לרבנן דאין אדם מעמיד עצמו על ממונו ואי לא שרית ליה אתי לאתויי ד' אמות ברשות הרבים: **ואם אין עמו נברי בו'.** האי יש עמו נכרי, לנכרי יהיב ליה, מ"ט חמור אתה מצווה על שביתתו, נכרי אי אתה מצווה על שביתתו. וכשמניח כיסו על החמור משתתשך מניחו עליו כשהיא מהלכת, כלומר לאחר שעקרה רגליה לילך דלא עבדה עקירה, וכשרוצה הבהמה לעמוד נוטלו מעליה, ולאחר שתחזור ותעקור רגליה לילך יניחנה עליה, כי היכי דלא תעביד הבהמה עקירה והנחה, דהי שביק לה למעבד עקירה והנחה והוא מחמר אחריה ומנהיגה נמצא מחמר אחר בהמתו בשבת ואסור, אף על פי שאינה טעונה אלא כל דהו דכתיב (שמות כ) לא תעשה [כל] מלאכה אתה ובהמתך, איזו היא מלאכה שנעשית בין האדם והבהמה, הוי אומר זה מחמר:

יד אברהם

1.

מִי שֶׁהֶחְשִׁיךְ בַּדֶּרֶךְ, — *If darkness overtakes a person* (lit. *one for whom it became dark*) *on the road,*

I.e., if one sets out on the road early in the day, not realizing that he will not reach his destination before nightfall, and darkness overtakes him, he may resort to the following devices delineated in the mishnah. Should he deliberately set out shortly before nightfall, however, none of these lenient rulings apply. He must, in that case, abandon his property (*Beis Yosef; Bach* 266; *Shulchan Aruch* 266:8 from *Rabbeinu Yerucham* 12:1; as regards the final halachah, see *Mishnah Berurah* 266:22).

נוֹתֵן כִּיסוֹ לְנָכְרִי; — *he may give his purse to a gentile;*

I.e., he may give his purse to a gentile before nightfall to carry for him (*Rav; Rashi*). Others permit it even after nightfall (*Rosh; Tur* 266; *Rambam, Hil. Shabbos* 6:22). Even though money is *muktzeh* (see preface to Chap. 21), the Rabbis permitted handling it in order to avoid incurring a loss (*Tos. Yom Tov; Maggid Mishneh* ad loc., *Beis Yosef* ad loc.). Some authorities reconcile both views by drawing a distinction between the preferred behavior and that permissible after the fact. Everyone agrees that when necessary one *should* give his purse to the gentile before the Sabbath sets in. If he did not do so, however, and darkness overtook him, he may do so even then (*Korban Nesanel; Bach*).

In any case, an element of leniency is involved in this ruling, since he is making the gentile his agent to carry his purse on the Sabbath, an act ordinarily prohibited (as above 16:6). Under these circumstances, however, the Rabbis permitted it because they realized that most people do not willingly part with their money, and that some people, unable to abandon their purses, would end up carrying them through a public domain on the Sabbath, where carrying a distance of four cubits is a capital transgression. To forestall this, the Rabbis permitted one to save his money by resorting to activities normally Rabbinically prohibited (*Rav* from *Gem.* 153a).

Even in places where there is no

1. If darkness overtakes a person on the road, he may give his purse to a gentile; if no gentile is with him, he may place it on the donkey.

YAD AVRAHAM

thoroughfare bearing the qualifications of a public domain (see General Introduction, p. 12), the Rabbis, nevertheless, permitted asking a gentile to carry the purse, rather than permit the Jew to carry it himself through a *karmelis*, since the latter is a more serious offense than the former (*Tif. Yis.* from *Magen Avraham* 334:3).

וְאִם אֵין עִמּוֹ נָכְרִי, — *if no gentile is with him*,

Or, if he does not trust the gentile who is with him (*Tif. Yis.* from *Magen Avraham* 266:4 from *Sefer HaTerumah*, Ch. 226).

מַנִּיחוֹ עַל הַחֲמוֹר. — *he may place it on a donkey.*

Where he has the option of giving it to a gentile, however, he may not place the purse on the donkey, but must give it to the gentile. This is because a person has a Biblical obligation to allow his animals to rest on the Sabbath (*Ex.* 20:10, 23; 23:12), while he has no such obligation towards a gentile. (The prohibition to tell a gentile to perform a *melachah* on the Sabbath is entirely Rabbinical.)

Since there is a Biblical prohibition involved in causing an animal to work on the Sabbath, it follows that even when one is permitted to place his purse on the animal, he must do so in such a way as to avoid any Biblical violation. [It is not within the power of the Rabbis to permit something Biblically prohibited. They can only allow special leniencies where the prohibition is entirely Rabbinical.]

The Biblical prohibition against causing an animal to perform *melachah* applies only to those acts which a person himself is Biblically prohibited to perform. Any act Rabbinically prohibited is similarly only Rabbinically prohibited to cause an animal to do it.

As has been explained in the General Introduction, p. 12, the *melachah* of *transferring from one domain to another* consists of two parts: *akirah*, picking up an article in one domain, and *hanachah*, depositing it in another. In the case of *transferring four cubits in a public domain* (a *toladah* of *transferring from one domain to another*) it consists of picking up an object in a public domain and depositing it a distance of four cubits away. Furthermore, the *Gemara* (3a) states that if one already has an object in his hand, moving his body from one place to another while carrying the object is tantamount to picking it up and depositing it. It follows, then, that if one places his purse on the donkey's back while it is at rest and allows the donkey to begin walking, the donkey is performing an *akirah*. Similarly, if one allows the donkey to come to a halt with the purse still on its back the donkey is performing a *hanachah*. If the donkey does both while traveling a distance of four cubits in the public domain, it has performed a *melachah* on behalf of the person,[1] and he has thus violated the Biblical commandment to allow his animals to rest. To avoid this, one must place the

---

1. One may allow his animal to perform a *melachah* which is for its own benefit. For this reason, one may allow his animal to graze, even though the animal is tearing out grass that is still growing (*Mechilta*, quoted by *Rashi, Comm.* to *Ex.* 23:12).

שבת כד/א

הִגִּיעַ לֶחָצֵר הַחִיצוֹנָה, נוֹטֵל אֶת הַכֵּלִים הַנִּטָּלִין בַּשַּׁבָּת; וְשֶׁאֵינָן נִטָּלִין בַּשַּׁבָּת, מַתִּיר אֶת הַחֲבָלִים, וְהַשַּׂקִּין נוֹפְלִין מֵאֲלֵיהֶם:

ר' עובדיה מברטנורא

הגיע לחצר החיצונה. מילתא באנפי נפשה היא ולא בדין כיסו מיירי: **לחצר החיצונה.** של עיר, שהוא מקום המשתמר ראשון, כשיבא לפרק החמור נוטל בידו כלים הניטלין בשבת: **ושאינם ניטלים מתיר את החבלים.** של אוכף שהן קשורים והשקין נופלים:

יד אברהם

purse on the donkey *after* it has commenced walking and remove it *before* it stops (*Rav* from *Gem.* 153b, as explained by *Rambam, Comm.* and *Hil. Shabbos* 20:6; *Tos. Yom Tov*).

Should the burden be too heavy for a gentile to carry, and also too heavy to remove and replace on the donkey, he must transfer ownership of the donkey to the gentile, or relinquish his ownership entirely. Since the commandment to allow one's animal to rest applies only to an animal one owns, by removing his ownership, he has circumvented the restriction[1] (*Magen Avraham* 266:2).

The lenient ruling of the mishnah applies not only to one's money but to all one's property. However, it does not apply to an object found in the street on the Sabbath. In such a case, one is not permitted to order a gentile to pick it up (*Gem.* 153a). Not only may he not do so in a public domain or a *karmelis*, but even in a yard furnished with an *eruv*, since the money is *muktzeh*. Since it was never his, the Rabbis did not fear that he might be unable to resist carrying it through the public domain. Therefore, no special leniency was granted (*Mishnah Berurah* 266:5).

If he acquired it before the onset of the Sabbath, it is regarded as his property, and all leniencies apply (*Shulchan Aruch* 266:1).

When he arrives home, he must remove the purse while the animal is still walking and throw it into his house in an unusual manner. [Since any *melachah* done in an unusual manner is only Rabbinically forbidden, the Rabbis here permitted it.] To bring it into the house in a normal way would constitute the *melachah* of *transferring from a public domain to a private domain (*Tos. Yom Tov* from *Gem.* 153b).

הִגִּיעַ לֶחָצֵר הַחִיצוֹנָה, — *When he reaches the outermost courtyard*,

I.e., when he reaches the first courtyard at the outskirts of the city in which it is safe to unload his bags (*Rav*).

This is not related to the first part of the mishnah, which deals with someone placing his purse on the donkey, but with a person who, while traveling on Friday with a donkey laden with packages, was overtaken by darkness (*Rav; Rambam, Comm.* and *Hil. Shabbos* 21:10).

נוֹטֵל אֶת הַכֵּלִים הַנִּטָּלִין בַּשַּׁבָּת; — *he may*

---
1. Although the obligation to allow an animal to rest applies only to an animal one owns, there is a further restriction against instigating even another person's animal to perform a *melachah*. Consequently, after placing his baggage on the donkey, he may do nothing to cause the donkey to begin moving, but must wait for it to move on its own accord (*Magen Avraham* ibid.). According to some, this restriction also applies to placing the purse on the donkey and removing it (*Shulchan Aruch* ibid.).

24 1 When he reaches the outermost courtyard, he may remove those objects that may be handled on the Sabbath; and [as for] those that may not be handled on the Sabbath, he may untie the ropes, and [allow] the sacks [to] fall of themselves.

YAD AVRAHAM

remove those objects that may be handled on the Sabbath;

I.e., those objects that are not *muktzeh* may be removed by hand from the donkey's back (*Rav*).

וְשֶׁאֵינָן נִטָּלִין בַּשַּׁבָּת — *and [as for] those that may not be handled on the Sabbath,*

[I.e., those that fit into any category of *muktzeh* (explained in preface to Chap. 17).]

מַתִּיר אֶת הַחֲבָלִים, — *he may untie the ropes,*

[I.e., he may untie the ropes by which the sacks are secured to the donkey. Since they are *muktzeh*, however, he may not directly handle them.]

וְהַשַּׂקִּין נוֹפְלִין מֵאֲלֵיהֶם. — *and [allow] the sacks [to] fall of themselves.*

[Since the bundles fell off by themselves, the person has not moved any *muktzeh*.]

If the load consists of breakable items, such as glassware that are *muktzeh* (e.g., cups used for bloodletting, which is forbidden on the Sabbath, and which, because they are repulsive, are not fit for any other use on the Sabbath), one may place blankets or pillows on the ground and let the load fall onto them.

This is permissible, however, only if the sacks are small enough to be removed from the pillows by pulling the pillows out from beneath the sacks, or tilting the pillows out from beneath the sacks, or tilting the pillows so that the sacks fall off (see above 21:2). If the sacks are so large and heavy that this is impossible, one is forbidden to place pillows or blankets beneath the sacks. Since the sacks are *muktzeh* and may not be directly handled, and since removal of the pillows from beneath the sacks by any other method is impossible, by dropping the sacks on the pillows, he would be *nullifying a utensil* (the pillow) *from its use* (on the Sabbath), which, as explained above (3:6), is prohibited. He must, therefore, try to let the sacks down as gently as possible. In any case, he may not leave the load on the donkey, because he would thereby cause suffering to the animal (*Rambam, Hil. Shabbos* 21:10; *Shulchan Aruch* 266:9).

Magen Avraham (266:11) raises the difficulty that since the animal generally pauses a moment before entering the courtyard, it is carrying the load from a public domain (i.e., from outside the courtyard, where it had come to rest as a result of the animal's pausing there) into a private domain (the courtyard in which the animal comes to a halt). As a result of this problem, *Mishnah Berurah* (266:23) quotes certain authorities who require that the donkey must be unloaded while it is still in motion in the courtyard (thereby avoiding having the donkey setting the sacks at rest by halting) or, removing it outside the courtyard before the donkey pauses, and then replacing it on the donkey's back after it has begun walking again (thereby avoiding having the donkey remove it from its state of rest in the public domain). In this latter case, he may unload it in the courtyard even after the donkey has stopped walking and is standing still. Since the donkey did not make the *akirah* (remove it from its state of rest), no Biblical violation takes place when it comes to a halt. (As explained above, *akirah* without *hanachah* or *hanachah* without *akirah* is not a Biblical violation.)

THE MISHNAH/SHABBOS — Chapter Twenty-Four: *Mi Shehechshich*

שבת
כד/ב

[ב] **מַתִּירִין** פְּקִיעֵי עָמִיר לִפְנֵי בְהֵמָה, וּמְפַסְפְּסִים אֶת הַכִּפִין, אֲבָל לֹא אֶת הַזֵּירִין. אֵין מְרַסְּקִין לֹא אֶת הַשַּׁחַת וְלֹא אֶת הֶחָרוּבִין לִפְנֵי בְהֵמָה, בֵּין דַּקָּה בֵּין גַּסָּה. רַבִּי יְהוּדָה מַתִּיר בֶּחָרוּבִין לְדַקָּה:

ר' עובדיה מברטנורא

(ב) **פקיעי עמיר.** קשין של שבלים שאגדן, מתירין אותן, דכל זמן שהן קשורין לאו אוכלא נינהו ומתירין אותן לשוינהו אוכלא, אבל פספום, לפזרן כדרך שרגילין לפזר עשבים לפני בהמה כדי שתריח ריחן ויהיו יפין לה לאכלן, אסור בפקיעי עמיר, דמאחר דאתעבידו אוכלא בהתר הפקיעין, והפספום אינו אלא לתענוג בעלמא, ומטרח בדבר שהוא כבר אוכל לא טרחינן: **ומפספסים את הכיפים.** ענפים לחים של ארז, מפזרים ושוטחים אותן לפני הבהמה שתריח ריחן, דבלאו פספום לא הוו אוכלא: **אבל לא את הזירין.** הן הן פקיעי עמיר, אלא שהפקיעין יש להן שני קשרים אחד בראשן ואחד בסופן, והזירין יש להן שלשה קשרים קשר אחד יתר באמצען. וקאמרה מתניתין שאין מפספסים את הזירין ואף על פי שהן דחוקים זה בזה ומתחממים והבהמה קצה בהן, אלא מתיר שלשה אגדיהן בלבד, דהתרת אגדיהן משוי לה אוכלא כפקיעין: **אין מרסקין את השחת.** אין מחתכין עשב של תבואה, והיא אספסתא, משום דטרחא שלא לצורך הוא: **רבי יהודה מתיר בחרובין לבהמה דקה.** שעניה דקות וקשין לה. ואין הלכה כרבי יהודה:

יד אברהם

2.

The following mishnah delineates permissible methods of preparing fodder on the Sabbath.

מַתִּירִין פְּקִיעֵי עָמִיר לִפְנֵי בְהֵמָה — *We may untie bundles of straw before an animal,*

(*Shenos Eliyahu* interprets this as fenugreek.) As long as the bundles are tied, the straw is not fit for the animal's consumption. Untying it, therefore, makes it edible. Making food edible for livestock is permissible on the Sabbath [as long as no *melachah* is violated] (*Rav*).

וּמְפַסְפְּסִים אֶת הַכִּפִין — *and we may scatter tender cedar boughs,*

These must be scattered before the animals, since when they are lying all together, the animals will not eat them (*Rav; Rashi*).

אֲבָל לֹא אֶת הַזֵּירִין — *but not triply bound bundles of straw.*

These are the same as the *bundles of straw* mentioned in the beginning of the mishnah, except that whereas those are tied only at both ends, these are tied in the middle as well (*Rav*).

The mishnah states that although these bundles may be untied, they may not be scattered. Although on weekdays it was generally the custom to scatter these (because, due to their being packed tightly by being triply bound, they become excessively warm and are not especially appetizing to the animals), since after untying them they are edible, they may not be scattered to make them more palatable to the livestock. This is regarded as an unnecessary effort on behalf of the

2. We may untie bundles of straw before an animal, and we may scatter tender cedar boughs, but not triply bound bundles of straw. We may not shred neither fodder nor carobs before an animal, whether [it is] lightweight or heavyweight. R' Yehudah permits [crushing] carobs for a lightweight [animal].

YAD AVRAHAM

animal and is prohibited for a food already edible (*Rav* in accordance with Rav Yehudah in the *Gem.* 155a).

Shenos Eliyahu interprets all three of the above terms as bundles of straw in different stages of hardness. When the straw was very tender, it was customary to bind it in bundles of three packets each, since its tenderness permitted it to be eaten in that manner. When it became harder, it was bound in bundles of two packets each, and when it became very hard and mature, each bundle was tied individually. Because of their hardness, these last were known as "cedars." Thus, the mishnah delineates the rulings for bundles in each of these three stages: We may untie double bundles of straw (in the middle stage of maturity) but we may not scatter them (untying renders them edible, whereas scattering is an unnecessary toil); we may even scatter bundles of hard cedarlike straw (since livestock will not eat them unless each bundle is separate); we may *not* even *untie* triple bundles of very tender straw (since these are edible even when tied). This explanation follows the reading of *Rif*, and is similar to that of *Rabbeinu Chananel*.

אֵין מְרַסְּקִין — *We may not shred*

I.e., we may not cut into small pieces (*Rav*).

לֹא אֶת הַשַּׁחַת — *neither fodder*

Straw from immature grain. This is soft enough to be eaten as is, and cutting it up therefore constitutes excessive toil (*Rav* according to Rav Yehudah).

וְלֹא אֶת הֶחָרוּבִין — *nor carobs*

The mishnah refers to tender carob-pods which are edible in their natural state and need not be cut up (*Tos. Yom Tov* from *Gem.*).

לִפְנֵי בְהֵמָה — *before an animal,*

[I.e., to make it easier for it to eat.]

בֵּין דַּקָּה בֵּין גַּסָּה — *whether [it is] lightweight or heavyweight* (lit. *thin or fat*).

[These are idiomatic terms used throughout Mishnah to describe the two categories of kosher animals generally raised for meat. Lightweight animals are sheep and goats; heavyweight animals are cattle.]

רַבִּי יְהוּדָה מַתִּיר בֶּחָרוּבִין לְדַקָּה. — *R' Yehudah permits [crushing] carobs for a lightweight [animal].*

R' Yehudah permits shredding carobs for small animals whose teeth are thin and who find difficulty in chewing even tender carob-pods. Thus, he is only making it edible. The halachah is not in accordance with Rabbi Yehudah (*Rav*).

We have explained the mishnah according to Rav Yehudah the *Amora* [not to be confused with Rabbi Yehudah the *Tanna*, just mentioned], who permits making a substance into food for livestock, and prohibits excesssive toil to make it more attractive or palatable. Rav Huna, however, prohibits making a substance into a food, since that involves creating something new. On

שבת
כד/ג

[ג] **אֵין אוֹבְסִין** אֶת הַגָּמָל, וְלֹא דוֹרְסִין, אֲבָל מַלְעִיטִין. וְאֵין מַאֲמִירִים אֶת הָעֲגָלִים, אֲבָל מַלְעִיטִין. וּמְהַלְקְטִין לַתַּרְנְגוֹלִין, וְנוֹתְנִין מַיִם לַמֻּרְסָן, אֲבָל לֹא גוֹבְלִין.

ר' עובדיה מברטנורא

(ג) אין אובסין. [אין] מאכילין אותו על כרחו ותוחבים לו בגרונו, ופירוש אובסין, עושין אבום בתוך מעיו: **ולא דורסים.** שדורס המאכל לתוך גרונה. ומיהו לא הוי כמו אובסין: **אבל מלעיטים.** שתוחב לו המאכל למקום שיכול להחזיר: **אין ממראין.** מפטמין, לשון וחלב מריאים (ישעיה א). ופירוש המראה, שתוחב לו המאכל לפנים מבית הבליעה במקום שאינו יכול להחזיר: **ומהלקטין לתרנגולים.** שתוחב המאכל לתוך פיו במקום שיכול להחזיר: **אבל לא גובלין.** אין לשין אותו במים:

יד אברהם

the other hand, if the substance is already fit to eat, he permits making the extra effort to make it more attractive for animals. Accordingly, he explains the mishnah as follows:

We may untie bundles of sheaves before an animal, and we may scatter them as well. Since they are normally intended for food, this preparation is not regarded as creating foodstuffs. Likewise, triply bound bundle of straw may be untied and scattered. [Rav Huna reverses the meanings of כיפין and זירין as given above. To him, כיפין

is *one triply bound bundle of straw*, while זירין are *cedar boughs.*] Since these are generally intended for kindling, untying or scattering them converts them into food, and is prohibited. We may not shred either hard fodder or hard carobs for animals, since they are not edible in their natural state until they are cut into small pieces. The end of the mishnah presents difficulty for Rav Huna, since R' Yehudah permits shredding carobs for small cattle who are unable to eat it otherwise (*Gem.* 155a).

3.

The mishnah now delineates those methods of feeding livestock that are permissible on the Sabbath and those that are not.

אֵין אוֹבְסִין אֶת הַגָּמָל, — *We may neither stuff a camel,*

The *Gemara* (155b) traces the word אוֹבְסִין to אֵבוּס, *a manger*, explaining that we may not make a manger in the camel's innards; i.e., we may not fill the camel's innards with food for several days (*Rambam; Meiri*); as expressed idiomatically, to the extent that "they become as wide as a manger" (*Rashi*).

Before setting out on a journey through the desert, it was customary to stuff the camel with enough food to last it for the duration of the journey. This was done by force-feeding, i.e., by stuffing the food down the camel's throat to a point from which he could not spit it out (*Meiri*).

וְלֹא דוֹרְסִין, — *nor cram it,*

This, too, is a type of force-feeding, but not in such large quantities as stuffing (*Rav; Rashi; Meiri*).

These are prohibited because of excessive toil on the Sabbath (*Meiri*). Alternatively, we fear that one may come to crush beans or knead flour for this purpose (*Tos. Yom Tov* from

3. We may neither stuff a camel, nor cram it, but we may put food into its mouth. We may not fatten calves, but we may put food into their mouths. We may put food into the mouths of fowls, and we may put water into bran, but we may not knead it.

YAD AVRAHAM

Rambam, Hil. Shabbos 21:35).

אֲבָל מַלְעִיטִין — *but we may put food into its mouth.*

If a camel is reluctant to eat, we may put food into his mouth, but only to a point from which he can still spit it out (*Rav; Meiri* from *Gem.* 155b).

[Since one is not forcing it down the camel's throat, but merely putting it deep into the camel's mouth, this is not considered excessive toil. It is only considered excessive if one has to force it beyond the point from which it cannot be spit out.]

וְאֵין מַמְרִים אֶת הָעֲגָלִים, — *We may not fatten calves,*

I.e., we may not force food down their throats to a point from which they cannot return it (*Rav,* in accordance with Rav Yehudah).

The *Baraisa* elaborates on this by explaining that the calf would be forced to lie down, its mouth would be held open, and it would be forced to swallow vetches and water simultaneously.

אֲבָל מַלְעִיטִין — *but we may put food into their mouths.*

I.e., we may feed calves in the usual manner, viz., by allowing them to stand upright and putting the vetches and water into their mouth separately (*Gem.* ibid.).

וּמְהַלְקְטִין לַתַּרְנְגוֹלִין — *We may put food into the mouths of fowls,*

I.e., the food may be inserted into the throat but only to a point from which the fowl can spit it out (*Rav*).

וְנוֹתְנִין מַיִם לַמֻּרְסָן, — *and we may put water into bran,*

[This too involves preparation of food for livestock.] The mishnah teaches us that merely adding water to bran does not constitute *kneading, one of the thirty-nine *melachos* enumerated above (7:2). One is not permitted, however, to actually knead this mixture, as will be explained below. The *Gemara* attributes this view to R' Yose the son of R' Yehudah. Rabbi [Yehudah HaNassi], however, rules that adding water to bran or flour is in itself the *melachah* of *kneading, although one has not actually kneaded the mixture.

Most authorities (*Rif; Rosh; Rambam, Hil. Shabbos* 21:34) rule in accordance with R' Yose the son of R' Yehudah (since the mishnah follows this view). Others (*Rabbeinu Baruch* in *Sefer HaTerumah,* Ch. 220; *Semag; Semak;* and *Hagahos Maimonios*) rule in accordance with Rabbi (whose views are generally accepted when in dispute with those of a colleague).

אֲבָל לֹא גוֹבְלִים. — *but we may not knead it.*

Rambam (*Hil. Shabbos* 8:15) rules that kneading substances that do not adhere, such as bran, coarse sand or ashes, is only Rabbinically prohibited. There is, however, no Torah prohibition involved in kneading such substances. For this reason, we may add water to bran; since adding the water

שבת
כד/ד

וְאֵין נוֹתְנִין מַיִם לִפְנֵי דְבוֹרִים וְלִפְנֵי יוֹנִים שֶׁבַּשּׁוֹבָךְ, אֲבָל נוֹתְנִין לִפְנֵי אַוָּזִים וְתַרְנְגוֹלִים, וְלִפְנֵי יוֹנֵי הַרְדְּסִיּוֹת:

[ד] **מְחַתְּכִין** אֶת הַדְּלוּעִין לִפְנֵי הַבְּהֵמָה,

ר' עובדיה מברטנורא

אין נותנין מים לפני דבורים. שאין מזונותיהן עליו, שיוצאין ואוכלין בשדה ומים מצויין להם באגמים: **דורסיאות**. יונים שגדלים בבתים. ונקראים דורסיאות על שם הורדוס המלך שהיה מגדל מהן בארמונו: (ד) **מחתכין את הדלועין**. התלושין לפני הבהמה, ואף על גב דסתמן לאו למאכל בהמה קיימי אלא לאדם: **ואת הנבלה**. שנתנבלה היום, ואף על גב דלא חזיא השתא לאדם, אף על גב דין השמשות היתה עומדת לאדם ולא לבהמה:

יד אברהם
---

never in itself constitutes the *melachah* of *kneading* (in accordance with the view of R' Yose the son of R' Yehudah), and since even if one did actually knead the resulting bran and water mixture he would not violate a Torah prohibition, the Rabbis saw no need to prohibit adding the water to bran (*Maggid Mishneh* ad loc.).

Most authorities, however, rule that there is indeed a Torah prohibition involved in kneading the above substances, for which one is liable to a sin offering. Nevertheless, since according to the view of R' Yose the son of R' Yehudah, adding the water to these types of substances is only Rabbinically forbidden — the Biblical *melachah* not occurring unless one actually kneads the mixture — the Rabbis did not prohibit adding water to bran because it is necessary to do so in order to feed livestock on the Sabbath (*Beis Yosef* 324 according to *Ravad, Tos.*, and others).

וְאֵין נוֹתְנִין מַיִם לִפְנֵי דְבוֹרִים וְלִפְנֵי יוֹנִים שֶׁבַּשּׁוֹבָךְ, — **We may not place water before bees or before doves that are in a dovecote**,

Since those creatures are not dependent on their keeper but have their own access to food and water, and since these substances are readily available to them, the beekeeper and the owner of the dovecote are not obliged to feed them. Putting water before them is, therefore, unnecessary toil (*Rav; Tif. Yis.* from *Gem.* 156b).

Accordingly, many object to the popular custom of putting out wheat or breadcrumbs for the birds on *Shabbos Shirah* [the portion dealing with the splitting of the Red Sea] (*Magen Avraham* 324:7, *Shulchan Aruch HaRav* par. 8). Some justify this practice on the grounds that it is done with the intention of fulfilling a precept, since, according to popular belief, the birds joined in singing the song of rejoicing and praise of Hashem after the crossing of the Red Sea. Others base this practice on the popular belief that Dathan and Abiram put manna outside on the Sabbath, in order to make Moses, who had stated that there would no manna on the Sabbath, appear to be a liar. The birds, upon spotting this morsel, quickly ate it up, thereby saving Moses' reputation. As a reward, we place wheat kernels outside for them on that Sabbath (*Likutei Mahariach*).

According to *Olas Shabbos* (§16), the restriction on feeding wild birds applies only to water, since it is readily accessible in ponds. Food, however, which may not be accessible, may be given to them. [Accordingly, there is no objection to feeding the

24 We may not place water before bees or before doves
4 that are in a dovecote, but we may place [water] before geese and chickens, and before Herodian doves.

4. We may cut up gourds before cattle or a

YAD AVRAHAM

birds on *Shabbos Shirah*. See *Beis Yosef* 324.]

אֲבָל נוֹתְנִין — *but we may place [water]*
[I.e., we may place food and water.]

לִפְנֵי אַוָּזִים וְתַרְנְגוֹלִים, — *before geese and chickens,*

We may feed geese and chickens since they are domesticated and do not fly outside their owner's domain to obtain water. One may do so, however, only for those he is responsible to feed [not for wild ones] (*Meiri*).

וְלִפְנֵי יוֹנֵי הָרַדְסִיּוֹת. — *and before Herodian doves.*

I.e., domesticated doves, called Herodian after Herod, who raised doves in his palace (*Rav; Rambam, Comm.*).

Rashi attributes the name to the place whence these doves originated.

4.

The following mishnah deals with preparing food for livestock from substances which before the Sabbath were not destined for this use, but rather for human consumption.

מְחַתְּכִין אֶת הַדְּלוּעִין — *We may cut up gourds*

This refers to gourds picked before the Sabbath. Despite the fact that these are generally put aside to be cooked for human consumption, not to be fed to cattle, the *Tanna Kamma*, identified by the *Gemara* as R' Shimon, does not consider them *muktzeh*.

Gourds which either fall off the plant or are picked on the Sabbath (by non-Jews for example) are *muktzeh*, even according to the *Tanna Kamma* (R' Shimon). Since the owner could easily have picked them prior to the Sabbath and did not, thereby consciously placing them beyond his reach for the Sabbath (since one is not permitted to pick produce on the Sabbath), it is considered as if he expressly made them unusable for the Sabbath, in which case even R' Shimon agrees

that it is *muktzeh* (*Tos. Yom Tov* from *Beis Yosef*; cf. *Shulchan Aruch* 310:2).[1]

Others explain that R' Shimon agrees there because fruits removed from the plant on the Sabbath are forbidden by Rabbinic enactment, lest a person be tempted to pick them on the Sabbath (*Tos. to Beitzah* 3a quoted by *Magen Avraham* 318:4).

This law is stated here to teach us that we may prepare food for an animal on the Sabbath. Although this has been stated above in mishnah 2, it is repeated here because of its similarity to the law of cutting a carcass, both dealing with cutting up food (*Tos. Yom Tov* quoting *Tos., Chullin* 14a; *Rosh ad loc.*).[2]

לִפְנֵי הַבְּהֵמָה, — *before cattle*

I.e., to feed cattle, even though it was

---

1. Although in a strict sense this logic applies only to produce owned by a Jew (which is his to pick) but not to that owned by a gentile, it was extended to that of a gentile, too, in order to avoid confusion (*Rashi* to *Beitzah* 24b).

2. *Tos. R' Akiva* suggests that the law of cutting gourds is related to the dispute concerning *muktzeh*, and resembles the dispute about cutting the carcass of an animal that died

שבת כד/ה

וְאֶת הַנְּבֵלָה לִפְנֵי הַכְּלָבִים. רַבִּי יְהוּדָה אוֹמֵר: אִם לֹא הָיְתָה נְבֵלָה מֵעֶרֶב שַׁבָּת, אֲסוּרָה, לְפִי שֶׁאֵינָהּ מִן הַמּוּכָן.

[ה] **מְפִירִין** נְדָרִים בַּשַׁבָּת, וְנִשְׁאָלִין

ר' עובדיה מברטנורא

רבי יהודה אומר אם לא היתה נבילה מערב שבת אסורה. דכל מידי דחזי לאינש לא מקלה ליה לבהמה. ואפילו חולה מט"ש, סובר שתתרפא. ואין הלכה כרבי יהודה: (ה) **מפירין** בעל לאשתו ואב לבתו: **ונשאלין**. לחכם: שהן לצורך השבת. כגון שנדר שלא יאכל היום. ונשאלין

יד אברהם

originally intended for human consumption (*Rav; Rashi*).

Since the gourds are hard, cutting them constitutes converting them into food, which is permissible according to Rav Yehudah, as explained in mishnah 2 (*Tos. Yom Tov* from *Gem.* 155b).

וְאֶת הַנְּבֵלָה לִפְנֵי הַכְּלָבִים — *or a carcass before dogs.*

I.e., an animal which died on the Sabbath [and whose meat is therefore fit only for dogs (since it did not die through *shechitah*, ritual slaughter)] may be cut up and fed to dogs, even though at dusk it was still alive, and therefore intended for human rather than canine consumption (*Rav*).

Although gourds that were not picked prior to the Sabbath may not be cut up for animals even according to the *Tanna Kamma* (R' Shimon), the carcass of an animal that was still living prior to the Sabbath may be cut up for dogs. This is because gourds do not usually fall off the plant by themselves. Therefore, by not picking them, one consciously places them beyond his reach for the Sabbath. A living animal, however, is likely to die by itself. Therefore, the possibility of feeding it to dogs on the Sabbath has not been precluded (*Tif. Yis.*).

Others answer that only produce which can be easily picked by anyone is considered having been consciously placed beyond reach by one's failure to do so. The proper *shechitah* of an animal is, however, not a skill available to all people nor is the proper knife. Consequently, by not slaughtering the animal before the Sabbath, one has not indicated his active disinterest in using its meat on the Sabbath, since his failure to slaughter may just as well be the result of his inability to do so (*Beis Yosef* 318).

The mishnah is dealing with tough carcasses, such as those of elephants, or with cutting up carcasses for small dogs, for whom any carcass is too hard to chew. (This is derived from the juxtaposition of the case of the carcass to that of the gourds. Just as the gourds are too hard to eat before being cut up, so is the carcass.) The mishnah, there-

on the Sabbath, mentioned below. There too, the animal, which was still alive before the Sabbath, was destined to be slaughtered after the Sabbath and used for human consumption. Therefore, just as R' Shimon permits cutting up the carcass to feed dogs (although it was originally intended for humans), so too, he permits cutting up gourds, even though they were originally intended for humans. Similarly, just as R' Yehudah prohibits cutting up the carcass (since before the Sabbath it was intended for human, not canine, consumption), so too, he prohibits cutting up gourds for dogs, since they too were originally intended for human consumption.

24
5

carcass before dogs. R' Yehudah says: If it was not [yet] a carcass prior to the Sabbath, it is prohibited, since it is not something that was prepared.

5. We may annul vows on the Sabbath, and we

YAD AVRAHAM

fore, is consistent with Rav Yehudah, who rules that making a substance edible is permissible, whereas unnecessary bother with something already edible is prohibited (*Tos. Yom Tov* from *Gem.* 155b).

רַבִּי יְהוּדָה אוֹמֵר: אִם לֹא הָיְתָה נְבֵלָה מֵעֶרֶב שַׁבָּת, אֲסוּרָה, — *R' Yehudah says: If it was not [yet] a carcass prior to the Sabbath, it is prohibited*,

R' Yehudah maintains that anything fit for human consumption is never intended to be used for animals. Consequently, an animal that was alive at the onset of the Sabbath is assumed to be set aside for slaughter after the Sabbath (since it cannot be slaughtered on the Sabbath). Therefore, it is *muktzeh* and must remain so for the rest of that Sabbath. (See above 3:6, the dispute between R' Yehudah and R' Shimon with regard to carrying a lamp whose flame has burnt out.)

לְפִי שֶׁאֵינָהּ מִן הַמּוּכָן. — *since it is not something that was prepared.*

[I.e., it did not stand to be used on the Sabbath.]

This clause seems superfluous. It is obvious that R' Yehudah does not deem it *prepared*. Otherwise, he would not prohibit cutting it up for dogs. *Tosafos*, quoting R' *Poras*, explain that without this clause, we would believe that a carcass is *muktzeh* only because when it was alive it was impossible to use on the Sabbath, since it could not be slaughtered. Should there be something set aside for human consumption which, however, is not subject to any prohibition preventing its use, we might be inclined to believe that, although fit for human consumption, it may also be handled to prepare it for animals. Therefore, the mishnah states explicitly, *since it is not something that was prepared*, to indicate that even something not requiring slaughtering, which was intended for human consumption, may not be cut up for animals on the Sabbath since it is not prepared for animals.

5.

The final mishnah of this tractate enumerates various Rabbinic prohibitions which were permitted in order to facilitate the performance of a *mitzvah*.

מְפִירִין נְדָרִים בַּשַּׁבָּת, — *We may annul vows on the Sabbath,*

The Torah states (*Numbers* 30:3) that if a man or woman utters a vow or oath, he is bound to keep it. He may, however, be released from that vow by applying to an expert Rabbinic judge or a lay court for a release. The court must then ascertain whether proper grounds exist for such a release. [The guidelines for these grounds are delineated in *Nedarim* Chap. 9.] As will be explained below, in most cases this may not be done on the Sabbath.

A woman, however, may be released in yet another way.

If a girl from the age of eleven [the lowest age at which her vows are binding] until the age of twelve and a half utters a vow or oath involving mortification of her body (e.g. not to eat), the father has the prerogative of annulling

[521] THE MISHNAH/SHABBOS — Chapter Twenty-Four: *Mi Shehechshich*

שבת כד/ה

לִדְבָרִים שֶׁהֵן לְצֹרֶךְ הַשַּׁבָּת. פּוֹקְקִין אֶת הַמָּאוֹר, וּמוֹדְדִין אֶת הַמַּטְלִית וְאֶת הַמִּקְוֶה. וּמַעֲשֶׂה בִּימֵי אָבִיו שֶׁל רַבִּי צָדוֹק וּבִימֵי

ר' עובדיה מברטנורא

דוקא קתני, דאילו בעל או אב מפר בין נדרים לצורך השבת בין נדרים שהן לצורך השבת, כיון שאינו יכול להפר אלא ביום שמעו בלבד. ונדרים שהן לצורך השבת אפילו היה לו פנאי להשאל עליהם קודם השבת נשאלין עליהם בשבת: **ופוקקין את המאור.** החלון שממנו האורה נכנסת, סותמין אותו בלוח או בשאר כל דבר שרגילים לסתום בו: **ומודדין את המטלית.** כגון אם היתה טמאה ונגעה בטהרות, מודדין אותה אם יש בה ג' אצבעות על ג' אצבעות לידע אם נטמאו הטהרות אם לאו, דמטלית פחותה מג' על ג' אינה לא מיטמאה ולא מטמאה: **ואת המקוה.** לידע אם יש בה אמה על אמה ברום שלש אמות. שאלו מדידות של מצוה הן לפיכך מותר למדוד אותן בשבת: **שפקקו את החלון וקרוי מאור שממנו האורה נכנסת.**

יד אברהם

this vow or oath.[1] However, he may do so only on the day he hears of it.

Similarly, if a married woman utters such a vow, or one affecting her relationship with her husband, the latter may annul it. Again, however, he may do so only on the day he hears of it.

The time allotted for this annulment is not a period of twenty-four hours, but only until the end of the day on which he heard the vow. Therefore, the actual time for annulment may range from twenty-four hours [if he heard at the very beginning of the day] to just a few minutes [if he heard just before the end of the day] (Nedarim 10:8). As in all matters of Jewish law, the day begins and ends with nightfall. Therefore, should the father or husband hear of the vow on the Sabbath, he has only until the end of the Sabbath to annul the vow. Since they will not be able to annul that vow after the Sabbath, the Rabbis permitted them to do so on the Sabbath (Rav from Gem. 157a).

The Gemara, however, quotes a dissenting view that a vow may be annulled for twenty-four hours after the time the father or husband hears of it, regardless of what day it is. Accordingly, there would still be time to annul it after the Sabbath. Those subscribing to this view, therefore, qualify the mishnah as referring only to vows inhibiting the proper observance or enjoyment of the Sabbath (Gem. ibid.).

וְנִשְׁאָלִין — and we may seek release [from vows]

I.e., we may apply to a Sage [or a court of three laymen (Shoshanim LeDavid)] to release us from a vow (Rav).

לִדְבָרִים שֶׁהֵן לְצֹרֶךְ הַשַּׁבָּת. — for things that are necessary for the Sabbath.

E.g., if one vowed not to eat on the Sabbath, he may be released from this vow on the Sabbath even if he had time to apply before the Sabbath (Rav from Gem. 157a).

However, one may not be released from vows that have no bearing on the Sabbath. Two reasons are given for this ruling: (a) Since either a Rabbinic judge or a court is required, it gives the appearance of being a litigation, which is prohibited on the Sabbath; (b) since there is time after the Sabbath, we may

---

1. According to Rambam (Hil. Nedarim 12:1), he may annul all types of vows.

24 may seek release [from vows] for things that are
5 necessary for the Sabbath.

We may stop up a window, and we may measure a patch or a *mikveh*. An incident occurred in the days of R' Tzaddok's father and in the days of

YAD AVRAHAM

not perform this rite on the Sabbath (*Ran, Nedarim* 77a). Since it can be done after the Sabbath, and it is not needed on the Sabbath, it is prohibited by the prophetic injunction of מִמְּצוֹא חֶפְצְךָ, *from seeking your personal wants* (*Isaiah* 58:13) (*Rosh Yosef* quoting *Tosefos Shabbos; Chidushei Chasam Sofer* quoting *Rosh, Nedarim*).

Tos. R' Akiva questions the first reason. As stated above, those who rule that vows may be annulled for twenty-four hours from the time the husband learned of them, regardless of the day, explain the mishnah as referring only to an annulment of a vow which in some way hinders Sabbath observance. Other vows may not be annulled on the Sabbath, despite the fact that such annulment would not require either a court or judge. Since annulment does not resemble litigation, and is, nevertheless, prohibited, it seems clear that it is prohibited because one has time to perform it after the Sabbath (the second reason).

פּוֹקְקִין אֶת הַמָּאוֹר, — *We may stop up a window* (lit. *a lit source*),

I.e., a window through which light enters may be stopped up with a board or the like (*Rav*).

This mishnah follows the opinion of the Sages (above 17:7) who permit stopping up a window with a shutter even if it is not tied or suspended from the window (*Rashi* and *Ran*). According to R' Eliezer, however, it is prohibited since it is regarded as adding to the building.

Rambam explains the mishnah as referring to stopping the window with a utensil which is not usually left in the window permanently. For this reason, it is permitted even according to R' Eliezer.

Rashi and *Ran* do not follow this explanation because they follow the view of *Tosafos* (126b) who state that R' Eliezer prohibits even a utensil because, having once been used to stop up the window, these too are sometimes left there permanently (*Tos. Yom Tov*).

וּמוֹדְדִין אֶת הַמַּטְלִית — *and we may measure a patch*

I.e., if a patch of cloth contracted *tumah* and subsequently came in contact with an uncontaminated food, the patch may be measured to determine whether it has the minimum dimensions for contracting and transmitting *tumah*. For a garment, this is three fingerbreadths by three fingerbreadths.

וְאֶת הַמִּקְוֶה. — *or a mikveh.*

A *mikveh* (ritual bath), in order to purify those who are *tamei*, must contain forty *se'ah* of water. This derives from the fact that a bath must measure at least one cubit in length by one cubit in width and three cubits in height in order for a person of average size to immerse his entire body in it at one time. The mishnah states that a *mikveh* may be measured in order to ascertain whether it has the minimum size.

Since these two instances represent measuring for the fulfillment of precepts, they are permissible on the Sabbath (*Rav*).

Measuring for any other purpose is regarded a *weekday activity* and is prohibited (*Tif. Yis.*).

שבת כד/ה

אַבָּא שָׁאוּל בֶּן בָּטְנִית, שֶׁפָּקְקוּ אֶת הַמָּאוֹר בְּטָפִיחַ, וְקָשְׁרוּ אֶת הַמְּקֵדָה בְּגֶמִי לֵידַע אִם יֵשׁ בַּגִּיגִית פּוֹתֵחַ טֶפַח אִם לָאו. וּמִדִּבְרֵיהֶן לָמַדְנוּ שֶׁפּוֹקְקִין, וּמוֹדְדִין,

ר' עובדיה מברטנורא

בטפיח. פך של חרס: **מקדה.** כלי חרס: **בגמי.** להכי נקט גמי שראלוי למאכל בהמה ולא מבטל ליה להיות קשר של קיימא: **לידע אם יש בגיגית פותח טפח.** כמין שביל קטן היה בין שני בתים שלא היה מקורה אלא גיגית שניגית מונחת על גבו, והיו חלונות פתוחות מן הבתים אל השביל, והיו חושיןן שמא ימות מת בבית אחד ותהא הטומאה בא מן החלון אל השביל ומן השביל אל הבית אחר דרך החלון הפתוח, לפיכך פקקו את החלון הפתוח לבית שהטומאה בתוכו בטפיח של חרס וגבו לגד השביל, וכלי חרס אינו מיטמא מגבו, וחוגר, כי חשבו שמא אין בסדק הגיגית פותח טפח ונמלאת הגיגית מחצלת על השביל והטומאה באה דרך השביל מבית זה לבית זה. אחר כך הולרכו לפתוח החלון וליטול אותו טפיח הפקוק בחלון, ובאו לידע אם יש באותו סדק של גיגית פותח טפח ואין שם אהל באותו שביל להבריח את הטומאה, שהטומאה יולאה מן השביל דרך סדק שבגיגית כלפי מעלה. או אין בסדק של גיגית פותח טפח, ונמלאת הגיגית השביל כאהל ומדיאה את הטומאה מבית לבית. ומדדו מקדה של חרס וקשרוה בגמי והושיטוה כלפי מעלה, לראות אם היה בסדק הגיגית פותח טפח אם לאו: **ומדבריהם למדנו שפוקקין וקושרין ומודדין בשבת.** ובלבד שלא יהיה קשר

יד אברהם

וּמַעֲשֶׂה בִּימֵי אָבִיו שֶׁל רַבִּי צָדוֹק וּבִימֵי אַבָּא שָׁאוּל בֶּן בָּטְנִית, שֶׁפָּקְקוּ אֶת הַמָּאוֹר בְּטָפִיחַ, — *An incident occurred in the days of R' Tzaddok's father and in the days of Abba Shaul ben Batnis, that they stopped up the window with an earthenware jug,*

Although most forms of *tumah* contaminate only through direct contact, a corpse also contaminates anything which is under the same roof as it (see above 2:3). However, a solid wall or other barrier prevents the *tumah* from spreading beyond it. If, however, there is an open window in this wall, the *tumah* exits through the window and contaminates anything under the ceiling or overhang on the other side of the wall. One who wishes to prevent the *tumah* from spreading to the far side of the wall must block the open window. He must, however, block the window with an object which is itself immune to *tumah*-contamination.

The incident to which the mishnah refers relates to two houses which were separated by a narrow path. Although the roofs were not connected, the gap between the roofs was spanned by a vat (which was split). In one of the houses lay a person near death. Anticipating his imminent demise, the people in the second house wished to prevent the resulting *tumah* from spreading from the first house, through its open window to the covered path and then into the second house, through its open window.

They did this by blocking their window with an earthenware jug. An earthenware jug cannot contract *tumah* unless its interior is exposed to the *tumah*. If only its exterior is exposed to the *tumah*, it is immune to contamination, and it therefore prevents the spread of *tumah* to points beyond it-

24.
5
Abba Shaul ben Batnis, that they stopped up the window with an earthenware jug, and tied a cup with a rush to ascertain whether a vat had an aperture of a handbreadth or not. And from their words we learned that we may stop up, measure,

YAD AVRAHAM

self. The jug was placed in the window of the second house with its mouth facing the interior of the house and its base facing the path (and the window of the dying man's house), thereby exposing only the exterior of the jug to the *tumah* (*Rav* from *Gem.* 157a, as explained by *Tos. Yom Tov*).

וְקָשְׁרוּ אֶת הַמְּקֵדָה בְגֶמִי — *and tied a cup with a rush*

Since rush is a substance used as animal fodder, it is not tied permanently to the cup. Consequently, there is no violation of the Biblical *melachah* of *tying*, as explained above (17:1). The Rabbinic prohibition is relaxed for the purposes of a *mitzvah* (*Rav*).

לֵידַע אִם יֵשׁ בַּגִּיגִית פּוֹתֵחַ טֶפַח אִם לָאו. — *to ascertain whether a vat had an aperture of a handbreadth or not.*

Later it became necessary to open the window previously blocked by the jug. This would, of course, result in the spread of the *tumah* to the second house (since the deceased was still in the first house). However, as mentioned above, the vat spanning the path was split. The halachah is that if there is a split in the covering, the width of a handbreadth, the two halves are not considered one roof, and the *tumah* therefore does not spread past the split. Therefore, before unblocking the window they wished to ascertain whether the split in the vat was a handbreadth wide. In order to determine the size of the aperture, they

tied a rush to a cup which was precisely a handbreadth wide, and thrust it up [with a stick] to see whether it would go through a crack in the vat (*Rav*).

Rashi's explanation is close to that of *Rav* except that he explains that the corpse was in the path under the vat. *Tosafos* prefer *Rabbeinu Chananel's* commentary, viz., that the corpse was in one of two connected houses. In the middle of the wall dividing the houses was a woven basket, closing up the hole. In this basket was a crack. It was not known whether the crack was a handbreadth wide. If it had those dimensions it would convey *tumah* to the other house. Since *Kohanim* wished to enter the house on that Sabbath, people went up to the roof and covered the skylight with an earthenware jug, so that, if the *tumah* was indeed conveyed to the house, those on the roof would not contract it when standing over the skylight. Then, they tied a rush around a cup and let it down to the opening in the basket, to determine whether the opening was a handbreadth long and a handbreadth wide.

וּמִדִּבְרֵיהֶן לָמַדְנוּ — *And from their words we learned*

[I.e., from their instructions to stop up the window, tie the cup and measure the aperture.]

שֶׁפּוֹקְקִין, — *that we may stop up,*

[I.e., we may stop up a window.]

וּמוֹדְדִין, — *measure,*

I.e., measure for *mitzvah* purposes or to learn a point of halachah, as in the case of measuring the aperture (*Rav* from *Gem.* 157b).

שבת כד/ה

וְקוֹשְׁרִין בַּשַּׁבָּת:

── ר' עובדיה מברטנורא ──
של קיימא, והמדידה תהיה של מצוה, או להתלמד על דבר הוראה:

יד אברהם

וְקוֹשְׁרִין בַּשַּׁבָּת. — and tie on the Sabbath.

This, too, is permissible only for mitzvah purposes (Tos. Yom Tov from Rambam[1],[2]) Furthermore, it is permissible only if one makes a tempo-

1. Tosefos Yom Tov points out that Rav seems to explain the mishnah as granting a leniency only as far as measuring is concerned. As far as tying is concerned, no special leniency is granted and only those knots normally permissible may be used, even for mitzvah purposes. Rambam (Comm. and Hil. Shabbos 10:6) and Tur (317), however, specifically state that this tying was permitted only for purposes of a mitzvah, thus granting a leniency to tying too. Beur Halachah (317) takes this to mean that even knots normally forbidden by Rabbinic decree are permitted for mitzvah purposes.

2. Since the cup was tied with a substance used for animal fodder, it would seem to be indicated that the melachah of *tying is applicable to foodstuffs as well; otherwise there

24 5 and tie on the Sabbath.

YAD AVRAHAM

rary knot. A permanent knot, being Biblically prohibited, can never be permitted on the Sabbath (*Rav; Rashi*).

We have stated that measuring is permitted only for the purpose of fulfilling a *mitzvah* or learning a point of halachah. Since measuring is prohibited only because it is a *weekday activity* (a Rabbinic prohibition), it is permitted for *mitzvah* matters. Stopping up a window, however, since it is in this case obviously temporary, involves no *melachah* at all and there is, therefore, no reason to prohibit it even for non-*mitzvah* purposes. Obviously, if it is meant to be a permanent addition, it is Biblically prohibited and one may not do it even for a *mitzvah* (*Tos. Yom Tov*).

would be no proof from here that Rabbinically prohibited knots may be made for the purpose of a *mitzvah*. This contradicts the statement of *Rambam* (*Hil. Shabbos* 10:4) that whatever is fit for animal fodder may be knotted on the Sabbath. *Chayei Adam* explains *Rambam* as meaning only such plant stalks or leaves which become brittle when they dry out. That being the case, a knot made in a fresh stalk will fall apart of its own accord once it dries. For this reason it is not considered a knot at all. (Cf. last *Beur Halachah* 317 and *Mishnah Berurah* ibid. 324:12.)

Appendix

~§ The Eighteen Decrees

The first nine decrees involve the purity of תְּרוּמָה, *terumah*, the share of produce due the *Kohanim*. The Torah enjoins us to be extremely scrupulous in preventing *terumah* from becoming טָמֵא [*tamei*], *ritually unclean*. To safeguard its ritual purity, the Rabbis of the Second Commonwealth enacted several measures, enumerated in *Chagigah* 2:7.

~§ Degrees of Tumah

The severity of contamination [*tumah*] and the ability of one contaminated [*tamei*] person or object to convey *tumah* to another are not uniform, but vary according to the degree of *tumah* and the class of object which has become contaminated.

The strictest level of *tumah*, אֲבִי אֲבוֹת הַטֻּמְאָה, *the most severe origin* [lit. father of fathers] *of contamination*, is a corpse. The next, and far more common, level is known as אַב הַטֻּמְאָה [*av*], *the origin* [lit., *father*] *of contamination*. This category includes: one who touched a corpse; a שֶׁרֶץ, one of the eight species of dead *rodent* or *reptile* [listed in *Leviticus* 11:29-30; see Commentary to 14:1 below]; נְבֵלָה, *the carcass*, of an animal that died by some means other than a valid ritual slaughter; or a *zav*, *zavah*, or *niddah* discussed in 1:3.

A vessel or food that is contaminated by an *av* is a רִאשׁוֹן לְטֻמְאָה [*rishon*], *first degree of contamination*. An object contracting *tumah* from a *rishon* is a שֵׁנִי לְטֻמְאָה [*sheni*], *second degree of contamination*. In the case of unsanctified food, contamination can go no further than a *sheni*; thus if a *sheni* touches another unsanctified food, the latter food acquires no degree of contamination whatever.

Due to the greater degree of stringency associated with *terumah*, it becomes *shelishi*, or third degree of contamination. But the *tumah* of *terumah* goes no further than this third degree. As a general rule, the word *tamei* is applied only to an object which can convey its contamination to another object. An object which cannot convey its contamination is called *pasul* [*invalid*], rather than *tamei*. For further details, see *Chagigah* 3:2.

The first three decrees deal with consuming ritually unclean foods and beverages. The following three people all become a second degree of *tumah* and render *terumah* invalid:

(1) **one who eats food which is a first degree of *tumah*,** or

(2) **a second degree of *tumah*,** or

(3) **one who drinks ritually contaminated beverages.**

The Sages decreed this in order to discourage *Kohanim* from consuming ritually contaminated food or beverages while eating *terumah*. They wised to prevent the *terumah* from coming in contact with the ritually unclean food while in the *Kohen's* mouth, thereby rendering the *terumah* invalid. The *terumah* would become invalid by Rabbinical enactment, since Biblically, one food cannot contaminate another.

The following two render *terumah* invalid on contact:

(4) **one who immerses his head and the larger part of his body into water that was drawn with a vessel (in contrast to spring water or naturally collected rain water) on the same day that he purified himself in a *mikveh*,** or

(5) **a ritually clean person over whose head and most of his body three *lugin***

of drawn water were spilled. These measures were enacted because people used to purify themselves in *mikvaos* of stagnant water which had become foul and then cleanse themselves by pouring מַיִם שְׁאוּבִים, *water drawn with a vessel*, over themselves.

So entrenched did the custom of rinsing oneself off with drawn water after coming out of the *mikveh* become, that people started thinking of the rinsing as the main part of the purification and the immersion in the *mikveh* as merely a preliminary to it. The Rabbis feared that people might eventually presume that only the drawn water was necessary to effect purification rather than a *mikveh*. In truth, however, drawn water is invalid for a *mikveh* and cannot effect purification. To discourage this practice, they decreed that one whose head and most of his body enter into drawn water *on the day of his immersion* invalidates any *terumah* with which he comes in contact. In order to assure compliance with this measure, they additionally decreed that if three *lugin* of drawn water should *fall* on a ritually clean person at any time, he, too, invalidates *terumah*. It was sufficient to decree that a clean person should become contaminated if drawn water *fell* on him (rather than if he immersed himself in the drawn water) since it was customary to shower (rather than bathe) after immersion in fetid *mikveh* water (*Tos.* 13b). Only on the actual day of the immersion in a *mikveh* did the Rabbis render *tamei* even one who immerses in drawn water.

(6) **Books of Scripture invalidate *terumah* on contact.**

At one time people felt that since *terumah* and Scripture are both holy it would be proper to store them together. Unfortunately, the *terumah*, being food, attracted mice and as a result the Scripture scrolls were damaged. To discourage this practice, the Rabbis decreed that Books of Scripture would invalidate *terumah* on contact.

(7) **Unwashed hands invalidate *terumah*.**

It is not fitting for *terumah*, being holy, to become soiled. Thus, in order to discourage the handling of *terumah* by unwashed hands, which inadvertently often come in contact with dirt, the Sages decreed that *terumah* handled by unwashed hands is rendered invalid.[1]

(8) **Liquids always become a *rishon* and cause foods to become a *sheni*.**

As explained above, the chain of *tumah* diminishes in severity as it moves further away form the original source. Thus an *av* will contaminate something and make it a first degree, which in turn will make it a second degree.

An exception to this rule is liquids. There the Rabbis decreed that *any* level of *tumah* which has the power to invalidate *terumah* renders a first degree, i.e., even a food, which is itself only a second degree, will (Rabbinically) render a beverage (with which it comes in contact) a first degree. (Since a second degree *tumah* invalidates *terumah*, it falls within this rule.) The reason for the more stringent attitude towards liquids is that Scripturally, liquids are more susceptible than foods to contracting *tumah*. Foods require הֶכְשֵׁר [*hechsher*], *prior preparation*, to become susceptible to *tumah*, i.e., they must first become wet. Liquids, however, require no prior *hechsher*, but contract *tumah* as is.

As a result, liquids that come in contact with unwashed hands, which are considered a second degree of *tumah* (see number 7), become a first degree and they, in turn, render *terumah tamei*.

(9) **Any vessel which becomes *tamei* through contact with a liquid which is**

---

1. The first one to enact a requirement to wash the hands was King Solomon, who instituted washing the hands for touching קָדָשִׁים, *sanctified food*. Later, Hillel and Shammai required it for *terumah*. Their enactment was, however, not accepted by the populace. It was again brought to a vote by their disciples, and passed (*Gem.* 15a). Later, the requirement was extended to unsanctified food, as well, either in order to accustom those who eat *terumah* to wash their hands or because of cleanliness (*Chullin* 106a).

tamei becomes a second degree of *tumah,* and can then invalidate *terumah.*

Scripturally, vessels can become *tamei* only from an *av,* i.e., a vessel can become a first degree but not a second degree. Nevertheless, the Rabbis decreed that *liquids* which were contaminated and have become a first degree (as explained above) do render vessels a second degree. These vessels, in turn, invalidate *terumah.*

The reason for this decree is that there are liquids which are Scripturally in the category of *av* and, therefore, are able to render a vessel a first degree. These liquids are the saliva, urine and issue of a *zav* or *zavah.* In order to avoid confusion between liquids, the Rabbis decreed that all liquids which are *tamei* can transmit *tumah* to vessels on contact.

The following nine (10-18) deal with miscellaneous matters.

(10) **The daughters of the Cuthites are considered menstruants from the cradle.**

When a woman senses blood issuing from the womb, she becomes *tamei,* ritually impure. This rule applies to female infants — in the rare instances when blood issues from them — as well, as the Rabbis infer from Scripture. The Cutheans,[1] however, did not accept the Oral Law and, consequently, did not observe the ruling concerning infants. In order to prevent the contracting of *tumah* from the children of the Cutheans, the Rabbis proclaimed all their females, including newborn ones, *tamei* — although the vast majority of them certainly never had blood issue from them.

(11) **Objects whose thickness have a circumference of one handbreadth transmit *tumah* as an *ohel*-tent.**

As mentioned above, a human corpse is the most severe type of *tumah,* known as *avi avos,* literally, *father of fathers.* In addition to conveying *tumah* through מַגָּע, *contact,* and מַשָּׂא, *carrying,* it also conveys *tumah* through אֹהֶל [*ohel*], literally a tent, i.e., if a tent or any other covering simultaneously shelters both the corpse and an object, that object contracts *tumah* from the corpse. According to the Torah, this is true only if the *ohel* is at least a handbreadth wide. The Rabbis decreed, however, that all objects shall transmit *tumah* if their thickness has a *circumference* of a handbreadth though the *diameter* (width) is less. The Sages feared confusion between circumference and width and therefore decreed that both convey *ohel* contamination.

(12) **Juice exuding from grapes being picked for the wine-press is considered a *hechsher,* or prior preparation rendering the grapes susceptible of contracting *tumah.***

Foods become susceptible to *tumah* only if they are first מֻכְשָׁר [*muchshar*], *prepared or made fit.* This occurs when the food becomes wet from any one of seven liquids: wine, bees' honey, olive oil, milk, dew, blood, or water (*Machshirin* 6:4-8).

There are certain exceptions to this however. One is a case in which the liquid is unwanted; e.g., juice oozing from grapes while in a basket. Since that juice goes to waste, the owner would prefer that it not ooze from the grapes. It therefore Biblically does not render the grapes prepared to contract *tumah.* The Rabbis, however, decreed that the juice exuding from grapes being picked *for* the wine-press shall constitute a

---

1. The origin of the Cutheans in *Eretz Yisrael* is mentioned in *II Kings* 17:24.

The non-Jewish citizens of Cutha were brought by the king of Assyria to settle the Samarian cities left desolate by the exile of the Ten Tribes. Although they converted to Judaism, as the result of a plague of lions which attacked them, there was considerable dispute as to the validity of their conversion (see *Kiddushin* 75b). When, at a later date, they were discovered to be idolaters, they were declared gentiles (*Chullin* 6a). Whatever their status, they remained a sect unto themselves — known as Samaritans because they lived in Samaria — and exhibited great animosity toward the Jews (see *Ezra* 4 for a description of their effort to prevent the construction of the Second Temple and see *Yoma* 69a for their attempt to have the Temple destroyed).

valid preparation for *tumah*, lest one pick grapes into pitch-lined baskets, which do retain the juice, in which case the grapes are Biblically prepared. Since he intends to press them anyway, the owner is satisfied with any juice which has oozed from them.

(13) The offshoots of seeds of *terumah* are considered to be *terumah*, even if the original seeds have disintegrated.

A Kohen who possessed *terumah* which was *tamei* was not permitted to eat it. He could, however, save the seeds for the planting season and grow new plants which would not be *terumah*, and which could, therefore, be eaten.

The Rabbis worried that in the interim he might inadvertently eat the forbidden *terumah*. They decreed, therefore, that the new plant also be considered *terumah*, and that it retain the contaminated status of the seeds, thereby removing any advantage in saving the seeds.

(14) A person who is traveling and cannot reach his destination or a safe resting place when the Sabbath arrives must give his purse to a gentile to carry for him, if one is available, rather than carry it less than four *amos* at a time.

It is prohibited to carry four *amos* [about six to eight feet] in a public domain on the Sabbath (see General Introduction, p.12). A traveler who finds himself on the road when the Sabbath arrives can either give his purse to a gentile[1] to carry for him or carry it himself making sure never to walk a full four *amos* without coming to a full stop.

The Rabbis preferred giving it to a gentile to carrying it himself lest he inadvertently carry it a full four *amos*.

(15) One may not delouse a garment by the light of a lamp on the Sabbath.

(16) One may not read by the light of a lamp on the Sabbath.

These two decrees are discussed in 1:3.

(17) The bread of gentiles, their oil, their wine, and their daughters are prohibited. (These are all listed as one because they all serve one ultimate purpose.)

Their bread was prohibited to discourage the use of their oil; their oil to discourage the consuming of their wine; their wine to discourage marrying their daughters; marrying their daughters to discourage idolatry (*Rav*).

Tiferes Yisrael criticizes *Rav* for citing a statement rejected by the *Gemara*. The final version of the *Gemara* is: They prohibited their bread and their oil because of their wine, and their wine because of their daughters; i.e., they prohibited the wine of gentiles to discourage Jews from socializing and eventually intermarrying with gentiles. They prohibited being alone with the daughters of the gentiles, lest we be influenced by them to worship idols.

The Mishnah (*Avodah Zarah* 2:6) tells us that R' Yehudah HaNassia[2] and his *beis din* [Rabbinic court] repealed the prohibition of the oil of gentiles. Concerning bread, too, the prohibition was modified not to include commercially produced bread of a baker, since commercial bread from a baker requires little or no social intercourse and will not lead to intermarriage as homemade bread may. According to some authorities, gentile bakers' bread is permitted even where Jewish bread is available. Some authorities, however, forbid it and it is therefore preferable to abstain from eating it

---

1. Although on the Sabbath one may not ask a gentile to do a forbidden labor, he may, however, ask him to do so before the Sabbath begins (*Rashi*). Others say that in this instance he may do so even on the Sabbath because if it were not permitted to tell the gentile, he might, in his anxiety over his money, carry it himself. The Rabbis, therefore, permitted this exception to the general prohibition.

2. *Tosafos* (ibid. 36a) quoting *Rashi* deletes this from the Mishnah because it is clear from the *Gemara* that this repeal was the work of R' Yehudah Nesiah who was the grandson of R' Yehudah HaNassi. See *Tosefos Yom Tov* who attempts to resolve this contradiction. Cf. *Doros HaRishonim*, vol. 5, Chap. 8.

(*Shulchan Aruch Yoreh De'ah* 112:2; see *Shach*, ad loc. 9). Where no bakers' bread is available, even a gentile's homemade bread may be eaten (ibid. 8). Of course, this applies only if the kashruth is not questionable.

(18) **A gentile child causes ritual contamination as though he were a *zav*.**
They enacted this decree so that a Jewish child should not associate with him for the purpose of sodomy (*Rav* from *Gem.* 13a-17b).

According to the Talmud (*Avodah Zarah* 36b), this applies only to a male child nine years old, who is capable of performing the sex act.

Others include in the count of "eighteen" the decree mentioned in mishnah 3, that "a *zav* may not eat with a *zavah*." Accordingly, they count the first and second measures as one, or the fourth and fifth as one (*Tos. R' Akiva* from *Tos.* 17b).[1]

---

1. *Rambam* lists three groups of *halachos*, consisting of eighteen each: (a) eighteen *halachos* concerning which Beis Hillel and Beis Shammai eventually concurred; (b) measures of Beis Shammai opposed by Beis Hillel, in which Beis Hillel were outnumbered; (c) *halachos* which were disputed by the two schools, but never came to a vote.

The first group consists of the *halachos* mentioned in the first three *mishnayos* as follows: (1-8) the four types of transferring from domain to domain for the one standing outside, and the four for the one standing inside; (9-13) the five prohibitions from mishnah 2, a person may not sit before a barber . . . a person may not enter a bathhouse . . . nor a tannery . . . nor to judge . . . nor to eat . . .; (14-18) The five prohibitions from mishnah 3, a tailor may not go out with his needle . . . nor a scribe with his pen . . . one may not delouse his garments . . . nor read by lamplight . . . a *zav* may not eat with a *zavah*.

The second group of *halachos*, those in which Beis Shammai outnumbered Beis Hillel, are as follows: (1-7) same as *Rav* [that is, the list expanded on the discussion above]; (8) combination of 8 and 9, listed by *Rav*; (9) If one forgets a vessel under a pipe, and water gathers in it, the water is considered as drawn water and can render a *mikveh* invalid (*Mikvaos* 4:1). This is the opinion of R' Meir, who maintains that Beis Shammai outnumbered Beis Hillel on this point. According to R' Yose, however, this dispute was not resolved and in its stead he counts the decree concerning the daughters of the Cutheans, listed by *Rav* as number 10. (10-13) coincides with 11-14, as counted by *Rav*; (14) bread of gentiles; (15) oil of gentiles; (16) wine of gentiles; (17) daughters of gentiles; (18) coincides with *Rav*. This count is also found in *Sefer HaMaor*, quoted from *Geonim*.

The third group of *halachos* where the two schools did not vote (or, as *Rambam* speculates, perhaps Beis Hillel gained the majority through some disciples of Shammai who voted along with Beis Hillel) are *halachos* mentioned in later *mishnayos*, viz. —
(1) We may not soak ink, (2) or dyes, (3) or vetch . . . from mishnah 5. (4) We may not place bundles of flax into the oven . . . (5) nor wool into a vat . . . (6) we may not spread snares for wild animals (7) nor for fowl, (8) nor for fish . . . from Mishnah 6. (9) We may not sell to a gentile, (10) nor help him load, (11) nor lift a load upon him . . . from mishnah 7. (12) We may not give hides to a tanner, (13) nor clothing to a gentile launderer . . . from mishnah 8. (14) One may not lend articles to a gentile before the Sabbath, (15) nor sell to him *chametz* before Pesach unless he can consume it before Pesach, (16) nor lend him money, (17) nor give him a gift, (18) nor send letters before the Sabbath.

The last five are mentioned in the *Gemara* 18b, and are discussed in the commentary to mishnah 7.

Meiri objects to the inclusion of the third series on the grounds that there is no indication in the *Gemara* that there was a series other than the eighteen decreed in which Beis Shammai were in the majority and the eighteen *halachos* in which they disagreed at first and later concurred.

Glossary

Amora, pl. **Amoraim,** (אֲמוֹרָא (אֲמוֹרָאִים: a Sage of the post-Mishnaic era

avodah zarah, עֲבוֹדָה זָרָה [strange worship]: any object of idolatry

baraisa בָּרַיְיתָא: statements of the *Tannaim* not included in the Mishnah

beis din, בֵּית דִּין: Rabbinical court of law

Chumash, (חוּמָשׁ) חוּמָשׁ: the Pentateuch or any of the five books it comprises (*Genesis, Exodus, Leviticus, Numbers, Deuteronomy*)

ephah, אֵיפָה: a dry measure equivalent in volume to 432 average size chickens eggs; halachic opinions regarding the modern equivalent range from 30 to 48 quarts.

Gaon, pl. **Geonim,** (גָּאוֹן (גְּאוֹנִים: (1) title accorded the heads of the academies in Sura and Pumbedisa, the two Babylonian seats of Jewish learning, from the late 6th to mid-11th centuries C.E.; they served as the link in the chain of Torah tradition that joined the Rishonim to the Amoraim; (2) later used to describe any brilliant Torah scholar

halachah, pl. **halachos,** (הֲלָכָה (הֲלָכוֹת (1) a religious law; (2) [cap.] the body of Jewish law

kares, כָּרֵת: a form of excision meted out by the Heavenly Tribunal, sometimes as premature death, sometimes by one being predeceased by his children

Kesuvim, כְּתוּבִים [Writings]: the section of Scripture comprising *Psalms, Proverbs, Job, Song of Songs, Ecclesiastes, Ruth, Lamentations, Esther, Daniel, Ezra-Nehemiah* and *Chronicles*

log, pl. **lugin,** (לֹג (לוּגִין: a measure equal to the volume of six eggs; halachic opinions regarding the modern equivalent range from 13.2 to 21.2 fluid ounces

meizid, מֵזִיד: the deliberate performance of a prohibited act

mikveh, pl. **mikvaos,** (מִקְוֶה (מִקְוָאוֹת: ritualarium; pool of water for the halachic cleansing of one who is *tamei*

Minchah, מִנְחָה: (1) the afternoon prayers; (2) the time period during which the afternoon prayer may be offered; this period is divided into *Minchah gedolah* and *Minchah ketanah*; (3) a flour offering in the Holy Temple; (4) the daily afternoon burnt offering

Mishkan, מִשְׁכָּן: the Tabernacle which traveled with the Israelites in the wilderness

Neviim, נְבִיאִים [Prophets]: the section of Scripture comprising *Joshua, Judges, Samuel, Kings, Isaiah, Jeremiah, Ezekiel* and the *Twelve* (minor) *Prophets*

posek, pl. **poskim,** (פּוֹסֵק (פּוֹסְקִים: halachic authority

reviis, רְבִיעִית: a quarter-*log;* halachic opinions regarding the modern equivalent range from 3.3 to 5.3 fluid ounces

Rishon, pl. **Rishonim,** (רִאשׁוֹן (רִאשׁוֹנִים: a Torah authority of the period following the *Geonim* and ending with the publication of the *Shulchan Aruch* (approx. 1000-1500 C.E.)

shaatnez, שַׁעַטְנֵז: a mixture of wool and linen; *Leviticus* 19:19 and *Deuteronomy* 22:11 prohibit the wearing of a garment made from a combination of these fibers

sheretz, pl. **sheratzim,** (שֶׁרֶץ (שְׁרָצִים: eight species of reptiles and rodents (identified in *Leviticus* 11:29-30) which, when dead, transmit *tumah* on contact

shogeig, שׁוֹגֵג: the performance of a prohibited act by one who is unaware of the prohibition

taharah, טָהֳרָה: a halachically defined state of ritual or spiritual purity, free of *tumah*-contamination

tahor, טָהוֹר: in a state of *taharah*

tamei, טָמֵא: in a halachically defined state of *tumah*-contamination

Tanna, pl. *Tannaim,* (תַּנָּא (תַּנָּאִים: a Sage quoted in the Mishnah or in works of the same period

Tanna Kamma, תַּנָּא קַמָּא: unidentified speaker of first opinion stated in a mishnah

tefach, pl. **tefachim,** (טֶפַח (טְפָחִים: a measure of length equal to the width of the four fingers of the closed hand; halachic opinions regarding the modern equivalent range from three to four inches

tevel, טֶבֶל: any commodity that requires that one or more tithes be removed from it is called *tevel* until the particular tithes have been set aside

tefillah, תְּפִלָּה: (1) prayer in general; (2) specifically the *Shemoneh Esrei*

tumah, טֻמְאָה: a halachically defined contamination inherent in certain people (e.g., a *niddah*) or objects (e.g., a corpse) that under specific conditions is transferred to another person or object

Yom Tov, pl. **Yamim Tovim**, יוֹם טוֹב (יָמִים טוֹבִים): a festival or holiday, specifically, those days, other than the Sabbath, on which labor is forbidden

This volume is part of
THE ARTSCROLL SERIES®
an ongoing project of
translations, commentaries and expositions
on Scripture, Mishnah, Talmud, Halachah,
liturgy, history, the classic Rabbinic writings,
biographies and thought.

For a brochure of current publications
visit your local Hebrew bookseller
or contact the publisher:

Mesorah Publications, ltd
4401 Second Avenue
Brooklyn, New York 11232
(718) 921-9000